HOUSING

HOUSING

JOHN MACSAI

Architect
Professor, University of Illinois
Chicago Circle

EUGENE P. HOLLAND

Structural Engineer
Lecturer, University of Chicago
Chicago Circle

HARRY S. NACHMAN

Consulting Engineer

JULIUS Y. YACKER

Attorney

Illustrator

ALFRED J. HIDVEGI

Architect

A WILEY-INTERSCIENCE PUBLICATION

JOHN WILEY & SONS

New York • London • Sydney • Toronto

Library of Congress Cataloging in Publication Data:

Main entry under title:
Housing.

"A Wiley-Interscience publication."
Includes bibliographical references and index.
1. Apartment houses. 2. Architecture, Domestic. I. Macsai, John, 1926- II. Hidvegi, Alfred

TH 4820.H68 728.3'1 75-38736
ISBN 0-471-56312-9

Printed in the United States of America

10 9 8 7 6 5 4 3 2 1

ACKNOWLEDGMENTS

If the purpose of ''Acknowledgments'' is to give due credit to all who directly or indirectly helped in the formulation of the material included in a book, then I should start with my students at the University of Illinois at Chicago Circle; their questions, their eager search for material when faced with a housing problem was a prime motivating force in writing this book. I should continue by expressing my thanks to two friends and colleagues, Stanley Tigerman and Ezra Gordon; their praise of the predecessor of this book—the textbook I prepared for my class, *High Rise Apartment Buildings/A Design Primer*—encouraged me to seek a publisher for an expanded study of housing design.

In the narrower sense, to acknowledge those who were involved with the book directly, my first thanks go to my coauthors Eugene P. Holland, Harry S. Nachman, and Julius Y. Yacher. In this connection I owe thanks to Leonard Korobkin who wrote the mechanical engineering section of the above mentioned textbook; he would have written it in this book as well had family illness not put prior demand on his time. I had to accept his withdrawal regretfully. I feel doubly fortunate that Harry S. Nachman agreed to step in and I owe him special thanks for an outstanding job.

My friend and partner Al Hidvegi is listed as illustrator of the book. He has been much more than that; he was truly my coauthor. His contribution, with ideas and suggestions, has been constant. The errors he discovered and that were eliminated are innumerable. The ones that remained in the book remained not because he did not point them out to me but probably because I did not listen to him.

I should also like to thank those unlisted coauthors who helped generously in specific fields. Frank Zimmerman of Westinghouse Corporation supplied most of the material in the chapter on elevators. Rein Pirn of Bolt, Beranek & Newman, Inc., researched the data in the chart and text on sound transmission ratings. Jerry Haag of National Loss Control Service Corporation prepared the report that appears in the chapter on fire protection.

ACKNOWLEDGMENTS

The numerous ''coauthors'' I quoted from, who are listed under Notes, also deserve thanks, especially so Oscar Newman (*Defensible Space*) and the Urban Design Council of The City of New York (*Housing Quality—A Program for Zoning Reform*) whose work is not merely quoted, but forms the core of many ideas in the book.

In a certain sense all the architects whose work is included in the book are coauthors. Their efforts in supplying me with photographs, plans, and data are much appreciated. It was a difficult job of selection when the size of the book limited me to 60 or so. Unavoidably some very good projects were left out.

In the truest sense the editors are coauthors. William Dudley Hunt, Jr., FAIA, at John Wiley and Sons, was most patient with my delays and constantly encouraging.

There is no way that this book could have been completed without the help of my secretary, Ms. Diane Kessler, who handled the seemingly endless correspondence with architects, photographers, and publisher. To her my sincere thanks.

Any practicing architect who is masochistic (and egotistic) enough to want to write a book needs more than anything else—support. My wife Geraldine not only read and corrected the architectural text (''translating'' from Hungarian to English would be the proper expression), but she, as well as my children, offered the kind of support without which architects, working evenings, weekends, and holidays, cannot get along. To her and to Pam, Aaron, Marian, and Gwen not only my thanks, but love!

John Macsai

Chicago, Illinois
October 1975

CONTENTS

Introduction, 1

1 DATA GATHERING by John Macsai 3

Building Program, 4
Location Data, 10
Zoning, 12
Building Code, 15
Budget, 18

2 COMPONENTS OF DESIGN—ARCHITECTURAL by John Macsai 23

The Apartment, 23
Separators—Connectors, 34
Fire Safety, 38
Stairs, 43
Elevators, 47
Other Core Elements, 51
Parking, 53
Loading and Refuse Removal, 62
Lobby, 65
Storage, 68
Laundry, 69
Recreation, 71

CONTENTS

3 COMPONENTS OF DESIGN—STRUCTURAL by Eugene P. Holland 75

Structural Frame Selection, 75
Structural Frames, 77

Cast-in-Place Concrete, 77
Other Concrete Schemes, 86
Structural Steel, 88
Midrise Structural Variations, 90
Wood Frame, 92

Lateral Loads and Resisting Elements, 92
Foundations, 96
Member Size Selection, 99

4 COMPONENTS OF DESIGN—HVAC by Harry S. Nachman 105

Heating and Air Conditioning, 105

Requirements, 000
Use of Fuel and Energy, 108
Equipment Location, 109
Fuel Converting Equipment, 112
Built-in Conservation, 115
Heating Media, 116
Cooling Equipment, 118
Heat Pumps, 122
Systems, 123
Independent Heating and Cooling Systems, 124
Central Heating and Cooling Systems, 129
Combined Heating and Cooling Systems, 137
Controls, 137

Ventilation, 139

Infiltration, 140
Exhaust Ventilation, 142
Supply (Makeup Air) Ventilation, 145
Ventilation Space Requirements, 147
Miscellaneous Ventilation, 148

Maintenance and Operation of Equipment, 148

5 COMPONENTS OF DESIGN—PLUMBING by Harry S. Nachman 151

Water, 000
Water Quality, 152
Water Pressure, 153
Water Heating, 1 56
Hot Water Circulation and Protection, 158
Water Piping, 159
Back Siphonage, 161
Waste Disposal, 163
Building Drainage, 164
Ground Water, 167
Below-sewer Drainage, 168

Plumbing Fixtures, 168
Location of Fixtures, 170
Fire Protection, 170
Plumbing Space Requirements and Costs, 174

6 **COMPONENTS OF DESIGN—ELECTRICAL by Harry S. Nachman** 175

Total Energy Plants, 176
Purchased Electricity, 177
Electrical Provisions Within a Residence, 178
Distribution and Service, 181
Emergency Light and Power, 186
Auxiliary Electrical Systems, 187

Safety, 188
Security, 189
Communication, 190
Enjoyment, 191

7 **DESIGN METHODOLOGY by John Macsai** 193

Highrise, 194

Central Corridor System, 197
Apartments, 198
Rythm, 203
End apartments, 212
Symmetry-sequence, 216
Corridor, 218
Framing, 219
Multicore System, 222
Point-Block System, 224
Exterior Corridor System, 229
Skip-Stop System, 231
Single Tower Sites, 234
Multitower Sites, 240
Exterior, 241

Lowrise, 266

Townhouse, 266
Core-Type Walk-Up, 276
Corridor-Type Walk-Up, 281
Mixed Walk-Up, 283

Midrise, 285
Lowrise and Midrise Exterior, 287
Lowrise and Midrise Sites, 291

8 **FINANCING by Julius Yacker** 303

Notes, 317

Projects, 319

Index, 457

HOUSING

INTRODUCTION

Architectural design is a multileveled process. The designer—in this case the designer of housing—must consider simultaneously a multitude of tasks, a multitude of options.

To reproduce this complex thought process in words, a medium in which one is forced to put down one thought at a time sequentially, is impossible. The designer's concurrent awareness of program, regulations, budget, functional possibilities, structural and mechanical options, and architectural form is not reproducible. At best, the components can be identified and dealt with separately but not at once, as the architect must.

How much space should be allotted to each component? Each is of sufficient importance to have often been the topic of an entire study. It is neither necessary nor wise to try to be all encompassing for the purposes of this book; components of housing are treated only in their capacity as design generators.

This book is not a designer's Sweets Catalogue. It simply hopes to be: for the colleague already well versed in housing, a refresher course to clarify ideas or something to criticize and take issue with; for architects not so well acquainted with housing, a guide when a housing commission materializes; for architectural students, a reference when taking a course; and for others, such as developers and housing officials, an insight into the way architects think and therefore a tool to make their association more positive.

Because there are few absolutes in architecture, I am quite aware that there is no statement in this book with which a colleague could not disagree, based on his own experiences or architectural attitudes.

Writing about design inevitably reveals one's own prejudices and limited experiences in facets of housing and the avoidance or brief treatment of these areas. My own dislike of curtain walls in apartment buildings, disregard of industrialized housing, and extreme brevity in discussing steel framing all spring from the above. Aside from these prejudices and limitations, I must admit to other shortcomings: megastructures are not included; specialized housing types such as student accommodations and apartment hotels are not covered; regional differences such as earthquakes and climate are at best only touched on; site planning is covered in a much briefer manner than it deserves; examples are limited to the United States.

I must conclude with a warning: building types and apartment prototypes are not meant to be recipes. They are merely illustrations to cast light on a problem. No catalogue of solutions could be a substitute for architectural design: from the options inherent in the task, from the choices we make in responding to the task, based on our own theory of space born of the limitless combinations and permutations possible, a unique and individual architectural solution will be reached that no book can—or should—influence.

"True originality is to be found by those who, standing on the limits of the sphere of the known, reach out naturally to some apprehension and understanding of what is beyond; it is the next step in an orderly development."[1] This book attempts to cast light on the orderly development of housing design in the hope that it will help some of its readers who are about to take that next step.

DATA GATHERING 1

John Macsai

''The process of designing a building is really a path which you begin to travel as soon as you possibly can, in terms of the problems''—Kevin Roche *Conversation with Architects.*[2]

What hides behind the simple expression ''in terms of the problems'' is a mountain of data that the architect must have at his fingertips in order to start the design process. Rare is the architect who can design well when information is missing, when programming is loose. The fact is that the more circumscribed the program, the more specific the data, the more challenged he feels, and the more likely he is to respond to the challenge.

Most good design will rise out of the specificity of the program data, which is peculiar to this client, to this user, to this location. When we claim that the building grows out of the particularity of its conditions, we naturally do not mean that this outgrowth is ''self-generated'' or that it happens ''in a sort of automatic pragmatism.''[3] Far from it. The architect's response to the problem will be much influenced by his theory of form. Obviously the same program data, the same site information, would be responded to differently by the offices of Mies van der Rohe and Davis, Brody & Associates. Obviously, and inevitably, the solutions by the same architect to two entirely different building programs would still carry that architect's stamp of theory.

The chance to utilize theories of spacial organization is, however, somewhat limited in the field of housing. The program data—user needs, site conditions, local regulations, and marketing and financing constraints—allow the architect a more limited latitude of options than other areas of architecture. If these program data do not predetermine an architectural solution, they at least carry in themselves the kernel of a solution. Thorough understanding of the program data is a prerequisite to uncovering this kernel.

DATA GATHERING

Naturally it is hard to avoid the temptation to ''design'' all through the process of data gathering. It is likely that the architect will concentrate on those data that, based on his experience, are most likely to affect design. More than that, he may try to influence the program data—at least those about which his opinion is sought, such as the mix—to lead to a more rational design solution. He knows that an even number of apartments on a typical floor is conducive to orderly exterior rhythm. He knows that pairing apartments leads to various economies. He will have had enough experience with certain apartment designs to know whether they fit readily into a particular building type.

All this is unavoidable. Nevertheless, maximum objectivity can have its reward. One is never sure what specific data, what hitherto unknown piece of information, will suggest a new approach, a new solution, completely different than all the preceding notions.

Compiling the data in the form of a checklist to which to refer when the next housing job materializes is a helpful procedure. Each situation will have its own peculiarities and each architect will group the data in his own way. However, five major categories emerge: building program, location data, zoning, building code, and budget.

BUILDING PROGRAM

When designing multifamily housing—spaces in which human beings raise families and communicate with one another in the most intimate settings—where they eat, sleep, relax, and make love— the architect naturally wants to know all about the people who will inhabit the buildings. Unfortunately he cannot meet, learn about, or interview the actual occupants. Rarely has he an opportunity to deal with a known group whose needs, desires, and idiosyncrasies he can sense in first-hand contact. Usually this information will be handed to him, and although he can personally verify site data, zoning, or financial figures his chances of double checking the correctness of the information regarding the users are minimal. The normally heavy social responsibilities inherent in the design of housing are made even heavier by scanty or irresponsibly put together information about the users and their needs.

On the one hand, programs prepared by various housing authorities are frozen in bureaucratic rule books that, if not already outdated when written, are obsolete by the time they are implemented. There are many reasons for this, but it is not within the scope of this book to delve into them. The sad fact is that although modern research tools are more than adequate to do a reliable job the best information becomes meaningless when inflexibly and heartlessly applied. Public housing—at least as we know it in the United States—traps the designer with its minimum standards. The program data for low- and moderate-income families reflect our social philosophy toward housing and the poor: low-income housing is equated with low-cost housing, for if you are poor you have not done well; therefore you do not deserve so much. The size and quality of the dwelling unit are not determined by human needs but by economic equations. As Anthony Pangaro stated in the June 1973 issue of *Architecture Plus,* ''We cannot continue to let land economics, in the realm of minimum standards and maximum saturation, determine the quality of life. This policy has clearly produced unsatisfactory results.''

On the other hand, when the client is a private developer, when bureaucracy is not in control, and there are no rule books, we expect more up-to date program data. This, however, is not necessarily the case. Few developers are large enough or sufficiently well organized to commission scientifically conducted market analyses.

Even if they were, it often happens that when the developer first approaches the architect he is gambling: he is not at all certain that the project will materialize. It all depends on whether he can obtain financing at the right terms. At the time he discusses the project with the architect he may not even own the land; at best he may hold an option on it. Until the mortgage is promised, he wants to keep his financial exposure to a minimum. He will pay minimally for the architect's preliminary design, which is necessary to obtain financing. Even worse than the negligible compensation, the lack of seriousness is often reflected in the scanty data with which the architect is provided. It is likely that at this stage no proper survey will have been made of the lot, nor will there be money to spend on soil investigation, and for the kind of housing the architect is to design, "why don't we just copy the units from the building across the street; it was successful, wasn't it?"

Because of the lack of reliable data in both the public and private sectors of housing, it is doubly important that the architect know what kind of information he will be given. Only thorough knowledge of these data will enable him to ask the right questions when he tries to drag the answers from the developer. As far as most housing authorities are concerned, he will need not only a thorough acquaintance with program data but also enough courage "to determine and then insist upon the set of amenities appropriate for a particular group in a particular context."[4]

The role of the architect as researcher to establish user preferences has been underrated. Although professional researchers are quite able to cull from questionnaires certain common desires among users, the architect—in full knowledge of the limitations of site, structure, and budget—will be able to formulate the available options far more precisely, and the users' responses, related to a tangible, visible choice will be more reliable. A case in point is Harmony House in New Haven, Connecticut, a series of townhouses designed by Louis Sauer. According to his own description, he acted as "an architect trying to identify who the user is, and how the architecture should be changed for a different lifestyle." After interviewing potential occupants, however small in number, facts were gathered that could

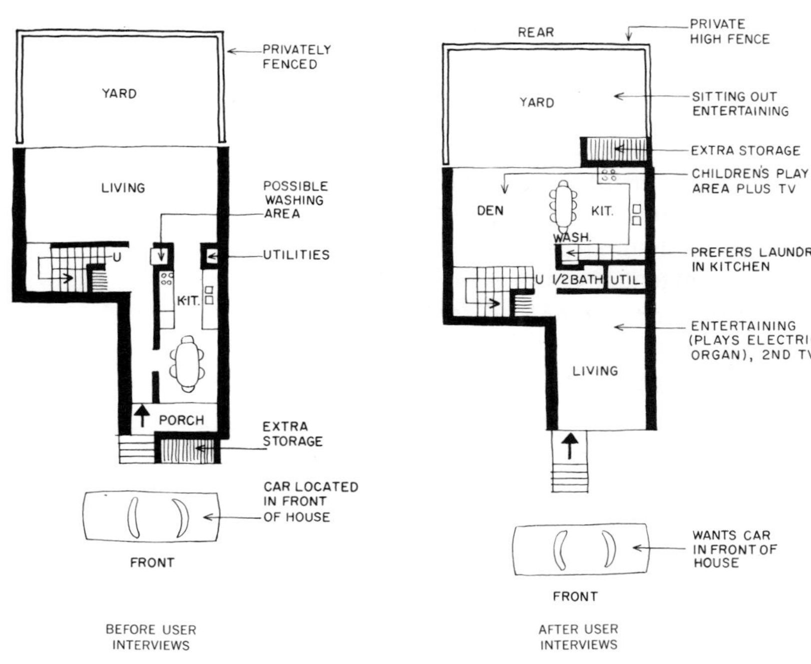

BEFORE USER INTERVIEWS

AFTER USER INTERVIEWS

be gained only by first-hand contact and seldom by "translation" by the sponsor. He found that the large kitchen-dining-family room was preferred to the large living room and that this family space should face the private yard instead of the street. The car right in front of the house was preferred to the hard-to-maintain "middle-class grass." Similarly, other preferences were established—storage in the private yard, laundry in the kitchen instead of the hall closet, and so on, which can be handled best by the architect as researcher.

Because the quality of human life is strongly influenced by the kind of housing he designs, the architect assumes an immense responsibility, and inhuman results simply cannot be blamed on the less than scientific developer or on the rigid bureaucracy. Obviously, in upper income housing this responsibility is lessened because the user can make his own choice, based on his ability to pay. In low-income housing the user has little choice under present socioeconomic conditions and the architect is indeed responsible for the quality of life that is possible in the building.

All of the data gathering categories are important, but the building program has to precede all other, for it answers the basic questions: for whom and what?

USER

1. AGE. Different age groups—young, middle-aged, elderly—will require not only different structures but different amenities and services.
2. FAMILY SIZE. Will the building serve singles, families with children, or both? If it serves both, in what mix?
3. OCCUPATION. Occupations of the users are often hard to predict with any certainty but useful in reflecting living habits and recreational needs.
4. LIFE STYLE. Life style may be related to income levels, occupation, ethnic background, or education. It is frequently neglected and most buildings are designed for the common denominator.
5. PREVIOUS HOUSING. Whether families are moving from the suburbs to the city, from slums to better areas, from farm life to urban existence, their needs, habits, and degree of sophistication will vary.

MARKET

1. SPONSORSHIP. Whether private developer or instutitional sponsor the architect deals with different rules, different requirements, different goals.
2. OWNERSHIP. Rental, cooperative, or condominium type will affect the design of individual climate control, parking space, or extent of common facilities.
3. RENT OR SALES STRUCTURE. Knowledge of the proposed rental or sales price brackets will suggest limits in the design.
4. COMPETITION. Investigation of similar projects in the vicinity will indicate market preferences as well as pitfalls.
5. FINANCING. Financing is in a separate chapter. Here it is important to note that private lending institutions occasionally and governmental financing sources inevitably have their own requirements.

DWELLING UNIT

1. MIX. The percentage of various apartment types such as efficiencies (sometimes called studios), one-, two-, three-, or more bedroom units.

2. UNIT SIZE. Gross square footage of the dwelling unit is not adequate. How it is defined should be clarified. Does it include exterior walls? (In condominiums, these walls should be included because they are owned by the buyer.) Does it include corridor partition or balconies?

3. ROOM SIZE. Room sizes should be given in approximate terms to keep design options flexible. It is also useful to state certain critical minimum dimensions. Height is currently assumed to be 8 ft from floor to ceiling unless specifically called for otherwise.

4. LIVING SPACE. Options should be defined: formal living room with certain activities elsewhere; combined family—living room for all functions. Where can activities for which no specific space is designated take place (sewing, studying, and so on)?

5. DINING. Alternatives should be clearly stated: combined with living room; defined alcove in interior zone of the apartment; defined alcove along exterior wall; combined with kitchen; completely separate room.

6. KITCHEN. Amount of counter space, amount of cabinet space (base as well as wall) in linear feet and types of appliance should be specified. Is eating space to be provided in the kitchen? Is it to accommodate other family activities?

7. BEDROOM. When more than one bedroom has been designated, should they be adjacent or split on each side of the living space? Should the use of bedrooms as living space be considered?

8. BATHROOM. How many? Complete bathrooms or powder room? Which should have shower stalls, which bathtubs? Compartmentalization? In case of multilevel apartments, on which level? Should the approach be directly from the bedrooms or from the common bedroom corridor?

9. STORAGE. Each type of storage space should be defined in terms of linear feet because depth is more or less standard.

10. ENTRY. Size and function of the entry should be stated. Will it serve any function other than reception?

11. EXTERIOR SPACE. Depending on whether the unit is on ground level or elevated, will there be a terrace or balcony and in what size? What provisions are necessary to create a sense of security and privacy?

12. SOUND SEPARATION. Criteria relating to degree of sound separation should be determined: between apartments, between apartments and other areas, within apartments.

BUILDING

1. TYPE. Preference such as low- or highrise, exterior- or interior-corridor, or multicore, is often stated by the owner before the architect prepares any studies.

2. PRIVACY VERSUS COMMUNITY. This is stated primarily in terms of the maximum number of units that will share a common corridor or lobby.

3. ORIENTATION. Should sunlight penetrate every unit? Is there a preferred view and to what extent should it be visible from what percentage of the units? Is special protection to be considered?

SERVICES

1. PARKING. Minimum off-street parking is generally determined by zoning, but the client may have additional requirements. Controls? Self- or attendant parking? One-way or two way traffic? Maximum walking distance from parking areas to units?

2. LAUNDRY. Will there be a washer/dryer in each unit or will a common laundry be provided? Where is it to be located? Is it to serve as a social magnet as well?

3. REFUSE. Methods of refuse handling and disposal should be determined.

4. DELIVERY AND PICK UP. Loading areas and controls should be defined; if the distribution is vertical, the location of service elevator should be discussed.

5. MAIL. Method of handling and distribution of letters, magazines, and parcels should be considered.

6. WINDOW WASHING. By resident or by management? If by management, access from inside the apartments or by scaffold? Decisions will strongly influence fenestration and type of operating sash.

STORAGE

1. TENANT. Type of tenant lockers should be specified; size and location in the building.

2. GENERAL. Purpose should be stated: maintenance, repairs, vehicle storage.

3. BICYCLES. How many and where to be stored; type of security?

4. BABY CARRIAGES. Storage for how many? Relation to the entrance lobby?

SOCIAL AND RECREATIONAL

1. GOALS. Is the purpose to ensure maximum privacy of units? To what degree should social intercourse between residents be promoted?

2. RECREATION. Various desired activities should be defined in terms of the user: adult, child, or mixed? In terms of location: indoor, outdoor? Extent to which nontenants can use facilities should be considered.

3. CHILD CARE. Local or state regulations should be followed governing these facilities if they are required in the program.

COMMERCIAL SPACE

To what extent does it depend on outside partonage? How to handle parking and deliveries? One or more than one tenant?

SECURITY

1. NEEDS. Locality and type of user will determine security provisions and surveillance required.

2. CONTROL. Human: doorman, resident caretaker, other attendants. Mechanical: intercom systems, closed circuit TV.

SPONSOR PECULIARITIES

1. BUILDER SKILLS. When the developer is also a general contractor, he may exhibit preferences based on available skills related to structural systems, materials handling, or construction logistics.

2. EXPERIENCE. Sponsor's history of success—or failure—in similar prospects will help to avoid mistakes.

3. MARKETING. Should model apartments be set up in the building proper or in a separate temporary structure? Sales office requirements? Visitors' parking and routing?

MECHANICAL

1. HEATING, VENTILATING, AND AIR CONDITIONING

   a. Fuel for heating: gas, oil, coal, or electricity?

   b. Central or individual apartment heating plant(s)?

   c. Exposure control: quantity of fenestration; ordinary or insulating?

   d. Insulation in walls and roof; importance of initial versus operating cost.

   e. Is humidification wanted?

   f. Is cooling wanted? If so, by central or individual residence plant(s)? The owner should understand thoroughly the possibilities and implications of heating and cooling controls, which range from manual, through simple overall building, to sophisticated room-by-room. The latter may be a prestigious point in rentals or sales but may also add substantially to maintenance costs and problems. In some types of all-electrical system, however, room-by-room controls may be a normal part of the equipment. Thus it behooves the owner to acquire a fair understanding of the many alternatives available. If cooling is desired, what should the inside temperature be? A straight 75 degrees for optimum comfort (or even lower?), or 10 to 12 degrees below the maximum outdoor temperature for minimum installation and operating costs?

   g. Energy source for cooling. If natural fuel is used, the owner should be made aware of the possibilities of absorption refrigeration, using the same fuel. If electricity is used for heating, the potentialities of the heat pump should be made clear to the owner.

   h. Will the owner, the individual occupant, or an organization of occupants pay fuel and energy costs for heating and/or cooling?

   i. If individual heating and/or cooling systems are used, who will be responsible for their maintenance and replacement?

   j. Ventilation for bathrooms and/or kitchens: central, individual, or a combination of individual control and central collection?

2. PLUMBING

   a. Water centrally metered or individually metered?

   b. Domestic water heating to be central or individual? Who will pay for the energy?

   c. Water closets to be flush valve or tank operated?

   d. Details of other sanitary fixtures; for example, lavatories to be free standing or cabinet type; kitchen sinks to be china or stainless steel; tub in every bathroom or shower only in some, quality of tub (cast iron or steel)?

   e. Laundry facilities: central or individual? If central, will there be a concessionaire, or will the owner operate the facility?

   f. Fire protection: should this be the minimum required by governing codes or does the owner want extra protection in the form of additional standpipes, fire extinguishers, and/or sprinklers? Will insurance charge reductions justify such additional costs?

3. ELECTRICAL

   a. Is an owner-operated ''total-energy'' plant feasible, in which the owner provides all his own electricity, heat, and cooling for the entire project?

   b. If purchased electricity from a utility company is opted, the owner should understand the possibilities of various rates for different intensities of use and the overall costs, both installation and operating, for all alternatives. Any subsidies offered by the utility companies should be included in the consideration.

c. Will purchased electrical energy be individually or centrally metered and paid for? (The latter option is not available in Illinois, for example.)

d. Are the heating and cooling systems to be electrically powered? The same question applies to domestic water heating.

e. Quality of specialties such as switches and receptacles. The usual decision, low installation cost combined with higher maintenance and replacement costs for minimum quality specialties or the converse?

f. Who will furnish and install lighting fixtures in the residential areas?

g. Electrical or gas ranges?

h. The range of choices of auxiliary electrical systems is broad:

Front (and rear) door bell signals.

Voice communication with remote entrance doors.

Closed circuit television surveillance of entrances.

Central television antenna system.

Intercommunication systems of varying inclusiveness.

Burglar alarm and similar security systems.

Emergency alarm for persons in trouble in their apartments (particularly applicable in housing for the elderly).

Panic alarm for elevators.

Smoke and fire alarm systems.

Should any or all of these features be combined with the public telephone system?

i. Emergency light and power. Should this be the minimum required by code or should such possibly noncovered uses as elevators, domestic water pressure pumps, heating boilers, and pumps be provided with standby power?

LOCATION DATA

The decision to discuss the building program before location data is arbitrary, and it can be fairly argued that location is probably the major contribution to the success or failure of any project.

The stigma attached to public housing in the United States is in no small measure due to location. Built in the most deteriorated parts of the urban ghetto, in areas in which delinquency and crime are rampant, these projects are doomed to fail even if all other conditions—proper tenant selection and education, concerned management, and well designed buildings—are properly met.

To realize the importance of location in the private sector of housing one only has to remember the often quoted statement by the developer who, when asked the secret of a successful apartment project, replied:

"The secret lies in three factors. The first is location, the second is location, and the third is location."

A successful development starts out with the search for land. Whether the site is urban or exurban, the astute developer has to know a great deal about the property, not only its physical and environmental conditions but also the stability of the area. This should be determined by scientific projection. Often it is by looking through a crystal ball.

For the architect the physical and environmental characteristics of the site become generators of design which, like the building program data, will narrow the choices and lead to a solution.

SURFACE

1. SIZE. Correct survey must be available showing lot dimensions, lot line angles. Special attention must be paid to such possible limitations as deeded restrictions and permanent easements.

2. BOUNDARIES. Property line conditions often carry hidden hazards: party walls, adjacent foundations or basements to be protected, and proposed street widenings.

3. TOPOGRAPHY. Terrain elevations should be available at regular intervals not only on the property but in relation to adjacent properties, sidewalks, and curbs.

4. ECOLOGY. Surface drainage pattern, surface soil, flora, and natural features such as rocks and water should be investigated.

SUBSURFACE

1. SOIL. Composition, stability, and load bearing capacity must be analyzed by a qualified soil engineer.

2. WATER. Knowledge of the current water table alone is not enough; predictable rise of water level should also be considered.

3. UTILITIES. Proper survey should include all utilities such as water, sewer (storm and sanitary), and gas and electric lines.

4. HINDRANCES. As far as possible— by soil borings or historical investigation— underground hazards, such as rock formations, underground streams, peat areas, fills, abandoned foundations or filled-over structures like railroad beds and wharfs, should be uncovered.

CLIMATE

1. TEMPERATURE. Knowledge of the extremes, duration, and humidity is needed to make decisions about environmental control systems.

2. PRECIPITATION. Maximum rain and snowfall will determine site issues such as drainage or snow removal.

3. SUN. Direction and angles throughout the year; shadows cast by adjacent structures are essential in locating and orienting buildings.

4. WIND. Awareness of direction, velocity, and unusual conditions created by adjacent structures will eliminate irreversible decisions.

HAZARDS

1. POLLUTANTS. Data on sources of smoke, fumes, and unpleasant odors in relation to wind direction are necessary for proper building placement.

2. NOISE. Train lines, truck routes, and proximity to airports or other noise sources will influence the location of structures as well as the intensity of sound insulation.

3. OTHER. Presence of unusual hazards such as high-tension lines, adjacent subway, atomic plant, flooding and shore erosion, wave action, vibration, and earthquakes should be investigated.

TRAFFIC

1. VOLUME AND DIRECTION. Maximum number of vehicles on adjacent roads at critical hours, one way streets, traffic lights, speed limits; any proposed change in traffic direction; any proposed street widening or introduction of median strips.

2. RESTRICTIONS. Width of permitted curb cuts, their minimum distance from one another and from nearest intersection; special curb cut visibility requirements.

3. PARKING. Conditions of on-street parking; availability of public parking facilities in the vicinity.

COMMUNITY FACILITIES

1. REDUNDANCY. Availability of recreational facilities such as parks, sport fields, or playgrounds will eliminate duplication in the project.

2. LINKAGE. Awareness of the location of educational and religious institutions, health and recreation facilities, commercial services, public transportation, and so on, will influence pedestrian networks, especially on larger projects.

VISUAL CONDITIONS

1. BUILDINGS. Character of neighboring buildings in relation to physical stability and degree of deterioration; their architectural style, scale, predominant material, and fenestration.

2. STREETSCAPE. Buildings viewed as a total composition: continuity, height, and character of street facades. Is the existing pattern worth reinforcing?

3. PANORAMA. Is there anything worth looking at during the day or at night? Conversely: significant view-channels of the neighborhood that will be influenced by the proposed project.

4. FEATURES. Significant structures, historical buildings, monuments, or natural features such as hills and forests worth relating to.

SERVICES

1. FIRE FIGHTING. Although building codes determine the minimum safety requirements, it is essential to know the character and availability of local fire-fighting equipment, especially in exurban locations. The project should be discussed with the local fire chief in a small community with a limited fire department.

2. REFUSE COLLECTION. Private or public; frequency; type of vehicle.

3. STREET. Frequency and method of snow removal, street cleaning, maintenance, and lighting.

4. MAIL. Frequency of delivery and collection; any specific governmental requirements?

5. MISCELLANEOUS. Various services such as tree protection or anti-insect programs.

ZONING

If there is any one rigid control that has the greatest influence on apartment house design, it is zoning. Although a community may realize the necessity of controlling land use to the best advantage of all, many of the zoning regulations are based on arbitrary standards and are fraught with political pressures. The objective is to provide controls so that residential living conditions will be at a high enough level to foster health, safety, and the public welfare, and to set a pattern for the orderly growth of the community in order to eliminate blight and congestion. But unless the zoning ordinance has a built-in process for adapting its provisions to meet changing conditions and advances in land planning, it can become archaic and defeat its very objectives.[5]

Unfortunately, after 50 years of zoning, blight is still with us. As David J. Mandel, eloquent and sincere advocate of no zoning at all, has said:

> Since zoning is only one of a host of forces shaping land use, it is difficult to measure its practical effects. There certainly is no evidence that the introduction of comprehensive zoning has improved the amenities of cities and substantial evidence that it has reduced them.[6]

A better understanding of the evolution of the zoning concept will clarify its purpose and spirit and encourage the architect to become concerned in shaping its future.

Zoning started in the United States in the 1920s and, simply stated, provided "all landowners with knowledge before the fact of what they could and could not do with their land."[7] It resulted in the simplistic subdivision of municipal areas into single-family, commercial, and industrial zones, with complete lack of preparation for future development. By the late fifties most cities had rewritten their zoning ordinances using a more sophisticated division (several density areas in the residential zone) and controlling bulk, density, light and air, off street parking, and loading by various formulas.

Unavoidably, the planners also formed an image that the ordinance was to achieve. Housing in the fifties—based on Le Corbusier's early vision of towers in in an urban park—lead to serious zoning problems, the most obvious of which was the destruction of streets and city matrix, the lack of reference points, problems of safety and surveillance, and ultimately repetition and monotony. This type of zoning in each residential district in effect built in a preconceived prototype and lead many to say that not the architect but the zoning ordinance designed the apartment buildings.

In this zoning "there is no sensitivity beyond generalized mapping for the various neighborhoods within the city. Both Greenwich Village and South Bronx are mapped R-6. No account is taken of the various geographic, social or economic conditions within these dramatically different areas."[8] High-density areas—with their high land values—are mapped to perpetuate existing real estate conditions and to protect and insulate the single-family areas. High-density housing along recent major rapid transit arteries, a development that would foster urban rejuvenation, becomes impossibly difficult under current mapping.

The social consequences of the zoning of the fifties are equally serious. The poor are segregated from the rich (by minimum lot size per dwelling), the old from the young (by allowing no apartment buildings for the elderly in zones in which their children live). Based on the old theory that the glue factory has a deleterious effect on humans, zoning removes housing from other areas of human activity, such as shopping, restaurants, and crafts, and results in dormitory districts with dull, unsafe, unfriendly, and lifeless streets "because there is seldom any active reason for a good cross-section of people to use them,"[9] thus robbing us of the richness of human interaction that has traditionally been a major attraction of the city. Looking at the cities of Europe, it becomes obvious that the strict separation of residential from other day-to-day activities is really not necessary and "zoning for diversity," as so admirably argued by Ms. Jacobs, will result in richer, safer, and visually more stimulating neighborhoods.

As if all this were not enough as a condemnation, the zoning of the fifties is obsolete and inflexible. It was based on knowledge and technology that tried to address itself to problems already decades old when the zoning plan was written. Not only was it therefore obsolete when it became law, but it was assumed to create an ideal world that would never need adjusting. Because the authors were looking through "clouded crystal balls,"[10] to use Babcock's term, zoning became a set of frozen rules.

To deal with this lack of flexibility several devices were introduced. One popular technique, still with us, was the special use permit, which allowed a review of each proposal that did not follow the existing ordinance.

A far more resilient instrument is the discretionary review, or the planned unit development, which eliminates the ad hoc quality of the special use permit. Each project, which usually requires a certain minimum land area, is judged on its own merit, in fact pre-empting existing zoning. "Pre-regulation gives way to negotiation."[11] The trouble with PUD is threefold: it requires an intelligent, flexible, architecturally sensitive, and politically independent staff to prevent zoning from becoming a political football; it is time consuming; the architect and the developer usually work with inadequate criteria, not knowing in advance what they will or will not be permitted to do.

Bonuses (i.e., rewarding the developer with larger building areas in exchange for various concessions such as larger apartments in Chicago or arcades and theaters in New York) did not make zoning more flexible.

The most imaginative approach in recent years came from the Urban Design Council of New York in their proposal for zoning reform in New York City. In contrast to current zoning practices, it does "not mandate all requirements nor offer voluntary bonuses for specific amenities. Instead, within given limits, the entire process would be elective, setting goals rather than minimum standards that effectively become maximum achievements."[12]

How does it work?

In order to put up a new residential building, a developer would have to earn a sufficient number of quality points in the four identified programs of quality; namely, neighborhood impact, recreation space, security and safety, and the apartment. The point system is delicately calibrated: different values are given for different elements and for varying degrees of compliance with each specific goal. For twenty-two of the elements, a minimum level of compliance is specified; extra points would be gained by going beyond that minimum. The degree of compliance of the other fifteen elements would be left to the discretion of the developer. Although minimum compliance with the twenty-two basic elements would yield a project of acceptable quality, the scoring has been established in such a way that there is always an incentive to achieve higher levels of quality to the mutual benefit of developer and tenant alike. By its flexibility, the proposed zoning would offer a free choice system that for the first time accurately mirrors the selective process of actual planning and design. A developer and his architect could choose to amass points by enlarging room sizes while sacrificing some degree of visual privacy, or by providing larger windows but deleting balconies.

The proposed Housing Quality Program recognizes the diversity of neighborhoods and the different needs of an already-developed as opposed to a predominantly vacant area. The present limitations on ground coverage would be removed so as to produce the opportunity for lower buildings and economic efficiencies. Recreation activities would now be encouraged not only outdoors, but also on rooftops and even within the buildings. Increased security is envisioned, for example, by making elevator lobbies visible from the sidewalks.[12]

Notwithstanding all sincere attempts for reform, the frozen rules are still around and it is essential for the designer to understand them. Failure of thorough zoning investigation can result in serious and costly problems. Because the language of bureaucracy is not always clear, interpretation must be requested from the officials before making assumptions. When zoning is by planned unit development, the architect has to be familiar with the overall plan and the intentions of the planners who will negotiate with him and his client and will give the final approval for the solution.

Zoning ordinances deal with land use, building bulk, density, light and air, parking, and loading.

LAND USE. Most cities are divided into residential, business, commercial, and manufacturing areas in which housing, commercial-building, or factory locations are designated. The residential, "R" districts (in some cities denoted as "H" for housing), are further subdivided into R-1, R-2, R-3, and so on, indicating a gradual increase in density and usage as the number goes up from single-family detached houses (R-1) all the way to high-density highrises.

DENSITY. The number of dwelling units—or families—permitted on any site, related to the size of the lot.

BULK. Most often the volume of the building is related to the lot size: land area multiplied by a floor area ratio which can vary from 0.5 in single family districts up to 10 or more in highrise districts.

Some cities offer bonuses in density and/or bulk allowing an increase in density or in bulk above the normally permitted maximum if the developer meets certain conditions; for example, in Chicago both density and bulk can be increased when the lot faces an open public space of a certain size; floor area ratio, therefore bulk, can be increased if the developer decreases the density below the allowable maximum, thereby encouraging the construction of larger apartments.

Bulk is sometimes determined vertically by limiting the height of the buildings and horizontally by yard setbacks and/or percentage of permissible ground coverage—in fact, providing an envelope within which the structure must fit.

LIGHT AND AIR. Light and air are provided by open space which is created by the distance between structures and the location of the building on the site. Zoning ordinances have various formulas to determine setbacks for front, side and rear yards or for distances between buildings. These formulas are related to the lot size and the building height.

PARKING. The minimum number of parking spaces to be provided, off the street, in relation to the number of dwellings.

LOADING. The minimum number of loading stalls to be provided, off the street, based on the number of dwellings or the total floor area of the building.

BUILDING CODE

Next to zoning ordinances, building codes represent the severest restricting force in the design process. The purpose of the code is to protect life, to ensure safety, and to prevent the ignorant or the unscrupulous from endangering the well-being of the user or the public. If zoning determines "what and where," codes tell us "how."

Although we can quarrel about the necessity of zoning, there is little doubt about the need for a code; we only have to look at the shoddily built houses and apartment buildings that are possible under relatively stringent codes to make us shudder at what would happen in the absence of regulations. A visit to one of the rapidly growing, corruption-laden South American countries is enough to convince most of those who oppose codes.

This is not to say that codes are either perfect or fair. They can be products of selfish local interests, politically strong local unions, and manufacturers' associations, In one city, for example, for many years run by politicians beholden to masons, exterior walls had to be thicker than anywhere else in the country. Similar self-serving regulations which were part of the code in another city protected lathers and plasterers and delayed the use of gypsum board for years.

Another shortcoming of building codes is their inflexibility. They, like zoning ordinances, reflect knowledge rooted in the past and are not adjusted and updated often enough to allow for the constantly appearing new materials and products.

The worst problem facing the architect regarding codes is the lack of uniformity from one city to the other. Some cities have adopted basic building codes. Others, usually large cities with adequate staffs, have written their own codes which may then be adopted by some of the larger suburbs that lack help. Many small towns and suburbs have highly inadequate and scanty codes. The periodic enthusiasm for a nationwide uniform building code that would still recognize unique regional conditions such as climate or earthquakes dies fast in the face of vested local interests.

Because of these variations, when the architect faces a task in a city in which he has never worked before, he is well advised to acquaint himself thoroughly with the code.

In spite of the fact that codes vary to such a great extent, there is enough similarity among them to distill the common design generators. A large part of all codes is taken up with regulations that deal with materials, their properties, and installation methods. Although ultimately they do affect design, they are beyond the scope of this study.

USE

All codes recognize the differences between buildings according to their occupancy and use. Among the various categories—factories, commercial structures, institutional buildings, and assembly buildings,—one is residential. Under this specific use codes define the rooms that are considered habitable and therefore in need of natural light and ventilation. What is the minimum ceiling height? What is the maximum travel distance to exits? What are the minimal exit dimensions based on maximum possible occupancy? In mixed use the required fire separation is stated, such as the separation required between the residential part of the structure and hazardous use (garage).

CONSTRUCTION TYPES

For each use-category different floor-area and height limitations are set according to their degree of fireproofing under four basic construction types. Some cities limit some of these construction types to stated "fire districts" in the municipal area. The following table reflects in general terms the relation between the number of floors, their size, and the particular construction for residential occupancy. It is a distillation of many tables, and although it is not valid in any particular city, it is an indication of the limitations set by most building codes.

LIGHT AND AIR

Codes define for all habitable rooms the minimum amount of light (glass area) and natural ventilation (operating sash area) required. This is usually a set percentage of the floor area of each room, generally 10% for light and 5% for natural ventilation; if the room is exceedingly deep, these percentages are increased.

CONSTRUCTION TYPES

Construction Type[a]	Fire Rating (hr)		Maximum Number of Floors[b]	Maximum Floor Area of Each Floor[c] (sf)
	Floors	Columns		
FIREPROOF All noncombustible with high rating of elements	2–3	3–4	7 and Up	No limit
NONCOMBUSTIBLE All noncombustible with lower rating of elements	1–1½	2	5–6	8,000–20,000
ORDINARY Combustible interior elements with protected exterior such as masonry	¾–1	¾–1	3–4	6,000– 8,000
FRAME Interior and exterior combustible	½	½	1–2	5,000– 6,000

[a] A separate table usually sets the rate of fire separation between different construction types such as a "fireproof" garage and the "ordinary" apartment building above it.

[b] Sometimes when a floor is below the level of adjacent street or grade it does not count as a "floor" according to the code, thereby increasing the allowable number of floors. However, it must be determined, probably elsewhere in the code, whether this below-grade floor can be used for habitation.

[c] Floor areas can be increased if adequate distance between the building and other structures provides accessibility for fire-fighting equipment. Some codes also permit an increase if the building is equipped with automatic sprinklers—a prohibitive cost in housing. However, sprinklers in the garage or portions of the garage falling under the residential section of the building are usually required by code even when the entire building has "fireproof" construction.

When windows required for light and natural ventilation are located in an exterior wall of a true court or a partial set back of the building, most codes define these courts as inner, through, or outer and regulate their size in relation to the height of the building.

EXITS

Exits are just one means of providing fire safety, an issue discussed in detail in a separate chapter. Here, we submit a brief summary of the exit elements, keeping in mind that codes vary in their requirements for maximum distance, dimensions and even kind and number.

CAPACITY. The width of doors, corridor, and stairs is related to maximum occupancy load determined by the number of square feet of floor area per person.

NUMBER OF EXITS. In most cases a minimum of two exits is required, but in low-rise buildings of certain construction type, height, floor area, and number of dwellings one exit may be permitted.

TRAVEL DISTANCE. Maximum distance between apartment entrance and stair doors is defined by travel distance. Codes also regulate the maximum length of dead-end corridors beyond the stairs. Inside the apartments the maximum distance betweeen the entry and the remotest part of the apartment is sometimes stated. In large apartments this might necessitate two entries.

STAIRS. Maximum riser height, minumum tread width, maximum number of risers between landings, landing width in relation to door swing, and fire rating of the stair shaft and its openings are defined. The code also determines whether any of the stairs can be open.

HORIZONTAL EXITS. The code regulates whether stairs on the ground level must open directly to the outside, whether they can have a horizontal fireproof corridor leading to the outside, or whether they can lead into a lobby.

RAMPS. In residential occupancies a ramp is a seldom-used means of egress. It is more important in the garage. The code limits the maximum degree of slope if the garage ramp is used as an exit.

SMOKEPROOF TOWER. A vestibule in front of the stair door which opens to an exterior balcony or to a vertical shaft that will draw the smoke from the corridor before it can enter the stair shaft proper. The code defines size and details of shaft and vestibule and determines whether both of the required exit stairs or only one must be a smokeproof tower and at what building height.

ENERGY CONSERVATION

Some codes have recently adopted energy conservation regulations that deal with the maximum amount of heat loss through the building envelope. Glass areas must be minimized and dual-glazed, and solid walls and roofs must have a high degree of thermal insulation. These regulations place severe limitations on exterior design, the consequences of which are far reaching.

Most codes have adopted special regulations to serve the handicapped. Some cities, or lending institutions, require that, in addition to the local code, the Life Safety Code (published by the National Fire Protection Association) be followed. Most cities—or the particular states in which they are located—have special regulations for the design of swimming pools and day care centers.

These rules by no means limit the agencies that may have jurisdiction over a project. They run from air pollution control to fire departments, street and highway departments, local park districts, and federal agencies such as aviation. When a building is constructed under federal mortgage insurance, minimum property standards must be followed. Regional HUD offices, state housing agencies, and local housing authorities have their own architectural staffs and consequently may have their own criteria for the architect to deal with.

Preliminary to understanding codes and regulations is the task of determining exactly what agencies have jurisdiction over a project and finding out whether they have set regulations.

BUDGET

It is easy to design a great museum or office building, but so very difficult to design good housing. I. M. Pei in *Architecture Plus*, March 1973.

It is difficult enough because of the severe limitations of function and the limited options of architectural form, but it is even more difficult because of budget. This is not to say that other types of building are not budgeted.

The apartment must be built to a lower cost per square foot than any other type of building except single-family houses and certain industrial buildings. As an example, a medium high-rise office building (without the office partitions) constructed by an owner-builder will cost at least 50 percent more than a medium highrise apartment project built also by an owner-builder, using the square foot or cubic foot basis as a standard for cost comparison. The apartment project will include all the partitioning as well as all kitchen and bathroom equipment. The reason why the builder can spend this difference on office buildings is that he can command two to three times the rent of an apartment project, again using the square foot as a comparable basis.[14]

Developers build apartment buildings in order to produce an income (or depreciation for tax calculations which for our purposes does not change the picture). The building itself is only one unknown, although the largest one, in a most complex economic equation, and slight variations of construction cost can have severe results in the last line of that equation called income.

The building must compete in the rental marketplace with all other living space being offered, and the only extra expense it may incur is for those items for which the tenant is willing to pay a premium. Although there has been a steady growth in apartments sponsored by nonprofit organizations, unions and religious groups, multi-family housing in the United States is profit motivated, and an attempt to satisfy this motivation must be made no matter what extra skill is asked in solving the problem. If the market analysis calls for an apartment that must rent for a maximum of $40 per room, any design that requires a potential rent of $50 per room is not economically feasible and must be revised to conform with the original rent limitation (assuming that the original rent limit estimate was an accurate and experienced one).[15]

In the semipublic or public sector budget is equally important. Buildings for which federally insured mortgages are provided at favorale rates and long amortization periods have an even lower construction cost limit than those that are privately financed. Budgets are somewhat higher in public housing because the equation does not have to show a return. One would hope that the lack of profit motivation would result in truly high quality public housing with sufficiently high construction budgets. This, however, is not the case, because public housing in the United States is not one of the main priorities and certainly must not give the impression of competing with the private sector.

Because cost of construction is so important, it is part of the data that must be looked at before the design process can start. Public agencies and well-experienced builder-developer clients will set bugdets without consulting the architect. Although this is unfortunate, it is essential that the architect be able to scrutinize these pre-established budgets unless he is planning to become a miracle worker. When budgets are set with the cooperation of the architect, he has no excuses.

At the top of the list is the proper definition of construction cost. Does it include the builder's profit, or in case of a builder-developer does it mean cost plus overhead only? By construction cost do they mean the bare building or are such items as appliances, corridor carpeting, landscaping, and furnishings in public areas included?

When a cost figure based on the square foot (the more common basis in housing) is established, it is usually related to the architect's or the developer's recent cost experience with similar building types, although we have to question how similar? It is certainly not enough that the building with which the cost figures were compared is also an apartment house. Before we can accept these cost figures, we have to consider all conditions to ensure that apples are not being compared with pears; for instance:

DATA GATHERING

1. One structure has small one-bedroom apartments and efficiencies and therefore a high proportion of partitions, kitchens, and bathrooms per square foot. It cannot be equated in cost with a building that contains larger two-bedroom apartments.
2. One project may need a large amount of site development, earth moving, and new roads; the other, on an urban site, will have few of these. In order to get a fair cost comparison, the cost of site development should be handled separately.
3. Soil and foundation conditions on two projects must be taken into consideration when comparing unit costs.
4. When we use the unit cost figures of a recent building of similar size, we still have to make certain that the two buildings—the recently completed and the proposed—will have similar mechanical systems, quality of exteriors, and amenities.
5. When two buildings are compared, they should also contain a similar size and kind of parking structure. A most important caveat! Because garage floors cost less than apartment floors, an apartment building with an enclosed, multilevel parking garage will cost less per average square foot (including garage area) than a similar building with open, on-grade parking, but the cost per apartment naturally will be considerably higher.
6. Comparison must be made in terms of location and time. Construction costs vary from city to city, a point that should be carefully considered. When we say that a building—on which we have based our estimate—cost so much, it is important to realize that we do not mean the year in which it was completed but the year in which it was bid or bought, probably two years before. Had it been bid at the date of completion, it is likely that it would have cost more. Similarly, the time that elapses between the setting of the budget and the actual date of bidding, or buying, is crucial, especially so because neither the architect nor the owner has control over the time it will take to obtain financing. Attention must be paid to a proper inflation factor.
7. When the cost of the building volume is discussed (per square foot or cubic foot), we must make sure that everyone concerned—owner, architect, and contractor—uses the same basis to establish the volume. The following tabulation illustrates a generally accepted way to deal with such controversial oddities as balconies, arcades, and developed decks.

When developers talk about the cost of an apartment building, for example 22 dollars/sf, they generally include in this figure the parking garage which has an ameliorating effect on the average square foot cost. In fact, the tower containing the apartments may cost as much as 26 or 27 dollars/sf, whereas the parking garage may only cost 10 or 12 dollars/sf.

It is equally important for the designer to be aware of how the average cost per square foot breaks down in trades or components of the building. Needless to say, this breakdown will vary from building to building. Two buildings are seldom identical. Still, though fraught with the danger of generalization, it is useful in order to show where the money goes.

Structural frame	22–30%
Plumbing, ventilation, heating, air conditioning, electrical	24–28%
Exterior skin	7–10%
Partitions	7–9%
Elevators	3–6%
Balance of trades	20–25%

The importance of design decisions regarding structural framing and mechanical systems cannot be overemphasized because the two together can constitute 50% or more of the building cost. In the balance the three major cost items that involve early and basic architectural decisions are the exterior skin, the partitions, and the elevators.

BUDGET

	Area	Floor Height	Volume
Penthouse	..............sf @	............ft =	..............cf
Tower			
a. Enclosed: Typical floor area × number of floors =	.............sf @	.............ft =	.............cf
b. Balconies: Floor area of all balconies on typical floor × number of floors; total multiplied by 0.5 =	.............sf @	.............ft =	.............cf
Intermediate Floor			
a. Enclosed floor area =	.............sf @	.............ft =	.............cf
b. Open area under tower multiplied by 0.66 =	.............sf @	.............ft =	.............cf
Base			
a. Enclosed floor area =	.............sf @	.............ft =	.............cf
b. Arcade floor area multiplied by 0.66 =	.............sf @	.............ft =	.............cf
Developed Roof Deck			
Area multiplied by 0.33 to 0.66, depending on extent of development =	.............sf @	.............ft =	.............cf
Basement Floor =	.............sf @	.............ft =	.............cf
Totals	.............sf		.............cf

Total square feet @ $... = total cost; total cost divided by number of apartments = cost per apartment.

COMPONENTS OF DESIGN—ARCHITECTURAL 2

John Macsai

Once the programming or data gethering has been completed the architect is ready to design. In the design process he will respond to the challenge of the program by utilizing his knowledge of the component elements of housing.

The more he knows about these elements, the easier his work will be. This is not to say that acquaintance with the component elements and experience in housing will ensure good design! However, to have the components at his fingertips will facilitate his design process considerably.

This knowledge is obtained in a variety of ways, from a variety of sources. Experience in housing, obviously the major source, is a storehouse of information. The less experienced designer will obtain his knowledge in study of other buildings, in books and magazines, and from his teammates and colleagues.

The purpose of the following chapters is to introduce these component elements. They are not a substitute for experience. They do not approximate the detailed data available in reference books. In the same manner, the structural and mechanical sections will not make the designer an engineer. They will, however, make his communication with the engineering consultants more meaningful.

THE APARTMENT

"If we believe that the object of architecture is to provide a framework for people's lives, then the rooms in our houses, and the relation between them, must be determined by the way we will live in them and move through them."[16] This statement is only partly valid. Only partly, for even though we research the potential users most carefully, we still do not know the persons who are to live there—as we try to know those for whom we may be designing a single family house. Individual families will live differently, even among the same economic, age, occupation, and ethnic groups. Therefore in an apartment building the spaces themselves must be simple and universal enough to adapt to a variety of life styles. As far as the movement through the apartment is concerned far more specific criteria can be established relying on basic circulation patterns that are valid for most living conditions.

A well-planned apartment provides maximum privacy for various activities and makes movement to any room possible without crossing another.

ENTERING THE APARTMENT

In inclement weather outer clothing should be taken off at the entrance and put away; umbrellas and boots should be stored to prevent dirtying the floors of other rooms; space should be provided to accommodate packages.

ENTERING WITH GROCERIES OR LEAVING WITH GARBAGE

Connection between entrance and kitchen should be as direct as possible; preferably through the entry hall and not the living space. A secondary entrance directly into the kitchen solves this problem ideally.

CHILDREN COMING IN FROM PLAY

Children should be able to reach the bathroom or their own rooms without crossing the living space.

DELIVERIES

Packages should be taken and paid for without having the delivery man enter the living space.

CHILDREN ENTERING WHILE ADULT ACTIVITY IS TAKING PLACE IN THE LIVING SPACE (OR VICE VERSA)

Children should be able to get to their bedrooms without crossing the living space.

PASSING FROM BEDROOM TO BATHROOM

It should not be necessary to cross the living space. Ideally, one should not be seen at all.

PASSING FROM KITCHEN TO BATHROOM

This should be done, if possible, without crossing the living space.

SERVING FROM KITCHEN TO DINING ROOM

Service should be as direct as possible without crossing any other space (except occasionally the entry hall).

Ideal circulation criteria are achieved by proper planning of the rooms around the core of the apartment, which consists of the entry hall and the bedroom corridor. In fact a well-planned apartment can be divided into two zones, living zone and sleeping zone, separated by the entry hall.

Neither this simple geometric division nor the ideal circulation pattern is always possible. Corner apartments, quadruplex walk-ups, and townhouses often require functional compromise to achieve economy.

Equally important as the relation of each room to the other is the relative position it occupies in relation to daylight and fresh air. Ideally, every room in an apartment should have exterior exposure to ensure light and air. To plan this way, however, would increase the perimeter of the building to an extent that no one could afford to build it. Therefore bathrooms, invariably, kitchens, often, and dining rooms, sometimes, are handled as interior spaces. This is possible because building codes allow bathrooms and kitchens to be mechanically ventilated, because an inside dining alcove is really an extension of the living space, and because the kitchen can be situated to borrow light from the living or dining room. Thus the apartment plan is divided into outer and inner zones. Naturally, units with double exposure—townhouses, duplex walk-ups, and exterior gallery-type buildings—can have kitchens and dining rooms in the outer zone without difficulty.

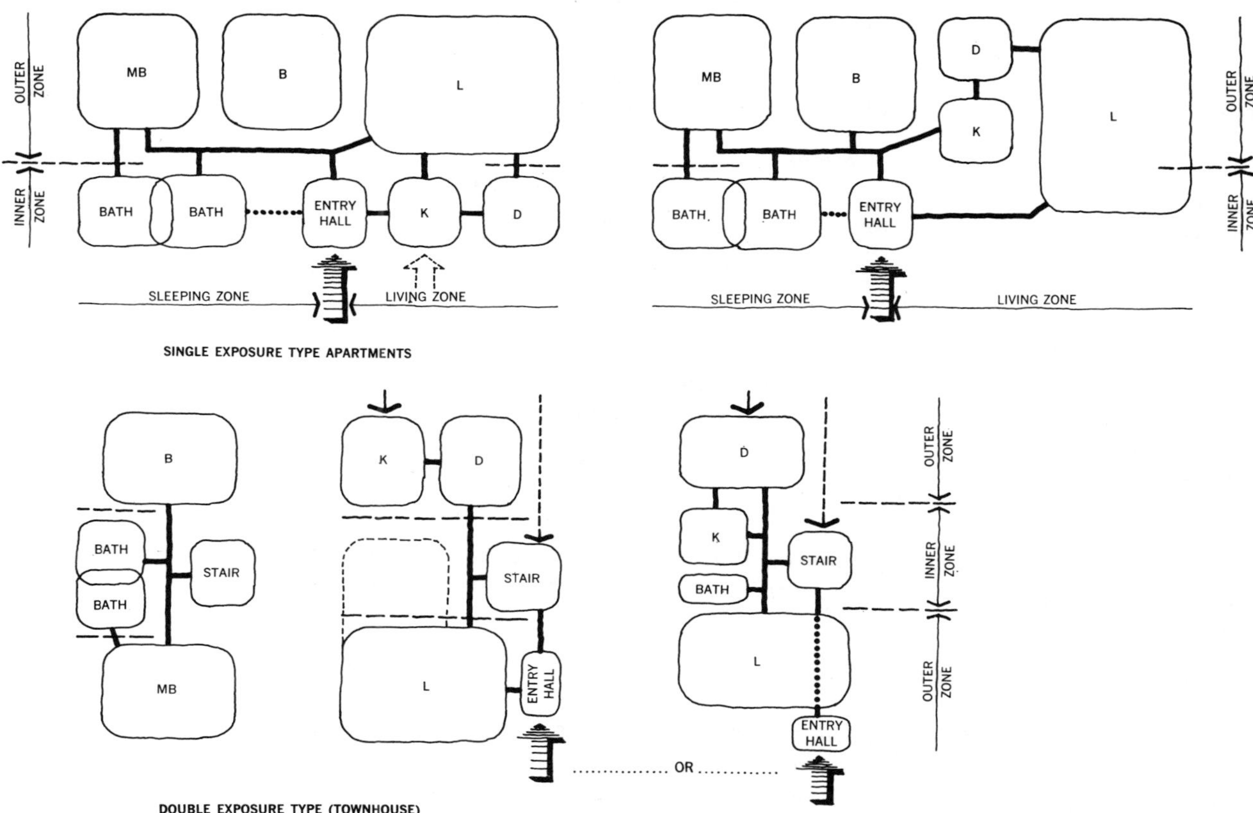

The approximate size and proportion of the rooms themselves must be included in the sponsor's program. Extreme care must be taken on public or federally assisted housing jobs because minimum dimensions given as guidelines cannot be accepted without scrutiny (see p. 26).

In the private building sector market conditions and competition are the best gauge of room sizes. Awareness of the local housing market is essential, for market conditions vary considerably not only from city to city but from neighborhood to neighborhood. As an example, the Chicago market demands a separate alcove as a defined dining space; in New York the entry hall is often substituted, thus serving a dual function and increasing the space allotted to the total living area. Considerably larger rooms are called for along Chicago's Lake Shore Drive than in Old Town, just a few blocks away.

The architect's most reliable guide is a thorough analysis of the function, furnishings, and circulation pattern of each space. In this respect HUD guidelines for minimum furniture requirements are quite reliable, assuming naturally that proper

Minimum Room Sizes

Name of Space	Minimum Area (sf)					Least Dimen-sion
	LU with 0-BR	LU with 1-BR	LU with 2-BR	LU with 3-BR	LU with 4-BR	
A. *Minimum Room Sizes for Separate Rooms*						
LR	NA	160	160	170	180	11′-0″
DR	NA	100	100	110	120	8′-4″
BR (primary)	NA	120	120	120	120	9′-4″
BR (secondary)	NA	NA	80	80	80	8′-0″
Total area, BR's	NA	120	200	280	380	—
B. *Minimum Room Sizes for Combined Spaces*						
LR-DA	NA	210	210	230	250	
LR-DA-SL	250	NA	NA	NA	NA	
LR-DA-K	NA	270	270	300	330	
LR-SL	210	NA	NA	NA	NA	
K-DA	100	120	120	140	160	

Abbreviations:

LU = living unit
LR = living room
DR = dining room
DA = dining area
0-BR = LU with no separate bedroom
K = kitchen
NA = not applicable
BR = bedroom
SL = sleeping area

circulation space is provided. To ensure comfortable use and adequate dimensions we can safely refer to *Time Saver Standards*, 4th edition (McGraw-Hill, New York, 1966).

LIVING ROOM (LIVING-DINING ROOM)

The living room should be conducive to general family life and should allow for group activities as well as individual relaxation: "entertaining, reading, writing, listening to music, watching television, and children's play."[16] HUD *Minimum Property Requirements* (1973 edition) calls for the following furniture as a minimum to be accommodated:

One couch, 3′-0″ x 6′-10″
Two easy chairs, 2′-6″ x 3′-0″
    (one for efficiency apartment)
    (three for four or more bedroom units)
One desk, 1′-8″ x 3′-6″
One desk chair, 1′-6″ x 1′-6″
One television set, 1′-4″ x 2′-8″
One table, 1′-6″ x 2′-6″

The living room is the most impressive and largest of all rooms in the apartment, which is why many developers like it to be visible from the entry hall.

To serve as a guide the living room in the average middle income two-bedroom apartment is about 260 to 300 sf; combined living-dining room is about 400 sf. When the living room is also used for dining, its proportions, with minimum waste, become critical. Typical square (20′ x 20′) living-dining rooms are far less efficient than the oblong (15′ x 26′) of the same square footage.

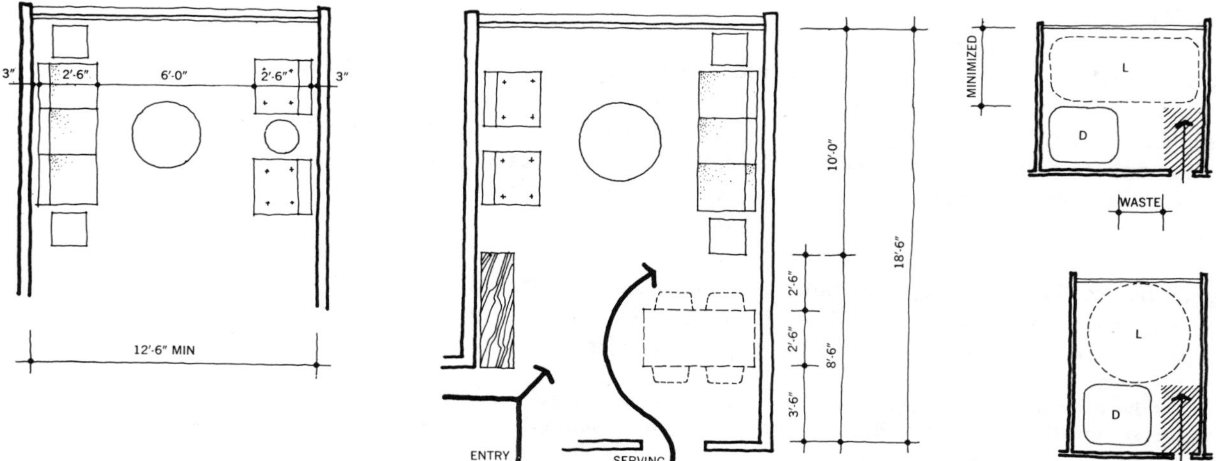

DINING

A truly separate dining room can be afforded only in townhouses or luxury housing. The most common arrangement takes the form of an alcove off the living room. Although this alcove can occupy an inner zone, a windowed area is preferable even though it creates a larger building perimeter and consequently increases costs. When a large group of diners is to be accommodated, the table must be expanded into the living room and space should be provided for it without having to move heavy furniture.

HUD *Minimum Property Standards* (1973 edition) calls for the table and chair requirements listed below. They should be considered not only with proper circulation space and pattern of food serving in mind but also in relation to space for storage.

Efficiency or one bedroom, two persons: 2′-6″ x 2′-6″
Two bedrooms, four persons: 2′-6″ x 3′-2″
Three bedrooms, six persons: 3′-4″ x 4′-0″ or 4′0″ round
Four or more bedrooms, eight persons: 3′-4″ x 6′-0″ or 4′-0″ x 4′-0″
Dining chairs: 1′-6″ x 1′-6″

In middle-income two-bedroom apartments an average dining alcove is about 100 sf and a separate dining room is about 140 sf.

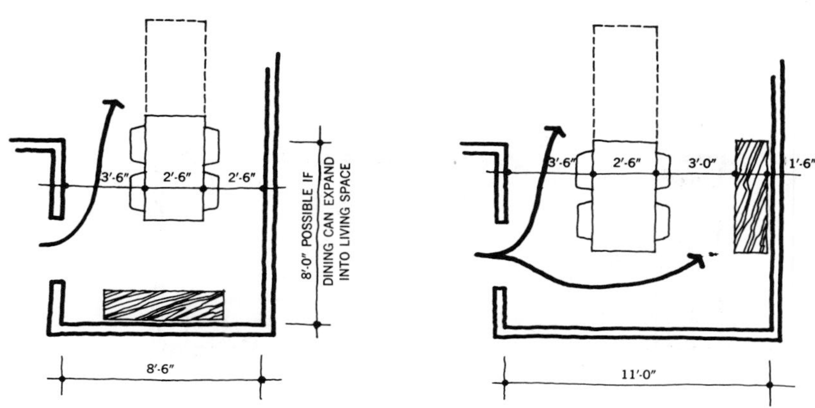

BALCONIES

There is much controversy about the need for balconies, which are costly, and it is questionable in profit-motivated housing whether they will result in increased rent or sales price. Besides the balcony's aesthetic factor (it allows strong articulation) and its symbolic significance (a visible indication of the presence of human beings), its functional role has pros and cons. Those who argue for it stress the delight of sitting outdoors when the weather is pleasant. Its proponents call attention to the visual extension of the living space, to extra storage space, and to the opportunity to grow plants. Those who oppose balconies claim that they cut off daylight, that they are dirt catchers and hard to keep clean, and in many regions can be used only part of the year. Balconies are most popular in Europe:

> . . . every dwelling should have some outdoor space—a terrace, loggia or balcony to enable the occupiers to sit or stay outside the enclosed living space. Even if the balcony can only be used for a few days or weeks of the year, it enables the town dweller, deprived of his association with the open countryside, to escape even in a block of flats from the artificial climate of his dwelling—albeit, as in inclement weather, for a moment only.[19]

Balconies must be wide enough for proper use (not less than 5 ft) and have adequate privacy.

KITCHEN

To provide for the most efficient food preparation, storage, and service, careful planning is required. *Architectural Graphic Standards* (6th edition) Ramsey and Sleeper (Wiley, New York, 1970) is an excellent guide and HUD *Minimum Property Standards* (1973 edition) contains useful information on dimensional requirements for counter tops, fixtures, and storage cabinets (see p. 29). Storage space normally provided in cabinets or utility closets can be expanded by the addition of shallow pantries: floor to ceiling shelving behind hinged doors.

Unless space is extremely tight, kitchens should be equipped with a small eating space to augment the regular dining room or alcove. When the kitchen is part of a combined kitchen-dining or kitchen-family room, the food preparation-cooking space should be screened from the dining or family area. When planning kitchens, the basic sequence of refrigerator-sink-stove, starting from the door and progressing toward the serving and eating areas, should be observed. The method of connecting with the dining room or alcove, pass-through or door, needs special attention. Well-planned kitchens in an inner zone should borrow daylight from the living or dining space to make working conditions in the kitchen pleasanter.

In a middle-income two-bedroom apartment an average kitchen with minimum eating space is about 100 sf.

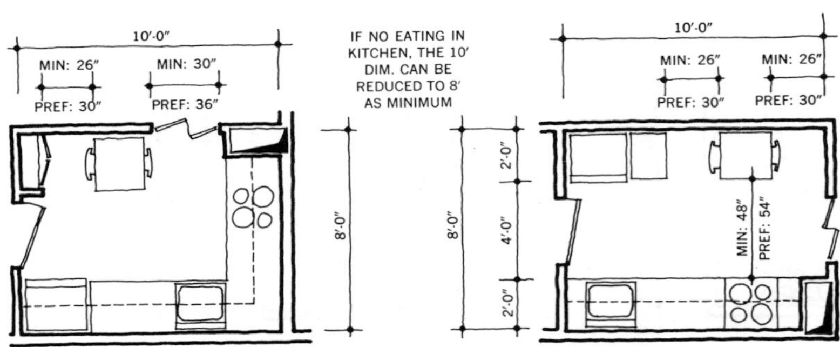

COUNTERTOPS AND FIXTURES

	Number of Bedrooms				
	0	1	2	3	4
Work Center	Minimum Frontages (lin in.)				
Sink	18	24	24	32[a]	32[a]
Countertop, each side	15	18	21	24	30
Range or cooktop space	21	21	24	30	30
Countertop, one side	15	18	21	24	30
Refrigerator space	30	30	36	36	36
Countertop, one side	15	15	15	15	18
Mixing countertop	21	30	36	36	42

[a] When a dishwasher is provided, a 24-in. sink is acceptable.

STORAGE AREA[b]

	Number of Bedrooms				
Square Feet	0	1	2	3	4
Minimum shelf area	24	30	38	44	50
Minimum drawer area	4	6	8	10	12

[b] Wall cabinets over refrigerators and shelves above 74 in. shall not be counted as required storage area.

BEDROOM

Each bedroom should have enough space for double occupancy unless the client specifically agrees to its single use. HUD *Minimum Property Standards* (1973 edition) calls for the following basic furniture:

Two twin beds, 3′-3″ x 6′-10″
One dresser, 1′-6″ x 4′-4″
One chair, 1′-6″ x 1′-6″
One crib, 2′-6″ x 4′-6″

It should be kept in mind that night tables must also be accommodated. Because the bedroom often serves as an extra work area, space for a sewing machine or writing desk is not a luxury.

In middle-income two-bedroom apartments average bedroom sizes (exclusive of closets are 150 sf for secondary bedroom and 180 sf for master bedrooms (see p. 30).

BATHROOMS

For the sake of economy a back-to-back arrangement of bathrooms is preferred either in the same apartment or with one that is adjacent. When there is only one bathroom, a tub and shower combination is standard equipment; when there are two, the second usually contains a stall shower. When an apartment has two or more bathrooms, one is customarily attached to the master bedroom; the others

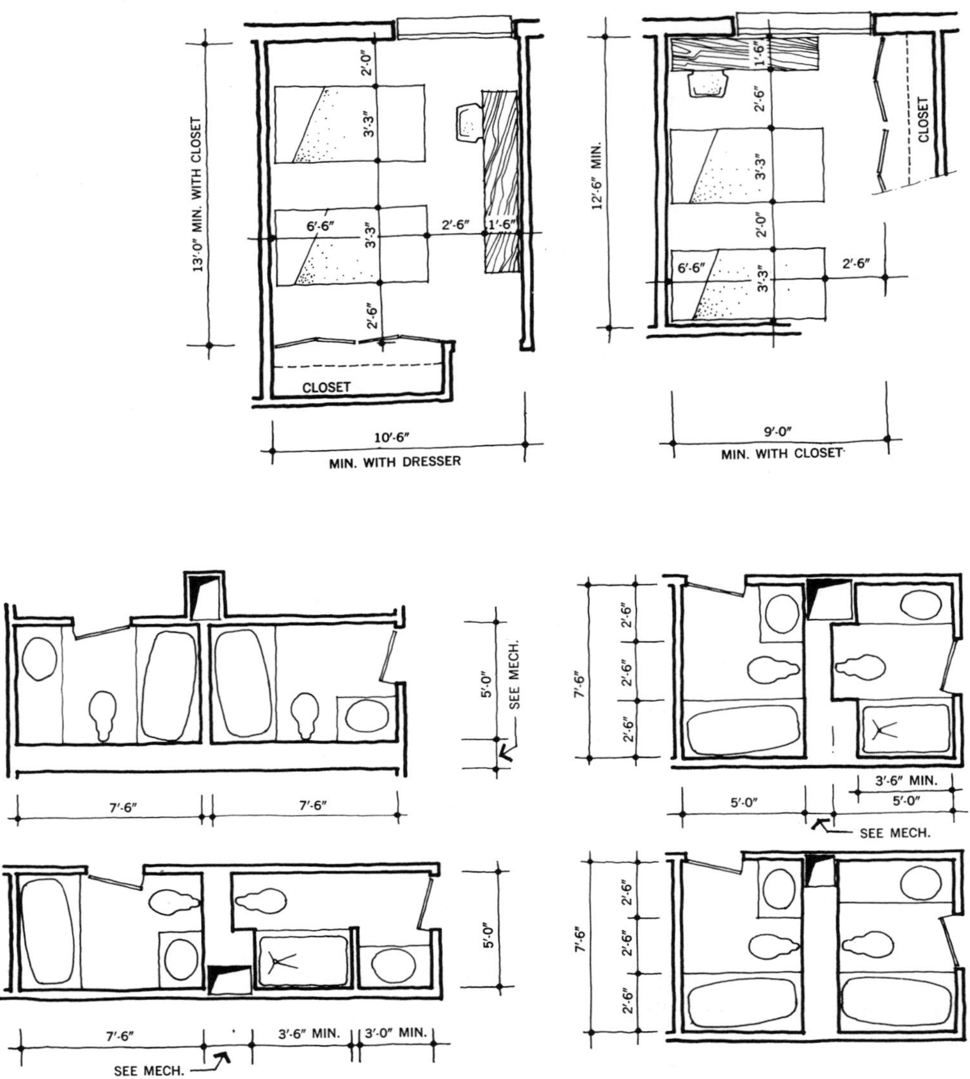

serve the remaining bedrooms. A powder room or lavatory is sometimes substituted for the second bathroom, although the savings are nominal compared with the convenience of having two baths. In luxury housing compartmentalization is an advantage that allows simultaneous multiple use. *Architectural Graphic Standards* (6th edition) Ramsey and Sleeper (Wiley, New York, 1970) is a useful planning guide; for innovative ideas Alexander Kira's *The Bathroom* (Grosset & Dunlap, New York, 1967) is unsurpassed.

CLOSETS

Although overall apartment size is stated in a client's program, few clients pay attention in the early design stages to the amount and kind of closet space that is provided. It is generally accepted however, that it is never enough for the tenant or buyer. The tabulation that follows is a guide to closet sizes at various rental levels.

	Depth	Length (linear feet)[a] Low Rental	Middle	Luxury	HUD minimum
Guest closet (in or near entry hall)	2′3″	3′	4′	5′	2′
Utility closet (in or near kitchen)	2′0″	2′	2′	2′	2′
Pantry (in kitchen)	8 to 10″	—	—	4′	—
Linen closet (in bedroom hall)	1′6″	2′	2 to 3′	3 to 4′	1′6″
Master bedroom closet (in bedroom)	2′3″	8′	10′	12′	5′
Second bedroom closet (in bedroom)	2′3″	6′	8′	9′	3′
General storage closet (in entry or bedroom hall)	2′0″	—	—	4′	—

[a] Or equivalent linear feet in a walk-in closet.

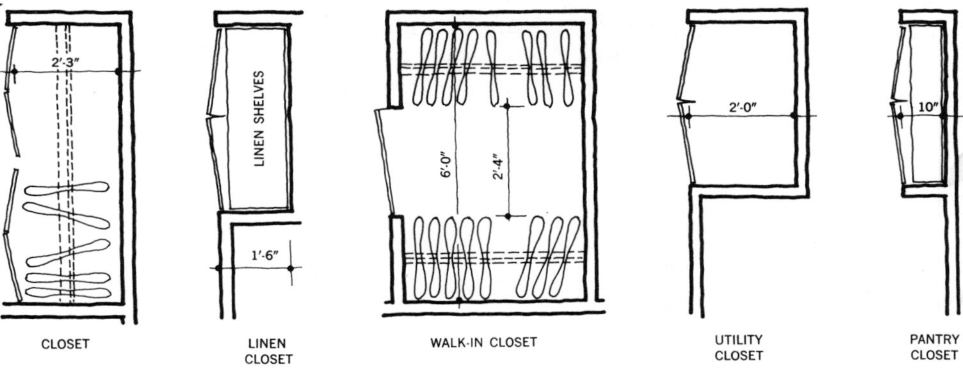

ENTRY HALL

The precise function of the entry hall should be stipulated. Is it merely for circulation or for other uses as well? For example, if it is to be used for telephoning, a small desk will be required. It might also become an extension of the living room and made large enough for dining.

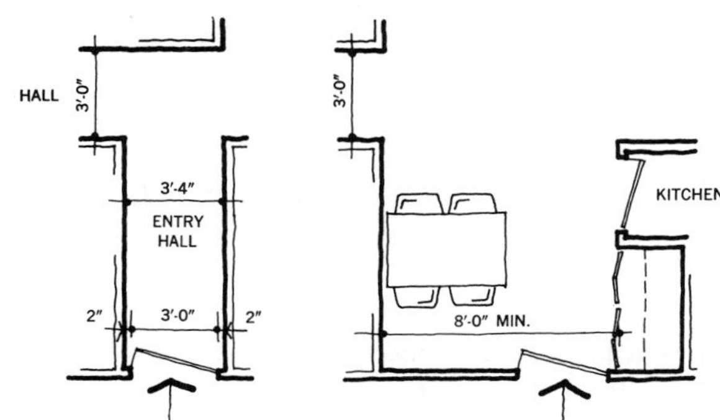

Certain building codes require that large apartments have two exits to the public corridor and that access be made easy to either one without having to pass through the bedrooms. The ideal location for the second exit is in the kitchen (though it may make its planning more difficult). In this case the connection between the regular entry hall and the kitchen may be eliminated. The second exit, depending on the local code, may also open directly onto the stair landing (with "B" label door), though not when the stair is a smokeproof tower.

EFFICIENCY APARTMENTS

In efficiency apartments not only room functions but circulation patterns present different problems. Because one space serves for living, dining, and sleeping, precise demarcation is difficult. Still, an attempt must be made to define these areas. The kitchen is usually considerably smaller than those found in regular apartments, and because there is no bedroom the bedroom-closet should serve as a walk-in dressing room.

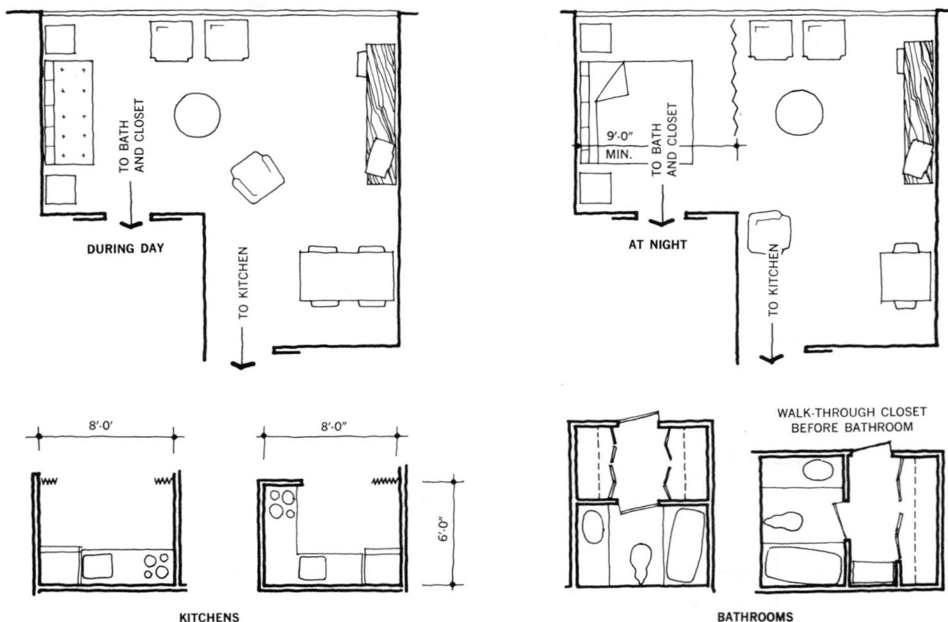

Obviously there is a close relation between room sizes and the total dimensions of the apartment. As a rule of thumb all room areas (living, dining, bedrooms), kitchen, bathrooms, (but not entry hall), and closet spaces can be added to reach a total that should constitute 80 to 85% of the gross size, leaving 15 to 20% for circulation (entry hall, bedroom corridor), walls, columns, and shafts. Efficiency apartments naturally have less circulation space. In two-story apartments the space occupied on each floor by the stairs should also be taken into consideration as circulation space. It should be kept in mind that the most efficient apartment is not necessarily the largest but one that has the largest rooms within the smallest gross square-foot area and therefore the smallest possible circulation space. Although good, differentiated circulation is important, it should be handled with a minimum of wasted space.

What one developer considers a small apartment another may find medium; what would be considered medium in a plush suburb may be placed in the luxury class in Greenwich Village. Nevertheless, it is possible within the broadest parameters to propose some guidelines (the HUD minimums in the following table were arrived at by adding up HUD minimum room sizes and closets and adding 20% to them for circulation):

	Gross Size			
Unit	Low	Medium	Luxury	HUD minimum
Efficiency (1 bath)	450	500 to 550	600+	380
1-bedroom (1 bath)	650	700 to 800	900+	580
2-bedroom (2 baths)	950	1100 to 1200	1250+	750
3-bedroom (2 baths)	1,250	1350 to 1450	1600+	900

It is useful to know how apartment sizes are figured: from the exterior face of the exterior wall (in condominiums) and from the interior face of the exterior wall (in rentals) to the center line of the corridor partition, and from center line to center line of party walls (partitions between the apartments). Balconies are not included in these dimensions.

Apartments for the elderly fall into a special category. These apartments are generally small (550 sf for one bedroom is not unusual) and are mostly one-bedroom units or efficiencies. This limited size demands taut, imaginative planning. Because of the frequent use of wheel chairs, wider doors (2 ft 8 in) are used throughout the apartment, including the bathroom, and bedrooms should be furnished to permit clear passage around each bed. Bathroom layouts are for ease of wheelchair manipulation and kitchen cabinets are built to be reached with minimum bending and stretching. Because many of the elderly are tied to their apartments for long periods, northern orientation—in which no sunlight can reach the interior—should be avoided. For general philosophy as well as details, *Housing the Elderly* issued by the Central Mortgage and Housing Corporation, Canada, is an excellent guide.

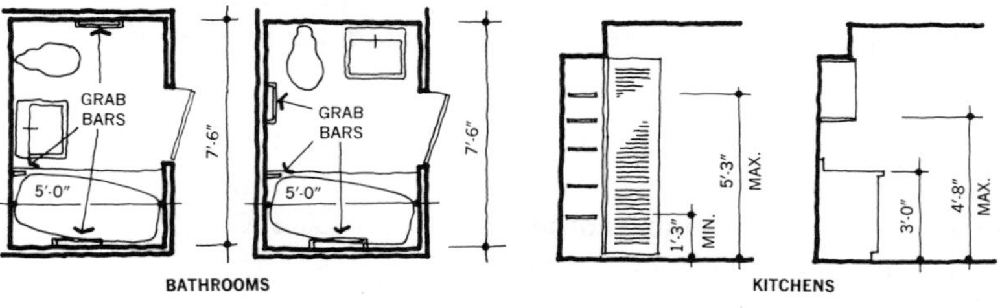

BATHROOMS

KITCHENS

SEPARATORS-CONNECTORS

Apartments are separated vertically by floors and horizontally by party walls. Their rooms are defined by partitions, the purpose of which is not only physical and visual demarcation, but also protection, at least for a specified period of time, in case of fire; they also reduce noise transmission.

The building code regulates the required fire rating of all floors and partitions. The publications of the Underwriters' Laboratories contain information that is based on various tests of floor and partition assemblies. Literature published by the manufacturers of gypsum-board partition systems, the most commonly used in housing today, provides additional data on fire ratings.

A far more complex problem is the reduction of noise transmission. The best planned, most generously sized apartment becomes unlivable and a constant source of irritation if its privacy is inadequate. Because proper sound separation results in increased construction cost, some builders have tried to minimize the problem, but many lenders set their own requirements in order to protect their investments.

Sound is basically of two kinds: airborne and impact. Airborne sound has its source in the human voice, television, and hi-fi and is transmitted through the air. Impact sound originates when an object in motion comes in contact with the structure and causes it to vibrate. The sound-isolating qualities of walls and floors are expressed in STC (Sound Transmission Class) for airborne sound and in IIC (Impact Insulation Class) for impact noise. Obviously the higher the class rating, the better the results.

As far as partitions are concerned, the danger lies in airborne sound. When heavy masonry walls were used to separate apartments, the problem was much simpler because mass or density is still the best control. In bearing-wall buildings the load-bearing partitions are excellent sound insulation, as are the reinforced concrete shear walls in highrises. In today's stud partition, with its small mass, the air space between the two layers plays an important role. Naturally, adding to the density of the gypsum board layers will improve the rating but under the law of diminishing return. The addition of sound-attenuating blankets in the air space helps considerably.

HUD *Minimum Property Standards*, 1973 edition, and manufacturers' literature recommend STC ratings. With HUD these ratings vary if the background noise is low or high; that is, if it helps to reduce the airborne sound. Background noise is a tricky problem. To be effective it must be steady. Although the difference in noise levels between a downtown and a rural location is unquestionable, an acoustical engineer must be consulted if one is to rely on masking. This, of course, is a wise procedure in general except under the most routine conditions.

In arriving at recommended STC ratings, some manufacturers rate differently for low-, middle-, and high-income families. Such differentiation is unacceptable because it equates tenant sensitivity with income. Privacy should be equally available to all occupants.

The following STC ratings and illustrations reflect good, generally accepted practice (when adjacent to noisy mechanical equipment STC should be increased by 5):

Between apartment and apartment (party wall)	55 STC
Between apartment and corridor	50 STC
Within apartment between bedroom and another room	50 STC
between bathroom and another room	40 STC
between other rooms	40 STC

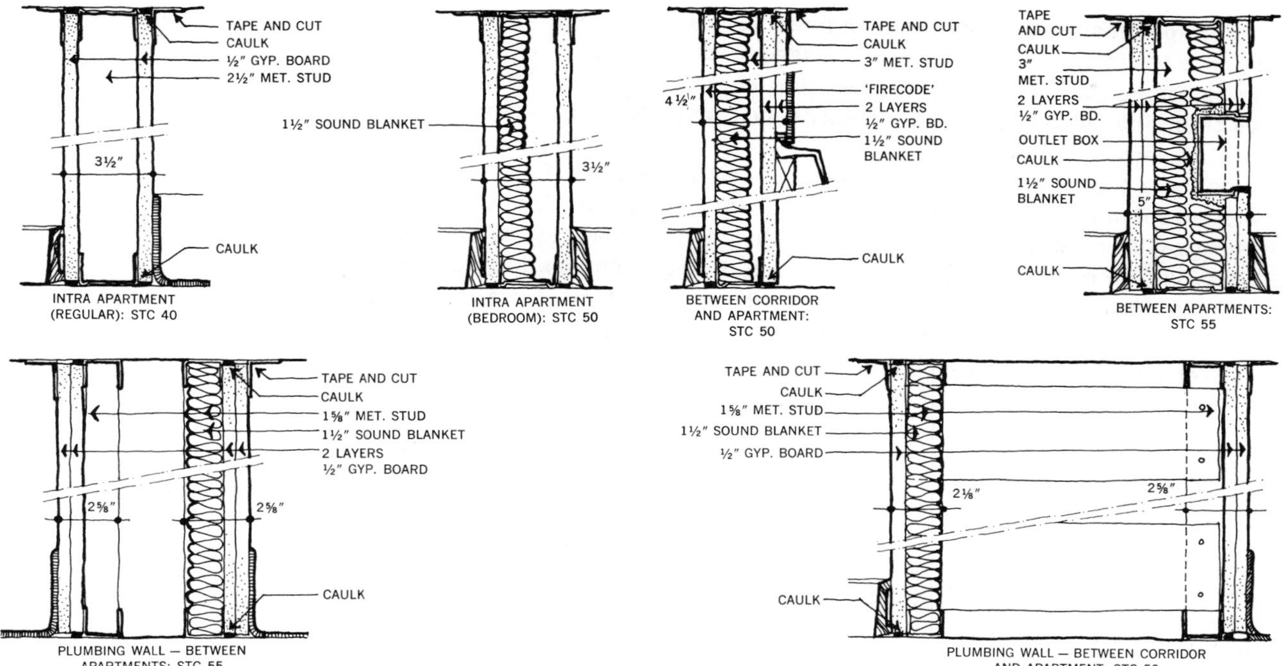

INTRA APARTMENT (REGULAR): STC 40

INTRA APARTMENT (BEDROOM): STC 50

BETWEEN CORRIDOR AND APARTMENT: STC 50

BETWEEN APARTMENTS: STC 55

PLUMBING WALL — BETWEEN APARTMENTS: STC 55

PLUMBING WALL — BETWEEN CORRIDOR AND APARTMENT: STC 50

The effectiveness of the best partitions can be destroyed by poor detailing and workmanship. Most critical are the boundary details where walls meet the floor and ceiling. Carefully placed caulking beads are essential. Another area of danger is wall piercing for pipes and electrical outlets. Outlets in party walls must be solidly caulked and should never occur back-to-back. The largest penetration of the wall takes place in bathrooms at the grilles of common exhaust ducts and at recessed medicine cabinets. These cabinets should be surface-mounted rather than recessed and sound baffles should be installed in the ducts between bathroom grilles.

In concrete highrises in which the exterior columns are exposed there is movement of columns and slab edges as the outdoor temperature changes. This structural movement, called racking, causes partitions to crack and separate from the structural slab, especially when they occur between exterior and interior columns (tied on both ends). This racking action is worse on the upper floors of highrises. Another cause of cracking and separation is midspan deflection. Both problems can be ameliorated by using slip joints between partitions and slabs and control joints between partitions and columns, thus allowing the structure to move independently and preventing cracks and shielding separation—that is, maintaining the integrity of partitions as sound isolators.

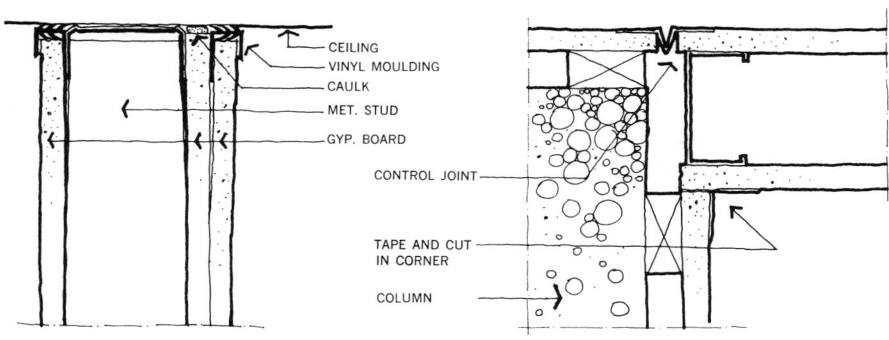

For floor construction the issue of mass versus air space in relation to airborne sounds is similar to the problems discussed in relation to partitions. Here, however, impact noise, caused by walking, dropping objects, or moving furniture, must also be taken into account. Mass or density is no great advantage in controlling it. The best remedy is cushioning.

As far as STC is concerned 55 is ideal but seldom reached. Ratings in the low 50s are acceptable, but in the high 40s complaints can occur. The low 40s are poor. The ideal IIC rating of 70 is hardly ever reached. Satisfactory results can be obtained with 60 IIC in bedrooms, 55 IIC in living and dining rooms, and 50 IIC in kitchens.

The following chart lists STC and IIC ratings for the most common floor constructions. The ratings are rather pessimistic, assuming not the highest quality of workmanship, especially in multilayered assemblies.

Construction Type		STC	STC With Blankets and Resilient Clips Added	IIC	IIC With Blankets and Resilient Clips Added
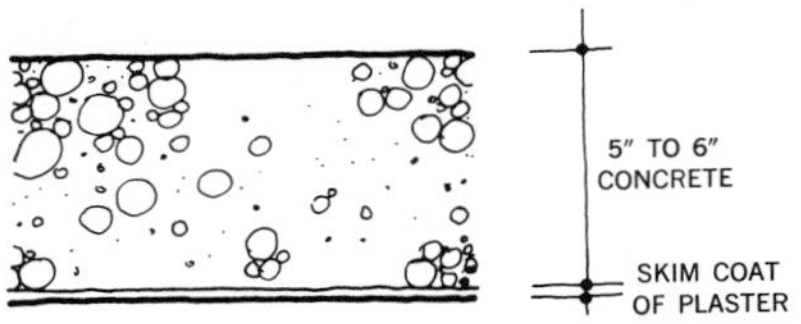 5″ TO 6″ CONCRETE; SKIM COAT OF PLASTER	w/carpet	48		65	
	w/⅛″ resilient tile on underlayment	48		40	
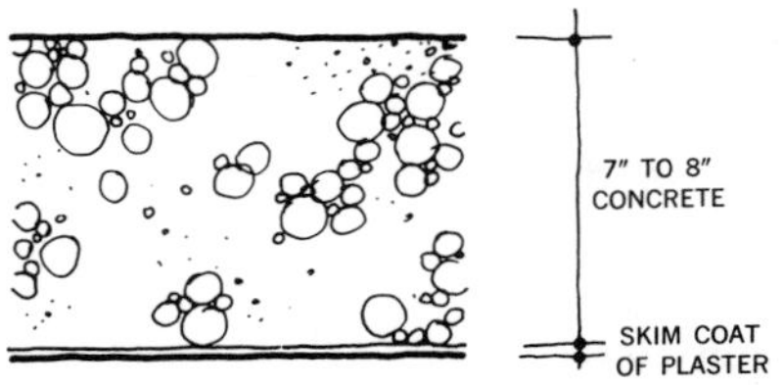 7″ TO 8″ CONCRETE; SKIM COAT OF PLASTER	w/carpet	51		66	
	w/⅛″ resilient tile on underlayment	51		44	
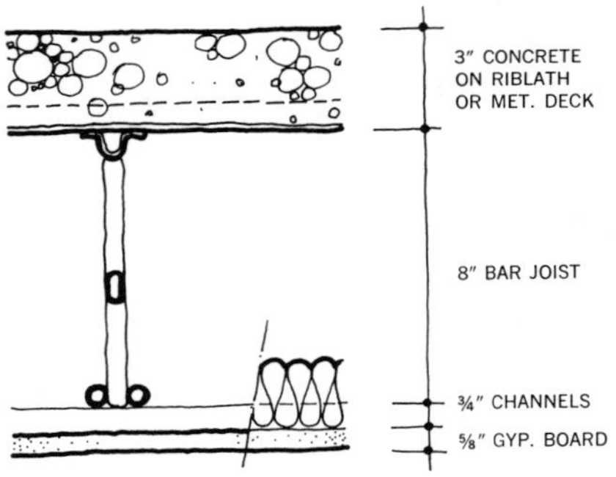 3″ CONCRETE ON RIBLATH OR MET. DECK; 8″ BAR JOIST; ¾″ CHANNELS; ⅝″ GYP. BOARD	w/carpet	48	56	63	68
	w/⅛″ resilient tile on underlayment	48	56	38	52
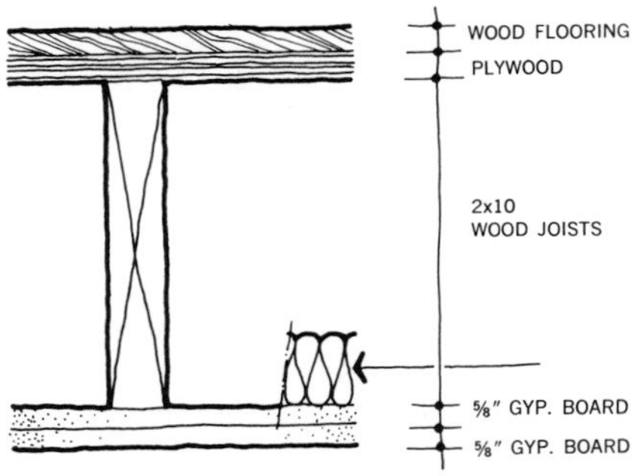 WOOD FLOORING; PLYWOOD; 2x10 WOOD JOISTS; ⅝″ GYP. BOARD; ⅝″ GYP. BOARD	w/carpet	40	52	55	63
	w/⅛″ resilient tile on underlayment	40	52	35	48

The danger of poor performance (especially STC) is greatest in multilayered structures involving joints: inadvertent leaks and rigid ties where connections are meant to be resilient. Best reliability is achieved with concrete slabs. Obviously the IIC ratings are greatest when the floors are carpeted. The figure given in the chart is a generalization and it should not be forgotten that appreciable differences exist between carpet-pad combinations and tile underlayments. STC is not affected by the floor finish.

As partitions are the separators between apartment spaces, doors are the connectors. They should function and be sized according to the purpose they serve.

Apartment entrance doors are generally 3 ft wide and most codes require a one-hour fire rating ("C" label) and self-closers. Bathroom doors are 2 ft 4 in. wide and doors to bedrooms are 2 ft 6 in. or 2 ft 8 in. wide. In plans for the elderly bathroom and bedroom doors are 2 ft 8 in. All are hinged. The door between kitchen and dining space presents a unique problem. Flexibility for swinging in each travel direction is desirable and a pair of double-acting doors is ideal in a 3 ft opening. Occasionally half doors ("dutch door," "bar door") borrow daylight from the dining space. Pocket-type sliding doors may save swing space but are hard to operate and should be avoided. The wall between kitchen and dining is sometimes entirely eliminated (based on market preference). This condition lends itself to the creation of a counter-type eating space and to an accordion-type door. Occasionally the connection between kitchen and dining is only a serve-through opening.

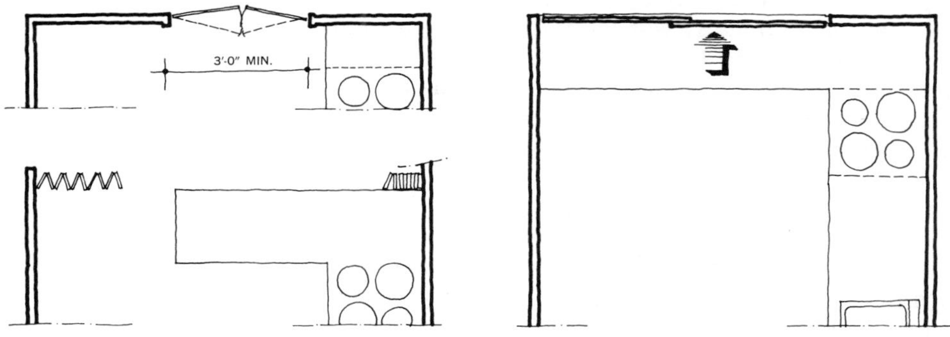

For closets the most commonly used door is the bifolding type (sliding doors limit the closet opening to half.) These doors, in contrast to standard hinged doors, do not require frames; a simple cased opening with ceiling track is adequate. Walk-in closets enjoy wide market preference; their standard hinged door width can be reduced to 2 ft 2 in. The walk-through dressing closets of efficiency apartments are generally equipped with bifolding doors in front of the hanging space.

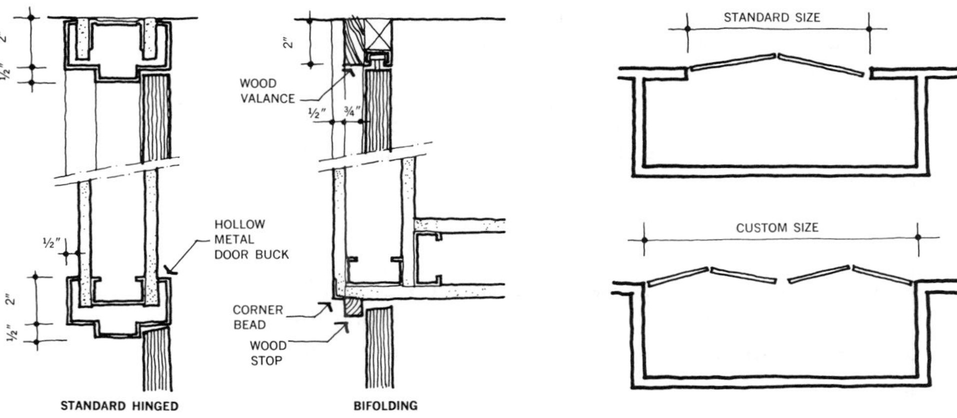

FIRE SAFETY

The floors of a multistory apartment building (and in this sense more than one floor is multistory) are connected vertically by stairs or stairs and elevators.

Although stairs in walk-ups and elevators in buildings of more than three stories serve both tenants and freight, they also play an important role when fire erupts: stairs provide an escape route for evacuation and elevators carry the firemen quickly to the source of the fire.

Fire safety is an ever-increasing concern when larger and larger numbers of people live in proximity and the threat to human life is heightened. Although statistically there has been far less loss of life by fire in highrises than in smaller buildings, the potential threat of a large number of people trapped in a highrise fire is ever-present. Notwithstanding the extensive fire safety regulations of present codes, most cities are in the process of writing special ordinances for highrises because of the panic caused by front-page publicity given the occasional highrise fire. The tendency has been to go overboard, whether for political reasons or to satisfy the sprinkler manufacturers' lobby, with little regard to the increase in already sky-high construction costs.

In order to understand the real need for stairs and elevators in a fire—and to help architects sitting on the committees that draft new ordinances—several excellent studies have been prepared by National Loss Control Service Corp., specialists in fire safety. Much of the foregoing is excerpted from their report (prepared in 1971 for the Twin Oak Towers in Oak Park, Illinois) with grateful acknowledgment.

In case of fire special problems are related to the highrise structure. It is "beyond the reach of fire department aerial equipment," it "poses a potential for significant stack or chimney effect (vertical air movement due to temperature differential)," and it "requires unreasonable evacuation time."

FIRE PROPAGATION AND SPREAD

"The problems associated with fire propagation and spread in a building are not unique to high rise buildings but apply to all buildings." These problems—compartmentation and protection of vertical shafts by fire-rated floors, walls, and doors, limitation of interior finishes, and so on,—are well covered by existing building codes.

SMOKE AND COMBUSTION PRODUCTS PROPAGATION

Unquestionably, smoke spread is the single most significant life hazard existing at the time of a fire in a high rise building. The movement of large quantities of smoke to areas remote from the fire is due to a number of factors including stack effect, ventilation system arrangements and interfloor leakage. Vertical shafts for stairs, elevators, and utilities are primary avenues of smoke spread. Smoke can cause serious physical effects on building occupants, can block exitways and obscure exit signs, and can force evacuation from portions of the building far from the fire with resultant overloading of exits and rescue problems.

Smoke spread can be expected even in buildings which have a complete installation of automatic sprinklers because of the normal time lag associated with the heat activated sprinkler heads and because the contents and furnishings of high rise buildings are capable of producing relatively large volumes of smoke prior to the operation of the sprinklers. Complete or partial failure of a sprinkler system is also possible due to closed water supply valves, painted heads, inoperative fire pumps, fire shielded from the sprinkler head discharge, etc.

There are several ways to remedy this situation. Overpressurization of public corridors will prevent the smoke from billowing from the apartment in which the fire has its source. Tamperproof automatic closers on all apartment entry doors will also help to keep corridors smokefree. This is in addition to making a smokeproof tower of one or both stairways, traditionally required by building codes.

OCCUPANT EVACUATION CONSIDERATIONS

At the time of a fire, a number of unique evacuation problems exist in a highrise building. In a residential building, the detection of a fire is frequently delayed as many of the occupants are either sleeping or at work a good portion of the day. Evacuation is further complicated by the fact that building codes do not require an effective means for notifying building occupants of a fire or, more importantly, what to do at the time of such an emergency.

Stairways, the traditional means for building evacuation, are normally designed to handle only a population load equal to the floor level having the highest number of persons based on the assumption that only a single floor needs to be evacuated. Thus, at the time of a fire, only a few floors can be simultaneously evacuated without seriously overcrowding the stairs. In addition, these stairs may become smoke filled due to the stack effect existing in the building.

It is also important to note that when a building height exceeds about twenty-five stories, total evacuation becomes impractical due to the excessive time needed to descend from such a height and the physical stress imposed on even a healthy individual.

Naturally, complete evacuation is seldom required. What is more important is an area of refuge. In fact, an apartment itself—surrounded by fire rated floors and walls—can be safe enough until the arrival of the fire department. Even greater safety is provided by balconies.

FIRE CONTROL PROBLEMS

Fire control in a highrise building can be effected either automatically, as by installed fire extinguishing systems, or manually, by the fire department. Usually fire department actions are also required to aid the automatic systems to effect extinguishment.

Automatic fire suppression has been utilized to only a limited extent to date in highrise buildings. While automatic sprinklers have been quite effective in controlling fires in many types of conventional buildings, their installation in highrise structures is relatively costly for several reasons and poses definite design problems, particularly for apartment buildings where a suspended ceiling is not normally provided.

The physical demands placed on a fire department in a highrise building fire are much more severe than that of a similar fire in a low building. Just getting to the fire floor high above the street level may be difficult or impossible if elevators are not available or are inoperative.

Ventilation of heat and smoke, an important fire control procedure, is often quite difficult in a highrise fire and greatly complicates firefighting operations.

Where effective means are not provided for communicating with building occupants, often the fire department must deploy already overtaxed manpower to individually notify occupants and direct evacuation. This can require more men than are needed for actual extinguishment of the fire itself. In addition, the internal communication system of the fire department may be ineffective because radio transmissions often will not reach outside the building due to the shielding effects of the structural frame.

Building codes call for water availability on the exterior of the building near the entrance (siamese connections) and standpipes with firehose in the stairways and corridors. Firemen, however, prefer to use their own hose; those along the standpipes may be old and brittle and at best are good enough only for fighting small fires until the fire department arrives.

Most codes do not include, but should seriously consider, the following equipment:

Sensors in every apartment with direct connection to the fire department.

A voice communication system on all floors capable of being operated either selectively or on all floors together, from a central location in the first floor lobby.

A system of sound-powered telephone circuits paralleling the standpipe risers for the use of the fire department for fire scene command and control purposes.

Elevator controls arranged so that actuation of an emergency switch on the first floor will cause all elevators to disregard any floor calls and respond only to the first floor and remain there until returned to service. A light indicating that the elevators are out of service should show on each floor near the elevator call buttons. The freight elevator should be designated for fire department use, with all appropriate manual controls.

Highly dependable secondary source of emergency power supply for:

a. Fire department elevator
b. Fire pump
c. Air handling units for corridor air supply
d. Exit signs and exit lighting
e. Internal communications system

An emergency Command and Communication Center for Fire Department use in the first floor lobby of each building and equipped as follows:

a. Fire detector annunciator panel
b. Emergency tenant communication system
c. Floor plans of each floor
d. Sound-powered phone handsets
e. Keys for stair doors
f. Elevator emergency controls
g. Standpipe water pressure gauge

The one factor, other than carelessness, that causes maximum loss of life is panic. Most tenants do not know what to do when fire breaks out in their own apartments or when they smell smoke from a neighboring one. Most are unaware that elevators are not to be used or that escape is to be made via the stairs—assuming that they know where the nearest staircase is located. Proper tenant education, rarely attempted by management, should be a requirement for renewal of occupancy permits!

Many cities from New York to San Francisco have already revised their building codes to include special sections on highrise fire protection, as have some states in which a central code covers all construction. Highrise in this context starts at 60 to 80 ft, depending on the reach of the fire department's equipment. Several cities which are considering revision and others which have not yet done so will be pushed toward adoption by the impact created by recent trashy though effective bestsellers and the movie "Towering Inferno." All this in spite of statistics (in Chicago "93 percent of fire deaths in 1973 occurred in buildings under 80 ft"), in spite of the fact that "the typical concrete apartment structure is divided into small one hour rated compartments already," that "each apartment has its own air-handling system, so smoke spread is far less of a problem than in centralized office buildings," and also that "windows are generally movable sash, so venting is possible."[20]

Some of the new requirements are wise: automatic closers on corridor-to-apartment doors, central control station for the fire department, automatic products-of-combustion detection system, automatic recall of elevators, voice communication system for the fire department, and emergency electrical systems. What does go overboard is the requirement that automatic sprinkler systems be installed.

Because of the high cost of sprinkler systems, most codes permit alternate methods of fire prevention or what is commonly called trade-offs; the most usual of which is compartmentation. It is essential that designers understand clearly what it means and how it is interpreted by local building officials.

What we have presented here about stair, elevator, and corridor design is valid in locations in which no highrise fire ordinance has been passed, and even when one has been adopted it is valid for buildings under highrise height (as defined by the fire ordinance).

In order to avoid confusion, though it may seem like jumping the gun, compartmentation possibilities are covered in this chapter with the caveat that later chapters on stair, elevator, and corridor design should be read with such requirements in mind when the building is covered by a special highrise fire ordinance.

Although the idea of compartmentation varies from code to code, there are some constants. The most common method of compartmentation calls for continuous vertical two-hour-rated partitions which divide each floor into two or more compartments in an area ratio not to exceed 3 to 1 and in which each area is not to exceed a prescribed square footage. In apartment buildings, by necessity of limited floor space, this means two compartments. Naturally each compartment must have a separate corridor air-supply system and each must contain one set of stairs, but because the code requires two means of egress the two-hour-rated partition, when it intersects the corridor, must have "B" label doors in each travel direction. These doors, if kept open, must have magnetic hold-open devices activated by electronic sensors responding to the products of combustion.

Because each compartment must have a separate enclosed stair case, the use of scissor-stairs in buildings covered by highrise fire ordinances is prohibited.

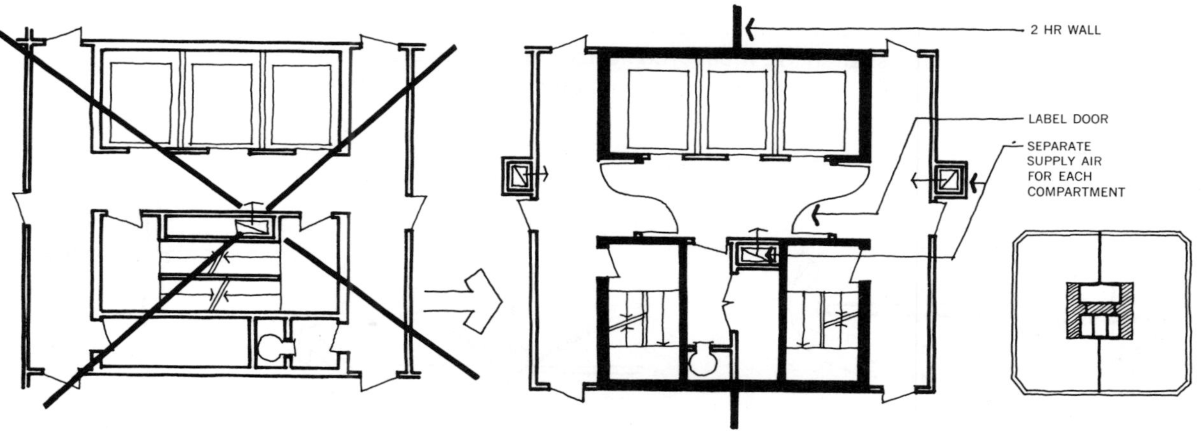

Some codes also require an elevator in each compartment, feasible, of course only in buildings with at least two banks of elevators.

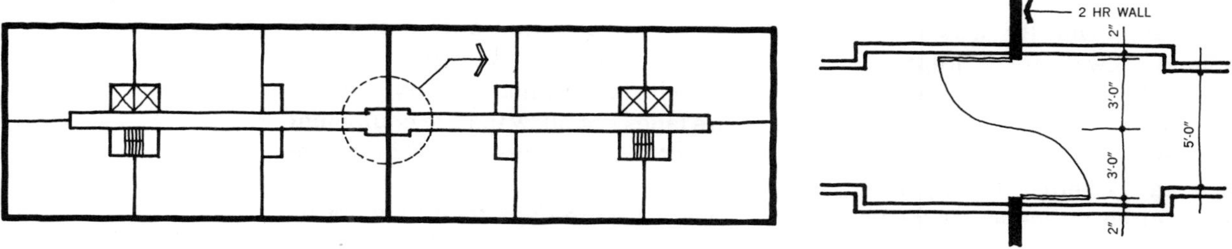

When there is only one bank of elevators, the code may permit handling it as an independent compartment in lieu of one elevator in each compartment. Other fire codes lean toward this third compartment by requiring that the elevator lobby at each level be separated from the remainder of the building by an effective smoke barrier.

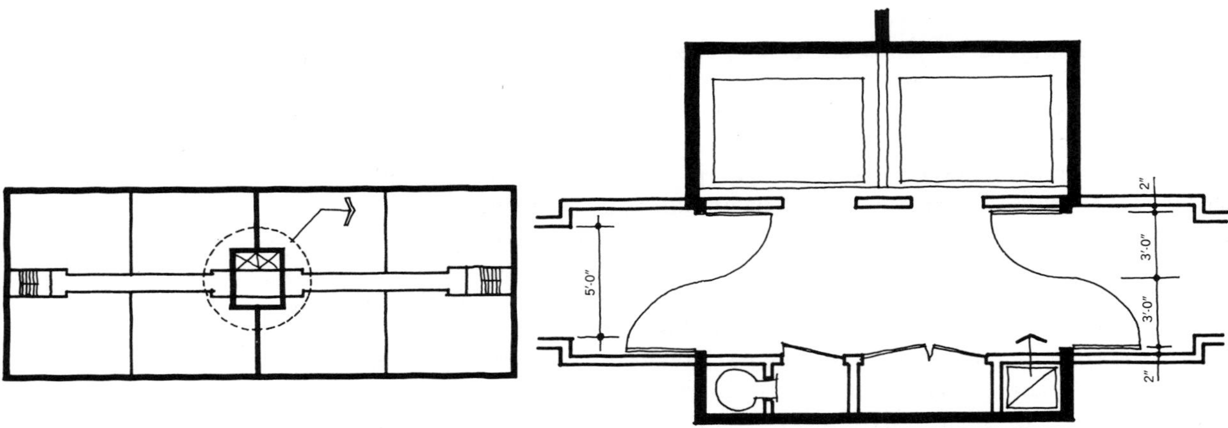

Some highrise fire codes specify that all openings in exterior walls located vertically above one another shall be protected by approved flame barriers extending 30 in. beyond the exterior wall in the plane of the floor or by vertical panels not less than 3 ft or so in height; also, all exterior openings adjacent ot the vertical two-hour partition must be located not less than 3 ft, measured horizontally, from the vertical, division wall. These stipulations pose severe limitations on the exterior options of the designer.

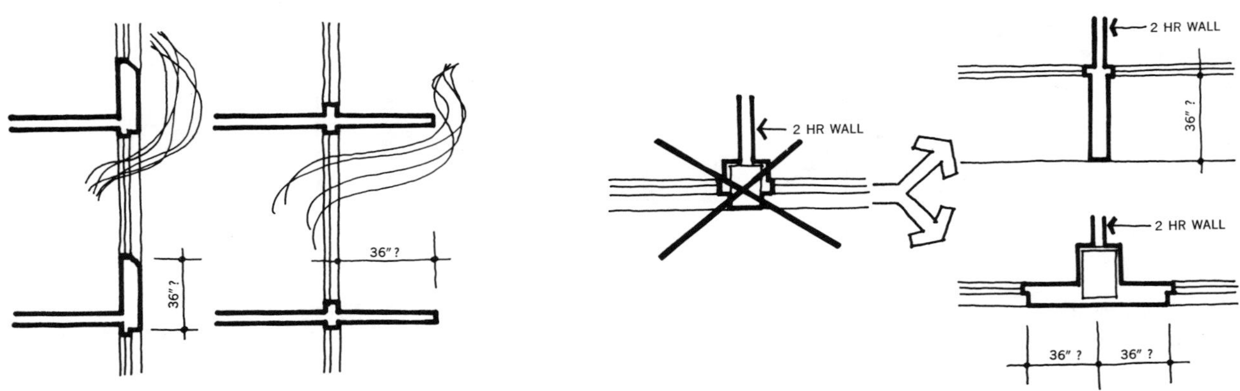

In dealing with lowrises the issue of fire safety is somewhat different. Codes demand a lower rate of fireproofing because complete evacuation is possible and because floors can be reached by the fire fighters with ladders and "cherry-picker." The problem is to provide adequate access—fire lanes—to allow the fire equipment to reach the buildings. This is particularly difficult in lowrise projects in high density areas. Whether driving isles, parking lots, or even the open space otherwise not required for vehicular traffic are to be used, the fire department should be consulted for the necessary turning radii and maneuvering space, distances between buildings (depending on building height and equipment reach), and location of fire hydrants. When it becomes impossible to plan roads or parking lots close enough to the buildings for the efficient deployment of fire equipment, areas that normally serve recreational purposes can be considered. The use of collapsible ballards will prevent normal vehicular traffic in fire lanes.

STAIRS

Stairs, required as escape routes in case of fire, are governed by codes. In apartment buildings with three floors—occasionally four—in which stairs are the only means of access their design is also determined by ease of climbing. In addition, stairs in walk-ups become important as visual architectural elements. In elevatored buildings, on the other hand, their main function is as a means of escape, and more generous design than that required by code is unnecessary and economically unfeasible.

In most cases codes require two exits. Buildings of a certain height (three or four floors), limited floor area, particular construction type, and serving a limited number of families per floor often have only one staircase, but there are ways of "stretching" the number of floors in which only one is still permitted: the ground floor depressed below grade may not count as a "floor," depending on code definition, of course. When building codes limit the single exit to buildings of three stories, a second exit can be created from the top floor by providing access to the roof, thus allowing the occupants to reach the next staircase. Both devices need careful code analysis. In lowrises in high-crime areas single stairs add to the security of the project.

The location of stairs varies with codes. The maximum travel distance is usually 75 to 100 ft from the apartment entry door to the remotest fire stairs. (This dimension can be increased by 50% if the floor is sprinklered, though not usual in apartment buildings.) The distance from the entry door to the furthest point in the apartment is generally a maximum of 50 ft. When apartments are large, two entrances are specified. There is much disagreement among codes regarding the question of dead-end corridors. Some allow none, others define it as 50% of the maximum travel distance, and some as 20 or 25 ft; HUD allows 35 ft. It is obvious that unless a third staircase is introduced travel distances determine the maximum length of the corridor, therefore the building.

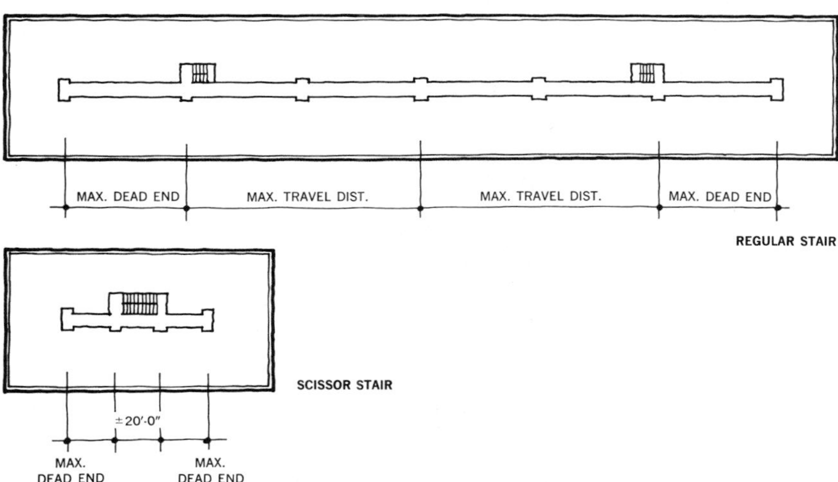

REGULAR STAIR

SCISSOR STAIR

Exit width is also set by code and depends on the population of the floor. Population is defined either as real (two people per bedroom) or by allowing 125 to 200 sf of floor area per person. Doors are generally 3 ft wide, two-hour-fire-rated "B" label with automatic closers. The minimum width of stairs is 3 ft on floors housing about 45 persons. Maximum required width is usually 3 ft, 8 in. The intermediate landing must be as wide as the stair itself. The width of floor landings is interpreted in a variety of ways, as illustrated. When it is more than the plan can take in that direction, it can be reduced by increasing the stair volume in the other direction and using the excess space for air supply ducts or something else.

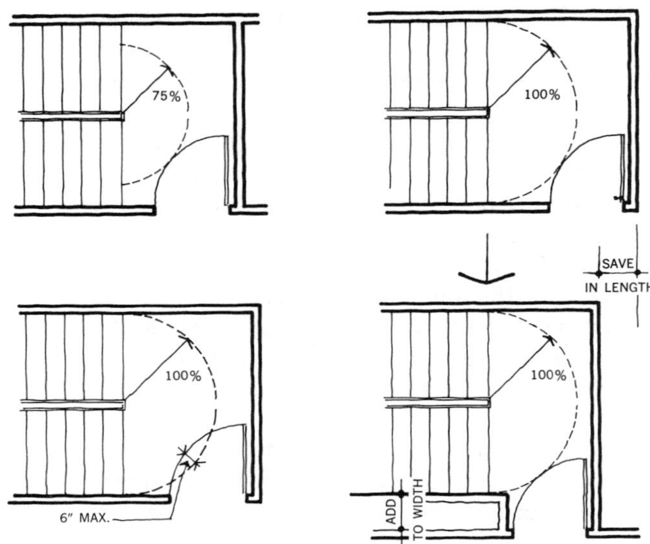

Winders in fire stairs are prohibited. The minimum number of risers between landings is three and the maximum vertical distance between landings is usually 12 ft. Maximum riser height is 7¾ or 8 in. Minimum tread width is 9 in., with 1 in. nosing. When the stair width is not more than 3 ft 8 in., railing is required on one side only, and the need for wall railings is eliminated. Railings may project 4 in. into the required stair width. Minimum headroom is usually 7 ft.

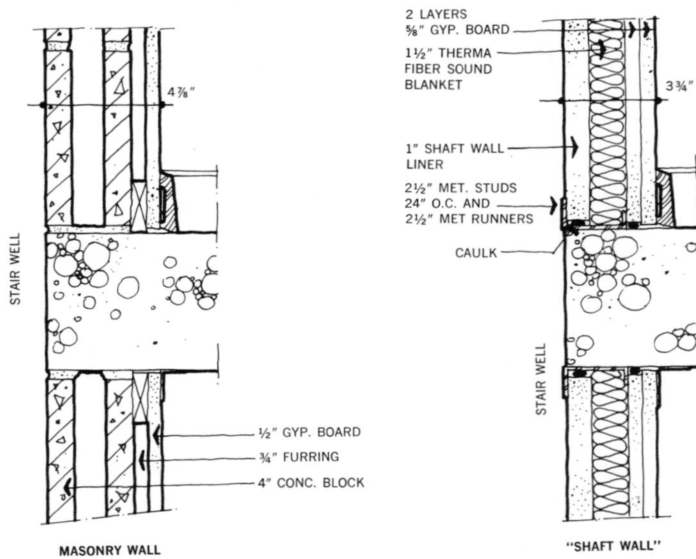

The construction of stairs, except in lowrises, is generally noncombustible. In highrises it is usually reinforced concrete. The stair-shaft enclosure must provide two-hour fire protection which is achieved by 4 in. concrete blocks with furred gypsum board on the apartment or corridor side or by a gypsum board assembly called a "shaft wall" which is only 3¾ in. thick, This shaft wall is not only thinner and more economical than masonry but often eliminates beams that may be needed under masonry walls around openings (see p. 44).

Exterior open stairs are limited to a certain building height or to the number of floors they are to serve; as a rule, only 50% of the stairs required for exit can be open. Exterior stairs lend themselves to visual variety.

Codes also define how stairs should lead to the outside at ground level: either directly or via a two-hour enclosed corridor, the horizontal exit. Sometimes the lobby will qualify in spite of its glass walls.

In order to provide two independent exits in a minimum floor area a special staircase, or scissor-stairs, is used in short corridors. Two completely separated stairs wind around each other in the same shaft like a double helix. Intermediate landings are eliminated. Each stair "runs" floor-to-floor without interruption. The length of a scissor-stair is greater than a regular stair but its floor area is less than that of the two regular stairs it replaces. The run dimensions obviously vary with floor height; the illustrations are based on an 8 ft 6 in. floor-to-floor dimension

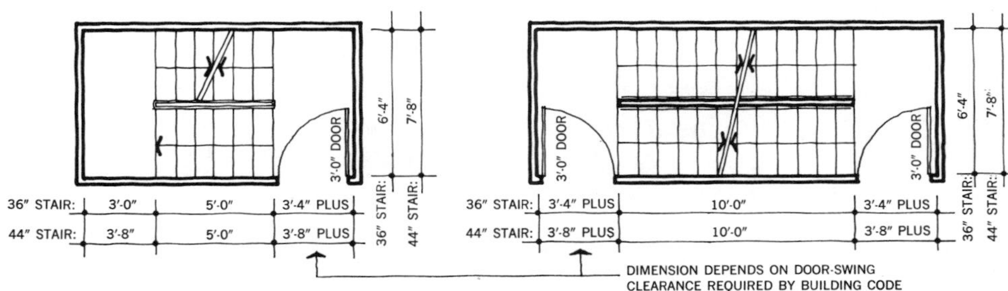

In tall buildings—the code defines the height limit—one or both of the required stairs must be a smokeproof tower to prevent smoke from entering the enclosure. This is done by providing a vestibule in front of the door to the stair so that when the vestibule door is opened—but before the stair door is reached—the smoke can be sucked out of the vestibule. The smoke is dispersed by opening this vestibule—like a balcony—directly to the outside or by a vertical shaft. The size of the shaft depends on whether it is mechanically exhausted or acts as a chimney to pull the smoke out naturally.

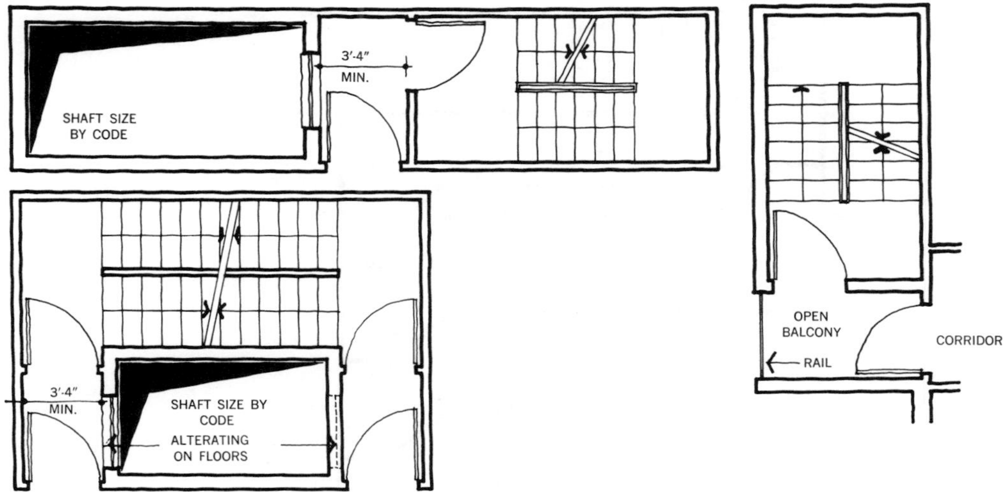

Special attention must be paid to stairs on the first floor. This floor in most apartment buildings requires more height than the upper floors not only because of aesthetic reasons, but also because of the space needed for air ducts, pipes, and so on. The increased height results in longer stair runs on the first floor which sometimes (when the shaft is bordered by shear walls) cannot be accommodated. The problem is avoided by introducing two intermediate landings instead of the customary one. If the typical floor height is 8 ft 6 in., the first floor height should be three times one-half the typical, or 12 ft 9 in. The problem is similar on other floors of increased height.

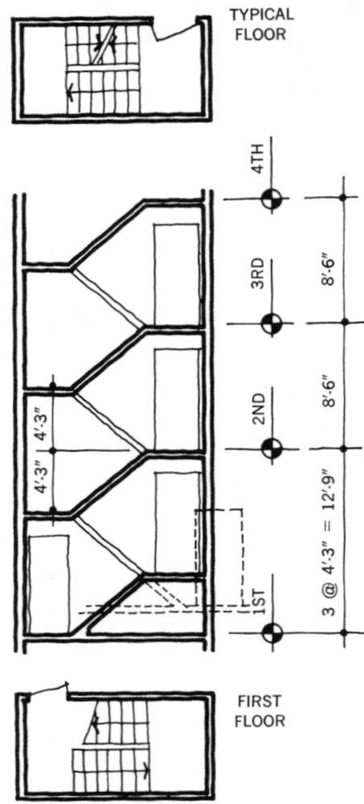

On occasion the function of the lower floors does not permit the stair enclosure to continue down in a straight line; the stairs will have to be transferred. Transfer can be a slight shift or a completely new location when the connection is made by a two-hour enclosed horizontal passage on the transfer floor.

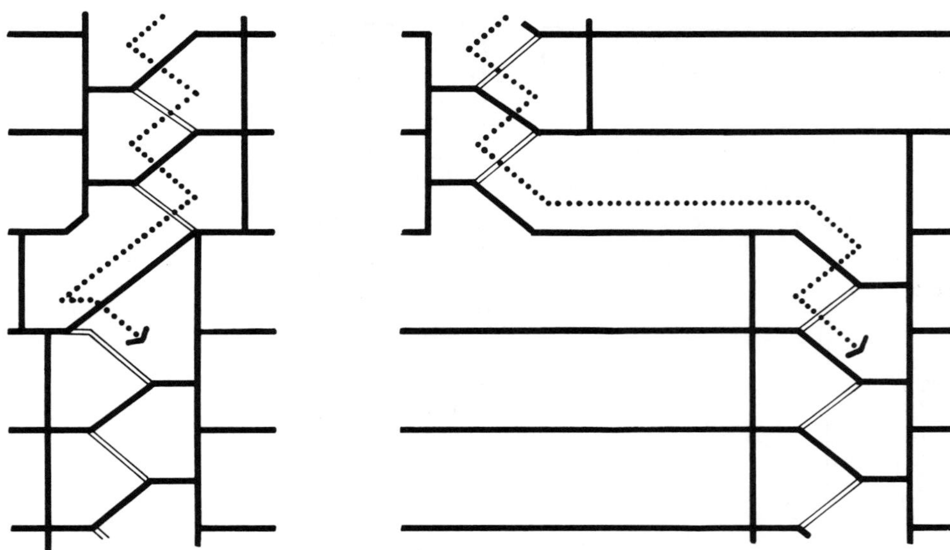

Code regulations are far more liberal for stairs that connect two levels of the same unit. Some, as in townhouses and other lowrises, might even have combustible construction; most, however, are allowed to have open risers and winders.

ELEVATORS

Elevator selection (the number, speed, and capacity of elevators) depends on a variety of interrelated factors such as population of the building, number of floors, number of stops, and speed of door operation. Because the calculations necessary to a reasonable decision are extremely involved and probability tables as well as empirical data must be used, the architect has to rely on the expert opinion of a consultant. Although years of experience will enable the designer to make some educated guesses, the responsibility is so heavy that a specialist should be called in in all but the simplest cases and certainly when the population of the building is more than 400.

Nevertheless the designer must have a schematic plan before he can call on a consultant. To prepare such a plan he can make some assumptions regarding the elevators. The following chart is no more than a number of ''rules of thumb'' to help in making these assumptions.

ELEVATOR TABLE FOR APARTMENT BUILDINGS

Number of Floors	Passenger Elevators (minimum 2000 lb; if used for service, 2500 lb)	Service Elevators (minimum 2500 lb)	Remarks
3–4	1 hydraulic (150 fpm)	1[a]	
5–6	2 hydraulic (150 fpm) or 2 electric (350 fpm)	1[a]	
7–12	2 electric (350 fpm)	1[a]	If population is more than 500, need more than 2
13–20/25	3 electric (350 fpm) or 2 electric (500 to 700 fpm)	1[a]	
20/25–40/45	3 electric (350 fpm) or 2 electric (500 to 700 fpm)	1 + 1[a]	
50–	2 banks of 3 electric (500 to 700 fpm)	2	

[a] Indicates that a passenger elevator can be used as a service elevator as long as its capacity is 2500 lb.

It is obvious that one elevator is adequate for three- or four-story buildings. If the elevator breaks down or is being serviced, it is still possible to walk up to the top floor without serious discomfort. In five- or six-story buildings electric elevators are a luxury that can hardly be afforded. When a building reaches six floors, however, a borderline is also reached concerning hydraulic elevators because of their low speed. In 12-to-45 story buildings the choice is between three regular-speed and two high-speed passenger elevators and much depends on availability of space in the floor plan.

Service elevator requirements are based on tenant turnover and travel distance (turnover in big cities runs 6 to 13% in the heaviest rental month; condominiums have minimal turnover but as a rule need more deliveries). As the chart indicates, buildings 20 to 25 stories get by with one service elevator which can also be used for passengers; buildings of more than this height will need two service elevators, one of which can also double for passengers. The distinct advantage of having a service elevator in the same bank with the passenger elevators for multiple use is obvious. It is also desirable to load in the basement or on the first floor through a rear door to avoid passing through the main lobby. Side doors are possible but expensive. When the freight elevator is not located in the passenger bank, it should open into a small anteroom on each floor. It is important that service elevator cabs be 10 ft high—or have removable tops—for carrying large objects. When this provision is not made, objects of unusual length will have to be raised on top of the cab, a cumbersome and dangerous method.

An apartment building will have adequate passenger service when the following criteria are met (these should be documented by the consultant):

1. It should be possible to move 6% of the population in less than five minutes.
2. The traffic interval should not exceed 60 seconds. (If the traffic interval is more than 55 seconds, the car should be able to make a full run from the top of the building to the lobby in 45 to 50 seconds.)

To understand the consultant's recommendations, the architect must be familiar with some of the terminology commonly used in traffic studies:

POPULATION. Population can vary from two persons per bedroom in low-rent housing to one-half person per bedroom in deluxe apartments. Recommended averages (not including public housing): 1 person per efficiency apartment of 350 sf or less and 1.5 above this size; 1.8 persons per one-bedroom apartment, 2.5 persons per two-bedroom apartment, 3.5 persons per three-bedroom apartment, and so on. Although the number of persons per elevator trip requires intricate calculations, the architect should know at least that a 2000-lb cab can hold 11 persons and a 2500 lb cab can hold 13 persons; maximum laoding is seldom achieved, however.

TRAFFIC INTERVAL. A traffic interval is an arbitrary time element calculated as follows: the number of stops (only the specialist can estimate it) multiplied by the sum of acceleration and deceleration time, plus door operation time, plus passenger loading and unloading time, plus other lost time. To this we add the round trip time of the elevator without stops. The total is then divided by the number of elevators to give the interval in seconds.

Example

Assume that 20 stories times 8 ft 6 in. is 170 ft; travel is in two directions, therefore 2 times 170 ft is 340 ft; an elevator that travels 350 fpm will make this run in approximately one minute, therefore for round trip assume 60 seconds.

ADD FOR EACH STOP

Acceleration and deceleration time of a 350 fpm elevator at each stop	2.35 sec
Time required to open and close the door at each stop	4.30 sec

(This time can be reduced by 1.4 sec if the door is center opening instead of single slide.)

Time required to load and unload passengers at each stop	2.00 sec
Other lost time: 0.1 × 2.35 (acceleration and deceleration) plus 0.1 × 4.30 (door opening and closing)	0.63 sec
	9.28 sec/stop
Assume 10 stops × 9.28 sec	92.80 sec
60 sec + 92.80 sec =	152.80 sec

152.80 ÷ 3 elevators = 50.93-sec interval; very good. If the interval is much shorter than 40, the building is probably over equipped.

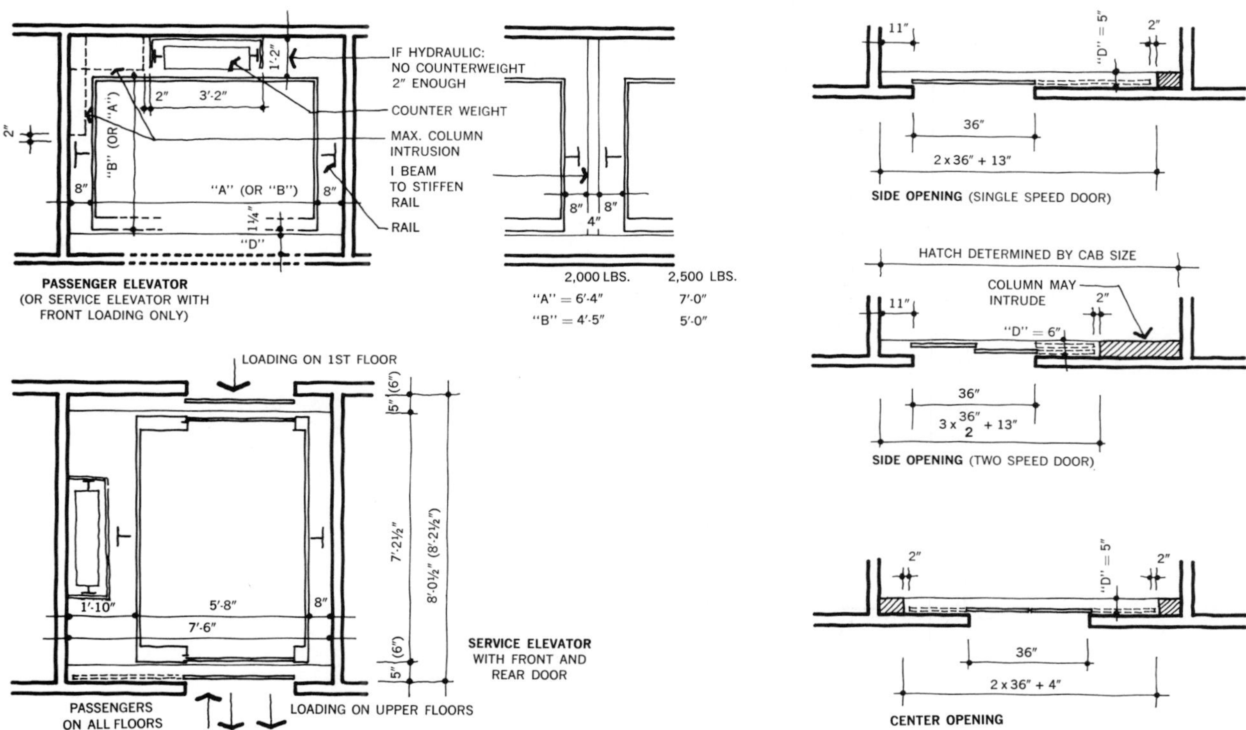

The hatch, cab, and door details illustrated here meet industry and building-code standards. Other cab dimensions may be used, but they can be costly and should be checked by the consultants.

The machinery (pump) for hydraulic elevators is housed in a small (approximately 8 × 10 ft) room near the lowest stop. A small (2 to 3 ft) protrusion on the roof accommodates overrun unless the top floor is higher than the average apartment floor, in which case the protrusion is eliminated.

Machinery for electric elevators (unless they are the underslung type hardly used in apartment buildings) is housed on the roof. The machine height *M* should be a minimum of 7 ft 6 in. for geared and 8 ft 6 in. for gearless elevators (those with speed in excess of 350 fpm). As the travel increases to 30 to 35 stories these figures should be checked by the elevator manufacturer or consultant.

Note that the dimensions given for the pit include space for the following: buffers to slow the car if it is approaching the bottom landing at full speed because of failure of controls. A space must be allowed between the car striker plate and the buffer for cable stretch, and a safety device is required under the car to allow for overspeed in the run. The car depth from platform to striker plate may be as much as 16 to 18 in. The code demands 2 ft under the compressed buffer to allow clearance for anyone caught in the pit under a falling car. In very tall buildings, which require higher speeds and more critical counterweight balance for landing, a form of cable compensation necessitates more pit depth. These facts will explain the need for the dimensions shown which may otherwise appear excessive.

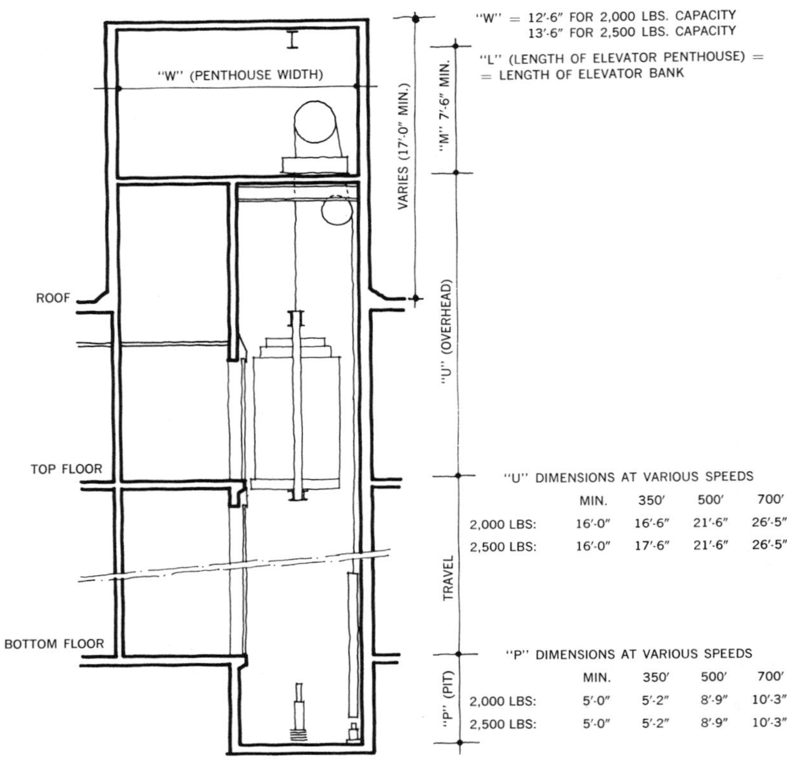

"U" DIMENSIONS AT VARIOUS SPEEDS

	MIN.	350'	500'	700'
2,000 LBS:	16'-0"	16'-6"	21'-6"	26'-5"
2,500 LBS:	16'-0"	17'-6"	21'-6"	26'-5"

"P" DIMENSIONS AT VARIOUS SPEEDS

	MIN.	350'	500'	700'
2,000 LBS:	5'-0"	5'-2"	8'-9"	10'-3"
2,500 LBS:	5'-0"	5'-2"	8'-9"	10'-3"

How passenger elevators connect with the lobby and how service elevators connect with the receiving area of a building is discussed in a later chapter. It will be seen that direct connection between the service elevator and the receiving area is not always possible, or only at considerable cost, and sometimes loading will have to take place in the passenger lobby. This compromise is not recommended for senior citizen housing, in which the service elevator is frequently used for stretchers, a disturbing sight for other residents who like to congregate in the lobby. For this reason one of the elevators should be deeper and have a rear door connecting it directly with the receiving area. Cabs for the elderly and handicapped should have handrails and a height of 2 ft 9 in. and control buttons should not be higher than 4 ft 8 in.

The waiting space in front of the elevators and its relation to the public corridor as well as the elevator and main lobbies on the first floor are treated in Chapter 7.

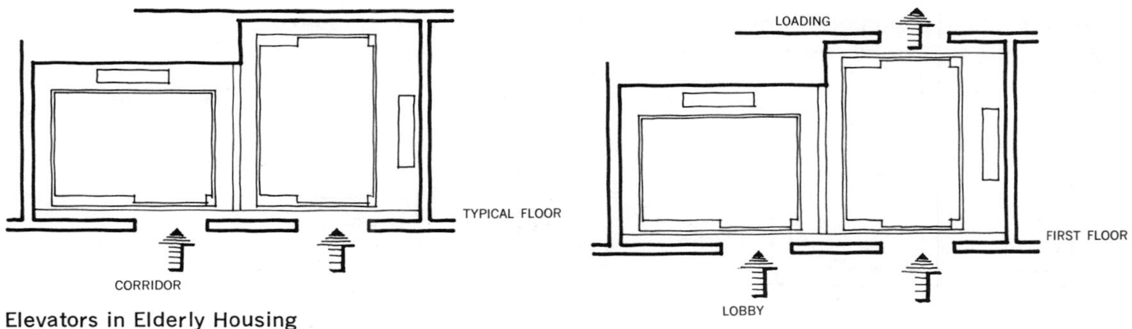

Elevators in Elderly Housing

OTHER CORE ELEMENTS

Stairs and elevators constitute only part of the vertical core of an apartment building. Other major core elements may include refuse chute, boiler stack, electric meter and transformer room, and corridor air supply duct.

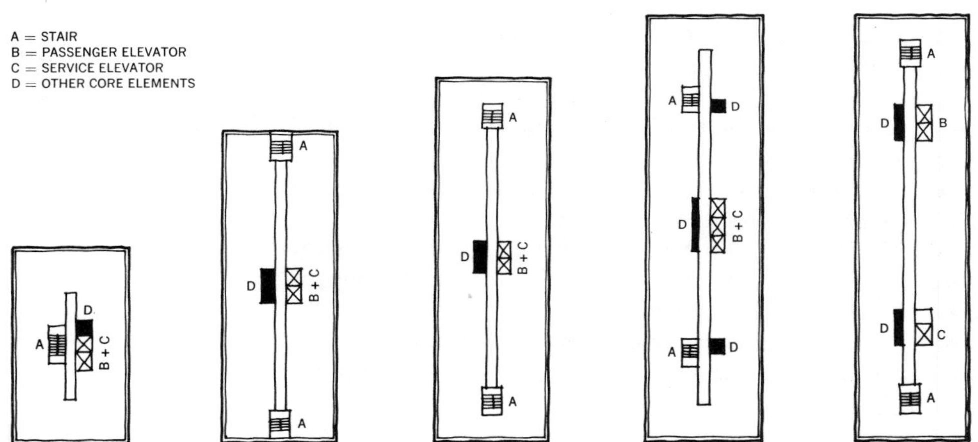

The location of these elements is an essential part of the planning process and is discussed in detail in a later section of this book. Location criteria, however, can be established in advance.

Stairs, as determined by building codes, must be as far apart as possible to fulfill the criterion set for travel distance. Elevators on the other hand, in order to provide equal distribution on the typical floor, tend to be placed in the center of the building, though ground level conditions may require off-center location.

The refuse chute, even when individual garbage disposals are standard equipment, provides the tenants with a way of getting rid of a variety of waste. The ideal location is also in the center of the building, thus minimizing the walking distance from any of the apartments. Building code regulations stipulate that refuse chutes must be installed in two hour fire rated enclosures (similar to stairs) with "B" label doors. It is advisable, when planning constraints permit, to provide a small room in front of the refuse chute for the temporary storage of items such as boxes that will not fit into the chute. When garbage is stuffed through the door of the chute, some small waste occasionally drops and remains on the floor; the anteroom will prevent the public corridor from becoming littered. HUD requires that this anteroom measure at least 20 sf.

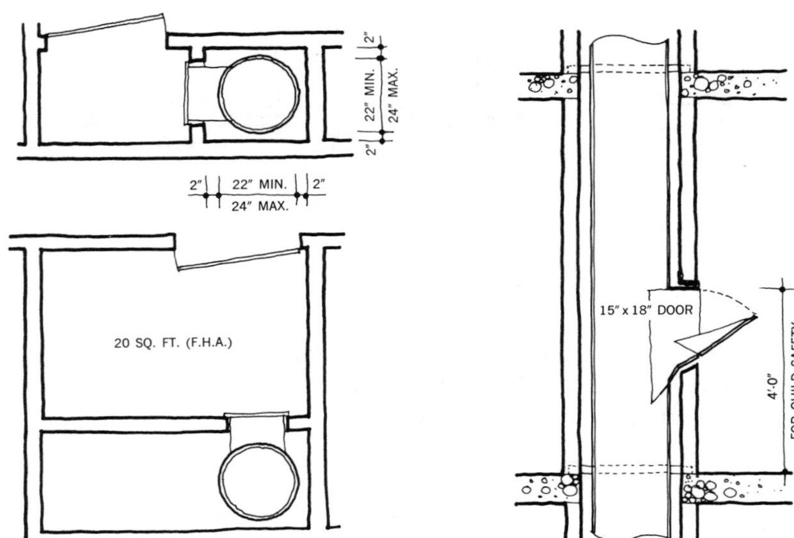

Unless the building is electrically heated or the boiler is located in the mechanical penthouse, the boiler room will be in the basement or on the first floor. The boiler stack, as part of the core, is ideally situated near the elevators because the stack must terminate above the elevator penthouse and it is easier to handle as part of that unit than as a separate element.

Electric meter and transformer rooms, with the electrical riser, are also core elements. Their size and configuration is discussed in the electrical section of this book. Ideally they are included in the building's core in order to provide short distribution lines in both directions (the exception is in long buildings in which two risers and two electrical rooms may produce a more economical distribution, enough to outweigh the cost of the extra riser and room).

Because it is necessary to exhaust interior bathrooms and kitchens, apartment buildings would be under negative pressure, even though there is always some leakage through the windows, unless the lost air were somehow made up. For this reason make-up air is forced into the corridors, through corridor supply ducts, and into the apartments along the jambs of the apartment doors. The fan equipment which pushes the air into the corridors is generally on the roof unless in buildings of more than 40 stories the system is split in two: the upper section is then supplied from above, the lower from below. The space required for corridor supply ducts is discussed in the mechanical section of this book. Location in the center of the building permits the supply fans to be housed in the elevator penthouse. In long buildings the corridor supply is achieved by using two ducts (space for them can be borrowed from an apartment closet) and two fan housings on the roof.

On occasion a restaurant may occupy a lower floor of an apartment building and its kitchen must be exhausted. If the site conditions do not permit exhausting the kitchen horizontally, the exhaust duct must penetrate the apartment tower. This duct is located wherever space can be found for it, assuming that the fan housing can be properly handled on the roof.

Although the various vertical core elements have their own location criteria based on function and economy, the roof housing required for this equipment will influence the design of the roof, an often neglected part of the building that is discussed in detail in Chapter 7, Design Methodology.

PARKING

Though many planners would prefer an automobile-free world, though malls and even entire city districts are being emptied of vehicular traffic, though those who live within walking distance of their jobs or along rapid transit lines can forego the automobile in getting to and from work, most people still rely on their cars for transportation. The automobile is an essential part of existence in the United States and it must be stored in conjunction with the dwelling.

As more and more families acquire two or more cars, it is becoming increasingly difficult to determine the amount of car storage required for a housing project. Although zoning establishes the minimum amount of off-street parking, the user's lifestyle, economic status, proximity to public transportation and other factors also play a role. Near-downtown housing may get by with 60% parking, condominium projects must have 100%, and on suburban sites the requirement can reach a 1:1.5 dwelling-to-car ratio. In housing for the elderly 20 to 30% parking is sufficient, and most authorities will permit it, even though the zoning ordinances require a higher ratio for regular housing.

The relation of parking to dwelling can be any of the following, depending on building type, site constraints, and budget:

1. On grade, open parking (most common with lowrise housing and low-income mid- and highrise buildings around which there is adequate space available).
2. On grade, under the building (most common with midrises).
3. In separate garage structures connected to one or several apartment towers (most common with highrises when land is plentiful).
4. In a garage under the apartment tower which forms its base (most common with highrises on limited land).

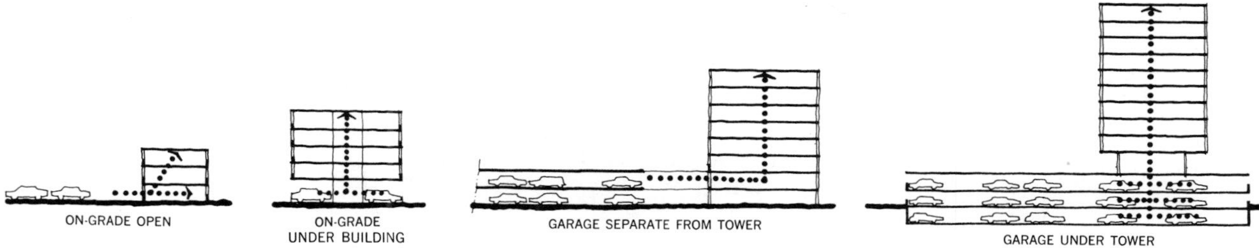

Dimension data developed by HUD can be very useful (see p. 54).

Whether along minor streets, in small compounds, or on large lots—other than the basic technical issues of surfacing and drainage, bumpers, and safe lighting—the visual aspects of handling these parking areas is of utmost importance. Large parking areas can become the familiar ''sea of asphalt'' and are quite unattractive, especially from upper floors. Smaller areas are more manageable. The partial

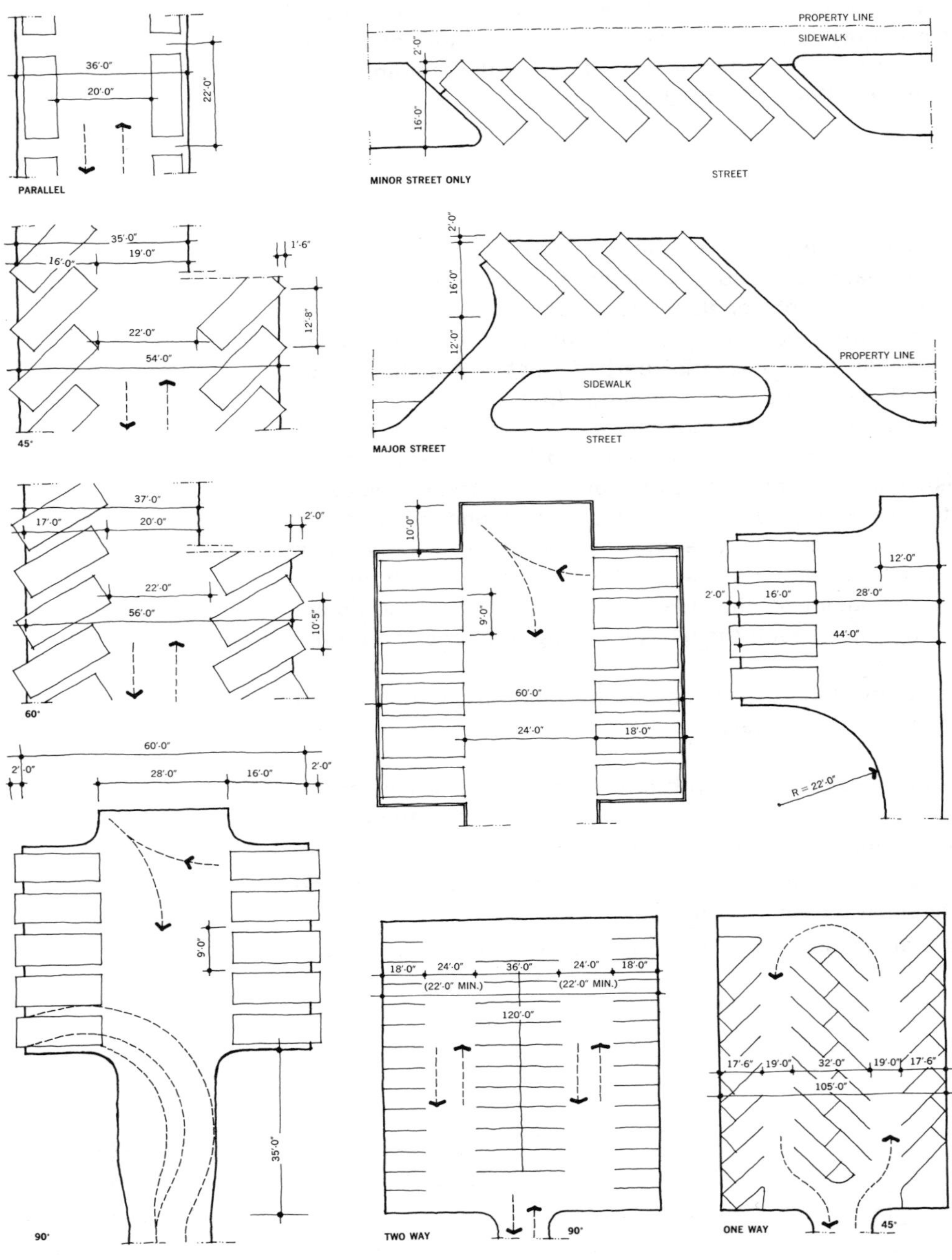

sheltering of cars with lightweight umbrella structures is generally too costly. Trees, particularly those with dense branchwork for winter shielding, are ideal and can be located to provide minimal interference with the parking layout. Proper protection, drainage, and selection of species suggests consultation with a landscape architect (see p. 55).

Horizontal shielding of parking areas, especially in high-crime locations, should be carefully weighed against the fact that they become less visible, therefore potentially unsafe areas. If shielding is decided on, it can be achieved in a variety

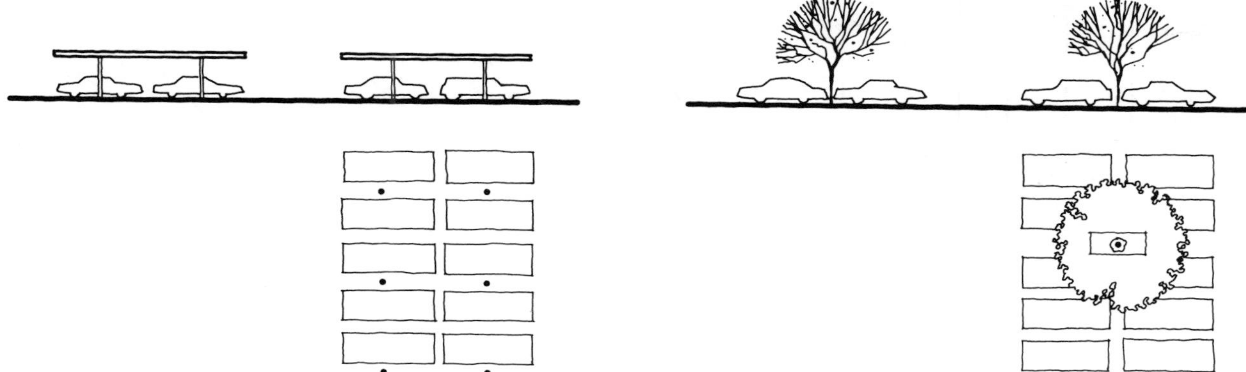

of ways: with fences, garden walls, dense hedges, or earth mounding if space permits; a partly depressed parking lot can achieve a similar effect. Oscar Newman concludes[21] that properly defined outdoor recreation area near the parking lot will add to the security.

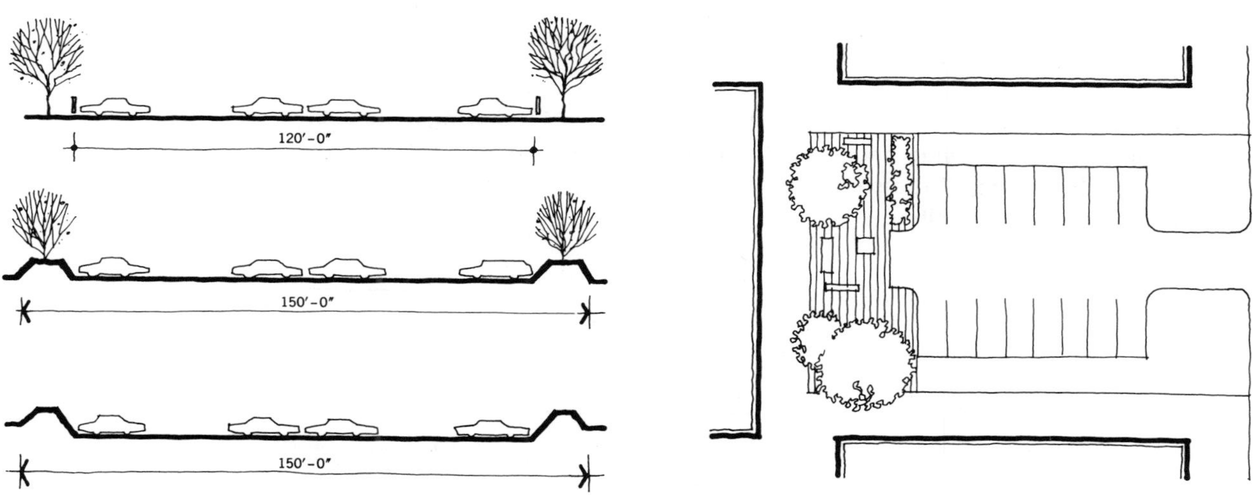

Because on-grade parking has the tendency to spread out, the distance between the automobile and the dwelling unit is critical. Even a visitors' parking space should not be farther than 200 ft from the dwelling, and for the resident 100 ft is preferred; 150 ft is maximum.

Garage parking is six or seven times more expensive than open on-grade parking and compact planning is essential. Special attention must be paid to the location of columns that will interfere least with parking. HUD recommended driving-aisle and parking-stall dimensions work well, especially when the parking structure is separated from the apartment tower (see p. 56).

On small sites, particularly when parking is beneath the tower, dimensions must be tighter. By moving the columns away from the driving aisle, the width of parking stalls can be reduced (see p. 56).

Generally speaking, 90-degree parking, with automobiles on both sides of the driving aisle, will result in the best utilization of the available space; 45- or 60-

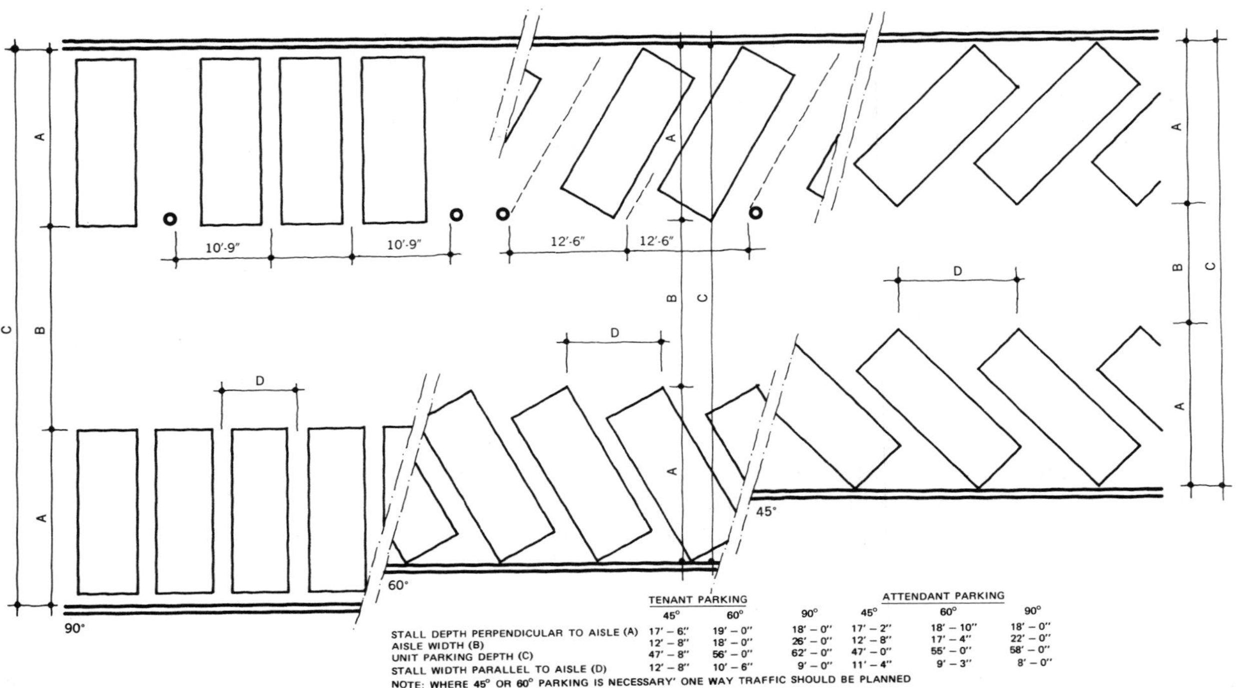

	TENANT PARKING 45°	60°	90°	ATTENDANT PARKING 45°	60°	90°
STALL DEPTH PERPENDICULAR TO AISLE (A)	17' – 6"	19' – 0"	18' – 0"	17' – 2"	18' – 10"	18' – 0"
AISLE WIDTH (B)	12' – 8"	18' – 0"	26' – 0"	12' – 8"	17' – 4"	22' – 0"
UNIT PARKING DEPTH (C)	47' – 8"	56' – 0"	62' – 0"	47' – 0"	55' – 0"	58' – 0"
STALL WIDTH PARALLEL TO AISLE (D)	12' – 8"	10' – 6"	9' – 0"	11' – 4"	9' – 3"	8' – 0"

NOTE: WHERE 45° OR 60° PARKING IS NECESSARY' ONE WAY TRAFFIC SHOULD BE PLANNED

degree parking requires one-way traffic, whereas the 22-to-24 ft driving aisle of 90-degree parking which is wide enough for two-way traffic produces more options. Even with the 90-degree, 22-ft aisle system, however, a one directional traffic flow is preferred whenever possible.

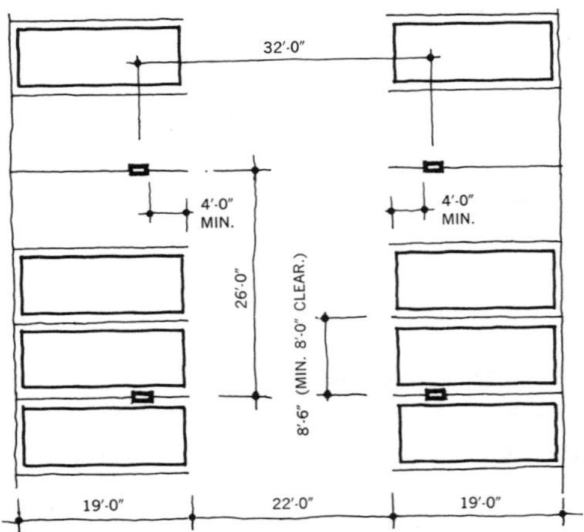

Before the preparation of actual layouts the parking capacity of a floor can be estimated. A typical bay in the 90-degree system is 26 × 60 ft or 1560 sf, which will accommodate six automobiles; 1560 divided by 6 is 260 sf per automobile. Taking into consideration cross aisles, space needed for ramps, stairs, and so on, no less that 350 sf should be allowed (300 sf is adequate for open on-grade parking). It should be kept in mind that attendant parking will improve this ratio. When attendant parking is provided, cars can be parked in double or even triple rows. It should be noted, however, that to satisfy zoning ordinances only those cars that are in the first row and directly accessible from the driving aisle can be counted among the required number of cars.

When parking is not under the apartment tower, 25-to-35-ft column spacing (with heavy 8-to-10-in. flat plate concrete slab and shear heads on the columns) is adequate. Parking under the tower itself presents a different picture. Here column spacing is dictated by economical apartment planning and not by the best parking layout. Though columns can be transferred under the tower, this procedure is extremely costly and ought to be avoided wherever possible. Therefore the 350-sf-per car ratio is only seldom achieved.

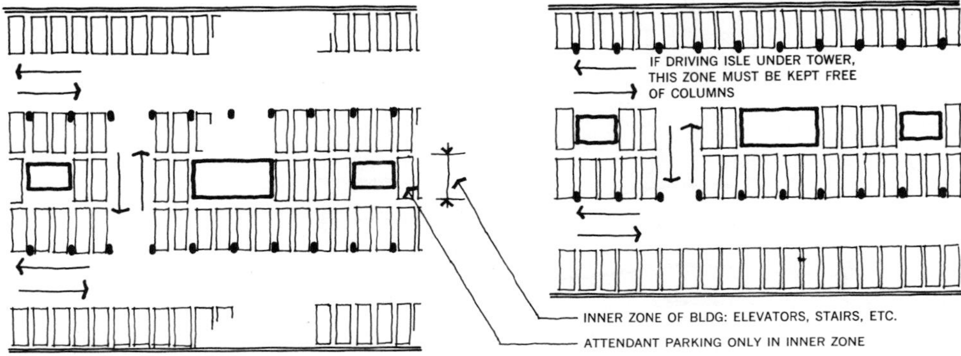

Apartment planning, especially with column rhythm along the exterior of the building, has serious consequences for the parking levels below. Everything else being equal, if there are choices of column location, parking is a factor that must be considered.

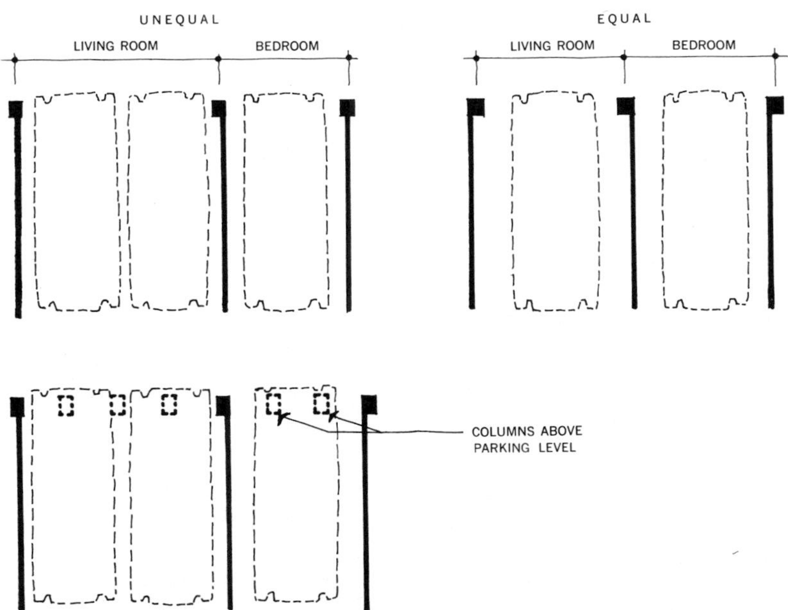

Ramps are the customary means of moving automobiles from level to level. When the lot is extremely tight, car elevators should be installed. Elevators are not only expensive but increase the operating costs, for 24-hour attendant service must be provided.

Ramp length, naturally, depends on floor-to-floor height. In determining this dimension, the need for sprinklers must be considered. Codes establish minimum headroom under sprinkler heads. Generally a 9-ft floor-to-floor dimension is adequate for structural slab and sprinklers. When the building code permits its use as a fire exit, the ramp must be less steep (maximum degree set by code) than when it is used only for driving. On circular ramps the minimum turning radius is 60 ft. Driving aisles used for turning on and off the ramp should not be less than 25 ft wide. It is possible to extend parking above the top and below the bottom level of a ramp as long as there is adequate headroom.

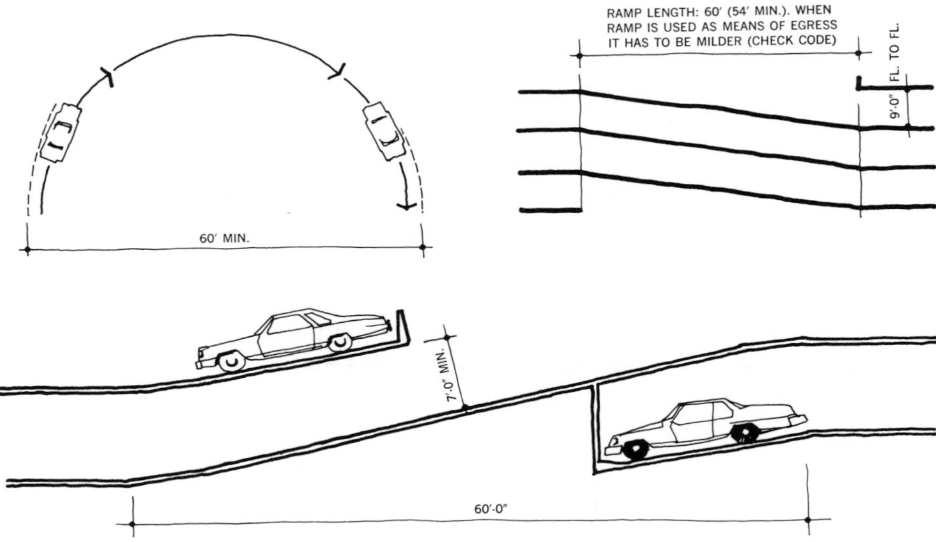

The difficult to handle ramp length can be reduced in two-level garages when they are depressed in relation to grade by half the floor-to-floor height.

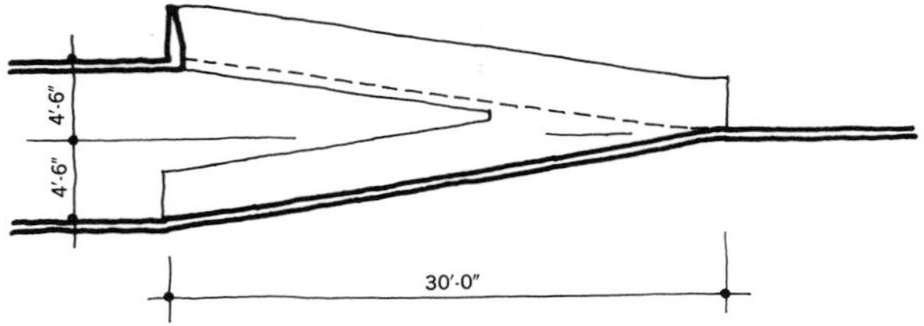

The following illustrations describe and give dimensions for a variety of ramp systems under apartment towers. It should be kept in mind that scissor ramps are costlier than normal ramps (see p. 59).

The principle of depressing the garage half a level below grade in order to shorten the ramp length can be applied to the entire garage. When all cars must be parked by the tenants, triple rows as shown in the diagrams, are not acceptable. Therefore

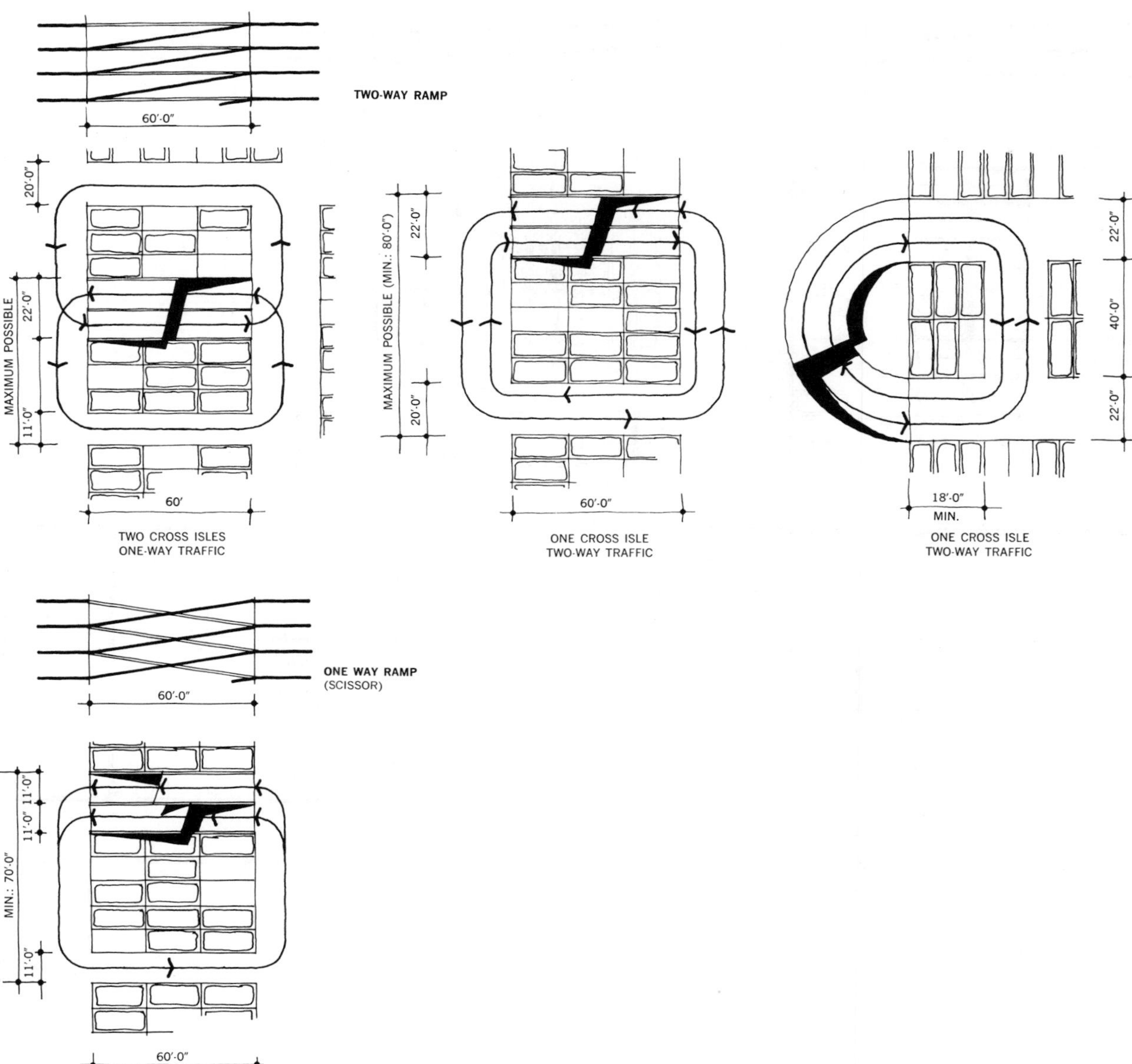

it becomes difficult to coordinate a 60 ft ramp with two stall lengths of 40 ft. However, the 40 ft length is more than adequate for a ramp spanning only half the regular floor-to-floor height. A further extension of this principle is the ramp garage in in which driving aisle and parking stalls form a continuous mild ramp (see p. 60).

The integration of parking and apartment tower requires special attention in highrise projects. On tight lots much of the parking will be directly under the building (reducing the number of cars considerably) and so will the ramp (requiring careful column alignment). Even when the site is not so tight the outer bay under the tower is often used for parking. On these larger sites there is a broader choice of ramp locations. Large sites, where the tower sits on the parking volume in the middle, will need column alignment for drive-through aisles. The most efficient parking structure is completely independent of the tower, connected to it by a bridge (see p. 60).

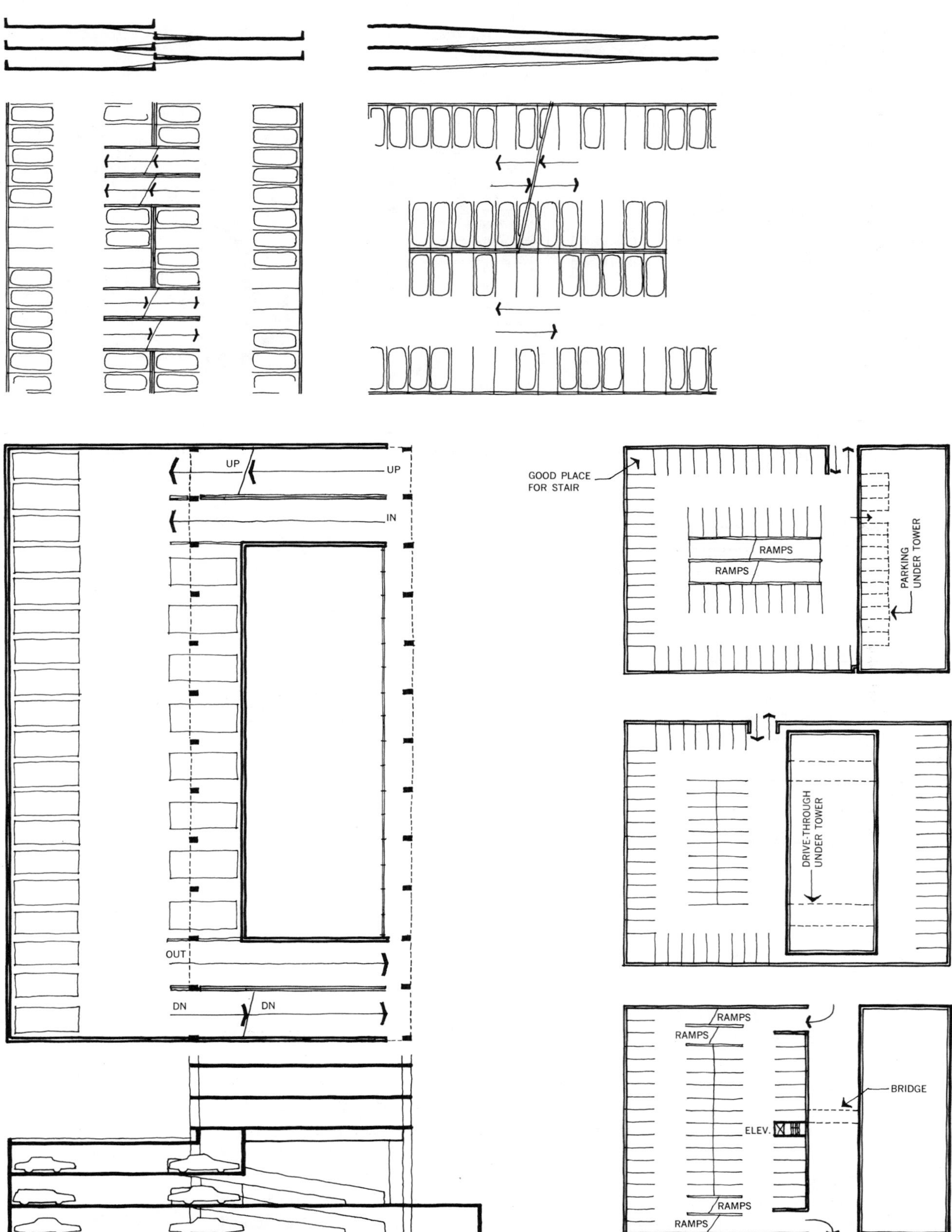

UP
UP
IN
OUT
DN
DN
GOOD PLACE FOR STAIR
RAMPS
RAMPS
PARKING UNDER TOWER
DRIVE-THROUGH UNDER TOWER
RAMPS
RAMPS
BRIDGE
ELEV.
RAMPS
RAMPS

No matter how the garage relates to the tower, vehicular entrance and exit must be easy. A thorough knowledge of local traffic conditions (direction, volume, pile-up conditions at traffic lights, maximum permitted width of curb cut, minimum distance of driveway from intersection, and so on) is essential. The basic criteria of good traffic flow can be summarized in three points:

1. A cab can drive to the lobby entrance (without driving into the garage proper), drop off or pick up the passenger (under canopy or arcade), and leave.
2. A tenant can drive to the lobby entrance, drop off his family, and drive on to the garage without having to go back into the street.
3. A tenant's car can be picked up in the garage (by himself or the doorman) and brought to the lobby entrance for loading without having to leave the property.

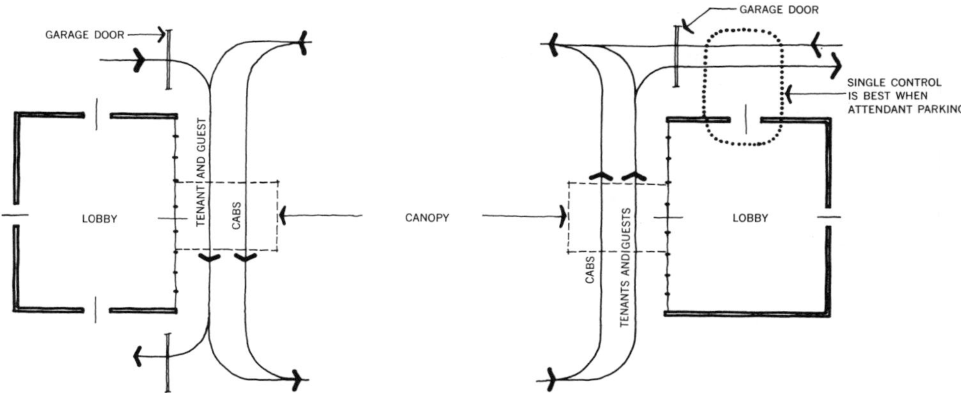

The required number of exits and maximum travel distance to the nearest exit are determined by the local code for garages. Under certain conditions the ramp can be used as one of the required means of egress and its maximum slope is regulated by code. Generally garages under apartment towers are required to be fully or partly (the part under the tower proper) sprinklered, and in this case the code usually stipulates more liberal distances between exits. When the garage is not extensive, the two stairs of the apartment tower proper may serve as exits for the garage as well. These stairs, like the elevators that connect the garage to the residential floors, must be separated from the garage by a fire vestibule of high rating, most commonly four hours with "A" label doors on both sides of the vestibule.

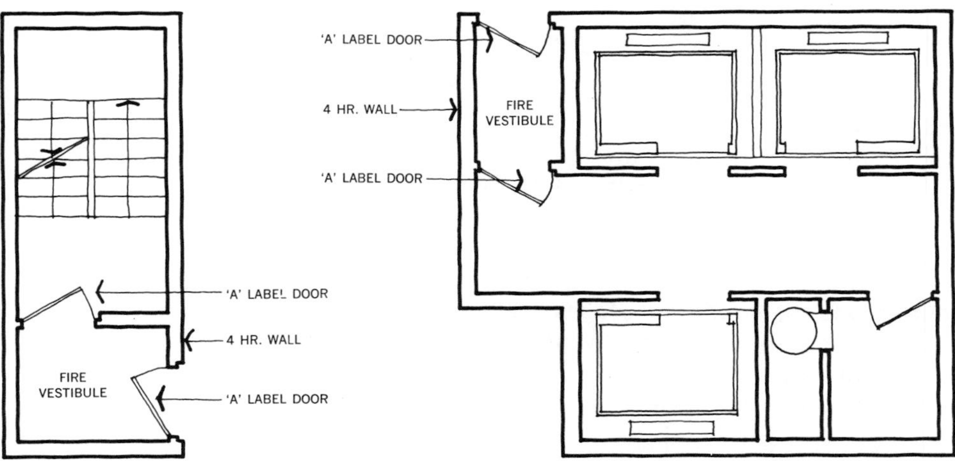

Garages are seldom heated. However, codes do require mechanical ventilation unless a required percentage, usually 50 or more of the exterior walls is open. When possible and aesthetically acceptable, open-sided garages are obviously more economical. The pattern of garage lighting, which can be otherwise neglected, needs special design attention in this case. Enclosing the garage, while adding to the cost, will minimize freezing temperatures even without heating. Some codes require periodic access openings in the walls of enclosed garages when those walls face a public way to be made accessible for the fire department.

Garage roof decks serve as excellent outdoor recreation spaces. In highrise projects this is not only the cheapest but often the only space for these facilities.

Lowrise projects, consisting of several buildings, normally have adequate ground for both open parking and recreation. When the property is inadequate, however, the use of the roof deck of the garage as an elevated grade for circulation and play areas between buildings is a solution. It is not so economical when compared with open parking but it is an answer when land is scarce. Properly sized and spaced openings to the parking area below provide natural ventilation and daylight, and trees can be grown in the wells rather than in boxes on the deck. The cost problem is aggrevated by code requirements for fire separation between parking and housing (concrete deck) as well as waterproofing and wearing slab or other hard surfacing of the waterproof membrane. These costs should be weighted against the obvious planning advantages of the scheme.

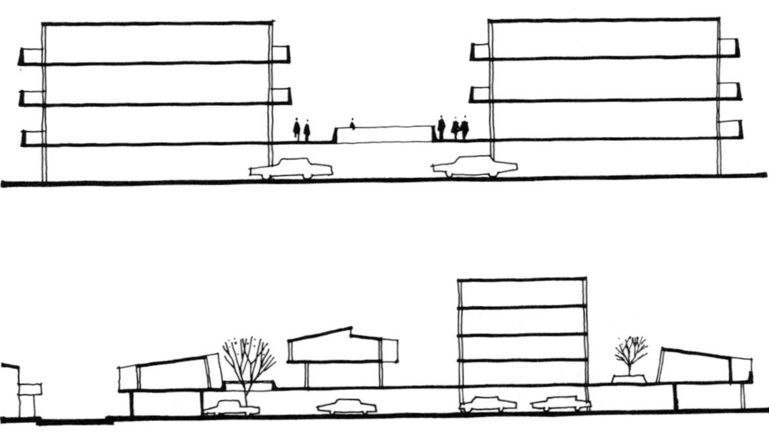

LOADING AND REFUSE REMOVAL

Apartment projects must allow for the delivery of goods and the disposal of refuse. The vertical movement of goods is handled by the service elevator and refuse is dropped into the refuse chute (except in walk-ups where both are handled manually).

The horizontal movement—goods in, refuse out—takes place on the ground level and both require vehicles: delivery and pickup vans and garbage trucks. Not only must the designer provide adequate space for parking these vehicles, but they must have access in some way to the service elevator of refuse room.

PICK UP AND DELIVERY

Zoning ordinances determine the number and size of off-street loading stalls on the basis of the number of dwellings served or the gross square footage of the buildings.

For the movement of pick-up and delivery trucks on large-site projects with open parking the driving aisles of the parking lot will serve well, provided that loading areas are assigned at strategic locations to avoid interference with parking or blocking pedestrian pathways. The loading areas, obviously, should be as close to each building as possible. In townhouse groups and other walk-ups with spread-out unit entrances ideal proximity is not possible.

Densely built sites with parking garages present an entirely different picture. Because of the minimum clearance of 14 ft required for trucks, to get the vehicles close to the freight elevator or to the refuse room is no small problem.

Many of these sites have limited access which sometimes is easiest through the garage, but its entire ground level would have to be raised to 15 ft, a terrible waste when 9 ft suffices for parking. To move the goods through the garage after unloading is a poor solution. Alternate possibilities are shown in the following illustrations.

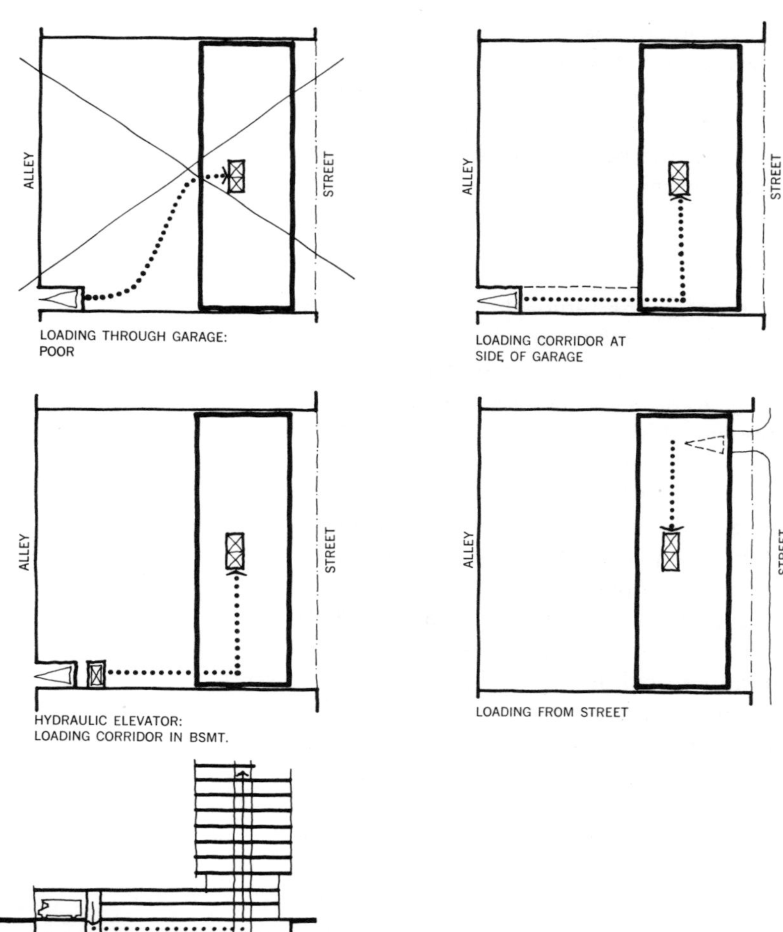

LOADING THROUGH GARAGE: POOR

LOADING CORRIDOR AT SIDE OF GARAGE

HYDRAULIC ELEVATOR: LOADING CORRIDOR IN BSMT.

LOADING FROM STREET

The best spot for loading is the area in which the garage volume meets the apartment tower and in which there is no interference with the garage nor any need to introduce loading vehicles at the front of the building near the lobby. Such ideal loading conditions are possible only on corner lots or large sites on which buildings are freely positioned.

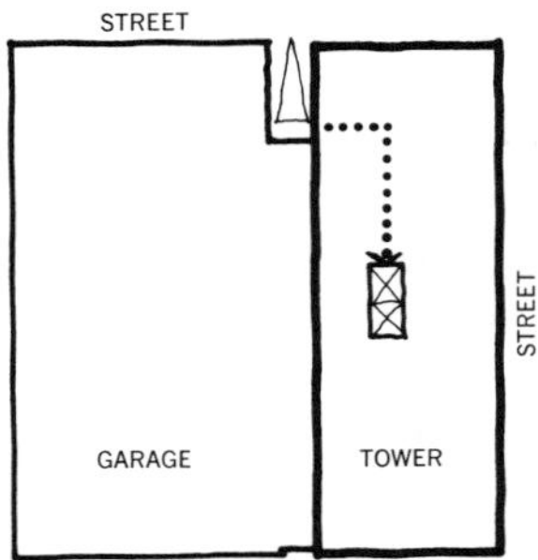

The loading area proper is either a level one or a traditional raised dock. Although the dock is preferred, it cannot always be achieved. In either case loading is done best under cover; if not fully enclosed, at least it should be under a canopy. With an enclosed dock the garage doors help further to seal off the loading activity from the weather. There should also be a receiving room adjacent to the loading area where goods can be held until picked up by the tenant. Visual control of the loading dock should be possible from this receiving room. For the purpose of security the door leading from the dock to the elevator should be manned or controlled by intercom.

REFUSE REMOVAL

The line of movement of goods is also adequate for the removal of refuse. Therefore on large sites with open parking the driving aisles that serve delivery vans will also serve garbage trucks. Trucks can park in the area designated for loading. Because it is not possible to provide an assigned area for each townhouse or walk-up, the distance between the unit entrance and the loading area is more critical for refuse removal than for moving goods. Refuse removal is a daily occurrence, and the distance the tenant must walk to the garbage collection area in no case should exceed 100 to 150 ft. Visual shielding, or fencing of these areas demands attention. An alternate solution is provided by enclosed by properly ventilated trash rooms strategically located in the building complex.

In mid- and highrise apartments refuse dropped into a chute lands in a compactor in which it is crushed and then removed in carts. Incinerators are prohibited in most locations because of their contribution to air pollution.

In addition to the size of the compactor, the number of bins or carts will determine the size of the refuse room. With a compactor of approximately 1200 cf volume capacity and 2-cubic yard capacity carts, a 100-unit apartment building will need two carts and once-a-week pick-up. A 200-to-250-unit apartment building with the same equipment will need two pick-ups a week or double the number of carts. Large projects should have more than one chute.

The chute and compactor should be joined by an ''accessible connection,'' which is not a permanent attachment, so that large items such as brooms and curtain rods can be removed.

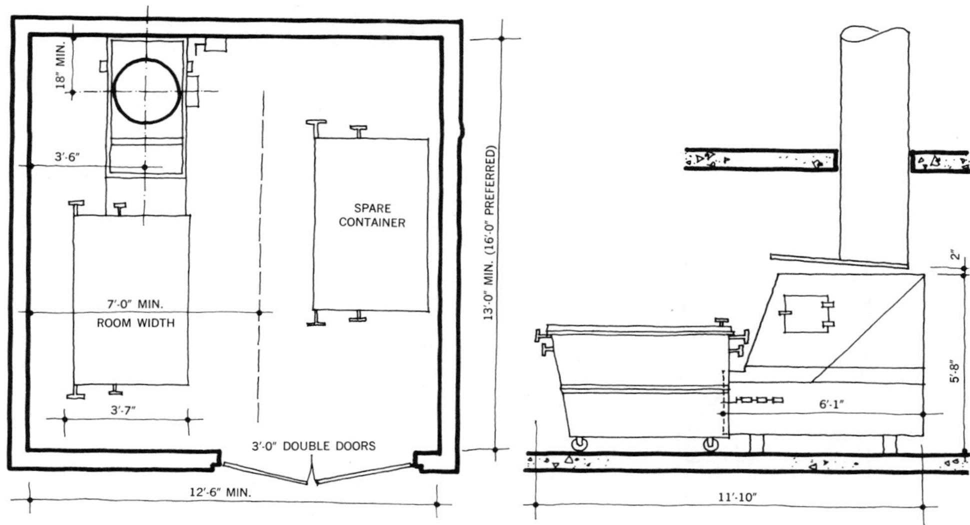

A service corridor usually connects the refuse room with the loading dock (the same corridor that connects the loading area with the service elevator). In large buildings it is especially important that space be provided on the loading dock for refuse carts.

The location of the refuse room, whether in the basement or on the first floor, is determined by the position of the refuse chute. Clogged angles or offsets in the chute are dangerous because they can cause the garbage to back up. Refuse rooms as required by code are generally sprinklered.

LOBBY

The lobby of an apartment building (except those with direct access to the units) is the major connector between the exterior and the stairs or elevators. It is the first space entered in which an immediate impression is gained of the interior quality of the building. Therefore it can be, and often is, a showplace. Developers sometimes try to make up for the lack of amenities elsewhere by providing lavish lobby decoration.

The lobby has several other functions: tenant directories hang on its walls and visitors can reach the occupants on an intercommunication device or wait for them to return. Here tenants can pick up their mail or whatever equipment they may have left in the storeroom.

There are no rules that indicate how large a lobby should be. Much depends on the sponsor's wishes. As a general rule, however, in walk-up buildings of limited magnitude the lobby is merely an oversized vestibule with intercom and mailboxes and usually without furniture. In midrises which have more apartments it is still a modest space but should be large enough to provide a small sitting area. In highrises that serve a large population the lobby can be quite elaborate with large waiting areas, plants, and artwork (see p. 66).

At all times the lobby is a security checkpoint. The visitor can ring the occupant or communicate with him (on an independent intercom or telephone intercom system) before he—by remote control—opens the door leading to the elevator lobby or stairs in walk-ups. Sometimes for visual recognition and added security a closed circuit television system is installed. When operating budget permits,

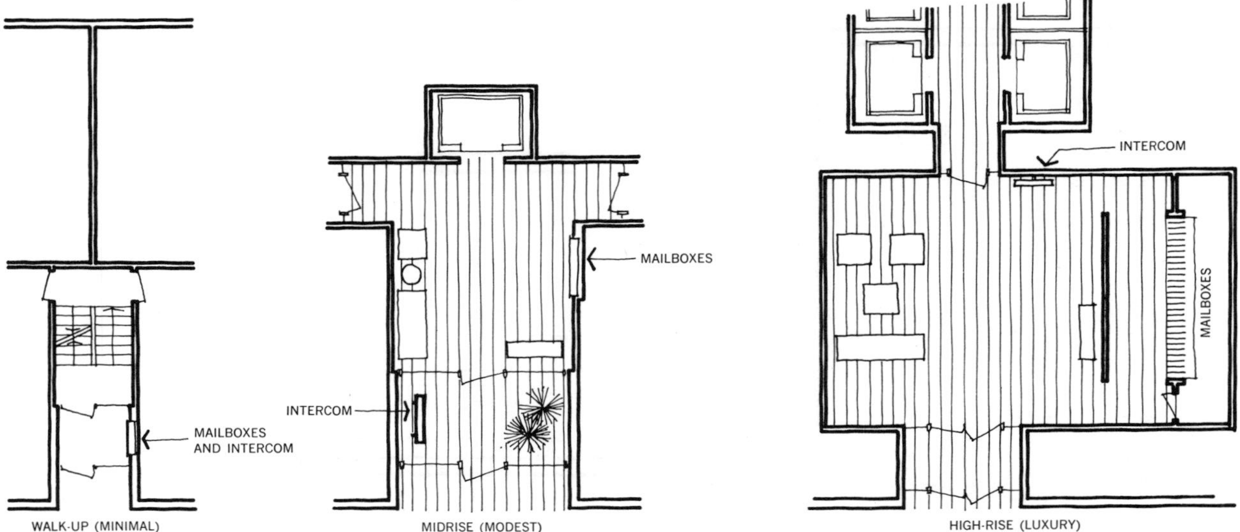

the best security is provided by a doorman on the premises. He not only helps with packages and directions but his mere presence is a deterrent to prowlers. Unfortunately, in low-income housing located in troubled areas in which the doorman would be most useful there is seldom an adequate budget for such "luxury." In these buildings a certain amount of security can be achieved, according to the defensible space principles of Oscar Newman,[22] by facing the lobby toward the street and making it as well as the elevator doors visible from the outside. The possibility of surveillance by the public acts as a deterrent to the potential criminal.

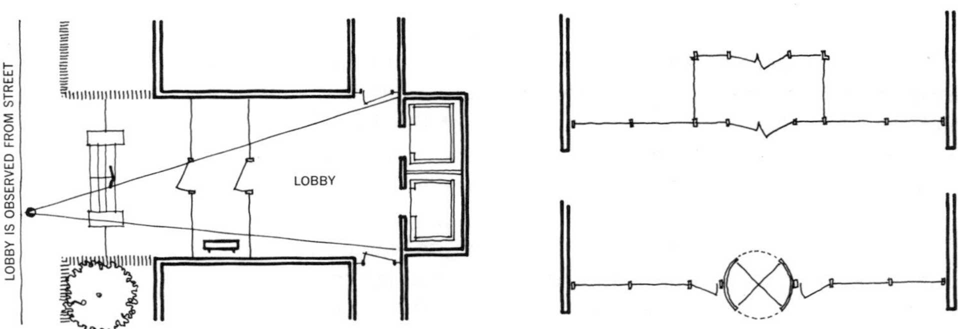

Because of frequent coming and going, the lobby needs a weatherbreak; that is, a vestibule or, in larger buildings, a revolving door. Because, however, the lobby may serve as a horizontal exit from the fire stairs to the outside, a hinged door is required in addition to the revolving door which can substitute for only a portion of the width of the code-required exit. The hinged door is useful also in relation to the delivery of packages that would not fit easily in a revolving door or for the handicapped for whom level passage between exterior and elevator must be provided. Most cities have ordinances for the handicapped that describe this on-grade passage (which can also be a mild ramp with rail) and the required door size.

The elderly as well have special needs. Because of the occupants' high incidence of sickness and accidents in addition to the customary intercom, an alarm system, which operates from both bedroom and the bathroom of the unit, should be connected with the manager's office, superintendent's apartment, or lobby counter. The lobby itself is a social center. The elderly enjoy sitting in the lobby and like to watch life in the street. Seating therefore should allow them to observe outdoor activities.

Although buildings with a relatively small number of units can be served with front-loading mailboxes, larger apartment buildings should have rear-loading boxes with a small room behind them where, on a shelf, the mailman can sort out the mail and load the boxes undisturbed. In planning the space for mailboxes, it is necessary to keep in mind the number of rows that be can reached comfortably in order to arrive at the horizontal dimension needed for the total number of mailboxes. The architect should be aware of the federal standards for mailboxes and, in larger projects, of the delivery and collection processes followed by the local postal service.

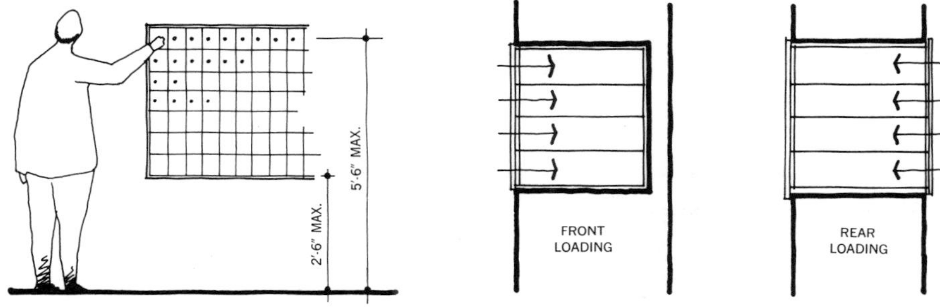

A constant problem is presented by packages or mail too large to fit into the mailboxes. When the addressee is not at home, the mailman can leave the package with the doorman or receiving clerk, if such person is on the premises, or take it back to the post office and leave a notice in the addressee's mailbox. When such personnel is provided, a secure area for packages must be located near the mailboxes or receiving room. In addition, a small closet or room near the doorman's stand is useful for various paraphernalia such as brooms, signs, and wheelchairs.

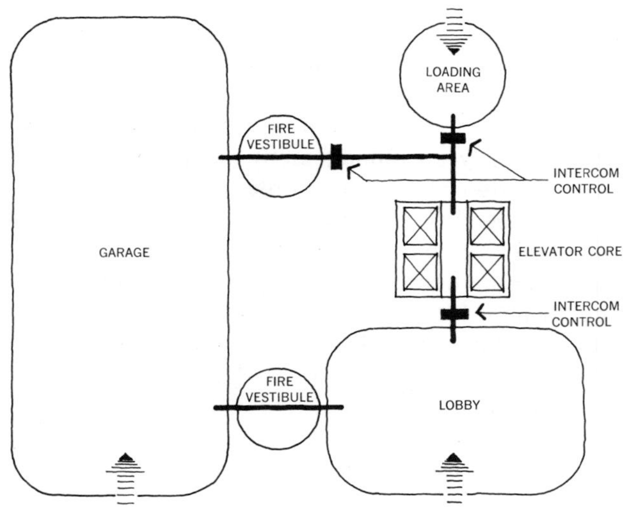

The perambulator storage (pram room) is closely related to the lobby function. The need for this space, and its size, depends on the type of occupancy. It should open from the vestibule, especially if the lobby is carpeted, so that prams do not have to be dragged through the lobby.

If there is a connection (through a fire vestibule) between the lobby and the garage, no separate intercom security is required. If, however, the garage connection is beyond the elevator lobby, an intercom security system similar to the one at the loading dock entrance must be installed (see p. 67).

When parking is by attendant it is necessary to provide a continually operating manlift, office and toilet for the manager and attendants, and waiting space for the tenants. This waiting space—approached through a fire vestibule—connects with the lobby. The entire complex should be designed to permit sufficient automobile pile-up space for both incoming and outgoing vehicles. It is usually a shabbily treated area between the utilitarian garage with its exposed concrete and the lavishly decorated lobby and deserves better design attention.

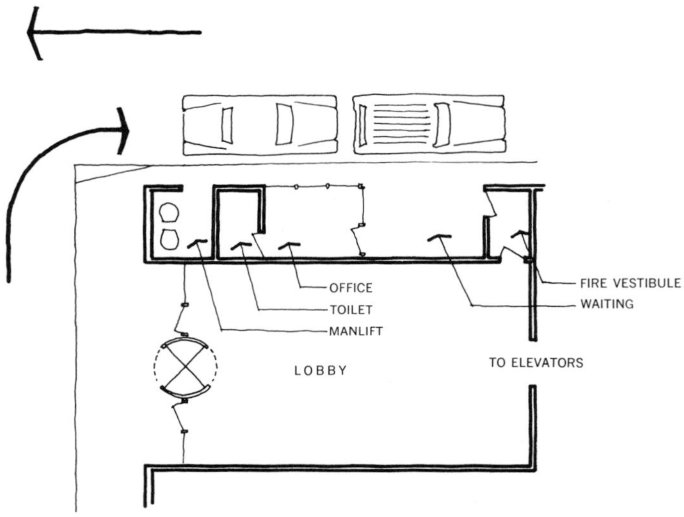

STORAGE

A large number of storage areas are needed in apartment buildings, the most forgotten of which is general storage used for all kinds of maintenance materials and at least a small amount of work space for in-house painting and repairing. The size of this area depends largely on management needs and practices. If large outdoor areas are to be tended and their maintenance is not separately contracted, general storage includes lawn mowers and snow-moving equipment. Consequently it is placed on grade level in contrast to small-site, highrise projects which do not need heavy ground equipment and whose storage can be in the basement or on ground level, usually near the mechanical equipment room. Large-site projects with several buildings may have general storage and maintenance facilities in a separate centrally located structure or central recreation building.

Storage for the use of occupants is provided in several sections of the building. Baby carriages are stored in the pram room near the main lobby, bicycles in a section of the garage, walled in or separated by wire partition, near the entrance.

Other tenant belongings that do not fit comfortably into the apartments—luggage, trunks, boxes, skis, tires, and so on—are stored in tenant lockers which are 3 × 5 or 4 × 4 ft spaces enclosed by partitions of metal frame and wire mesh, located in rows on each side of 3 ft aisles in a locker room. (Lockers may be planned one above the other, but each must have at least an 80-cf capacity.) For estimating the floor area needed for tenant lockers a minimum of 25 sf per apartment should be allowed (this includes locker as well as proportionate aisle space). The locker room, can be located anywhere in the building as long as it can be reached by the service elevator; it must also have two means of egress. The usual locations are on the top floor of the tower, an unused part of the garage, or the basement in highrises, the first floor or the basement in midrises, and the basement in walk-ups. Sometimes tenant lockers are located on the same floor as the apartments. This is a rather special case which occurs when the building configuration results in "wasted" space on the typical floor, space that cannot be otherwise utilized or when, because of site restrictions, no space can be found for lockers on the lower levels.

LAUNDRY

Some developers consider the laundry as an amenity, but like proper storage facilities, the laundry is a necessary adjunct of housing.

Although its purpose is tenant convenience, its provision, like so many other things in housing, is dictated by economy. The ideal arrangement which would provide every apartment dweller with a washer/dryer is the general parctice in townhouses, but in other multifamily housing it can be implemented—due to cost and space limitations—only when the market can absorb the extra expense. When laundry facilities are part of each apartment, they are located in the kitchen or, more commonly, in a closet opening on the entry hall or bedroom corridor. The ultimate in luxury is a small utility room near the kitchen.

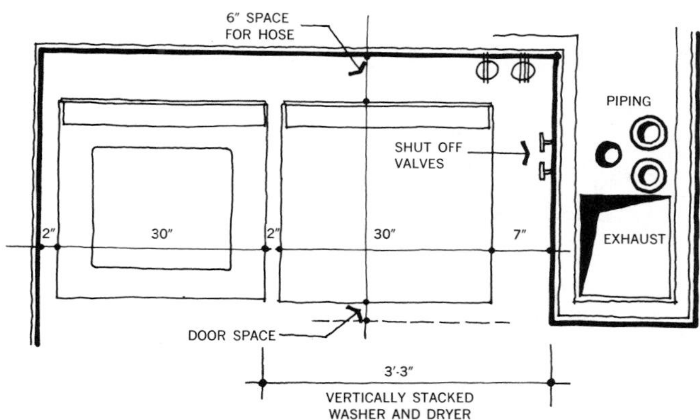

The next step, a small laundry room on each floor with one or two pairs of machines, is a distinct convenience. However, the use of such a small number of machines requires tight scheduling, a problem eliminated by a central facility equipped with many machines. Also, in addition to being uneconomical, a laundry on each floor is a source of odors and vibration. Only in housing for the elderly is this system occasionally used, but even here it is a luxury, for the elevator provides a perfectly acceptable means of access to the central laundry.

Obviously economy dictates the installation of a central laundry facility. Many pros and cons relate to its location and the decision must depend on the type of occupancy. For families with many young children a room near the play area is ideal because it affords excellent supervision. When there are only a few youngsters in a building and recreation facilities are more formal, the laundry should not be part of the recreation complex. For the elderly the laundry provides an opportunity for socializing and its proximity to other recreational facilities is an advantage.

Physically the basement is the least desirable location. The ground floor is preferable because it can have daylight, and the recreation deck is even better because it interrelates with other community and recreational activities. The top floor is the ideal location not only because of its good view but also its accessibility to the roof terrace. It is important, however, that the service elevator stop at this floor.

Projects with several small buildings but a large enough site may have laundry facilities in a separate centrally located community building.

Regardless of its location, the central laundry should be near the elevator, should have toilets nearby, and two means of egress. In addition to washing machines and dryers (coin-operated in larger projects) the laundry room should be equipped with laundry sinks, space for folding tables, and a sitting area (with vending machines, coin changer, and soap dispenser). A 3 ft service space is required behind the dryers and 1 ft 6 in. for plumbing between the rows of washers.

The number of washers and dryers is proportionate to the number of apartments. In projects of 20 families, a washer and a dryer for every seven apartments; 20 to 50 families, a washer and dryer for every 10 apartments; between 50 and 100 families, a washer and a dryer for every 15 apartments; for more than 100 families, a washer for every 20 apartments and a dryer for every 40 apartments. To determine the size of the laundry room, 25 sf of floor area should be allowed for each machine.

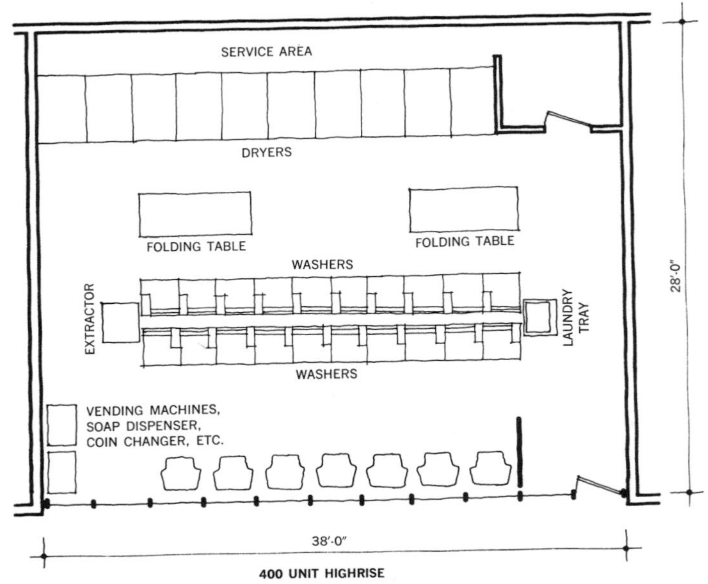

400 UNIT HIGHRISE

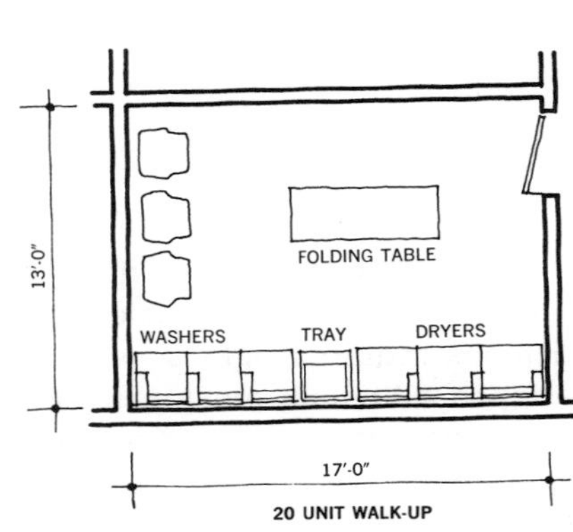

20 UNIT WALK-UP

RECREATION

The most ambiguous of all housing requirements is the space needed for recreation facilities. There are no useful standards to guide the architect in deciding the kind and quantity of recreation space to provide in a particular project. Zoning ordinances do not address themselves to this problem. At best they set ''open space'' requirements.

Because there are neither adequate guides nor meaningful regulations, developers tend to provide only as much recreation space as is needed to make the project marketable. This approach results in a relatively high level of recreational amenities for upper income housing, where the renter or buyer, through his pocketbook, can exercise his options. In public or federally assisted housing it is minimal, but even the upper income renter has only limited choices in a seller's market.

In all recent attempts to define recreational needs the one most sensitive to the problem is described by The Urban Design Council of the City of New York in ''Housing Quality—A Program for Zoning Reform.'' It proposes that certain recreation facilities be made mandatory in all housing.

> Any proposed housing development will accommodate, within predictable limits, a fixed number of children and/or adults. Based upon these projections, specific types of recreation space must be provided for the exclusive benefit of the various age groups. The required recreation space is based upon a reasonable minimum need per person in the development, and may not be impinged upon for any other purpose, such as parking.

The New York proposal then defines what should be considered as recreation space. Its major innovations occur in its definitions. It considers public stoops, terraces, and laundry rooms as adult recreation areas and advocates that properly developed roofs be made available for the use of residents. The general requirements of the program are the following:

> The proposed development should provide child use space, mixed use space (children and adults) and adult use space in relation to projected tenancy characteristics. Computation is as follows:

a. Compute the building occupancy according to the following schedule:

Apartment	Occupancy
Studio	1 Adult
1 BR apt.	2 Adults
2 BR apt.	2 Adults & 1 child
3 BR apt.	2 Adults & 2 children
4 BR apt.	2 Adults & 3 children

b. Compute the amount of recreation space required according to the following schedule:

- For child use space multiply the number of children by 20 S.F.
- For mixed use space multiply the total number of residents (children plus adults) by 25 S.F.
- For adult use space multiply the number of adults by 100 S.F.

c. The facilities permitted to fulfill space requirements are:

Children	Adult	Mixed
Tot Lot	Passive	Swimming Pool
Intermediate Playground	Rooftop Terrace	Handball
Nursery Daycare (Public)	Health Club	Tennis Courts
Nursery Daycare (Private)	Terrace	Basketball
	Laundry Room	Meeting Rooms
		Volleyball
		Shops—Craft
		Shops—Automotive

Within these categories the developer can fulfill recreation requirements in relation to user characteristics and demands. Unfortunately this proposal, like all categorizations, has built-in rigidities; for instance, there are areas in which buildings containing two-bedroom apartments will be without children and consequently need no child-oriented recreation spaces. Also, some kinds of tenancy such as the elderly, demands special recreation space.

The greatest difficulties appear to be in the square foot requirements, on the basis of which a luxury condominium of 500 apartments in Chicago would need more than 140,000 sf in combined recreation space! This particular building, in which the residents are well satisfied with the area provided, actually has two open pools, two tennis courts, a putting green, shuffle boards, an enclosed handball court, saunas, daycare facilities, game rooms, and large community rooms and devotes altogether approximately 40,000 sf to recreation, far less than the 140,000 estimated in the New York guide. The figures in the New York proposal seem valid for smaller projects, but as the number of apartments increases the proposed space requirements are excessive; taking into account simultaneous use, they should be proportionately decreased.

The grouping and definition of facilities in the New York proposal have wide validity with minor adjustments and amplification:

CHILDREN

In open-air tot-lots and intermediate age playgrounds careful differentiation between young children and teen-age groups with proper activities and identification for each is essential. It is important that these areas be observable. A level connection between the elevator stop and the tot lot is a necessity.

Daycare or nursery facilities require space for supervisory personnel, storage, special toilets, and cooking facilities. For minimum requirements the regulations of local health boards or state agencies must be consulted. These agencies also regulate the necessary adjacent outdoor play area per child.

ADULT

Open air sitting and quiet areas must have some sort of shading, landscaping, lighting, and outdoor furniture.

Gardening plots are sometimes provided in housing for the elderly. The location of tool storage must be considered in this case.

A rooftop terrace must have an elevator stop at terrace level. It also needs proper surfacing, lighting, and screening from stacks, exhausts, and strong winds. Part of it should be covered to provide shelter from rain and sun, and public toilets must be nearby.

The laundry room, as a social magnet, can be counted among recreation spaces. The lounge area must be adequate for furniture grouping and public toilets should be accessible, but to be considered at all it must have daylight.

The health club contains sauna, dressing rooms, showers, and toilets, for men and women and is usually located near the swimming pool. An exercise room—sometimes with massage tables, sleeping rooms, and even a steam bath—can be located between the men's and women's section of the sauna, making possible the use of a single facility by men and women in alternate schedules. As a rule of thumb, a health club consisting of sauna, showers, dressing space, and toilets (but not exercise room or steam bath) for each sex requires the following square footage: for 100 apartments, 8 sf per apartment; 100 to 250 apartments, 5 to 6 sf per apartment; 250 to 500 apartments, 3.5 to 4 sf per apartment.

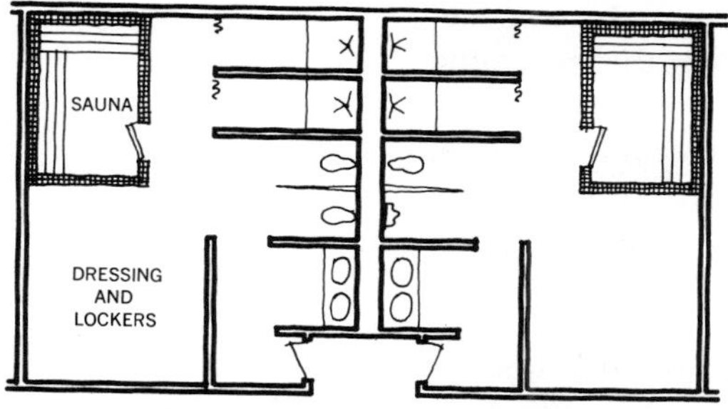

APPR. 800 SQ. FT. HEALTH CLUB: 250 APTS.

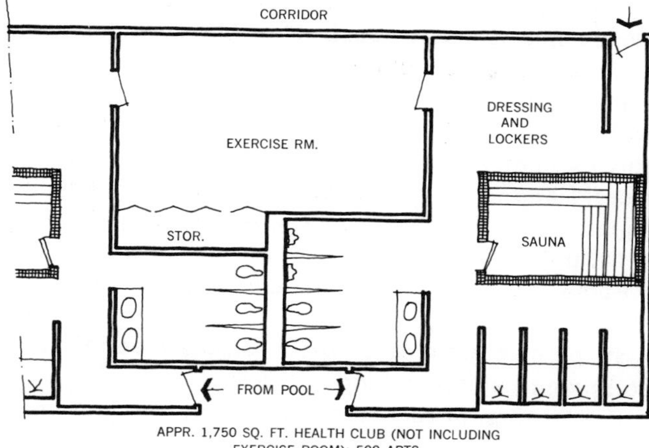

APPR. 1,750 SQ. FT. HEALTH CLUB (NOT INCLUDING EXERCISE ROOM): 500 APTS.

MIXED

Sports such as tennis, handball, basketball, and volley ball are usually played in the open air unless a high budget permits enclosures. Dimensional stardards, orientation, height, proper finishes, and lighting must be checked. Toilets, showers, and dressing rooms are needed for each sex, and can double as pool facilities. Sometimes a small spectator space is provided.

An open-air putting green needs no adjacent facilities.

A swimming pool can be enclosed or in the open. When covered, the height of the space depends on the diving board, and an open-air sun bathing terrace must adjoin. The season for open-air swimming pools in northern climates can be extended by providing wind shielding around the deck. State health regulations will determine toilet and shower requirements as well as such details as gutters around the pool, foot bath, and filtering. Storage space must be built for deck furniture.

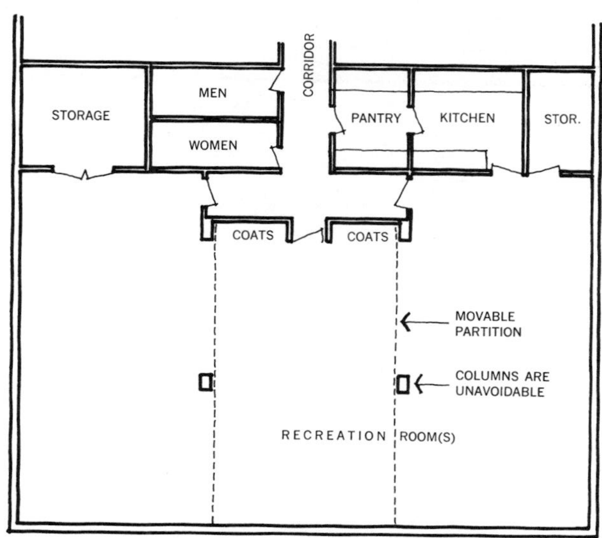

APPR. 3,200 SQ. FT. RECREATION FACILITY: 500 APTS.

Meeting rooms must have space for impromptu community gatherings or special events on a scheduled basis. Movable partitions permit multiple use of the space. Separate toilets should be installed because the floor of the toilets that serve the sauna or the swimming pool is usually wet.

Meeting rooms also require coat space, storage for furniture, small kitchen, serving pantry for catered parties. In estimating meeting room space (including storage and kitchen) 15 sf per apartment is needed for buildings of 100 units. The square footage can be proportionately reduced to 8 sf per apartment for buildings of 500 units (see p. 73).

Game rooms for cards, pool, and ping pong are usually located near the meeting rooms.

Shops or craft rooms, also near the meeting rooms, require storage, special equipment, and plumbing.

The location of recreation space depends not only on functional requirements and interrelations but on the physical character of the project it serves. The locations available for recreation depend on the type of project and the site.

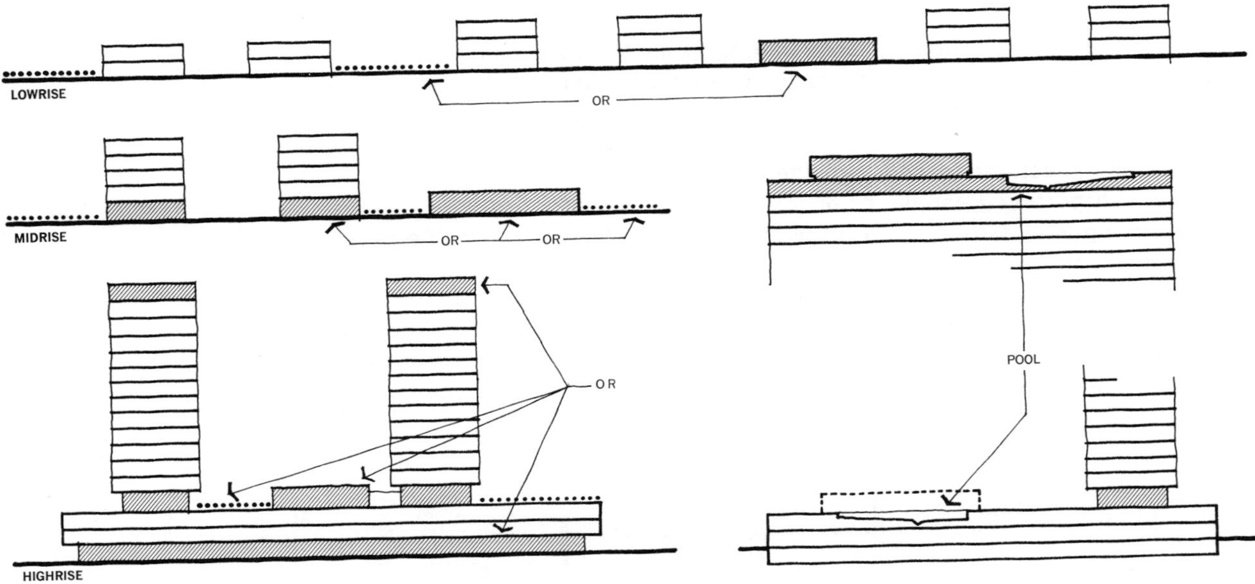

COMPONENTS OF DESIGN—STRUCTURAL

3

Eugene P. Holland

FRAME SELECTION

The selection of the frame must result in the most economical structure within the bounds of the building function. The final product must be serviceable as well. What does "serviceable" mean? Deflection of floors and vibratory conditions must be within reasonable limits; architectural elements interfacing with structural elements must suffer minimal distress; building drift must be limited to minimize partition cracking or crushing and must be so minimal that adverse human response to building movement will be eliminated.

Unlike mechanical equipment, hardware, doors, or cabinetry, the structural system has no range of economic decision. The same well-designed structure could be used in minimal housing or in the most exclusive apartment construction. Having satisfied strength and serviceability, there is no way to make the structure "better." Additional quantity adds only to cost, not to quality.

Selection of the structure is bound by a multitude of interacting parameters. The program established by the building's sponsor tends to dictate the general type of structure. The number and type of desired units requires a specific expanse of building. Walk-up apartments are generally limited to three or four stories. Within this range, if allowed by code, the wood frame has most frequently proved to be economical from a first-cost standpoint. Aside from walk-ups, the number of apartments may be achieved by utilizing a large floor area and few floors or a smaller floor area and a greater number of floors. The choice is generally limited by the building code, zoning, and site conditions. If tolerance is allowed, the former will usually result in a more economical structure.

FLOOR AREA

A structure with a floor area of less than approximately 8000 sf cannot utilize a concrete crew efficiently; therefore a steel frame, site or plant precast, or other "prefabricated" structure is generally competitive.

HEIGHT

A structure of less than about seven stories high generally requires no significant lateral-load-resisting provisions. The gravity load elements of the building will be adequate to resist lateral loads with only slight modifications. Above this height consideration must be given to the integration and additional cost of bracing, shearwalls, or moment connections. The use of a concrete flat plate requires about 8 ft 5 in. floor-to-floor, whereas a steel frame needs about 9 ft 6 in., a signicant difference in multistory structures. Accordingly, more stories may be developed within the same overall building height with a flat plate. A good example is Chicago's requirement that a smokeproof tower be provided in buildings more than 264 ft high. Within this height four more stories could be provided by using a thin concrete flat plate instead of steel. Careful consideration of cost must also be given to the increased exterior wall surface, longer stair runs, increased pipes, and mechanical ducts in a structure with greater floor-to-floor heights.

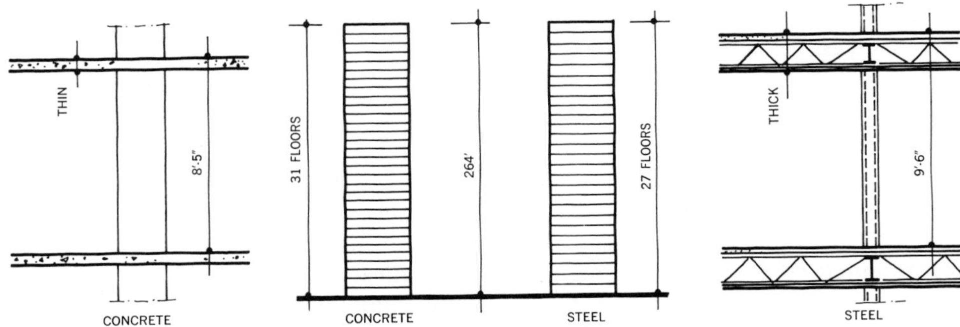

COLUMN SPACING AND ARRANGEMENT

Columns may be arranged in a rigid grid pattern or "scattered"—their placement determined by the best apartment plan. The rigid grid is ideal for a structural steel frame and is advantageous for a concrete frame in which "flying" forms are utilized. The "scattered" column layout, however, allows almost complete architectural freedom in apartment planning.

Except for a few cases, column spacing in apartment structures need not exceed 15 or 16 ft (maximum living room width). Thus in contrast to office buildings a short-span framing system becomes possible. The small span will result in additional columns; however, unless foundation considerations are critical, the added cost is minimal when compared with the positive cost advantage of shorter spans.

COLUMN TRANSFERS

Parking under the tower portion of the building requires careful coordination to avoid problems with the column layout. Column transfers are extremely costly and should be avoided. The most economical parking is outside the tower itself. The same problem exists for ''air-right'' projects in which clear open spans at the lower levels are required. If major column transfers become unavoidable, the lightest frame possible should be used: either structural steel or lightweight concrete should be considered.

FOUNDATIONS

Similar consideration is required when foundation material is poor. If very deep foundations, such as piles, are recommended, the added cost must be taken into account when comparing structural frames.

MATERIALS

The availability and cost of materials may dictate the choice of structural frame. Especially in times of material shortages, the structural engineer must maintain current knowledge of material supply and up-to-date relative costs. The time element in obtaining materials may also effect the decision. If the owners' financial commitment is generating inordinate interest costs, the choice of a more expensive structural frame that is available for earlier construction may be offset by the savings in interest and sometimes earlier occupancy.

CONSTRUCTION SEASONS

Seasonal variation in construction depends on the building's geographical location. In cold-weather country the brevity of good construction time in the winter season may dictate the use of a frame that can be erected without regard to climate. Many winter days do not permit on-site casting of concrete, whereas structural steel or precast concrete can readily be placed.

LABOR

Union and other labor practices may effect structural frame choice. A prime example relates to the variation in union rules concerning casting concrete. In the Midwest the same concrete crew may be required to stay with the casting process. If the concreting extends beyond the normal work day, the contractor is obligated to pay double and sometimes triple hourly rates. This minimizes the cost advantage of concrete. On the other hand, labor unions in other areas of the country permit entirely different crews to work the second and even third shifts of the work day, thereby allowing the contractor to complete the work in a shorter time without the ''overtime'' penalty. Another example relates to the tieing of reinforcing steel. Certain regions permit the iron worker to carry the tie wire with him; others require him to go back and forth from a designated tie wire storage area. Before selecting the framing system, the structural engineer therefore must review union regulations and also standard practices in the building's locale. The results may tip the scale in the selection of the frame.

STRUCTURAL FRAMES

CAST-IN-PLACE REINFORCED CONCRETE

The cast-in-place reinforced concrete flat-plate structure is the most widely used system for highrise apartment structures in the United States. It is estimated that approximately 90% of all apartment buildings of more than 10 stories are so constructed. Reasons for this high percentage are numerous.

1. Reduced building height, thereby reduced mechanical and electrical runs, facade, and wind loadings which minimize lateral load-resisting elements and foundations.
2. Contractors have become adept at this type of construction.
3. Finishes are simplified, with paint or skim coat of plaster for final ceilings.
4. Fire rating is automatically provided with concrete. Normal slab design thicknesses satisfy most building-code fire requirements.
5. Architectural planning is not hindered by consideration of rigid column layout because scattered columns may be used. Partition layout is not controlled by beams extending beneath the slab.

SLAB THICKNESS. Maximum economy is obtained when structures that require materials working the least to resist applied loads are devised. The object therefore is to minimize slab span by maintaining close column spacing. Additional columns do not substantially increase cost but thinner slabs will decrease it. All but the most luxurious apartment structures can accommodate column spacings of about 15 ft. This span, measured from face to face of the columns requires a slab thickness of 5 in. Increased spans require increased reinforcing steel, the prime measurement of economy in a concrete structure.

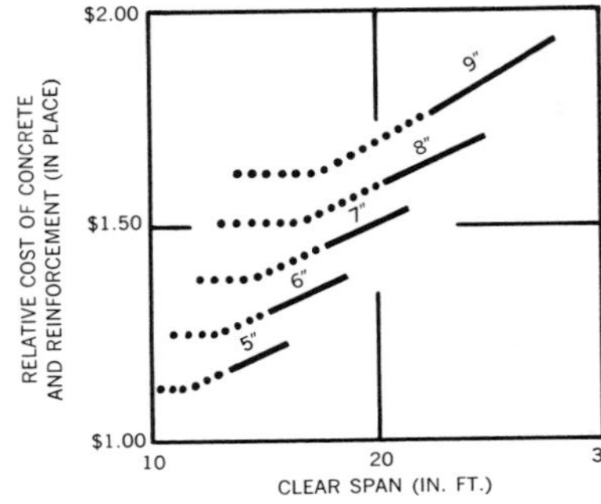

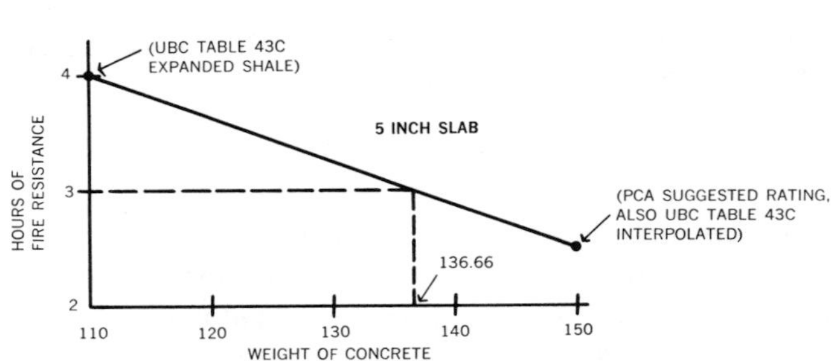

The rule of thumb for slab thickness provides that the span length in feet, when divided by three, will give the slab thickness in inches. In other words, the slab thickness must increase ½ in. for each 1.5 ft increase in span.

A slab thickness of 5 in., using normal weight concrete, will satisfy the majority of building-code fire requirements; however, some codes require a three-hour vertical separation which necessitates using a lighter weight concrete or a thicker normal weight slab. The curve above shows that a 5-in. slab of 137-pcf (pounds per cubic foot) concrete will satisfy the three-hour requirement. A 5½-in. slab of 150-pcf concrete would also be adequate.

MECHANICAL, ELECTRICAL CONSIDERATIONS. Slab penetration for pipe chases, shafts, and duct work should be accomplished without adverse effect to the structure and a minimum increase in structural element size. Larger shafts for elevators and stairs should be ideally located in the center half of the bay. To achieve this condition lightweight wall assemblies (shaft walls) are best. Lightweight walls avoid the need for edge beams. (Masonry walls could be used without edge beams, provided that the masonry passes the slab with adequate lateral ties or that it is allowed to span from column to column with only minimal load bearing on the slab span.) The most critical areas for openings are at or near columns. Openings at columns generally require an increase in column size to maintain equivalent slab capacity. The opening size and position greatly affect this condition. If large openings (stairs or elevators) are located at columns, it may be necessary to frame the opening with walls or at least additional columns.

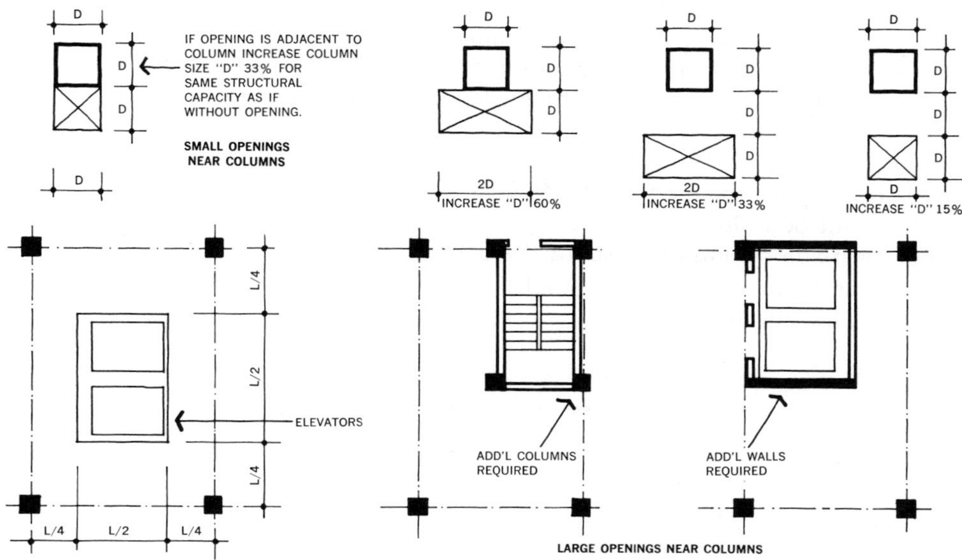

IN-SLAB CONDUITS. The use of sleeves for pipes and vents, in lieu of totally open chases, offers considerable structural advantage. Electrical conduits in the plane of the slab (including crossovers) should never be greater than one-third of the slab thickness and should always be placed between the bottom and top layers of reinforcing material. If possible, the grouping of conduits, especially at columns, should be avoided. If this is not possible, the grouped conduits must be considered as creating an entire opening in the slab.

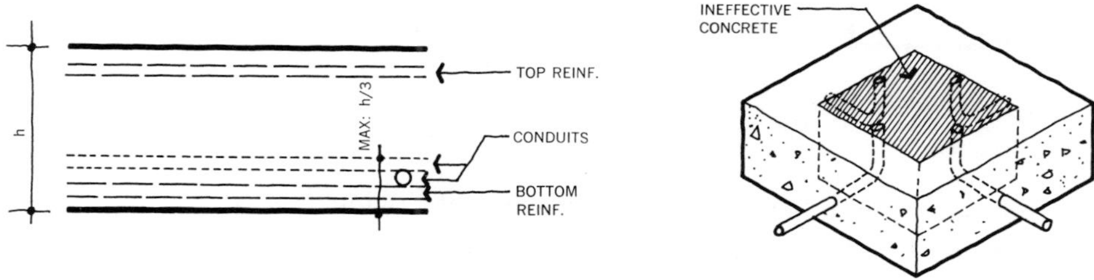

PLUMBING. To fit within the floor slab standard plumbing traps require a minimum slab thickness of about 6 in. With a 5 in. slab the standard fittings project below the slab. The result is a suspended ceiling or some other architectural solution to disguise the trap. A fixture that discharges above the floor avoids the problem, as do the shallow traps that have been used on 5-in. slab projects in conjunction with prefabricated stacks.

SOUND CONSIDERATIONS. Concrete flat plates provide excellent resistance to airborne transmission. As far as impact noise is concerned slab thickness does not discernibly influence the effectiveness of the floor. The major influence is the type of floor covering. With the same floor covering the difference between a 5-to-6-in. slab and a 7-to-8 in. slab is 3 (STC) and 1 (IIC).

COLUMN CONFIGURATIONS. Columns are usually square or rectangular and, on occasion, circular (usually when free standing). The square column requires the least formwork and is therefore the most economical. Square and especially rectangular columns are generally more adaptable to apartment layouts than the round. Long narrow (6 to 8 in. wide) columns may be used to good advantage in limiting projections into rooms, fitting well into closets and corners and also minimizing slab spans. Unless the reduction of column sizes offers an extreme architectural advantage, columns should be reduced only every 10 to 15 stories. This reduction, however, need not be made symmetrical about the column centroid. Maintaining at least one flush face throughout the building height will eliminate dimensional problems and allow efficient form use.

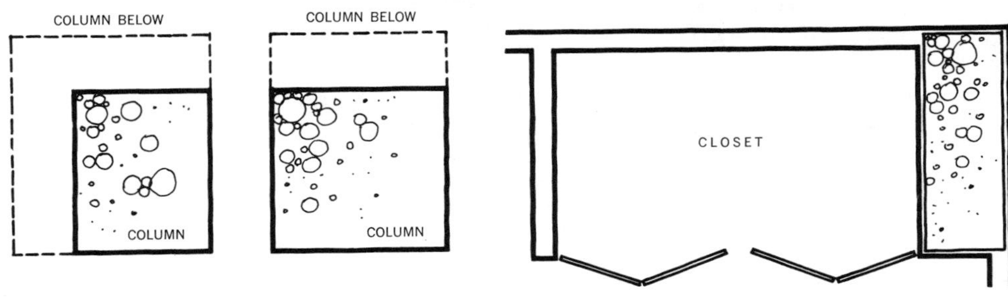

Architectural considerations can lead to a variety of column configurations and shapes on the exterior.

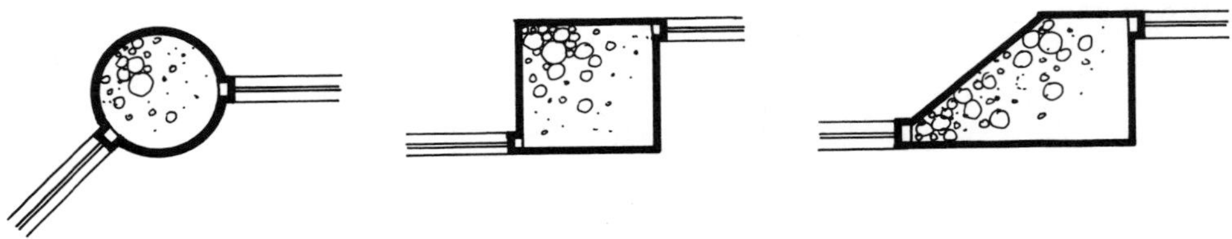

RIGID COLUMN PATTERN. The rigid column layout allows for the use of "flying forms" (entire sections of shores and forms are lifted intact from story to story). Unfortunately the completely rigid layout generally requires longer spans and thicker slabs, therefore defeating or at least seriously affecting the forming cost advantage.

SEMIRIGID COLUMN PATTERN. The "semirigid" grid with shorter spans (none longer than the 15 ft, dictated by living room width), which combines ''flying forms'' and ordinary forming may prove to be advantageous: column placement is not so rigid and inflexible that it hinders the floor plan and regularity provides uniformity in construction procedures, details, and reinforcing.

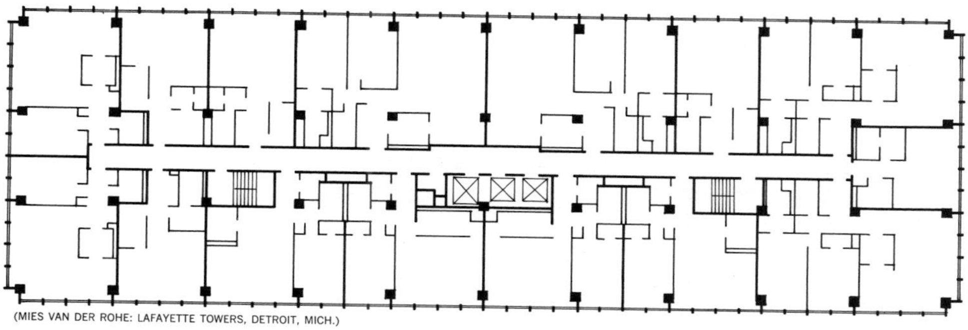

(MIES VAN DER ROHE: LAFAYETTE TOWERS, DETROIT, MICH.)

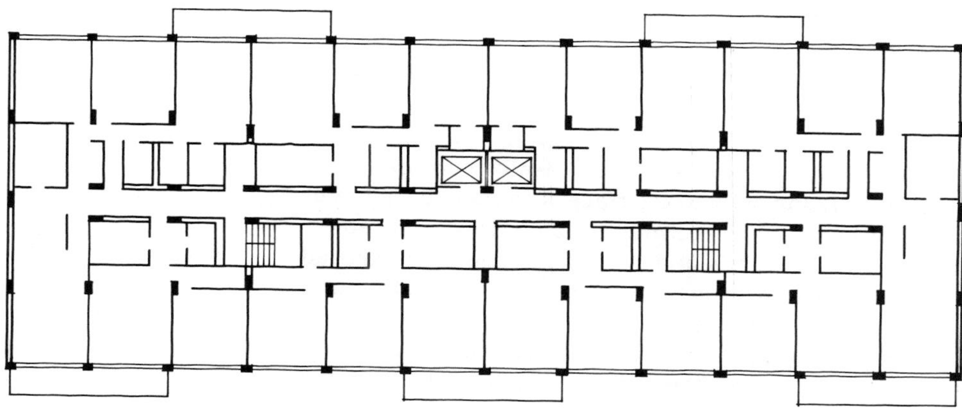

SCATTERED COLUMN PATTERN. The ''scattered'' column layout eliminates architectural restraints and allows placement of columns where they fit into the plan best. It is often advantageous to use long and narrow rectangular columns to minimize slab spans and even decrease the total number of columns.

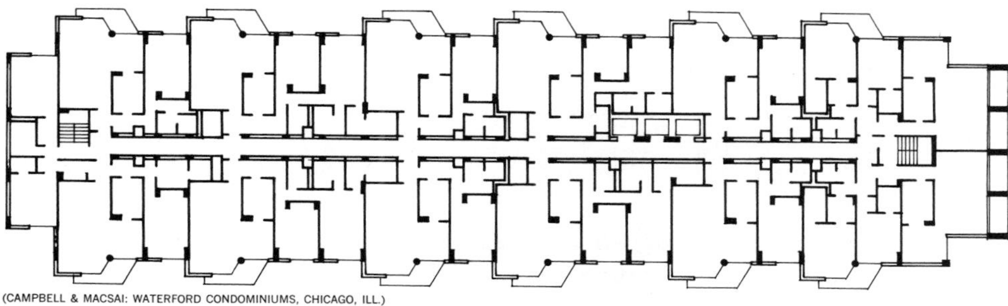

(CAMPBELL & MACSAI: WATERFORD CONDOMINIUMS, CHICAGO, ILL.)

EXTERIOR COLUMN SPACING. Exterior column spacing is generally dictated by the exterior skin. To avoid problems of deflection and/or excessive cambers, close spacing is often needed to support the weight of a heavier exterior such as precast concrete or masonry. This closer spacing replaces spandrel beams, which should be avoided unless essential from an architectural standpoint. Exterior spans with a lightweight facade should be limited to 15 ft for thin slabs (5 in.+) and 21 ft for thicker slabs (8 in.+). Heavyweight facades limit the span to about 12 ft and 18 ft for thin and thick slabs, respectively.

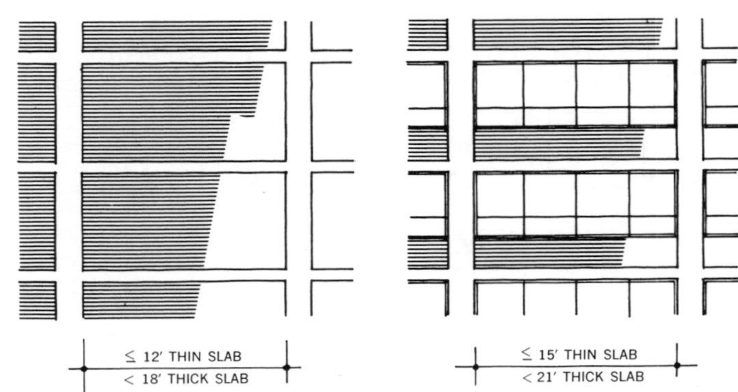

Architecturally exposed exterior columns require special design considerations for both column configuration and slab-to-column interface. The transfer of forces require sufficient slab "bite" to the column. Thermal movements of exposed exterior columns need special structural analysis and construction details: exposed concrete may change vertical dimension by an inch or more in a 50 story structure.

Exterior column spacing may also be influenced by interior partition locations. A closely spaced column grid allows greater flexibility in partition layout. Close spacing of exterior columns, discussed later, offers a further structural advantage concerning lateral loads.

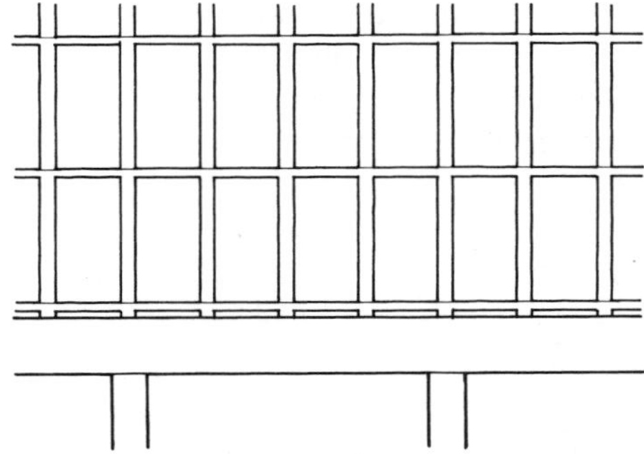

CANTILEVERS. Apartment structures are often designed with cantilevered balconies or projecting bays. The basic structural consideration is to maintain a cantilever span-to-slab thickness relationship that will prevent misbehavior in the form of deflections and flexibility. This is particularly true for projecting bays enclosed by walls at the free edges. The slab thickness-to-cantilever-span ratio shown may be extended with the understanding that serviceability may be impaired. The slab thickness, however, may be decreased at the end of the cantilever to provide drainage. (Caution should be exercised in arriving at the minimum thickness because of the anchoring requirement of railings.)

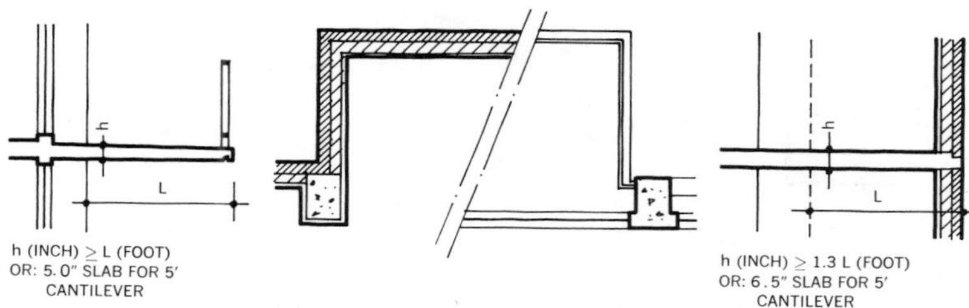

A curb may be provided to prevent water intrusion, although some argue that it is dangerous or at least inconvenient. However, it has been used satisfactorily on luxury apartment buildings under sliding doors. Somewhat less efficient but eliminating objections to the curb is the ¾-in. break in the slab proper. Efficient but costly is the balcony that utilizes a spandrel beam.

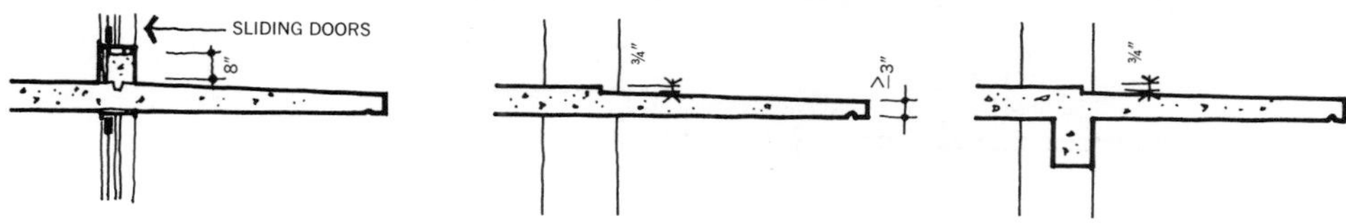

Continuous, exposed exterior balconies or corridors, popular in warmer climates, require considerations for thermal movement generally satisfied by the use of joints. Joints are normally placed in the range of 10 to 15 ft, depending on the architectural plan and balcony extent.

COLUMN TRANSFERS. The interruption of column continuity is often desirable at the lower levels of apartment structures: the need is for larger spans at entrances, community rooms, and lobby areas or parking and driving aisles under the

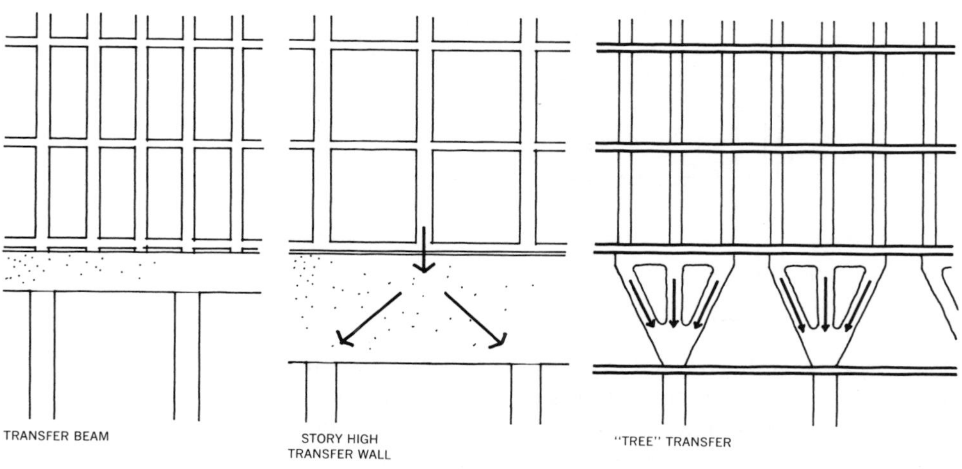

tower. The best solution is to avoid the problem; when unavoidable, however, the methods generally employed utilize transfer beams, transfer walls, or transfer "*trees*." The last two are preferable because of their structural efficiency in force transfer.

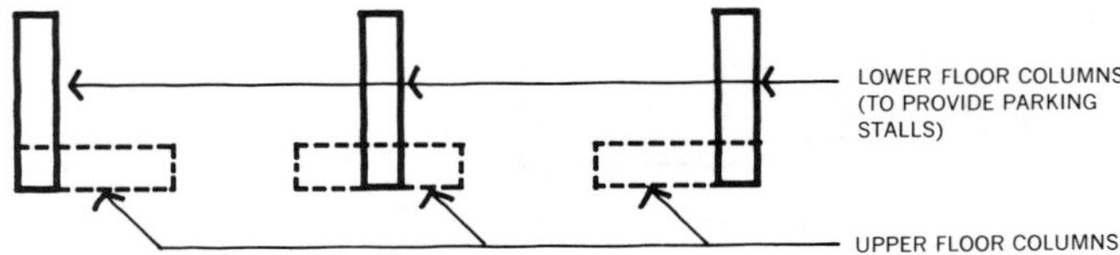

Occasionally the increased space on the lower level may be accomplished by changing the orientation of the columns.

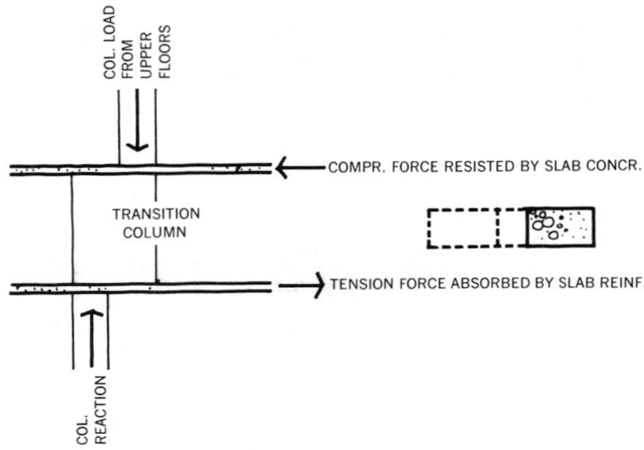

In addition, a complete offset in column location from upper to lower floors is made possible by using a "transition" column and utilizing the floor slabs to provide a resisting couple against the moment created by the eccentric load.

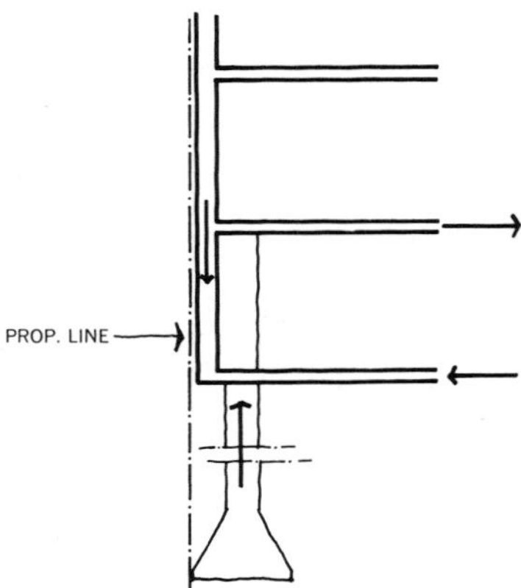

The same structural action may be readily adapted to other eccentric loads. The scarcity and cost of land in urban areas require the full use of the available property and structures are often designed to extend from property line to property line. To prevent foundations from encroaching on adjacent property they must be set back from the lot line, thereby creating an eccentric load.

FLAT PLATE—FORMS AND SHORES. Although construction remains the contractor's responsibility, it is necessary to elaborate on the procedures required to form and shore a flat plate structure safely.

Careless shoring and early shore removal have resulted in numerous cases of nonlevel floors and, on occasion, catastrophic failures. The contractor must be made aware of the fact that ''green'' concrete has only a limited carrying capacity.

The problems can be minimized by removing only small portions of forming and reshoring as the forms are removed or utilizing ''trapped'' shores (shores that remain in place when the forms are stripped automatically become the ''reshores'').

The casting cycle is the primary factor in determining the number of shored and reshored floors required. Generally, the following sequence is necessary as a minimum shoring criterion: the first structural slab must be completely shored. The second structural slab must also be completely shored when the concrete is placed. When the second slab has gained at least 70% of its 28-day compressive strength and the first slab has gained at least 85% of its 28-day compressive strength, the first slab shores may be removed and reshores placed under the first slab. The second slab shores must remain in place. The third slab shores are then set and the third slab cast. When the third slab has gained at least 70% of its 28-day compressive strength and the second slab has gained at least 85% of its 28-day compressive strength, the second floor shores may be removed and reshores placed, and so on. The compressive strengths required are best determined by test cylinders cast and cured by the same procedure used in the actual slab construction.

For a three-to-four-day casting cycle this ''formula'' results in the need for four sets of forms. Three floors are always fully shored and one set of forms is in transit. Three additional floors are reshored. A very large floor area (greater than about 16,000 sf) allows for staggered casting of half floors, thereby minimizing the required forms and maximizing the casting cycle. In other words, reinforcing for half the slab is being placed while the other half is being cast, and so on.

The contractor usually knows that certain deflections will occur and generally provides a small camber in the slab forms. Most contract specifications require the contractor to provide camber in accordance with ACI 347, ''Concrete Formwork.'' This document outlines the responsibility of the contractor to provide camber for shortening of shores, mud sill settlement, and form deflection. It does not require camber for elastic deflections following shore removal nor for long-term creep deflections. This is the structural engineer's responsibility, and, if deemed necessary, requirements must be contained in the contract documents.

EXPANSION JOINTS. Changes in volume of concrete due to variations in temperature and moisture content must be recognized as a detriment to the structure's serviceability. Exposed vertical concrete elements such as columns or shear walls will change dimensions when subjected to temperature variations. In highrise structures this dimension may be an inch or more. Slabs and partitions interfacing such elements will suffer distress if not detailed to allow for this movement.

Exposed horizontal concrete spandrels, balconies, walls, and roofs, require expansion joints to provide for length changes due to temperature. The spacing of expansion joints in roofs is dependent to a great extent on thermal roof insulation. Requirements for expansion joint spacing vary between 150 and 250 ft on roofs and a lesser distance in exposed concrete; particular attention must be paid to offsets. To be totally effective expansion joints should extend vertically through the building. They are not required, however, when structural elements supporting the subjected concrete are flexible enough to deform with the temperature movement; for instance, slender columns supporting a concrete roof may be flexible enough to drift with the expansion of the slab without deleterious effects. Expansion joints are also used on roofs of buildings with nonlinear plan geometry; Y-, T-, or L-shaped buildings with long or dissimilar wings should have expansion joints at the building core separating the wings. Joints that allow for differential settlement are required at the meeting of the tower columns and garage slabs.

GARAGE FRAMING. Parking under the apartment tower offers many nonstructural advantages: reduced land coverage, shorter walking distance to the elevators, and increased security. With the most efficient 90-degree parking system, 20-to-22-ft aisles are used and therefore large spans and heavier slabs are required. Small spans, however, preferred from the point of view of structural economy, result in thinner slabs in the tower and transfer columns to facilitate parking, a rather costly solution. Methods of transfer have already been discussed. Cost advantages of close column spacing in the tower may be totally maintained if coordination of apartment layout and parking allow the apartment columns to continue down through the parking area without transfer. This, of course, requires other than 90-degree parking; for instance, with a 13 ft 6 in. one-directional travel aisle and 45-degree parking the close spacing of tower columns may not hinder a reasonable parking layout. Parking outside the tower area is more advantageous from a structural standpoint and produces the most efficient parking layout.

The framing system of the garage is dictated by column spacing. In concrete mild reinforced or post-tensioned flat slab with column capitals, ribbed slabs (pan joist or waffle), or precast, prestressed double-tee sections are used. The recent relaxation of fire-rating requirements for parking structures permits steel frames with concrete slabs to be considered more often.

Ninety-degree parking with 20-ft driving aisles requires 22 to 27 ft between columns. With an 8 ft 6 in. or 9 ft parking-stall width, columns in the transverse direction may then be spaced at a multiple of the stall width; for example, 18 or 27 ft. From these choices various column layouts may be selected. For a square (or nearly square) grid with minimum column spacing the flat slab with column capitals is generally the most economical and may be mild reinforced or post-tensioned. A two-way grid (waffle slab), also applicable, utilizes material to its best advantage; however, form costs (steel or fiberglass) are high. For a rectangular 18 by 27 ft bay pan joist spanning in the long direction with a wide flat beam (in depth equal to the joist) in the 18-ft direction has proved to be economical. Narrow (8 to 12 in.) rectangular columns limit infringement on the parking spaces. Prestressed precast and structural steel frames are generally applicable to rectangular bays with much larger spans.

OTHER CONCRETE SCHEMES

Although in highrise apartment construction mild reinforced, cast-in-place concrete predominates, other methods of concrete use are becoming prevalent.

POST-TENSIONED SLABS. When the building's function requires larger spans (greater than about 22 ft) cast-in-place concrete slab with post-tensioned strands is competitive. Because of the post-tensioning, slab thicknesses may be less than those required for mild reinforced slabs. The slab forming and casting procedure is the same as already discussed. The slab concrete, however, must reach a specified strength before stressing the high-tension strands. This necessitates leaving shores and forms in place longer or using a higher concrete strength to develop early strength gain.

SITE PRECAST, ERECTED BY CRANE. Cast-in-place concrete requires scores of laborers and craftsmen, alternating between work accomplished by fits and starts and waiting their turn. In addition to this inefficient utilization of labor, about 30% of the cost of the structure is spent on forming and shoring. Precasting, on the other hand, eliminates forming and can be organized in a rational, assembly-line fashion and results in a smooth flow of work.

If, however, we think in terms of the usual precast floor elements—voided planks 2, 4, or even 8 ft wide or double tees—various drawbacks become apparent. Neither the ceiling nor the floor is smooth or level. The architect may decide to live with this or spend money on camouflaging the ceiling and topping the floor. There is nothing anybody can do about the unidirectional structural behavior of these elements. They must be supported along lines, beams or walls, as opposed to flat plates, which because of their two-way structural action require only point supports, that is, columns. To support planks or tees, beams amounting to an entire set of new structural elements must be introduced or bearing walls must be used.

A way to combine the advantages of precasting without the disadvantages of the unidirectional elements is to use large precast floor panels, each equal to several rooms in size. Thus the joints are hidden in the partitions, and the top and bottom surfaces of the panels are smooth and ready for floor finish and paint, respectively. These panels can be designed to provide two-way structural action; the panel does the job of the planks in one direction and the beams in the other. Moment continuity across the joint is not necessarily required, but it can be provided.

The panels are precast on the job site in layers. Casting beds are mud slabs, tennis courts, parking lots, or the first floor of the building. The slabs are lifted into place by crane. Readily available equipment can handle large and heavy panels economically.

The best way to ensure proper fit of the panels when on-site space is available is to fit-cast them on a single bed for an entire floor. Simple edgeforms and dividers between the panels, both raised for successive layers, are the only forming material needed. Special joint details, which provide for a grout key between panels in addition to bolted connections, produce an exact fit. They also transform the individual panels into a diaphragm needed for lateral stability of the building. This stability is otherwise achieved in a manner similar to the cast-in-place scheme.

Columns may be steel or precast concrete. Lateral loads are resisted by shear walls, shear panels, or steel bracing.

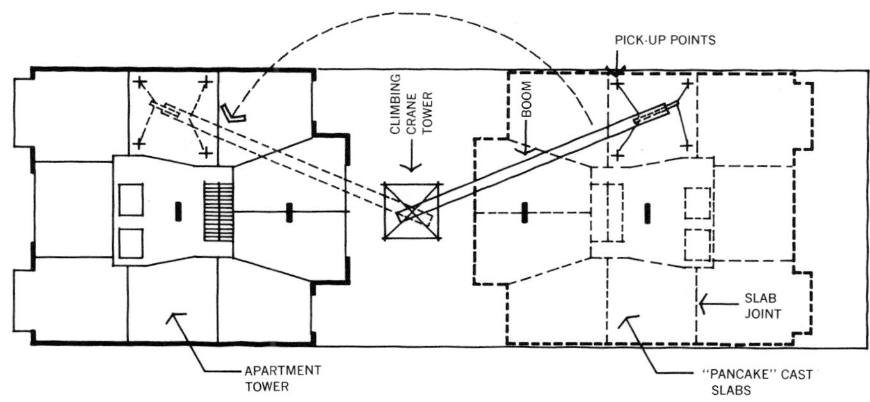

SITE PRECAST, LIFT SLAB. The advantages of this precast scheme in relation to poured flat plates are also inherent in the "lift slab" approach. Rather than casting the slabs adjacent to the building, they are pancake-cast on a ground-floor slab in their final plan location. Sophisticated hydraulic lifting devices and procedures are necessary to raise the slabs at all lift points at an identical rate of climb.

PLANT PRECAST. Numerous plant-precast structural products are available, from individual elements such as hollow-core slabs, double tees, columns, and ledger girders to entire structures. Although most often applied on low-rise buildings in conjunction with steel-frame or bearing masonry walls, their use in highrise apartments is increasing. Structures of almost any height become feasible with precast wall panels and floor elements with proper connections. As on-site construction costs increase, and assuming demands large enough to make precasting worthwhile, totally precast construction is becoming more and more competitive.

STRUCTURAL STEEL

Compared with concrete, relatively few apartment buildings of more than 10 or 12 stories have been constructed of structural steel. The advancement in structural design techniques, changes in code fireproofing requirements, higher strength steels, and ease and speed of erection are factors that are increasing the competitiveness of steel.

A rigid rectilinear column layout is normally required. Two or three column rows are used, depending on the width of the building and on the span and depth requirements of the secondary floor members and whether parking space is provided inside the building. A secondary member span of 20 to 25 ft is reasonable. Spacing of columns at about 20 ft on center in the longitudinal direction produces an economical beam design.

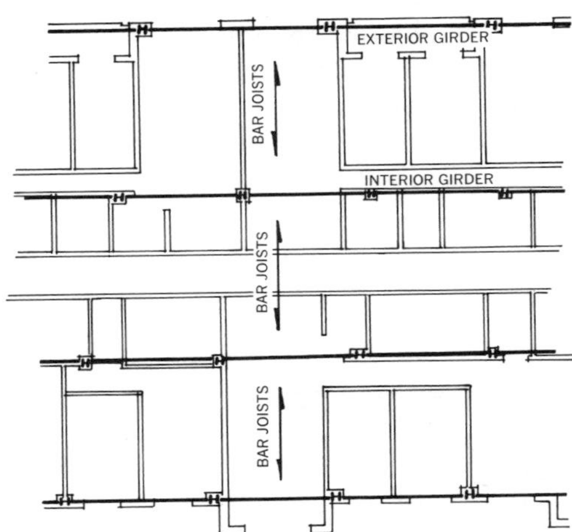

The small floor plan of fewer than about 8000 sf is most competitive when structural steel is used. As already discussed, pouring concrete for such a small area is inefficient, and prefabricated steel frames allow rapid erection and ease of materials handling. Columns are usually wide-flange sections, although steel tubes and pipes have been employed. The size of structural steel columns may be small when compared with concrete (even after fireproofing) because high-strength steels may be utilized in the design.

Most steel-frame structures use bolted connections, and high strength A325 bolts predominate. Welded connections are a simplified means of creating continuity of beams and columns which may be required for lateral loads and also minimize the weight and size of the flexural members. The testing of welded connection, however, is rather complicated and costly and the acceptance criteria is vague, whereas simplified procedures are available for testing bolted connections.

Open web steel joists 14 in. deep suffice for the spans discussed above, but simplification of the framing and ease of ceiling installation require that the joists be 2 in. deeper than the steel beams. With the 14-in. joist, therefore, a 12-in. beam should be used. For shorter spans a 12-in. joist and a 10-in. beam will satisfy this condition.

Joists are spaced at 20 to 30 in. on center. The greater spacing provides for more efficient use of the corrugated steel deck above. This deck, with 2½-in. cast-in-place concrete, is the most commonly used floor. A particularly critical design consideration relating to the use of bar joists is the minimization of vibrations. This flexible joist is likely to create a condition of adverse human response. Joist depth-to-span ratios that satisfy these conditions are discussed later on.

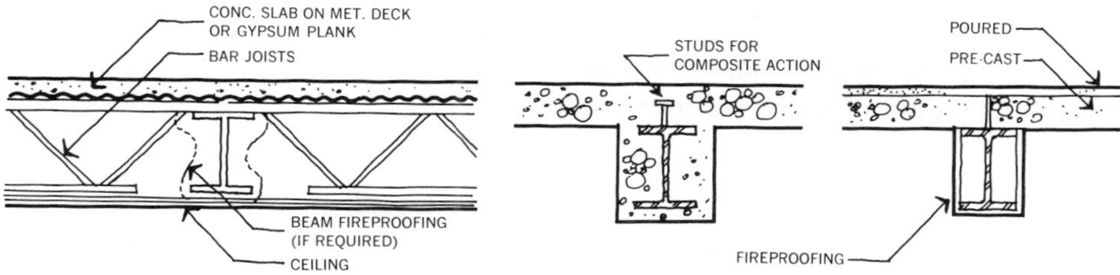

In addition to steel deck and cast-in-place concrete, gypsum planks spanning between joists that are spread to 48 in. on center may be used. A ¾-in. mastic is applied to the top of the gypsum plank. Reduced weight tends to decrease the structural steel considerably. The total savings, however, will depend on the number of floors.

Prestressed precast members spanning between steel girders may also be used. Hollow-core planks and double tee sections offer the advantage of long spans. Concrete topping is required to level the floor and allow for placement of electrical conduits.

FIREPROOFING. Fireproofing requirements are constantly in a state of flux. The requirements for highrise structures in many codes have been or are in the process of being revised. "Trade offs," such as compartmentation in lieu of sprinklers, will help the competitive status of structural steel because compartmented (or sprinklered) structures do not require the usual three-hour fire separation between floors according to the most recent highrise fire codes. Modern methods of fireproofing in the form of spray-on materials have also lessened the cost of protecting structural steel. Cementous, vermiculite, and perlite are used with the spray on technique. Fire ratings may also be obtained by boxing the structural members with gypsum board. Gypsum board or plaster ceilings can also be used to develop floor-system fire ratings, and the newer fireproofing paints or coatings, such as Albi-Clad, offer great promise. Underwriters Laboratory have rated this type of fireproofing for columns. A 3⁄16-in. thickness will provide one hour, ½-in., two hours, and 1 1⁄16 in., three hours.

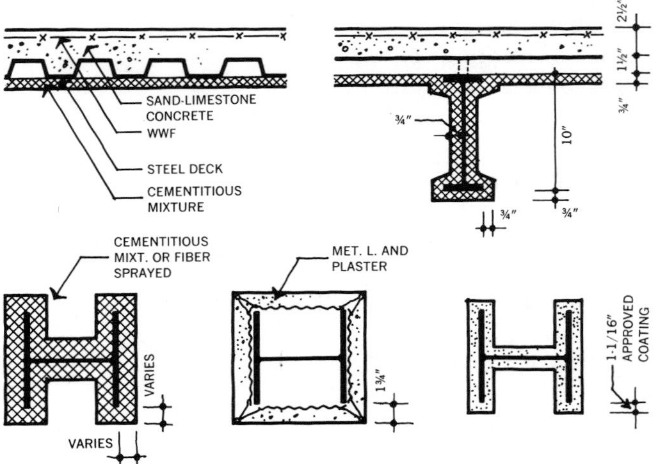

STAGGERED TRUSS. A fairly recent development in structural steel for highrise apartment buildings is the "staggered truss" system. Story-high trusses supported on columns at the exterior span the width of the building. The trusses are arranged in a staggered pattern on adjacent column lines. Typical secondary members frame between the trusses. This scheme is particularly advantageous if there are air rights to consider or a substantial amount of parking under the tower.

MIDRISE STRUCTURAL VARIATIONS

Although the preceding framing systems are generally applicable to structures four stories or taller, apartment buildings in the 4-to-10 story range (and occasionally even walk-ups) may employ other combinations of steel, concrete, and bearing masonry walls more economically.

MASONRY BEARING. Floor-framing systems (joist, precast elements, and cast-in-place concrete) are often supported on masonry walls. Reinforced masonry-bearing wall structures have been constructed to a height of about 18 stories and 8-in. nonreinforced masonry has been used in 12-story buildings. The fact that the masonry-bearing wall may function as architectural enclosure as well as structural support offers economic advantages. Structurally, the wall is designed to serve two functions: acting jointly with the floors as a horizontal diaphragm, both gravity and lateral loads are resisted.

For years masonry design was dictated by rule of thumb and nebulous conservative code restrictions, primarily because of a lack of research. However, with the advent of design criteria established by the Brick Institute of America and the National Concrete Masonry Association both major materials, clay brick and concrete block, may be engineered by a rational approach. Hence the use of engineering masonry for midrise buildings is now a more viable solution.

Precautions must be noted, however. Although design criteria have been established, construction expertise is lacking in engineered masonry buildings. Masons must be made aware that this type of structure requires greater control of the use of materials and construction techniques. Specifications necessary to ensure construction in accordance with design must be enforced. Mortar cubes and/or prisms (units + mortar) should be tested to ascertain that materials conform with those specified. In addition, cold-weather precautions, moisture-content limitations, and total filling of collar (slush) joints are required.

The most common application of masonry bearing walls is the double-loaded corridor, in which one or both corridor walls and the exterior walls are bearing, or a combination of exterior bearing wall and interior steel columns. If the apartment layout is repetitive, the party walls may be used for bearing.

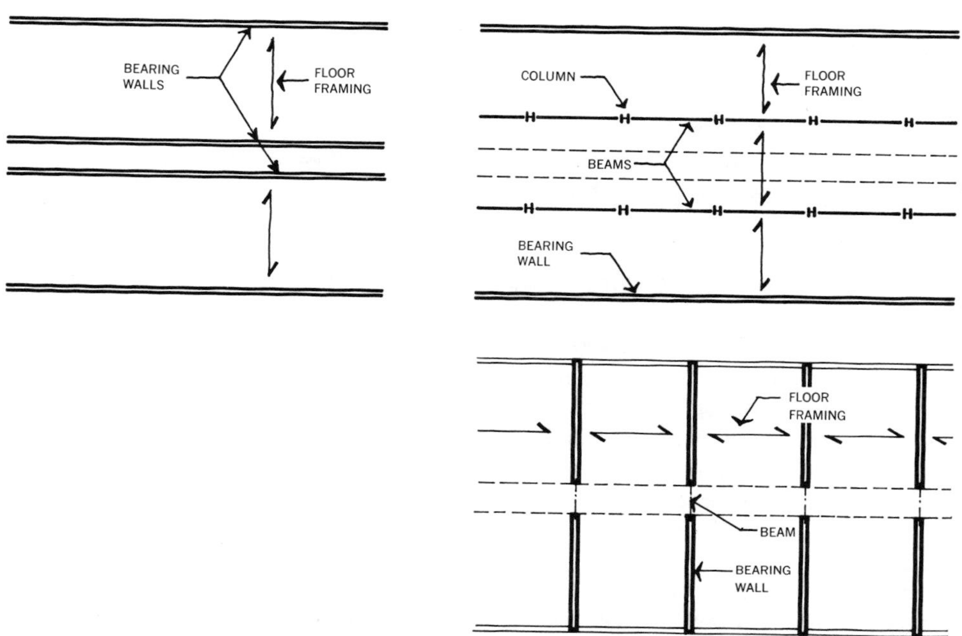

FLAT PLATE/PIPE COLUMN. The flat plate/pipe column system consists of cast-in-place or precast (on-site) thin slabs supported on pipe columns. Pipes 3 in. in diameter allow placement within standard stud partitions. This system has all the advantages of concrete construction. When more than two-hour fire rating is required for the columns, narrow (4-to-6-in.) cast-in-place or precast columns are used; otherwise the gypsum board will provide one-hour rating of the steel pipes. Lateral loads are resisted by braced bents, masonry walls, or shear panels.

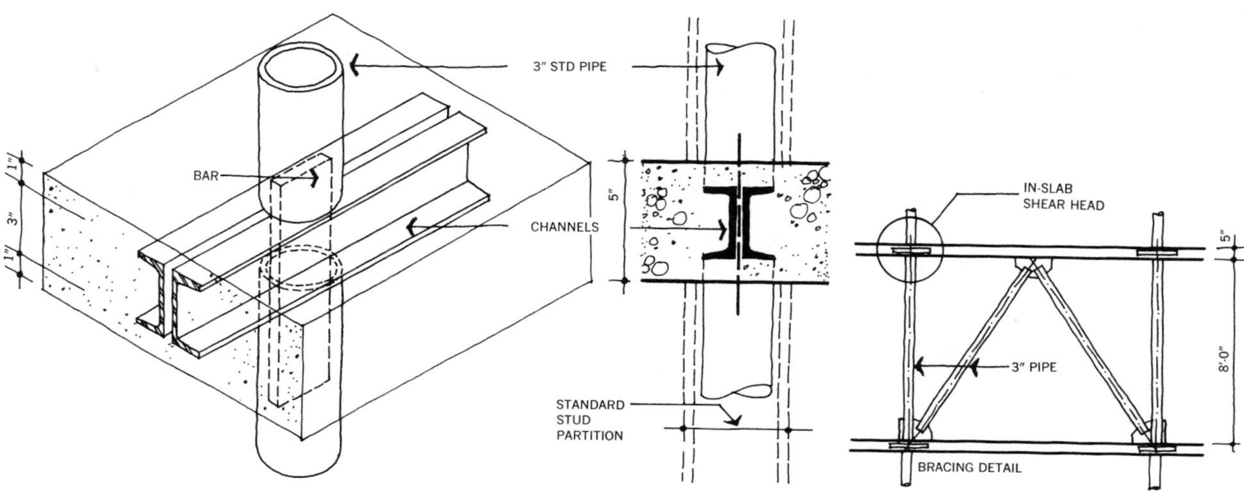

Because column spans are kept at a minimum so that these slabs can be used, they generally do not work well in parking areas if parking is under the tower. When this happens, a thick concrete slab above the parking floor will transfer the scattered pipe column loads to the regularly placed concrete columns. Concrete walls in the first apartment level have also served this transfer function.

WOOD FRAME

Wood frame apartment construction (often termed ''ordinary construction'') is usually restricted by code to walk-ups or elevator buildings of limited height (four stories). In this construction bearing walls and partitions and floor and roof framing are wholly or partly of wood. Exterior walls may be masonry veneer or bearing masonry. Partitions may be constructed of metal studs but most often wood 2 x 4's spaced at 16 or 24 in. are used. Light gage metal joists in lieu of the standard wood joist are gaining acceptance. The roof members are often lightweight prefabricated wood trusses.

Most wood frame structures are not ''structurally designed,'' and sometimes this leads to misbehavior and occasionally to structural failure. Nailing and other details of construction are usually left to the carpenter. Because of the lack of moisture control, some wood members, especially when subject to load, exhibit considerable creep and shrinkage, evidenced by partition and ceiling separation of disturbing magnitude and unsightly drywall cracking at locations such as lintels where varying load conditions are present. The result is expensive maintenance. Bearing of wood-floor members on stud walls at one support and masonry at the other leads to floors that slope from the ''rigid'' masonry support to the shrinkage-prone stud support. These and numerous other serviceability problems could be minimized by using balloon framing in lieu of the standard stacking of stud on joist on stud, which results in cumulative shrinkage. Unfortunately the cost of balloon framing (first cost) is often prohibitive (probably because of a lack of the knowledge of carpentry in this method of construction). Another remedy is the use of a hybrid system that combines wood floor joists and steel columns and beams. Naturally the proper solution is engineering design even of the ''simple'' wood framing.

LATERAL LOADS AND RESISTANCE

Requirements for lateral load resistance depend on two basic factors—the building plan and height. The shape of the building may inherently provide increased lateral load resistance. Long and narrow structures offer poor resistance to lateral loads on the broad face but are extremely stiff in the opposite direction.

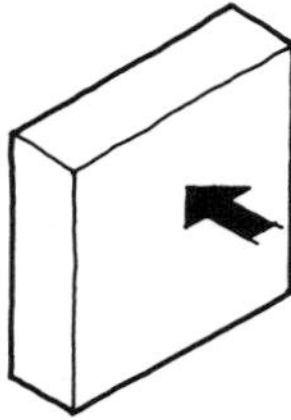

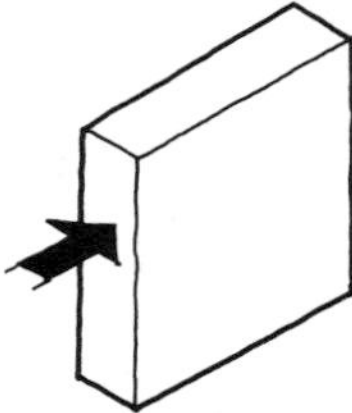

Combining rectangles to form more structurally efficient plans provides good but unequal resistance in both directions.

A square plan with equal resistance in both orthogonal directions is obviously the better solution. A circular plan has less applied wind load because of its shape and the result is a more economical shape in regard to wind resistance.

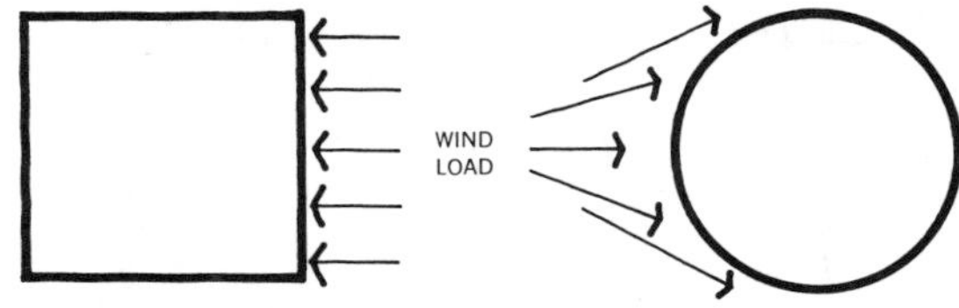

CONCRETE RIGID FRAME

The building height dictates the means of the most economical resistance to lateral loads. From the point of view of lateral loading the concrete frame (columns and slabs) is efficient to a height of about 10 stories, for within the limitation of this height the addition of nominal reinforcing is sufficient to satisfy the bending requirements caused by the lateral force.

To use only the frame to resist wind in higher structures requires increased reinforcing and often increased slab thicknesses in the lower floors. This means of resisting lateral loads (due to the flexible frame action) creates possible problems with the interaction of structural and architectural elements. It necessitates special joinery to prevent the partitions from crushing and cracking and special detailing for pipes and ducts that may be in contact with the structure.

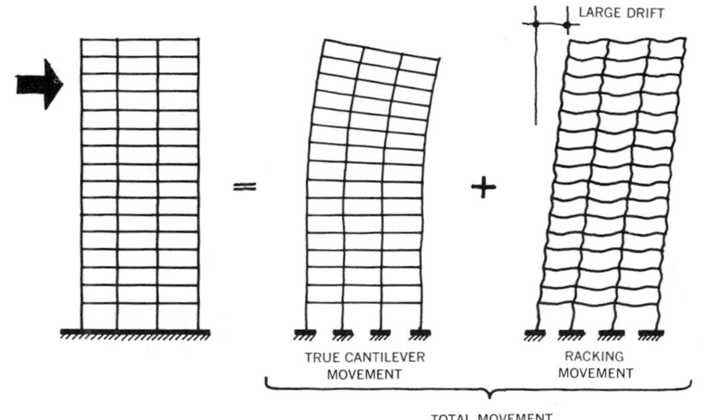

CONCRETE RIGID FRAME AND SHEAR WALLS

Between 10 and about 40 stories economy requires the addition of stiffer elements to supplement the frame resistance. Shear walls generally satisfy this function. The lateral loads are distributed through the slab which behaves as a deep, thin beam in the horizontal plane (diaphragm) and transfers the lateral loads to the shear walls and frame according to their relative stiffness. Vertically continuous shear walls are thought of as vertical cantilevered beams, restrained at the foundations, and resisting both axial (gravity) and lateral loads. The efficiency of the shear wall is dependent to a great extent on the amount of gravity load applied. (See shear panel discussion below).

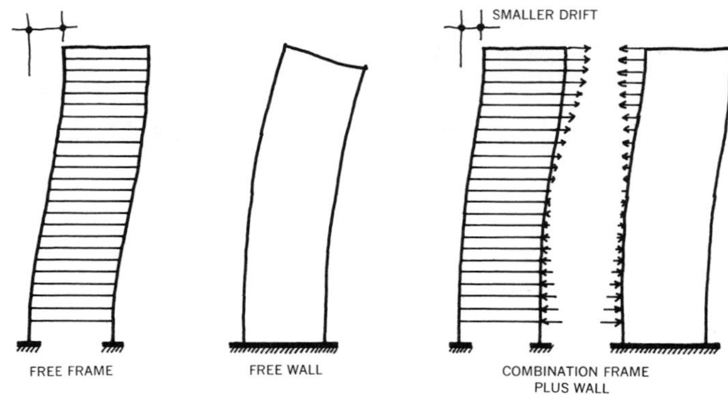

CONCRETE SHEAR PANELS

The primary difference between the shear wall and shear panel is the purposeful vertical discontinuity of the shear wall, supported on columns, and placed strategically throughout the plan to mobilize the maximum amount of gravity load possible. In fact, the total horizontal force is distributed about evenly among all the structural elements of the building. The increased gravity load counters the panel tension forces (uplift) created by lateral loads. Naturally the number of shear panels increases on the lower floors according to the increasing lateral load forces. Shear panels also minimize the diaphragm span.

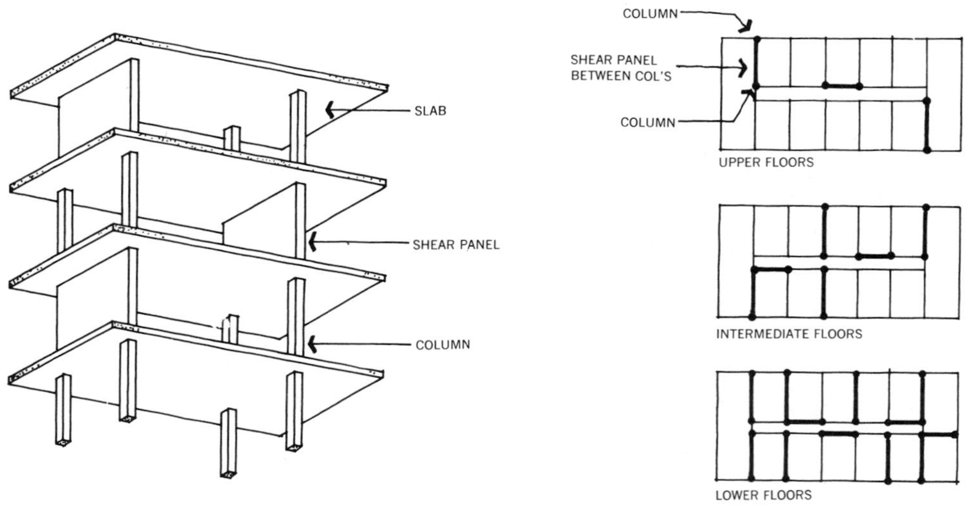

SHEAR ELEMENT LOCATIONS

The location of shear walls or panels is dependent on the floor plan. Generally the more economical locations are corridor or apartment separation walls (due primarily to the relative ease of forming, when compared with exterior walls). Using shear elements as apartment separation offers an excellent barrier to sound transmission. When exterior (end walls) and core shear walls are used, cost should be seriously weighed. Increased forming considerations for this type of wall decreases its economic advantage. However, core walls with special forming systems (slip forms) have proved to be most efficient as shear-resisting elements with point-block type structures in the 60-story range.

CONCRETE TUBES

Exterior concrete bearing walls which form a tube provide a uniquely efficient structural system. Variations in the tube have been used economically for apartment structures in the 40-to-60-story range. The extent of window openings dictates the structural behavior. Smaller openings allow a closer approximation to the pure tube behavior, with stiff columns and spandrels providing the tube effect. Increasing the size of openings diminishes the column and spandrel stiffness and the structural response tends to approach frame action.

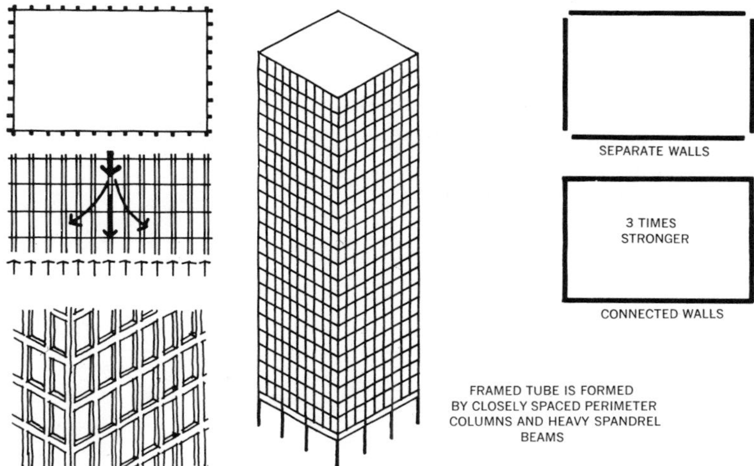

FRAMED TUBE IS FORMED BY CLOSELY SPACED PERIMETER COLUMNS AND HEAVY SPANDREL BEAMS

SEPARATE WALLS

3 TIMES STRONGER

CONNECTED WALLS

The tube effect becomes more efficient if a diagonal truss system is employed instead of vertical (column) and horizontal (beam) members. The diagonal members function as columns to resist gravity loads and as a deep truss cantilevered from the foundations to resist lateral loads.

Economical lateral load resistance for apartment structures of more than 60 stories requires interaction of the exterior "bearing wall" and interior shear resisting elements generally consisting of the core walls. To provide the necessary interaction stiff framing elements between the interior and exterior structure are required. These interconnecting elements need not occur at every floor but only as required to distribute the lateral forces.

The shear resisting elements of a highrise can also be constructed of steel when the basic system is structural steel framing or a combination of concrete and structural steel. The rigid frame and tube structures are readily obtained in steel by providing moment connection between columns and girders. Equivalent shear walls or shear panels are provided by bracing between columns with angles, channels, wide flanges, plates, or pipes.

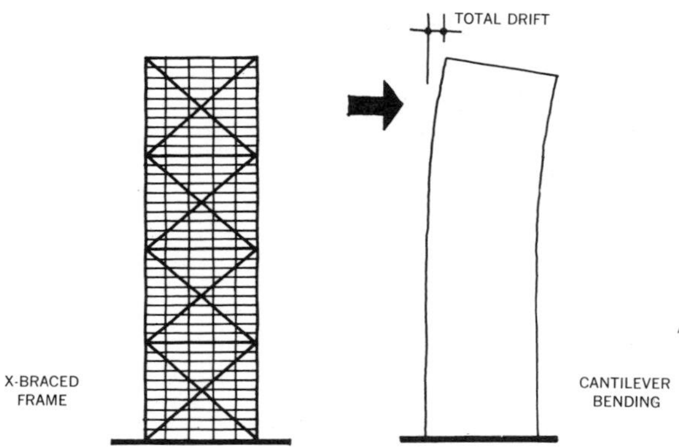

EARTHQUAKE CONSIDERATIONS

The preceding discussion of schemes for lateral load resistance should be *generally* applicable to seismic conditions as well as wind loading. Code restrictions, however, on the use of a ''box type'' structure (shear walls or tubes) have limited their use in seismic regions. However, recent proposed code limitations on building drift (to minimize architectural element distress during an earthquake) will require even stiffer structures. The existing code provisions which demand a ductile moment-resisting space frame to resist 25% of the earthquake force (in addition to the shear walls resisting 100% of the earthquake force) necessitate thicker slabs, thereby negating the cost advantages of a thin flat plate.

FOUNDATIONS

Selection of the appropriate substructure for an apartment building depends on the available soil bearing capacity and a multitude of other parameters including building height, column spacing, superstructure weight, water-table level, adjacent structures, and underground utilities.

SOIL REPORT

Complete soil investigation should be made on any proposed building site. A report prepared by a soil engineer on the basis of his investigation is required to determine the foundation type intelligently and economically. The architect and structural engineer generally prepare a project description for the soil engineer which includes information pertinent to his conclusions such as building height, bay sizes, and column loads. The number and depth of borings should be left to the discretion of the soil engineers. The boring logs contain grade elevations, classification of each soil strata, water-table elevations, blow count, unit weight, water content, and unconfined compressive strength of the various materials encountered. The soil report contains the logs and recommendations for foundation types, soil bearing elevation, and anticipated settlements and construction abnormalities.

SPREAD FOOTINGS

Spread footings are considered the most economical and have been used for structures of about 20 stories. They may be plain or reinforced concrete. Column loads from the superstructure are generally transferred by concrete piers extending to footings at an adequate bearing strata. Continuous footings usually support the walls, whereas individual spread footings support isolated columns.

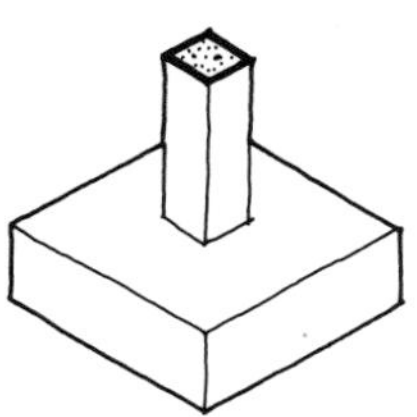

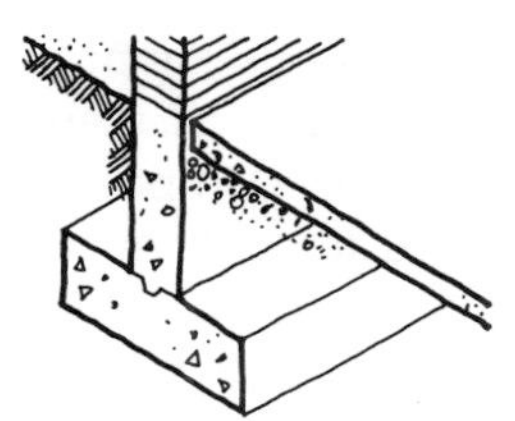

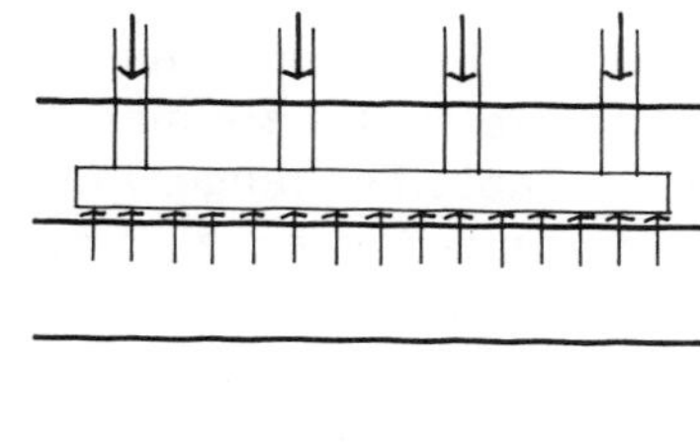

MATS

Low bearing capacity and/or the possibility of differential settlement suggests the use of a mat foundation, which is simply a continuous slab of reinforced concrete that supports the columns as well as walls and is designed as an inverted flat plate with the soil pressure loading the "flat plate" and the columns providing the reactions.

DEEP FOUNDATIONS

When adequate bearing capacity is substantially below surface elevation, deep foundations are used. Drilled piers (sometimes defined as caissons) are employed when a bearing strata of hardpan (stiff clays) or bedrock is available. The shaft is generally augured by mechanical means, and if bearing on hardpan "bells" are formed at that level to increase the bearing area. Straight shafts are used when bedrock is reached for bearing strata. Temporary steel liners are used in the upper soft materials and anchored into stiffer clays to allow drilling without fear of cave-ins. The liner is generally withdrawn as concrete is cast. Permanent steel liners sometimes required by code or soil conditions prevent sloughing of the soil into the hole and may also be used as part of the load-carrying capacity of the caisson.

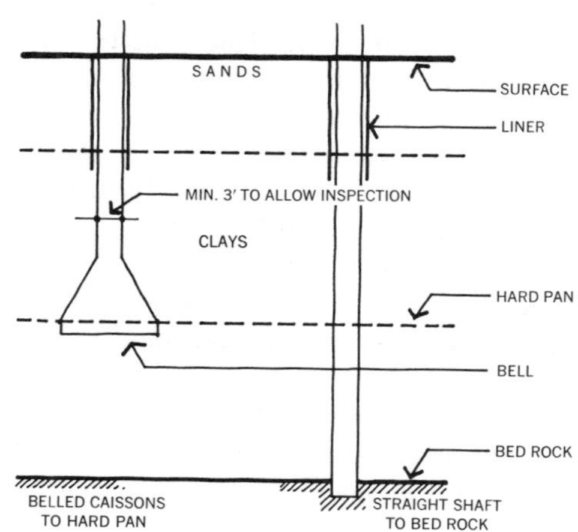

Piles are used when soil conditions and/or cost considerations do not warrant caissons. They develop their capacity to support the superstructure by skin friction and end bearing. The type of pile selected depends to a great degree on the soil being penetrated and the loads to be carried. Recommendations to this effect are given in the soil report. Depending on required capacities, piles may be used singly or in groups. Although column loads are directly applied to caissons, piles require a reinforced concrete cap which greatly influences the economies of this type of foundation.

Piles may be driven, vibrated, or placed in prebored holes. Treated timber piles are used primarily for lightly loaded structures; their capacity is limited to about 25 tons. Precast-prestressed concrete piles are manufactured in various shapes, with tapered or parallel sides. Capacities range up to 200 tons. Structural steel piles (H sections) can develop capacities equal to precast concrete. Composite piles are a combination of more than one material and often lead to economical solutions. Steel shell or pipe driven in and filled with concrete, precast with steel sections embedded, timber with cast-in-place concrete, and various other combinations can be used.

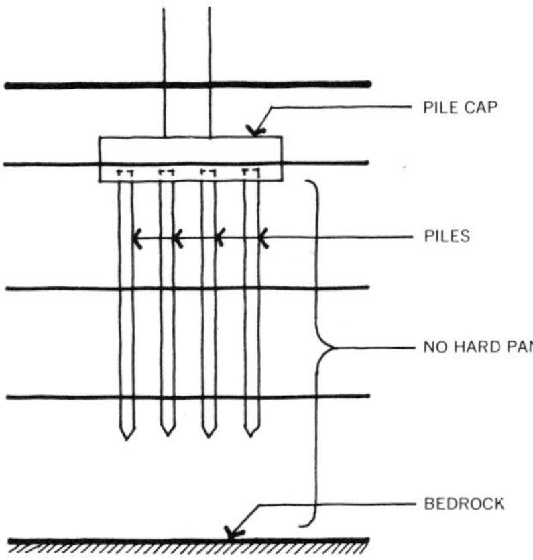

HYDROSTATIC PRESSURE

Basements, parking garages, and pits to be constructed below the water table require special attention to counteract hydrostatic uplift. Construction procedures are complicated because of the need for pumps and well points to lower the water table temporarily to allow working "in the dry." Needless to say, this type of construction is costly and should be avoided if at all possible.

An accurate determination of the high water-table elevation is difficult because water fluctuates with the seasons and because means are lacking to separate the actual water-table measurement from trapped water (water trapped between earth seams). Therefore the high water table "design" elevation is usually conservative.

A highrise apartment structure with a mat foundation will readily resist a considerable uplift force due to its gravity load; for instance, a 30-story structure with 5-in. normal-weight concrete slabs developed a total dead load of about 1900 psf (pounds per square foot). To overcome this load would require about 30 ft of hydrostatic head; the weight of one 5-in. concrete slab is equal to 1 ft of hydrostatic water pressure. If the structure's column loads are supported by deep foundations, the lowest floor slab would be required to resist the uplift forces between columns.

This may be accomplished by structurally designing the floor slab to resist the pressure or by providing a massive concrete slab, or a combination of the two. Deep foundations adequately serve as a ''hold-down'' to prevent buoyancy. In parking garages and other lightly loaded structures deep foundations designed specifically to resist uplift forces are required.

Instead of using the structure to resist uplift, mechanical means of relieving hydrostatic pressures are sometimes used. Under-floor and perimeter drain tiles in conjunction with pumps to maintain a lower water level may prove to be more economical although not ''fail safe.''

Structural or mechanical design for uplift is only a portion of the problem created by construction beneath the water table. Waterproofing is essential and costly to attain. All walls and slabs below the water table must receive membrane waterproofing applications. All joints must have water stops. To protect the waterproof membrane ''mud-slabs'' are often needed as a base for applying the waterproofing before casting the final structural elements.

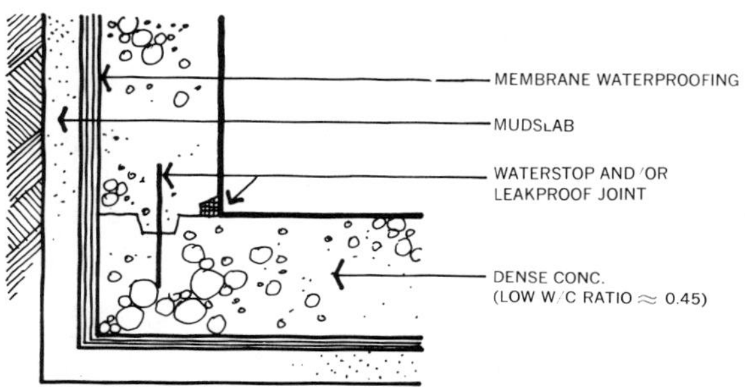

MEMBER SIZE SELECTION

The following simplified equations allow a rapid determination of *approximate* structural member sizes. The formulas are based on apartment loadings and are *not* to be used indiscriminately for all conditions. A slight variation in limiting parameters may substantially change the required value; therefore extrapolation should not be used. Span lengths are in feet and resulting member depths in inches.

CAST-IN-PLACE CONCRETE

1. *Solid slab supported on all sides* by walls or stiff beams. Span range is 15 to 30 ft (recommended for heavier live loads):

$$\frac{L_1}{L_2} < 2 \; (L_1 \text{ longer span})$$

Slab thickness:

$$h = \frac{L_1 + L_2}{7.5} \geq 4 \text{ in.}$$

Example: $L_1 = 25$ ft, $L_2 = 20$ ft

$$h = \frac{25 + 20}{7.5} = 6 \text{ in.}$$

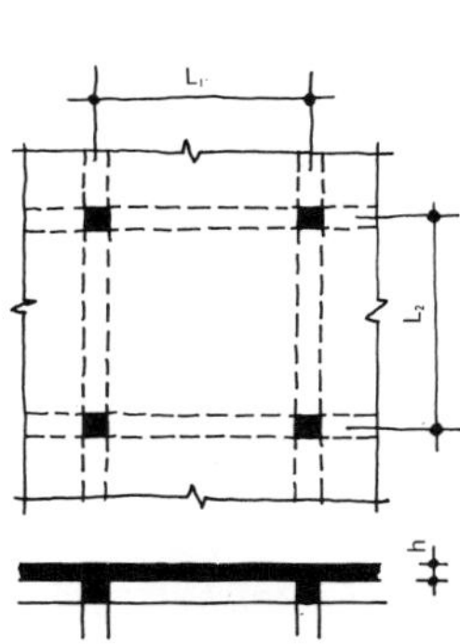

2. *One-way solid slab* supported by walls or stiff beams. Span range is 5 to 20 ft:

$$\frac{L_1}{L_2} \geq 2 \text{ (L_1 longer span)}$$

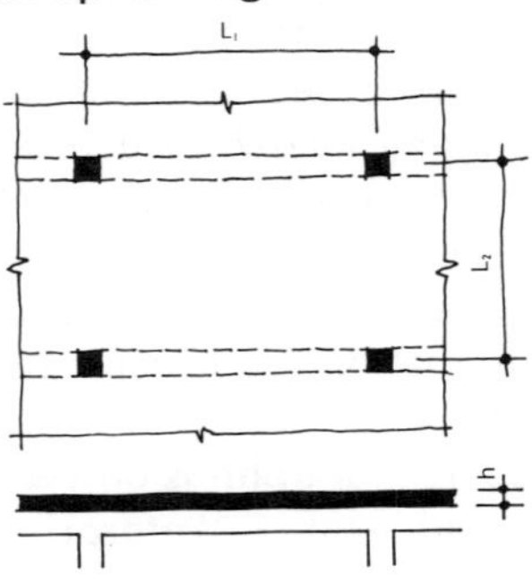

Slab thickness:

$$h = \frac{L_2}{2.8} \text{ (continuous spans)} \geq 4 \text{ in.}$$

$$h = \frac{L_2}{1.8} \text{ (simple span)} \geq 4 \text{ in.}$$

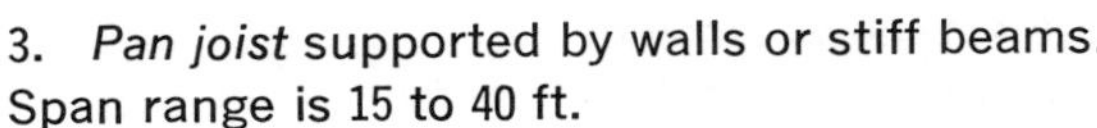

3. *Pan joist* supported by walls or stiff beams. Span range is 15 to 40 ft.

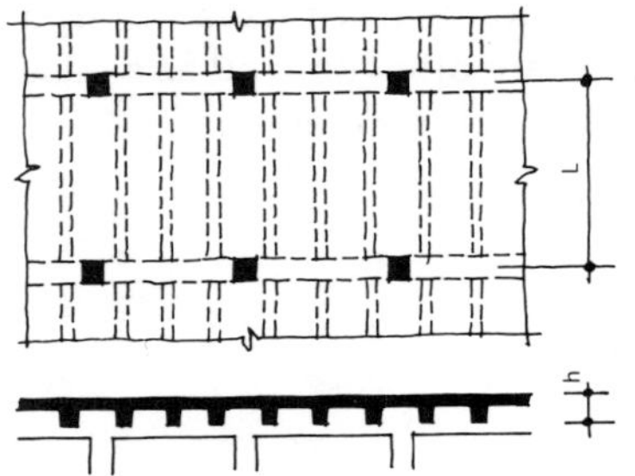

$$h = \frac{L}{2} \text{ (continuous spans)}$$

$$h = \frac{L}{1.5} \text{ (simple span)}$$

4. *Flat plate* supported only on columns. Span range is 14 to 22 ft:

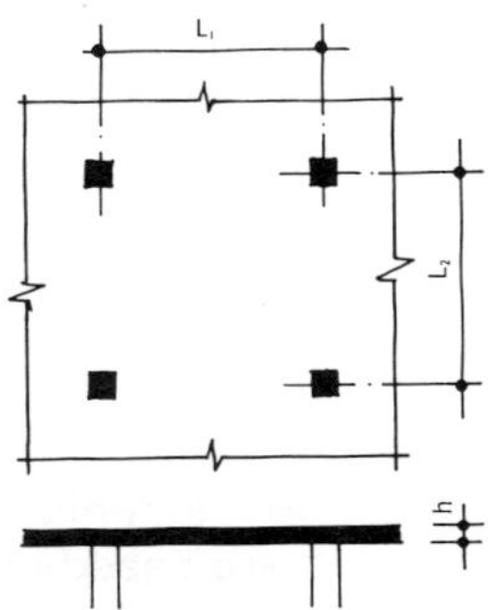

$$\frac{L_1}{L_2} < 1.50 \text{ (L_1 longer span)}$$

Slab thickness:

$$h = \frac{L_1}{3} \geq 5 \text{ in.}$$

5. *Flat slab* supported only on columns. Span range is 18 to 30 ft; recommended for heavier live loads:

$$\frac{L_1}{L_2} < 1.50 \text{ (L_1 longer span)}$$

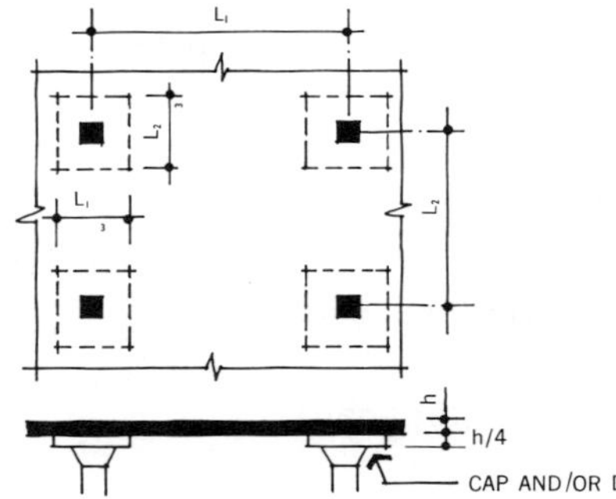

Slab thickness:

$$h = \frac{L_1}{3.3} \geq 5 \text{ in.}$$

6. *Beams:*

Beam thickness

$$h = \frac{L}{2} \text{ (continuous spans)}$$

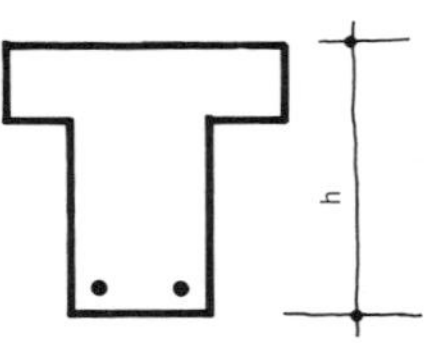

$$h = \frac{L}{1.5} \text{ (simple span)}$$

$$h = \frac{L}{0.8} \text{ (cantilever span)}$$

PRECAST PRESTRESSED CONCRETE

1. *Beam:*

   Beam thickness

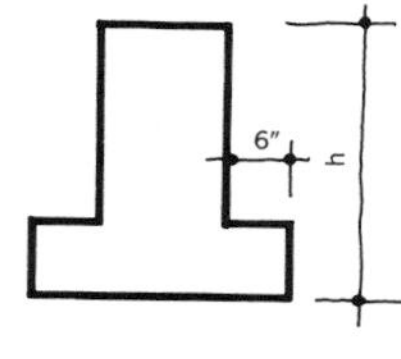

$$h = \frac{L}{2.5} \text{ (continuous spans)}$$

$$h = \frac{L}{2.0} \text{ (simple span)}$$

$$h = \frac{L}{1.0} \text{ (cantilever span)}$$

2. *Secondary member* (hollow-core slab and tee):

   Member thickness:

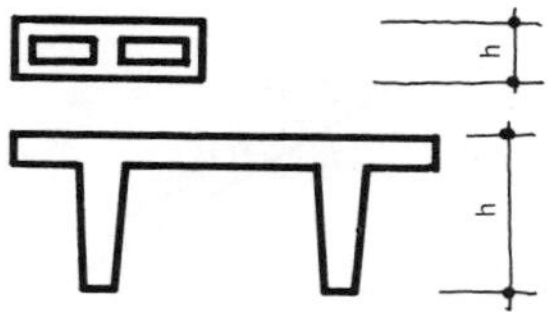

$$h = \frac{L}{3} \text{ (floors)}$$

$$h = \frac{L}{3.5} \text{ (roofs)}$$

CONCRETE COLUMNS

The building is assumed to be completely braced.

Example

Assume an 18-story apartment building. Normal weight concrete: 24 x 24 ft bay size. Enter chart at 18 supported slabs, extend a line horizontally to intersect the solid (normal weight concrete) diagonal line for 24 x 24 ft bay size. Drop a vertical line to intersect the ''economical'' and ''uneconomical'' lines. Move horizontally and read column area. The top value (870 in.^{2}) is an economical column size. The lower value (570 in.^{2}) is an uneconomical column size. Both, however, satisfy structural conditions and either one or an area between the two may be used (see chart on p. 102).

STRUCTURAL STEEL

1. *Girder*

   Girder depth:

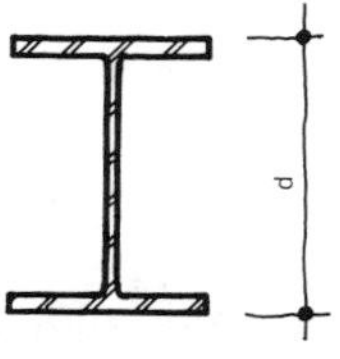

$$d = \frac{L}{1.5} \text{ (floors)}$$

$$\frac{L}{2} \text{ (roofs with adequate slope for drainage)}$$

2. *Beam*

   Beam depth:

$$d = \frac{L}{2} \text{ (floors)}$$

$$\frac{L}{2.5} \text{ (roofs with adequate slope for drainage)}$$

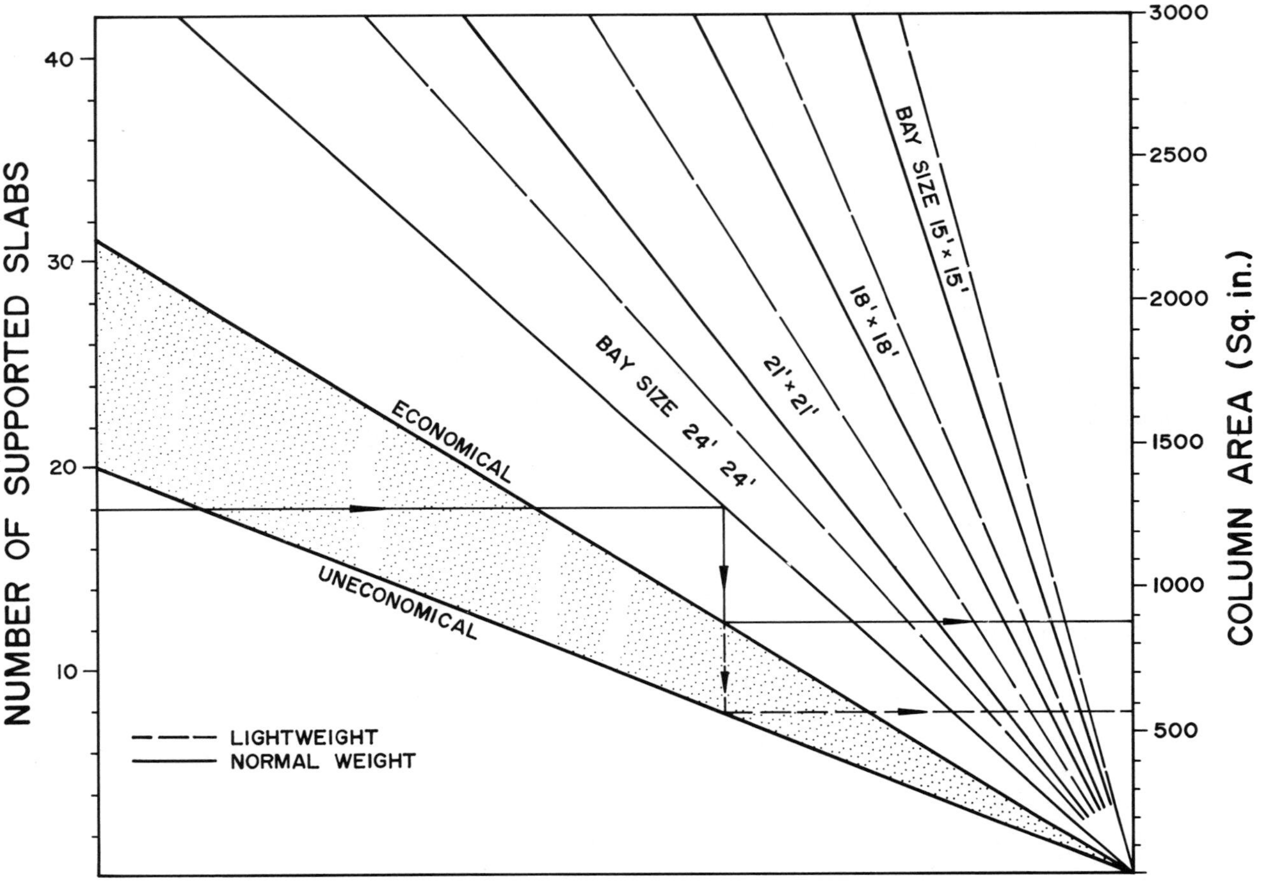

NUMBER OF SUPPORTED SLABS

40
30
20
10

3000
2500
2000
1500
1000
500

COLUMN AREA (Sq. in.)

BAY SIZE 15' × 15'
18' × 18'
21' × 21'
BAY SIZE 24' 24'
ECONOMICAL
UNECONOMICAL

LIGHTWEIGHT
NORMAL WEIGHT

CONCRETE COLUMN SELECTION CHART

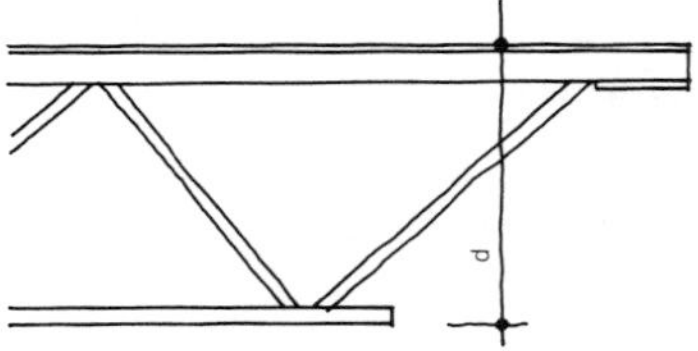

3. *Bar joist* (spacing—24 to 30 in. floors, 48 to 96 in. roofs)

   Joist depth:

   $d = \dfrac{L}{1.4}$ (floors with no partitions, i.e., churches, offices)

   $\dfrac{L}{1.6}$ (floors with partitions, i.e., apartments)

   $\dfrac{L}{2.0}$ (roofs with adequate slope for drainage)

STEEL COLUMNS

Building is assumed to be completely braced.

Example

Assume a 24-story apartment building. Floor dead load: 80 pounds per square foot; tributary area to column, 500 ft[2]; enter chart at 24 supported slabs, extend a line horizontally to intersect dead load = 80 diagonal line. Drop a vertical line to intersect tributary area = 500. Move horizontally and read column size required = W14 x 211.

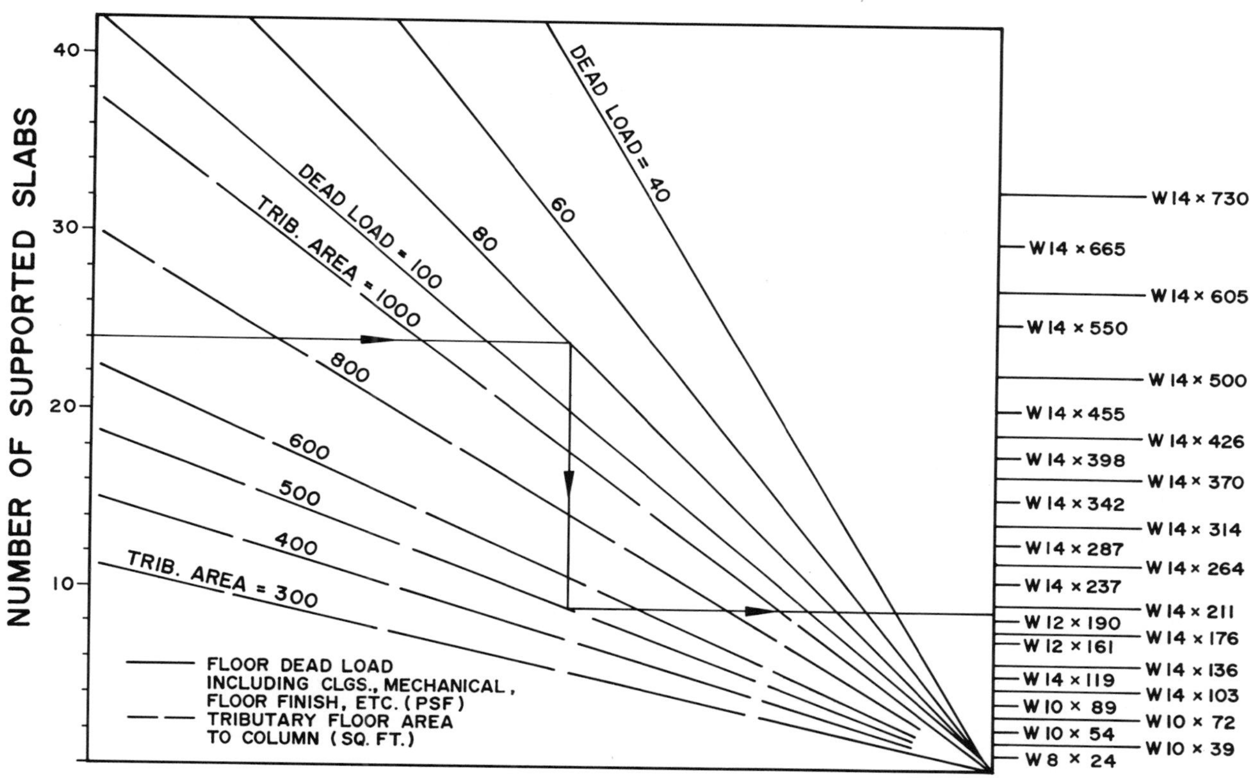

STEEL COLUMN SELECTION CHART

COMPONENTS OF DESIGN—HVAC 4

Harry S. Nachman

HEATING AND AIR CONDITIONING

The chapter heading, "Heating, Ventilating, and Air Conditioning," is really redundant. Air conditioning, correctly defined, is the science that deals with controlling temperature, humidity, cleanliness, and distribution of air in enclosed habitable spaces. Therefore the real name of our subject is "air conditioning." Somehow, however, this term has become equated with "cooling" in the public consciousness, and because of it we may as well employ the time-honored "HVAC" to avoid misunderstanding.

Stating the definition has not been an empty exercise in semantics. It reminds us that temperature is not the only factor of importance in our living environment. We may ignore humidity, cleanliness, and distribution for a number of perfectly acceptable reasons, but our selection of building air conditioning systems should be made only after considering all four factors. If we neglect one or more, that neglect should be deliberate, not inadvertent.

The necessity for *heating* in buildings is not universal. There are favored parts of the earth in which the temperature never falls below the comfort level and others in which outdoor temperatures under that level are so infrequent or so little below it, that no heating equipment is required. A critical need in all building plans is a history of climatic experience in the area. The important historical facts in regard to heating are those that set the lowest temperature likely to occur in any year. In most parts of the world records are kept over periods long enough for this minimum, called "design heating temperature," to be predicted. If that temperature is above 60°, it is reasonably safe to say that no heating is necessary. If the design temperature is above 50°F, with the further proviso that this level is held almost always at night, another factor which may be expressed as the expectations of the occupants or, more brutally, as "how much does it cost to live there," will influence the decision. Low-cost owners and low-rent tenants may be expected to put on sweaters against the evening chill. Their more affluent neighbors may demand heating to dispel the possibility of even mild discomfort. As a minimum in mild climates, fireplaces may heat the major rooms, if fuel is available.

In areas in which the heating design temperature is below 50°F, mechanical heating must be part of the building plan.

The temperature to which homes should be heated varies somewhat with custom, age, physical condition of the occupants, and personal preference. As worldwide diminution of fuel and energy supplies become more and more serious, pressure is being applied to reduce indoor design temperatures. In England many people have been accustomed to house temperatures of 65 to 68 degrees. In the United States accepted design has been 70°–72°, but it is no secret that thermostats are commonly set to 75 degrees and higher. Elderly persons usually demand temperatures some 5 degrees higher than ''normal'' design. Finally, air humidity, discussed later, has some effect on the comfort level.

When we turn to *cooling*, the emphasis is quite different. Although there are large parts of the earth in which heating is necessary for the survival of the human organism, there is almost no place on the globe in which temperatures are so high that people cannot live. Thus the ''necessity'' for cooling takes quite a different dimension, which is largely that of expectations and economics, discussed above. Even lacking accurate statistics, compare the number of residences cooled in an area of the United States with those in areas of similar size and climate in Africa or Asia.

Wherever cooling has become customary the same considerations of weather history and duration of hot spells apply. Cooling design temperatures are established by the records, which reflect the air temperature and the amount of moisture it carries. The latter factor is critically important to human comfort, as everyone knows. ''It's not the heat, it's the humidity!'' Consider what that cliche actually says. If the air is at 80°F and contains 2.2% water vapor (moisture), all of us will feel miserable, but if outside air at the same temperature contains only 1% moisture most of us will call it a pleasant summer day. Therefore our climate history must include a gauge of maximum atmospheric moisture to be anticipated as well as the highest temperature. Humidity is usually expressed as ''relative'' humidity; that is, the actual quantity of water vapor present compared with the maximum amount the air could carry. This proportion is conveniently measured and expressed as ''wet bulb temperature.'' The regularly recorded air temperature is known as ''dry bulb temperature.''

If a family is building a new house, whether to cool is a matter of a few simple questions: How much will it cost to install cooling? How much to operate it? How often will we use it? In short, what is it worth to us? When a builder is planning multiple dwellings for sale or rent, the state of the market becomes crucial. Will the prospective tenants demand cooling? Will they pay the purchase or rental price made necessary by the installation cost? In rental housing who will pay the operating cost? If the owner is to shoulder this burden, will the rental market level cover his expense? If the tenants pay, will they accept this ''hidden'' rent, and will tenants in high exposure dwellings (such as the top floor of a multilevel building or an apartment with windows facing south and west) accept higher utility bills? The answers to some of these questions may be obvious, but they should still be checked off in the planning stage to make sure that the ground has been covered.

Ventilation is comparatively noncontroversial. Natural ventilation, in the form of windows or louvers, is mandated for residences by building codes and furthermore is an aesthetic consideration in the design of residential buildings. Mechanical ventilation is required for interior-occupied areas such as bathrooms and kitchens in which odors and quantities of water vapor may be generated. Interior spaces such as closets and dressing rooms usually do not require ventilation, but common sense consideration of special circumstances may sometimes dictate special treatment of these areas.

Mechanical ventilation of kitchens and bathrooms has long been understood to mean the removal of air from the subject space and expulsion of that air to the outdoors. A combination of building-code requirements and experience dictates that the removal rate should be such that a volume equal to the total cubic contents of the room be expelled at least every five minutes. For kitchens in high-cost or high-rental dwellings, in which occupant expectancies may correspond to the cost-rental level, the air change rate might be every two minutes.

It must be kept in mind that for every cubic foot of air exhausted from a building a cubic foot of air must enter. This replacement could be leakage around doors and windows, or it may be introduced in a controlled and purposeful way, but there is no escaping the necessity of having it come in. Of course, in winter that makeup air must be heated and in summer, if the building is cooled, that air must be cooled.

Fuel and energy restrictions have lent and will continue to lend impetus to a means of reducing the expenditures for treating the replacement air. One dramatic method which removes odors from the exhausted air and then discharges the cleaned air back into the room instead of outdoors has been accepted by some building codes. Emphasis is laid on the word ''remove.'' It has been found that chemically activated charcoal absorbs and stores particles in the air that cause odors; the exhausted air is then passed through activated charcoal before being returned to the room. After a period of time, usually three months to a year, the charcoal will have absorbed all it can store and must be replaced or regenerated. This process is in contrast to one that masks unpleasant odors by use of perfumes, small quantities of ozone, or the like, and which is unacceptable for residential ventilation purposes.

The use of odor control and recirculation of exhausted air, however, is not a complete solution for ventilating needs. Activated charcoal does nothing to remove accumulations of moisture due to cooking and bathing nor to replace the oxygen. Therefore ventilation of some kind is still needed either by leakage from the outdoors due to wind pressure or by mechanical means.

The subject of *humidity* has already been touched on. It is generally understood that air can hold more moisture at high temperatures than at low and that comfort is tied to *relative* humidity. Examine an illustration. Assume that outside air at 0°F and 100% relative humidity is holding as much moisture as it possibly can. As that air into is introduced into a building and heated to 70°F without the addition of any moisture, its relative humidity falls to approximately 7%!

One reaction to that revelation might be ''So what?'' What is bad about very low or very high relative humidities?

Extremely low humidities cause dryness of skin and other body surfaces such as the nasal passages. Many people, including many of those trained in medicine, believe that this nasal dryness adds to a person's susceptibility to respiratory disease. Skin dryness connotes the rapid evaporation of body surface moisture, which has a cooling effect. This is not a critical effect, but it does mean that an individual in a room at 70°F and 7% relative humidity may be no more comfortable than at 67°F and 30% relative humidity. It is significant that by the judicious addition of moisture lower inside design temperatures may be tolerated and fuel saved.

Other objections to low humidities concern their effect on materials such as wood and fabric, which may become warped, embrittled, or damaged in similar ways.

Excessive humidities, on the other hand, can cause discomfort by inhibiting evaporation of moisture from the skin, leaving an oppressive or overwarm feeling. A familiar effect of high humidity is condensation on cold surfaces, particularly windows, although this occurs only in climates in which outside temperatures are low. In mild climates or in periods of prolonged high humidity anywhere wood and fabrics tend to rot.

In the design of residential air conditioning low humidity in winter is the primary concern. High humidities resulting from warm and moist outside conditions are reduced by the very fact of cooling the building. If there is no cooling, the occupants will have to live with the humidity as well as the temperature. Low winter humidities can often be improved at low cost in equipment and operation. Here, again, the factors of occupant expectations and return on investment should be weighed and should be decisive.

A note of caution is in order regarding winter humidification. Optimum relative humidity for comfort in the home is about 40% for most people. That level, however, will cause severe condensation on cold surfaces. In regions that have low outside temperatures double-pane glass, wood or tubular metal window frames, and well-insulated walls and roof will prevent this condition. If it is impractical to avoid some cold interior surfaces because of construction costs or other factors, a compromise can be reached by maintaining lower than optimum relative humidities in the 20 to 30% range.

USE OF FUEL AND ENERGY

When western mankind entered into the nineteenth century's industrial era, the passage was made possible by the exploitation of seemingly unlimited supplies of natural fuels. Burgeoning industrial development called for, and produced, new discoveries in fuel and energy sources. Despite a few voices citing obvious arithmetic facts, the earth's stores of fuel were gobbled up with little thought of the future. "They" would find a way when new energy sources were needed. "They" still may do so, but the present generation has suddenly confronted the unthinkable. Some day the well has to run dry.

That day is probably still quite distant, but the realization of it has added a new dimension to the selection of fuel and other energy sources for building heating, cooling, and other power needs. Best obtainable estimates of availability and cost trends during the expected life of the residential project must be weighed against immediate supplies and prices and hopefully the final decision made with some deference to the common good as well as to the advantage of the individual owner.

Let us list the sources of energy available to us, both practically and theoretically; they are placed in alphabetical order to avoid any hint of bias.

	Strength	Drawbacks
1. COAL	a. Large reserves still exist b. Safe to use; nonexplosive c. Moderate cost at this writing d. Simple machinery needed to burn	a. Bulky; large storage requirements b. Dirty in handling and burning c. Difficult to ignite and extinguish d. Abrasive; short life of handling equipment e. Large equipment space needs, in addition to storage space

	Strength	Drawbacks
2. ELECTRICITY	a. No storage facilities required b. Easy to control c. Safe to use; nonexplosive d. Silent e. Clean f. Simple equipment; generally lowest capital investment; minimal space requirements	a. High cost per energy unit b. Lowest efficiency in use of natural fuels for generation of electricity, *except* if the natural flow of water can be used
3. GAS	a. Low cost at the time of this writing b. Simple equipment; generally modest capital investment c. Clean d. No storage facilities usually required	a. Potentially explosive b. Potentially toxic c. Reserves will probably be depleted before coal reserves
4. NUCLEAR FISSION AND FUSION.	At this time we cannot simply list the advantages and disadvantages of nuclear power. It is legally impossible for operators of residential building projects to own or use nuclear energy plants. Atomic fusion is not yet developed to the point at which its energy can be converted into useful heat or generation of electricity, although there are hopeful prospects. Atomic fission is being used for these purposes but only in large plants operated by major producers of energy federally licensed in the United States. The disposal of radioactive by-products has not been solved on a permanent basis and future pollution problems exist. The danger of explosion and other failure is small, but the results could be catastrophic. Fissionable material is limited. Equipment costs are enormous.	
5. OIL	a. High calorific value per unit weight b. Can be stored underground. c. Low explosion potential	a. Uncertain reserves. b. Pollution possibilities in handling. c. High cost at this writing, due to monopolistic control d. Large storage requirements e. Not notably clean-burning f. Complex burners compared to coal and gas
6. SOLAR ENERGY	a. Supply inexhaustible b. Clean c. Quiet d. No cost at present	a. Dependent on weather conditions c. Conversion equipment very bulky and space consuming at this time d. Available supply is minimum at time of maximum need.

EQUIPMENT LOCATION

From the designer's standpoint the space to be allocated for fuel storage and fuel utilization equipment is very important. It is particularly important that the selection of the source of energy be made early in the design process so that carefully drawn plans will not have to be scrapped or radically altered to accommodate unforeseen hundreds of square feet of mechanical equipment area. At the same time that the area is allotted its location in the building should be fixed.

Heating, ventilating, and cooling equipment may be at the bottom, the top, or at some intermediate location in a building, preferably near the center. This revelation, though a fundamental, may not be startling, but the fact of flexibility should always be borne in mind, whether the building is a lofty skyscraper or a three-story walkup. A second fundamental is that, regardless of the location of the HVAC machinery, there must be space for mechanical and electrical equipment in the lowest level of the structure. Specifically, water service entrance and pumping equipment, electrical service entrance equipment, fuel storage if needed, gas service entrance piping and meter if gas is used in the project, and a means of garbage and rubbish disposal all require space "downstairs." It is sometimes sensible to combine these area allocations for mechanical and electrical equipment in one block, which must then be in the lowest level. An exception to "lowest level" can be the refuse collection room, which may be at ground level for ease of transportation, even in buildings with basements. Let us consider some of the pluses and minuses in the different locations.

1. *Lowest Level*

ADVANTAGES:

Weight of equipment can be carried directly on the earth.

All equipment can be located in one area.

Equipment can be installed and placed in operation at earliest possible time.

Electrical feeders are usually short because the major equipment is close to the electrical service.

Depending on building design, there may be intervening floors between equipment rooms and the nearest living space, thus requiring less sound isolation of the equipment and consequently lower expense.

Major equipment can be installed early, checked out in operation, used for such purposes as temporary heat during construction, and even for heating and cooling to allow partial building occupancy.

Inflow of rental or sales cash may begin months before the building is finished.

DISADVANTAGES:

If there is no basement, a potentially valuable first-floor area is surrendered to nonrentpaying equipment.

If there is a basement, substantial cost may be added to the building, particularly if soil and/or ground water conditions are unfavorable.

If natural fuel is burned, provision must be made through the entire height of the building for a chimney.

If there is a cooling tower which must be on the roof, long condensing water lines are needed at considerable cost. See the later discussion on cooling towers.

2. *Intermediate Level*

ADVANTAGES:

In high rise buildings this location can sometimes serve as the logical level at which to change the typical floor plan (e.g., the upper floors may command higher rentals or prices and may consequently call for larger or more luxurious units). This change may also be used to create a visual break on building elevations.

Pipe sizes for HVAC systems may be reduced, with the result that pipe riser spaces may also be reduced. This may be a trifling gain, but, on the other hand, it may permit a pipe riser space width, for example, to fall in line with a column depth or partition thickness, thus saving useful space in the entire plan.

DISADVANTAGES: Rentable space is being lost at a usually desirable level in the building.

Special precautions must be made to avoid the transmission of sound, heat, or vibration both above and below.

Space must be allowed for a chimney, although only in that part of the building above the equipment room.

If natural fuel is used, it must be transported up to the level. For gas this becomes a minor factor, for oil a major nuisance, and for coal a negating fact. In other words, the coal burning equipment must be at the bottom of the building.

Although it need not be the case in a well-managed building, an "out of sight, out of mind" maintenance philosophy can creep in. The more remote the essential equipment, the more easily neglected.

Distress due to vibration and sound of moving machinery must be designed and guarded against with special care, often at substantial expense.

3. *Roof Level*

ADVANTAGES: No boiler chimney is required, thus reducing construction cost and freeing space on each living floor.

Often a basement is not necessary, and, if no basement has been included in the plans, valuable ground floor space is released.

If the building has a central cooling plant, the water-saving device (cooling tower or aircooled condenser, discussed later in this Chapter) is usually best located on the roof. Thus, if the major HVAC equipment is also at the top of the building, the refrigeration machinery will be close to the water-saving equipment, shortening piping and electrical connections.

If the building is a highrise, an elevator machinery penthouse structure is required. Increasing this space to accommodate an equipment room is comparatively low in cost and can be an aesthetic improvement to the building.

DISADVANTAGES: Weight of heavy major equipment must be carried down through the building's structural system, partly offsetting the cost saving realized by elimination of the chimney.

Systems cannot be completed for operation until the building is structurally complete. This usually militates against early occupancy of lower floors and makes it impossible to use the permanent facilities for temporary heat (or cooling) during construction.

The cost of piping the major part of the fuel supply to the top of the building also cuts into the chimney saving. If the fuel is oil or gas, there is still the additional cost of electrical energy to lift it.

The same ''out of sight, out of mind'' maintenance danger cited above may exist.

Electrical supply and makeup water, both of which services enter at the bottom of the building, must be run all the way to the top.

Distress due to vibration and sound of moving machinery must be designed and guarded against with special care, often at substantial expense.

FUEL CONVERTING EQUIPMENT

Fuel, natural or electrical, is converted into heat in furnaces or boilers in most residential applications. The exceptions are those that use electric heat directly in the areas to be heated. The preponderance of installations are those that burn what we have called ''natural'' fuels (also frequently characterized as ''fossil'' fuels). These fuels require oxygen to support the combustion and a means of removing the waste gases, which are the products of that combustion, after they have yielded as much as possible of the heat they gained in the burning process. Electric central furnaces and boilers differ only in that they need no oxygen and produce no waste gases.

A furnace, in the nomenclature of residential heating, is a device in which air to be heated passes directly over a chamber in which the fuel is burned or the heat of electricity is released. The air is warmed by contact with the chamber walls and is then distributed to the spaces requiring warmth. The furnace is usually an assembly that includes air filters, a blower, and a motor to move the desired quantity of air, a burner to mix air (containing the requisite oxygen) with the fuel if natural fuel is being burned, a smoke outlet to release the products, and a fireproof steel housing to contain all of it, including the combustion chamber itself. Depending on optimum convenience in the residence being heated, the furnace may be built with its greatest dimension vertical, the heated air discharging through the bottom or top, or with its longest dimension horizontal, with the heated air discharging through one end. Vertical furnaces are usually selected for installation in closets or basements, where a minimum of floor space is to be surrendered. Horizontal furnaces find application in attics or wherever headroom is sufficient to permit suspension of the furnace and leave occupiable space beneath it.

In any application that burns fuel it cannot be stressed too vehemently that there must *always* be an unobstructed supply of air, continually replaced, to support combustion, as well as a flue to carry the combustion products safely outdoors. Failure to allow combustion air to reach a furnace or boiler is literally a life-and-death matter.

''Boiler'' is more often than not a misnomer. The name came from the boiling of water into steam, but in residential work in particular there are far more devices that just heat water for circulation than there are those that boil it. Nevertheless, all are called ''boilers.'' They include a burner to mix fuel and air, if natural fuel is used, a combustion chamber, a container in which the water to be heated is held (and in the upper part of which steam collects, if it is a steam boiler), passages and an outlet for the gaseous products of combustion in fuel-burning boilers, and, again, a steel or cast-iron housing for the entire assembly. Depending on the space available, there is some latitude of selection in the type of boiler used. Some are long but relatively low. Others, when the floor area may be at a premium but there is plenty of height, are short and high. They may be long and narrow or nearly square. Some are built in sections and assembled on locations, which is particularly convenient when a structure has been completed and no special doors have been provided for the movement of equipment.

In general, boilers not only contain the weight of the water but must also be strong enough to withstand some water pressure. Therefore they are much heavier than furnaces of like capacity and cannot be suspended. Their weight usually means that any other than a location at the lowest level of the building calls for structural strengthening beyond that required for normal loads.

Again, as in fuel-burning furnaces, there is an urgent reminder that fuel-burning boilers *must* have an adequate and unobstructed flow of air for combustion.

How many boilers or furnaces does a residential project require? Most often, a single residence heated by air will have one furnace, although larger houses not infrequently will boast of two, one for the general living quarters and one, perhaps, for the "bedroom wing," or one for the northern exposure and one for the southern. Almost invariably, if heating is by steam or water, a house will have only one boiler.

The question of the number of heating machines in multiple residential buildings is usually concerned with boilers only. An air-heating system, with a furnace, almost never serves more than one residence. In some localities it would be illegal and in all cases inadvisable to risk transmission of disease, cooking odors, or other perils and nuisances that could come from sharing an air distribution system.

With occasional exceptions, the fewer boilers installed, the lower the construction cost of a project, somewhat balanced by a generally higher operating efficiency realized by more and smaller boilers. If cost alone is to be the criterion, the first advantage would usually dictate the selection of one boiler in the largest size commercially available for the project to be served. Obviously there is a major danger in using one boiler, for in the case of any malfunction, failure, or accident which would incapacitate the single machine the project would be without heat. Of course, a similar failure in a single small boiler serving one residence would leave its occupants just as cold and vulnerable as any of the tenants in a thousand-unit project. So it seems that the question is not whose ox is gored but how many.

The decision when to use multiple boilers may depend on many factors: climate, rental or sales value of the residences, type of occupancy expected, and legal requirements. Clearly, a cold climate, high cost housing, and a large proportion of elderly residents would militate for multiple boilers. In regard to official requirements, some guidance may be found in the rules of the Federal Housing Administration of the United States, which has decreed that any project of 60 or more dwelling units must have more than one boiler, and that if two are used the capacity of each must be at least two thirds of the calculated heating load of all spaces served.

This appears to be a minimal requirement for multiple boilers. A project with 59 residences seems rather large to be served by only one boiler. Project planners here must use their best judgment in assaying the other factors involved, some of which are mentioned above.

In the following tables some rough rules of thumb are listed for sizes and space requirements for heating plants. There are, of course, too many variants to permit a complete tabulation. One of them is the use in large plants of many boilers of quite small size, which permits close correspondence of the fuel burned to the actual heating load at any time. This kind of installation requires substantially more space than the conventional arrangement of a few large boilers, and its installation cost is usually not lower and frequently higher. It is not included in the space tabulation but often warrants serious special consideration in buildings in which there may be plenty of floor space allocable to a boiler room, often at the top of the building.

In the table a single boiler is designed to have a capacity equal to 100% of the actual heating load, two boilers are at 67% each, and three boilers at 33⅓% each.

APPROXIMATE HEATING LOADS, BTU PER HOUR PER SQUARE FOOT OF FLOOR AREA FOR RESIDENTIAL OCCUPANCY (AVERAGE WINDOW AREAS ASSUMED)

Winter design temperature	30°F	20°F	10°F	0°F	—10°F	—20°F
Heating load, Btu/sf [a]	21	26	31	36	42	47

APPROXIMATE SPACE REQUIREMENTS FOR HEATING EQUIPMENT, INCLUDING ACCESS FOR SERVICING

	Vertical Furnace			Horizontal Furnace		
Heating Load (Btu/hr)	Length[b] (ft)	Width (ft)	Height (ft)	Length (ft)	Width (ft)	Height (ft)
A. Furnaces						
50,000	4.5	3	6.5	7.5	4.5	4
150,000	4.5	5	6.5	9	5	4

Minimum Boiler Room Dimensions

		One Boiler			Two Boilers			Three Boilers		
Heating Load (Btu/hr)	Head-room Avail-able	Length (ft)	Width (ft)	Height (ft)	Length (ft)	Width (ft)	Height (ft)	Length (ft)	Width (ft)	Height (ft)
B. Boilers										
1,000,000	Low	20	11	8.5	12	14	8.5	Not Recommended		
1,000,000	High	16.5	10	10.5	12	14	8.5			
5,000,000	Low	31	15	12	27	25	11	24	28	10
5,000,000	High	25	13	15	22	21	13	21	23	11
10,000,000	Low	42	17	14	31	28	12	30	31	11
10,000,000	High	30	15	19	25	24	15	25	26	13
20,000,000	Low	Not recommended			42	30	14.5	34	35	13
20,000,000	High	Not recommended			30	26	20	31	34	16

Note. For electrical heating one electric watt provides 3.41 Btu of heat, or, looking at it from another point of view, 1 kilowatt hour on your electric bill has given you 3410 Btu of heat for one hour, whether you used it for heating or for light, television, or an electric toaster or blender.

[a] Gross area of residence itself, not including public spaces.

[b] Reduce length by 2 ft if furnace can be serviced through the door to the furnace closet.

The following illustration shows typical equipment-room layouts for a moderate-sized project and gives two of many possible arrangements, depending on space available. Note that tube servicing areas can be combined or "transferred" by use of doors or removable panels. The illustration implies that the equipment is not at the top of the building. If it were, the boiler flues would probably go directly through the roof.

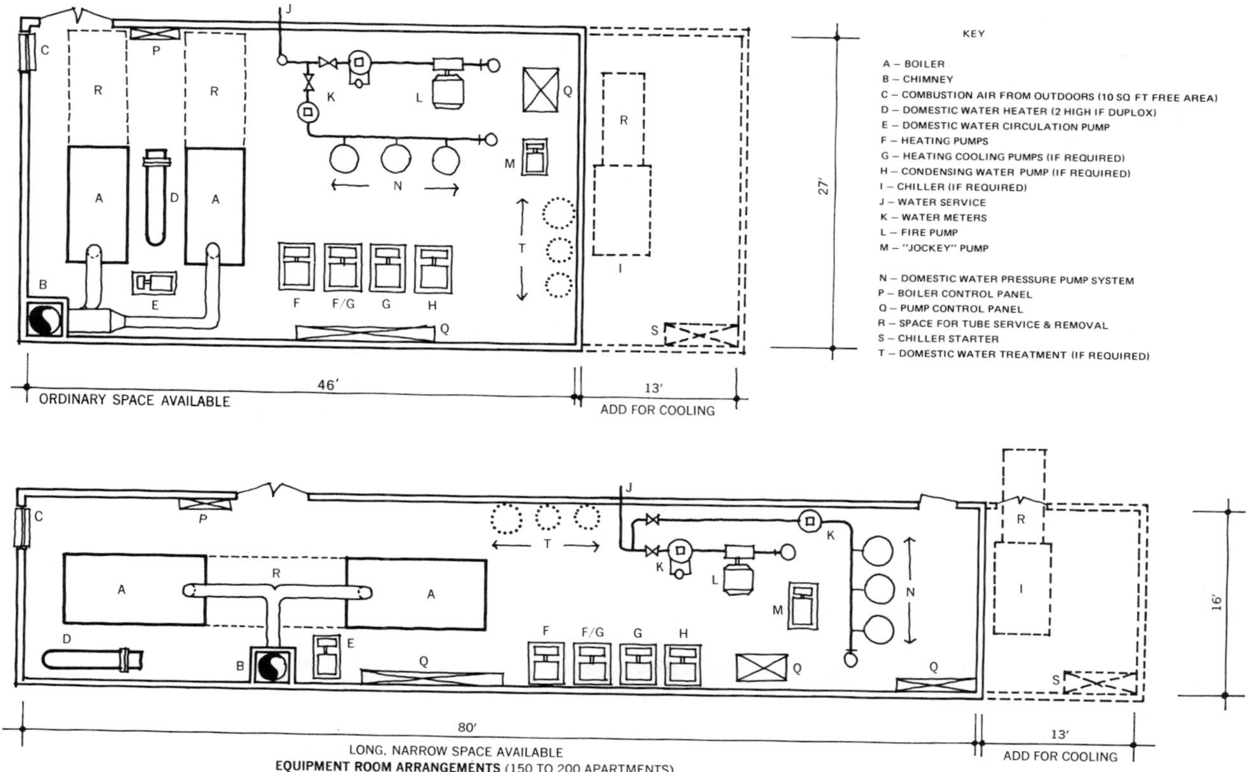

EQUIPMENT ROOM ARRANGEMENTS (150 TO 200 APARTMENTS)

BUILT-IN CONSERVATION

Building owners, architects, and designing engineers who have not yet expressed concern for the depletion of this planet's supply of energy will have to face reality, and soon. A few common-sense rules, observed wholly or even in part, can materially reduce the energy consumed for heating and cooling in the life of a building.

1. FENESTRATION. The glass worship characteristic of midtwentieth-century architecture, whether for genuine design reasons or, covertly, for cheaper construction cost, has been an insatiable energy gobbler. Let us cool it, literally.

2. ORIENTATION. If a choice is at all possible, face each building so that its major glass exposure is least exposed to sun and prevailing winds when cooling is involved. If, on the other hand, a building must be heated, judicious solar exposure is obviously a benefit in energy consumption. The compass direction of exposures is not the only way to employ orientation. The presence or absence of hills, trees, and other buildings are also factors to be considered.

3. INSULATION. Insulation should be used both as an adjunct to the building's exposed surfaces and in consideration of the material of which they are made. Lightweight concretes and special mixes, including insulating substances, air spaces, insulating glass of the double-pane type, tinted glass that blocks out part of the solar input, prefabricated panels which include factory-installed insulation, and the use of wood in lowrise buildings are some of the design and construction decisions that will pay their way in fuel savings and, even more important, help to conserve a dwindling global supply.

4. REFLECTIVE SURFACES. Color and finish of surfaces, especially those directly exposed to the sun, are important. When cooling is the prime consideration, the roof and walls should be as light as possible to reflect solar radiation, and windows, too, should be tinted or coated for the same purpose, whenever feasible. Conversely, dark surfaces and clear glass are helpful when heating is the greater concern.

5. OVERHANGS. The perimeter wall of a ground floor is often set in for architectural reasons from the wall line of the building above. This creates an overhang at the second-floor level. If the overhung floor is occupied, that is, if it is not storage space, it can pose a critically important problem in a climate in which heating is required. A cold floor contributes to miserable living. Therefore a ceiling should be dropped over the open area below the second floor to create a dead space which must be well insulated. In addition, the dead space should be warmed by the general heating system so that the second floor will benefit from the same temperature as every higher floor in the building. This policy applies, of course, wherever there are overhangs.

HEATING MEDIA

Wood-burning fireplaces or stoves that were fired by wood, coal, oil, or gas heated the rooms of former days and many up-to-the minute electrical heating devices and methods have returned to this old principle of direct exposure. Otherwise, a medium must be provided through which heat will travel from the fuel source to the location of need. Our common media in buildings are steam, water, and air. Their various attributes and drawbacks should be compared with respect to the project being served and a selection made to suit. A designer should not be typed as always choosing any one of them. Different problems do not necessarily call for different solutions but careful study will at least promote a logical solution.

In our consideration of steam, water, and air noise is not discussed as a factor. A properly designed and constructed distribution system for any one of the three will be quiet. A badly conceived or built piping system can be noisy, whatever the medium. Furthermore, fuel efficiency should be comparable with any of them. Installation cost, oftener than not, will favor air; steam is more expensive and water frequently the highest in cost. Varying circumstances, however, may upset this order, and it behooves us to continue our examination of the merits of all three.

Steam releases approximately 960 btu/lb of the medium, which compares with 10 to 50 Btu/lb of water and 5 to 15 Btu/lb of air. These figures also illustrate one of the two strong points of steam as a heat-conveying medium: its ability to heat quickly and raise a cold room to the comfort level in a hurry. This advantage is not so dramatic, however, as the above numbers would seem to show because there is a limiting factor in the ability of the heating device to transmit all of this sudden warmth.

The second attribute of steam is its rapid distribution without expenditure of mechanical energy. Little more fuel than that required to make steam in a boiler will raise its pressure to a level that will cause it to travel to the far reaches of a piping system in short order, and with reasonably even distribution, so that all parts of the building will receive their share. The condensed steam may have to be pumped to force it back into the boiler or to expedite total circulation in a very large building, but the steam itself moves under the impetus of its own pressure.

Against these two advantages of steam are two drawbacks. The first, and most serious, has to do with its narrow temperature range. In small simple steam-heating systems the temperature of the medium is always within a degree or two of 215. Whether the temperature outside is 50 degrees, requiring just a touch of heat, or 15 below zero, demanding full throttle, the heating medium is the same—not a very satisfactory performance factor. In the most sophisticated systems there may be a range of 190 to 215 degrees, but it, too, does not begin to reflect the variance in requirements.

The second consideration against the use of steam is its somewhat corrosive effect on pipes and other vessels containing it and the comparative complexity of adjuncts to the system, such as traps and thermostatic vents, whose exact functions need not be discussed here.

Water has the great advantage of wide temperature variability. In 50-degree weather the water temperature may be as low as 80 degrees, just enough to send up a little warmth. That temperature can readily be raised to 220° when it drops to subzero outdoors, making water really responsive to load demands. The principal weakness in the use of water as a heating medium is its temperamental behavior in a pumped piping system. Most water systems are pumped, or "forced" in the trade expression, despite the fact that there are many highly successful gravity flow installations in single and duplex residences which balance themselves out quite well. Installations of any considerable size require pumped systems, and for many years the large pipe sizes required for good gravity flow have militated against gravity systems even in small buildings.

Forced water systems, no matter how carefully designed, can be difficult to balance correctly to give every space its intended share. Parallel to this problem in distribution is the surpassing importance of keeping water pipes free of air. Comparatively small air accumulations can impede or stop circulation in small or major parts of a building, with resultant failure to heat.

Unlike steam and air, water is virtually incompressible. When it is expanded by rising temperatures, as most substances are, a chamber called a compression tank, which allows the expanding water to compress a volume of entrapped air, is introduced into the system. Compression tanks are usually mounted on the ceiling or an otherwise noncritical space. For small buildings and systems this tank will often be found on the boiler room ceiling. In tall buildings there is an advantage in locating the compression tank at or near the top of the system because a much smaller tank up high will do the work of a large tank located down below. Therefore, in high-rise buildings the compression tank will often be found tucked away in the elevator machine penthouse or some other inconspicuous space in that area of the building.

Air offers the advantage of great flexibility of temperature, ranging from 75 to 130 degrees in forced systems and as high as 175 degrees in gravity systems. It has, by definition, a ventilating effect that changes the ambience and helps to create an atmosphere of comparative freshness, although it must be conceded that an air system can also spread unpleasant cooking odors to rooms remote from the kitchen. Another talking point for this medium is the ease with which it may be used to humidify by picking up moisture from the heating equipment and conveying it directly where it is needed. In addition, system leaks cause no damage, an advantage not enjoyed by steam or water.

Finally, a strong advantage is the ease with which cooling and summer dehumidification can be added to an air-heating system, whereas steam or water heating may require an entirely independent cooling system. We shall see that large building installations which combine central water distribution and local air supply can also offer heating and cooling in a single system, frequently without need for any distributing ductwork.

Mention has been made of gravity air systems, which are in the same category as gravity water, confined to small installations, and rapidly disappearing even there.

The disadvantage in the use of air is the space it requires. The ducts for air distribution are substantially larger than water or steam piping, and space must be arranged for them in the construction. To a somewhat lesser extent air heating equipment also requires more space than water or steam boilers of comparable capacity. In general, heating or heating-cooling air systems are practical only for single residences. Multiple dwellings can be served by multiple systems, but when the number of homes in one building exceeds six air systems require too much space when centrally located outside the living areas. If, on the other hand, each system is installed in the residence it is to serve, there is no limit to the number per building. There are other considerations, however. If fuel is used for heating, flues become a difficult problem, and the space required for each piece of equipment subtracts from the rental or salable area.

Electricity is not really a medium for the transmission of heat; it is a fuellike source. Its direct use, however, makes any other medium unnecessary, and at this point it may logically be compared with steam, water, and air. On the favorable side its transmission requires the least space in the way of piping and may often be combined with electrical energy for other uses. It is easy to control and lends itself readily to room-by room thermostatic guidance. Often there are "no moving parts," a simplicity that results in minimal maintenance costs.

Disadvantages in electrical heat, in addition to the cost factor already cited, are found principally in temperature inflexibility; there is no way to get reduced electrical heat in mild weather. This is somewhat overcome by dividing the heating elements, particularly the large ones, into several separately controlled stages. The high temperature of electric heating elements, far above that associated with steam, water, or air, poses some hazard of fire or personal injury but safeguards built into equipment, and intelligent control of materials in environs of electric heaters makes dangerous incidents quite infrequent.

COOLING EQUIPMENT

The temperature of Lake Superior, largest of the Great Lakes of the United States and Canada, is said never to rise above 52 degrees, even at the height of summer. A home or a residential complex built on the shore of that lake could be comfortably cooled by use of water drawn from the nearly inexhaustible source, passed through air cooling equipment, and returned to the lake slightly warmed by the experience. Some sort of societal control would have to be exercised so that this source of virtually free cooling could not be overexploited, thus raising the lake temperature and spoiling it for everyone. Because the water temperature is just as important as the quantity, a level is quickly reached at which the temperature is all-important. For comfort cooling in most of the world it is necessary to squeeze some moisture out of the air. Water temperature above 55 degrees is useless for dehumidifying air for almost all cases.

It follows, therefore, that for any favored site that can boast an adequate supply of water from well, river, lake, or rain cistern colder than 55 degrees and whose availability can be predicted to last into the indefinite future *natural water* is Nature's gift for cooling, to be seized eagerly. Unfortunately there are not many areas in the planet whose air temperatures require cooling and which can boast of a supply of such cold water.

There is one other natural recourse for cooling, also applicable in limited areas only. It is called *evaporative cooling*, which can be successful in deserts or desert-like regions, whose outdoor relative humidities are extremely low, below 10%, specifically, even when the temperature is above 100°F. In these rare cases water at any ordinary temperature for domestic supply can be sprayed into this hungrily dry air. Some of the water will evaporate, thus raising the humidity but reducing the temperature. If the rate of evaporation is controlled, the result will be air cool enough and not too moist for a comfortable environment.

Mechanical refrigeration must be resorted to for cooling in the overwhelming majority of cases, when conditions for natural water cooling or evaporative cooling do not exist. The first half-century of air conditioning has produced three basic types of refrigerating machine, used in various situations according to their suitability. Before considering the comparative strengths and shortcomings of these machines, let us examine the mechanics of the refrigeration process as it applies to air cooling.

The purpose of refrigeration is to remove heat where it is not wanted. Heat is a form of energy that cannot be destroyed and, at the level at which it is extracted from the air, cannot be put to useful work. Consequently, the second function of the refrigeration plant is to dispose of this heat in a way that will not create a nuisance. If these two basic functions are kept in mind by nontechnical people, they will find much of the mystery of refrigeration cleared away. Now to translate the principles into machinery.

The medium that removes the unwanted heat is called a refrigerant, a substance chosen because it has the property of absorbing heat. Refrigerants are expensive, too expensive to discard when they have picked up their quota of heat. Thus the process is a continuous cycle, designed to use the same refrigerant over and over again. The following is the basic cycle and the refrigeration equipment that implements it:

1. The refrigerant absorbs the unwanted heat from the space to be cooled.
2. The refrigerant is placed into a state in which it can easily dispose of the heat it has absorbed. Changing its state requires mechanical work or more heat in a compressor or concentrator.
3. The unwanted heat (plus heat added to the refrigerant in Step 2) is separated out of the system in a condenser.
4. The condensed refrigerant is restored to a condition in which it can best absorb heat, through an expansion valve, orifice, or metering device. The cycle then goes back to Step 1 and repeats itself.

Basically, this is equipment for convenience, not efficiency. Work is expended just to move heat from one place to another.

Refrigeration systems are classified as direct or indirect. In direct systems, often called ''direct expansion,'' air blows over finned tubes in which the ready-to-absorb-heat refrigerant is circulated. Indirect systems are those in which the refrigerant chills water; the water, in turn, circulates through finned tubes over which the air to be cooled is blown. Direct systems are confined to small-capacity installations such as room coolers and air conditioning systems for stores and offices of modest size and to larger installations in which the refrigeration plant is located close to the air processing unit (at most the plant may serve two units).

At this point let us insert a word about refrigeration capacity. The American industry is married to a term that goes back to the original mechanical cooling plants whose sole purpose was to make ice. The measure of capacity is the rate of cooling required to produce 1 ton of ice in 24 hours. It is called a ''ton'' of refrigeration and can be remembered as 12,000 Btu/hr. To be more specific, direct refrigeration systems range from ½ ton (6000 Btu/hr) room coolers to about 75 ton (900,000 Btu/hr) "packaged" rooftop units. Indirect systems may overlap at the lower end of their range, from 25 tons for a small office complex up to thousands of tons for a huge residential or office building, or convention hall. Building codes often fix the size of direct refrigeration systems, particularly for residential use, far below the upper limit we have cited and should always be consulted on this point if direct systems are being contemplated. Most systems for multiple residential use are indirect, and those for single rooms or single residences may be one or the other.

Step 3 in the refrigeration cycle, as described a little way back, refers to the condenser. This does exactly what its name implies; it condenses the refrigerant from gaseous to liquid form, in which process the refrigerant releases all the heat. To do this the condenser uses a large quantity of coolant, of which the most readily available and least expensive is air. Next in line is water. These are the two condensing substances generally used. The reason for Step 2 can now be revealed. The refrigerant was put into its new state at that time in order that air or water at the actual available temperatures could condense it.

Air is free for the purpose, but it is a poor conductor of heat, and therefore large quantities of it must be moved over correspondingly large surfaces behind which the condensing takes place. Water, comparatively, is an excellent conductor of heat, thus more desirable but often expensive to use and becoming scarce and too precious for air cooling. Refrigeration technology has worked out a compromise.

Water is circulated as the condensing agent (this water having no direct connection whatsoever with the ultimate process of chilling the air in the residential area). The water thus circulated picks up the heat and, of course, becomes warmer. This water is then sprayed into an outdoor air stream, in which a small part of it evaporates into the air, cooling the remainder of the water which is then recirculated through the condenser. The part that has evaporated must be constantly replaced with fresh water, but it amounts to only 2 to 4% of the total circulated. The equipment in which the condensing water is sprayed into the air stream is called a cooling tower. An alternate piece of equipment combines the "tower" and the condenser and is called an evaporative condenser. The functions of these items of machinery are identical. The cooling tower or evaporative condenser must be located where it can take in large quantities of outdoor air, used to evaporate the small amount of condensing water. Often the best place is the roof, remote from occupied areas, for some noise is associated with the movement of air and water and the moist air discharged is unpleasant. If the roof location is chosen, the equipment, which is quite large, should be architecturally integrated with the elevator penthouse. If a roof location is impractical, often for aesthetic reasons, an on-the-ground spot must be found at some distance from any building. The last alternative, location inside the building, is possible but quite expensive and with numerous possibilities for annoyance and damage.

Location of a condenser that uses air as its only condensing agent follows the same rules as those laid down for location of cooling towers and evaporative condensers.

Types of condenser usually applied to various sizes of refrigeration plant are listed as follows:

1. Water-cooled condensers, in which the condensing water is discharged to the sewer after having passed through the condenser once, are becoming rare as water supplies are threatened by rising population and proliferation of air conditioning. Their use now is virtually confined to 7½ tons and smaller and only when circumstances make installation of air-cooled condensers impossible.

2. Air-cooled condensers are widely used, ranging in capacity from the ½-ton familiar "window" room cooler to 75 ton plants and occasionally even larger.
3. The cooling tower or evaporative condenser equipment applies to the larger plants. Their sizes may drop into the air-cooled condenser range, but they are usually placed in the 100 ton and indefinitely upward capacities.

The three types of refrigeration machine referred to bear the formidable names of reciprocating, centrifugal, and absorption. Some strange facts of industrial life are illustrated in the use of these machines:

1. RECIPROCATING. This is the most mechanically complex of the three kinds of equipment, the most subject to wear and the need for replacement of its multitude of moving parts. Yet it is by many hundredfold the most commonly used. Reciprocating machines have the field to themselves in sizes smaller than 25 tons and are virtually unopposed at 25 to 100 tons. The smallest units, 5 tons and smaller in capacity, sell in vast numbers for such applications as room and apartment coolers. Manufacturers have been motivated to build them to be quiet and with their normal vibration well contained. The larger machines, however, tend to be noisy and shaky and to require a comparatively high quantity of energy to operate. As a rule they are driven by electric motors, but occasionally gas engines or turbines serve the purpose.

2. CENTRIFUGAL. This basically simple, turbinelike machine is built in capacities of 50 to 1000 tons, driven by electric motor or steam or gas turbine. Maintenance and replacement of parts should be minimal, noise level is moderate, and little vibration is apparent. The centrifugal compressor is not competitive in installation cost with reciprocating machines for capacities smaller than 200 tons; for example, two 75-ton reciprocating machines will usually be less expensive than one 150-ton centrifugal.

3. ABSORPTION. This type of equipment uses heat instead of the work of a motor or engine to power the refrigeration cycle. It is often selected when natural fuel is freely available and cheaper than electric energy. In some localities this is particularly true in summer; inducements are offered to encourage off-season use of fuels in order to smooth out the annual demand curve. Absorption machines offer the advantage of quiet vibration-free operation. The only moving parts are small auxiliary motor-driven pumps, one of which helps to maintain the extremely low vacuum that must be held inside. A small machine, of the 25-ton size uses gas directly for its heating medium, but for many years the trend has been to large units, ranging from 100 to 1500 tons, with steam or high-temperature water (240° or more) providing the heat. The principal disadvantages of absorption machines are in the somewhat temperamental nature of the refrigeration cycle and in the comparatively bulky size and weight of the unit. The "nature of the cycle" is such that a comparatively slight irregularity can put the machine out of commission and in such a way that it takes half a day or longer to get it working again.

Refrigeration plants can, or course, contain more than one machine. For machines of the same type it is an almost invariable rule that the overall installation cost of a single large machine is less than multiple units of the same aggregate capacity.

If the criterion is reliability rather than cost, the question must be viewed differently. For a critical industrial process requiring 1000 tons of cooling, the best solution might be three 500-ton machines; full capacity would be available even in the event of failure of one piece of equipment. For a residential installation, in which continuous cooling is desirable but not vital, a 1000-ton load might call for two 500-ton machines on the theory that if one broke down the other would be able to do at least part of the job and some cooling should be more palatable than none at all. In many cases, however, the lowest first cost determines the issue, and the single machine is installed with acceptance of the obvious risks of resident alienation.

Selection of cooling towers offers similar choices but different parameters. A tower or evaporative condenser is a comparatively uncomplicated piece of equipment, less likely to collapse in action. It is quite large in physical size, and two units might overflow the available space. On the other hand, this equipment costs much less, ton-for-ton, than refrigeration machinery, and duplicate units do not pose so severe an economic problem.

The following table offers minimum space requirements for refrigeration plants of various sizes:

Gross Living Area[a] (sf)	Tons Capacity	Number and Kind of Machine	Space Length, Including Servicing Area (ft)	Width (ft)	Height (ft)
110,000	200	2 reciprocating	25	17	7.5
110,000	200	1 centrifugal	32	13	7
110,000	200	1 absorption	34	12	8.5
275,000	500	1 centrifugal	33	16	8.5
275,000	500	1 absorption	45	14	10
275,000	500	2 centrifugal	32	22	7
550,000	1000	1 centrifugal	40	24	13
550,000	1000	1 absorption	61	16	12
550,000	1000	2 absorption	40	24	10

[a] The ratio used here of square feet of actual residential area (including closets, bathrooms, and interior halls, but excluding public corridors and stairwells) per ton of cooling is 550. This is a fair average but will obviously vary according to climate, building construction, direction of exposure, and similar factors.

The approximate space requirements predicted in this table are in addition to those approximated for a central heating plant. Occasionally the total can be reduced by combining servicing areas for the major items of equipment; that is, making the servicing lengths common. If this is possible, the length of the refrigeration plant space can be reduced by one-third. That reduction can also be realized sometimes by providing servicing doors at one end of each refrigeration machine, permitting its tubes to be removed to space outside the equipment room. With respect to space saving in combining heating and cooling plants, however, one possible code restriction may govern. Some localities prohibit refrigeration and fuel-burning machinery to be operated in the same room. This must be ascertained before combined equipment rooms are arranged.

HEAT PUMPS

Refrigeration equipment has been defined as taking heat from where it is not wanted and disposing of it where it will cause no nuisance. A reversal of the refrigeration cycle permits the same machinery to perform the opposite function, to take heat from where it is not needed and transfer it to where it is; in short, to act as a heat pump. The reversal is not mechanically difficult to do. It is accomplished by operating appropriate valves in the refrigeration cycle piping. It happens that reciprocating machines operate in a range of pressures and with a refrigerant that makes heat pumping most feasible. Therefore this type of machinery is used for heat pumps. A striking heat pump advantage is that it has a coefficient of performance of 1.8 to 1 up to 2.8 to 1, which means that it will deliver that much more heat from the source than the heat equivalent of the electricity used.

What limits the use of this technique is convenient availability of heat. To illustrate, in a locality in which outside temperatures never fall below 35°F the outdoor air itself can serve as the heat source for the comparatively small heating requirement in such a climate, even though air is a poor conductor. Important impediments crop up in colder parts of the world, however. First, more heating is required and, second, heat becomes progressively more difficult to extract as the source air gets colder. These facts have limited the widespread use of heat pumps.

There are, of course, other heat sources. The earth itself is one, but it, too, is not a good conductor of heat. This means that such a large tract of earth must be used for the source that the method is impractical. Another potential heat source is underground or surface water in large quantities and at moderate temperatures. The latter is a requisite, of course, because heat can be removed practically from water only down to its freezing point, and if the water is rather cold to begin with not a lot of heat is available. Water conducts heat well; it is comparatively noncorrosive, easy to pump, and altogether a desirable heat source.

SYSTEMS

There is no invariable rule of order in which decisions can be made to define the HVAC system for residential occupancy. Heating and cooling requirements, fuel and energy selections, heating and cooling media, and equipment types and locations have been touched on. Certainly no less important is the determination of the kind of distribution system to be used within each dwelling unit, a decision that might also fix the larger project distribution system, if one is required, to bring heating and cooling to each residence.

There is a fairly wide range of systems of heating, cooling, and combined heating and cooling from which to choose. The first guidepost to be fixed must be whether the overall plan is to make each residence independent unto itself, to design a complete central system to serve each dwelling unit in the project according to its needs, or to provide some combination of the two whereby each residence is served by its independently operated subsystem but draws some kind of basic central-plant service to make its subsystem operative. What factors decide which of these categories fits the project being planned?

INDEPENDENT SYSTEM. There are two principal categories of multiple dwelling projects whose natures point to entirely separate heating and/or cooling plants for each residence. The first is the ''tract home'' project in which single units, attached in groups or completely detached, are scattered about a comparatively large site. Here the costs of central distribution are often prohibitive and the building for a central plant obtrusive and out of character.

The second is the condominium in which each dwelling unit is its owners' castle, and fewer shared services and expenses mean fewer opportunities for friction and misunderstanding. If the condominium is in a single large building or a number of smaller multistory buildings, it is often found that an electrical heating (and cooling) system answers the need, for there is no problem of fuel distribution or collection of flue gases. This does not always have to be the case, however. Gas-fired equipment has been developed which can vent its products of combustion through a wall and, when local codes permit, single dwelling units in a multistory building can use this kind of furnace and/or cooling unit. Practical considerations would seem to confine this technique to lowrise buildings, up to perhaps as many as six floors, but no more.

The independent system has a clear plus-minus standing on its mechanical merits. The plus factor is that it is overall breakdownproof. Complete failure of one system will have little or no effect on any other. The countervailing disadvantage is that there are many small pieces of equipment to be maintained and thus more numerous service calls to be contemplated. Whether the cost of these calls is to be borne by the user or by the project as a whole is a factor that enters into the making of the first decision on which system to use. A closely related question is that of length of equipment life and replacement cost. Perhaps it should not be so, but it is a fact of industrial life that mass-produced small heating and cooling units have predictable operating life spans one-half to one-quarter the length of more carefully made central machines. Over the long run, this usually balances out any first-cost advantage the individual furnaces, boilers, or compressors may have.

CENTRAL SYSTEM. The central heating and/or cooling system is particularly attractive economically in a single large building or a group of large buildings. The ''large'' building might be a low- or midrise, seven floors or fewer, covering a great land area, or a highrise of eight floors or more. The highrise structures offer several factors that make central systems particularly advantageous, although when the height exceeds 30 stories certain drawbacks begin to appear.

One of the chief benefits of a central system lies in the minimal space needed for equipment in or adjacent to the residential areas. Because it is the highest value space in the building, it is well saved. Clearly, however, a major drawback in central systems lies in their interdependency. Trouble in Apartment 17-D may have repercussions in Apartment 18-D and above but even more often in Apartments 16-D and on down.

COMBINED SYSTEM. The combined system offers some of the advantages of each of the others but it also contains some of their drawbacks. Its design usually contains the same kind of buildings that were proposed as good subjects for central systems, and its heating and/or cooling air supply units and distribution system serve one residence only. It receives some central service or services from a project plant which might eliminate fuel distribution, flues, refrigeration compressors, condensers, or heating units, or some combination of them, from the individual residences.

As in most compromises, the system combines some of the strengths and weaknesses of the two it amalgamates. There is comparatively little interdependence, but there is some, with the attendant risks, and there is little, if any, saving in space. On the other hand, the number and cost of service and replacement calls should be materially fewer than for the independent systems.

INDEPENDENT HEATING AND COOLING SYSTEMS

Electrical heating lends itself readily to independent, residence-by-residence heating. Fed by electrical energy from the dwelling unit's own power service, often metered and directly charged, the actual method of heating may take any one of several forms.

''Baseboard'' electrical resistance heaters are designed to simulate ornamental baseboard trim. Their dimensions are not much greater than standard baseboard trim (generally two and a fraction inches maximum depth by six and a fraction inches high). These heaters provide a continuous curtain of low-level heating, preferably along the outside wall of each room. Controlled by their built-in thermostats or by a central thermostat mounted at a strategic location in the room, they offer a simple and effective means of heating. Their capacity per unit length is somewhat limited unless their physical size is so increased that they cannot pretend to look like baseboards. In a sense, however, this limitation is a healthy one. It dictates that attention be given to maintaining moderate heat losses, which means good insulation, reasonable glass areas, and control of air leakage from outdoors.

Electric convectors can be thought of as concentrated baseboard heaters. They are analagous to the old-fashioned steam or hot-water convectors or radiators and provide the total heat needed in a room in one or very few locations, preferably under a window or windows. Sizes vary greatly according to heating capacity, but an average dimension would be 25 in. high by 48 in. long by 6 in. deep. The device might be recessed or partly recessed into the wall construction, in which case particular care should be exercised that it is well insulated on the rear and exposed sides.

Electric radiant panel heating has proved successful in many residential applications. Like all radiant heating systems, it provides a large source of low-level heat which produces a comfortable environment. Like other radiant systems, however, it has the disadvantage of being unable to concentrate a proportional amount of its heat at the outside wall line of greatest heat loss, and there is likely to be a narrow uncomfortably cold zone in that part of the room. Electric radiant systems do boast one advantage over the wet systems. By their nature they have less construction bulk to warm up or cool down and are much more quickly responsive to changing load demands. It is in the nature of heating that loads do fluctuate, often very quickly. The sun swings around its daily course, outside temperatures change, lights go on and off, and people come in and out.

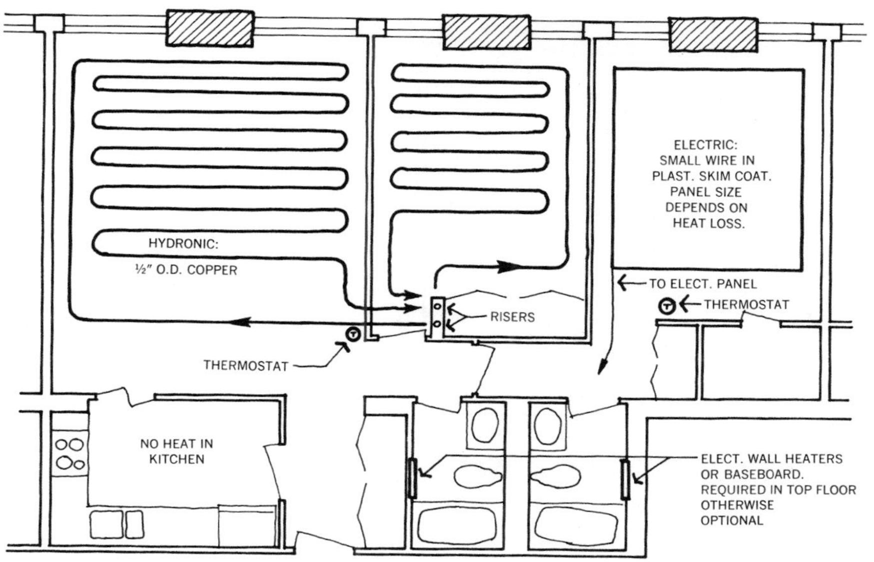

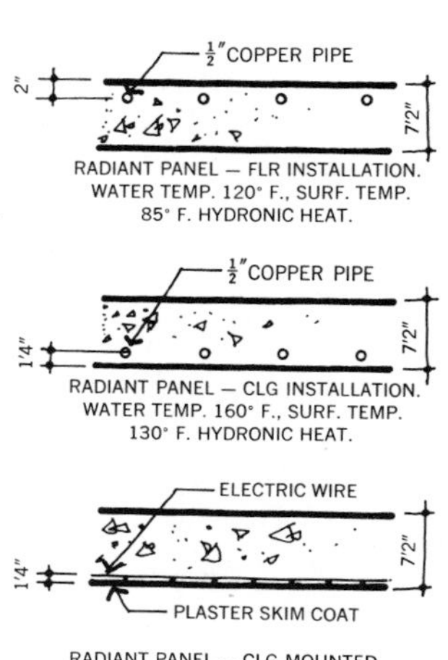

Electric radiant panels are invariably installed on the ceiling in one of two forms. The ceiling itself may be made up of factory-manufactured panels in which electrical conducting-resisting materials have been imbedded, each panel rated for its electric input and therefore heat output. The panels are heavily insulated on the up-facing side, nearly all the heat goes in the direction in which it is wanted. The other common method is the one usually applied to concrete slabs in multistory buildings. After the slab has set and the shoring has been cleared away, electric conducting-resisting cable is applied to the underside of the concrete in long serpentine loops in which adjacent lengths of cable may be 2 to 6 in. apart, depending on the room heating load. Cable is secured to the slab at intervals close enough to prevent its drooping, and the thinnest possible "skim" coating of plaster, usually $\frac{3}{16}$ to $\frac{1}{4}$ in. thick, is applied to hide the cable, distribute its heat over the entire area, and give a finished ceiling appearance.

Electric furnaces fall into the category of residential fan-coil units, a prolific kind that is prevalent in the central and combined systems as well as in the independent systems now under discussion. The fan-coil unit description is similar to that of the heating furnace, and like the furnace the fan-coil unit may be horizontal or vertical in its major aspect. Briefly, then, it includes a small blower or tandem blowers, driven directly or by pulleys and belt from a fractional horsepower electric motor or motors, and assembled with filters and heating and/or cooling finned tube coils in a steel casing. If instead of coils there is an electrical resistance heating element, the unit is called an electric furnace.

Fan-coil units may be of such capacity that one unit will serve a single room, a group of rooms, or an entire residence. If the fan-coil is combined in a single housing with a refrigeration machine, it is called a self-contained unit. A well-known example of self-contained equipment which also includes the refrigeration condenser is the through-the-wall or "window" room cooler, which takes in outdoor air directly, uses and expels some of it for condensing purposes, and mixes a small amount of it with recirculated room air to help ventilate the room being cooled. This machine is sometimes furnished with a built-in, electrical resistance heater and thus can cool, ventilate, or heat the space when required. Dimensions of an average unit are about 17 in. high by 16 in. deep and 25 to 42 in. long.

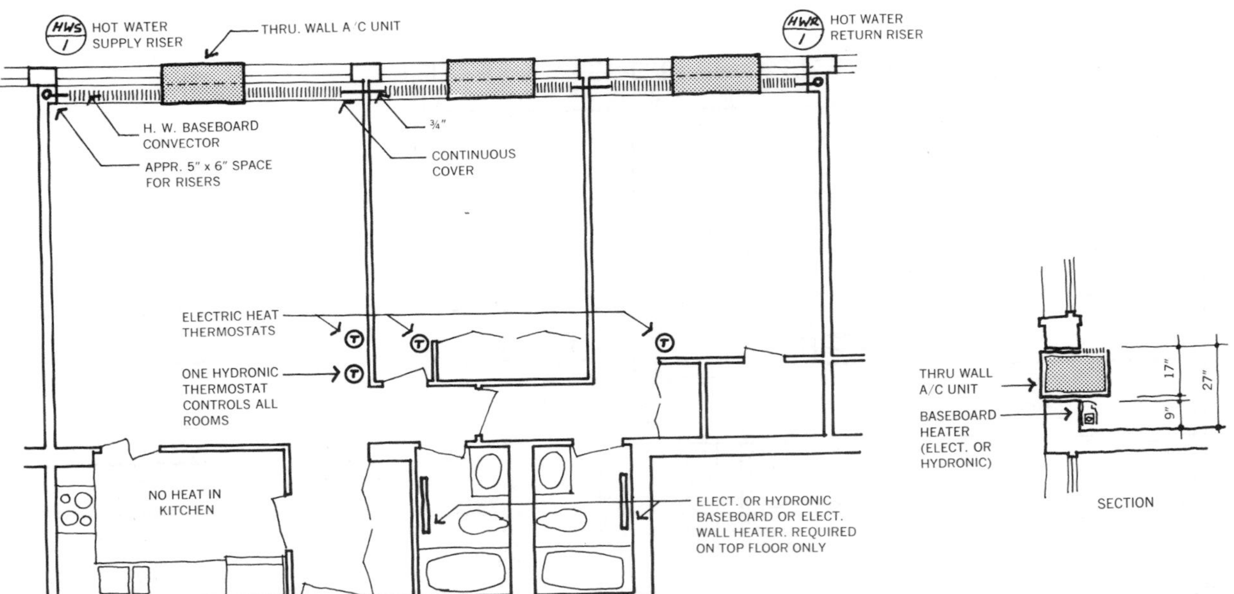

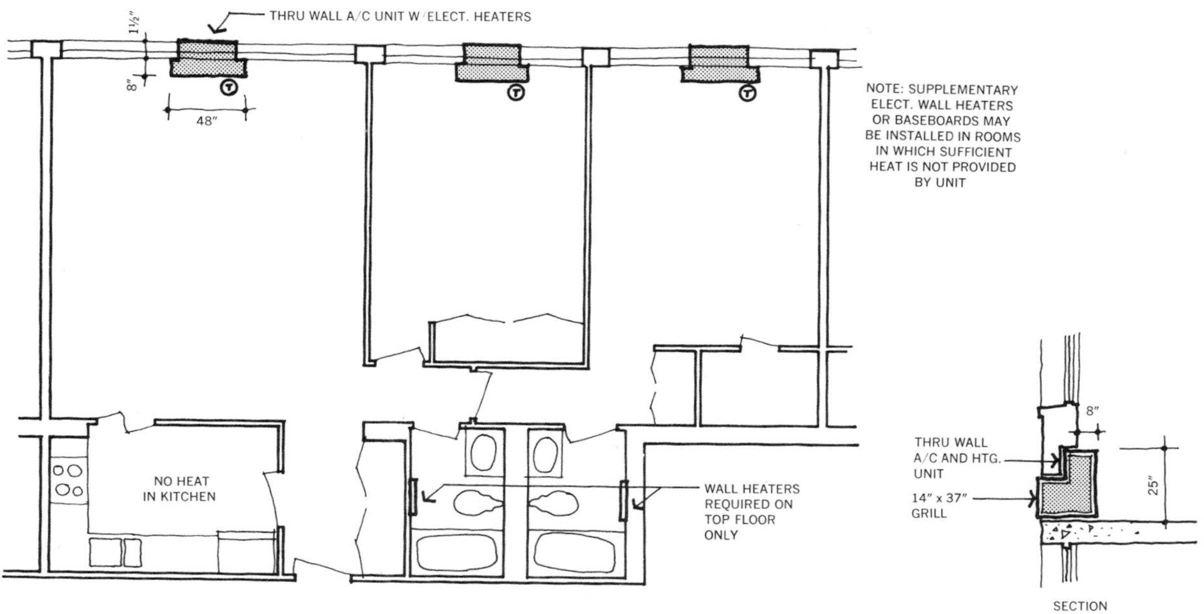

Similar self-contained fan-coil units are available in sizes to heat and cool an entire dwelling in conjunction with appropriate air distribution ductwork. These units are too large to be spotted casually in a wall or window opening and are usually floor mounted at an outside wall, where condensing air is readily available. This arrangement, however, uses up an appreciable amount of premium living space and has found little favor.

What has gained widespread use is the split independent system rather than the self-contained. Here the horizontal or vertical fan-coil unit is mounted or suspended in an interior closet, entrance hall, or similar living space of lower desirability, and the refrigeration compressor-condenser is mounted as a unit on the outside, thus moving a source of noise and vibration away from the dwelling quarters. In one- or two-story residential buildings space for the refrigeration machine can often be found on the ground outside, partly shielded by planting. In three-to-five or six-story buildings the refrigeration assemblies may be mounted on the roof with careful vibration isolation and structural provisions. If the method is at all practical in multiple-story buildings, it will be by the use of balconies, at least one for each dwelling unit, on which the refrigeration equipment hopefully can be located so as not to spoil the balcony entirely for recreational purposes.

In all these installations small copper refrigerant lines are run between the outside refrigeration machine and the inside coil, and in all cases this leaves the problem of heating to be solved. For one- or two-story residences a natural fuel furnace can be introduced as an adjunct to the fan-coil unit or a refrigeration coil can be installed in conjunction with a standard furnace. Although the flue problem becomes difficult, these arrangements can be used for buildings as high as five or six stories. For higher buildings the furnace problems become too serious to cope with and heating must be done electrically. This may be done by a resistance heater installed in the fan-coil unit or its ductwork or, if the climate is suitable, by the use of a heat pump as an embellishment of the refrigeration machine. Recall that if the heat pump can be used it will return about two and one-quarter times as much heat per electrical watt as the straight resistance heater.

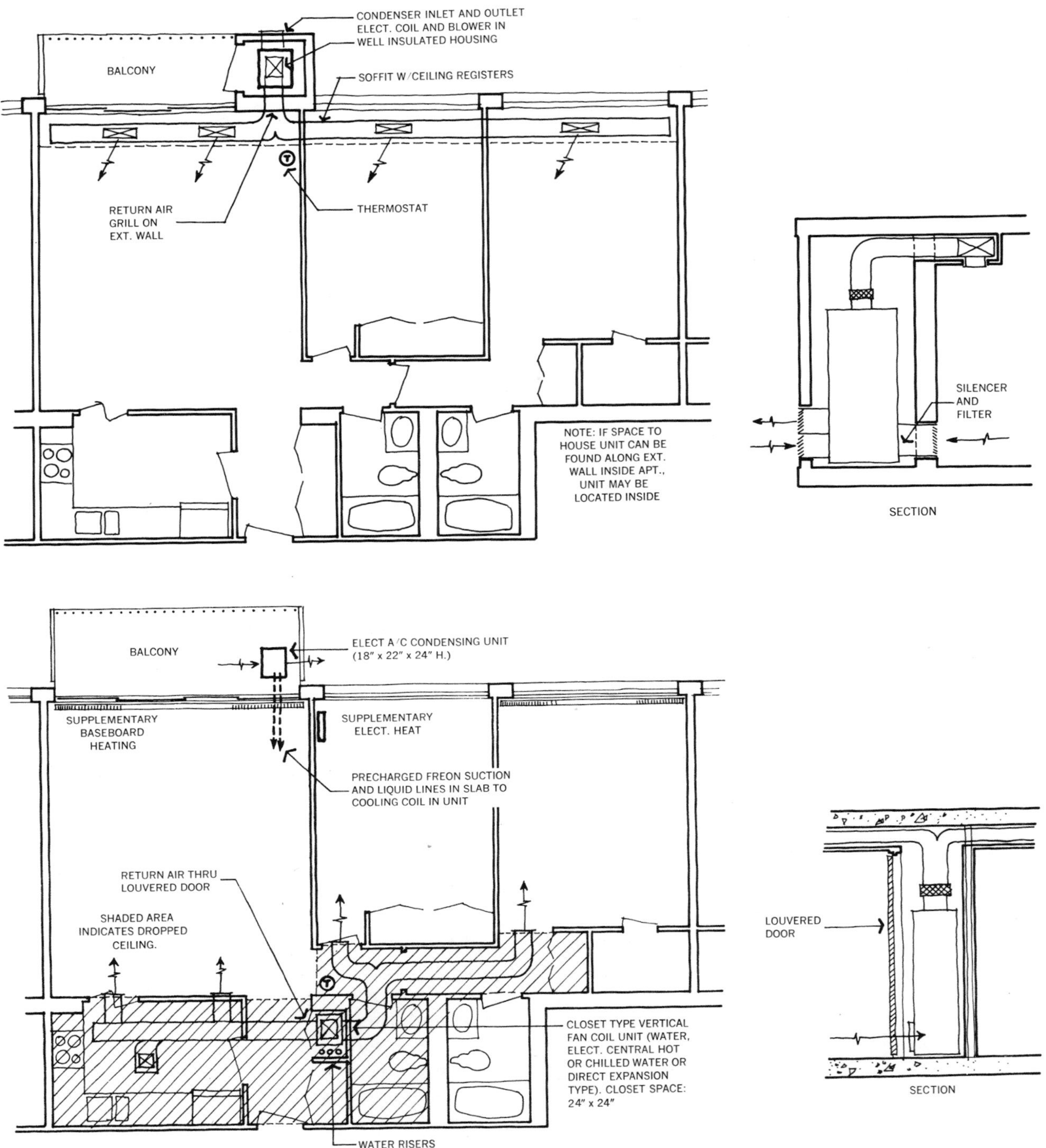

Two practical rules should be inserted here to govern the installation of these types of equipment. First, if the fan-coil unit is used for cooling, a drainpan must be incorporated in the unit to catch moisture condensed from the conditioned air by the coil and a drainpipe must be run from the pan to conduct the condensate to a sewer or drainage outlet. In ''window'' units this condition has been met in most units by draining the pan to the fan which moves the outside air used for condensing purposes. When enough condensate accumulates, the fan blades pick it up and fling it into the atmosphere with such velocity that it becomes mistlike and is absorbed into the air. Occasionally when the adjustment is not quite right, passers-by are made aware of it by what seems to be a light drizzle on a sunny day.

The second rule is that the cooling coil should be after, or downstream of, a fuel-burning furnace. If the coil is first in line, the chilled air off the cooling surface will pass through the furnace. In summer the products-of-combustion side of the furnace's heat exchanger is in direct contact through the flue with the hot, humid air from outdoors, and the cold on one side of the furnace metal will cause condensation of moisture in the hot weather air on the other side. That moisture will rust the heat exchanger. If it is impossible to avoid an arrangement of cooling coil first, the furnace must be made of stainless steel, which is expensive but will not rust.

There is a final word of caution regarding installation of fan-coil units serving more than one room, especially if the unit is mounted outside the house itself; for example, in a utility closet. Layout of supply ductwork conveying the warmed or cooled air is an obvious requirement in the design, but sometimes an unwary designer will forget that air must be recirculated from the living quarters back to the fan-coil device. If this calls for ductwork or for the use of construction space above suspended ceilings or soffits, it must be made certain that no other construction such as masonry fire-separation partitions shuts off the duct or passage. If there is an impediment of that nature, a legal way must be found to go through or around it.

CENTRAL HEATING AND COOLING SYSTEM

The hallmark of the central system is a mechanical plant in which heating and/or cooling capacity is sufficient to serve an entire building or project and a water piping distribution system that connects the plant with every part of the residential area. Elements of the heating and cooling plant have already been considered, and the piping systems are no less important. They must be designed with at least equal care. An understanding of their potentialities, problems, and comparative values reveals possibilities and requirements, particularly structural requirements, associated with the various piping arrangements.

Pipe systems for central residential heating and cooling are described as one-, two-, three-, and four-pipe. The two-pipe system is the most widely used. There is a further classification into direct and reversed return.

One-pipe systems are used only for heating. When they are feasible, they are favored for low cost and minimal space requirements. Water is pumped through a single main which feeds a number of heating devices such as baseboard convectors or standard convectors. At each heating device a specially designed tee fitting whose size is selected for the particular application extracts as much water from the main as that device needs. That part of the water passes through the heater and then returns to the main, downstream of where it was taken off. In multiple-story buildings one-pipe systems can often be mixed with two-pipe, which are reviewed next. Anticipating a moment, two-pipe (separate supply and return) vertical risers with one-pipe horizontal mains between them can serve a number of heating devices on the same floor level, a useful arrangement because it minimizes the locations in a building at which risers must be allowed for in the construction.

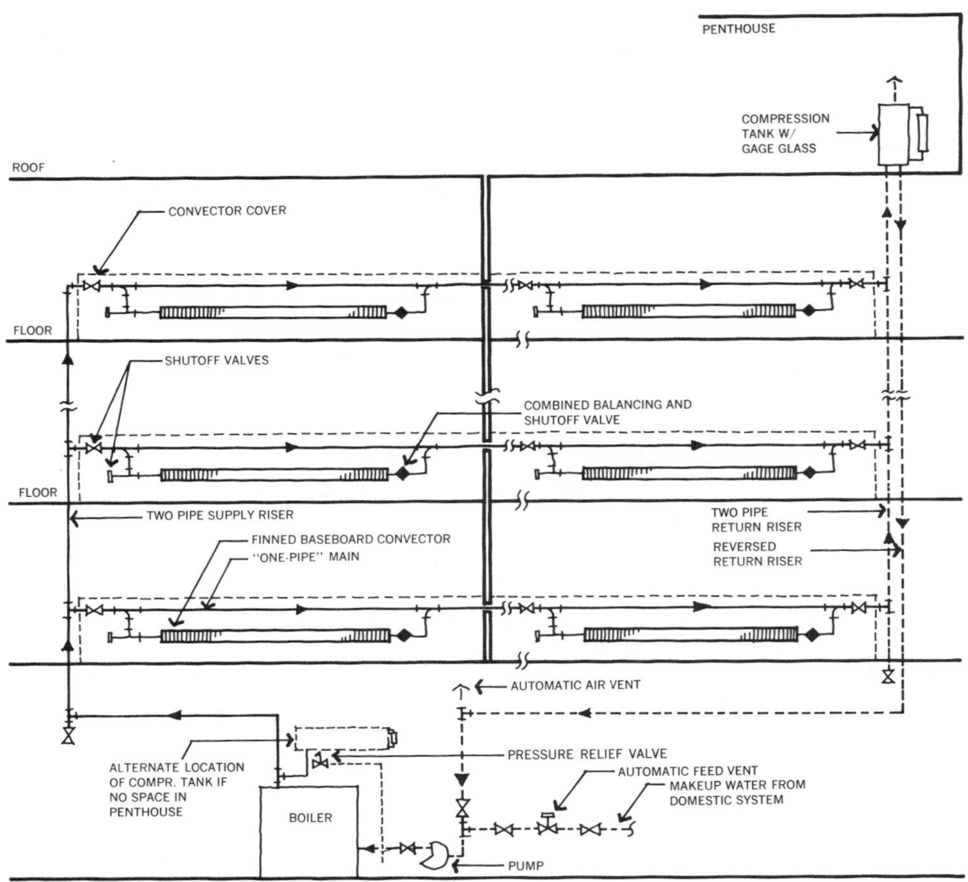

TYPICAL WATER HEATING PIPING DIAGRAM (SHOWING 1-PIPE AND 2-PIPE SYSTEMS)

One-pipe systems also apply to steam heating, particularly in old buildings. The use of steam for heating, in residential applications particularly, has been reduced to the vanishing point in new building design and new one-pipe systems are rare. They can work, however, in buildings of modest height. Steam is supplied to radiators or convectors in a vertical riser pipe, and after it has given up its heat in the heating device and condensed to liquid form the condensate water returns down the same pipe. That pipe must be large enough to permit simultaneous passage of steam and water. In three-story buildings the riser can even feed up from the lowest floor so that steam and water are traveling in opposite directions! In taller buildings, up to 10 floors, steam is piped under the roof, from which risers feed down, and steam and water move in the same direction. For taller buildings the one-pipe system is simply not practical. Too much steam and water are in the risers and the design becomes unmanageable. Economy of installation is the reason for one-pipe systems. Their great drawback is that the heating device must be all on or all off; throttling a valve will impede return of the condensate.

Two-pipe systems provide separate channels for supply and return water, either or both for heating and cooling purposes. When applied to steam heating, the two-pipe system permits throttling of the steam supply when the heating load is light, for example, in mild weather, and only part of the heating device is supplied with steam, thus reducing its capacity commensurate with the demand on it.

Two-pipe water systems for heating and cooling have a serious drawback, best illustrated by an example that applies to the climate in large parts of the world.

Early in the morning of a spring or autumn day the outdoor temperature may have fallen to 50°F and a little heat is needed. Water at 90°F may be circulated to meet this mild need. By noon of this sunny day it is 75°F outdoors, and cooling is being called for, particularly on the southern exposure (in the northern hemisphere) where the sun is streaming into the huge modern windows. Cooling needs water at about 50 degrees. The manufacturer of the equipment has probably warned that no water warmer than 80 degrees should ever be run into his machine, and so the distraught building operator has had to run his 90-degree early-morning heating water through the building until it naturally cooled down to 80°F and then run that through the chiller until it dropped to 50 degrees. If the project is a large one, it is well on in the afternoon by the time all that has been accomplished and almost time to start heating again for the approaching cool evening.

This very real operating trial can be lessened by dividing the project piping and pumps into separate zones, so that the exposures that face the sun in the cool mornings may be supplied with chilled water much earlier than those that get no sunlight at all or get it later in the day. This piping is not easy to arrange in buildings of irregular or complex shape, and even in square or rectangular buildings perfectly compass-oriented the operator must respond to the weather, the cloudiness of the day, the actual temperature swing, and so on. Therefore the zoning method has its own pitfalls.

Even zoning in a two-pipe system cannot solve another common problem. Occupants of one dwelling expect a large group of friends in for Sunday afternoon cocktails and need cooling at once. Their elderly neighbors, occupying an identical apartment with the same exposure, are spending a quiet afternoon at home. Noting that the outside temperature is 50°F, they invoke the lease provision that entitles them to heat. There is no way in which a two-pipe central system can satisfy both sets of tenants or apartment owners, and someone must take on the unpleasant task of breaking the news to one or the other.

An obvious answer is the four-pipe system in which there are separate and independent piping systems and pumps for heating and cooling that make these services available simultaneously throughout a building or project, at least in intermediate weather when one or the other may be needed at any time. Equally clear is the drawback to the arrangement. It is an expensive installation that requires extra unusable space in the habitable areas. It is a luxury that is sometimes found in the highest room-rate hotels but much less often in residential buildings.

In an attempt to compromise between the inflexibility of two-pipe distribution and the high cost of the four-pipe arrangement, a three-pipe system has been introduced. Separate heating and cooling piping and pumps characterize it, and common return mains are associated with each pair of supply pipes. Used to its full potential generally in the intermediate seasons, its theory is that enough diverse calls will be made for heating and cooling simultaneously and that the mixture of return water will not be too warm for the chiller nor too cold for the boilers. Introduced with fanfare, the systems have met with some success, but they have proved to be temperamental in operation and conducive to problems in the central plant. Sales pressure for their use noticeably diminished a few years after their introduction.

Reference has been made to direct and reversed return piping systems which apply to water distribution and can be simply illustrated. Assume a central plant and pumps in the lowest floor of a building (the effect is exactly the same wherever the location and this assumption merely ties down the example). Warm or chilled water is distributed to this multiple-story building by a number of two-pipe risers. Consider one of these pairs of pipes—supply and return. The simplest way to run the piping would be floor by floor through a branch supply pipe at each level, diminishing the supply riser as it goes up because it carries less water floor by floor. The return would be the same, starting at the top with a minimum size riser from the uppermost floor, increasing as it gets down back to its source. The problem here is that water takes the easiest flow pattern it can find. The heating-cooling unit on the lowest floor offers the shortest path for its supply and return water and will tend to grab an undue share. The same pattern will exist all the way up, and the unit at the top, where the exposure is probably the worst, will get only the leavings.

One way to even things out is to provide easily adjustable indexed valves called balancing fittings, through which artificial resistance can be added to the nearest units' branch piping so that each will get a fair share. In a riser that feeds a large number of units the adjustment of these balancing devices becomes an extremely sensitive and time-consuming procedure. They can be manufactured and factory preset to allow a theoretically calculated flow of water through each one, but they are more suitable to laboratory control than to the uncertainties and irregularities of a construction project. If the job is to be done the right way, it will require considerable field time, which may cancel out the first-cost advantage of this piping method, known as "direct-return."

Its counterpart is the "reversed-return" piping method (see preceding illustration). To use the same illustration, the supply risers are identical, but the return risers start at the lowest floor of the building and pick up water, floor-by-floor, going up, as its companion supply riser is dropping it off. When the now full-size return riser reaches the top of the building, it joins all the other returns and goes back down in one large return main. The theory here is that the heating-cooling unit whose water has the shortest supply path has the longest return path, and vice versa; pressure losses through all the units are almost identical, and the system is substantially self-balancing. Balancing cocks are usually provided at each unit as a safety precaution, but the reversed-return system often requires no balancing whatever.

The additional cost in the reversed-return system is the cost of the one big vertical main, the height of the building, which is at least partly offset by the cost of sophisticated balancing devices and balancing time required in the direct-return arrangement. There is a warning here, however. If, for some architectural, structural, or aesthetic reason, the building design does not permit gathering the return risers at the top, then each pair of supply and return risers will have to have its own associated reversed-return riser running all the way down, to be gathered at the bottom in the space also used for the distribution of the supply risers. This means multiple reversed-return risers and more space at the riser locations. It may also be a serious cost impediment to the use of this relatively foolproof reversed-return system.

Engineers differ on the hazards of the direct-return arrangement. There is general agreement that for five story structures the simplest direct-return system is not too hard to balance. For 6 to perhaps 16 stories many engineers will consider preset balancing fittings without too many misgivings. For taller buildings engineers will generally insist on reversed-return piping.

In any long piping runs, whether risers in tall buildings or horizontal mains in large lowrise buildings, the effects of pipe-length expansion and contraction must be allowed for. Such allowances may be in the form of pipe configuration, often a large "U" in the run of the pipe, of fabricated expansion joints constituting bellows that squeeze or relax to accommodate movement, or, when the general arrangement permits, provision for movement in branches taken off the main to compensate for movement in the parent pipe by controlled movement in the subordinate.

The "U" bends are often feasible in horizontal mains. The bellows expansion joint is most useful for risers. A serious cautionary note here is that this kind of device must be accessible for maintenance and replacement and that the necessary access panels may be aesthetically undesirable.

The branch takeoff flexibility serves both horizontal and vertical mains and is generally a well advised piping design feature even if the other cited methods of expansion allowance are employed.

There is no sacred rule governing the length that the piping must be when special expansion provisions are necessary. It depends on the circumstances of each system. A fair estimate of a maximum length would be 75 ft.

When pipe risers are located close to columns, it is mandatory that mechanical and structural engineers coordinate their designs so that connections of horizontal structural members with the columns will not be endangered. In the following illustration arrangement (c) is usually preferable on that count.

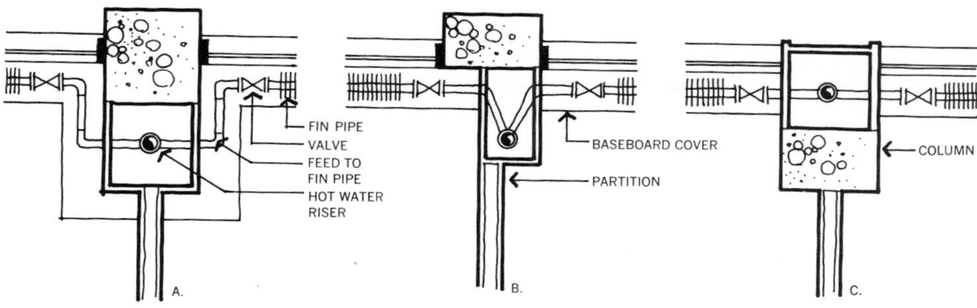

The heating and cooling devices used in conjunction with central systems are similar in type to those in independent systems. For heating only, there are radiators, convectors, and radiant panels. Radiators are usually cast iron and have comparatively large areas of exposed surface which approach the temperature of the water or steam contained within them. They emit heat by a combination of low-level radiation from these hot surfaces and convection, or continual rising of air warmed by direct contact with them, up through air spaces in the radiator. Old-fashioned cast-iron radiators put together in sections, with feet supporting the end sections, are still seen in many old buildings, but they are no longer made. Present-day radiators are still assembled in sections, but they offer a smooth front appearance with patterned designs for the convected air passages and are more pleasing aesthetically. They have much smaller dimensions than the old ones, particularly in depth, but correspondingly lack the enormous heating capacities boasted by the old monsters.

Convectors, both the baseboard and more concentrated types, are similar to those described under electrical heating for independent systems. Steam or water baseboard "wet heat" convectors are made in a larger range of sizes and output capacities. The smallest residential types are akin to the electrical baseboard described, but for severe load applications they may go to nearly 4 in. deep and 10 in. high. When baseboard convectors are used in conjunction with a one-pipe distribution system, as already described, their cabinet height can sometimes be increased to accommodate the one-pipe main concealed in the cabinet and feeding a series of baseboards. The designer must always remember that the last convector in line is getting the coolest water and its length must be increased to suit (see the illustration above).

When balconies are in the picture, baseboard convectors must be designed carefully to avoid an excessive step up at the balcony door.

Radiant panels, too, are similar to those described for electrical systems. Serpentine tubing, which carries warm water, can be laid directly in a concrete floor or ceiling slab or applied and covered with plaster after the slab or other flooring is completed. The tubing is usually copper, ⅜ in. in diameter, and will require cement plaster to a thickness of about 1 in. for adequate cover and distribution of heat. Plaster expands with heat at about the same rate as copper, and there is little cracking of plaster for this cause. It is essential that a new system be started with very slow increase of water temperature and with safeguards against drafts. Plaster which dries too quickly will crack.

Fan-coil units for central systems have in common the fact that they are fed with the project's warm and chilled water in season. For two-pipe distribution systems each unit will have one finned coil. For three- and four-pipe systems each unit may have one coil with appropriate valving in the pipe branches to select between warm and chilled water or two coils with separate supply (and return in four-pipe distribution) branches from the warm and chilled water risers. The fan-coil units differ primarily in shape, which depends on where and how they are to be mounted.

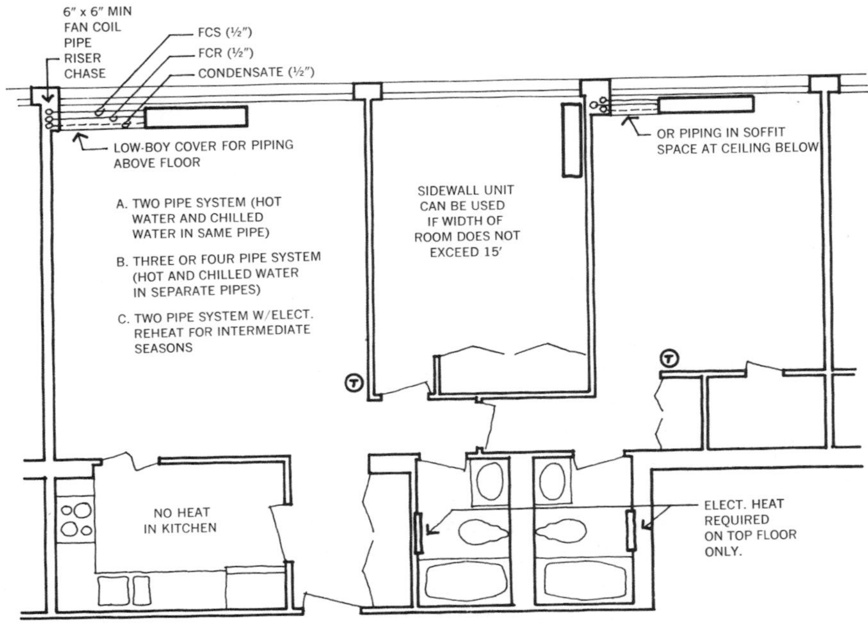

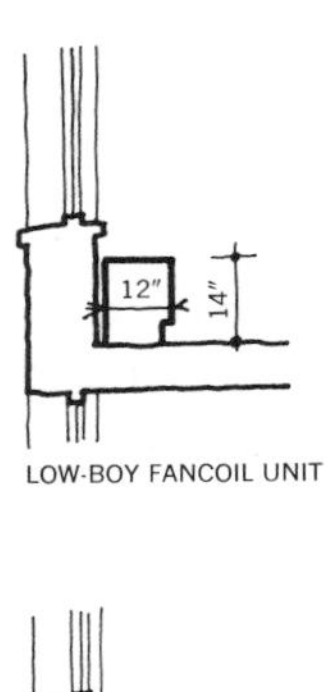

LOW-BOY FANCOIL UNIT

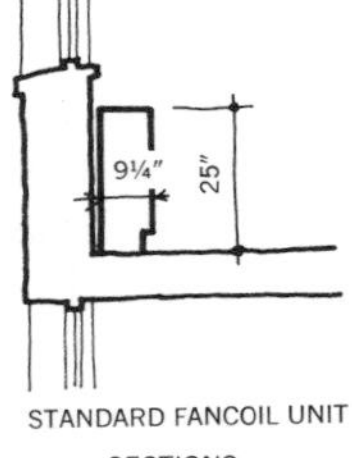

STANDARD FANCOIL UNIT

SECTIONS

The first fan-coils to be developed simply copied the concept and appearance of the long familiar convector. Housed in a rectangular casing about the size of a convector, although a little deeper because of the dimensions of the fans, these units were intended to be mounted under windows and to discharge their air upward to blanket the area of greatest heat exchange with the outdoors. In multistory buildings, the only kind in which fan-coil units make economic sense, space is generally found for risers in partitions or walls running perpendicular to the outside walls, and branches from risers to fan-coil units are concealed in the outside wall construction or in special horizontal chases which are part of the designed wall elevation. It is also possible to leave the pipe branches exposed, as was often done with runouts to the old fashioned radiators, but this alternative finds little favor. The pipes are unsightly and subject to damage. If they are to be concealed in the outside wall construction, care must be taken to insulate them and ensure flow through them at all times, if the locality is one in which subfreezing temperatures can occur.

The fan-coil system was found to be a quiet, readily controllable, and effective method of heating and cooling, and the under-the-window units were soon supplemented by larger, suspended units capable of supplying an entire apartment by ductwork or construction air passages, and by vertical, floor-to-ceiling units, which contain the entire riser systems by which they are fed. The latter found considerable favor soon after their introduction into the market because of the substantial labor savings that can be realized with them and their lower overall installation cost. The units themselves are comparatively expensive, but when wheeled into place, set up, and a few quick piping connections made at the top or bottom the entire job is done. Their housings enclose not only filters, fan, coil, discharge and intake outlets, insulation, controls, and two-, three-, or four-pipe risers but cooling condensate drain risers as well. Their height of a little less than 8 ft is selected to fit the standard residential ceiling height, with enough margin to get them into place. Their location is, of course, of paramount importance. For most applications they should be at the perimeter of the building to be effective where the heating or cooling load is greatest. If the planning is done properly and in advance, both the building elevation and room layout can be made to accommodate the necessary space. Frequently one vertical fan-coil unit can be made to serve two rooms if control is not needed in each. Conversely, if a room has a long perimeter with continuous glass, necessitating unit mounting at the outside corner, one fan-coil may not be able to distribute heat and cooling for the entire exposure length, and two units, one in each corner may be required. Of course, they may be designed to supply the adjoining rooms as well.

When fan-coil risers are placed at a building perimeter, a high degree of design coordination must be observed. The pipe openings through the floor slabs must not in any way weaken the structure by interfering with beams or reinforcing bars.

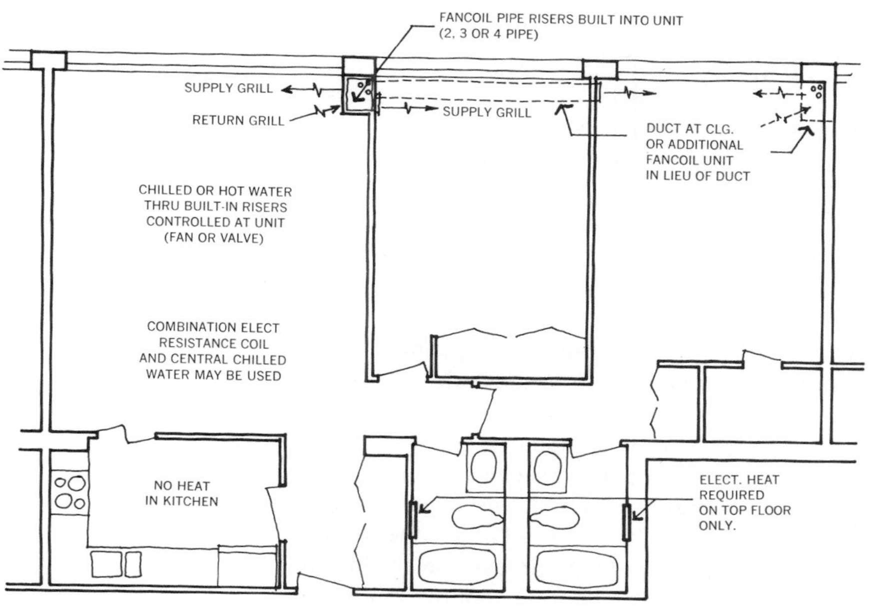

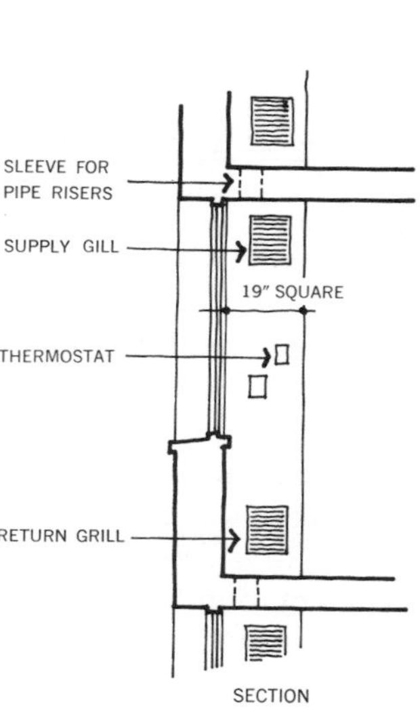

Suspended fan-coil units are usually concealed above a lowered ceiling, located in a part of the residence in which a clear ceiling height of 7 ft or a little less is not objectionable. This may be in a bathroom, utility space, hall, or closet, and convenient access for servicing filters, motor, blowers and coil must be provided. Suspended units in particular, but even floor-mounted fan-coils which serve an entire residence or section, usually discharge air through ducts or construction spaces at ceiling level. In multistory buildings it is often not feasible to provide duct space outside the bounds of the floor and the structure at or above the ceiling. In such cases it may not be possible to supply air or to pull recirculated air at the critical locations for heat loss and heat gain (i.e., under windows or continuous glass area). It is particularly important that these places of maximum exposure be protected by heat in cold climates. Without that design precaution, convection of air cooled by contact with the frigid glass surface will cause that air to fall along the outside wall and sweep across the floor as a chilly draft, a source of major discomfort to occupants. There are cases in which the perimeter configuration of the building will simply not allow for fan-coils at the perimeter, and suspended units in the interior are the only solution. In such circumstances a split system in which baseboard radiation along the perimeter handles enough of the heat load to obviate the cold draft curse may be necessary for comfort; the fan-coil will pick up the rest of the heating load and, of course, all the cooling requirements.

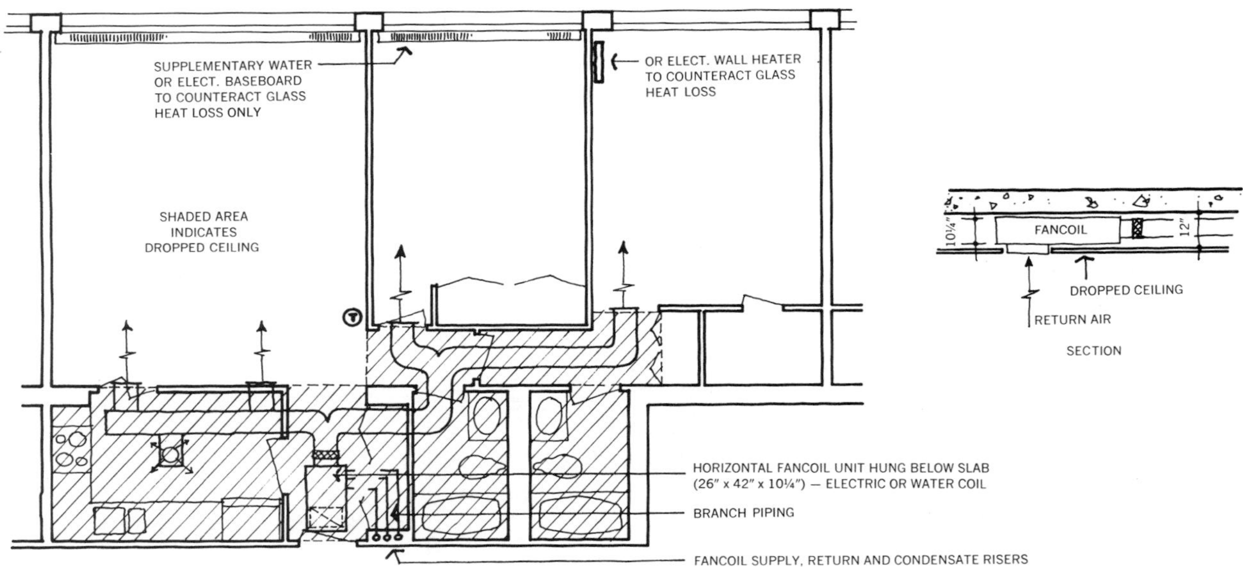

There are modifications of the fan-coil unit principle that find occasional use in residential buildings, particularly multistory structures of 6 to 20 stories. One is the induction unit which uses the aspirating power of comparatively high pressure air, instead of a motor driven fan, to move room air to be heated or cooled across a finned coil. The high pressure air is produced in a central air conditioning unit in which it is warmed or cooled as the season demands, filtered, and sent through a system of round ducts and risers to the induction units mounted under the window in each room. An aspirating effect permits a quantity of high pressure air to induce several times its own volume of room air through the heating-cooling coil in the unit. This induced air does a major part of the heating or cooling, which enables the designer to minimize the quantity of primary (high pressure) air and thus keep the duct riser sizes to a minimum as well. The induction unit system requires a primary air duct riser in addition to the pipe risers at every location. Condensate drain-riser pipes are sometimes omitted in this system because all the dehumidification is supposed to be accomplished in the primary air and there is no moisture left to be squeezed out in the occupied spaces. Accidents and malfunctions can occur, however; moist outdoor air can blow into a room through windows left open, and dehumidification can occur at induction units under particular circumstances. Some designers choose to avoid any possibility of grief by providing condensate piping against the remote danger. Others play the percentages and save the cost.

The primary air in induction systems is usually all taken from the outdoors, and no air is recirculated from dwelling to dwelling. This offers an advantage in the presence of constant fresh-air ventilation. An equal volume of air is removed from the premises by bathroom or kitchen exhaust ventilation. All in all, the system is an excellent one but expensive to install and consequently has found limited use in residential projects.

COMBINED HEATING AND COOLING SYSTEMS

A common combined system, embodying individual operation and central services, is usually the lowest first-cost installation of heating and cooling in a residential building. It is a central hot-water heating plant with baseboard convectors, and through-the-wall room coolers operated by the residents (see the illustration on p. 126). The project pays for the heat, occupants pay only for the cooling in their apartments, and complications are at a minimum. The same division can be made by using standard convectors or radiant panel heating combined with through-the-wall coolers.

Particular circumstances can reverse this arrangement. If a highrise residential building is to be combined with commercial use, it may be advantageous to expand a central chilled-water plant to provide cooling for the residential section, perhaps through a fan-coil system, but then require each occupant to pay for electric heat in conjunction with each fan-coil unit.

An ingenious combined system has been developed which offers energy conservation and consequent low operating cost in multiple dwellings. The independent element is a self-contained unit for each residence, with blower, motor and drive, filters, coil, housing, and a heat pump refrigeration compressor. The central part of this system is a two-pipe water circulating system which can serve all self-contained units, and in whose supply main 85°F water circulates the year round. This water is used for condensing purposes in the cooling season and as the heat pump source in cold weather. In the intermediate seasons, houses requiring cooling at a given time will be putting heat into the circulating water, whereas houses whose exposure asks for heating would simultaneously be extracting heat from it. When everybody requires heat, a central boiler plant will replace the heat that has been extracted from the water by the heat pumps. When all residences are being cooled, a central cooling tower installation will remove all the heat from the water that has been added. Clearly, there can be times in spring and autumn when the demands for heat and cooling will balance one another. Refrigeration machinery in southern exposures puts as much heat into the water as northern exposures extract from it, and neither boilers nor cooling towers have to do any work at all.

CONTROLS

Heating systems are designed for the coldest expected day combined with an adverse wind. Cooling systems are sized for the hottest, most humid anticipated weather, with the sun shining brightly, at least normal occupancy, and some use of indoor heat-producing functions such as lights, television sets, and cooking. Because these "design" conditions are rarely encountered, it follows that heating and cooling systems have more capacity than they need most of the time and would thus make a house warmer or colder than comfortable, all of which is a roundabout way of stating a rather evident truth—that HVAC systems must be controlled in order to function satisfactorily most of the time.

Controls can vary to a great extent, depending on the construction budget, the importance of operating cost, the sophistication of the occupants, and their likelihood to be demanding. Consider the following list of controls in rising order of complexity and cost.

1. Manual valves, which reduce or shut off flow of steam for heating or flow of water for heating or cooling to each radiator, convector, or fan-coil unit. Because every unit should be provided with a shutoff to permit its being repaired in any event, this primitive method of control adds no cost to the installation. It is a poor control, however, because it requires frequent attention and considerable skill on the part of the occupant.
2. Water temperature control, for heating systems only. Water temperature is adjusted automatically according to outside temperatures and wind conditions; the warmest water is supplied when it is coldest outside and vice versa. This system can be further refined if the water piping is arranged in zones so that different exposures will receive different water temperatures at any time, based on wind direction and solar exposure. The counterpart of this control in steam systems is one by which steam is supplied to the heating elements for a greater or lesser proportion of the time, based on the need dictated by outside conditions. In either case, if the system is well designed and the control well calibrated, the occupants will find that little or no adjustment of manual valves is necessary.
3. Fan speed control for fan-coil units. Typically, each fan-coil is factory-provided with a motor that may operate at two or three speeds to produce commensurate volumes of air. High speed would answer the need for cooling and/or heating on the "design" day. The lower speeds might suffice for most of the rest of the time. The occupant learns what unit operation best fits the need and sets the switch accordingly. The switch should also have an OFF position, but the danger in this should be cited. If an occupant leaves for a summer vacation and turns the switch off, normal leakage of outside air into the house may permit humidity to build up to outdoor levels. The fan-coil unit has the fan turned off, but chilled water is circulating steadily through the coil. Soon the steel housing around the coil will become quite cold because there is no air passing through the unit to prevent it. The moist room air strikes the cold metal surface and moisture condensed from the air runs down the housing onto the floor. The returning vacationer is greeted with a wet, stained, and moldy carpet. This is by no means a theoretical story. Enough water can be generated this way over a period of time to run along the floor until it finds a way to leak into the apartment below. To avoid this peril prudence dictates that in addition to the fan speed switch there should be an electric valve on the chilled water supply line; when the fan is off, water flow will stop or very nearly stop because there can be another kind of danger (in horizontal fan-coil units). If the resident leaves for a long winter vacation and turns the fan off, thus closing the valve, a severe cold snap could conceivably cause the trapped water to freeze in the fan-coil unit. To circumvent it a tiny hole can be drilled in the electric valve to permit a slight flow of water, enough to prevent freezing but not enough to chill the housing and cause condensation in summer. These little horror stories illus-

trate the importance of considering all the implications of whatever controls system is chosen.

4. Factory built-in thermostatic control for through-wall room coolers. This is the first mention of thermostatic controls, which sense the temperature in the room and operate the cooling system automatically to suit. If electric heat is built into the fan-coil unit, a room-heating thermostat should likewise be provided in the factory. In addition to room coolers cited in the preceding paragraph, simple fan-coil units can also be factory-supplied with thermostats that sense room-air temperature and thereby actuate an electric valve that governs the water supply to the coil. This valve may be the ON-OFF type, two-position, either-or, or gradual acting, which regulates water flow in close accordance with the actual requirement at any time. The thermostat obviously must have characteristics suitable to operate the kind of valve selected.

5. Self-actuating valves for heating or cooling devices. Usually these valves are not factory-installed but rather are separately purchased and mounted in the field. They require no electric operation, sense room temperature at the heating or cooling unit itself, and take a position that permits a flow of water commensurate with the load.

6. Remote room thermostats. A thermostat that is separated from the heating or cooling device can be mounted in any location in the room. Often careful consideration in the design stage will produce a location best suited to provide optimum comfort in the room, a location better than adjacent to the heating or cooling device, as described in (4) and (5) above. This remote thermostat can operate a fan-coil unit blower or a valve for a heating convector, fan-coil unit, or induction unit. It requires an electric box, wiring and, perhaps a conduit and is thus a more expensive installation than those cited. It almost always does a better job of temperature controlling to justify the cost.

7. Zone controls. Residences heated and cooled by ductwork in single HVAC units can enjoy separate zone control in at least two arrangements. One may be an independent coil in the duct to each room or group of rooms; the water flow to the coil is regulated by a room thermostat mounted in the area served. In this context one group constitutes the bedrooms and the other contains the living, dining areas. In a second and more common zoning method motor driven air volume dampers, one in each zone duct, are operated by room thermostats. If an air unit provides both heating and cooling, there must be an automatic or manual method of reversal according to season. In summer high room temperatures call for more air, in winter, less, and the automatic volume dampers must operate with seasonal instructions.

A third zone-control method is by multizone systems, much more common in office and commercial air conditioning than in the residential. In this system the volume of air circulated to each zone remains constant but its temperature is varied according to need. In summer this is done by mixing cooled and uncooled air for each zone; in winter, by mixing heated and unheated air.

VENTILATION

If the word "ventilation" conjures up visions of fans and intricate duct systems, that really is taking the long way around, at least for residential conceptual thinking. What should come to mind first is simply "windows."

Windowless buildings, and that term includes those with perimeter glass that cannot be opened, have become a twentieth-century phenomenon which followed the development of air conditioning, but their use has not spread to residential projects, where codes require window areas that open in living spaces. With rare exceptions, even the most sophisticated heating and air conditioning systems anticipate some contribution by window ventilation.

One dictionary definition of the word "ventilate" is "to admit fresh air into." Under atmospheric conditions in some of the world's industrial societies, that adjective "fresh" is more than a little suspect. Nevertheless, the need for changes in air content in an enclosed space requires little explanation. Occupants reduce oxygen quantity by their physiological processes. Likewise, equipment that burns fuel extracts oxygen from the building's air to do it and in the process removes a quantity of air from the building. Odors are created by food preparation and bodily functions. Humidity is increased by cooking and cleaning processes that release moisture. Without changes and replenishment of the air content an enclosed space would very quickly become uninhabitable.

1. Infiltration

The simplest residence is one in which kitchen and bathrooms have windows to the outdoors. Thus exhaust fans to remove air from those spaces are not needed. Assume that a house is heated by electricity or by steam or water from a remote plant. In neither case does air needed for combustion purposes have to come from the residence. Finally, say that the day is cold and that the occupants do not choose to open the windows, even a crack. How then is any kind of ventilation to be achieved? The embarrassingly unscientific answer is that outdoor air must leak in—an effect called infiltration.

The mere fact that windows and doors must be movable in order to perform their functions creates junctions in the construction of a building. Construction processes and materials are not so perfect that these junctions are absolutely tight; for example, like two machine-polished surfaces in an engine. Their imperfections take the form of cracks through which outdoor air is forced. Moreover, every time an outer door opens outside air mixes with room air right at the entrance by the very motion of the door. In these crude ways basic ventilation is achieved.

Complete reliance on leakage must, however, be accompanied by some warning. By the installation of storm windows and supercaulking infiltration can be reduced to a dangerously low level. An invalid or recluse may use the door infrequently. Finally, windows and doors must face more than one exposure. If the wind blows from the north for a week and the only openings are on the south, what can leak in? This question brings to mind a typical apartment building in which there is a central corridor with apartments on both sides whose windows have only one exposure. In such a building the apartment doors to the corridor must not be tight fitting. In the example cited above air will leak into the north facing apartments. The pressure of this air will be exerted through the building via the doors so that an equal volume will exit through the south windows. It may be contended that the south apartment is really not being ventilated; it is only getting used air from the north apartment through the corridor. The fact is that the life-and-death need for oxygen replacement calls for a really surprisingly small quantity of air, and leakage through the north apartment windows is far more than the vital needs of residents on both sides of the corridor. The explanation is that when we breathe we do not by any means use up all the oxygen in the air we have taken into our lungs. Actually, we reduce oxygen content by only about 4% in every breath. So it is only when people are literally packed together without significant ventilation, as in the infamous Black Hole of Calcutta, that oxygen deficiency can quickly become dangerous.

As well as being a positive good for ventilation, infiltration must be considered for all its effects. One is that it obviously imposes a load on the heating system of a building in winter and on the cooling system in summer. These loads are much harder to predict than the easily measurable loads of heat loss or gain through walls, windows, and roofs. The type of window (or door) and frame to be selected and the quality of workmanship in the construction are imponderables that the designer must estimate in planning a heating or cooling system. Prudence dictates that a dim view be taken, and that the design be based on a higher rate of leakage than the designer hopes can be obtained. The odds here are all in favor of reasonable conservatism. The factor is almost never a large proportion of the heating or cooling load and somewhat overestimating it adds comparatively little to the size of heating or cooling equipment. Underestimating it, on the other hand, can lead to extremely unhappy occupants and perhaps disastrously expensive corrective measures.

An aspect of infiltration not touched upon when considering it as ventilation is that it brings in outdoor air as is. If the atmosphere is dusty, dirty, or filled with industrial odors, that is the way the interior will be. Mechanical ventilation, it will be seen, can help correct some of those problems.

Finally, infiltration causes a phenomenon known as ''stack effect'' in tall buildings and can be an unpleasant feature. In planning a highrise building, the designer should be aware of the danger of stack effect and take precautions to minimize its nuisance value. There is no way to eliminate it entirely. Consider what makes it happen.

Think of a tall building on a cold day. Inside the air is warmed to comfort temperature. Outside is cold air which is heavier, volume for equal volume. The temperature variation is enough to create a noticeable difference in weights of the air, and the taller the building, the greater the total amount of that difference, called the stack effect.

This effect causes the outside air to try to enter the building at or near its bottom and escape at or near its top. Designers should discourage the process emphatically. Why? Because unless the stack effect is controlled the unbridled leakage of outside air in the lower part of the tall building will cause the first floor lobby and perhaps the lower floor apartments to be cold; it will produce a most unpleasant and unmelodious whistle caused by incoming air rushing through the entrance and elevator door cracks and may even be so strong that many people will be physically unable to open out-swinging doors at the lobby level. The problem occurs as long as it is colder outside than in, and the colder the weather, the worse the nuisance. Practically speaking, it is usually of little concern when the temperature is above freezing outside.

What can be done about it? Simply to impede vertical motion of free air up through the building in every way possible. It is not possible to close off the vertical passages in a building completely. There are elevator shafts, pipe and duct shafts, stairways, and, in some buildings, smoke towers, but attention to detail can minimize the chimney effect of these necessary vertical risers. Elevator doors can be of better than the cheapest construction, well-fitted and permanently well operating. Pipe and duct entrances into mechanical shafts must be thoroughly and permanently sealed, and to secure them further the shafts themselves must be sealed securely at periodic intervals in the building's height. Doors on the various floors leading into the exit stairways must be kept closed and should be tight fitting, weatherstripped, and with solid thresholds. These measures should not be considered an unnecessary or burdensome expense. They can reduce stack effect materially. Dampers that permit smoke towers to discharge their intended function of smoke removal must be well made, and close fitting, tightly sealed when closed. If permitted by code, the main entrance doors should be revolving, which work better against leakage and are easier to operate against whatever stack effect remains after all the precautions have been taken. Front entrance and rear service doors should open into vestibules whose depth is great enough that the likelihood of inner and outer doors being open at the same time is reduced, although this possibility, of course, can never be eliminated entirely.

If the designer has successfully completed these steps, stack effect will be at a minimum, and whatever remains will have to be accepted on the premise that the planner has done all that is reasonably possible.

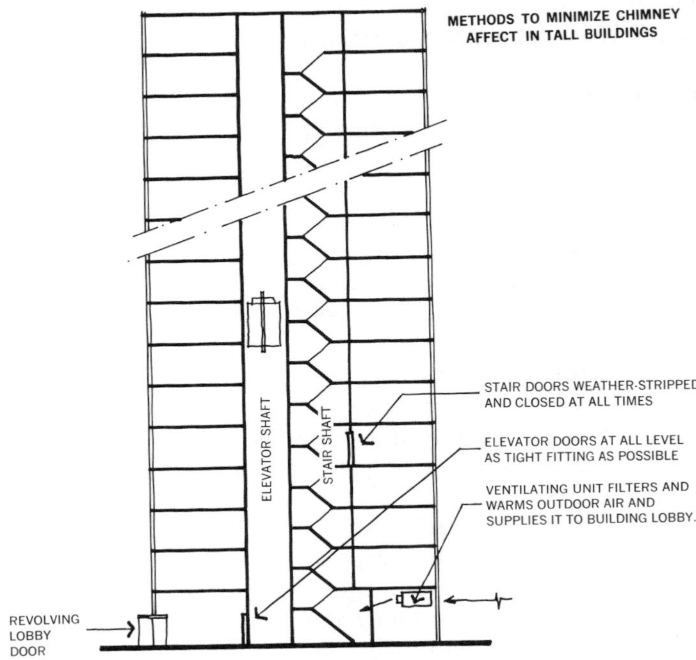
METHODS TO MINIMIZE CHIMNEY AFFECT IN TALL BUILDINGS
STAIR DOORS WEATHER-STRIPPED AND CLOSED AT ALL TIMES
ELEVATOR DOORS AT ALL LEVEL AS TIGHT FITTING AS POSSIBLE
VENTILATING UNIT FILTERS AND WARMS OUTDOOR AIR AND SUPPLIES IT TO BUILDING LOBBY.
ELEVATOR SHAFT
STAIR SHAFT
REVOLVING LOBBY DOOR

EXHAUST VENTILATION

Odors and excessive moisture generated in kitchens and bathrooms are best positively removed. In the preceding examination of infiltration the assumption was made that kitchens and baths had outside walls and windows and thus required no positive ventilation. The conclusion is valid according to most building codes but does not necessarily represent good practice. Even when there are bathroom windows, they will seldom be opened in cold weather, and if the wind is wrong kitchen odors may be spread all over the house rather than evacuated through an open window.

If either of these rooms is interior, as they so often are, there is no question. Whatever the code, it will require positive exhaust ventilation.

Exhaust systems may be individual, central, or a combination of the two, a situation similar to that discussed for heating and cooling systems. First, individual systems call for an exhaust fan or blower for each kitchen and usually for each bathroom as well, although it is possible to combine exhausts from two or more bathrooms through ductwork to a single exhaust fan serving one dwelling unit. Kitchen and bathroom exhausts should never be combined. The kitchen exhaust fan is controlled by a switch of its own and is used as the occupant wishes. If each bathroom is served by its own fan, it may be controlled by a switch or wired to operate when the light is turned on. In interior bathrooms it is particularly important that the fan be built with motor overload protection, so that failure in the motor will be safeguarded electrically and will not cause coincident failure of the bathroom light. Bathroom exhaust fans discharge outdoors, probably through small ducts in the ceiling construction or directly through an outside wall. Each has a self-closing damper to permit air to flow out when the fan is running but to prevent outside air from blowing back in when it is not. Another desirable feature is a time delay relay that lets the fan run for a short time after the light is turned off. Kitchen exhausts usually discharge in the same way, with one exception. A kitchen exhaust system has been developed in which a hood, usually of finished and pleasing design, is mounted over the cooking range to entrap most of the fumes. The hood is an assembly that includes a blower and a combined filter and odor remover. The filter removes grease and dirt. The other component is activated charcoal or a similar substance which has the property of adsorbing minute particles that cause odors. The air thus treated is relatively clean and odor free and is discharged right back into the kitchen rather than outdoors. This process, of course, does nothing to remove kitchen heat, but it very materially reduces the need for makeup air in a multidwelling building. The saving in heating and cooling costs corresponds. The odor-removing substance will finally adsorb to its saturation and must be replaced or regenerated, an operation that is necessary, depending on the characteristics of the material used, once to four times a year.

Central systems are for multidwelling buildings and are particularly applicable to highrise concrete construction in which individual systems offer structural problems. Tiers of bathrooms or kitchens are served by duct risers, built with inlets from each bath or kitchen. Space must be found in the apartment plans for these duct risers, which usually increase in size as they near the central blower. Often these ducts can be located within the space that contains the plumbing riser pipes, especially since that space is always contiguous to the kitchen or bathroom. If the building is more than a few stories high, inclusion of duct risers will necessitate an increase in the size of the pipe shaft, which means loss of usable space in the dwellings, but the total shaft increase in actual area lost to the apartments is often more than justified by convenience, appearance, and construction cost.

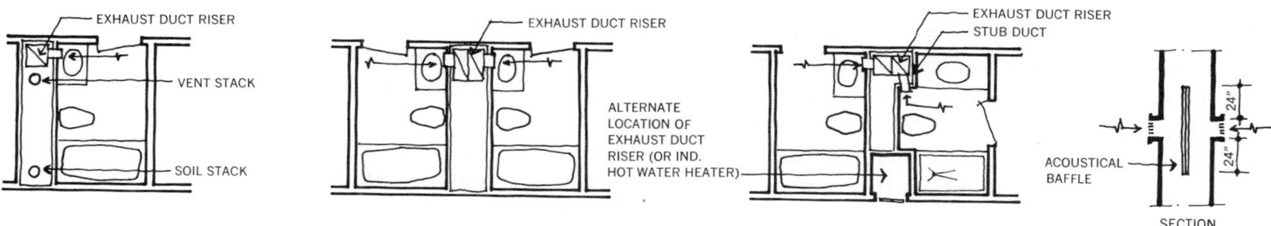

The central system duct risers may feed individual exhaust fans, usually roof-mounted directly above the riser. A number of risers may be grouped above the topmost ceiling to be served by one exhauster on the roof. If there is adequate space between the roof and the top-floor ceiling for plumbing, heating, and cooling pipes as well as exhaust ducts (usually 3 ft will do), all the risers may be picked up by ductwork mains running in that space and feeding central blowers, separate for kitchen and bathroom exhaust, mounted in the elevator machine penthouse. The decision will usually be based on cost preference, although other factors may enter. If a large part of a roof is used for recreational purposes, the individual exhausters cannot be used, and a single large blower hidden in the penthouse is preferred. One point should be clarified at this time. The exhaust risers do not have to move air to the top of the building. It is usually most practical to discharge it there, away from the likelihood of causing a nuisance, but sometimes it may be more convenient to move air downward to a point of discharge not far above the ground. This might apply in particular to a very tall building, more than 30 stories high. The size of riser ducts, and thus the shafts in which they are concealed, can be kept from growing out of hand by splitting them, taking the upper half of the building to the roof and the lower half down to an above-grade discharging blower.

An important caution in central systems is that noise from one dwelling must not be transmitted through the ducts to another. Carefully designed acoustical baffles at the register inlets in each apartment, and also in the riser itself, will obviate this hazard. In fact, with proper precautions it is quite practical to serve back-to-back kitchens or bathrooms in separate residences with a single riser, thus saving space and cost. A last practical precaution is especially important in systems with individual roof fans for the risers. Here the fan is close above the exhaust register in the top-floor dwelling and must be selected carefully. The acoustical lining of the riser and the fan mounting curb provided, will prevent the fan noise from being heard through the nearby register.

Central systems operate continuously or blowers are controlled by timers on a fixed schedule to operate certain hours of the day and night. If operation is continuous, heat and cooling are pulled out of the building, whether or not ventilation is needed in a particular room, an expensive waste of fuel and energy. If operation is timed, the waste is reduced, but will still exist, besides which exhaust may not be available when occupants with unusual hours need it most.

The combined exhaust system attempts to use the strength and discard the disadvantages of the individual and central systems. There are two principal types, both of which feature the common risers of the central system. In the first, each kitchen or bath is equipped with its small fan or blower, as in the individual system, but they discharge into the common riser, each through a self-closing damper that permits air to enter the riser but not to back up out of it when the fan is not running. The system has the advantage of controlling use when needed, with consequent energy savings and some saving in the size of the riser itself. In this system the direction of air in the common riser should always be upward.

In the second combined system each exhaust outlet is equipped with a motor-driven damper instead of a fan of its own. The light switch or ventilating switch in the bathroom or kitchen opens this damper and exhausts the room when needed. Otherwise the damper is tightly closed. This system requires an added area of sensitivity, which militates for the use of one large exhaust blower for the bathroom and one for the kitchen. If 19 out of 20 dampers are closed, the central blower must not be engaged in trying to pull the capacity for all 20 out of that one open damper. It must respond to the load. This response can be accomplished by pressure-sensing devices in the main air stream, which will close specially designed dampers at the blower itself or open them as necessary to maintain nearly constant pull throughout the system.

Either of the combined systems, but especially the second, will usually call for higher construction cost than the individual or central systems. When operating costs are considered, as they should be especially in these days of dizzying increases in energy fees, the payback will be rapid and the first investment more than justified. There is one advantage to be cited for the energy-wasteful central exhaust system, however. It has the minimum of moving equipment and will thus engender the lowest maintenance time and costs. By the same token, of course, if there is a breakdown in the central system or in the damper-type of combined system, all or a substantial number of dwellings will be without exhaust.

SUPPLY (MAKEUP AIR) VENTILATION

For every cubic foot, cubic inch, centimeter, or molecule of air exhausted from a building, an equal volume will enter. This can happen by leakage through cracks around windows and doors, one of the less desirable effects of which is the simultaneous entrance of dirt. Even beyond that, a high rate of suction through window cracks during a heavy rain can actually pull water into the rooms in sufficient volume to drench carpeting and damage furniture.

As long as windows and doors have to be opened and as long as winds blow, there will be air leakage, but it can be held under some control by the deliberate introduction of outside air into the building by some method of supply ventilation. Here are some of the options. In every case it is to be understood that the air introduced must be filtered and warmed or cooled to conform with building requirements.

1. Individual room coolers are equipped with small openings to permit them to take in from the outdoors a portion of the total air circulated. They are usually fitted with manually controlled dampers, and the occupant can decide whether makeup air will be introduced—a rather haphazard method.
2. The same kind of manually controllable outdoor air intake can be furnished with fan-coil units, either individual room or full residence type. In regions in which freezing temperatures are encountered it is unusual and dangerous to open to the outdoors fan-coil units that are centrally fed with warm and/or chilled water. No matter how carefully the controls are designed and installed, the dangers of freezing and bursting a pipe in any one of a great many units is too great a risk in view of the amount of damage that can be caused. If, however, an apartment unit has direct expansion cooling and electric heat, in which there is nothing to freeze, it may be a good way of bringing makeup air into the building. This reasoning does not hold only for multidwelling buildings. A residential furnace system with or without direct expansion cooling can be equipped with an outdoor air connection. All too few are.
3. In multistory buildings an effective way to admit outdoor air is in a central supply system which draws it into all the public corridors of the structure. A way must then be found to direct the air from the corridors into the apartments, where it will make up their exhausted air. This can be done by deliberately creating gaps around the apartment doors and inserting rubber bumpers in the door frames to perform the dual function of permitting air to get in around them and at the same time decreasing the noise of closing doors. The bottom edges, however, should be sealed to prevent discoloration of carpets. Distribution of corridor supply air is not critical. Unless the corridor is unusually long, air supplied through a grille at one location will find its way to the points at which it is needed to make up exhaust. Besides apartment ventilation, an advantage of this system is that corridors are at a higher air pressure than the apartments, which helps to make corridors odor free and should eliminate the transmission of odors from one apartment to another. Even more important, smoke from a fire in one apartment will tend to be contained there if the public corridor is under pressure. If the building heating and cooling system features apartment fan-coil units in equipment rooms adjacent to the pub-

lic corridor, they can take in corridor air for makeup purposes. It is possible also to introduce central supply air directly into the apartments through supply risers of the same nature as the exhaust risers, but this method is quite expensive to construct and loses the advantage or pressurizing the corridor. If a central supply system has been installed in a building with variable exhaust, the supply blower(s) should be synchronized with the exhaust. If exhaust blowers operate on a timer, the supply blower should also be controlled in that way. If the system is the combined type with individual motorized kitchen and bathroom dampers and total volume control of the main exhaust blowers, the supply blower should be controlled in parallel. That parallel will usually be with the kitchen exhaust blower because it generally handles more air than the bathroom exhauster.

4. Another good way of bringing ventilation and makeup air into a building is by an induction system, which has already been described. The primary air is 100% outdoor air.

5. What quantity of makeup air should be introduced into a residential building by its supply ventilation system? There is a range of possibilities rather than firm rules.

   a. Supply a volume exactly equal to the air exhausted to put the building in balance.

   b. Supply 10 to 25% more than the exhaust quantity to pressurize the building and reduce (or eliminate) infiltration and stack effect.

   c. Accept the fact that there will be some infiltration leakage due to wind, regardless of building pressure, and design the supply system to provide the difference between the total air exhausted and calculated normal leakage.

   d. Arbitrarily select a proportion of the total air exhausted, between 40 and 75%, and let that be the capacity of the supply system(s).

Options (a) and (b) appear to be most logical, but experience tends to show otherwise. Winds are variable. On still, cold days (b) may pump in and heat far more air than is needed. On windy days there will probably be substantial leakage on the windward side in either case. Option (c) provides the designer with the comforting knowledge that the design is defensible, but (d) works just as well, especially when used by engineers experienced in multidwelling planning.

In a discussion of air supply systems a word should be said about air filtering. On a rising scale of excellence we discuss first the filters provided by manufacturers in induction system units. They are thin fibrous screens, which can keep only the coarsest lint from getting to the induction unit's water coil. The primary air, however, has been thoroughly and effectively filtered in its central unit, where it was also warmed or heated and put under pressure.

Filters for apartment fan-coil units and for individual room coolers are also furnished by the manufacturer and are a small step above the quality of induction unit filters. Because a blower does move the air through them, they can offer a bit more resistance and do a little better filtering job.

Filters for entire residential units, such as apartment fan-coils or residential furnaces, are usually better quality and more effective in air cleaning. They may be the disposable type that uses fiberglass or a similar filtering medium, for single use only, or the cleanable type of steel fiber or like construction which can be washed clean and reused. At the highest level of filtering efficiency now available are the extremely effective units that attract dirt particles by electrostatic charging. They are particularly favored by sufferers from hay fever and other allergies because they free the air of tiny pollen particles that the ordinary filters cannot trap.

For large central air units, such as corridor supply or induction primary air supply, the disposable, permanent, washable or electrostatic filters described above are applicable. The favorite, probably, is still another type. This is a roll of fiberglass or similar filtering material that is motor driven to move slowly through the air stream. When the entire roll has unwound itself, it is discarded and a new one installed. The maintenance is much easier than is required to change a large number of filter cells.

VENTILATION SPACE REQUIREMENTS

Crucial in the planning of multistory residential buildings is the space that must be allocated to duct and pipe risers, lost space in the architect's view, but nonetheless necessary. Varying code and load requirements in different localities make it impossible to set hard and fast rules, but a few principles can be supplied, and an example or two may help to show how to apply them.

1. For each apartment bathroom air should be exhausted at a rate of 10 to 15 air changes per hour; that is, the volume of air exhausted in an hour should be 10 to 15 times the room volume. Assuming that the room height of 8 ft, this translates to an exhaust rate of 1.33 to 2.0 cubic feet of air per minute (cfm) for each square foot of floor area.
2. For each kitchen allow 12 to 18 changes per hour. On the 8-ft ceiling height basis, this equals 1.6 to 2.4 cfm per square foot of floor area.
3. For *individual* exhaust systems these quantities set the sizes of the small exhaust fans. For *central* systems the total of all bathroom quantities defines the required capacity of the bathroom exhaust fan (and the same for the kitchen), whereas the subtotals of the various tiers and collections of tiers determine the duct sizes to serve those subdivisions. The main ducts of the *combined* systems are sized like the central system ducts, except that use factors may be assumed because all apartments will certainly not be exhausted at any one time.
4. Duct sizes are determined by a simple formula:

Area (in square feet) is the air volume (cfm) divided by air velocity in feet per minute (fpm).

The smaller the air quantity, the lower the permissible velocity. This is a physical truth based on friction and noise levels, and, to avoid a lengthy excursion into physics, should be accepted on faith in this treatise. To be specific, for basic central systems the following rules can be used to give first approximations of duct sizes for a designer's layout assistance.

Air quantities up to 1500 cfm, velocity up to 1000 fpm.
Air quantity from 1500 to 2800 cfm, velocity up to 1100 fpm;
from 2800 to 4000 cfm, velocity to 1200 fpm;
from 4000 to 7000 cfm, velocity to 1350 fpm.
above 7000 cfm, velocity to 1500 fpm.

Having proposed some guiding rules, let us immediately list the exceptions. First, exhaust outlets whose design incorporates built in acoustical treatment which effectively dampens air flow noise in ductwork have been developed. The outlets themselves are comparatively expensive but they save at least part of their cost by permitting higher riser air velocities and thus smaller duct sizes. They also save space. If these outlets are used, the recommended riser velocities may be increased 50%. Second, if the combined exhaust system is used, risers and collector mains should be sized to take advantage of their diversity at any given time.

The first half of each riser, considered in the direction of air flow, should be sized for 100% use; the next quarter at 80%; the final quarter plus collector mains and the blower itself at 70% of the total capacity of all the inlets. Finally, corridor supply risers can be greatly reduced by going to high velocity with acoustical air valves to control noise.

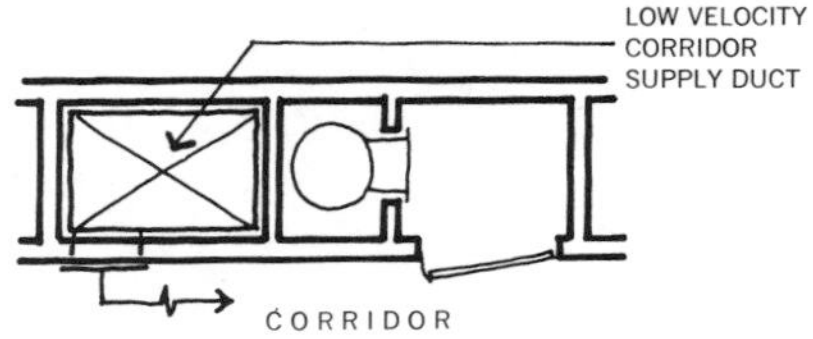

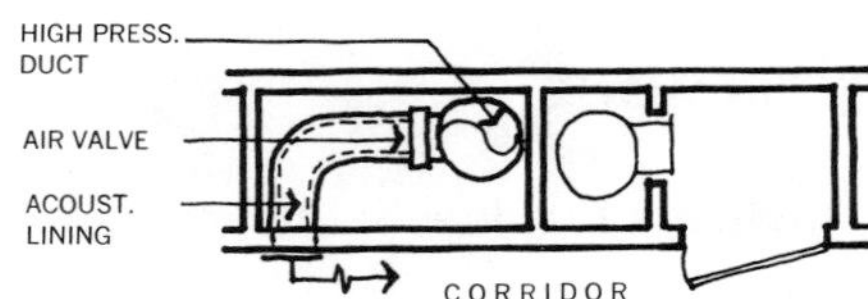

MISCELLANEOUS VENTILATION

The discussion on ventilation has centered around the residential units themselves, as the most important. Only mention need be given to miscellaneous requirements, some or all of which may be found in any project.

1. Indoor automobile parking facilities. Removal of engine exhaust fumes, with provision for makeup air, warmed or unwarmed, depending on whether the garage is heated.
2. Commercial areas, such as shops, restaurants, and grocery stores require their own complete HVAC systems, which may or may not be served, fully or in part, by the apartment building system. See the following section for further discussion of these options.
3. Building service areas. Typical are the rubbish room, where garbage and trash are accumulated before being burned or baled, the elevator machine penthouse and electrical transformer rooms, where excess heat must be removed, repair shops, service shops (such as valet services), and the manager's office, all needing some combination of cooling, heating, air supply, and air exhaust.

MAINTENANCE AND OPERATION OF HVAC EQUIPMENT

In concluding this section on heating, ventilating, and air conditioning, let us give consideration to important factors in design and planning that concern the ultimate success and economical use of whatever systems have been chosen. The purpose here is not to remind the user that motors must be lubricated and filters cleaned or changed. Nor is it to estimate actual operating costs of a project. There are too many variable factors to make a general estimate practical. What is intended is to bring out factors that an owner or developer forgets only at great peril to the project.

First it is vital that all equipment be placed in such a way that every part of it can be reached and serviced. This may be self-evident, but in their zeal to make maximum living use of space all too many planners crowd equipment so unmercifully that it is dangerous or even impossible to maintain and operate properly.

Next are general considerations of operating costs. Who pays for what? Fan-coil systems have proved their worth, yet there is a small motor in every fan-coil unit which may run all or nearly all of the time. It is a small cost per hour, but over thousands of hours each year that cost is significant. Does the occupant pay this cost on the comparatively high individual electric rate or does the project pay on its much lower bulk rate? If the occupant pays, has that fact been made clear? Has the kind of small motor in these units been carefully considered in the light of its electrical efficiency? Specifically, one type of motor may cost 10 dollars more than another. In a building with a thousand fan-coil units that means an initial expenditure 10,000 dollars greater, a sum of money nobody gives away. The efficiency of the more expensive motor, however, may be such that the initial cost will be paid back in a year or less in lower bills for electricity.

Another electrical bill item that may weigh in the planning process is the "demand charge." Prudent equipment planning may provide a small refrigeration unit, for example, for mild weather use, saving hundreds of dollars in electrical bills for such months as April, May, and October. Higher installation cost may thus be returned in a few years. Such a unit might serve commercial areas only.

The use of various fuels for heating and different motive powers for cooling have been discussed as alternatives. Each project deserves a careful analysis of initial installation and long range operating costs attributable to each fuel and each method of powering refrigeration. There is no set answer that suits all cases. This year's project may show results quite different from last year's. Only after such an analysis can a fair opinion be reached and implemented.

COMPONENTS OF DESIGN—PLUMBING 5

Harry S. Nachman

Water is a necessity of life. In the design of buildings, particularly of residential buildings, we expect without possibility of exception that all residents will have free access to a water supply adequate to their basic needs. In fact, our laws make this mandatory.

"Basic needs" have expanded beyond the use of water to sustain life, to encompass sanitation and frequently fire control. That sentence just about provides a definition of plumbing as applied to buildings. Somewhat incidentally the distribution of fuel gas is often included in the plumbing trade but has come to pass merely by custom and some resemblance in appearance rather than because of any relationship.

So the quest for water has determined the location of camps, settlements, and cities throughout human history and is the first problem to be disposed of in the planning of a housing project, whether a single residence or a tract of thousands. There are two categories of water source, individual and communal, and at least one must be available before any further planning can take place.

Individual sources of water may be subterranean streams or strata tapped by wells, a nearby river or lake, or rainfall which is collected and saved. Surface water is becoming more generally polluted and rainfall is usually not reliable.

For the most part, therefore, individual sources of water are sought in wells. There is no known rule or principle for predicting the depth or potential yield of an underground stratum of water to be tapped, but the best guide is experience in the area. The more wells drilled, the better the chance of locating an additional adequate source. By the same token, the more wells drilled, the more water extracted from the stratum, and the greater the danger of exhaustion or serious depletion. Occasionally a stratum is under sufficient pressure in the earth to force its water to the surface with enough pressure left to allow it to flow in volume. The well that taps this kind of source is called artesian, but most wells require pumps to lift the water to the surface and to add enough pressure to make it flow.

A well is dug by drilling a circular hole in the earth to whatever depth is required to find an adequate supply. A pipe of material impervious to corrosion is forced into the hole to provide a permanent channel for the upflow. The bottom sections of this pipe constitute a perforated circular screen, usually of brass, which is imbedded in the water-bearing stratum. Its perforations permit water to flow into the pipe and are designed to exclude as much clay, sand, and gravel as possible. For most residential projects the well pipe will range between 4 and 8 in., although larger developments may require larger pipe sizes. The well pump is built to fit into the well pipe. The pump shaft is driven by an electric motor or gas engine at the top of the well and must be protected from the weather or other harm by an adequate enclosure. Depending on the location of the pump house, heat may be required in a climate in which subfreezing temperatures occur. The water will not freeze when it is flowing from underground, but overnight or at any time when there is no flow the danger exists.

The second water-source category is municipal. One of the first services that identifies a hamlet, village, town or city as a viable community is a water distribution system consisting of a network of corrosion-resistant pipes called water mains. The network is generally located under or adjacent to streets and public alleys; it is well-mapped and can be tapped by users under conditions controlled by the municipality. "Municipality" in this sense may be misleading. The control of a water system is often vested in a private, profit-making water company operating under a municipal franchise. In any case, the user expects a reliable flow of pure water whenever it is needed. This is one of the fundamental reasons why people band together into communities.

WATER QUALITY

Purity with respect to organisms dangerous or deleterious to human and animal life is the first criterion of water quality. In municipal systems this purity is part of the agreement, expressed or implied, between the supplier and the user. In private systems safety is the responsibility of the user, whose purification treatment is administered according to official regulations and regularly and frequently monitored by the supervising authority. The basic treatment generally consists of adding small quantities of chlorine sufficient to kill harmful organisms, but limited to minimize the unpleasant taste associated with this gas.

Another chemical additive is fluorine. Discovery of a phenomenally low incidence of tooth decay in a particular area of the Southwest led to an analysis of the local water supply and the discovery of an unusually high (although still miniscule) concentration of fluorides. Further testing convinced many dental authorities that a definite relationship existed, and many communities have begun to introduce this compound into their water supplies. There has been some objection to this practice on socioreligious grounds and some questioning of the long range side effects that still remain uncharted.

Certain chemicals and compounds found naturally in water contribute to a quality called "hardness." The property of hardness is not a threat to life or health, but "hard" water becomes undesirable on two counts. First, it is difficult to use soap effectively, for hardness inhibits the formation of lather. Second, when water is heated, the compounds it contains are rapidly driven out and deposited on the heating surfaces. This deposit builds up until it forms a highly effective insulating layer, which at best will impair the effectiveness of the heater and at worst destroy it. Not all of this deposit remains in the heater. Some will build up in the pipes until, after the passage of years, they may be completely clogged.

Water hardness is expressed in the proportion of the hardness-producing compounds in a volume of water. A convenient scale is parts per million (ppm); that is, molecules or grams of compounds per million molecules or grams of water. On this scale water will usually range between 75 and 700 ppm.

A process predictably called ''softening'' is used to treat water whose hardness is high enough to endanger heaters and piping and to make soap ineffectual. How hard is hard enough? A reasonable rule is that water whose hardness is measured at less than 140 ppm needs no softening for ordinary use; between 140 and 350 ppm at least that portion of it to be heated should be treated and at more than 350 ppm all the water should be softened. The process of softening is a chemical treatment in which the addition of certain salts will hold the hardness-causing compounds in solution and prevent their precipitation, thus neutralizing their ill effects. Tanks and vessels to contain the salts require space and maintenance, and the planning of equipment rooms must be done with the knowledge that treatment will be required. The hardness of water to be used can be determined from data available at the community water source or, in the case of private supplies, by testing first samples of the well water found.

The softening process must be controlled, preferably limited, to maintain hardness in the 50–to–75–ppm range. Soap lathers so well in soft water that removing it becomes difficult, and water with zero hardness can become corrosive to certain kinds of pipe.

In the foregoing discussion of water quality two implicit assumptions have been made. When purity is the issue, it is assumed that the water is to be used for direct consumption. When the issue is hardness, it is assumed that cleaning is the primary consideration, either for hot or cold water. In residential buildings these are the major uses of water, but there is at least one more common need and that is for irrigation, generally lawn sprinkling. A cleaning chore in which hardness is unimportant and in which the water quality is usually of no consequence is the hosing down of stairs, walks, or windows. The cost of softening and/or purifying it is wasted, and it should be removed from the general water service upstream of such processes. A warning to remember here is that no unpurified water be permitted to mix with that certified for drinking purposes. To carry that precept one more step, it is even more important that water that has been used for sanitary purposes by no mischance be allowed to re-enter the water supply system.

WATER PRESSURE

The planner must investigate not only the quality of the water to be received but also the pressure at which it will be delivered. Pressure is needed for three purposes. First, for convenience. Pressure at the last point of use must be strong enough to provide a brisk flow of water in order, for example, to fill a bathtub in less than an hour. Second, the pressure must be sufficient to overcome flow friction encountered by the water as it passes through water meter, pipes, heater, faucets, and any other fittings in the plumbing system. Anything moving has to fight friction, and water is no exception.

The third factor determining pressure is the height of the building. Water has substantial weight, and in order to lift it to its highest point of use there must be enough pressure at the bottom to hold its weight in the vertical pipe.

To put this into numbers, water pressure is often expressed in pounds per square inch (psi). Each floor of an ordinary residential building will require about 4 psi just to lift the water to that level.

Let us use these principles in a practical example—a 20-story apartment building. For proper action in the showers and waterclosets on the top floor the manufacturer of plumbing fixtures recommends a pressure of 15 psi. After the piping system has been designed we are able to estimate pressure loss due to friction on the meter, pipes, and fittings at 20 psi. The calculation for total pressure required is simple:

Factor		Pressure Required
Pressure at top of system		15 psi
Allowance for friction		20
Twenty-story height		80
	Total	115 psi

Few public systems maintain pressures at so high a level. Therefore the available pressure must be supplemented by a pressure-increasing system.

Let us consider a typical municipal water system in which the delivery pressure at a given location does not fall below 50 psi. How much pressure will the interior booster system have to add to the main pressure?

Pressure required	115 psi
Pressure available in the main	50
Necessary addition by booster system	65 psi

To provide this pressure boost mechanical pumps, usually driven by electric motors, must be employed, although gas engines or turbines or steam engines may fill the need in rare cases. Three systems are found in common use:

1. OVERHEAD STORAGE TANKS. One or more tanks, of a capacity that approximates the building's estimated full-day water supply, are located high enough above the top floor to produce, by the weight of the water, the pressure required at the top-floor fixtures. Pumps of comparatively small volume which fill these tanks throughout the night and during the midday low-use hours, keep the tank level high enough to serve early morning and evening peaks. Steel tanks should be lined with a corrosion-resistant substance and checked periodically to ensure the integrity of the lining. Tanks also are often made of wood, which is impervious to water corrosion, but their joints can leak.

The advantages of this system are counted in the small pump size and correspondingly small maximum demand for electricity and in the storage capacity of a day's supply in the event of pump or power failure. The disadvantages are spatial and structural. The tanks are large and, to produce the needed pressure at the top of the system, must stand high above the top floor. Using the figures developed before, 15 psi at top-floor fixtures require that the lowest operating level of the tank be about 34 ft higher, necessitating a penthouse structure substantially taller than that usually required for elevator machinery and override. The structural consideration concerns the larger penthouse and the weight of the filled tanks, a load that must be carried down the height of the building into the foundations.

2. THE HYDROPNEUMATIC TANK SYSTEM. This approach was developed to avoid the added penthouse requirements described above. Intermittently operating pumps, sized to deliver the maximum flow of water anticipated, pump into a tank of moderate size, kept about half full of water and half of air under pressure equal to that needed to serve the building. The air "cushion" permits a part of the tank's water to be drawn off for use before the air pressure drops low enough to start the water pumps. The cushion and tank dimensions are selected so that

the pumps will not run oftener than 12 times an hour during peak use and may mean only a few operations in six hours at night. Over a period of time the air cushion is slowly absorbed into the water; therefore a small air compressor must be part of the installation.

In both systems two pumps should be considered a necessity, each large enough to assume the entire load. Water supply is too important to entrust to a single mechanical device. The pumps should be used alternately to keep them in running condition and the wear equal.

3. PUMPING SYSTEM. Begrudging even the reduced space required by the hydropneumatic tank, engineers have developed improved valves, controls, and pumps to produce the constant pumping system. In apartment buildings it contains three pumps. One small one, called the "lead" pump, is sized for about 25% of the maximum expected demand and is on the line constantly or nearly so. The other two, equal in size, may be planned to serve 55 to 75% of the anticipated demand. Automatic controls shift the pumps into and out of action as dictated by load requirements, and control valves regulate output between the capacity steps represented by the pumps; for example, if the actual demand is 10% capacity, the lead pump will operate alone and its control valve will throttle its output from its 25% potential to the 10% demand. For periods of zero demand, such as the night hours, the system may be able to shut down entirely.

The great advantage of the constant pumping arrangement, known as the instantaneous system, lies in its saving of space and tank costs. These savings may be accentuated if the lead pump is eliminated and a two pump system is installed. Less sensitive to fluctuating demands, this even more simplified system subjects the two pumps to much more operation at low capacity against heavily throttled control valves and is widely used when construction first cost completely outweighs longer range operating costs and problems.

Drawbacks in the instantaneous system are higher electrical costs because of the constant or nearly constant operation and greater maintenance costs consequent to the comparatively complex and fine-tuned controls.

In a very tall building a serious pressure problem of which planners should be aware is created by the very nature of the structure. Note in the foregoing example of the 20-story building that a pressure of 115 psi is required at its base. This approaches the 125-psi maximum safe pressure rating of standard valves and pipe fittings and faucets and other fittings assembled in plumbing fixtures. (Actually, United States government standards call only for an 80 psi rating for fittings, which compounds the problem.) The latter are critical. Whereas extra strong pipe fittings and general service valves are commercially available at premium prices that are not punitive, special fittings for mass-produced plumbing fixtures would, if available at all, be prohibitively expensive. Therefore, if the height of a building exceeds 22 living floors above the lowest living floor (often the second floor of the building), steps must be taken to protect the fixtures on the lower floors.

If the bulding height is only a few floors more than the safe maximum, these provisions may take the form of pressure-reducing valves in hot- and cold-water lines which serve the endangered lower floors to keep their supply within the safe limit. If the number of stories greatly exceeds the safe maximum, the number and arrangement of reducing valves will become awkwardly large and difficult to locate and service, and a "zoned" system is used in preference; for example, in a 40-story building the top 20 floors will be served by one pressure-boosting system, the lower 20 by a second. If overhead tanks are used, one set will be located in the penthouse as usual and will feed down only to the twenty-first floor. Space will have to be found at about the twenty-fourth floor for a lower zone tank system to supply the lower floors. If hydropneumatic tanks or the instantaneous system are used, the lower zone will be fed by one system in the basement, the upper zone by a second system operating at the required high pressure. The pipes distributing water from the high-zone pump system pass through the lower 20 floors without any connections made to them. The pipes and fittings, and any valves required, are selected for the pressure encountered and are commercially available, as mentioned before. By the time these "express" risers reach the twenty-first floor the pressure due to height will have been sufficiently reduced to suit the fixture fittings.

In tall residential buildings particular care must be exercised to control water pressure in public laundries. Washing machines are manufacturer-rated for quite low pressures, compared with sanitary fixtures, and no matter whether the system is zoned the laundries will require pressure-reducing valves unless they are at the top of the building or at the top of a pressure zone.

Another consideration in tall buildings is the pressure required on the ground floor. Often substantial water is needed for lawn sprinkling and car washing, and sometimes the laundry is located on that floor. To avoid the energy expense of pumping this water up to the pressure required to reach the top of the building (and then possibly reducing the pressure again for the laundry) it may be worthwhile to use direct main pressure, even though this method may require additional piping. Water is taken off the building service line before it goes to the booster pump and used for first-floor needs at main pressure. If this is done, however, the technique must be carried through into the hot-water system as well.

WATER HEATING

A good rule for domestic water heating keeps it at the lowest temperature acceptable to the residents. It has been noted that corrosion and mineral deposits are both accelerated with rising temperatures. A temperature of 140°F is considered maximum for general use to avoid discomfort or scalding. If residents will accept temperatures 10 to 15°F below that level, so much the better. For special uses that require hotter water, such as apartment dishwashers in a residential building or large commercial dishwashers in a public restaurant located in the building, local booster heaters must be provided with the machines. It is not advisable to operate an entire domestic hot-water system at 160°F because apartment dishwashers need that temperature to operate safely and are not equipped with booster heaters by the manufacturer.

Boosters in private dishwashers are usually electrically heated. For general purposes domestic water heating follows the pattern of the comfort heating plant. If, for example, individual heating-cooling plants "fueled" by electricity are decided on, apartment water heaters are often consistent with the purposes of the individual heating-cooling plant; that is, the operating expense is allocated to the user's direct account.

If, on the other hand, a project has a central heating plant, domestic hot water will most frequently be generated as part of that plant, usually, although not invariably, using the same fuel. Then there is the matter of deciding whether domestic water is to be heated by the heating plant boilers, by independent heaters, or by a combination of the two. If a project maintains only one heating boiler, the domestic water should be heated independently. A boiler should be taken out of service for thorough inspection and refurbishing once a year; therefore a single-unit plant would have this done only at the expense of occupants who would be deprived of hot water for a few days each summer, an unnecessary annoyance.

In a plant of two or more boilers the advantages of heating domestic water in common with the space heating may be found in saving boiler room space and, quite probably, in a lower initial installation cost. It must be emphasized, however, that water heating does not come free. There is the idea that heat is being generated in winter anyhow, so why not use some of it for heating domestic water? The fact is, of course, that the more work done, the more fuel needed to do it, and that heating boilers must be increased in size if they are to heat domestic water as well. The size increase index given in the following table is subject to considerable variation, depending on building exposure, entering cold water temperature, and similar factors.

Outside Design Temperature (°F)	Total Boiler Load Required for Domestic Water Heating (%)
−10	20
+10	25
+30	33

The more boilers in the plant, the more efficient the summer operation for heating domestic water. If there are two boilers of equal size, both will be much larger than required by the summer load, except in very mild climates. If there are five, one will be efficient for summer water heating in a rather cold part of the world.

The mechanics of heating domestic water from boilers are simple. The most popular heat exchanger is a steel shell that encloses a bundle of small-diameter copper tubes. Steam or hot water from the boiler passes over the tubes, and the water to be heated passes through them. The heating medium is controlled by the temperature of the heated water to maintain a reasonably uniform output regardless of the demand. The great advantage in the use of this heater is the small space it requires. As an example, a 200-unit project's hot water needs would be met by a steam-fed exchanger a little more than 8 in. in diameter and 7 ft long. This device can be tucked away conveniently in a boiler room. If the project can afford the moderate additional expense, it is always advisable to install two exchangers on a full standby basis, alternate them in operation, and have one ready at all times to take over when the other requires service. This amenity is sometimes omitted in the interest of first-cost economy on the premise that short-term lack of hot water is not a disaster. Even then it is well to have a spare copper tube "bundle" on hand for quick installation. Several days or weeks of delay in getting replacement parts for a single heater are hard on owner-occupant relations.

Separate domestic water heating may take the form of a boiler and heat exchanger used only for that purpose. More often, the process is combined into one vessel, or a battery of vessels, in which the fuel heats the domestic water directly, without an intermediate exchanger. The fuel may be gas, oil, or electricity, and the heater may contain some storage capacity for heated water. The subject of hot-water storage is further explored after a brief mention of combining boiler-powered heat exchangers and independent heaters in a single plant, a combination that can sometimes be justified as an economical means of standby availability. If, for example, gas is used for domestic water heating, but not for space heating, a project may be equipped with one gas-fired hot-water heater for normal use and a standby heat exchanger off the oil- or coal-fired boiler.

Hot-water storage capacity acts as a bank in which deposits are made in times of surplus to be drawn on in times of need. This reasoning stems from the fact that the use of water is far from uniform during a day. Peaks occur in the early morning and evening hours. A slightly oversimplified example illustrates the point. Suppose that the total use of hot water in a day is calculated at 4800 gallons, an estimate based on published studies which have proved over many years to be accurate, though leaning toward the conservative side. Furthermore, the maximum consumption is expected to be 900 gallons between 7 and 8 A.M. Two extreme positions may be taken. In one position heating capacity is selected for the maximum hour's use, that is, sufficient to heat 900 gallons per hour from the entering temperature of the domestic cold water service to the utilization temperature of 125 to 140°F. The other extreme provides just enough heating capacity to make up the full day's use by working through the full day. That would be 4800 gallons divided by 24 hours or 200 gallons per hour. The storage bank would have to be large enough to make up the greater requirements during the peak hours. The most demanding hour requires 900 gallons, during which the heater will produce its regular 200 gallons. The bank, therefore, must be able to disgorge the balance of 700 gallons.

One last proviso completes this example. The "bank" referred to is almost always a cylindrical steel storage tank. As hot water is drawn off during the tank's contribution periods, that water is replaced by cold makeup water. About 75% of the contents of a properly piped hot-water storage tank can be drawn off before the colder mixture begins to affect the temperature of the draw-off. Therefore the tank must be sized so that the calculated contribution is only 75% of the full tank capacity. In the above example that means that the full size of the tank would be 930 gallons.

There is a substantial advantage in the use of a storage tank for a central plant system. The smaller heater means a smaller boiler, a smaller chimney, and more efficient operation because the heater is in full use for a high proportion of each day. There are important disadvantages also. The tank is space consuming and expensive. Its installation cost is often considerably higher than the incremental cost of the largest heater needed for a no-storage system against the heater calculated for a full storage system. The tank will, in time, become corroded, need repairs and, finally, replacement. There is no universal rule for choosing between the two extreme systems or of any compromise position (larger heater, smaller tank) between. Each project must be examined on its own merits.

HOT WATER CIRCULATION AND PROTECTION

During the late night hours, when there may be little or no need for hot water in a residential building, the temperature of the water lying dormant in the distribution system will fall to nearly that of the building, some 60°F below its desirable delivery temperature. The first resident looking for hot water in the morning will be faced with a pipeful of cool water to be drawn off before the hot water arrives.

The solution to this problem is the installation of a secondary piping system that will permit water to return to the heater from the farthest point of utilization at a flow rate rapid enough to prevent the water from cooling in the pipes. The circulation may be by gravity produced by the difference in weight between the warmest water and the slightly cooled water which has traveled through the pipes, just as the gravity water-heating systems operate, described in an earlier chapter. Frequently, the circulation is urged along by the installation of a pump at the gathering point of all circulating lines.

A final note on water heating is concerned with safety. As water is heated above 39°F it expands. It will be seen in the following discussion of water piping that air chambers in the system provide a means of cushioning this expansion, but if there is excessive expansion or the air chambers are filled with water it will be necessary to provide a pressure relief valve that will open automatically and without fail to expel enough water to prevent unsafe pressures from building up. Usually the release of a small quantity of water will lower system pressure. A second danger is in the failure of the heater controls, which could permit water temperature buildup to scalding levels. This, too, can be met by the installation of a relief valve that will permit the escape of the excessively hot water before it reaches the users.

The two functions are usually combined in one valve, called a pressure and thermal relief valve. If the valve discharges at all, it may do so unexpectedly at any time, and for protection of personnel the discharge outlet should be piped to a safe point of disposal, preferably immediately above a drain. This is a point to be remembered particularly when individual water heaters are installed in single dwelling units. The relief valve discharge must be directed to a place where it cannot hurt anyone nor do any damage by releasing water where it will not be disposed of quickly and safely.

WATER PIPING

Water piping must resist erosion and corrosion—erosion caused by the flow of the liquid and corrosion by chemical action; for example, when air is also present, and all water supplies contain some entrained air, water reacts with iron to form iron oxide compounds called rust. Thus, when used for water distribution, steel pipe is protected by the application of an electroplated zinc coat (zinc has high corrosion resistance) in a process called galvanizing.

Other common materials used for the purpose are copper and brass, cast iron, an asbestos-cement compound, and a number of plastic compounds. Copper is expensive but easily handled and joined. When available, it is a great favorite for the manufacture of water pipes. Despite the tendency of its base to rust, cast iron undergoes changes in the casting process that make the material resistant to corrosion, and it is frequently used for underground water piping, particularly in 3-in. sizes and larger, for which copper is expensive. The great weight of cast iron makes it less useful inside buildings, in which its support becomes a serious problem.

Asbestos-cement pipe, too, is heavy and not easy to work. It has also been most useful in underground applications. Plastic pipe materials have gained rapid popularity in recent years because of their moderate cost and ease of joining; they not only resist corrosion but also the flow of electrical currents that can sometimes cause problems in metallic pipes. One serious limitation of plastic pipes, which are readily available on the market, is their unsuitability to high temperatures. They must not be located near a boiler or flue which could produce a temperature above 160°F in the material. Thus their use for ordinary domestic hot-water conveyance is cause for some nervousness, for if the water temperature controls fail and permit water temperature to rise unduly, to the danger of scalding users is added the peril of serious damage to the piping system!

The arrangement of water piping in a building has a familiar treelike pattern. An entering service is analagous to the tree trunk, and branches and twigs spread out to the various points of use. In large buildings especially the branches should be disconnectable by valves, so that repairs can be made in any part of the system with a minimum of interruption in the rest. If water pipes are concealed, as they often are in residential construction, it is mandatory that access be provided to the valves by suitable panels or openings and that the valves be well identified with the part of the piping system they serve.

The general distribution of a piping system is categorized as upfeed or downfeed, the importance of which is that space must be allowed accordingly in the building for distribution either (or both) at the top or bottom. In a building whose height permits the use of available water pressure without pumping the cold water will almost always be fed up, with a distributing main at the low level and risers feeding the plumbing fixtures above. If an overhead tank is used for pressure boosting, the cold water will be downfed from the tank, and a pipe attic or similar space must be provided under the roof to accommodate the distributing main.

Hot water can also be upfed or downfed. In a building six stories high the water is often upfed in each tier of plumbing fixtures. At the top of each hot-water riser a return circulating line is connected and brought down alongside. The circulating lines are connected by a collector main running parallel to the hot-water distribution main and returning to the heater. If the building is taller than six stories, the length of the doubled riser piping becomes a serious expense, and it is sometimes possible to extend each riser a few feet into the pipe attic or top ceiling space, collect these extensions at that level, and return in a single circulating riser to the heater, an arrangement that can be reversed. A single hot-water supply riser may be brought up to the top of the building, distributed at that level, the individual risers downfed and extended a short distance downward to the ceiling of the lowest level, where the collector main picks them up and returns them to the heater. In all cases each return riser should be fitted with a manually adjustable balancing valve to make the circulation flow reasonably consistent throughout the system. These balancing valves, as well as the riser shutoff valves, must be accessible wherever they are located, and for this reason it may be necessary to run longer piping than would be needed only for distribution.

A brief unscientific note must be inserted here. In tall buildings it has been my experience that downfeed hot-water systems operate much more satisfactorily

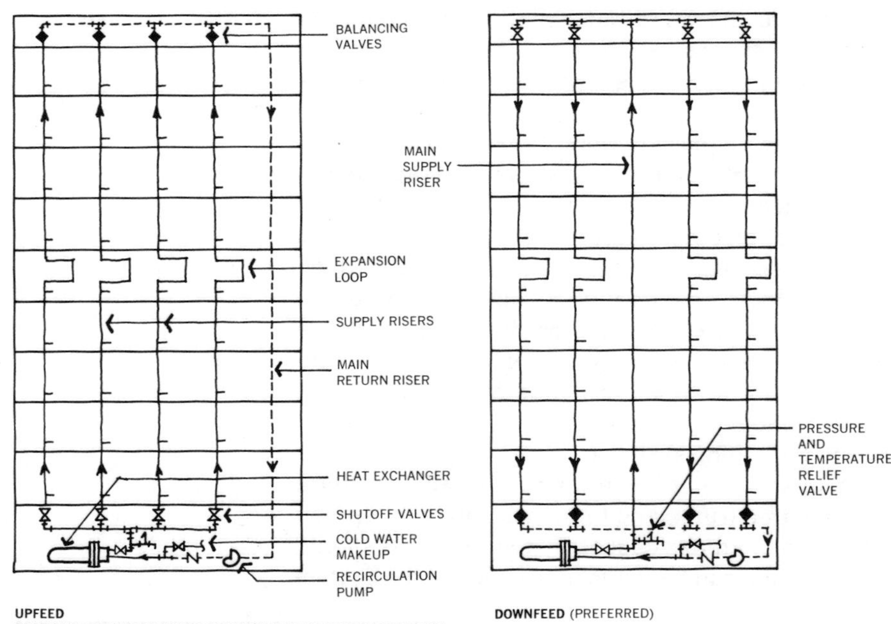

UPFEED **DOWNFEED** (PREFERRED)

DOMESTIC HOT WATER PIPING SYSTEMS (WITHOUT STORAGE TANKS)

than upfeed systems in their consistency of hot-water flow and availability. There seems to be no theoretical reason for this, and a moment's reflection will show that the installation is a little more expensive because the main riser that runs the full height of the building is the large total supply riser in the downfeed system, but the much smaller circulating riser in the upfeed system. Nevertheless, experience should not be denied, and the downfeed system is recommended.

Two dangers of damage to water pipes must be guarded against . The first is in the expansion and contraction of long runs, particularly in hot-water pipes. Expansion provisions for heating water pipes as previously described must be made, and all branches must be taken off mains and risers with a configuration of turns and bends that permits the branches to ''give'' as the main moves. This takes extra space, but it is absolutely essential disaster insurance.

The second peril is ''water hammering.'' When a user opens the faucet of a plumbing fixture, water flows out and sets in motion an entire column of water in the branch, riser, and main. When the faucet is closed, usually abruptly, the momentum of the moving column must stop just as abruptly. Water is incompressible, as anyone can attest who has landed flat while diving, and reacts to the sudden flow interruption by slamming against the closed end of the pipe with destructive force. Not only does this produce an alarming noise, but it can cause damage to the pipe or adjoining portions of the construction. The cure for this hammering is to create air pockets in the piping system so that the water momentum can be spent by compressing air rather than by banging solid pipe. Every riser should be extended as much as possible beyond its highest branchoff, up to 2 ft, a dead length that remains as it was when installed, full of air. This air chamber serves as the needed cushion. Similarly, every branch should have its air chamber, perhaps half the length of the riser chamber. Some plumbing codes require that every plumbing fixture pipe connection be fitted with its own air chamber.

Hot-water piping should be insulated to minimize waste of heat. In cold weather, of course, the heat may not be wasted because it supplements what the heating system puts into the building, but in warm weather the loss of heat is a waste and possibly an annoyance. If the building is cooled, it adds to the cooling load and expense. Sometimes, parts of the hot-water piping system are left uncovered, but this ''economy'' is a first-cost saving only and will ultimately be lost in operating cost. Cold-water piping may have to be insulated for a different reason. If the water-supply temperature ever falls below the ''dew point,'' condensation will appear on the exterior of the pipes (this is inelegantly called ''sweating'') and drip off and cause annoyance or damage to whatever or whoever is below. Thus, unless the water-supply temperature is certain to be high enough that sweating will never occur, insulation must be applied in a thickness sufficient to prevent it. Dew point of pipe surfaces is that temperature at which the air surrounding the pipes can no longer hold all the moisture it contains. So, as it is cooled by contact with the pipes, it deposits the excess moisture onto the cold surfaces as ''dew.'' The insulation simply presents much warmer surfaces to the surrounding air.

BACK SIPHONAGE

If in extreme need or merely a larcenous mood you want to siphon gasoline out of your neighbor's automobile, you set a pail below the gas tank level, insert a tube into the tank, suck sharply on the other end of the tube until gasoline begins to flow, and then drop that end into the pail. Flow will continue as long as there is liquid in the tank or until the pail is full and you pull the tube out. The pressure phenomenon that causes the flow to continue is called siphonage.

A parallel plumbing situation. I am washing the windows in my house. My pail of dirty water is half empty and I drop the hose into it and walk over to turn on the hose cock at the side of the house. The pail begins to fill when suddenly, down the street, a fire truck that has just arrived opens a fire hydrant wide. The enormous outflow of water at the hydrant causes the pressure at my end of the water main to drop suddenly to nothing. The disappearance of pressure causes the water in the pipes in my house to begin to flow backward down to the main that is below the level of my basement floor. This reversed flow starts a siphon from the pail through the open hose cock, and before I realize what is happening the dirty water has been siphoned out of the pail and into the water system, perhaps clear down into the main. When water pressure is restored, my neighbor (whose gasoline I have already stolen) may be drinking the water used for washing windows! The possibility may seem so far-fetched that it could not happen. Nevertheless, there have been occurrences of this kind, the liquid siphoned has been much more toxic than dirty window water, and in documented instances serious illness has resulted. It is imperative therefore that siphonage be prevented.

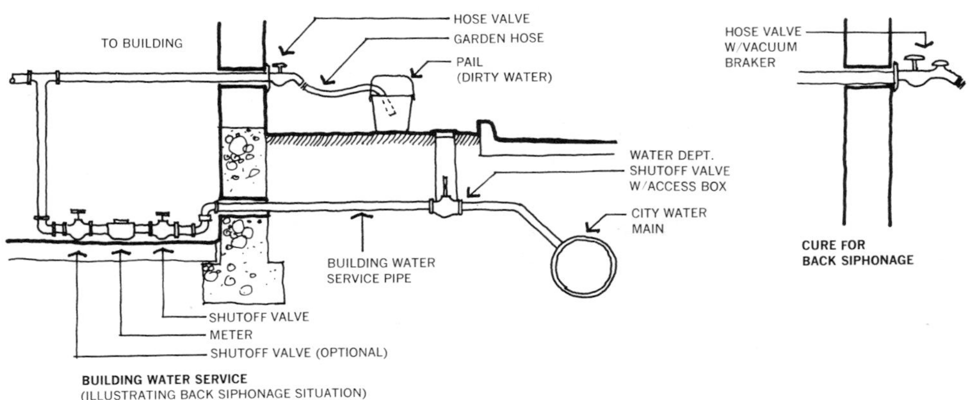

BUILDING WATER SERVICE
(ILLUSTRATING BACK SIPHONAGE SITUATION)

CURE FOR
BACK SIPHONAGE

The first easy answer is to be sure that wherever possible water faucets run water from above the fixture; for example, some old-fashioned bathtubs and lavatories had spouts that admitted water low in the body of the fixture. The foregoing example of siphonage could then occur while the tub or basin was being filled if the water level was above the submerged spout. In tubs, lavatories, and sinks this possibility can be circumvented by placing the spout safely above the fixture's rim so that the water level cannot engulf it.

For washing machines, hose cocks, and toilets with flush valves the water cannot be introduced by free fall from above the fixture and ''vacuum breakers'' must be installed. These devices are simple valves kept tightly closed by water pressure. When that pressure is released the device opens to permit air to enter, and air is the natural enemy of siphons. The siphoning cannot begin and there is no back flow. Plumbing codes now require vacuum breakers for use whenever over-rim supplies are not possible.

Antisiphon protection is required not only to protect the water supply from wastes, but from mixing with ''process'' water as well. Codes consider water used for heating, cooling, or refrigeration condensing as process water, which must be separated by an air gap from the domestic water.

WASTE DISPOSAL

For disposal purposes plumbing wastes are classified as storm and sanitary. Stormwater waste is rainfall or melted snow from building roofs and adjoining paved areas such as driveways, walks, and recreation pads. Sometimes the stormwater classification also includes moisture that seeps into the ground and collects under foundations and subgrade floors, where it can do damage. Sanitary drainage may be defined as everything else.

The purpose of stormwater disposal is to direct these wastes into natural watercourses without damage to land or construction. The purpose of sanitary disposal is to separate out the toxic and offensive solid or liquid matter and direct the remaining cleansed water into the natural watercourses. This definition is really quite modern and reflects growing awareness and concern for the pollution of natural water supplies. It was not so long ago that sanitary wastes were channeled directly into the nearest lake, river, or ocean, a practice by no means universally ended, but time is beginning to run out, especially as the worldwide people count continues to rise.

Akin to water supply, waste disposal may be private or communal. An important consideration in property selection is the presence of public sewer facilities. Private means of sanitary waste disposal are expensive in installation cost and require maintenance attention throughout the life of a housing project, whether a single residence or thousands. Stormwater drainage may require great lengths of large disposal pipe and, if property is not markedly higher than the watercourse, expensive pumping equipment will be needed to lift the rainwater. A careful appraisal, including a survey when necessary, should be made of this situation for every piece of property, preferably before a purchase is made. In developed nations private storm and sanitary waste disposal systems are usually under rigorous state control for adherence to legal standards.

Private sanitary sewage disposal of small residential projects containing only a few dwelling units may often be accomplished by simple seepage systems called tile fields. The sanitary wastes are first carried to a relatively large buried container called a septic tank. Because of its size, the tank retains incoming waste material so long and it moves through so slowly that solid matter drops out and sinks to the bottom. There is another and even more important effect. Certain kinds of bacteria thrive in these wastes and multiply by absorbing components toxic to higher forms of life. So thoroughly do these minute creatures do their feeding job in a properly designed tank that the liquid leaving the other end is nearly free of toxicity and actually contains some nutrients for soil. From the tank it passes through a charging device called a dosing tank which, operating on a siphon principle, discharges intermittently to the tile field. The field consists of a grid of pipes laid in such a way that the water seeps out into the ground and finally finds its way to the surface, where it evaporates, or down into the subterranean water table. The tile pipes are generally laid about 30 in. below the surface, and their number and length depends on the character of the earth itself in the location of the field. If it is sandy, seepage will be quite rapid, and the length of pipe will be comparatively short. If the ground is dense clay through which water seepage is difficult and slow, the pipe length will be correspondingly great. A careful analysis of the ground, called a percolation test, must be made before a system is designed. The number of dwelling units that can be served by the simple tile field system depends on the area of property devoted to the field and the results of the percolation test. It may also depend on the local situation as a whole. In some rapidly developed areas, particularly in suburbs, in which unlimited use of tile fields finally overloaded the seepage abilities of the ground, irrespective of percolation tests, backyards became marshes in rainy weather.

When the size of the project or local conditions preclude the use of tile fields, a private sewage disposal plant is the alternative. This may require a major investment, allocation of space at a place in which sewage flow can be conducted with the least pumping or other difficulty, and careful design so that odors accruing from the process of separation do not become a nuisance or a hazard. The last step in private disposal systems, from the simplest septic tank and tile field to the most elaborate plant, is removal of the accumulated solid sludge that is resistant to bacterial action in the tank or chemical attack in the plant. This sludge may sometimes be sold as fertilizer material.

Municipal or other communal sewers offer great convenience for the owner of a project. By their purpose sewers are classified as storm or sanitary sewers. In some localities a single system, called a combined sewer, is provided for both purposes. In others only sanitary sewers are offered, and storm drainage runs into and over the ground as it would if there were no buildings. Still others modify that arrangement. A storm sewer is provided for streets and paved walks and driveways. It is not large enough, however, for building roof drainage which must be permitted to spill on the ground and be soaked up. Under that kind of system a minimum unpaved ground area may be required in relation to the roof area that spills onto it. In any event, the planner must make the building and project design conform to the sewer system in the locality. Some localities, concerned by the ever-increasing load imposed on their storm sewers as buildings and paving multiply, require retention ponds as part of major construction projects. These accumulate rainwater and release it slowly to the storm sewer after the major part of the rain has ended.

Materials commonly used for underground sewers are cast iron, vitrified clay tile, reinforced concrete, and asbestos-cement. There is some use of plastic piping which may well increase as it becomes more familiar and more widely accepted in plumbing codes. Because of its great strength and corrosion resistance, cast iron is favored in unstable ground or where heavy loads can be imposed. Tile and concrete pipe are much cheaper and entirely satisfactory for most applications that are not underneath buildings or other great weights. Their limitation is that they do break under stress, particularly at joints. The pressure of tree roots will sometimes crack a tile pipe joint so that the root can grow right into the pipe. There, nurtured by the passing sewage and moisture, the root may thrive until its growth blocks the pipe entirely and the result is a backup of sewage until the trouble can be cleared.

All sewers are subject to clogging over a period of time. Even storm sewers may carry a load of rain-borne dust, roof surface dirt, and leaves from trees. So every sewer installation must have cleanout provisions that allow access to every portion of the pipe. This ''access'' may be obtained through vaults called manholes that permit personnel to get right down to sewer level and work, through small pipe extensions to grade called cleanouts, or by a combination of the two. Manholes are both more expensive and more satisfactory for the purpose. In either case, access permits insertion into the pipe of an extensible tool designed to clear obstructions.

BUILDING DRAINAGE

The simple task of conducting sewage through pipes is complicated by one fact. The pipe is large enough to carry the maximum volume of waste expected at any time, but most of the time it will be empty or nearly empty. Ultimately it connects to a sewer in which there is, has been, and will be waste material that at best emits unpleasant odors and at worst dangerous organisms. The empty pipe is a direct conduit between the sewer and the inside of the residence through the drain openings in the plumbing fixtures.

The protection, of course, is in the familiar trap, which holds a plug of water in the drain pipe just below the fixture. That water shields the interior of the building from the sewer and must be inviolate at all times. There is a danger, however, of loss of entrapped water, and against this possiblity an entire system of auxiliary piping called the venting system is employed in all buildings.

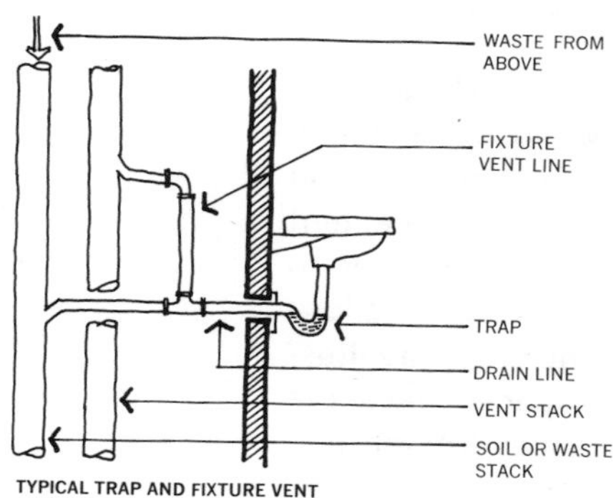

TYPICAL TRAP AND FIXTURE VENT

Consider a trap, with its proper complement of water, that connects into a drain pipe into which other plumbing fixtures drain. Somewhere up the line a toilet is flushed or a bathtub is opened and a rush of liquid comes along the common pipe, pushing air before it, building up air pressure in its path. That pressure pushes the water up on one side of the trap. No great peril there, but now the big volume of water passes the point at which the fixture branch connects to the main pipe and the air pressure is reversed; air is now being sucked after the departing mass. The reversal pulls the water up the other leg of the trap and its momentum may carry it beyond the crown to start flowing toward the main pipe. This can set up the siphon situation already described. Once the flow begins the rest of the trap will be siphoned out and the protection is lost. The living areas may then have direct contact with foul-smelling and possibly toxic sewer gases.

The enemy here has been air pressure, and the venting system is designed to prevent important changes in air pressure from occurring in the pipes. Air balancing connections are made at each fixture or each group of fixtures, the practice depending somewhat on local code requirements. The individual vent pipes are connected to provide an integrated pressure balancing system. The major vent pipes finally connect with the atmosphere by extension through the roof. The major waste pipes are connected to the main vents at sufficient intervals to ensure no undue pressure changes; for example, in a tall building each main waste riser will be connected to its companion vent riser at the top and bottom and at intervals of five or six stories between.

Cast iron, galvanized steel, copper, and plastic pipes are common materials for waste and vent pipes. Cast iron and copper are expensive but virtually permanent. Galvanized steel seems to have a life-span of perhaps 40 years when used in vent piping in which, interestingly enough, corrosion seems to be worse than in drainage piping. Because the first points of failure in steel piping with screwed joints is usually at the threads, where the metal is thinnest, a combination of steel pipe lengths and cast iron fittings into which the pipe is caulked is an effective compromise. The use of plastic piping is still somewhat new at this writing, but signs point to its increasing adoption unless presently unsuspected defects are discovered after years of use.

The observations on pipe material apply in equal measure to sanitary pipe and to interior rainwater conductors from the roof, called downspouts. For buildings whose roof drainage descends on the exterior the collection gutters and vertical leaders to the ground are usually sheet metal—galvanized steel, aluminum, or copper—the first two lower in cost and the third much longer in life. It has been implied before that the rainwater conductors may spill onto the ground, which should be protected at the point of spillage by a splash block or gravel bed to avoid erosion, or they may empty into underground sewers leading to a stormwater or combined disposal system.

Sizes of drain and vent pipes are predicated on the number of fixtures they serve and the maximum flow expected at any time. Sizes of downspouts and rain leaders are chosen by the maximum rate of rainfall expected in the area, based on records kept. Pipe sizes are codified in plumbing drainage practice to the extent that it is usually necessary only to count fixtures and to measure roof areas to select the pipe from the governing code tables. The tables show the minimum allowable sizes, used in all but rare cases and with uniform success. The following illustration shows typical dimensions of horizontal cross-section pipe spaces that serve fixtures in a variety of circumstances. Included here are allowances for venting, water risers, necessary expansion, and cases in which toilet room exhaust ducts are enclosed in the same shafts as the plumbing risers. From a piping standpoint it is advantageous to place the lavatory between toilet and tub if all three are in the same room, but the arrangement of the toilet in the center is often better for design. Interior downspouts can sometimes be accommodated in sanitary riser pipe shafts. In other designs the downspouts may be taken down independently. In multiple-residence buildings there are usually fewer downspouts than plumbing pipe shafts.

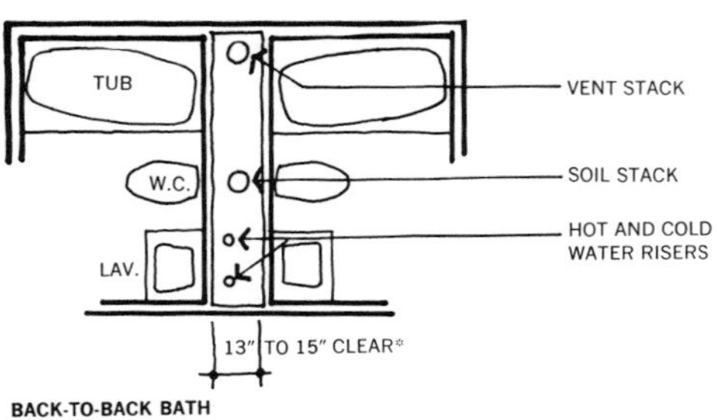

BACK-TO-BACK BATH
(EXHAUST ELSEWHERE)
*PIPE SPACE WIDTH VIRTUALLY THE SAME FOR SINGLE BATHS OR KITCHENS

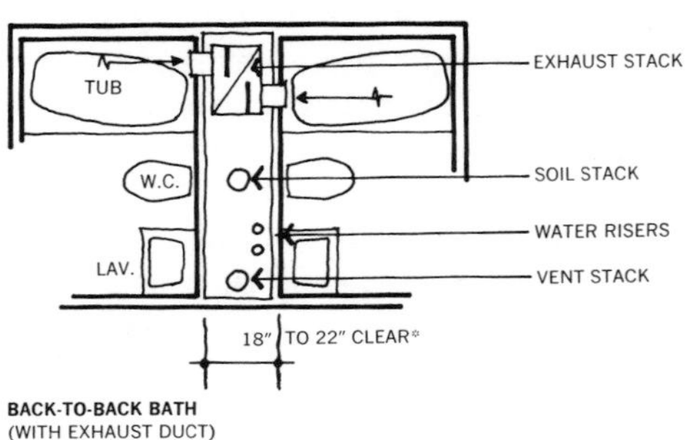

BACK-TO-BACK BATH
(WITH EXHAUST DUCT)

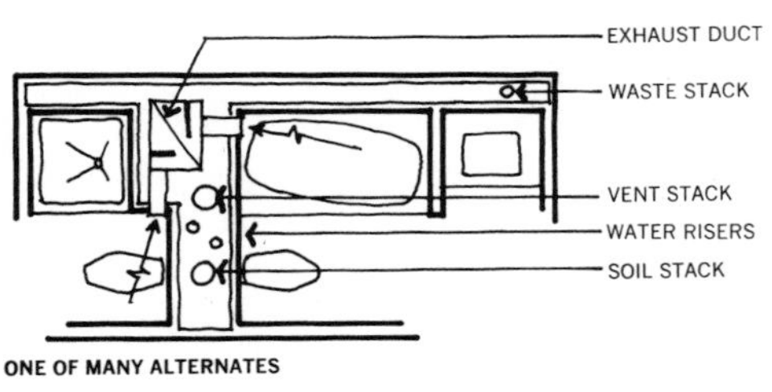

ONE OF MANY ALTERNATES

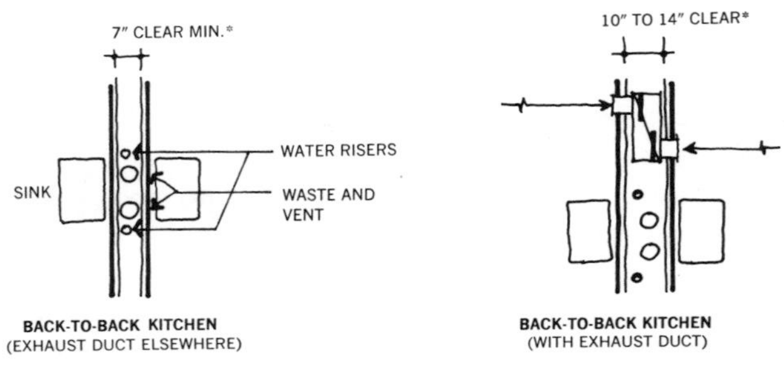

BACK-TO-BACK KITCHEN
(EXHAUST DUCT ELSEWHERE)

BACK-TO-BACK KITCHEN
(WITH EXHAUST DUCT)

Kitchen wastes require a separate word. Cooking grease and food wastes must be disposed of. The latter may be in ground-up form, the result of the work of garbage disposal units installed as part of the kitchen sink assembly. The grease may be dissolved in hot water only to solidify as the water cools and be deposited in the piping system. Grease can be removed in a fairly effective fashion in specially designed traps, fittingly named grease traps, installed in conjunction with each kitchen sink. Codes in different localities take varying views of this problem, some seeing none at all. The individual grease traps keep plumbing lines comparatively clean, but they must be treated periodically, an unpleasant task in a private kitchen or anywhere else for that matter. Some codes require that the kitchen waste lines be separated from all other wastes in the building, gathered and run through a central grease separation vault called a grease basin, and then joined with other sewage. Under this code, when a kitchen and bathroom share the same plumbing stack, there must be two separate waste pipes, although a common vent is permitted.

Another special provision affecting kitchen waste stacks in tall buildings should be mentioned. When detergents were first introduced for dishwashing, they created a volatile foam in the waste pipes. By the time this waste reached the base of the riser in a 10-story or taller building, it was so frisky that the turn in the riser to join the horizontal sewer running out of the building created an almost explosive foaming situation. Frequently the foam would back up right through the trap water below the sinks of a floor or two and their occupants had a sinkful of someone else's foam. The most satisfactory solution to this distressing situation was quickly found to be a second waste riser, which received the discharge of two or three lower floor sinks and joined the main riser only after they had both run parallel for perhaps 10 ft. The main stack still created foam when it turned, but the foam did not back up to the fourth or fifth floor where the lowest sink was connected. The second stack, aptly called a "detergent stack," was not high enough to produce a serious foaming situation. In the years that followed detergents were improved by their manufacturers to reduce the amount of foaming and materially lessen the problem. Some plumbing contractors report that it is now safe to omit the detergent stack, and simply waste the very lowest sink into the bottom of the vent stack (which is legal). Others continue to prefer a detergent stack as a comparatively inexpensive insurance feature.

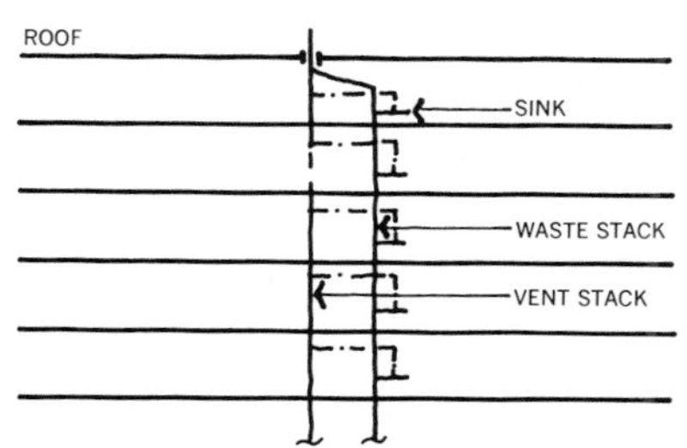

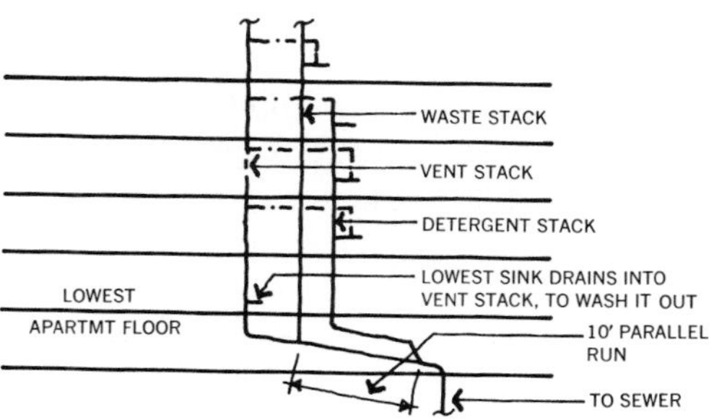

GROUND WATER

If the usual level of ground water is high enough to pose any danger to the stability of building foundations or below-grade floors, or even if this level is reached only during a rainy season, a system of subsurface drainage should be installed. Borings into the soil and any other available data should be studied to determine the necessity for this precaution. When a basement floor is well below ground, and data are incomplete for any reason, it is well to provide drainage for safety's sake, since the cost is comparatively low.

Tile piping similar to that described for small private sewage disposal tile fields is used, in this case to admit seepage rather than to discharge it. The tile leads to a gravel settling basin to prevent sand, gravel, or dirt that may become entrained by the water seepage from entering the sewer. The water discharge from the basin is conducted logically to a storm sewer, although some code jurisdictions prohibit any connection other than direct rainwater drainage to their storm sewers.

The location for drain tile usually preferred is just outside the foundation walls, slightly above the level of the bottom of the footing. If the system becomes clogged, it is comparatively easy to dig in that location. There are three instances in which a location just inside the foundation walls may be selected. In the first, when one or more of the foundation walls are at the property line, pipe cannot be installed on the property of another. In the second, when excavation discloses a water spring beneath the lowest floor slab, the water must be drained off before it reaches the underslab level. The third might be in a building of large groundfloor area, in which some engineers prefer to supplement perimeter drain tile with interior laterals connected to the perimeter drains at fairly wide intervals. In the last two cases it is well, if feasible, to have both exterior and interior perimeter tile lines.

BELOW-SEWER DRAINAGE

If the elevation of subgrade plumbing fixtures or subfloor drainage tile is such that they cannot drain by gravity, allowing for a flow grade in the building drain line of at least 1% and for an additional reasonable margin of safety, such drainage must be pumped into the sewer. First it is collected in a large underfloor tank, called a sump. A float switch in the tank starts a lift pump when the tank capacity is approached. If toilets or other fixtures discharging solid materials are handled, the pumps and/or their piping must be large enough that the solids will not clog them. This type of pump is called an ejector and is not required if only clear liquid is to be lifted. The piping is arranged so that the pump cannot place the receiving sewer under pressure but lifts the discharge high enough to allow it to flow by gravity into the sewer.

If removal of drainage is in any respect critical, alternative (duplex) pumps should be installed for maximum protection against pump failure and with suitable automatic alarms to signal high-water level or pump outage.

Sumps are made of cast iron, cast fiberglass, or concrete, with tight fitting steel covers and access provisions to permit cleaning.

PLUMBING FIXTURES

Selection of plumbing fixtures for residential use is based on considerations of first cost, longevity, maintenance and operating costs, and aesthetics. The latter includes the selection of color, usually at a small addition to the cost of the standard white fixtures.

TOILETS (WATERCLOSETS). The principal choice here is between flush-valve and flush-tank operation. A flush valve is a large orifice valve that passes enough water in a short time to cleanse the bowl thoroughly and refill the built-in trap. A flush tank is a storage device that accumulates enough water between flushes to achieve the same result. As a rule, the flush valve produces more water-movement sound than the tank. It requires larger water connections and larger main water pipes because of the greater instantaneous rate of flow. With fewer moving parts, it needs less maintenance. If exposed, it is unsightly, but if concealed its maintenance becomes difficult.

In localities with cold service water moisture can condense on a tank's exterior and antisweat provisions must be made. On the other hand, the top surface of a tank can act as a convenient shelf while the bathroom is inuse, although it must never be considered a permanent counter; it must always be removable for servicing the working parts inside.

If flush valves are installed, it is wise to oversize the cold water risers and even wiser to run an entirely independent riser for each bank of valves. The reason for these precautions is that the high rate of water drawn tends to drop pressure in other fixtures in simultaneous use, thus reducing the flow of cold water in them and, changing the temperature of the hot-cold water mixture. These effects can be eliminated by correct pipe sizing and arrangement. All in all, the use of flush tanks has been preferred in most residential projects.

LAVATORIES (WASHBOWLS). Will the lavatory be free standing or will it become part of a counter-bowl-cabinet assembly? Will it be made of china, impervious to corrosion but subject to possible (although unlikely) breakage, or steel or cast iron with hard-baked enamel coating, much lower in first cost but limited in lifespan, for eventually the protective coating must chip and expose the metal? Should the faucet have a single handle, two handles and spout combined in one fitting, or the somewhat more elegant separated handles and spout? In any event, the fitting should include a lever-operated lift connected with the drain plug by which the entire action is controlled. The old-fashioned rubber drain stopper with chain is no longer in favor.

BATHTUBS. The style, length, and material are at issue here. Style is a subjective matter of personal selection. Tubs, too large to be cast successfully in china, are made of metal. The better tubs are enameled cast iron, the cheaper ones enameled steel. The comparison is the usual story; the battle between low first cost and longer life. In tubs, as in lavatories, the drain operator should be combined with the faucet controls. The most widely used tub length is 5 ft, which often determines the width of the bathroom. Luxurious installations may call for tubs 6 in. longer, but bare-bones minimum housing may dictate the same amount shorter than the norm.

SHOWERS. The primary choice here is whether the shower will have its own stall of be combined with the bathtub. In multibathroom houses there may be a combination, one bathroom boasting a tub with shower, the other only a shower stall, or perhaps the master bathroom may contain a tub and separate shower stall. Another consideration is water control. A simple two-valve hot- and cold-water mixer, manually controlled, may be adequate, but in the event of its use the general water-piping system should be generously sized. Otherwise simultaneous use of hot or cold water in neighboring fixtures can alter the mixture to the shower, with accompanying annoyance or possibly even danger to the user. Thermostatic mixing valves, although rather expensive, automatically maintain a set temperature, regardless of changes in supply, and thus provide security against scalding or chilling. Pressure-balancing valves are considerably less sensitive but also cost less. They are made safe against scalding or chilling by balancing a change in pressure on one side (hot or cold) with a corresponding change on the other by action in the valve.

KITCHEN SINKS. Few free-standing sinks are installed in present-day housing. A sink that becomes part of the kitchen counter, with the space below it arranged for storage, makes good planning sense. As noted before, the sink may be fitted with a garbage disposal unit, and a dishwasher mounted alongside can use the same water and waste connections that serve the sink. Single-handled faucets are a great convenience in this application, because hands are usually well occupied in the kitchen. The sink material itself can be stainless steel, enameled cast iron, or enameled steel. The stainless steel is virtually corrosionproof and should last indefinitely. The other finishes have the familiar possibility of ultimate chipping and corrosion of the exposed metal. Stainless steel has one disadvantage in appearance, however. It is difficult to keep it clean looking, no matter how clean it actually is. Water leaves spots on the surface which take work to remove.

LOCATION OF FIXTURES

One dictum in building design is so well known and well understood that it needs to be mentioned here only as a reminder of its universality. Whenever a floor plan can possibly accommodate them, plumbing facilities should be "backed up" to one another so that a minimum number of drainage and water mains can serve a maximum number of fixtures. This is especially important in multiple-story buildings, in which the length of duplicate risers makes the cost so much the greater, but the rule is still applicable in one-story buildings. Even though some pipe sizes may increase for multiple service, that cost is inconsequential in comparison with duplication of the pipes. Obviously, the workability, rentability, or saleability of the residences is more important than piping economy, and no floor plan should be compromised. If bathrooms or bathroom and kitchen can be arranged to share common pipe space without such a compromise, there is no reason that it should not be done.

In the same line of thinking, it is desirable to locate and face fixtures to allow their water and drain branches to serve from the same pipe space. It is occasionally convenient that a lavatory, for example, occupy another wall than the toilet and tub. If this must be, it is not a disastrous expense, since it involves only an additional set of waste, vent, and water risers or branches. But if extra care and ingenuity in space layout can avoid that expense they should be exercised.

FIRE PROTECTION

The fundamentals of fire protection lie in the materials of construction, divisions of the building, and access to and number of exits. These rules are discussed in earlier chapters. Fire warning equipment is described in a later delineation of electrical systems in residential buildings. Within the context of plumbing, fire protection has to do with the preparation of the project's water supply system for availability in emergencies merely for the reason that water is an effective fire-extinguishing agent.

The most useful "tool" for fire fighting is the local fire department. Every building project, residential or otherwise must plan for fire hydrants to be connected to the water supply system, located so that the pumping and hose equipment can reach every part of the building or buildings. Therefore one of the earliest planning steps must be taken with the local fire authorities so that all regulations can be followed, that available hoses will fit the hydrants, and that the flow of water will be sufficient. Without this cooperation the project cannot and should not be built at all.

In two general areas the fire department's facilities may have to be supplemented by permanent fire-fighting installations in the project itself. First is that of instantaneous response—that is, when the time needed to summon the fire trucks and for them to arrive is deemed longer than minimum safety dictates; second, when the height of the building is beyond the reach of the department's pumping equipment with enough residual pressure to operate a hose effectively or at all.

LOCAL HOSES. One quick response agent is in hoses permanently connected to the water supply system, mounted in strategic locations. In buildings of more than one story the "strategic location" should be in or immediately adjacent to a stairway; for example, in the event of a fire near the stairway at one floor level a hose from the floor above or below can be used to work on it. The hoses must be fed by a system of water piping that is independent of the domestic water system, at least back to the building's water service entrance; thus fire-fighting pressure will not be influenced by the number of people who happen to be taking showers at the time the water is needed. Pipes that feed the hoses are called standpipes, and more particularly wet standpipes, because they are filled with water at all times. Many building codes require that a second valve be at each hose connection to each standpipe to which the fire department can attach its own hoses. Whether or not the code demands it, this provision should be made.

Wet standpipes must be terminated on the outside of the building at a place readily accessible to fire department pumpers and with protected threaded inlets to which their hoses can be connected. To minimize the possibility of loss of this vital fire-fighting feature by damage to hose threads or similar mischance, duplicate inlets, the familiar "Siamese" twin fitting, should be installed and protected by threaded caps. At each fire department connection it is necessary that a check valve be provided as well so that water can be pumped into the building but will not come pouring out. This is mentioned to point up the need for space inside the building wall for the pipe and valve, both of which are of substantial size and need room.

SPRINKLERS. The quickest response to a fire can be an automatic sprinkler system. The standard sprinkler is a fused valve connected to a well-supplied water source. Fire adjacent to the sprinkler will melt the fuse to release the valve and hopefully douse the flames. Sprinklers are spaced 9 to 13 ft apart in both directions; this spacing is intended to blanket an entire area and provide quick action before a fire can spread. It should always be remembered, however, that nothing is foolproof. Valves can be left closed, sprinkler heads painted shut, or pumps may fail to function. Call the fire department for every fire.

In residential buildings areas that have long been protected by sprinklers are rubbish/garbage collection rooms, rubbish chutes, garages and parking facilities, workshops such as carpenter shops, paint-storage areas, and restaurant kitchens. There has been some restiveness among fire-prevention officials and experts concerning fire and smoke hazards that can endanger the occupants of highrise buildings, whose means of escape, especially from the upper stories, may be arduous and slow. Construction provisions such as compartmentation and self-closing doors have been discussed in earlier chapters. In addition, pressure has been brought to add residential area sprinklering as a code requirement in certain circumstances. This may range from a single sprinkler inside the apartment door to prevent spread of fire into the public corridor, to full coverage of the entire area, or to sprinklers only in the public corridors and stairways. Developments are unfolding rapidly and every local change should be followed closely by planners and designers.

Another factor affecting the decision whether to provide sprinklers may be economic. A reduction in the annual cost of fire insurance may pay for a sprinkler installation in very few years. Accurate data should be secured in advance of planning and the decision made on the basis of complete understanding.

Sprinkler piping is subjected to little interior corrosion because the water inside seldom if ever flows. Ordinary steel pipe, without galvanizing or other particular protection against corrosion, is generally used because of its comparatively low cost. Plastic pipe is not likely to become a substitute because in its present development it cannot withstand temperatures likely to be present even in the early stages of a fire. Space requirements for sprinkler piping have to do with headroom and, to some extent, appearance; for example, if dwelling spaces are to be sprinklered, public acceptance will dictate concealed piping with only the sprinkler heads visible. The means of concealment would depend on the method of construction, and it is even possible in some cases for the reverse to occur. Floor construction might be designed to accommodate the sprinklers, by use of steel construction rather than concrete, especially in buildings of moderate height.

On the other hand, in portions of the building that don't "show," such as workshops, parking areas, and rubbish rooms, where sprinklers may be required, the piping is usually best left exposed and clear headroom below it becomes important. Requirements for clearance between the head and the ceiling above, in order to distribute the water evenly throughout the area served by the head, the height of the head, its connection to the main pipe, and the diameter of the pipe itself add to a total of 10 to 12 in. which impact on the clear usable headroom in a sprinklered space.

DRY STANDPIPES. In some jurisdictions the fire department requires the installation of standpipes that are not attached to any water system. They are empty risers in the usual standpipe locations, with hose valves and/or hoses at each floor level. The lower end of this "dry" standpipe is extended through an outside wall above grade, with a Siamese fitting for connection to the fire department's pumper. The dry standpipes may be in place of or in addition to the wet.

FIRE PUMPS. When the height of a building requires pressure greater than that made available by the fire department's equipment to serve the top floor's hose, the building must have its own pressure-boosting system. This is exactly analogous to the need for pressure-boosting pumps already discussed in connection with domestic water systems. Fire pumps must be completely independent of the pumps for domestic water in some jurisdictions. In others the same pumps may be used for both purposes, with appropriate automatic valve operation to close off domestic water use during a fire. When fire pumps are separate, buildings of extraordinary height require zones for the fire system like those for the domestic water, so that excessive pressures are not encountered at the lower floor hose outlets.

Buildings of such great height are built of noncombustible materials and only the contents can burn. Smoke can spread readily through such a building, but fire itself is contained in limited areas. For this reason the fire pumps are designed with the expectation that they will have to supply water for only a few hoses at a time. In a building more than one zone high the lower zone pumps will usually supply water not only for the hoses in their own zones but also for the intakes of the upper zone pumps. Thus the upper zones need pressure-boosting capacity only for their own zone's height, not for the entire height of the building up to the top of that zone.

The fire department connection on the outside wall of the building permits the department's pumper to help supply water to the fire pumps. It is often extended and adapted by arrangement of the piping to achieve the opposite effect; that is, the fire pumps in a building may be used to augment fire department equipment in fighting a fire in a nearby building or in a hard-to-reach area of the protected building itself.

Fire pumps are controlled automatically by pressure in their discharge lines held high enough to operate the topmost hose. As soon as a hose valve is opened and water rushes out, the line pressure drops and the pump starts. By the same token, if there is a leak in a standpipe or other fire line, the pump, sensing only loss of pressure, will start. If the leak is tiny, oozing a spoonful of water a month, at one joint in a farflung piping system, it may be impossible to locate it because that amount will evaporate as quickly as it leaks. Nevertheless, when a couple of spoonsful have been lost, the fire pump senses a drop in pressure and on it goes, alarms sound and a full-scale production takes place just as if there were a fire. Because fire pumps operate only in emergencies, they are not selected for quiet operation, and if all this excitement occurs in the middle of a night it becomes a decidedly unpleasant experience for the residents.

To combat this by no means unusual chain of events a tiny booster pump called a ''jockey'' is installed in conjunction with each fire pump. It is set to operate at a pressure a little higher than that which will start the fire pump. Then, if there is a small leak in the system, the jockey pump will replace the miniscule amount of lost water to maintain system pressure and prevent the big pump from running.

Fire pumps must be as reliable as it is humanly possible to make any mechanical device. If the pump is driven by an electric motor, as it frequently is, the electrical service for the pump must be independent of any other electrical service and should run underground from outside the building directly to the pump and its control. Sometimes fires start in the electrical service area, and it would be disastrous to have fire-pump service vulnerable to a fire! It is also feasible to make fire pumps completely independent not only of damaged building electrical service but also of electrical power failure in the entire area by driving the pumps with gas engines or turbines or gasoline or Diesel engines. Needless to say, special caution must be taken in piping the gas or storing liquid fuel for such a purpose.

Fire pumps should be tested regularly by running them to make sure that they are always in condition to operate in case of need.

FIRE EXTINGUISHERS. Fire hoses and sprinklers throw an enormous quantity of water and are intended for fires of serious magnitude. For wastebasket fires, fires in appliance motors, or similar limited blazes, the water thrown by a hose might do considerably more damage than the fire could. In such cases it is convenient to employ small portable extinguishers, mounted in a prominent and accessible location. There should be at least two on every residential level, or more if the building is large. Extinguishers should also be hung in the elevator machine room, workshops, mechanical and electrical equipment rooms, and parking facilities. Great care must be exercised in the selection of extinguishers for a given location. On residential floors probably the best kind is one charged with water under pressure. When a fire is likely to be electrical in nature, such as in an elevator machine or electrical service room, a carbon dioxide fog or dry chemical spray, which are agents that cannot conduct current back to the handler, should be used. Water cannot be applied, of course, when there is any danger of freezing.

Like fire pumps, extinguishers must be checked frequently to ensure their constant good operating condition.

PLUMBING SPACE REQUIREMENTS AND COSTS

Various illustrations show typical space requirements for pipe riser and connection areas, heaters, and pumping equipment.

Typical in multiple residential projects is an arrangement which by the project as a whole has only one water service and the total consumption is measured by one meter for payment by the single owner or combine of residents. Depending on local water department rules, the meter may be located in a vault outside the building or mounted inside. The vault location is more expensive, but the other requires valuable space in the mechanical equipment room. In either case there must be an accessible valve outside the building so that the water department can remove the meter in the event of malfunction or in the unlikely case of nonpayment of the water bill. If the water supply stems from a private well, meter requirements are, of course, nonexistent unless for any reason it is desirable to determine the water consumption.

Water provided for fire fighting is usually not metered directly because the meter introduces noticeable resistance in the service pipe, and every bit of available pressure is needed when a fire breaks out. To protect against unauthorized use of water from the fire system for other purposes, however, a detector meter is often installed in the fire service. Mounted in a small line piped alongside the fire service line, it senses flow in the main line and records the flow.

In projecting operating costs for a proposed (or actual) residential building project, plumbing charges must be considered by the planner as part of the building's total burden. These charges will include some or all of the following, which can be measured directly or estimated with reasonable accuracy by the designing engineer:

1. Domestic water consumption.
2. Sewer tax. When imposed, it is often equated to domestic water consumption.
3. Cost of heating domestic water.
4. Fire department connection tax.
5. Cost of operating pumps for domestic water supply, hot-water heating, hot-water circulation, sewage, and groundwater ejection.
6. Maintenance costs for pumps, charging fire extinguishers, and so on.

COMPONENTS OF DESIGN—ELECTRICAL 6

Harry S. Nachman

Inspection of a luxurious home built in the nineteen twenties might well reveal construction quality, details, and finishes superior to anything that could be found today. Fifty-year-old plumbing could still fall in the same category, If warm-air heating had been designed, a replacement heat exchanger might have been installed in the furnace over the years, but the system would probably be functioning as well as ever and with plenty of excess capacity built in. There would have been no cooling, but that could have been added without too much difficulty. All in all, the old home would still be more than a suitable place for gracious living, except for one thing.

By present-day standards the electrical installation would be a disaster. The number of receptacles (people often call them ''outlets'') in each room would be completely inadequate for the number of lamps and appliances now deemed necessary to everyday living. The size of the electrical service would be between one-half and one-third of that required in the last half of the twentieth century. Facilities for communication, security, and auditory recreation would be absent, at least in the sense of having been built into the structure. As a final damning blow, a 50-year-old residence subject to building code inspection based on the present-day code in its area would probably pass with flying colors in every category except the electrical!

What is demanded by electrical codes in today's residential construction? First, a minimum size of entering service to accommodate not just the electrical load when the building is new but to anticipate reasonable future trends that will increase it. It costs comparatively little to increase service size when a house is built but a great deal more to rip it out and replace it with a larger service when a few years' experience has proved it to be inadequate.

What happens when electrical service, or any part of the electrical distribution system, is too small? First, it must be understood that electricity is different in its behavior under stress from the other major services we bring into residential buildings—water and gas. When the load gets too heavy, the last two just give up.

COMPONENTS OF DESIGN—ELECTRICAL

You can push just so much water or gas through a pipe with a given pressure and, if more is needed, it simply will not come. Electricity is suicidal. The more asked for, the more will flow until the conductors carrying it become so overloaded that the heat due to their condition consumes them by burning or melting. Only then, when there is nothing left to carry it, does the electrical flow stop.

Now, of course, human ingenuity has found a way to prevent electrical systems from destroying themselves by overloading, whether careless, thoughtless, or accidental. Weak links are deliberately placed in the distribution chain in readily accessible locations. Before an overload approaches the point of danger, the weak link breaks and protects the rest of the chain. There are two types of "weak link" in common use—fuses and circuit breakers. A fuse contains a compound with comparatively low melting point which actually destroys itself when overloaded. A circuit breaker is an automatic switch which opens and interrupts its electrical circuit when its temperature rise indicates an overload. Fuses, or at least the melting compound in the fuse, can be used only once and must be replaced after every overloaded condition. Circuit breakers can be manually restored to operating position. Of course, neither should the fuse be replaced nor the circuit breaker restored until the condition that caused the interruption in the first place has been located and corrected.

Circuit breakers are favored in present-day electrical construction, both residential and other, because they make it unnecessary to carry a stock on hand. They are also easier to work with, although fuses have one important technical advantage, of which the building planner should be aware. It sometimes happens that an accident occurs which produces an enormous surge of electrical power in the lines. This may be caused by lightning striking the lines, by two major conductors touching each other as the result of a storm, or of insulation wearing through. The magnitude of the current in such an event may be so great and the time in which it builds up so unimaginably quick that the "switching" action of a circuit breaker is overwhelmed, and before the breaker can open its parts melt together to form a channel through which the current continues to pass until something else melts that was not intended to and a fire results. Fuses can be constructed to operate under these major "short-circuit" load conditions; that is, to melt and vaporize as intended and not to melt into a mass that keeps the circuit intact. These are standard, readily obtainable fuses, and it is good practice to use them at the point at which service enters a building even if circuit breakers protect every point thereafter. The enormous overloads can come only from power company lines, and only the power company can tell the designer how much the worst surge of current from its equipment can possibly be. Fuses at the point at which that surge would enter the building are then selected to match the heaviest possible current.

The assumption in the preceding paragraph should be examined promptly; that is, that building electrical service comes from a power company, either publicly or privately owned and franchised to operate in a given area by the government's representatives. In the vast majority of cases this is true, but there are exceptions. Let us consider them.

TOTAL ENERGY PLANTS

A power company usually has an exclusive franchise for selling electricity in its area but it has no monopoly on the technology of generating its product. The developer of a thousand-unit tract housing site or of a huge highrise apartment-complex might find it feasible to build a generating plant for that project. To make such an owner-built generating station pay every possible bit of heat from the generator engines must be used for other purposes. In residential buildings the "other purposes" are heating and cooling of the spaces and heating of domestic water. The reclamation consists of passing the exhaust gases from the generator engines through heat exchangers, which may take the form of boilers, furnaces, or some combination of the two.

The more electricity generated at any time, the more hot gases discharged from the generator engines, and the more heat available for other uses. For residential work this offers certain problems because the maximum or minimum use of electrical power does not necessarily coincide with the greatest need for heating, cooling, or domestic hot water; for example, on a cold winter night the lowest outside temperatures often occur in the early morning hours when poeple are asleep; minimum electricity is required but enough heat should be supplied to obviate waking in frigid rooms. For this kind of contingency the owner-operated plant must be equipped with auxiliary fuel burners to help out when the generator exhaust gases are not sufficient to do the job.

The owner-operated generating plant is often called a "total energy" plant because it serves all the energy needs of the project. Needless to say, it represents a major investment and should never be undertaken without a painstaking comprehensive, and wise analysis of the economics involved.

PURCHASED ELECTRICITY

Most residential projects purchase electricity from franchised power companies. A discussion of the company's equipment which most impacts on the planner of a residential project requires, first, a brief semitechnical review of some simple electrical facts.

The measure of electricity we care about is power. Power lights the lights and drives the appliance motors. Power is measured in watts. Electric power is produced by the quantity of current flowing, measured in amperes, multiplied by the pressure that causes it to flow, measured in volts. Finally, resistance to electrical flow, discussed below, is measured in ohms. Now this is a simplified statement. Other factors enter, but these salient points are sufficient for our purposes.

It follows that for a given quantity of power the larger the pressure (voltage), the smaller the current (amperes). It is not difficult to see that the size of electric conductors is determined chiefly by the current flow (amperes). It is like water pipe in this respect. The size of the water pipe is measured by the maximum volume of water expected to flow at any time, and the water pressure determines the thickness of the pipe wall. Similarly, electrical pressure determines certain properties of the material to withstand the pressure, whereas the size of the conductor depends on the current flow. There is a second factor as well. As in water, there is electrical friction or resistance to flow. The longer the conductor, the greater the friction; therefore in long distances of conductor run it is necessary to increase the size in order to reduce total friction.

An electric power company transmits large quantities of power over long distances. In order to keep the transmission cables to a reasonable size and cost, the transmission voltages range from 2400 volts for overhead lines in residential areas to as much as 300,000 volts in cross-country major lines. Voltages entering our homes must be at a level that is not lethal in the event of accident. Early in the age of electricity it was found that the maximum pressure at which shocks would be only unpleasant but seldom worse than that is 100 to 150 volts. For standardization electric lights and small motors have consequently been made to operate at approximately 115 volts in some parts of the world and 230 volts in others. Most of the current available in places of habitation today is at one of those voltages. As explained later, the 230-volt systems usually expose occupants to no more than 115-volt shocks.

So we have thousands of volts in the power lines outside and one or two hundred volts inside our dwellings. The device that makes the reduction is called a transformer. The power company generally furnishes the transformer or transformers for a residential project. If the power transmission cables run overhead on poles, it is likely that the transformers will be pole-mounted as well, which is both unsightly and unwelcome. Many power company distribution systems have gone underground in recent years, and even when most of the mains are overhead, it is often possible to pay a fairly modest premium to have them run underground in a residential property. Power-company requirements that transformers fed by underground mains be in underground vaults outside or inside the buildings served inhibited the development of underground service for years. The vaults were large and expensive to construct outside or wasteful of space inside. Recent improvements in transformer design have seen the development of compact, steel-housed units which are safe to mount on small protective concrete pads at ground level and whose size is such that the transformers can often be hidden by bushes and other plantings in a way that will make them quite inconspicuous. They must, of course, be accessible. For large projects it is often economical to scatter several rather small units in key locations rather than to concentrate the service in one place. In very large highrise apartment buildings in crowded city areas an underground or in-building vault may still be necessary.

The use of transformers is not restricted to electric company installations. In total energy plants it is usually practical to generate and distribute at voltages higher than the 120 volts finally utilized; 480 volts is common for this purpose. Standard commercial motors built for this voltage are fed directly by service at that level, and the power needed for lighting and small appliances is taken from small transformers distributed throughout the buildings.

This practice is also widespread in utility-company-served highrise buildings in which low voltages would require large distributing conductors. Power is taken from the company transformers at 480 volts and used and transformed as described above.

Our discussion of electrical systems centers on alternating current (ac) only. The only present-day use of direct current (dc) is for speed and smooth acceleration control of high-grade elevators, for which the direct current is generated within the elevator equipment itself, using ac power from the building service.

ELECTRICAL PROVISIONS

Practice and code requirements governing electrical construction are aimed at safety against shocks suffered by contact with current carriers and safety against fires, a danger already discussed in the use of electricity. First, of course, is that conductors must be insulated. Most conductors in residential work are cables, either copper or aluminum, insulated with a tightly adhering nonconducting covering based on plastic or rubber material. For large scale distribution, particularly in highrise buildings, the major carriers may be copper or aluminum bus bars, insulated by sheet-steel housing. The housing and bus-bar assembly is called a bus duct. Copper conductors have a higher current-carrying capacity per unit of area than aluminum and maintain better and tighter connections than aluminum conductors. Nevertheless, aluminum is becoming more widely used because of the higher cost and growing scarcity of copper. Aluminum is finding favor in bus-duct applications and in the larger sizes of wire conductors rated above 40 amperes. Most of the wiring in residences is in smaller conductors, rated at 20 or 15 amperes, and in these sizes copper is still the favorite because it holds the pressure of screw-type connections better than aluminum.

Insulated wires are further protected against rubbing or other damage to the extent that the insulation could be broken. Electrical codes are unanimous in their regulation of this protection for service conductors in garages, basements, on the outside of buildings, or in similar exposed areas. These conductors are enclosed in steel or aluminum pipe called conduit, which differs from pipe used for most other mechanical services in its malleability, and can be easily and neatly bent on location into turns and offsets required to clear obstructions. Because of its light weight and consequent ease of handling, aluminum conduit is gaining great favor, especially in the larger sizes. One caution must be observed, however. Aluminum conduit should never be imbedded in concrete because a reaction set up while the concrete is setting causes it to deteriorate.

Electrical codes differ regarding the protection of wires other than service conductors in residential work. Some codes require that all wires be in conduit. Other codes permit the use of flexible cable consisting of two or more insulated conductors with an outer sheath of moisture-resistant, flame-retardant nonmetallic material. This cable is not to be embedded in masonry or slabs, but it can be run through hollow construction, such as stud walls or partitions, at much lower overall cost than conduit and wire. Armored cable, in which the insulated conductors are run in a flexible metallic sheath rather than the nonmetallic cover, is also available, but it is more expensive. If the governing code allows conduit to be omitted, the nonmetallic sheath is favored due to its lower cost and greater flexibility.

A word must be inserted here about grounding electrical systems. If the insulation on a wire in a lamp or appliance rubs through or if a defect develops in a terminal connection, ''leakage'' of current will result. This condition may go undetected until someone touches the lamp or appliance, and at the same time has contact with a radiator or plumbing fixture. The current will then pass through the body of the toucher (a shocking experience) and the heating or plumbing system all the way to the point at which the water service pipe enters the building before running to earth. In this way the leakage will have been ''grounded'' to the detriment of the intervening body. To avoid this hazard, which can be lethal or merely annoying, electrical systems are artificially grounded, and leaking currents can take a route other than the human body to dissipate itself. Grounding consists of providing a path from the farthest end of the system to the ground by way of the water service pipe or, if that is inconvenient, through copper rods driven 10 ft or so into the earth. The terminal grounding connection is made right at the entering electrical service equipment to water main or ground rods. From the ends of the electrical system to the service equipment the path is kept continuous by uninterrupted conducting metal. If the entire system is run in conduit or in armored cable, the conduit pipe or metal armor sleeve will serve as a satisfactory grounding conductor, provided that connections are made and kept tight throughout. If nonmetallic sheathed cable is used, an extra conductor must be run inside the sheath, to serve as the continuous grounding conductor. Even so, this installation is lower in cost than conduit or armored cable.

In addition to insulation, wire protection, and grounding, the chief safety device in wiring practice is the electric box. The final connections to every lighting fixture and every receptacle or other convenience device must be protected in a sturdy box, usually of steel rustproof construction. The box has five solid faces, but the sixth is open to permit access to the wiring connections. The open side is ultimately covered with a finished plate which faces the living area. Some or all of the five sides are punched with easily detached caps called knockouts to provide passage for incoming and outgoing conductors. The size and depth of the box are determined by the number of conductors entering it.

Boxes mounted in masonry require that it be cut out to accommodate them unless the wall is finished with furring strips and plaster or wallboard. The furring should be designed to allow for the depth of the boxes, thus avoiding the expense of cutting the masonry. Boxes mounted in concrete columns or slabs must be set in the forms and cast into the concrete. They must also be of heavier construction suitable for that service.

Wherever possible, wires should be run without breaks between their point of origin and the box in which they terminate. When the length is so great that this cannot be done and the wires must be extended by splicing, a box must be provided where the splice is made.

Unflagging care must be used in mounting boxes straight and true and the wall opening must be large enough only to accommodate the box. Boxes on opposite sides of the same wall should be at least 6 in. apart, measured along the wall length, if the wall is in a single residence, 12 in. if it separates two dwellings. The penalties for failure to observe these precepts are the ugly appearance of crooked cover plates, dirt streaks set up by air currents from loose-fitting openings, and sound transmission from room to room or, even worse, apartment to apartment.

Returning for a moment to the high quality residence of the twenties, whose electrical failings led off this section, we would find one element of electrical construction more strongly represented than in present-day practice. There would probably be ceiling lights in each bedroom and bathroom, ceiling fixtures and bracket lights in the living room, and an imposing chandelier in the dining room. Taste 50 years later favors individual selection in lighting by much greater use of floor and table lamps. There will still be a ceiling light in the dining area and kitchen, inside each entrance, and in every major closet. Unless the bathroom is quite large, a light over or flanking the mirror will meet the need. A light directly above the kitchen sink often supplements the kitchen ceiling light. Utility rooms, garages, basements, and hallways must have service lights. Balconies, outside entrances, public areas, and walkways all require lighting consonant with their uses and with the general tone of the environment.

It is often preferable that the builder provide light outlet boxes and leave the selection and purchase of the fixtures to the occupants. If this meets renter or buyer resistance, a reasonable allowance can be made for their cost, beyond which the occupants will pay for their own taste. Even when this option is elected, the designer and builder should retain control of exterior entrance and balcony lighting and of all the other exterior fixtures that affect the visual aspect of the buildings.

All lights should be operated by switches located at the door to each room. This may sound like an obvious statement, but sometimes cost corners are cut by using pull-chain switches for closet lights, a nuisance in all respects, and occupants are much better served by door switches, which turn on the light whenever the door is opened. Another convenience to be commended is the installation of multiple switches for rooms in which there is more than one entrance.

The paucity of electrical outlets in our home of the twenties has been corrected by modern codes. The old order of only one or two outlets in a room gave rise to the "octopus" effect of plugs on adapters connected to those outlets and spawning a growth of cords draped around the room, to be tripped over, to be subject to insulation damage, and to be a general nuisance. The new codes require receptacle boxes at frequent intervals, usually no farther apart than 12 ft measured on the room's perimeter, thus leaving no more than 6 ft to reach any point with a cord. The general thrust is to have unused receptacles rather than a lot of cords.

The receptacles themselves are familiar. Despite the comparatively large number required by present-day codes, each almost always has two distinct points of attachment and cost no more than single outlets. All receptacles must be the grounded type identifiable by the small third opening, centered between and slightly set off from the two prong openings.

In rooms that are not equipped with fixed ceiling or bracket lighting fixtures at least one receptacle must be switched from the door to permit safe entrance in the dark. It behooves the occupant to connect a lamp to a switched outlet and it is likewise incumbent on the designer and builder to switch an outlet to which a lamp will logically be connected. Sometimes only half a duplex receptacle is switched to permit a clock or other device requiring constant power to be connected to the other half.

Receptacles, like switches, should be mounted at a convenient height for normal use. Sometimes they are set into the base of the wall to make them as inconspicuous as possible, but this necessitates cutting the trim. They are usually mounted 8 to 12 in. above the floor. However, there are at least two important exceptions to this practice. In housing for the elderly receptacles are mounted at twice that height to minimize stooping, and wherever there is baseboard heating they should be carefully located, of course, to avoid placement behind the heating element. In addition to that obvious precaution, they should also be placed so that cords will not come in contact with the convectors, the heat of which will dry out and embrittle the insulation.

DISTRIBUTION AND SERVICE

Some discussion is needed of electrical distribution in residential buildings, not in the way of a treatise, but to clarify space and access requirements for this vital facet of building construction. First, electrical distribution shows much of the treelike pattern already alluded to in water distribution. The main trunk is the incoming service, large and strong enough to support and nourish all its branches, but not so big as all of them added together. What should its size be?

Sizing the service required in a factory is easy. Add the requirements of all the motors that will be running at the same time, the lights that will be in use, plus any special electrical processes known in advance, put in a safety factor for the new and unforeseen, and there you have it. A residence is another matter. How many lights and appliances will be in use at one time? Will a load be plugged into every receptacle, all going merrily or madly at once? Is there an electric range and, if so, will it ever be in use when the air conditioner is turned on (the answer is yes)? Even more difficult, if a hundred identical residences are connected to the same service, must it be a hundred times as large as the service to one residence (the answer is no)?

The best answer to these questions lies in experience. Over the years experience has been codified into minimum standards published for virtually all localities. This is not to say that an experienced designer cannot select larger service and distribution sizes than the code standards. Codes are based on a vast storehouse of records and observations and incorporate more than adequate safety factors to minimize the likelihood of a service being undersized. Therefore their minimum standards are usually selected as actual service sizes.

Take the service selection for a typical residence from a typical electrical code (the National Electrical Code, published by the National Fire Protection Association of the United States and widely used throughout the States). First a little about voltage. It was stated earlier that a common domestic pressure is 115 volts. The most economical method of providing this voltage is by three conductors, two of which are traced all the way back to the electrical generator, and the third is grounded in the earth. The electrical pressure, or voltage, between the two "live" conductors is 230 volts. By a phenomenon whose explanation is beyond the scope of this discussion the voltage between either of the live wires and the grounded, wire is exactly half that, or 115 volts. This procedure is relatively safe because accidental contact between a person and the electrical system will almost always involve one wire, one loose connection, or one side of a receptacle, and the worst shock that a person can get is by acting to ground that one live wire. That puts 115 volts through the body. The only way the much more dangerous 230 volts can be experienced occurs when the victim deliberately makes himself a conductor between the two live wires. With this in mind, choose the service size for a 2500 ft^2 residence from the National Electrical Code.

ESTIMATED LOAD	
2500 ft @ 3 W/sf	7,500 W
Two kitchen appliance circuits @ 1500 W each	3,000
	10,500 W
Actual use estimate:	
First 3000 W @ 100% use	3,000 W
Remaining 7500 W @ 35% use	2,625
FIXED LOAD	
Electric range, total capacity, 12,000 W; maximum use predicted at any moment	8,000 W
Electric clothes dryer	4,600
Electric heat, 25,000 W	
Air conditioning, 15,000 W	
Control these appliances so that they cannot operate simultaneously; use the larger figure only	25,000
Total load	43,225 W

Harking back to the earlier formula that volts times amperes equals watts, we find our service size in amperes:

$$\text{Amperes} + \frac{\text{watts}}{\text{volts}} = \frac{43{,}225}{230} = 188 \text{ amperes.}$$

In a final bow to conservatism and safety in choosing a service, the code says that no service switch may be loaded to more that 80% of its rated capacity. In our example that means that the switch size would be 188 ÷ 0.80, or 235 amperes. Unfortunately, there is no commercially made switch rated between 200 and 400 amperes, and we should have to choose a 400-ampere switch, protected by 250-ampere fuses, for that is the nearest size above our 235-ampere calculation. The service conductors would accordingly be sized for 250 amperes.

The service size for a large building or complex follows the same pattern, with appropriate variations. The "use estimate" factor, which simply reflects the expectation that everything will not be running at once, becomes lower the more residents served. The electrical loads for motor-driven elevators, pumps, ventilating fans, and cooling towers must be added, together with public corridor, lobby, and outdoor lighting. The service voltage may well be 460 instead of 230, and the service will undoubtedly be "three phase" instead of the "single phase" we have used in the example without talking about it. Use of three-phase current is much more economical in service size and in any event is virtually mandatory for large motors. To complete the picture let us say that in the final ampere calculation of three-phase service the voltage in the denominator is multiplied by 1.732. Therefore, if our residence in the example were operated with three-phase 230-volt service, the calculation would have read

$$\text{amperes} = \frac{43{,}225}{230 \times 1.732} = 109 \text{ amperes}$$

which requires a 200-ampere switch only. However, technical complications dictate that a single-residence service will usually be single-phase. This follows through in multiple-residence buildings, in which the total service is three-phase but the branch service to each dwelling is still single-phase. The various dwelling services are balanced among the three available phases.

Now we know the size of the tree trunk. We have, incidentally, already mentioned that every service entering a building must have a main switch (or a group of switches totaling at least the calculated amperes) where the service conductors immediately enter the building. The remaining distribution consists of filling in the rest of the tree. In a residence of modest size there may be only a few branches.

For safety and convenience outlets are combined in groups called branch circuits, fed by a pair of conductors and protected by a single circuit breaker or fuse. The groups are arranged so that no circuit is expected to carry more than 1400 watts, at worst loading conditions. A moment's reflection shows that this is a respectable load. A television set pulling 550 watts, a 300-watt lamp, and five 100-watt lamps can live happily on one circuit. On the other hand, a typical room air conditioner at 1300 watts must have a circuit of its own, and a large air conditioner, pulling 2100 watts, needs a special oversized circuit breaker and larger wires to suit.

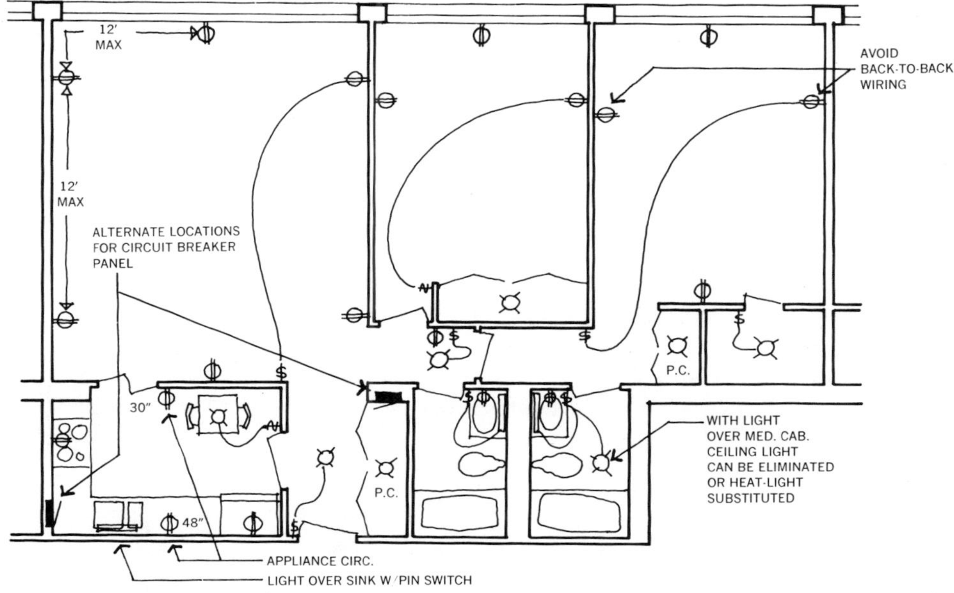

TYPICAL APARTMENT LIGHTING AND WIRING

All these circuits with their attendant circuit breakers are brought together in a distribution panel, which is just an oversized electrical box containing the necessary bus bars, circuit breakers, and wire connection terminals in a neat, easily serviceable arrangement. In a residence of moderate size the box may contain the main service switch as well. The entire distribution center is in one place, where the electric service enters the dwelling; the main switch and the circuits for lights, receptacles, kitchen appliances, air conditioners, electric range, clothes dryer, and electric heat. The total may vary from four circuits in an apartment for the elderly to 24 in a large house. It may be convenient and economical to divide the circuits into two or more small distribution panels, one perhaps to serve the bedroom wing and another, the living area. The main switch feeds a main distribution panel adjacent to or combined with it. The main distribution panel, in this example, contains two circuit breakers large enough to protect the wires called feeders, and has a capacity large enough to serve the distribution panels. The panels themselves are mounted in inconspicuous but readily accessible locations and are recessed in hollow partitions in order to conceal the conduits or sheathed cable leading to and from them. Panel boxes have a depth of about 4 in. and the thickness of the partition must be made to cover them completely, leaving only their fronts accessible and visible. See Fig. 132 for a typical apartment arrangement.

On a larger scale this kind of division of distribution serves highrise buildings as well. The details differ but the pattern remains. There is the incoming service from the transformers and one or more service switches. The main distribution panel, which contains breakers or fused switches for large pump and fan motors, public lighting, elevators, and bus duct risers which in turn feed the apartments, now becomes quite large. The main distribution panel may feed, in addition to the bus duct risers, subdistribution panels scattered through the building. They, in turn, serve the various public motor and lighting loads.

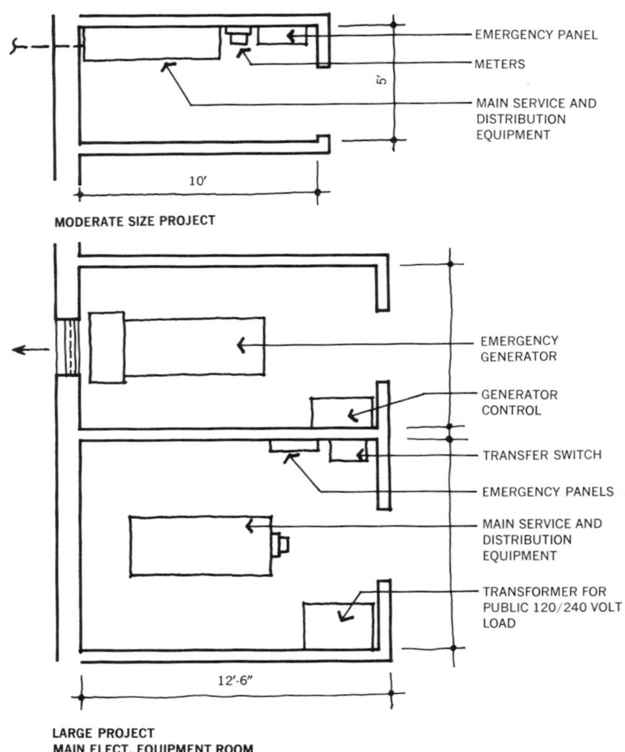

LARGE PROJECT
MAIN ELECT. EQUIPMENT ROOM

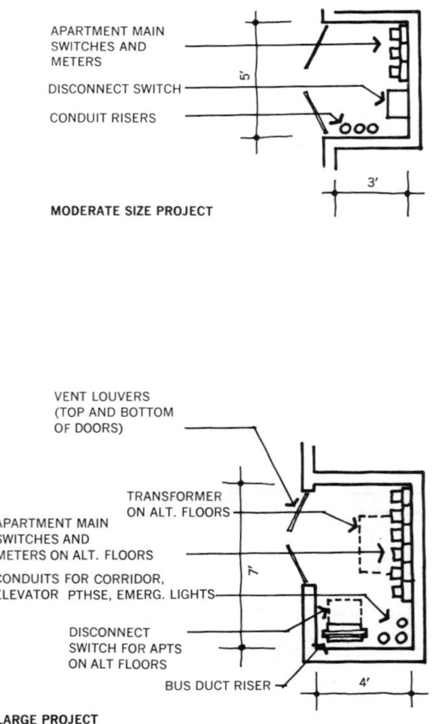

LARGE PROJECT
ELECT. CLOSET ON TYP. FLOORS

Arrangement of service to the individual residences in multistory buildings depends on the aspect of the building. Up to six stories it is often found economical to feed tiers of apartments with a vertical distribution pattern. Each apartment's distribution panel is located in a closet, kitchen, or passageway, one above the other. The lower panels are built to permit the feeders for the upper apartments to pass directly through. There are as many conduit risers as there are apartments.

In taller buildings a more economical solution relates to a single-bus-duct riser which passes through an electrical closet off the public corridor on every floor. In the buildings that are very large in area as well as tall, there may be more than one bus riser, each serving 8 to 12 apartments per floor, this requiring as many electric closets as there are risers. In buildings that combine separate apartment towers in one structure, it is impossible to reach all public corridors from one bank of elevators, and a riser is required for each tower, even though it may serve only one or two apartments per floor. In such cases, depending on the total load size, there may be a cost advantage in choosing wire in conduit rather than bus duct. Electrical closet arrangements have numerous possibilities. In general, the elements included are the riser, a submain switch or circuit breaker for the feeder which, tapped off the riser, serves the apartments on a given level, and an apartment main switch to protect each apartment feeder. The apartment feeders are concealed in the construction, from the electrical closet to the apartment circuit breaker panels. One closet arrangement finds all of these elements on each floor. In a building with 460-volt distribution, transformers are needed for the apartment loads. Space for the transformers can often best be provided by alternating them with the apartment main switch assemblies. Thus, on the second, fourth, sixth, and all even-numbered floors transformers large enough to serve every two floors may be mounted in the electrical closets. Correspondingly, on the third, fifth, seventh, and all odd-numbered floors assemblies of main switches will be located to serve the apartments on the two floors. Other arrangements are feasible, depending on the number of apartments, closet sizes, and similar factors. In some electrically heated buildings the main risers carry as many as 12,000 volts. These and the accompanying transformers will not be housed in the same closets as the apartment switches because of the hazard of the high voltages but rather in an adjoining locked closet, to which only authorized personnel has access.

In the descriptions of distribution systems no mention has yet been made of measuring the quantity of electricity used by the occupants. That may or may not be necessary.

If the project produces its own electricity and charges each occupant for its use or if it is served by a power company and residents pay the project owner or the power company for the amount consumed, the distribution system must include a meter for each dwelling. The meters are usually mounted in factory-fabricated assemblies along with the apartment main switches and require little, if any, more space than the main switch assemblies. Public light and power must be separately metered, generally at the main distribution center, where public and residential services are separated. If current is to be resold to the occupants, the main meter will measure the entire input, and the difference between this total and the consumption in all the individual dwelling units is the public use. If the project is a condominium or cooperative, the cost of public electricity will be shared by agreement.

The computation of electrical charges can be a most interesting task. It is possible that the dawning era of energy restrictions will change the practice, but until now it has been accepted that the large users pay lower average rates. This encourages use and, in a sense, makes the small user the subsidizer of the large. However, it is not all gravy for the latter, for his rate includes not only the direct cost of the energy used but another factor called ''demand charge,'' which reflects peak usage. Its philosophic base is that the power company must provide enough plant capacity to serve this maximum load, even if it is seldom reached.

Special rates have been offered by electric companies to promote and encourage electric heating, which often requires separate meters, and appreciable additional initial cost of installation. Before that extra cost is undertaken the load should be thoroughly analyzed. It may be that another rate, even without the bonus for heating, may actually be cheaper, in which case use it!

EMERGENCY LIGHT AND POWER

In the event of failure of electric power occupants of one or two-story buildings will be inconvenienced. People living above the second floor of midrise buildings will be seriously inconvenienced, and anyone living above the fourth-floor level of a highrise will be threatened. If the power interruption is due to fire, the two last categories of occupants will be *seriously* endangered.

To lessen the peril, most codes require at least minimal emergency lighting in mid- and highrise residences. This lighting is supposed to remain on during service failure and thus must be independent of the other services. Minimum emergency lighting usually includes illuminated signs clearly marking stairways, visible from all parts of the public corridors, and exit signs on the ground level from the stairways to the outside. It further includes enough lights in the public corridors and stairwells to enable people to use them safely when all other light has failed.

Many codes have permitted the use of separate services on the same electric power company lines that provide the main service on the theory that major problems will occur within the building confines and not in the electric company's system. The companies have set up admirable networks for distribution, and failure in one part of a system will often be corrected almost immediatley by transferring the load to another. That word ''often'' is looming larger and larger as complexity of systems increases and perhaps quality of maintenance and workmanship in the manufacture of components deteriorates. Whatever the reason, power failures seem to be more and more frequent, without any noticeable likelihood of a reversal of this trend. What that means, of course, is that an electrical outage in the main service of a project, if it stems from a larger failure in the power company network, will also knock out the emergency service derived from the same lines.

One cure for that problem is in the use of phosphorescent lights, which continue to glow for a time after the electric lamp has failed. This is useful for exit signs, whose glow in the dark acts as a guide to stair doors and outside exits and lasts long enough to permit evacuation of almost any building. The intensity of glow is faint, however, not nearly enough for illumination of halls and stairs, a function of emergency lights.

So an answer must be found for emergency lighting needs. One is available in the form of the battery-switch lamp pack. A storage battery is connected to the regular building source of power by a standard receptacle. This power keeps the battery charged and also registers at the ''brain'' of the pack. If the regular power source is interrupted for any reason, the brains operates a switch in the assembly, which turns on a low-wattage, high-intensity lamp (or lamps) that will illuminate a considerable stretch of corridor or stairway—that is, enough to permit safe passage of personnel even under panic conditions. For the sake of appearance and avoidance of the possibility of vandalism the packs may be remote from the lamps, locked in a closet or behind a locked panel. The batteries do wear out in time, with or without use, and must be checked and replaced periodically. There are three common types of battery available, and, needless to say, the lowest cost unit lasts the shortest time. The best batteries are expected to last 8 to 10 years between replacements.

Exit signs and emergency lights are not the only potential needs in the event of power failure. Fire-alarm systems and firemen's communication systems, discussed later, should be powered at all times. Power failures may not go back to the supplying utility. There may be a burnout in a transformer that supplies all or an important part of a project's service. Replacement of a transformer may take many days. If this should happen in winter in a cold climate (and it usually does!), must the residents move out and all the water in the pipes be drained to prevent them from freezing? More and more pressure is being exerted to provide emergency generating plants at least for major housing projects. If the project has its own total energy generating station, it would be a small auxiliary plant. When power is purchased from an electric utility company, the plant would be independent and project operated, fueled by gas, gasoline, or Diesel oil, the latter two safely stored on the premises. Local code requirements must be ascertained before a fuel is selected. Such a plant would be sized to perform some or all of the following functions:

1. Operate exit signs.
2. Operate emergency lights.
3. Operate one domestic water pressure pump.
4. Operate a fire pump or pumps.
5. Operate one or more boilers and heating pumps.
6. Provide power for at least one elevator. This has several values:
   a. An elevator is available for firemen if the interruption is caused by fire.
   b. An elevator is available for upper floor residents if the outage is of long duration.
   c. If a sudden power failure leaves one or more elevators stranded between floors, there will be power to move them, one at a time, to a floor landing, where the occupants can be taken off.
7. Operate a fire alarm system.
8. Operate communication systems for firemen, from elevators, and for residents in general (especially in housing for the elderly).

Items 7 and 8 can be served by their own storage battery systems if there is no emergency generator or if it is deemed preferable to separate them from the emergency generating system.

Emergency generators sufficient to these needs are available commercially. They require space, ventilation, and sometimes water for cooling and should be tested regularly under load to ensure their readiness at all times. They are expensive and noisy, but as more and more people move to tall buildings and more ugly incidents are recorded there is less excuse to build without this kind of vital precaution for the safety and well-being of the occupants.

AUXILIARY ELECTRICAL SYSTEMS

Light and power are the primary electrical systems. Ancillary systems are required for safety, security, communication, and pleasure. The explosive advance in electronic technology by which today's marvels are superseded by tomorrow's miracles makes the listing of techniques or facilities out-of-date before a manuscript can go to press. Thus, much of the discussion of security and communications is of a general nature that suggests the kinds of information that might be transmitted without detailing all the potentialities.

SAFETY

Structural design and site planning address themselves to the safety of residents against such natural hazards as earthquakes, high winds, and floods. Safety in the electrical context protects against fire or smoke inhalation, which can be as lethal as fire. The subject was opened in the discussion of fire protection, which has to do with extinguishing fires underway. Here we consider methods by which fire-fighting personnel and building occupants can be informed of danger in its early stages. The first order of business, of course, is to determine the minimum requirements of governing codes. Beyond that base, additional precautions may be deemed well worth their cost.

1. FIRE ALARM SYSTEMS

a. The alarm can be transmitted in one or more ways:

By direct electrical connection to the local fire department, by all odds the best, applicable only when the department has the electronic gear necessary to receive and identify the signals.

By connection to an independent security agency, which will relay the message to the fire department.

By an audible alarm in a location in the building that is within earshot at all times.

By an audible alarm outside the buiding.

By a general alarm audible inside the building. A drawback is the possibility of disturbing residents (possibly to the point of panic) for a minor incident in the middle of the night. A two-stage alarm, first sounding a limited warning and only after sufficient time for exploration going to a general alarm, is sometimes a good answer to that problem.

By a zoned alarm, audible only in the threatened area.

b. The alarm can be initiated by various agents:

By a water flow alarm. If an automatic sprinkler goes off anywhere in the building or if someone uses a standpipe hose, the alarm is energized.

By a smoke detector. This is a sensitive electronic device which detects smoke of greater intensity than that caused by a cigar or pipe and often before smoldering rags or paper burst into flame will send out a warning of impending danger. Detectors can be placed in unattended areas like equipment rooms, electrical closets, storage rooms, and stairways. One or more detectors can also be placed in every residence.

By a heat detector. Operating like smoke detectors, these devices send out signals in the event of abnormal temperatures or of a sudden abnormal rise in temperature, which will be picked up before it reaches a dangerous level. These detectors are less sensitive then smoke detectors.

By manual "pull" stations, the familiar fire alarm boxes mounted in public exits. Their use with a general or local alarm system should by viewed with caution. They offer too tempting an outlet for creating a nuisance.

Signal systems should always contain a trouble circuit, which automatically sends out a special trouble signal, distinguishable from an alarm signal, when any break or other electrical interruption occurs anywhere in the system. In buildings of any great size or complexity the signal system should also contain an annunciator board, which will identify the area from which the signal emanates. Alarm systems must always be powered by the best in emergency circuitry in order to function under any circumstances.

2. FIREMEN'S SAFETY SYSTEM.

   In highrise buildings in particular an auxiliary voice communication system physically parallel to the standpipe water installation enables firemen to communicate from various levels of the building. This system must extend to the fire department's Siamese connection on the outside.

3. OCCUPANTS DISABILITY.

   A pushbutton system, by which occupants of a multiresidential project can signal for help when illness or other incapacity strikes, is a valuable adjunct particularly in housing for the elderly. It is vital that the signal be transmitted to an annunciator board that gives both audible and visual notice monitored at all times. Signal buttons which will register on the annunciator board should be located in each bathroom and each bedroom. This system is valuable in multidwelling buildings and in single-dwelling tract-type housing.

4. ELEVATOR TROUBLE.

   In the event of elevator failure, the elevator installation includes an emergency button that sounds an alarm bell in the building. In addition, each elevator cab should carry a telephone on a special line. Occupants in a stalled elevator may tend to panic, and a reassuring voice that will give instructions of procedure and reports of repair progress can ward off serious consequences.

SECURITY

In a perfect world doors would serve only to keep the weather out. In our much less than perfect society not even door and window locks are enough to make us feel safe, and we are forced to go to electric and electronic systems of varying sophistication to help protect our homes and persons.

1. DOOR SIGNAL AND RELEASE SYSTEMS

   a. Pushbutton and buzzer, bell or chimes. The button is located at the front and rear doors. The rear signal is sometimes omitted in multiple-occupancy buildings, in which the buttons are grouped in a lobby inside the entrance and usually require an accompanying directory for identification. Often the buttons and directory are combined with mailboxes, an assembly usually purchased and installed by the electrical contractor.

   b. In multiple residences there will be an independent voice communication system in conjunction with the signal system to permit an occupant to identify the button pusher. Each occupant controls a release button in conjunction with the speaker, which opens the main door if the identification is satisfactory. If a building has 24-hour service, the door release is unnecessary, and the signal and voice communication are taken care of by the doorman.

   c. Television surveillance of the entrance areas on a closed circuit has proved to be a valuable security tool. A specific channel is set aside which permits each occupant and/or the building staff to check the identity of everyone who signals. It may also give the building manager an opportunity to monitor the entrance areas against loiterers.

d. Electronic burglar alarm systems further protect residents. Windows and doors are protected by wiring, such that forcible entry sends a signal to a central watch station or trips an audible alarm. In highrise buildings, in which the only point of entry to an apartment is the door to the corridor, the system can be arranged so that the resident sets a key when leaving. If the door is subsequently opened in any unauthorized manner, an alarm sounds and an annunciator shows at a central watch point, usually in the building. In all burglar alarm systems it is important that the occupant be taught to ''unset'' the alarm on returning home to avoid sending out signals when someone admits a neighbor or opens a window for air.

COMMUNICATIONS

1. First in electronic communications is the telephone. Telephone companies, operating as a franchised public utility, usually provide the instruments and the cable that connects them to the central system. In single residences of days gone by all the cable ran exposed along the basement ceiling, turning up into walls to reach the boxes that served the instruments. This method is still practiced in low-cost housing, but concealed conduit through which the cable can be pulled has become much more common, especially since basements have been eliminated in so many houses. The conduits from all telephone outlets are gathered together at a terminal cabinet or box in a closet or utility area, from which they are fed by the outside service cable. In multiple and highrise buildings, the arrangement is merely enlarged. A terminal cabinet feeds an entire building. Two to six apartments may be fed by a single cable in a riser conduit, which returns either directly to the terminal cabinet or to a central telephone major cable riser that leads from the terminal cabinet. The cabinets themselves are easy to locate because they

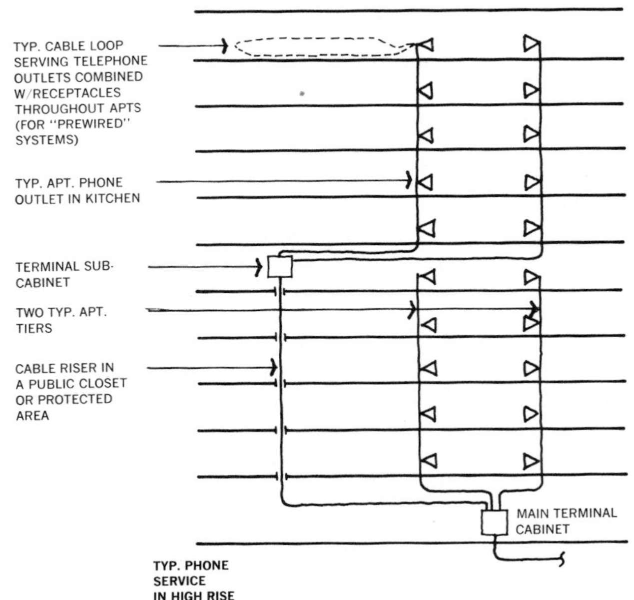

TYP. PHONE SERVICE IN HIGH RISE

are only about 4 in. deep. A cabinet of that depth, 2 ft wide by 4 ft high, will serve quite a large building. In concrete slab buildings a system of prewiring which has found favor eliminates the larger part of the conduit but conceals the cable. Cable is laid in the concrete forms, starting from a steel telephone box located as a rule in the apartment kitchen, and looped around the apartment to possible points of connection in boxes combined with electrical receptacles in most or all of the rooms. An entire loop is made back to the box in the kitchen. Therefore a single break in the cable which could occur while the concrete was poured would still leave both halves of the line alive. The advantage is in the large number of locations at which telephone extensions may be attached, depending on the resident's needs and furniture layout. This flexibility is gained at absolutely minimal cost, because the telephone company provides the cable and the boxes and the only cost to the building is the comparatively small labor charge to loop the cable around the forms.

2. Private voice communication systems can also be provided. Front and rear entrance talk-and-listen systems, already described can be extended so that residents can call the project's central office, the garage, the commissary, the swimming pool or gymnasium, or one another, if the system is extended to that degree. Called intercommunication, or "intercom," systems, they may be completely private or adjunctive to the outside telephone system. Many telephone companies make an earnest effort to sell these systems to housing developers because they are attractive rental or selling features. Obviously they must also be profitable to the company. A private system generally represents a substantially higher first cost and requires that the maintenance expense to be borne by the project, but unless the housing is designed with the idea of a quick sale in mind the greater investment and maintenance costs will be paid back in a few years by operating cost savings, especially if good equipment is selected and well installed.

3. A continually expanding field that embraces communications of a sort, along with safety and security, in an integrated package is the electronic marvel that gathers and disseminates data. The possibilities are many. A system may communicate the results of monitoring many factors of building operation, along with all the alarms for fire, smoke, personal distress, and security. What kinds of "factors of building operation"? Fuel and electrical consumption, temperatures of cooling water, outside temperatures, temperature of elevator motors and generators, temperatures of boiler flue gases, domestic water pressure, fire-pump operation, and timed operation of corridor supply and kitchen and toilet exhaust systems. The possibilities are as broad as the imagination. The data can be recorded, or it can be used to sound an alarm when some operation departs from the normal. Use of electricity can be automatically measured and invoiced for a large number of residents. The installation costs of these wonders fall as the techniques are improved and expanded, and the future probably offers developments we cannot even imagine at this time.

ENJOYMENT

Central systems for the improvement of radio and television signals are the principal electronic methods that enhance recreational facilities.

1. Underground cable companies, franchised as public utilities, serve buildings by bringing in a multitude of channels for commercial television, public and educational television, local and community programming, and FM and AM radio. The cable is carried through the buildings in a system of conduit risers (if preparations

are made when the building is planned) to feed boxes in all apartments. Occupants decide individually whether to tap the cable passing through their boxes and pay a fee if the decision is affirmative. Boxes are located at key places in each residence, one in the living room and at least one in the bedroom. If there are multiple bedrooms, boxes should be located in partitions between them, in order that one cable can serve two locations.

2. In areas in which cable utilities are not available, multistory buildings still provide central systems to eliminate an unsightly forest of television antennas on the roof. A single mast, designed to receive all locally available channels, serves a private cable which is distributed through the building in much the same way of the public cable. An electric power outlet from the building system, at 120 volts, is needed to energize the system. Often the building owner or a licensee will make this private service available for a fee. In other cases, a fee is charged for the initial connection to the private cable but no rent is levied thereafter.

3. The use of centrally distributed music in public areas of a residential project, such as the elevators, lobby, swimming pool, and commissary, must be listed under the heading of enjoyment for those who like it. To me it is a sour way to conclude the section on electrical installations because I hold strongly to the opinion that this is one of the minor curses of twentieth-century life. However, even the most unwilling member of the captive audience must acknowledge that this ''pleasure'' exists, and that it must be listed as available, either from a commercial source at a fee or over the private intercommunication system.

DESIGN METHODOLOGY 7

John Macsai

Although the technique of data gathering or programming and the familiarization with and sorting out all the components is an orderly process, putting it all together, the design phase, is hardly ever orderly.

The best program, the most thorough knowledge of components, will not ensure good design. Good architecture will depend on the designer's talent, his ability to respond to the challenge, and his unrelenting patient search for a solution. A multitude of avenues will have to be traveled and many will turn out to be dead-ends before the answer is found. The designer works simultaneously on many levels; he considers plan, structure, mechanical system, and exterior form, to mention only the main categories of his thought. These categories cross-influence one another; the limitations of one will open new options in the other and vice versa. Design is a complex process.

Design seems altogether too mysterious to be rationally analyzed and that is the stated purpose of this book. Design methodology is the rationalization of the design procedure. It does not eliminate the "mystery" that makes a building good architecture. On the contrary, the purpose is to cast light on the inherent possibilities of each housing type, therefore helping the "mystery" to happen.

The chapters in this section deal with the design methodology of housing types that are grouped under the headings of high-, mid-, and lowrise. There is no generally accepted definition of these categories. In this book lowrise is a walk-up without elevators (two to three stories, maximum four); midrise is defined as a building that uses hydraulic elevators and consequently is limited in height (four to six or seven stories); highrise starts when electric elevators must be substituted for the hydraulic and the maximum number of floors is limited only by current technology.

To develop the analysis from small toward large, from lowrise toward highrise, seems logical at first glance. A different approach was elected, however; highrise apartment buildings are discussed first. The highrise, because of its vertical repetitiveness, requires the strongest restraint and discipline; therefore it serves as an ideal introduction to design methodology by pointing the way from the most limited (highrise) toward the most permutable (lowrise) with an intermediate range (midrise) which can have the characteristics of both. Many issues and problems occur in all three categories. Because highrise is the first to be discussed, the issues already covered—to avoid repetition—are only alluded to under lowrise or midrise.

Each category is considered as a valid option to the solution of a housing problem. Currently fashionable social judgments are avoided as much as possible; for example, studies indicate that the highrise as a housing type is more of a problem creator than solver for low-income families. The studies deal with highrises built in the last 20 years, built without our present awareness of the need for "defensible space" so lucidly advocated by Oscar Newman. The fact is that these highrises, so justly criticized, were badly designed. Further, in most cases—howbeit well designed—they would have been doomed to fail, if we consider the crowding together of broken families with large numbers of children, with a minimum of economic and an even less than minimum of social assistance. In the belief that cures for our social ills can be found, rather than blaming them on highrises these housing types are discussed as valid options under the proper circumstances for all social groups.

HIGHRISE

The vertical repetitiveness of the highrise demands considerable design discipline, which means, naturally with exceptions, that all apartment floors are identical (typical) and that the mix of apartments on a typical floor reflects the total mix of the program.

Because it repeats so often, the shape of the typical floor has significant influence on cost. Exterior walls are expensive and every break in the floor configuration not only increases the perimeter of the building but multiplies this increase by the number of floors. Consequently the advantages gained from varied configuration should be carefully weighed against added cost.

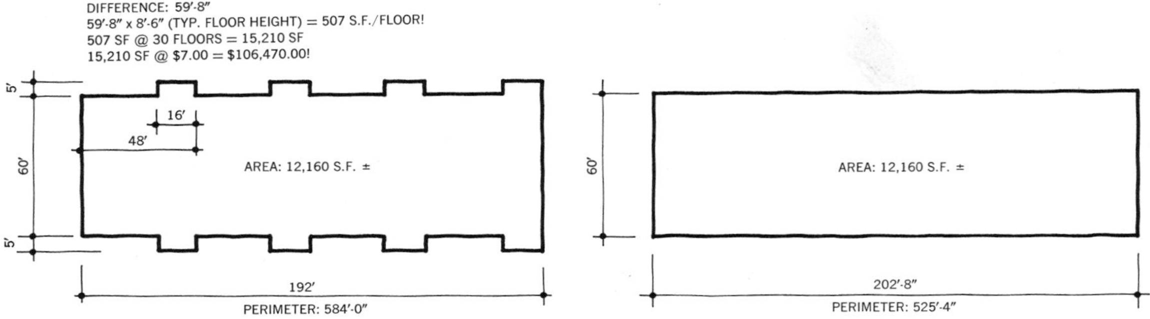

Not only is the shape of the typical floor significant economically but so is its size. This is especially true in relation to reinforced concrete framing which is the most commonly used structural system for highrise apartment buildings today. Because building codes require heavy fireproofing of the structural frame, concrete—particularly flat plate with randomly placed interior columns—has many advantages over steel and these have been discussed in detail in the structural chapters. Briefly, flat plate provides a ready ceiling surface, whereas steel construction, unless it is a combination of steel beams with concrete slabs, often requires suspended ceilings without any mechanical need for the space created by the suspension; floor thickness, less in concrete, results in a lower building, less exterior wall, and shorter stairs; random column spacing is adaptable to good apartment layout and liberates the plan from the restrictions of the column grid; columns and beams once poured are finished, whereas in steel they must be covered and fire protected. Because there are enough advantages to concrete framing to make it a prevalent construction type, the typical floor of a highrise should be such (or it should be subdividable into such areas) that it most efficiently utilizes the daily productive capacity of the concrete framing and pouring crew. Pouring sequence and "ideal" floor size, as described under structural framing, must be taken into account.

The maximum length and configuration of the typical floor is also influenced by the available construction technology (crane reach, material handling, and so on).

Current technology, together with the structural system, will have an effect on the building height as well. As the building gets taller and the distance between the ground and the top of the building increases, the longer it will take to transport workmen and materials and pump water. As the building becomes very tall, the more likely it is, depending on when construction started, that it will run into below-freezing weather and costly winter protection will be required.

The elevators are another factor that influences height. Sometimes it makes good economic sense to stay below the maximum height if an added floor or two would necessitate a more expensive elevator system or an additional elevator.

Smokeproof towers are also a factor. The building height or the number of floors at which code requires the introduction of smokeproof towers should be watched. Smokeproof towers mean added cost, nonutilized floor area, and larger, consequently harder to plan, stair shafts. If increasing the typical floor is possible on the site and will result in a building under the height necessitating smokeproof towers, much will be gained economically.

All the caveats about floor size and building height would indicate, paradoxically, that the higher the highrise, the costlier it becomes, or conversely, savings occur when the number of floors is smaller and the typical floor plan is larger because more apartments share the costly vertical elements such as stairs and elevators.

To these general rules must be added the efficiency ratio of typical floors which is also valid for all highrises with the exception of the exterior corridor types. The nonrental area of a typical floor is generally between 10 and 15% of the gross floor area. The lower this percentage, the more efficient the plan. When the total of nonrental spaces (public corridor, stairs, elevators, refuse chute, stack, electrical room, and corridor air supply ducts) is more than 15% of the gross floor area, not including balconies, the plan should be seriously re-examined!

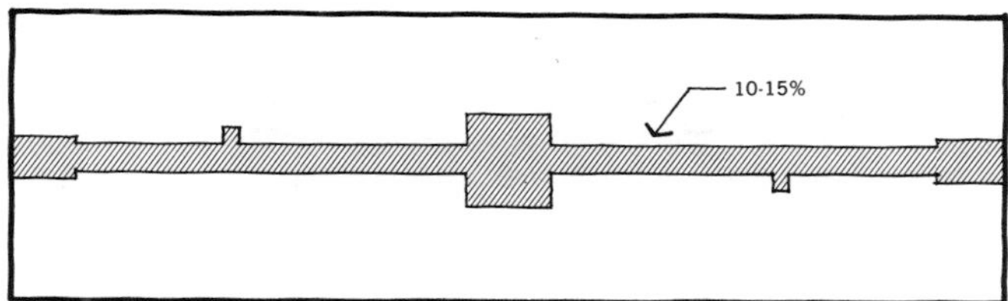

Knowing this efficiency ratio will help the designer to do some fast calculations before drawing a single line.

Example

THE CLIENTS MIX CALLS FOR

⅔ — 2 BR apartments @ 1200 sf
⅓ — 1 BR apartments @ 900 sf

THE SMALLEST GROUP THAT REFLECTS THIS RATIO

2 — 2 BR @ 1200 sf =	2400 sf
1 — 1 BR @ 900 sf =	900 sf
Total net	3300 sf
ADD FOR NONRENTAL	
13% of 3300 =	430 sf
Total	3730 sf

For concrete-pouring economy 3700 sf is obviously not a viable area. Double 3730, or 7460 sf, is better but still under the approximately 9000 sf ideal minimum. Triple 3730, or 11,190 sf, will suffice for concrete pouring, but one hopes for—if possible—an even-number multiplier. Therefore four times 3730, or 14,920 sf, appears to be ideal, and the typical floors would then have four 2 BR-1 BR groups, or 12 apartments per floor. This figure should be tested against a variety of criteria.

Zoning: Is 14,920 sf of ground coverage allowed? The total number of apartments permitted by zoning density should be divided by 12 to determine the number of floors needed; if this number is multiplied by 14,920 sf and the common area (lobby, recreation, and so on) are added to the result, is this above or below the total floor area permitted by zoning? *Site conditions*: 14,920 sf divided by the average apartment building width of 60 ft will result in a building 250 ft long; will this fit on the site with all the required setbacks? *Code:* Is 14,920 sf below the maximum permitted for the construction type already determined by the number of floors? Within allowed travel distances, will two exits be adequate? *Aesthetic:* What is the proportion of the volume, the length of which is 250 ft and the heights as calculated above? What is the impact of this volume on adjacent open space and buildings?

Problems of height, floor area, and floor efficiency are valid for every highrise. Beyond them, however, each building type has its own logic. Many approaches have been used to group highrise apartment buildings into prototypes. Perhaps the most universally accepted approach is the grouping by apartment access and vertical and horizontal distribution systems.

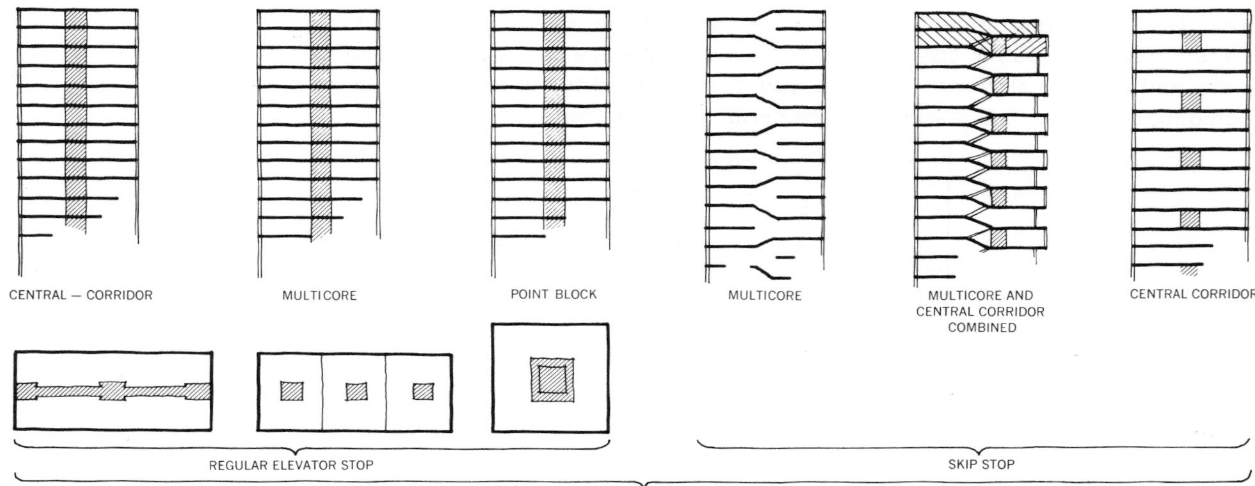

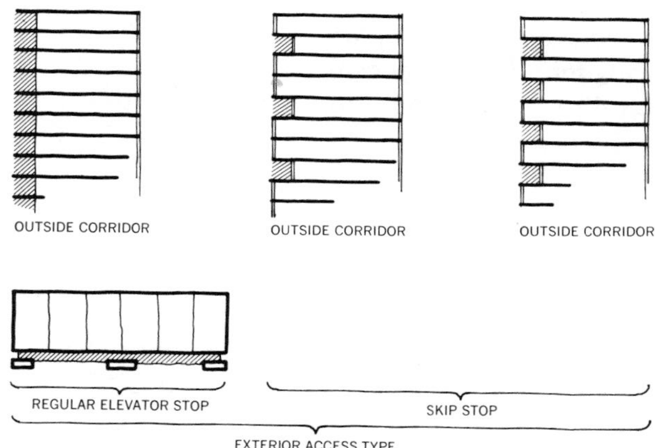

CENTRAL CORRIDOR SYSTEM

The central corridor system (also called "inner corridor" or "double-loaded corridor") is considered the most economical highrise apartment building **(1 to 15, 36 to 39).*** This is easy to understand when we consider that every square foot of public corridor serves two apartments instead of one, as in exterior corridors. It becomes even more obvious when we compare central corridor to point block. In the first maximum gross floor area is possible with a minimum number of stairs and elevators; in the second the floor area is limited by the core size. The comparison is even more favorable in the multicore type with its large number of elevators and stairs.

The economic advantage is not without concomitant problems. A central corridor system results in a long corridor which, unless broken up or daylighted if not at the elevators at least on the ends, can be barren and inhuman **(9, 11, 13, 14, 37** to **39).** Very long corridors are counterproductive as far as fostering a feeling of community or "knowing your neighbors." Surveillance, a deterrent to crime, is extremely difficult in long corridors.

When a preferred view occurs on one side of the building, almost half the apartments cannot enjoy it in a central corridor type. The situation is somewhat improved when the building parallels the view direction; an angled view is an acceptable substitute for a direct view and the living rooms could project out of the main volume to improve the angle.

When budget prohibits the use of air conditioning, the highly desirable cross ventilation becomes impossible in the central corridor building.

These disadvantages should always be kept in mind, and if they cannot be completely eliminated an attempt should be made to ameliorate them.

The central corridor building which is only two-directional (has solid end walls) grew out of tightly built-in urban conditions when the building was fitted between two adjacent structures. Its use on large sites in which such restraints do not exist is the result of structural considerations **(16, 21).** For many years it was common practice to utilize the end walls as wind-resisting shear walls that at best could be penetrated by small "punched" openings. It was found that these end shear walls are hard to form; consequently they are rather costly. The use of interior shear

* Boldface numbers in parentheses refer to the projects at the end of the book.

walls or shear cores and the increased use of scattered shear panels allows the designer to open up the end walls completely. The resulting four-directional central corridor building is the most common type today unless site conditions prevent its use.

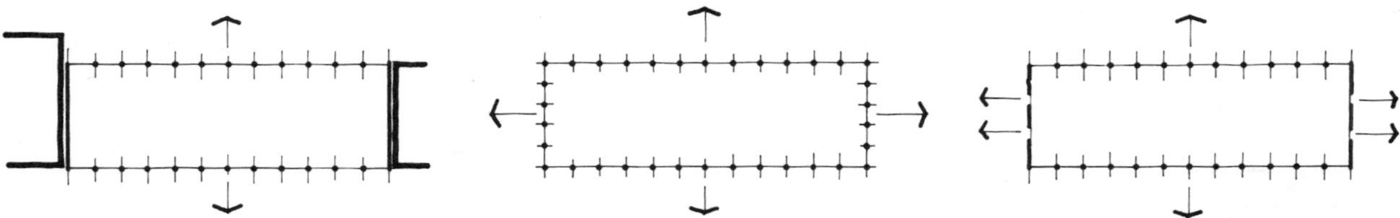

CENTRAL CORRIDOR SYSTEM: APARTMENT

Each building type has a modifying effect on the apartments placed within its confines. The central corridor type, once its other limitations are accepted, restricts the apartment minimally. What determines the kind of apartment the designer is able to work out is the total building length and depth.

In order to be economically feasible the typical floor should contain a maximum number of apartments. Given the minimum room widths determined by the program, just so many apartments can fit into the available building length. The number of apartments in this length can be improved on if each apartment is arranged—keeping the gross area constant—with shorter exterior exposure and increased depth. Naturally, this will put constraints on the apartment. Dining space along the exterior wall is out of the question. Bedrooms become so narrow that dressers and desks must be placed along the exterior wall, thus eliminating the option of floor-to-ceiling fenestration. The inner ends of the rooms become darker. In spite of all this, buildings with narrow, deep apartments tend to be more economical: using the same gross square foot area, they have smaller perimeters and less exterior wall.

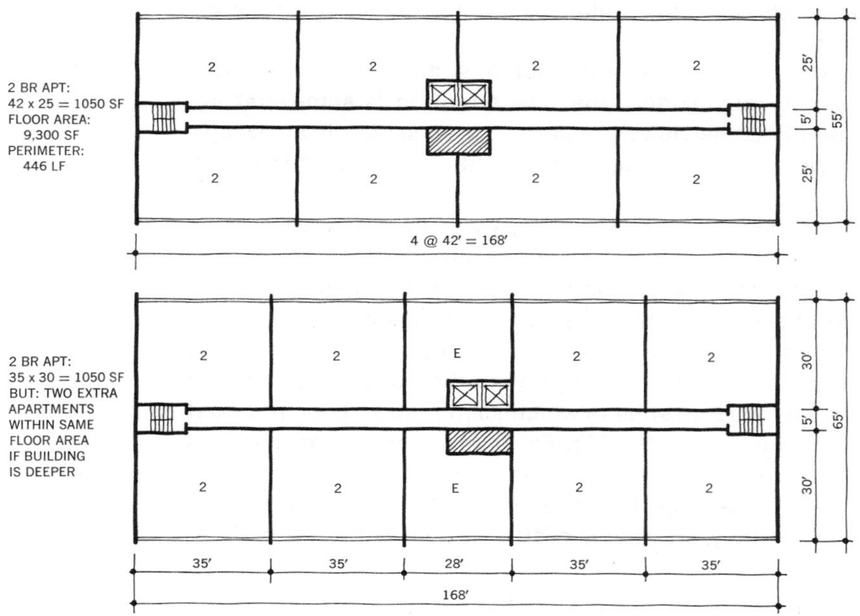

The apartment plan is not independent of the other elements of planning, the vertical cores, elevators, and stairs. It is possible to plan these vertical core elements independently when site conditions and economy permit more than simple building configurations **(6 to 9, 11 to 14, 37)**. In tight, compact, economy-minded plans the core elements have to bite into the apartment space proper or, to use another term, borrow space from the apartment **(1 to 5, 10, 15, 36)**. About 60 to 70 sf is as much borrowing as any plan can take easily and this area is just about equal to half the area of an average stair, to a single elevator shaft, or to an electric room and refuse chute.

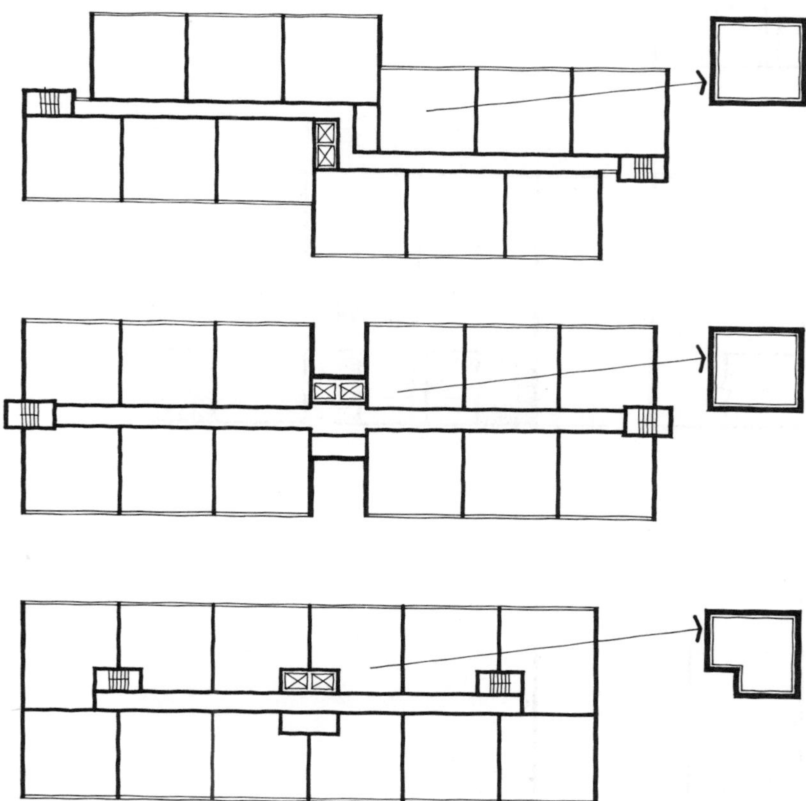

The illustrations show one-bedroom, two-bedroom, three-bedroom, and efficiency apartments with average depth and exterior exposure as well as with increased depth and reduced exterior exposure. They show the consequences of using some of the apartment space ("borrowing") to fit elevators, stairs, and other core elements along the central corridor.

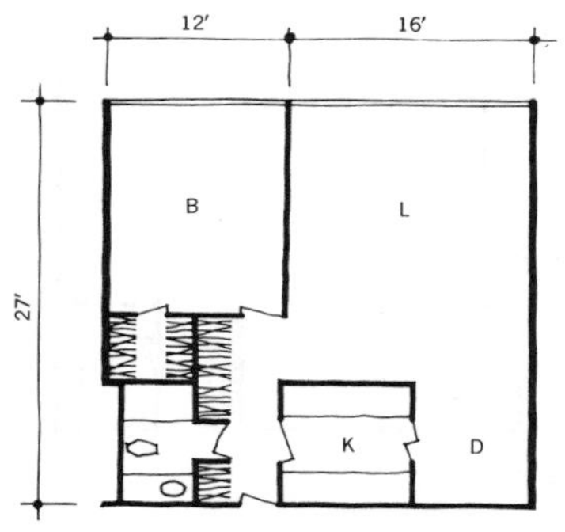

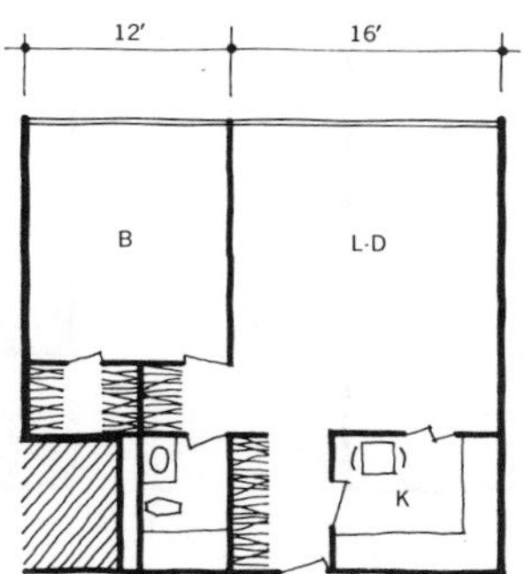

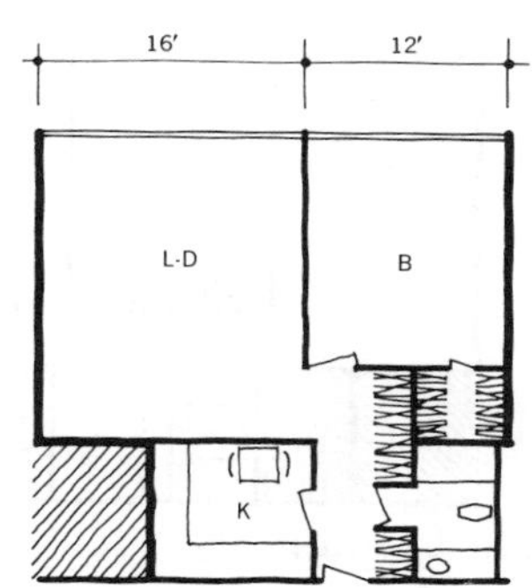

AVERAGE DEPTH — ONE BEDROOM APARTMENTS

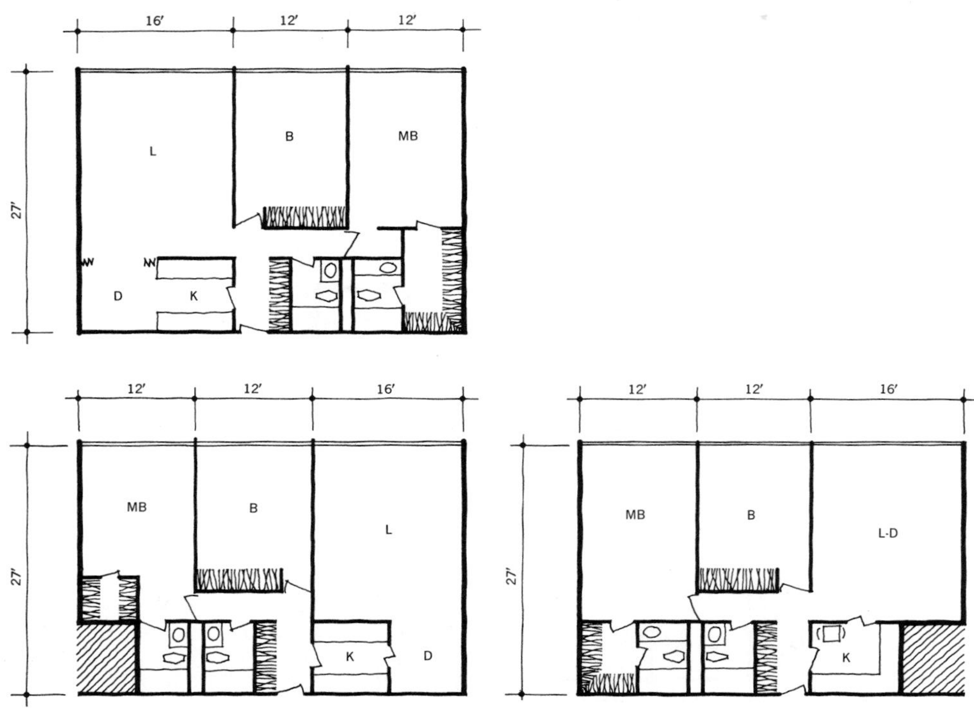

AVERAGE DEPTH — TWO BEDROOM APARTMENTS

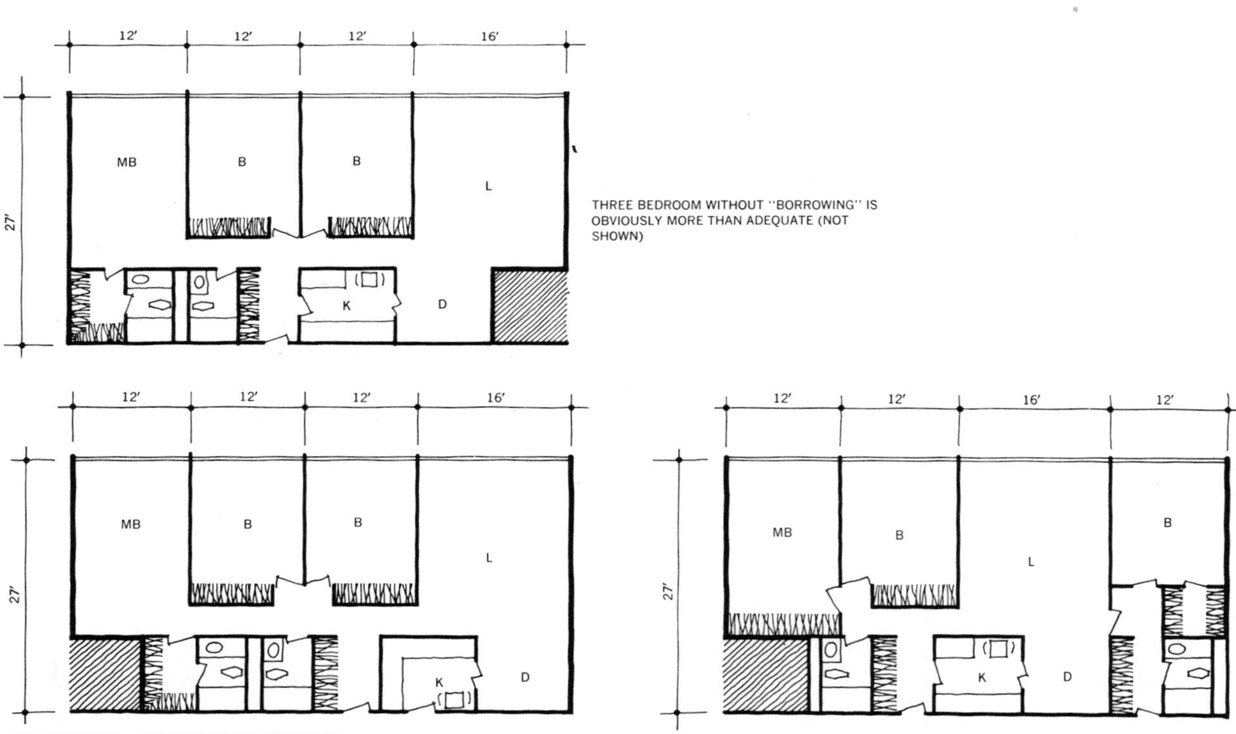

THREE BEDROOM WITHOUT "BORROWING" IS OBVIOUSLY MORE THAN ADEQUATE (NOT SHOWN)

AVERAGE DEPTH — THREE BEDROOM APARTMENTS

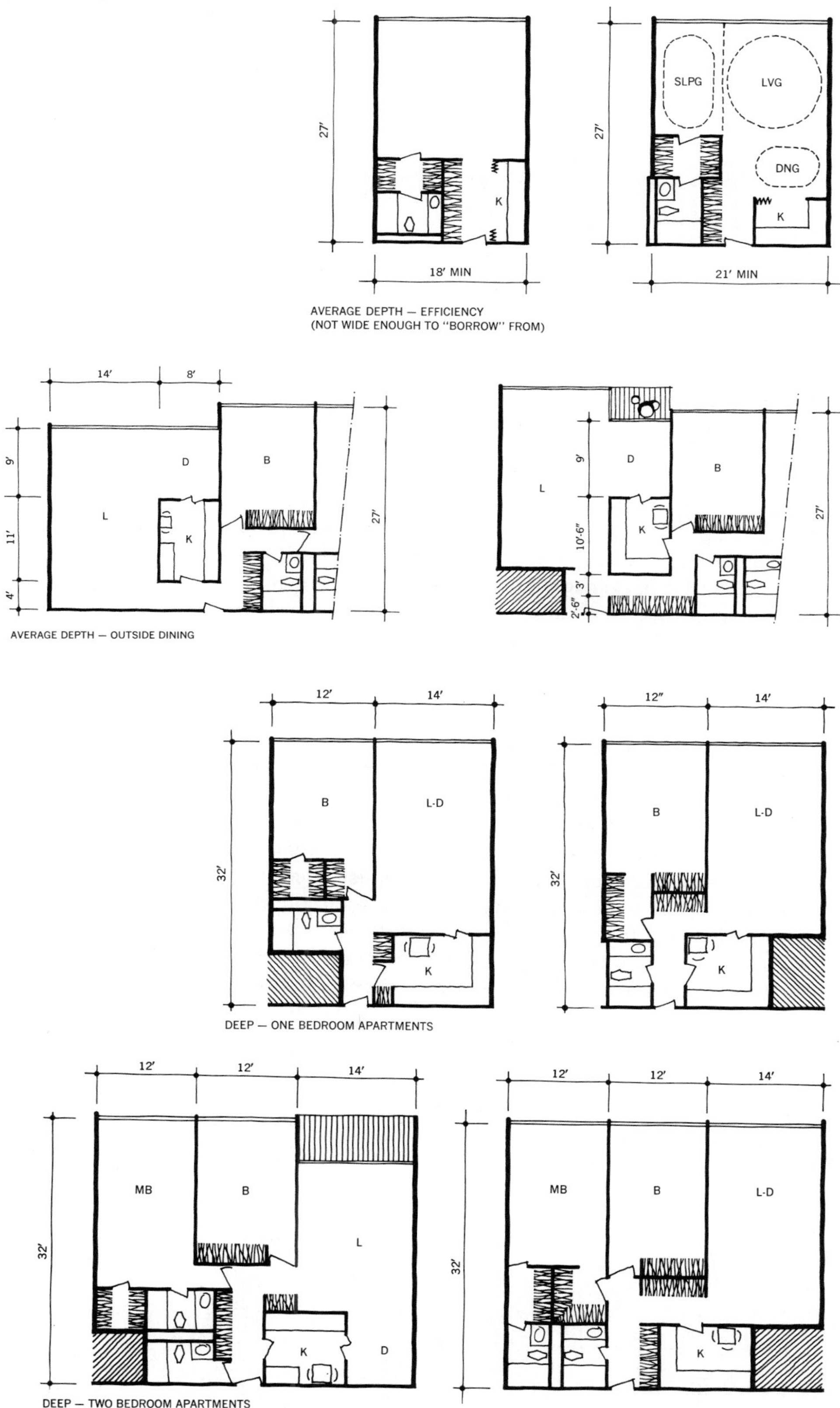

AVERAGE DEPTH — EFFICIENCY
(NOT WIDE ENOUGH TO "BORROW" FROM)

AVERAGE DEPTH — OUTSIDE DINING

DEEP — ONE BEDROOM APARTMENTS

DEEP — TWO BEDROOM APARTMENTS

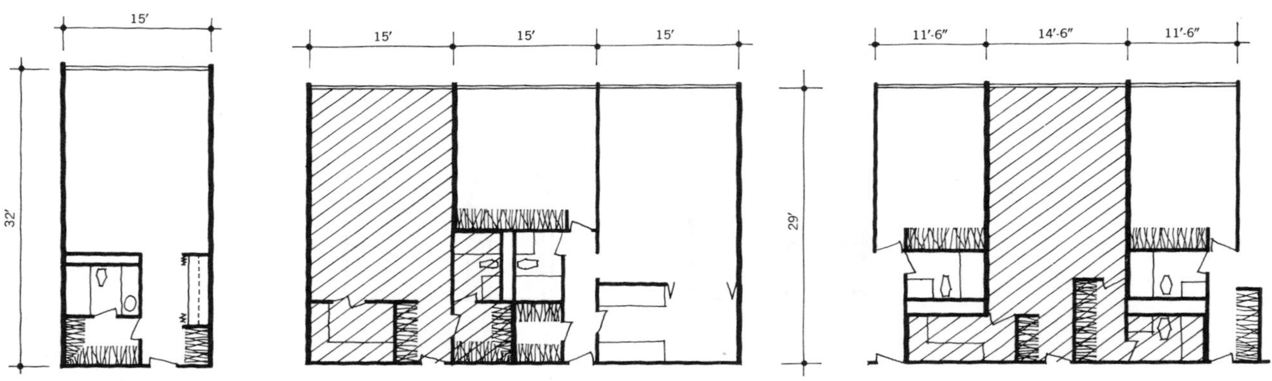

DEEP — EFFICIENCY

It is important to be aware that the apartments illustrated above are averages reflecting more the marketing conditions than living styles. As these conditions change, as the users' living style is more and more recognized, prototype plans must undergo a metamorphosis.

Even before that, the prototypes themselves—the results of economic equation, of emulating past successes, and lack of experimentation—should be recognized as laden with shortcomings. Bedrooms, attempting to use minimum exterior wall, when occupied by two children cannot be subdivided to provide privacy; therefore the apartment is not flexible enough to accommodate family growth. One wonders if sleeping has to take place in a room along the exterior wall. With advancement in mechanical ventilation a change in our building codes might liberate the exterior zone for activities that need daylight instead of using it as bed containers. Dining rooms in most prototypes can be used only for small formal meals and are not adaptable as family rooms, although it has been proved that family activities such as young children playing, studying, or watching television tend to take place near that great family magnet, the kitchen. Master bedrooms do not get multiple use in most current arrangements, and their location adjacent to the living room, instead of in the far corner, could open up the living space for large parties or varied activities in defined but not completely isolated groups when not in use as a bedroom. The more frequent splitting of one bedroom from the others would allow a separate exit and would permit the use of this room for young adults or for the elderly living with the family. The improvements are many. Their concomitant economic consequences, in most cases increased building perimeter, could be balanced by other savings.

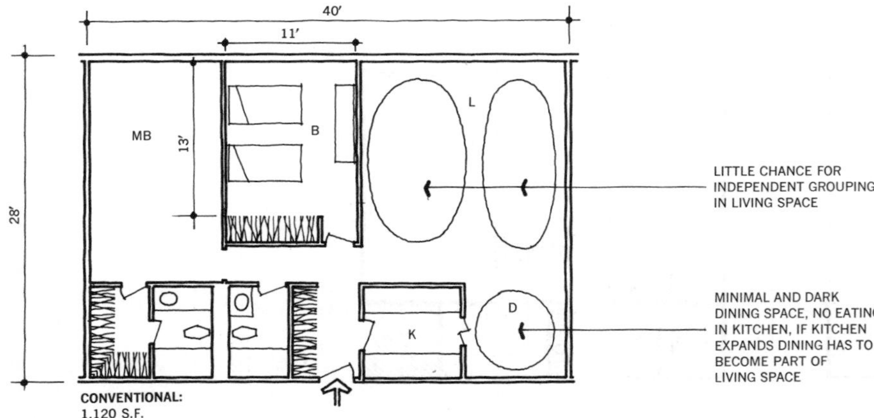

CONVENTIONAL:
1,120 S.F.

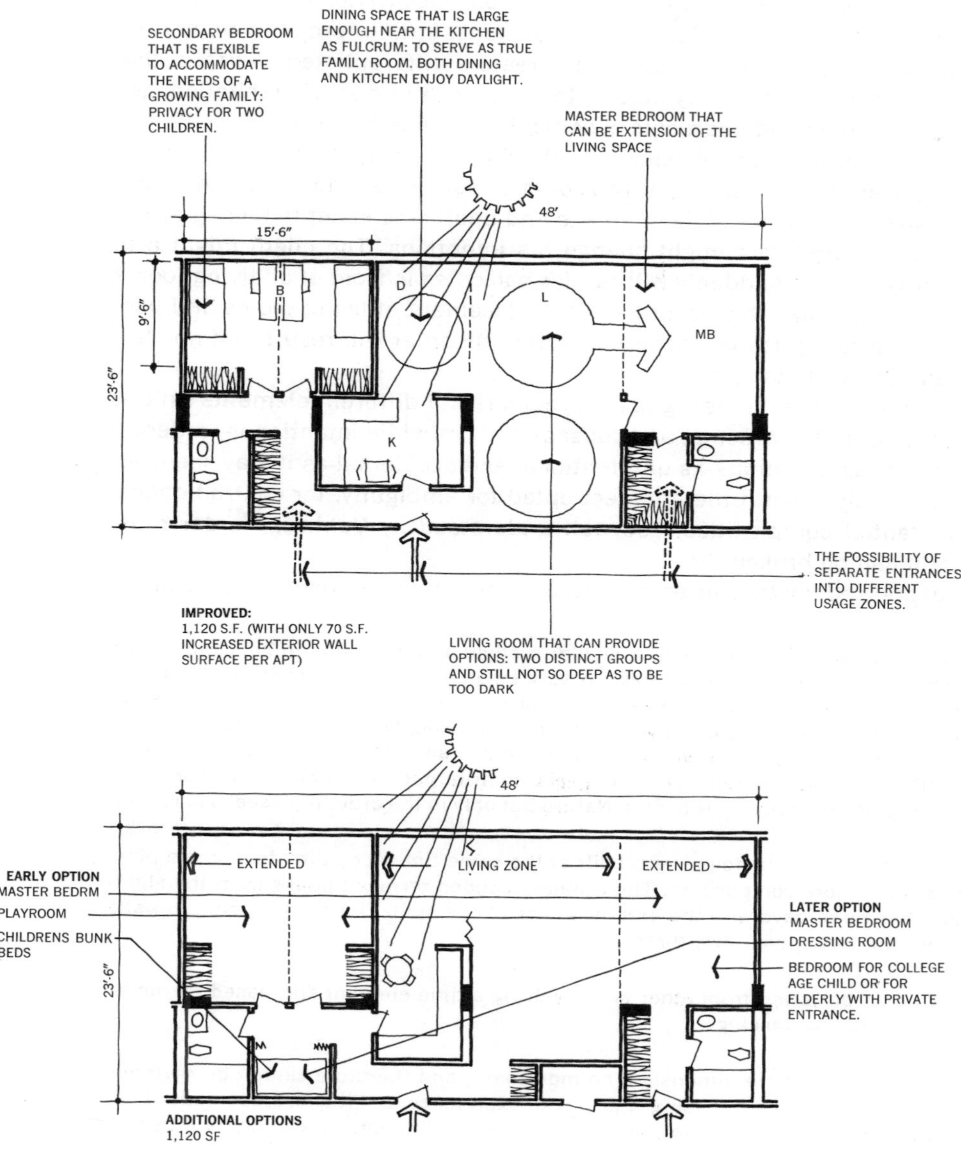
SECONDARY BEDROOM THAT IS FLEXIBLE TO ACCOMMODATE THE NEEDS OF A GROWING FAMILY: PRIVACY FOR TWO CHILDREN.
DINING SPACE THAT IS LARGE ENOUGH NEAR THE KITCHEN AS FULCRUM: TO SERVE AS TRUE FAMILY ROOM. BOTH DINING AND KITCHEN ENJOY DAYLIGHT.
MASTER BEDROOM THAT CAN BE EXTENSION OF THE LIVING SPACE
48′
15′-6″
9′-6″
23′-6″
B
D
L
MB
K
THE POSSIBILITY OF SEPARATE ENTRANCES INTO DIFFERENT USAGE ZONES.
IMPROVED:
1,120 S.F. (WITH ONLY 70 S.F. INCREASED EXTERIOR WALL SURFACE PER APT)
LIVING ROOM THAT CAN PROVIDE OPTIONS: TWO DISTINCT GROUPS AND STILL NOT SO DEEP AS TO BE TOO DARK
48′
EXTENDED
LIVING ZONE
EXTENDED
EARLY OPTION
MASTER BEDRM
PLAYROOM
CHILDRENS BUNK BEDS
23′-6″
LATER OPTION
MASTER BEDROOM
DRESSING ROOM
BEDROOM FOR COLLEGE AGE CHILD OR FOR ELDERLY WITH PRIVATE ENTRANCE.
ADDITIONAL OPTIONS
1,120 SF

Ultimately plans could be conceived in which only the perimeter walls of the apartment are fixed together with bathrooms, kitchen plumbing, and exhausts, structural columns and certain electric risers. This arrangement would permit the long-term lessee and certainly the condominium owner to place walls, with limitations naturally, to fit his needs and life-style.

CENTRAL CORRIDOR SYSTEM: RHYTHM

The moment apartments are placed next to each other a major design decision is in the making, one that will have unalterable consequences for the total design of the building. Regardless of whether the architect opts for a grid of exposed structural framing, for a masonry-clad exterior with punched openings, or even for such a homogeneous and anonymous exterior surface as a curtain wall, the apartments placed along the exterior will form a definite rhythm.

When it is the architect's intention to express on the exterior the living spaces as different from the bedrooms (with different fenestration, projections, and indentions or by the use of balconies) and to create a differentiated elevation that at least symbolizes, if not clearly states, the presence of human habitation, the rhythm of living rooms and bedrooms is self-evident **(10 to 12, 16, 30).**

Even if such intention does not exist, even if living rooms and bedrooms are identical in width, even if their differing width could somehow be hidden behind identical column bays, the rhythm of living rooms and bedrooms is not to be neglected. To begin with, the architect might change his intentions. The client might also change his program and suddenly will call for balconies in front of all living rooms **(3).** When something like this occurs and the placement of living rooms and bedrooms is not in a recognizable rhythm, a kind of disorder will result that no ''exterior design'' can camouflage.

Exterior rhythm means the recognizable regularity of different elements (in this case living rooms and bedrooms) and consequently must be intentional—ordered. Even irregularity as a rhythm—as unintentional and accidental as it may seem—is planned. Ultimately, even if the architect opted for ambiguity, for contradictions, or ''circumstantial complexities,'' so well understood by Venturi, ''order must exist before it can be broken.''[23]

Nobody expressed rhythm in architecture more poetically than Rasmussen.

> The architect is usually forced to create a regular method of subdivision in his composition on which so many building artisans will have to work together. The simplest method, for both the architect and the artisans, is the absolutely regular repetition of the same elements, for example solid, void, solid, void, just as you count one, two, one, two. It is a rhythm every one can grasp. Many people find it entirely too simple to mean anything at all. It says nothing to them and yet it is a classic example of man's special contribution to orderliness. It represents a regularity and precision found nowhere in Nature but only in the order man seeks to create.
>
> When a number of one-family houses are built at the same time according to a single plan, the rhythm is often more complicated. The ordinary London terraced house from the eighteenth century has three bays with the entrance door at one side. There they stand, in waltz measure: one, two, three, one, two, three.
>
> The term rhythm is borrowed from other arts involving a time element and based on movement, such as music and dancing.
>
> Architecture itself has no time dimension, no movement, and therefore cannot be rhythmic in the same way as music and dancing are. But to experience architecture demands time; it also demands work—though mental, not physical, work. The person who hears music or watches dancing does none of the physical work himself but in perceiving the performance he experiences the rhythm of it as though it were in his own body. In much the same way you can experience architecture rhythmically—that is, by the process of re-creation already described. If you feel that a line is rhythmic it means that by following it with your eyes you have an experience that can be compared with the experience of rhythmic ice-skating, for instance.[24]

The importance of rhythm in planning can be best illustrated by example. The exercise that follows is in a sense restricted; the site is bordered on adjacent property lines by existing structures with solid end walls and zoning is such that there is really only one logical way to position the building. Although this type of situation is not the most common, it was selected to highlight the issue and not further complicate it by options of varied configurations or by the possibilities of four directionality. The principles of rhythm are applicable on any site and building with any program mix.

Example

PROGRAM MIX

25%—1 BR apartments @ 700 sf
50%—2 BR apartments @ 1000 sf
25%—3 BR apartments @ 1400 sf

SITE CONDITIONS

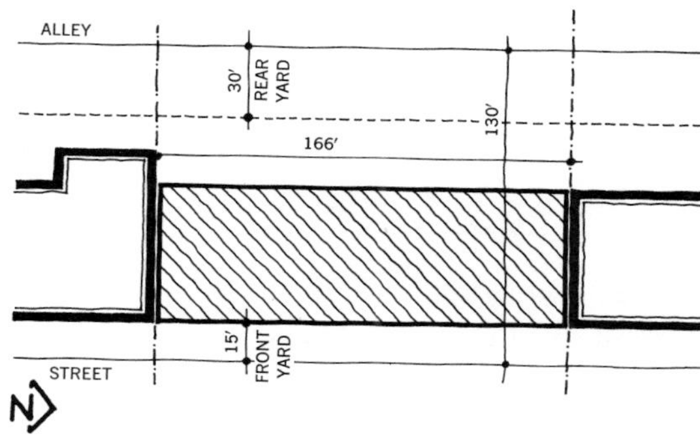

PRELIMINARY CONSIDERATIONS, ZONING CHECK. Based on front and rear yards required by zoning and no side yard requirements, the only viable option is a building 166 ft long. Thus site and zoning determines the typical floor volume. (This restricted condition was selected for our example because it helps to focus attention on procedure rather than providing a wide range of options in which other factors—not yet discussed—would come into play.) Assuming an average building width of 60 ft, the typical floor area becomes 9360 sf, a reasonable size for concrete pour.

THE SMALLEST GROUP THAT REFLECTS THE PROGRAM MIX

1 (25%)—1 BR @ 700 sf	= 700 sf
2 (50%)—2 BR @ 1000 sf	= 2000 sf
1 (25%)—3 BR @ 1400 sf	= 1400 sf
Four apartments	4100 sf
Add for nonrental 13%	533 sf
Gross floor area for 4 apartments	4633 sf

9360 sf ÷ 4633 sf = approximately 2

THEREFORE ON A TYPICAL FLOOR

2 × 1 = 2—1 BR; 2 × 2 = 4—2 BR; 2 × 1 = 2—3 BR

Based on the above, the number of spaces that require exterior exposure is as follows:

2—1 BR × 2 (1 living room + 1 bedroom) =	4 rooms
4—2 BR × 3 (1 living room + 2 bedrooms) =	12 rooms
2—3 BR × 4 (1 living room + 3 bedrooms) =	8 rooms
Total	24 rooms

The building has two exposed faces: therefore 24 ÷ 2 = 12 rooms on each face; 166 ft length minus 1 ft for end walls equals 165 feet; 165 ÷ 12 = 13 ft 9 in. Before any further steps can be taken exterior options and their consequences on room sizes must be kept in mind.

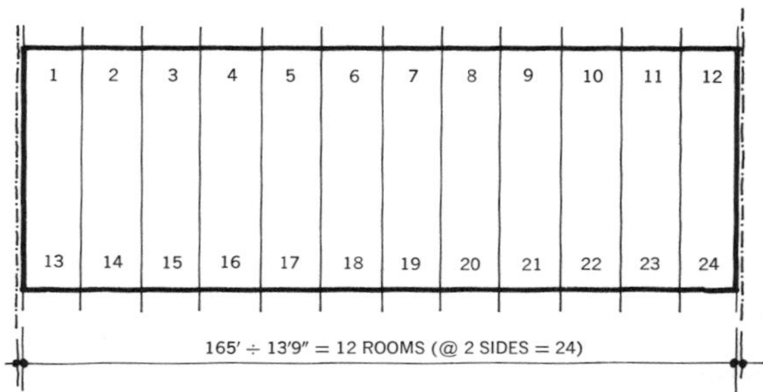

The 13 ft-9 in. module can be accepted as an expression of equal column bays, provided the columns are wide enough so that by shifting partitions behind the columns the living room width can be increased and the bedroom width can be reduced because 13 ft 9 in. (less partitions) is too much for a bedroom when the extra space can be better used in the living room.

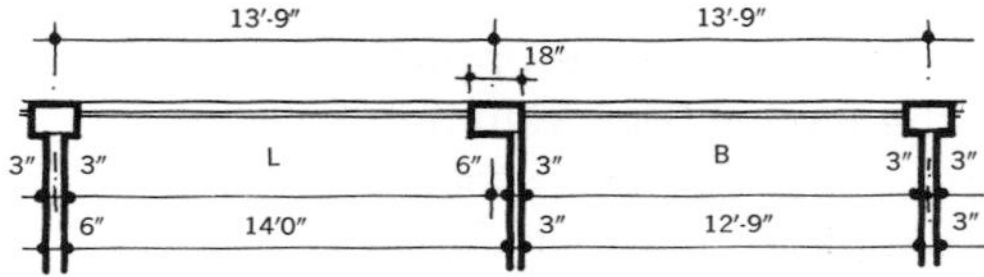

The columns can be rearranged to reflect the wider living room and the narrower bedroom, presuming that an acceptable rhythm of "L" bays and "B" bays can be found. In this case a 2 bedroom apartment has three rooms @ 13 ft 9 in. or 41 ft 3 in. However, 41 ft 3 in. also equals one living room @ 16 ft and two bedrooms @ 12 ft 1½ in.

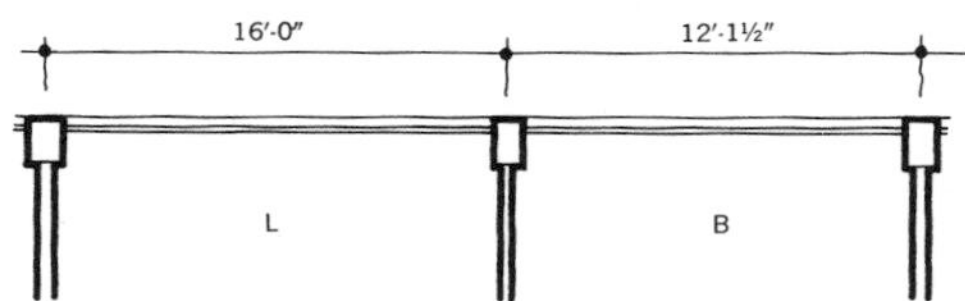

A masonry clad exterior with punched window openings, if that is the designer's choice, allows an even rhythm of windows on the exterior, whereas in the interior the living rooms are wider and the bedrooms are narrower. Fenestration that expresses this room width differentiation is certainly no problem at all.

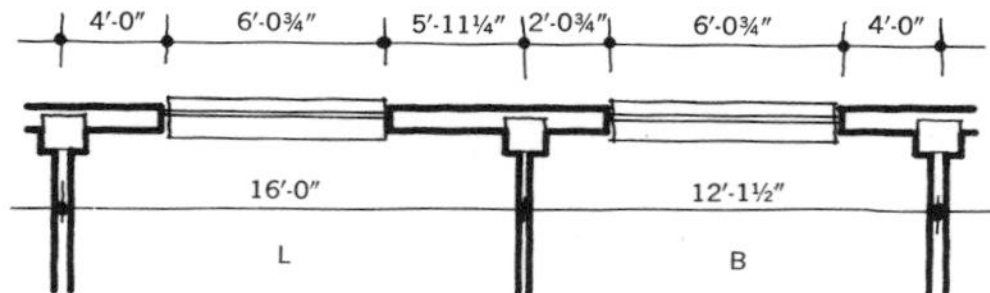

With curtain wall or load-bearing concrete mullions a grid can be found that consists of modules, four of which make up a living room and three, a bedroom. Using the 41 ft 3 in. two-bedroom apartment, 41 ft 3 in. ÷ 10 = 4 ft 1½ in. module; 4 @ 4 ft 1½ in. = 16 ft 6 in. living room, 3 @ 4 ft 1½ in. = 12 ft 4½ in. bedroom.

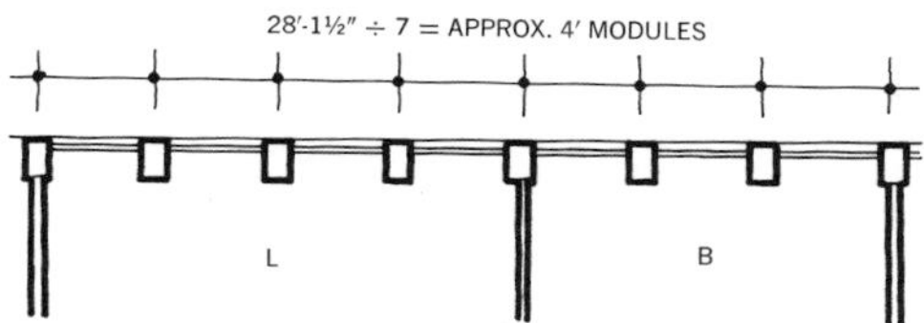

Using longer spans (20 ft 7½ in.) in which a bay equals one living room or two bedrooms has its problems because the bedrooms are too narrow compared with the living room size. Cutting the span in half provides no added flexibility.

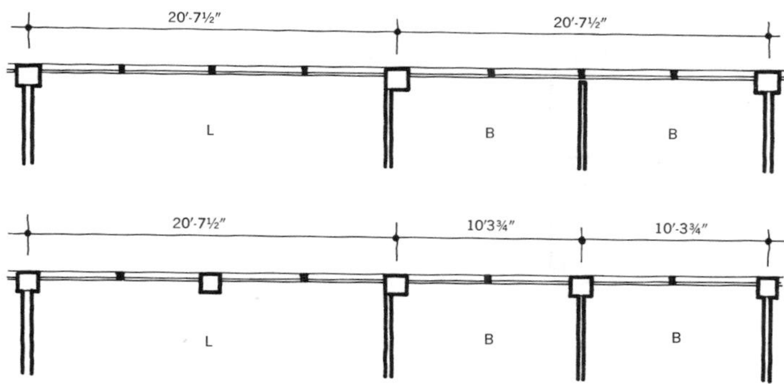

Disregarding their effect on parking, any of the above options—at least at this point—are possible and for the sake of early studies we are safe to use the 13 ft 9 in. module as a grid until a basic scheme is achieved.

What are the possible layouts? (Balconies are shown in front of all living rooms to emphasize the question of rhythm.)

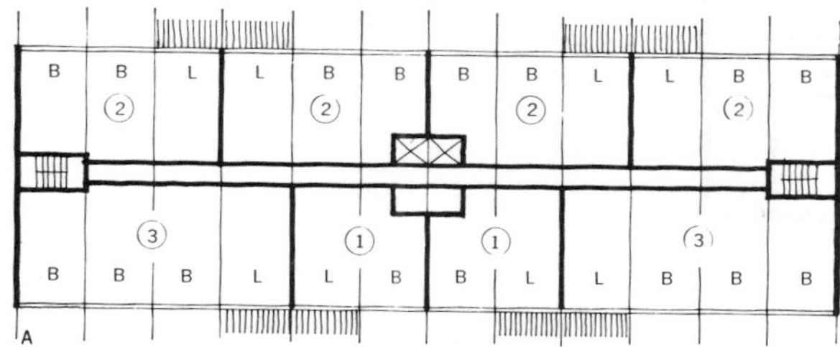

SCHEME A: Core elements are borrowed from the sleeping zone; the rhythm is good. (If the building has open ends, the living rooms should be at the end.)

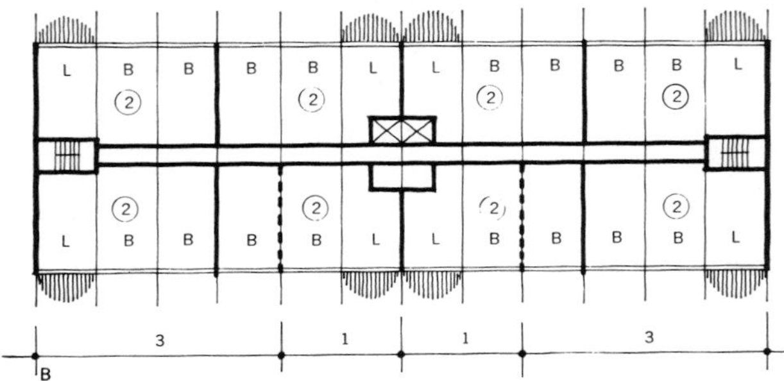

SCHEME B. The core elements are borrowed from the living zone; the rhythm is poor (pairs of balconies are fighting with single balconies); the pairing of apartments along their sleeping zones provides built in flexibility: out of 2 two-bedroom apartments a one-bedroom and a three-bedroom apartment can be created.

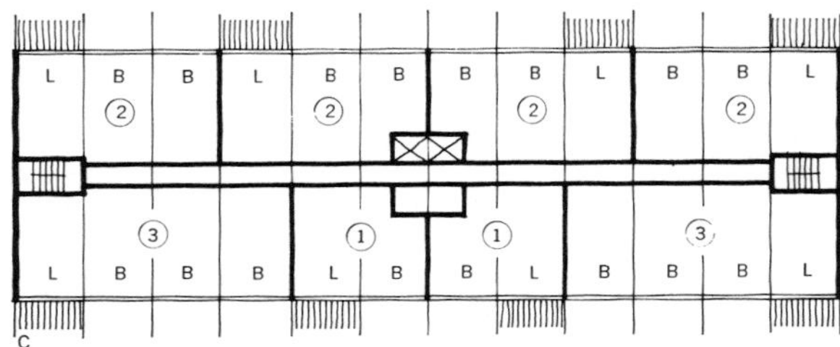

SCHEME C. The core elements are borrowed from both zones; this scheme tries to remedy the rhythm problem by using all single balconies; the rhythm is good. Assuming that there is a preferred view toward the east, the number of apartments facing the view—at least from their living rooms—can be increased by having end apartments occupy both sides of the building (''wrapping them around'').

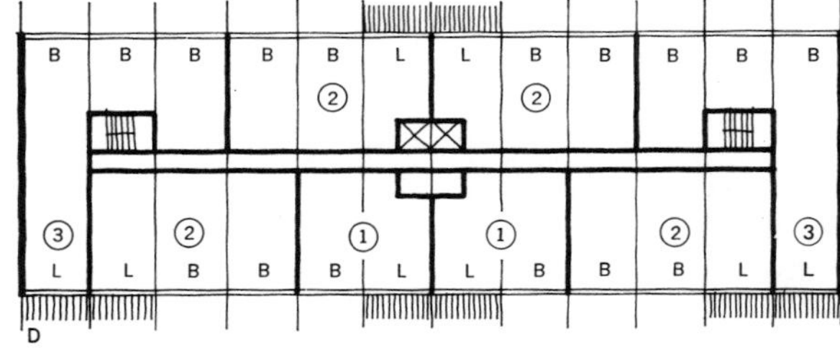

SCHEME D. Six out of eight apartments face the preferred view; the core elements are borrowed from the living zone; the balcony rhythm on the west elevation is poor; symmetry by itself is not rhythm.

SCHEME E. Rectifies the rhythm problem; borrowing from the "wrap-around" three-bedroom apartment poses unique problems on this scheme as well as on the preceding one.

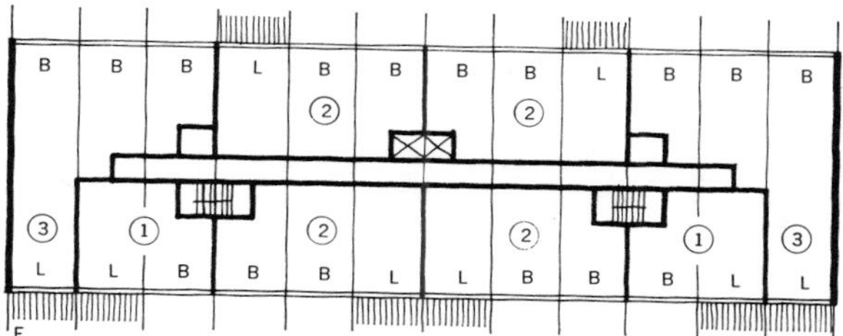

SCHEME F. Eliminates the difficulties of the three-bedroom apartment, but a price must be paid; the core elements that would function better in the center are dispersed because it is exceedingly difficult to borrow from both zones of a two-bedroom apartment of average depth.

The program mix and apartment sizes fit rather easily without leftover space in the 166 × 60 ft floor area dictated by site conditions and zoning. If the property were 180 ft long and the program stayed the same, 180 ft minus 1 ft for end walls = 179 ft; 179 ÷ 12 = approximately 15 for each room. This is obviously adequate for living rooms but far too large for bedrooms. Shifting partitions behind columns will not reduce the bedroom width sufficiently. Three times 15 ft makes up a two-bedroom apartment equaling 45 ft. This is just about what is needed for a two-bedroom apartment with dining along the exterior wall (14 ft living room, 8 ft dining alcove, 11 ft 6 in. bedroom, 11 ft 6 in. master bedroom). Presuming that these improved apartments (a two-bedroom becomes 1,180 sf) can be marketed, this is an acceptable alternate.

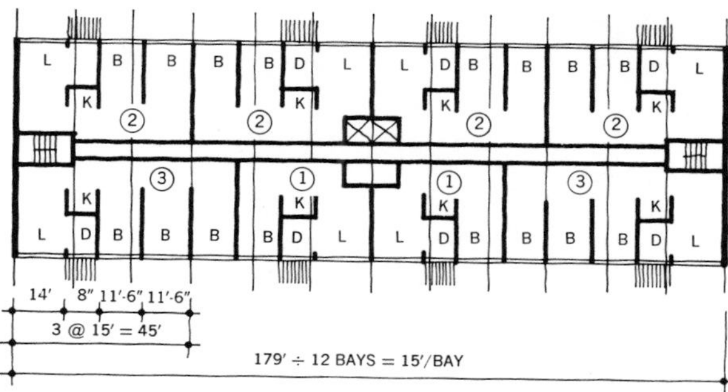

What if 1180 sf (two-bedroom) with exterior dining is too luxurious? The options on the new property using the preceding module of 13 ft 9 in. are 179 ÷ 13 ft 9 in. = 13 modules on each side of the building; 13 × 2 = 26, but the eight apartments on the floor need only 24 modules! There is an excess of two modules that equals a one-bedroom apartment, making a total of nine apartments per floor and changing the mix to 2 three-bedroom (22.5%), 4 two-bedroom (44.5%) and 3 one-bedroom (33.25%) apartments. Even if the client were to agree to this modified mix, the odd number of modules (13) and the odd number of one-bedroom apartments do not lead to an orderly disciplined solution as long as there is an intent to express living rooms differently from bedrooms. There is, however, a way out, if a uniform, undifferentiated exterior is acceptable.

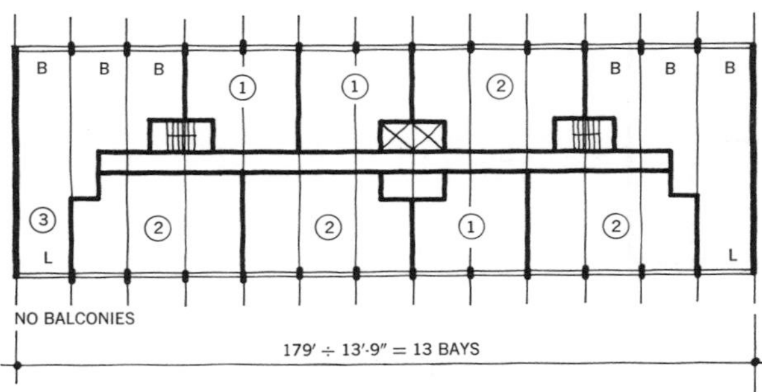

If 13 ft 9 in. results in an odd number of modules, what happens to the room sizes with the next even number? 179 ÷ 14 = 12 ft 10 in. per module. This means, approximately, a 14-ft living room and 12-ft bedrooms and is acceptable. However, with 28 modules the mix changes substantially from the one given in the program: 2 three-bedroom (20%), 4 two-bedroom (40%), and 4 one-bedroom (40%) apartments.

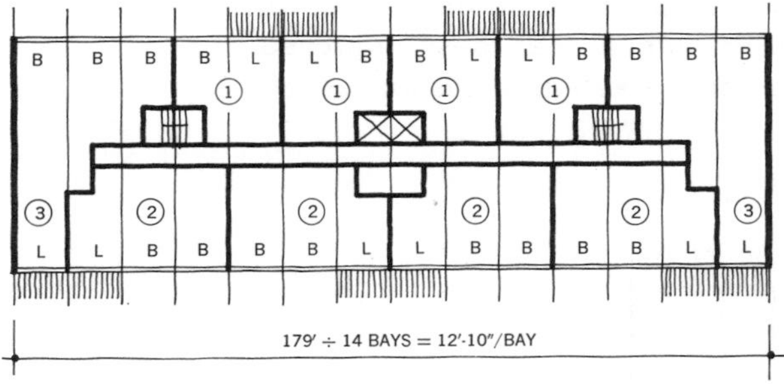

Is it possible to stick to the original program mix and the 13 ft 9 in. module on the 180-ft property?

Assuming that the issue of the preferred view is not an important one, the simple way to handle the extra two modules is not to use them at all or to use the extra modules for the vertical core elements in the center, strongly articulated.

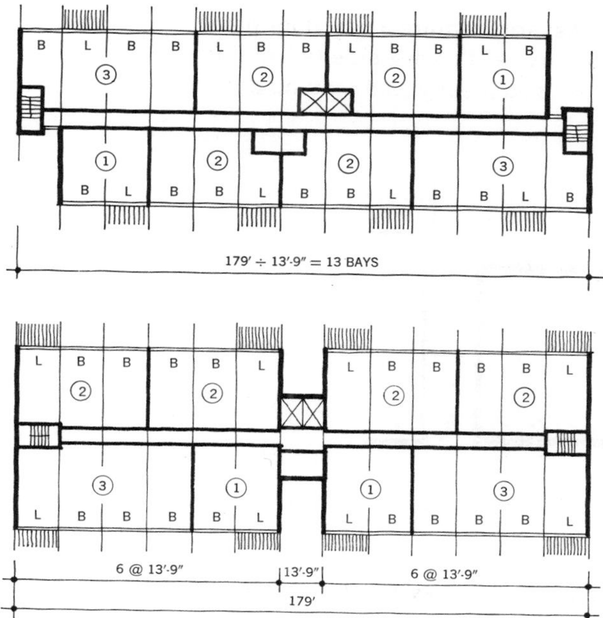

If the preferred view cannot be neglected, the preceding scheme can be modified. The price is poor balcony rhythm or no balcony for the one-bedroom apartment.

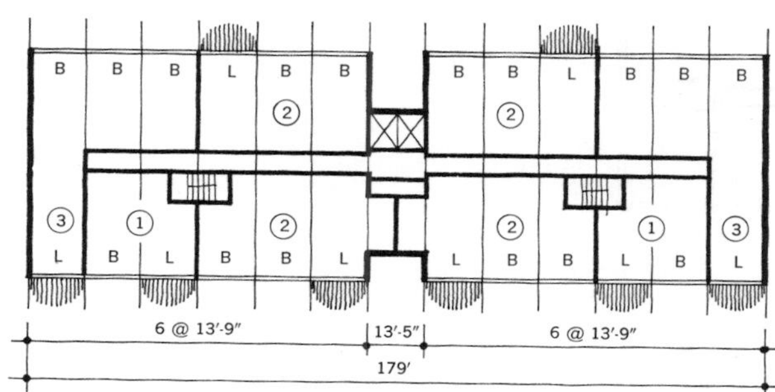

If the wrap-around three-bedroom apartments can take some added luxury (approximately 300 sf), the extra modules can be split between them.

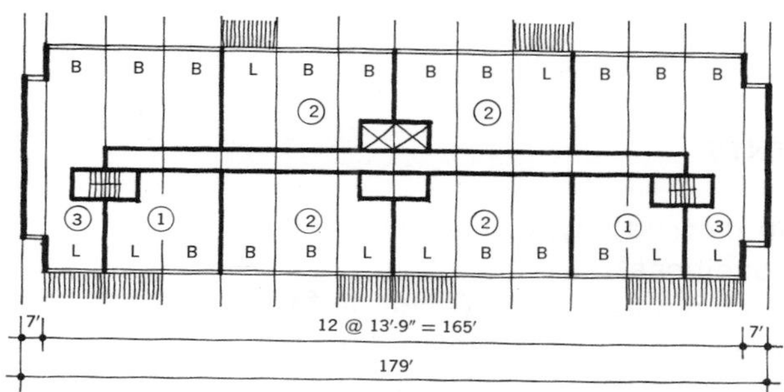

Finally, the increased property size does not necessarily require a new floor plan. The building can stay as it was, leaving a 14 ft voluntary yard on one side (assuming hat it is in accord with the zoning laws) that can be used ideally as a loading dock.

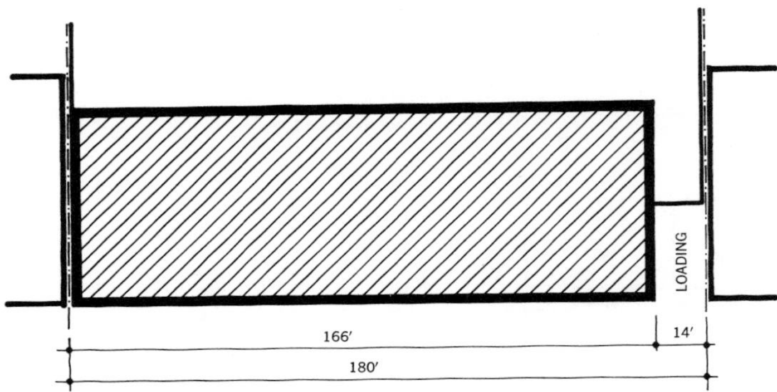

Throughout this example a small-span concrete framing was used. Large (20 ft 7½ in.) bays pose different problems. As long as the view issue can be disregarded, the system works well. Wrap-around apartments at the ends to increase the number of those who can enjoy the view create considerable difficulty because of the inflexibility of the large-span system on a restricted lot.

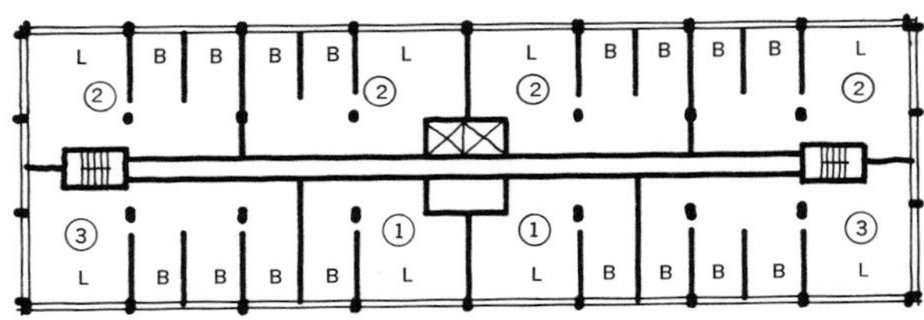

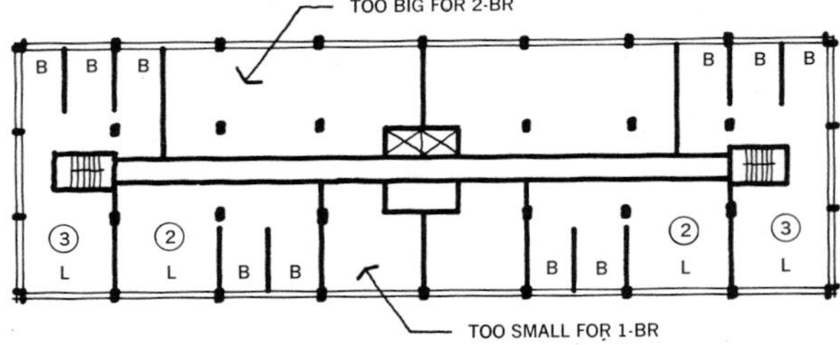

CENTRAL CORRIDOR SYSTEM: END APARTMENTS

When dealing with the end apartments of a central-corridor-type apartment building, the designer is faced with a set of special conditions.

Unless the stair shaft is pulled out of the main building volume (when, in fact, the end apartment is not different from any of the typical apartments) or the stair is positioned at the very end of the building centered on the public corridor (when the end apartment is minimally altered), the typical unit undergoes a serious metamorphosis when it becomes an end apartment.

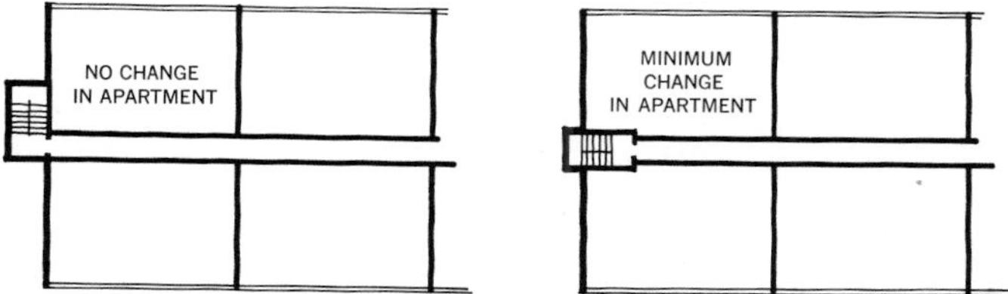

It is always advisable to reduce the travel distance and minimize the length of the corridor. When the stairs are pulled in from the end of the building to achieve this, part of the corridor (now behind the stair) can be added to the end apartments. In this manner, by decreasing the nonrental space the efficiency of the floor plan is increased.

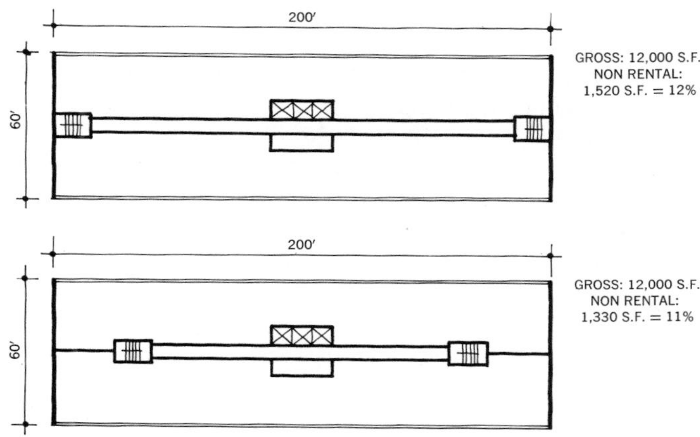

The part of the corridor that now becomes part of the apartments permits larger kitchens and/or dining spaces. When the building is free standing (in contrast to the example in the preceding chapter), fenestration of these dining areas will improve the apartments considerably **(3).**

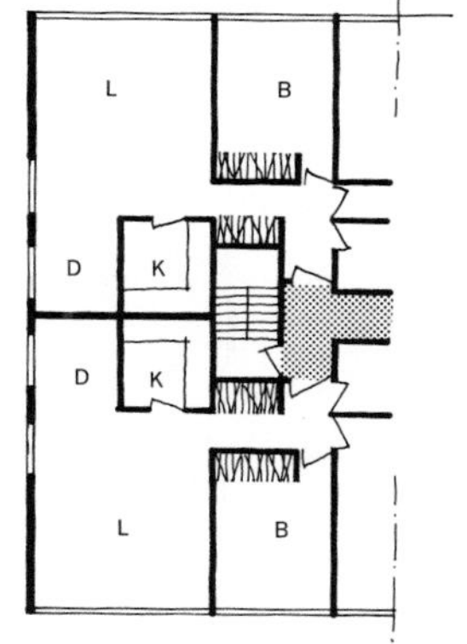

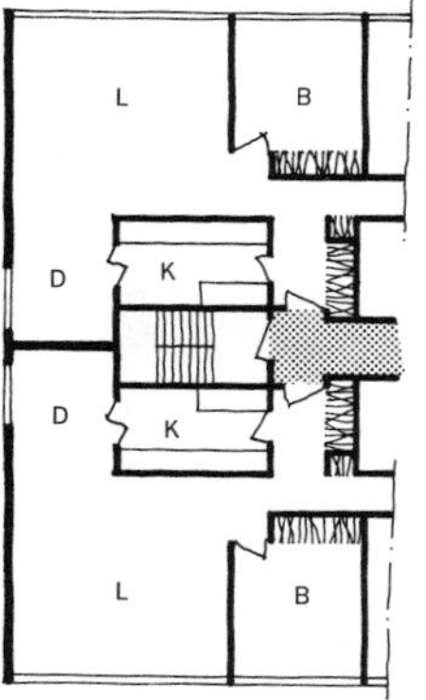

Wrap-around apartments—the result of preferred view conditions—open up a completely new set of possibilities. When the building has solid ends due to the restrictions of the site, options are limited **(16, 40).**

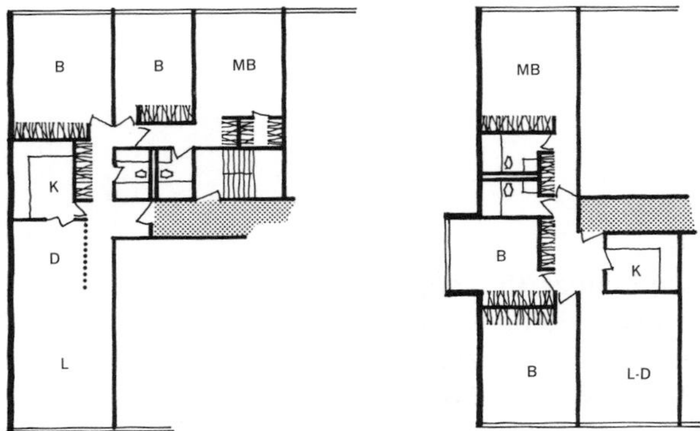

When the structure can open up on its ends, it becomes a four-directional building, it is possible to place one of the bedrooms instead of the kitchen along the end wall, assuming that the building is deep enough **(1, 6, 36).**

A three-bedroom apartment must have a minimum of four exterior spaces (living room plus three bedrooms) occupying four modules. When one of these rooms is along the end, the module requirements of a three-bedroom apartment are reduced to three. The chances to increase the number of apartments on the typical floor, within the same length but with a slightly increased depth, have improved **(37).**

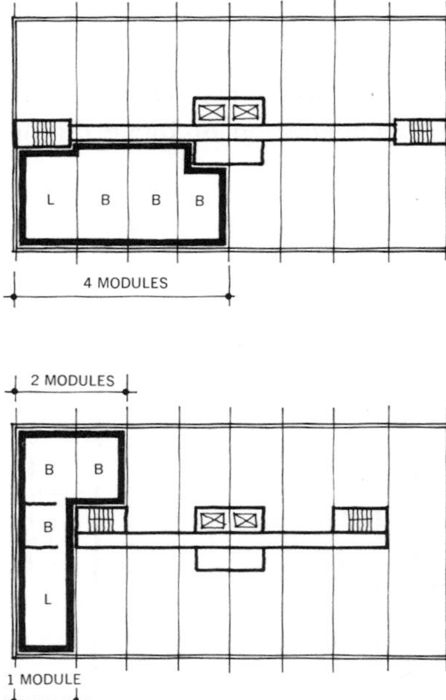

Depending on the depth of the building and on the bedroom-size requirements, it is possible to plan two, three, or even four bedrooms that front exclusively on the end wall **(4, 8, 10).**

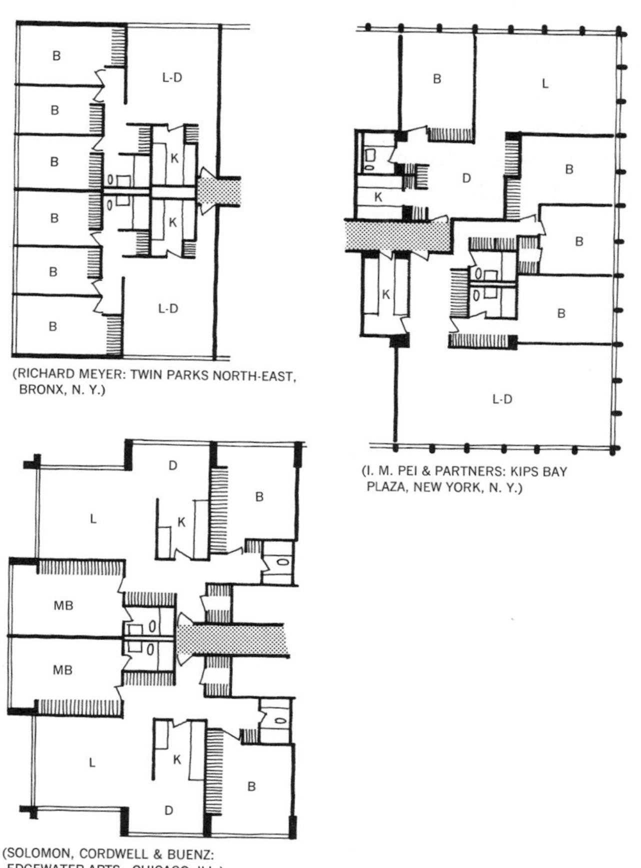

(RICHARD MEYER: TWIN PARKS NORTH-EAST, BRONX, N. Y.)

(I. M. PEI & PARTNERS: KIPS BAY PLAZA, NEW YORK, N. Y.)

(SOLOMON, CORDWELL & BUENZ: EDGEWATER APTS., CHICAGO, ILL.)

More than accommodating an extra bedroom or two, a complete efficiency apartment or if the depth is adequate even an entire one-bedroom unit can face the end of the building without using any of the modules along the building length **(1, 2, 5).**

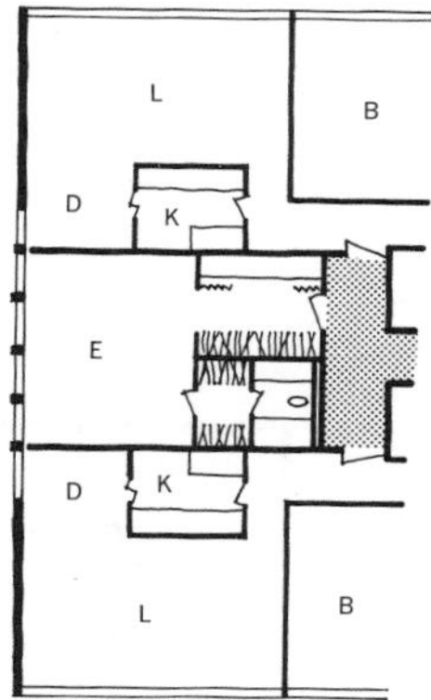

The economy of deep buildings (with narrow but deep apartments) becomes quite obvious when the possibilities inherent in the use of ends of the building are also exploited.

CENTRAL CORRIDOR SCHEME: SYMMETRY—SEQUENCE

The location of vertical core elements will influence the typical floor significantly and could limit its options severely. The most critical as an influencing factor is the elevator. Logically the elevator tends to be located in the center of the building, equidistant from apartments on each side. The result is a strong central element from which planning proceeds to the right and left **(1, 2, 3, 5).** The symmetrical process is further perpetuated by the desire to deal with apartments in symmetrical pairs: to increase the chance of switching a bedroom from one apartment to the other (2—2 BR = 1—3 BR + 1—1 BR) to back up, when possible, the kitchens or bathrooms of adjacent apartments.

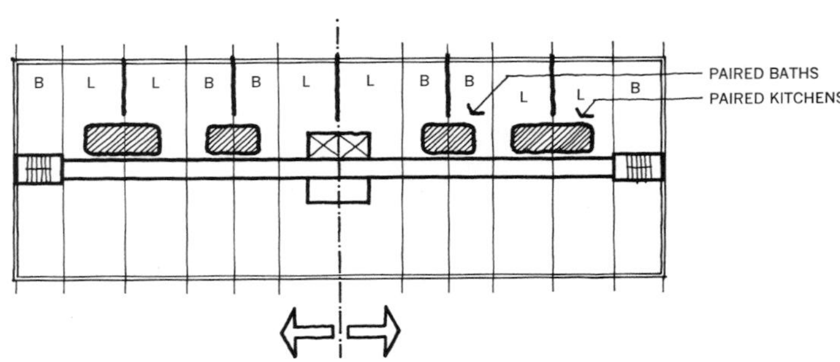

As the example in the preceding chapter illustrates, symmetry in itself is not rhythm, certainly not good rhythm. Sometimes the articulated core will solve the rhythm problem by splitting the building into two separate rhythmic entities **(12).**

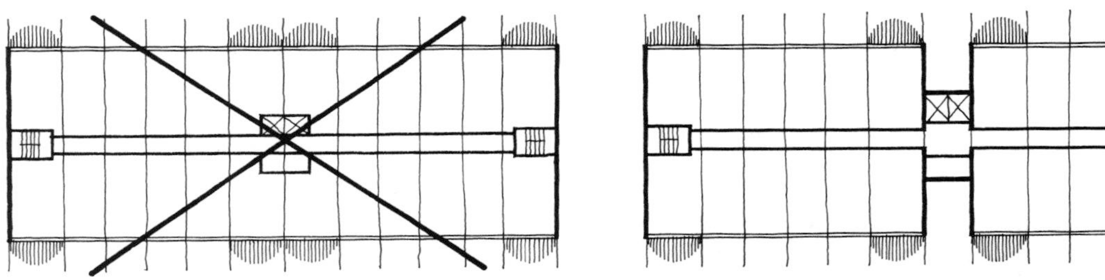

Site limitations, traffic conditions, or program considerations on the ground level may dictate the noncentral location of passenger elevators or, if there is a separate one, the service elevator. The total of vertical core elements may still be symmetrical **(36).**

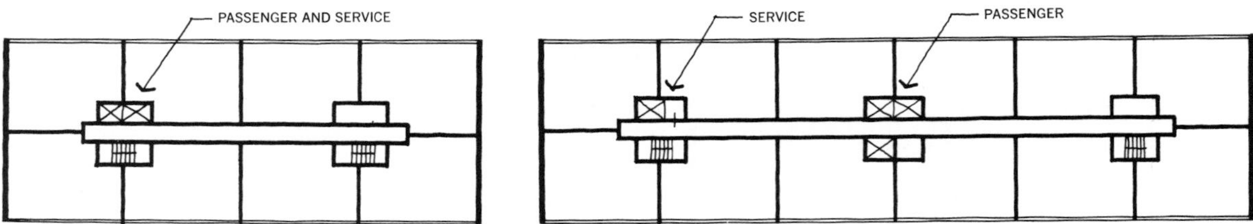

Core elements may become so large that the space for them cannot be comfortably borrowed from two adjacent apartments. This is common with three or four elevators in a group and with smokeproof towers that have a gravity type exhaust shaft of considerable size. In order to arrange the apartments around these large cores, part of each apartment may have to protrude beyond the simple oblong of the plan. The sense of rhythm will dictate that the plan be molded in such a manner that protrusions will occur rhythmically, whether or not all of them are justified by enlarged cores.

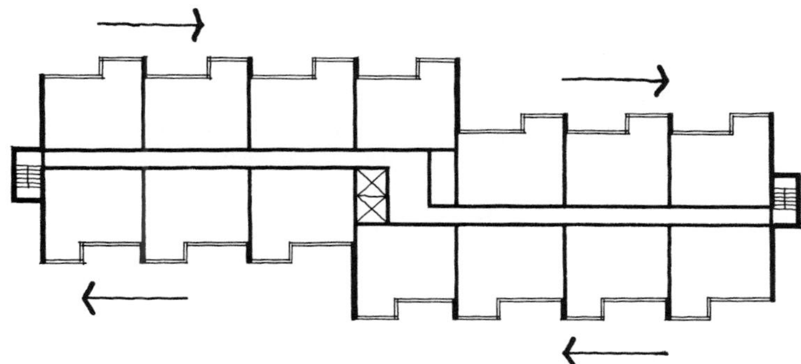

When the central vertical core elements are handled so that no borrowing from the apartments is necessary, the pairing of the units is not required from the start. Having eliminated the restraint of planning from the central axis can result in sequence instead of symmetrical planning **(11, 13, 37, 38).**

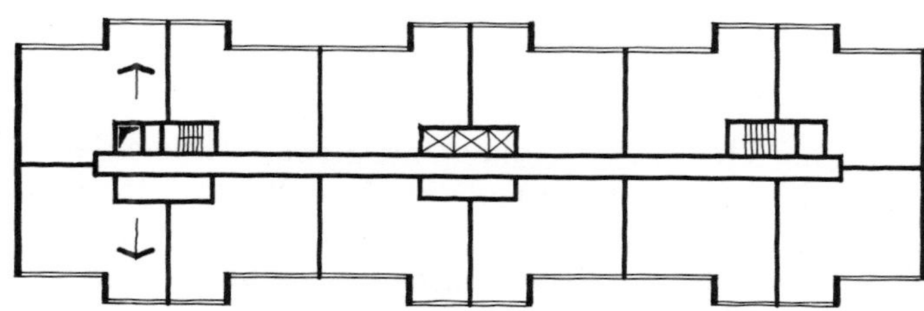

Another generator, probably the strongest one, of sequence planning is a proper view from every unit of a central-corridor building, achieved only by the protrusion of the living room. Only sequence arrangement will prevent a tenant from looking into his neighbor's bedroom from this pulled-out living space. Planning in sequence works best when all apartments are identical or when not more than two different apartment types occur.

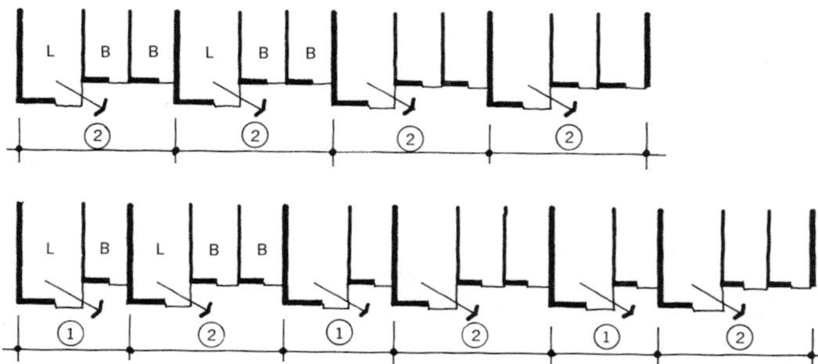

CENTRAL CORRIDOR SYSTEM: CORRIDORS

Public corridors are the most difficult to design and the most neglected elements of central-corridor apartment buildings. The best apartment will be degraded in the minds of the occupants who, on entering the lavish lobby and ascending in a plush elevator cab—perhaps with piped-in music to enhance the illusion further—will step out into the long, narrow, grim corridor.

Buildings with broken volume solve these problems by cutting the visual length of the corridor in half. Widening the waiting space is easily possible with this scheme, and a small increase in the perimeter and the building length can give the corridor adequate light, a view during the day and perhaps at night **(9).**

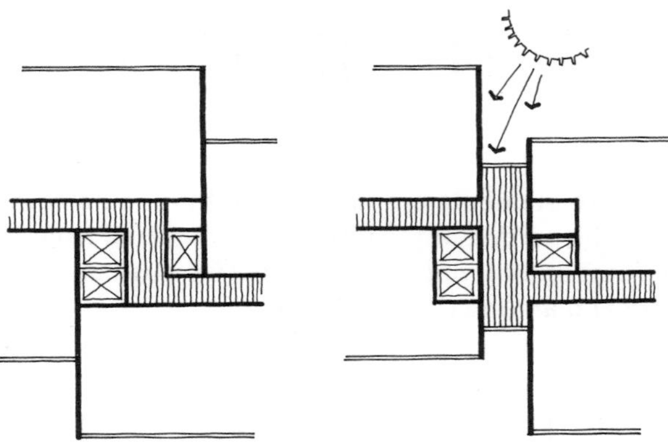

The customary unbroken-volume, central-corridor scheme must provide at least a wider space in front of the elevators than the standard 5-ft corridor width **(1, 3, 10, 12).** Not only will this widening make waiting for the elevators pleasanter, but it will suggest a different visual treatment (carpeting, ceiling, and lighting). Although the actual length of the corridor is not changed, its effect will be minimized. See also chapter on fire safety: how compartmentation necessitated by new high-rise fire codes influences elevator vestibules.

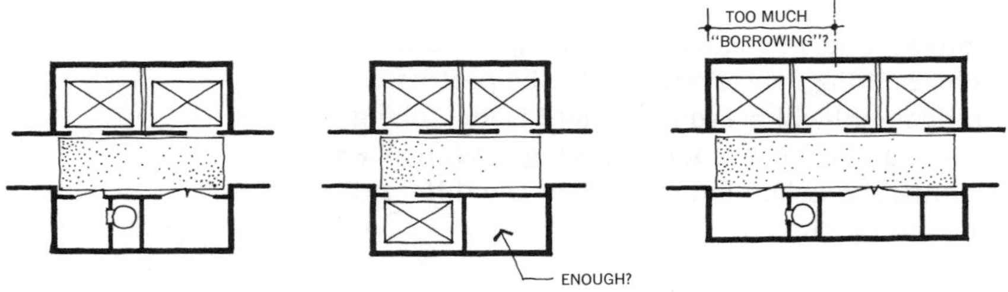

The vertical core itself can also be utilized to block the long corridor view, at least in part. This works best with two elevators or with three when the other core elements (refuse chute, electrical room, and so on) are located elsewhere. If the core is too long, it will result in excessive borrowing from the adjacent apartments.

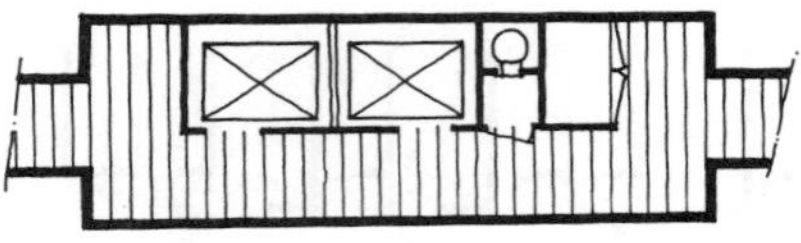

In extremely long buildings it is not unusual to have two independent elevator cores. A pair of doors in the center, working in both travel directions, will cut the corridor length effectively. When the building is so long that the maximum travel distance permitted by code necessitates a third means of egress, this third stair can act as a corridor break.

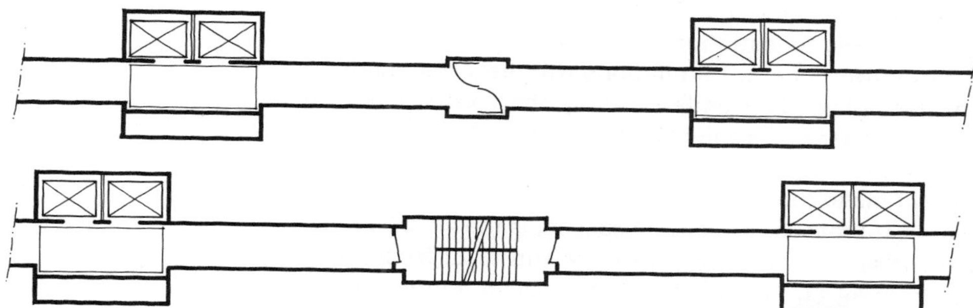

The part of the corridor in front of the elevators offers many possibilities, which is not the case with the rest of the corridor. When the apartments are not laid out symmetrically around the corridor center line as an axis, there is no rhythm of apartment doors. The regularly spaced corridor lighting relates poorly to these irregular door locations. When doors are regularly opposite each other, indenting them and treating the floor differently will help to ameliorate the effect of the long corridor **(6).** If the indentations are made wide enough, it is possible to reduce the width of the public corridor.

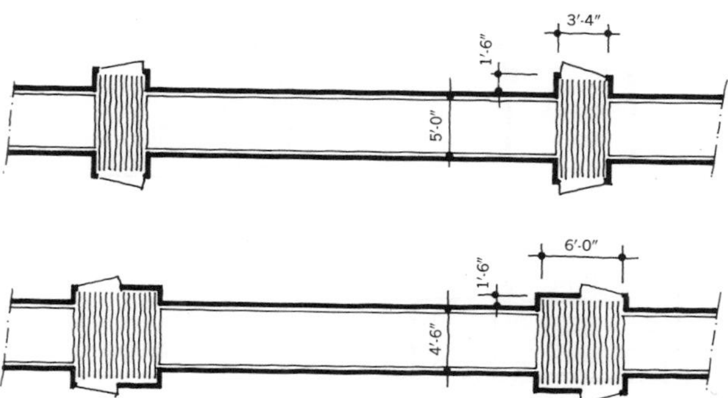

Under any conditions the corridor as the major horizontal channel of distribution merits close attention. It involves the waiting area in front of the elevators, corridor length, door rhythm, and lighting. For the elderly handrails should be provided at a 2 ft 9 in. height.

CENTRAL CORRIDOR SYSTEM: FRAMING

Framing options have been discussed in detail under the chapters of structural components. Exchange of ideas and exploration of possibilities with the structural engineer cannot take place soon enough. Nevertheless, the designer, though no structural engineer himself, needs to have enough structural sense to recognize the applicable framing principles at the moment he starts thinking of the solutions, even before he and the engineer are ready to get together.

The program conditions and the architect's own desires at this point have already started the selection process. The major masses of the project have been studied and the relation of the garage to the apartment tower has been established, suggesting column placement in relation to or independent of parking. Soil conditions and the need for caissons have been investigated. Exterior form has suggested exposed frame, complete coverup, or partial cladding (with masonry or curtain wall). All the variables of the typical floor plan have led to a determination of the possible exterior rhythm of form, framing, and fenestration.

Each framing system with its own inherent limitations will leave its stamp on the molding of the typical floor plan. Only understanding the consequences of each on planning and on economy permits a selection to be made. Prevailing practice and the limitations or desires of the contractor, if at this stage a contractor already has been selected, will make the decision easier.

Concrete framing, for a variety of reasons already discussed, is the most common of structural systems for highrises. When used with large (up to 22 ft) spans, it closely approximates steel framing **(1, 2)** except that it provides more liberties than steel in adapting column shapes to floor plans. Interior columns are not on an absolutely rigid grid **(3, 6, 10),** and even if "flying forms" are used adaptation is possible. The large span system, resulting in 7 in. or thicker slab, is more expensive than the small. It has its advantages, however. Standard plumbing traps can be buried in a 7½-in. slab, whereas thin slab requires other provisions such as special traps, furred ceiling in bathrooms or thickened slab in limited areas. Large span is more adaptable to a good parking layout and column transfer is less likely to be needed. The tripartite division of the tower width makes the outer bays useful as driving aisles on the garage floors.

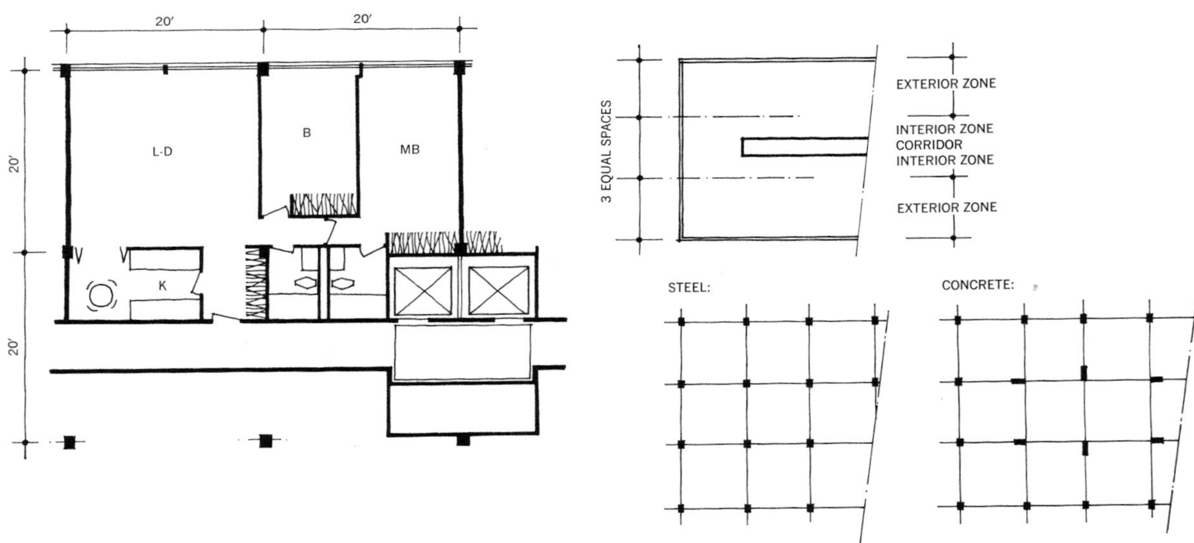

The small span system (maximum 15 or 16 ft) is quite economical because of the resulting thin slab (5 to 5½ in.) and the reduced floor reinforcing. The cost of the increased number of columns is outweighed by the savings in slabs. Its disadvantage is the increased number of caissons needed, unless pairs of columns can be easily supported on a caisson or spread footing can be used. This is a system that is not ideal when parking is directly below the apartment tower. The small bay can accommodate only one automobile with a lot of space left over and can be remedied only by costly column transfer. As costly as this is, it should be weighed against the savings gained by thin slabs on a large number of typical floors. The great planning advantage of the small span system is its complete flexibility in column placement **(13).** In fact, instead of forming a grid around which the plan must be molded, columns can be located after a preliminary plan has been worked out, presuming, however, that the widest room, the living room, does not exceed the span maximum of 15 or 16 ft.

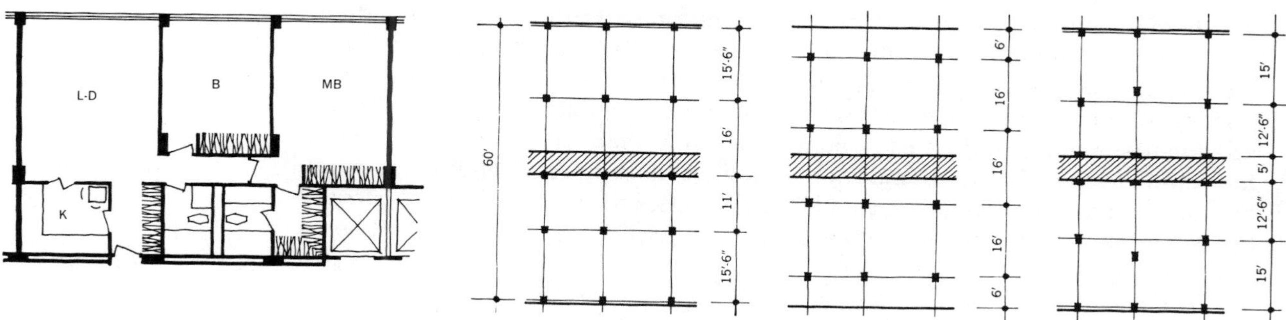

Load-bearing walls, masonry or precast concrete, with cast-in-place or precast concrete slabs, can be used for highrises up to a limited number of floors. Spans pose no particular problem with either slab type. Walls can be accommodated within the plan, although a certain discipline in planning is required. The system is best expressed when the load-bearing walls are perpendicular to and penetrate the transparent exterior wall. The drawback in this type of framing is not only the limited height (because of which it is best suited for midrises) but the inflexibility of planning the parking and common areas on the ground level.

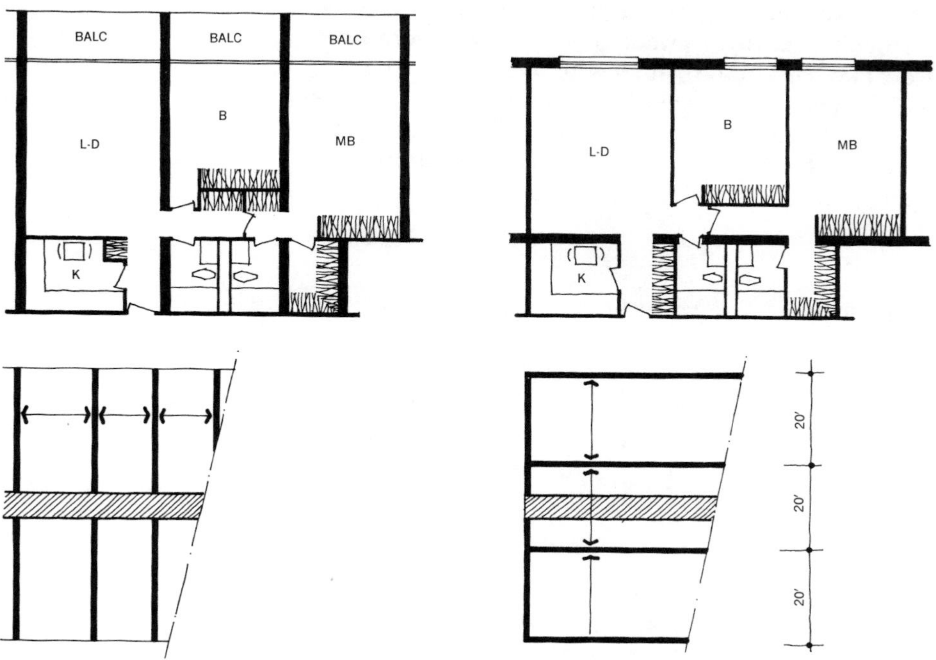

MULTICORE SYSTEM

The multicore apartment building can result from a variety of factors. Site conditions are the primary: the presence of a significant view and the requirement on the developer's part that a maximum number of apartments should enjoy it **(16, 17, 40).** The multicore type which also answers the desire for short corridors in upper income projects provides a sense of seclusion and in low-income housing a sense of community and improved surveillance. The multicore type exhibits a very human approach but is undeniably costlier than a central-corridor building.

To illustrate the evolution of this building type, it is best to return to the example that recalls the hypothetical condition of preferred view toward the east.

It was found in the example that when wrap-around end apartments—or through apartments—were introduced the number of units that could take advantage of the view increased. Through apartments are possible only at the ends of a central-corridor scheme. If the building could be cut up into several short central-corridor buildings, each with its own vertical core, the chances for through apartments would multiply.

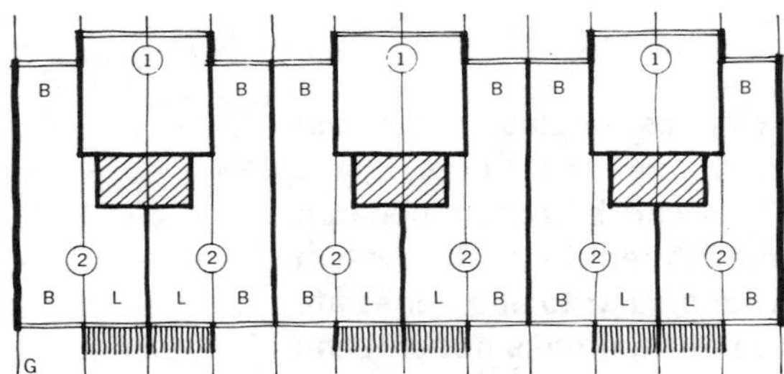

SCHEME G: The majority of the apartments, six out of eight, face the preferred view. Rhythm is excellent. Because each segment of the multicore needs two means of egress (usually a scissor stair), two elevators, refuse chute, electrical room, and corridor air supply duct, this scheme is costly. (It would be less so if it were a mid-rise project with hydraulic elevators. One could get by with one elevator per segment because hydraulic elevators need less servicing and tend to break down less often; when they do, the 5- to 6-story climb in an emergency is still manageable compared with highrises.) (See the chapter on fire safety: how new highrise fire-codes will substitute two independent stairs instead of scissor stairs.)

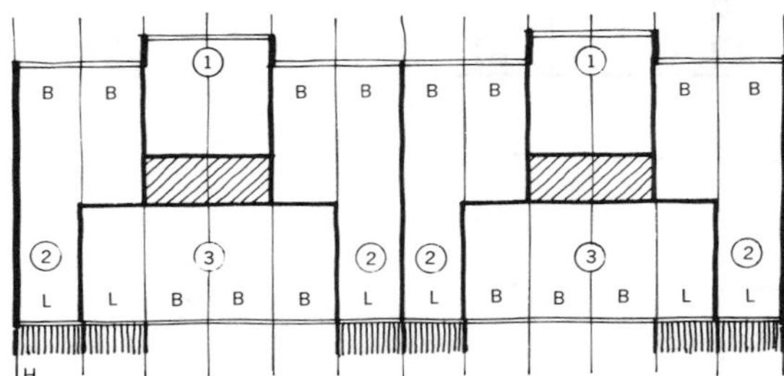

SCHEME H. Helps to reduce the number of cores without changing the number of apartments with preferred view. Rhythm is equally good. It still has more core elements than the central-corridor scheme and for the same mix and size of apartments requires a larger floor area (10,690 sf) than the equivalent central corridor type (9960 sf). It is important to realize that although the size and cost did increase, so did the efficiency ratio of the plan because the long corridor had been eliminated. In the central-corridor type with through apartments at the ends there is 1100 sf of nonrental space (11%); in the multicore, 910 sf of nonrental space (8½%).

The concentration of corridor and all the vertical core elements results in an area too large to be easily borrowed from the adjacent apartments. Consequently parts of the apartments, or entire apartments, might protrude from the building envelope **(16, 40).** Arrangement of the core elements depends on the number of apartments around the core.

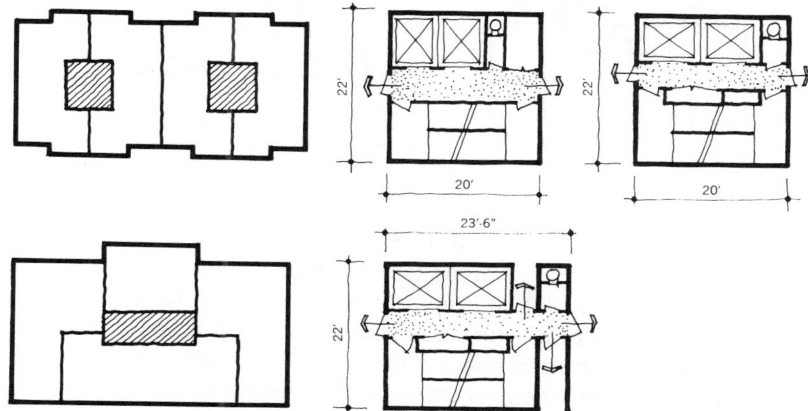

Because the multicore type consists of independent building segments, it lends itself to architectural forms not easily achieved with a central corridor. The independent segments, site conditions permitting, can be clearly articulated by a variety of means even by sliding the segments along their common wall. Similar sliding, so often desired to reduce long corridors or to break up the volume, requires additional building length on central-corridor types to solve the ''break'' of the corridor at the sliding access.

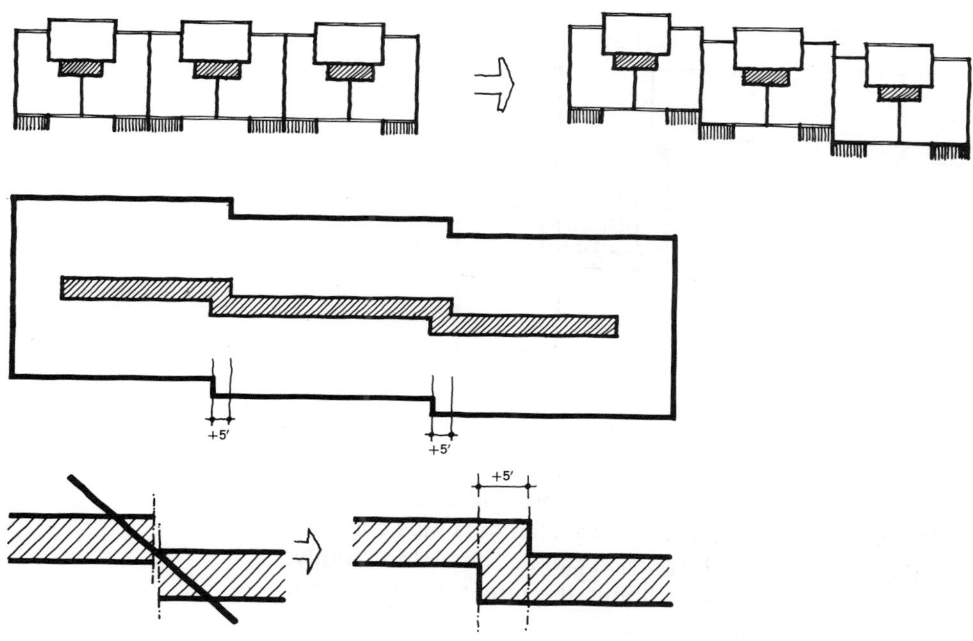

POINT-BLOCK SYSTEM

The borderline between a central-corridor apartment building and the one commonly called point block is sometimes hard to define. A short but deep central corridor scheme actually could be considered as a point block **(4, 5, 21, 24).**

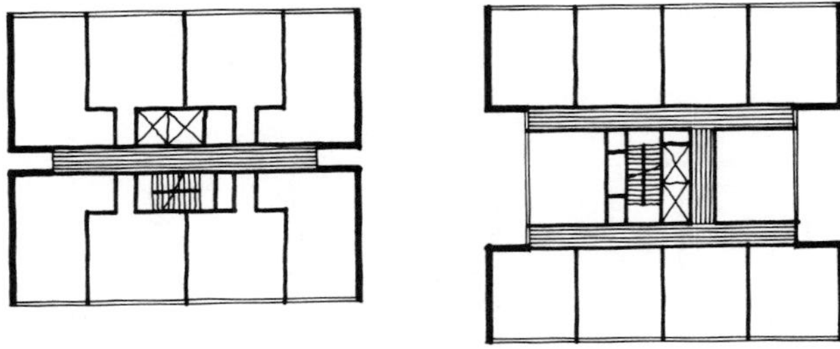

One thing is true about most point blocks that is not necessarily true about the central corridor: it has at least four (or more) directions **(18–29).** Whether the end is open or not, a central-corridor scheme is planned linearly, parallel to the long sides. The point block is schematically a square (or near square) and the apartments are planned along all sides in a ring pattern around the core. The limits of a point block lie in this circular planning. The central-corridor scheme can be extended almost endlessly (except that stairs must be introduced because of travel distance restrictions) and its number of apartments per floor are theoretically unlimited. The point block expands radially in four (or more) directions. Assuming a maximum useful depth for any apartment, the radial expansion is limited: as more apartments are placed along the circumference, the radius will grow, and at one point the space inside of the apartment ring will be more than is necessary for the vertical core elements and the corridor.

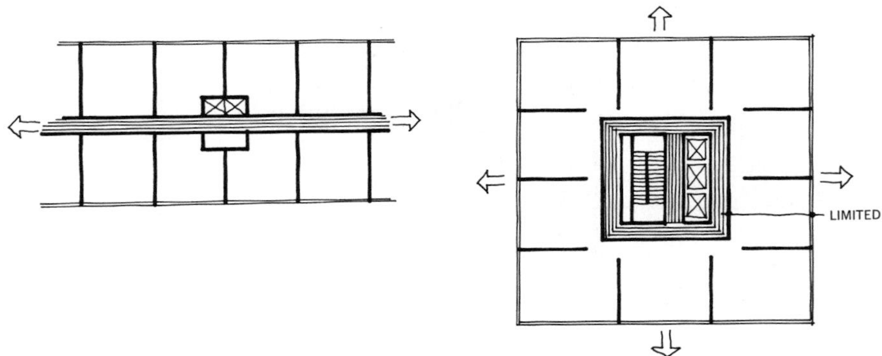

Because the efficiency ratio of 15% maximum nonrental is true for the point blocks as well, we could say that the maximum useful core will determine the maximum size of the point block. If the core (vertical core elements plus corridor) is equal to 15% of the gross floor area, the rental portion can be calculated readily. This also means that the taller the point block building, the larger it can become because its core will be larger (more elevators and smokeproof tower instead of regular stairs).

How the core relates to rental space in the point block plan is best illustrated with an example.

The assumption is a core containing two elevators and a scissor stair in a 30 by 30 ft grid. (See the chapter on fire safety: how new highrise firecodes will influence the use of scissor stairs.)

Each 900 sf square of the grid is adequate for a good one-bedroom apartment. The core (900 sf) to gross floor area (8100 sf) ratio is excellent: 11.3%. The difficulty lies in the corner apartments that are hard to enter.

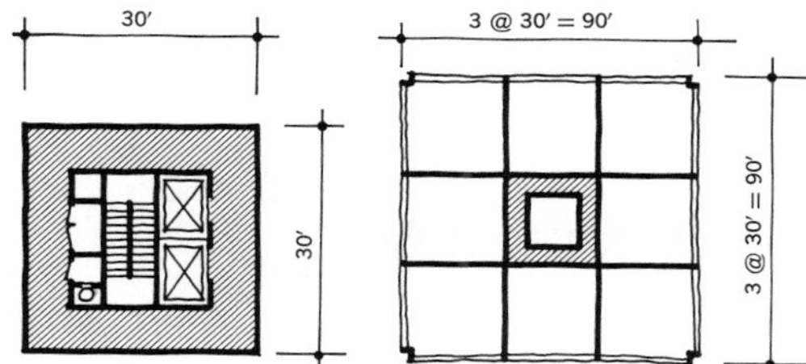

To remedy the tricky entrance problem branch corridors have been added in a pinwheel pattern. This not only helps to solve the apartment entry but provides the corridor with light and view. It has, however, proved to be too luxurious:

Original gross floor area	8100 sf
Increase	+600 sf
Total gross	8700 sf
Original core area	900 sf
Increase	600 sf
Total core:	1500 sf = 17.24% of gross!

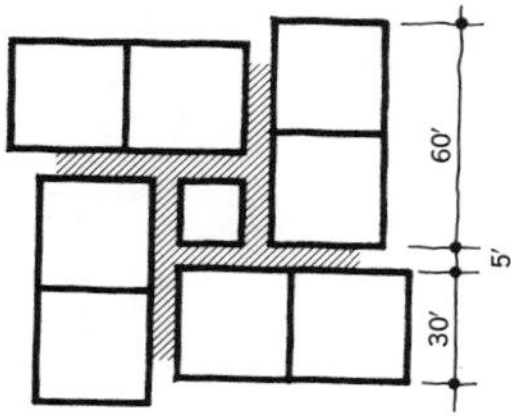

The apartment entry problem could be solved without the luxurious corridor system, thus considerably improving the floor efficiency:

Gross floor area	8200 sf
Core area	1000 sf = 12.2% of gross

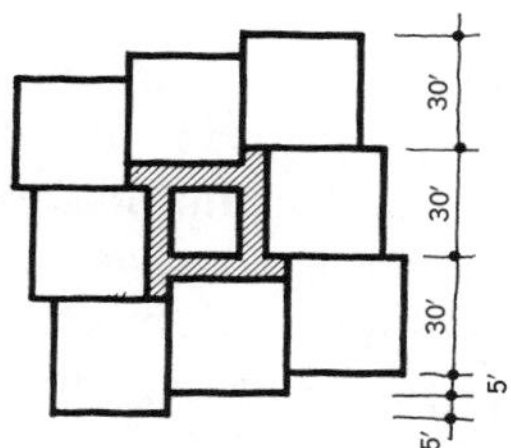

Returning to the original grid, half of the one bedroom apartments could theoretically turn into two-bedroom units by simple extension. The core (900 sf) to gross floor area (9900 sf) ratio is too good to be true: 9.1 percent. The problem is that the plan hardly functions due to the difficulties of entering the two-bedroom units.

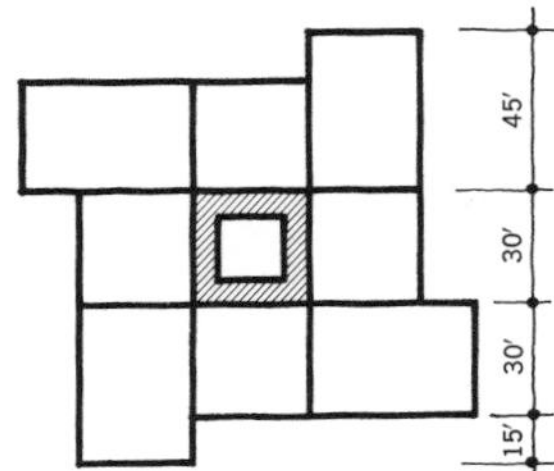

Again, branch corridors can remedy the situation by adding light and view to the core.

Original gross floor area	9900 sf
Increase	+600 sf
Total gross	10,500 sf
Original core area	900 sf
Increase	+600 sf
	1,500 sf = 14.3% of gross

There is no need to eliminate the light and view created by the extended corridor as it was necessary to do in the one-bedroom plan. The increased gross floor area can take an increased core without losing efficiency.

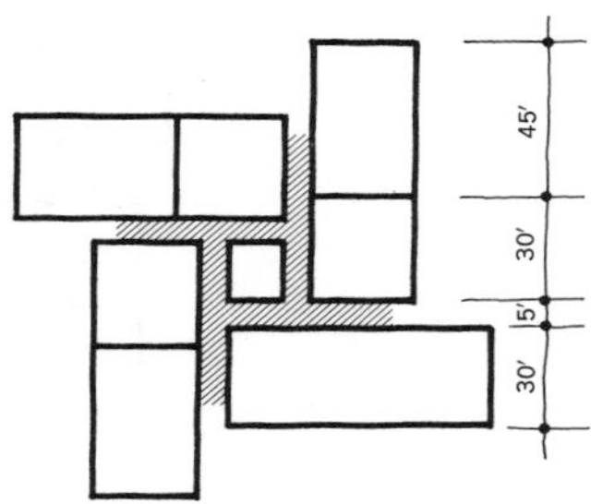

It is quite apparent that with a given core size, determined by the height of the building, the more rental square footage surrounding the core, the more economically efficient the plan will become. Deep plans with narrow exterior exposure can maximize this efficiency.

It is not necessary that the public corridor form a ring around the vertical core elements **(18, 28).** Depending on where the surrounding apartments can be entered, the amount of corridor, and consequently the total core area, can be reduced. Splitting the vertical core elements and using an "H"-shaped corridor is more efficient than the ring **(19, 22, 29).** To serve more than six apartments the wings can be extended, but the maximum dead-end corridor permitted by code must be kept in mind. When no dead-end is allowed, a ring corridor is the only answer.

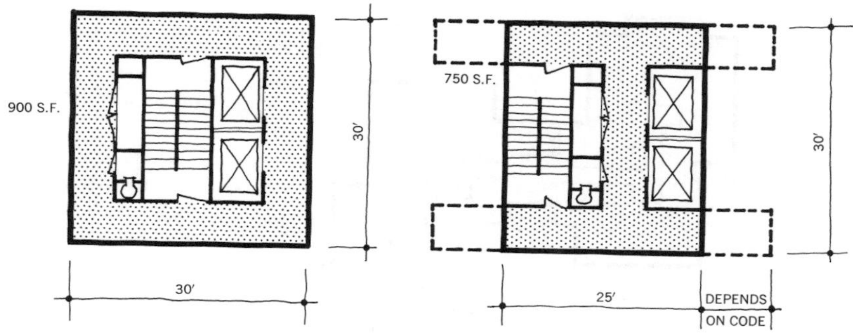

When a large number of apartments constitutes the typical floor and the core becomes bigger than needed for stairs, elevators, refuse chute and so on, the extra space can be filled with tenant lockers **(22)**. This is well justified when no other inexpensive space is available in the building for these lockers or when the proximity of lockers to apartments results in major marketing advantages. Otherwise, locating the lockers on expensive floor space makes little sense.

Point blocks can take many shapes, each of which has its own inherent limitations. The classic pinwheel is a sequential dynamic shape, most conducive to experimentation and invention **(27, 28)**. Less dynamic but still quite free is the "inverted symmetry" type. Axial plans can be symmetrical around a single axis, double axis, or four axes, leading to the circle with its unlimited number of axes and the difficulties of pie-shaped apartments **(18, 19, 20)**. Very tall buildings with considerably increased cores can be well fitted into triaxial arrangements and triangle- or tripod-shaped plans **(25)**.

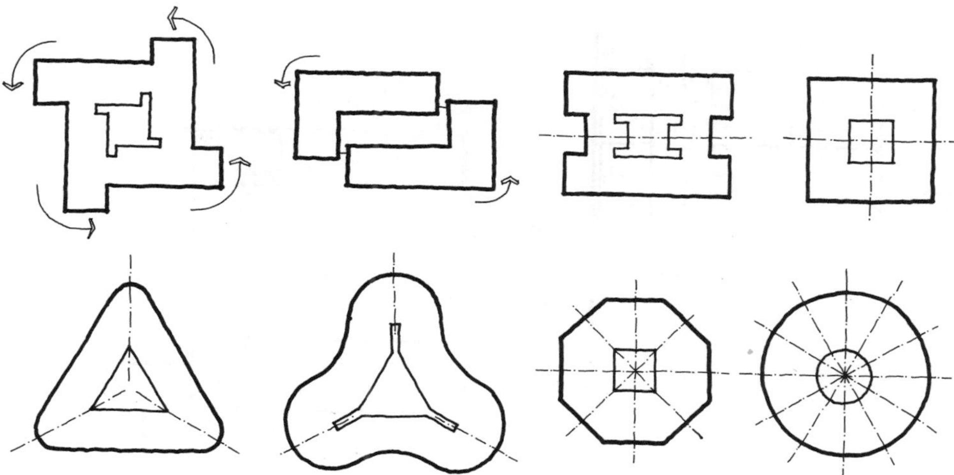

Another form is the linking of two point blocks to form a kind of multicore point block so imaginatively used by Davis Brody & Associates in New York. When the link is used to house the elevator core as done by Hoberman & Wasserman, sizable savings can be realized and, in fact, a complete circle will have been traveled: point blocks linked by an elevator core are nothing but central-corridor buildings with bold articulation **(26)**.

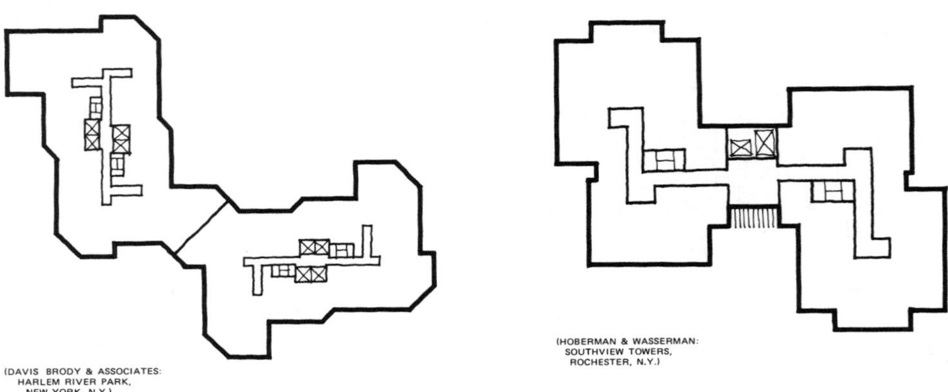

(DAVIS BRODY & ASSOCIATES:
HARLEM RIVER PARK,
NEW YORK, N.Y.)
(HOBERMAN & WASSERMAN:
SOUTHVIEW TOWERS,
ROCHESTER, N.Y.)

The principles of apartment planning described for the central-corridor scheme are valid for point blocks as well, but difficulties generally occur in corner apartments. Unless the corridor is extended—thus greatly increasing the nonrental space—these apartments are hard to enter, especially when corner living rooms with maximum light and wide-angle views are most marketable. The passage from entrance to living room inevitably bypasses the sleeping area. Imaginative planning should make this passage as direct and bright as possible. When the living room is pulled away from the corner, the problem will have been eliminated.

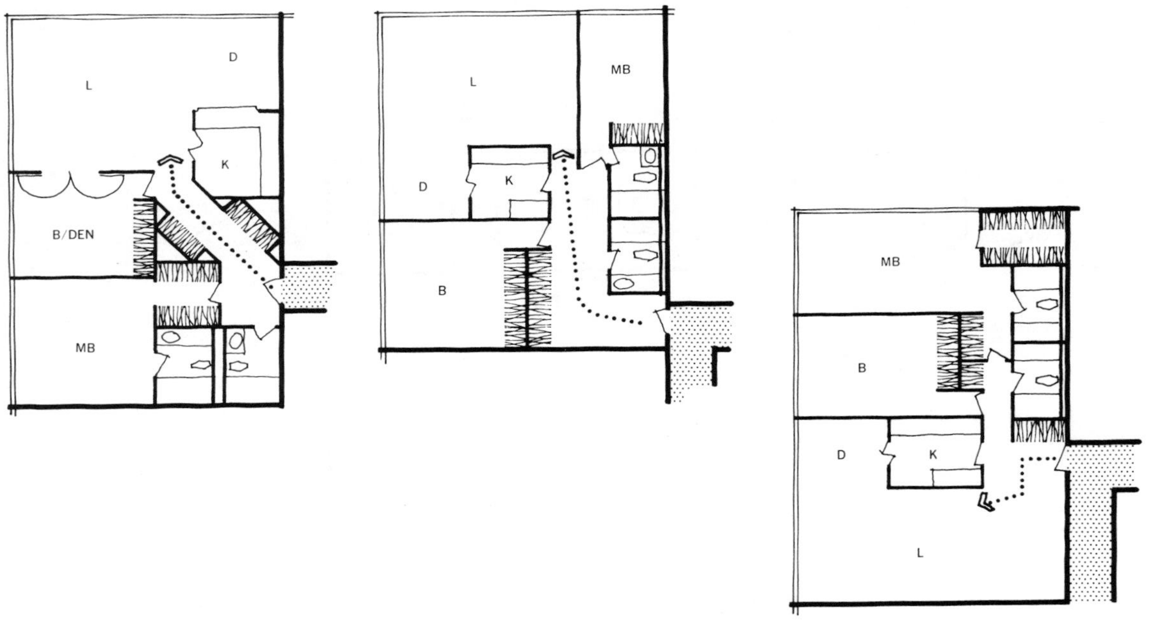

Structural principles already discussed do not change when a point block is planned. What happens, however, is that the vertical core elements concentrated in the center can act as a structural core, and the corridor, plus the normal apartment depth, creates two manageable bays in which the column line coincides with the line between inner and outer zones.

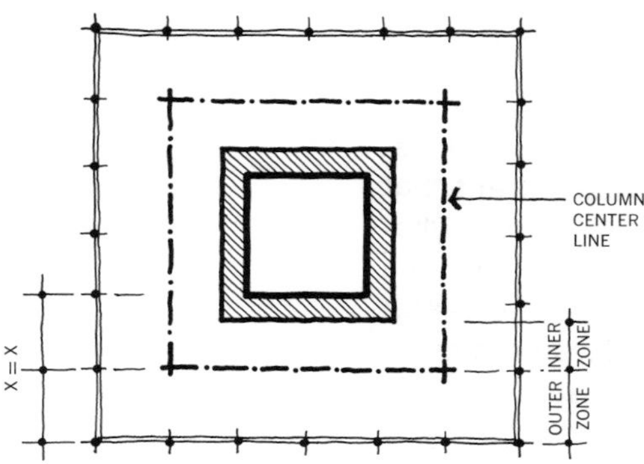

EXTERIOR CORRIDOR SYSTEM

The major generator of the exterior corridor scheme is that all apartments can have two exterior zones because of this form of access **(15, 31, 33)**. Its logical use is in moderate climates, in which advantage can be taken of the double exposure for cross ventilation. In northern latitudes the corridor exposed to the elements is far from ideal; it becomes icy, windswept, and snowpacked. The use of the exterior corridor scheme for low-cost housing, regardless of the climate, has been justified because of the outdoor area it can provide adjacent to the dwelling and because the open corridor is easily observable, at least up to a reasonable number of floors **(31)**.

It is not an economical type of housing. Each of its apartments carries twice the amount of corridor cost of the central corridor scheme. What is true about the cost of the corridor is also true about the vertical core elements; compared with the central corridor solution, their cost is absorbed by half the number of units. To accommodate the same number of families as a central corridor apartment building on the same area of ground, the outside corridor building will be twice as tall and less wind resistive as a result of its narrowness.

Aside from the question of wind resistiveness, the same structural principles apply as to the central corridor building. The ubiquitous outside corridor is generally handled as a cantilevered slab, although when the corridor is long columns along its edge can create added scale and articulation.

The same apartment types can be used with this scheme as the inner corridor, except that the principle of borrowing is seldom applicable, for the vertical cores can be separated easily and handled as independent elements.

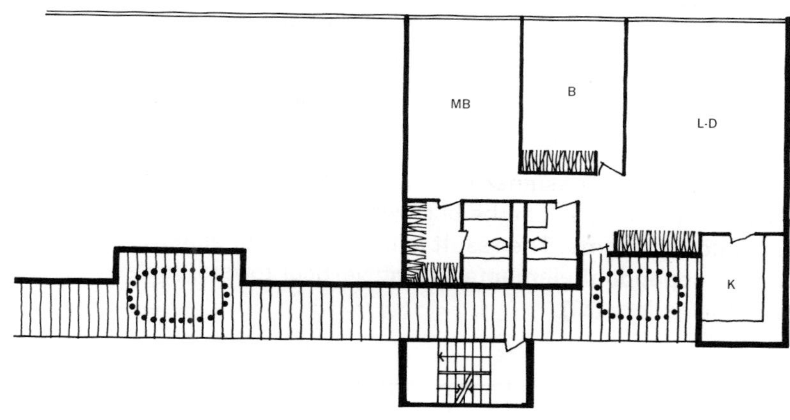

When the apartment types of the central corridor scheme are reused with an outside gallery, the real significance of the exterior corridor system is lost. The double exposure of this scheme demands a different approach to apartment planning, one that takes advantage of the fact that rooms can face in two directions. Naturally, this is not quite true. The gallery side of the apartments—except that of the last one—really faces a public walk which presents serious limitations. Bedrooms cannot face this way unless they have clerestory windows which, with the gallery overhanging, provide poor light. Again there is the question of climate; it may be a good solution in extremely bright semitropical regions. On the other hand, living rooms, dining spaces, and kitchens can get by with less privacy. Placed along the corridor they provide an added degree of surveillance that may be desirable.

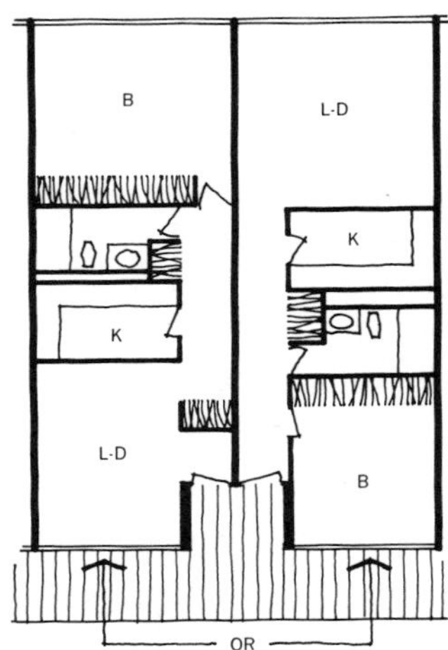

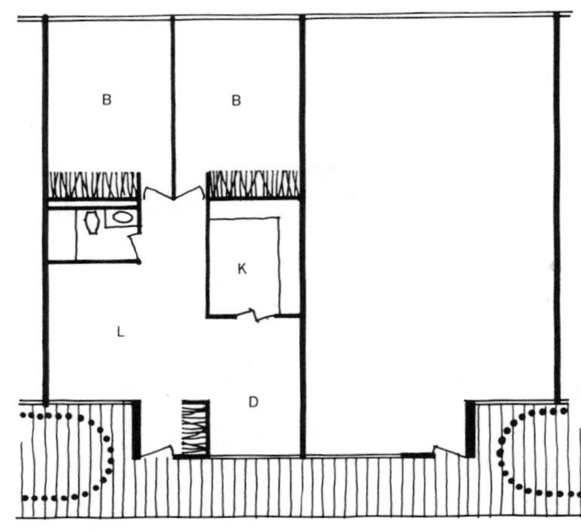

When significant indentations are called for in the plan or when the entire gallery is made considerably wider than necessary for mere passage (sometimes to accommodate out-swinging screen doors), well-observed play areas for small children and sitting areas for adults can be created. Some kind of symbolic separation, however,—level change or low fencing—is necessary between the passage and these areas if they are to serve as porches or verandas and to create a sense of private territory and "ownership" by the occupant.

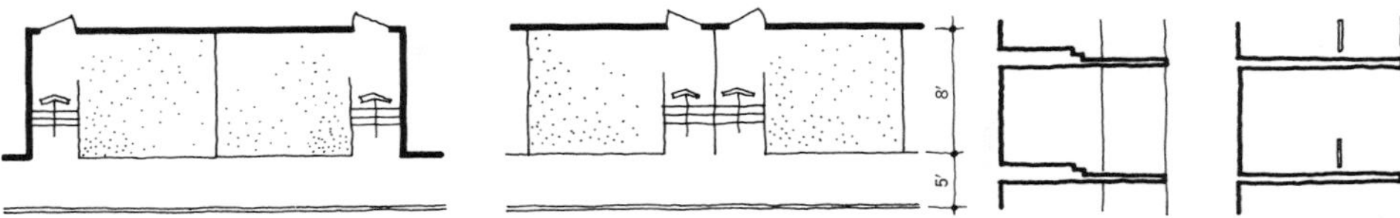

The vertical core elements provide the designer with a variety of options in exterior corridor buildings. To begin with, they can be borrowed from the apartment and handled as part of the building volume. The result is long, powerful galleries. They can be handled also as independent elements, strong vertical towers, juxtaposed to the horizontality of the gallery **(33).**

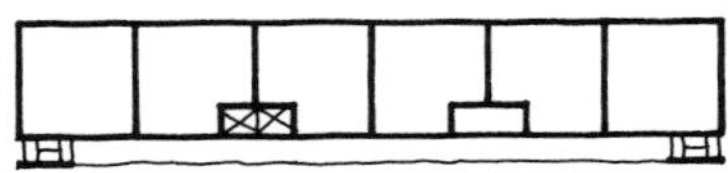

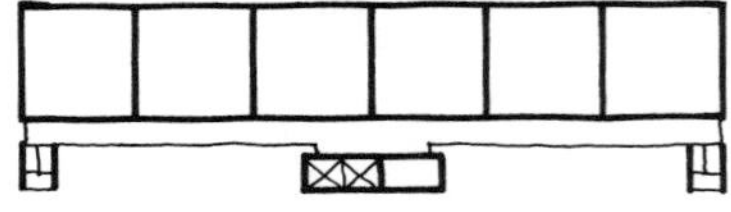

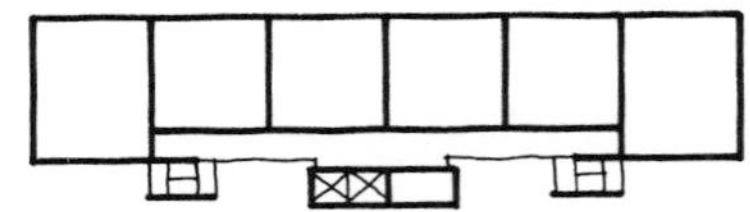

It has been advocated that galleries, especially when they serve as major traffic channels between buildings, be considered as "streets in the sky." This concept will remain an unrealized dream, for without shops and community spaces, both prohibitively costly on upper decks and commercial space is not self-supporting—there are no viable streets. "It seems that once the presence of shops, views of outside community life, and the automobile have all been taken away, the thing that remains is only a corridor."[25]

SKIP-STOP SYSTEM

Central corridor, multicore, point block, exterior corridor type—all are generated by differing horizontal distribution channels. These terms, in their common use, suggest regular elevator stops at every floor. However, when the plan is such that only every second or third elevator stop is necessary, we are talking about a completely new category, the skip-stop system **(15, 17, 30 to 35),** which can also be central corridor, exterior corridor, multicore, and, very rarely, point block.

What is even more important than the alternating elevator stops in this system is the fact that most or all apartments are on more than one level; hence the name "multilevel apartment scheme" often used for skip-stop.

In addition to regular (one-level) apartments, skip-stop schemes generate three basic multilevel apartment types:

1. Regular apartments that are entered on the floor above or below by way of a two-story interior stair hall.
2. Apartments on two or three levels. The levels relate to one another with one-half floor difference.
3. Truly two-story apartments with interior stairs.

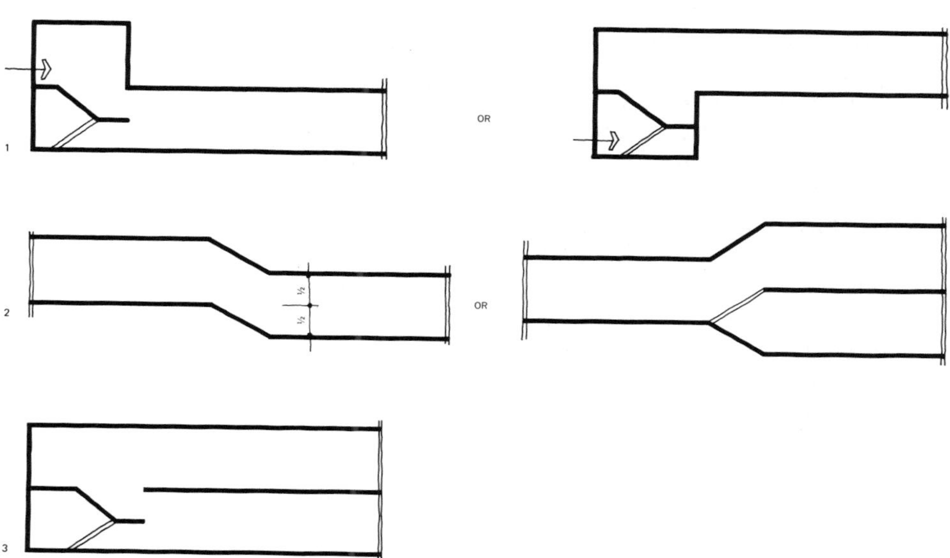

Stairs, the connectors between the various levels, play a relatively minor role as an aesthetic element in the first two types. They are not free standing and are surrounded by walls on two or three sides. In the third type the stairs can become the major element of spatial excitement when carefully handled and displayed. To gain maximum aesthetic pleasure not only from the stairs but from the interrelation of the two levels, this is possible only when the living space becomes truly two stories high and when the upper space appears as a mezzanine within the high space.

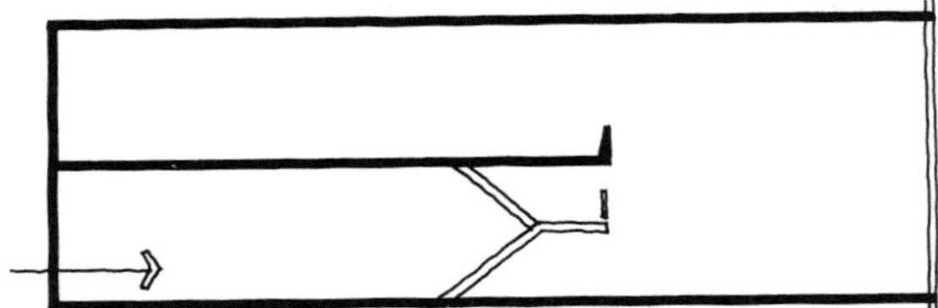

Combining the three basic types with regular apartments permits almost unlimited combinations (see p. 233).

Multilevel apartment schemes require careful analysis of the building code. Does the code require a separate exit into a public corridor for each floor of a two-story apartment? What about the exits for a trilevel scheme? Careful attention must be paid to framing the breaks in the floors and to the vertical alignment of plumbing shafts and exhaust ducts. When the kitchen occurs above the living space of the floor below, there is no kitchen carpeting that would help to minimize impact noises; a special liner must be used under resilient flooring.

These are just some of the major difficulties and caveats. Multilevel apartments are costly and their design must be justified. The justifications are varied: view problems, market requirements for unusual interior spaces, space for simultaneous but conflicting activities, maximum separation between sleeping and living zones, and so on, not to mention the variety that can be introduced on the exterior. Admittedly every designer is challenged by the idea, and, if it can be worked out within the budget, why not?

In weighing the cost problems, it should not be overlooked that, as in multicore schemes, the elimination of corridors on alternating floors will increase the rentable space. According to a recent study by the Urban Design Group of the New York City Planning Department (*Architectural Record*, April 1971), in a skip-stop prototype worked out by the group "the total structure creates about 25 percent less gross cubic feet of building than do 'normal' corridor-every-floor projects having the same number and size of apartments."

It is also possible to create two-story apartments or level changes in apartments without a skip-stop elevator scheme **(14, 16).** In the same way that the designer is free to mold the plan horizontally, he can slide portions of an apartment along a vertical axis and thus introduce more than one-floor elevation. It is a costly proposition compared with the level slab and is usually warranted only in high-rent housing. The increased cost is primarily in the special framing around the depressed portions of the floor.

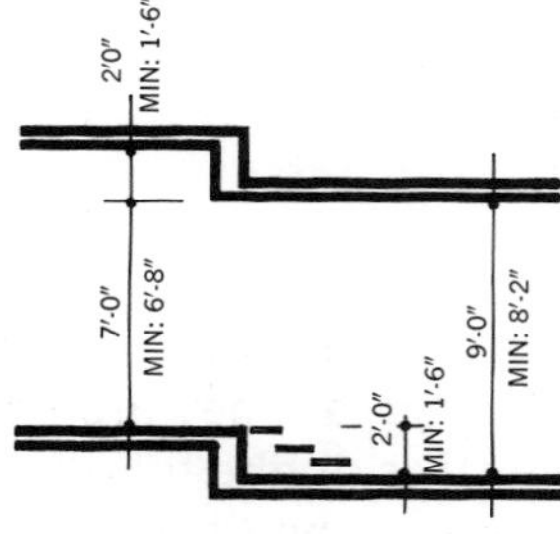

SKIP-STOP SYSTEM

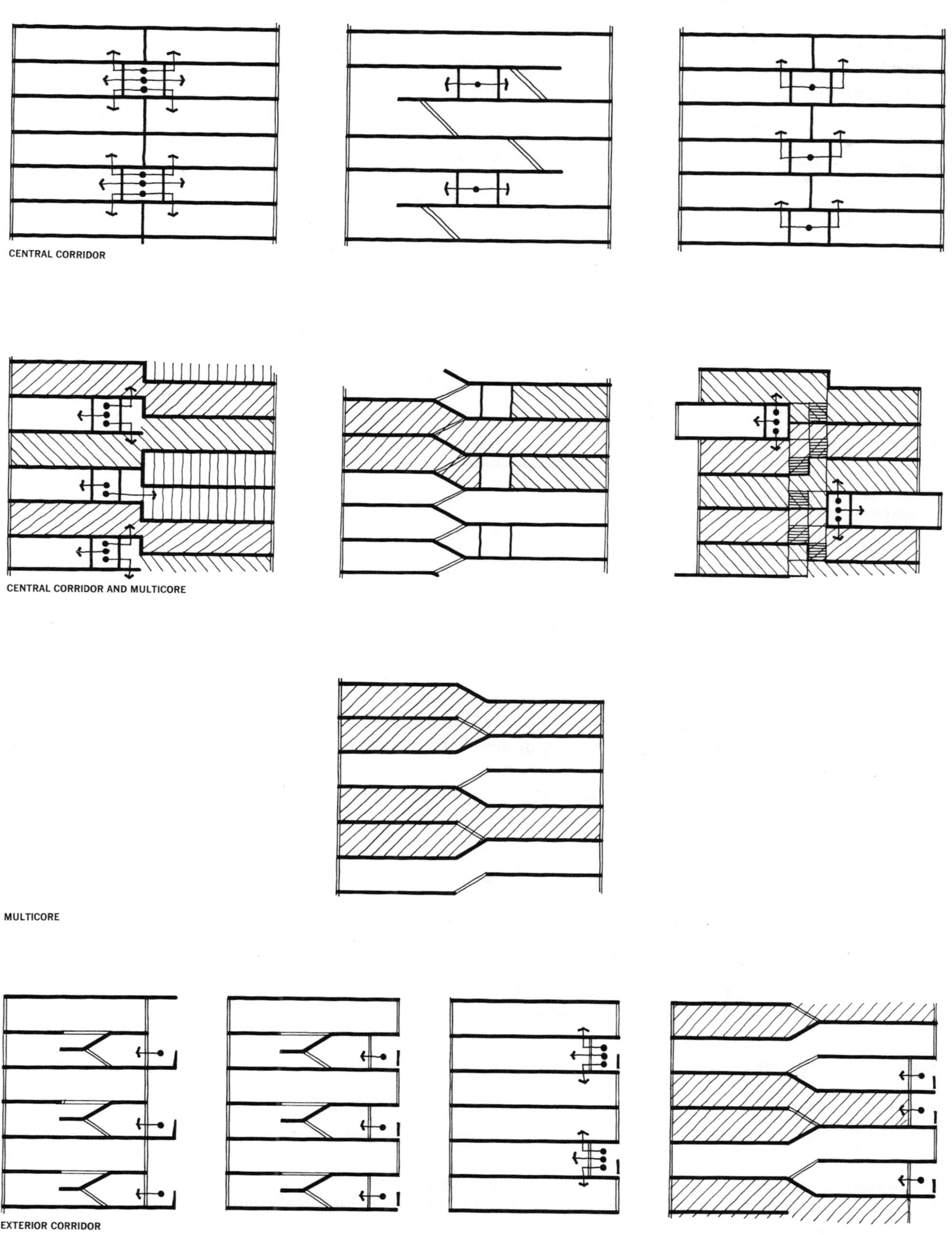

The simplest form of level break is the depressed living-dining-kitchen complex. In another form the living room alone is depressed, thus giving the dining space an elevated appearance. In this way though in the interior zone, it is well defined **(16).**

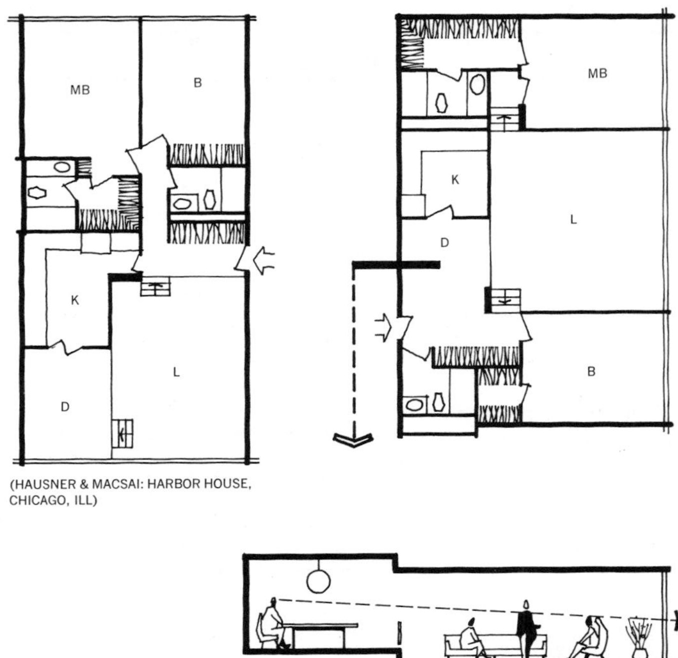

(HAUSNER & MACSAI: HARBOR HOUSE, CHICAGO, ILL)

To break the level between living and dining space the dining area must be more than adequate in size, for level breaks eliminate the possibility of expansion. The break itself can be handled with a railing or simply as an open step.

In addition to the spatial variety created in the interior, the change of floor levels opens up exciting new possibilities on the exterior of the building when properly expressed.

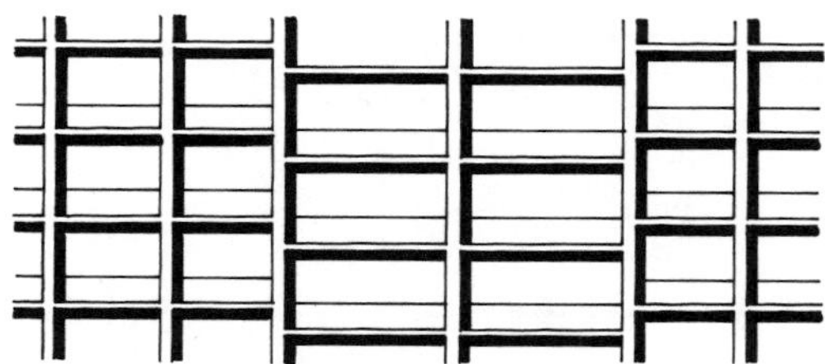

SINGLE-TOWER SITES

Having discussed the components of the apartment building and the basic systems of organizing the units into a vertical container, we are faced with the question whether there is a way of putting it all together in logical progression.

Needless to say, the number of variables is so immense that there is no foolproof formula, one that would cover all cases, for no two problems have identical conditions. Nevertheless, some broad directions are valid.

Again an example will best illuminate the issue. There is a client who wants to build a middle- to upper income condominium containing two-bedroom units of approximately 1050 to 1100 sf. The site is an urban one with a definite view that not only will help to market the units but does so at higher sales prices. Setbacks and density, determined by zoning, allow 240 dwellings (about 170 units per acre, or 265 sf of land per dwelling unit).

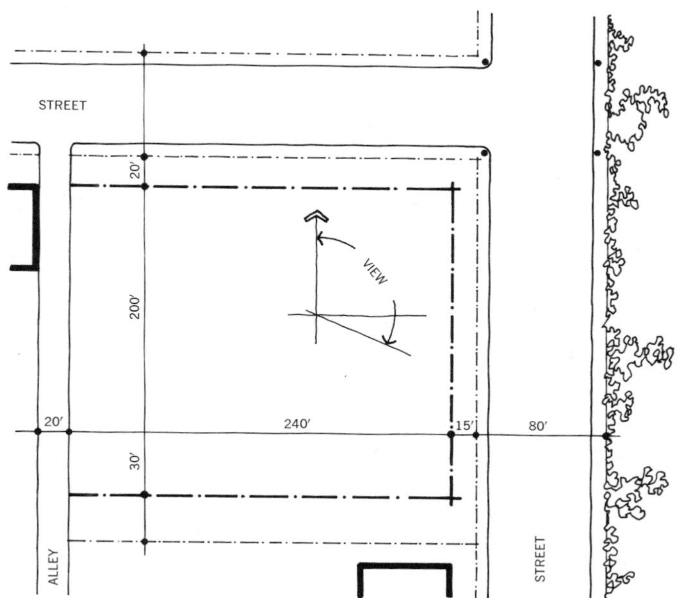

Lot dimensions and view will strongly influence the system of apartment organization. Even before considering the site, however, two of the possible systems (central corridor, multicore, point block, exterior corridor, and skip-stop) can be eliminated immediately—the exterior corridor because of climate and cost, the skip-stop because of cost, and local market resistance to stairs within the apartment. This leaves central corridor, multicore, and point block as valid options.

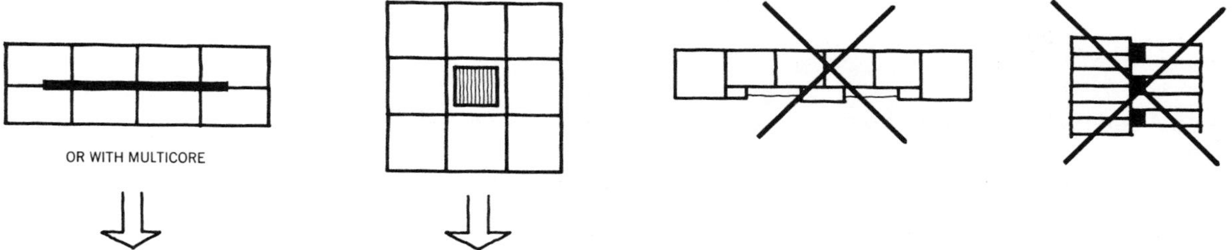

What are the possibilities of this site? Scheme A is a central corridor solution far enough from the highrise to the south to allow good angled view even from the farthest apartment. It has a large number of units, 12 per floor, and uses concrete construction economically. Scheme B is also a central corridor solution but solves the view problem unsatisfactorily and can be discarded. Scheme C, a multicore that requires a fourth elevator, is a modification of B that would improve the view.

There are 10 units on a floor. Scheme D is a point block with 8 units on a floor and a good view from most. Because of the small number of units per floor, it is taller than the others and requires a smokeproof tower (at least under our imagined code).

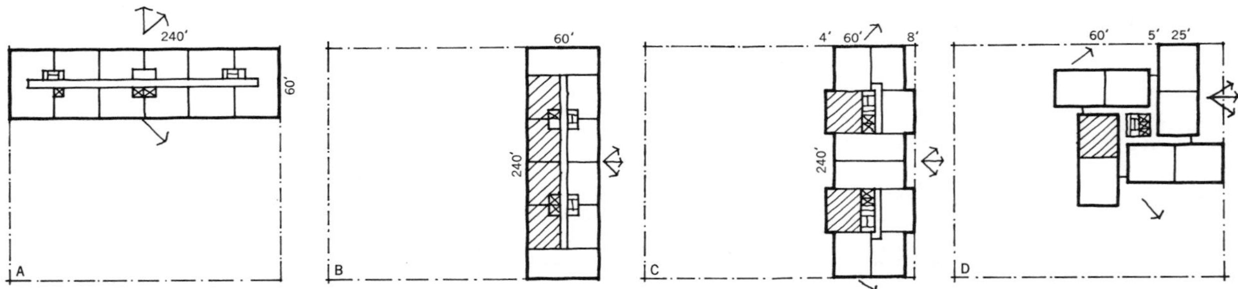

A comparative analysis of these schemes should help the choice of one of them, at least until the next step. Which has the smallest area for 240 apartments? Which has the least exterior skin? Which has the smallest nonrental-to-gross ratio? Which has the maximum number of apartments with view? At least two of the schemes score acceptably in some of the categories.

Category	Scheme A	Scheme B	Scheme C	Scheme D
Size of floor in sf (and number of units) @ number of floors = gross tower area in square feet for 240 units	14,400 (12) @ 20 = 288,000[b]	12,000 (10) @ 24 = 288,000[b]	12,960 (10) @ 24 = 311,000	10,880 (8) @ 30[a] = 326,400
Perimeter per floor @ floor height @ number of floors = skin in square feet	600 @ 8.5 = 5100 @ 20 = 102,000[b]	520 @ 8.5 = 4420 @ 24 = 106,000[b]	570 @ 8.5 = 4845 @ 24 = 116,280	550 @ 8.5 = 4675 @ 30 = 140,250
Nonrental per floor in sf = percent of gross	1640 11.4%[b]	1360 11.3%[b]	1540 11.8%[b]	1530 14%
Percentage of apartments with view	100%[b]	60%	80%[b]	87.5%[b]

[a] Added cost of smokeproof tower.
[b] Acceptable scores.

Scheme A seems to score well from every point of view with the exception of one major drawback—the long corridor that will have to be dealt with. Scheme B is equally economical; its corridor is shorter but it does not solve the view problem. Scheme C costs more but has unique advantages in its multicore setup. Scheme D is obviously uneconomical. On another site for another market scheme D could still be the answer (in any case it should be kept, at least for the sake of comparison, through the next step). Each scheme has its own exterior possibilities and limitations. Regardless of all the rational comparisons, the impact of the tower mass, so different in each scheme should be studied; the way in which each scheme lends itself to the designer's intent on the exterior should be considered at this point.

How do the towers relate to the common elements of the building—parking, storage, laundry, and recreation? Parking, the largest of all common elements, with strong functional requirements that cannot be easily disposed of, should be the first to be examined. The type of ownership (condominium) necessitates one-to-one parking regardless of zoning requirements. In this case the sponsor's program calls for self-parking.

Among the remaining three solutions D cannot accommodate the required 240 cars on two levels as the others can. The third deck adds so much to the cost that this fact together with other cost problems will permit the final decision to discard it. Both A and C have more than 240 stalls in this schematic study. Considering that parking spaces will be eaten up by the swimming pool—if it is on the deck—and that the loading dock and stairs will further cut into them, scheme C is tight, whereas A presents an easy parking solution.

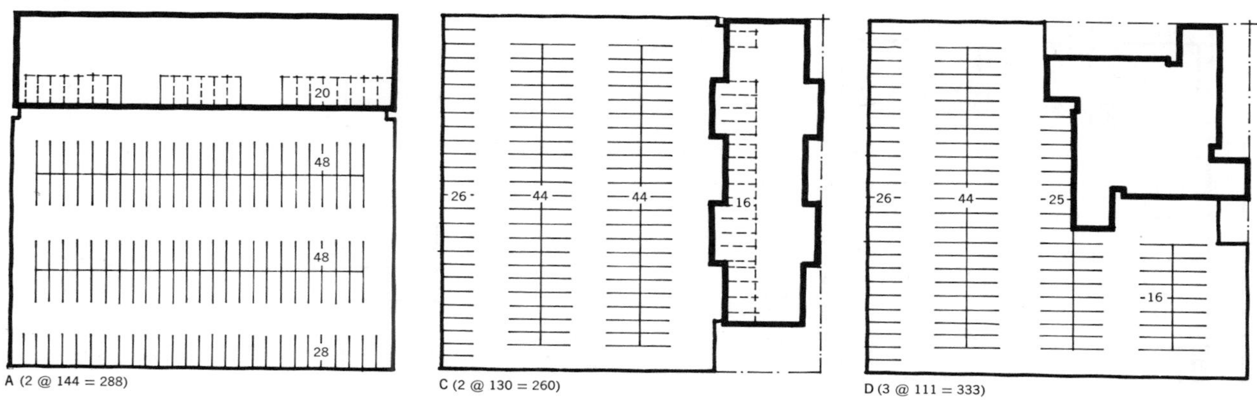

A (2 @ 144 = 288) C (2 @ 130 = 260) D (3 @ 111 = 333)

Traffic conditions on the site also favor scheme A. Because of the heavy traffic on the north-south street and the possibility of a pile-up at the traffic light, entry and exit appear to be easier on the less traveled east-west street. Loading from the alley, possible only in scheme A, is also preferred. Loading for scheme C—regardless of the street—is rather cumbersome because this scheme has two vertical cores and the loading path must reach both.

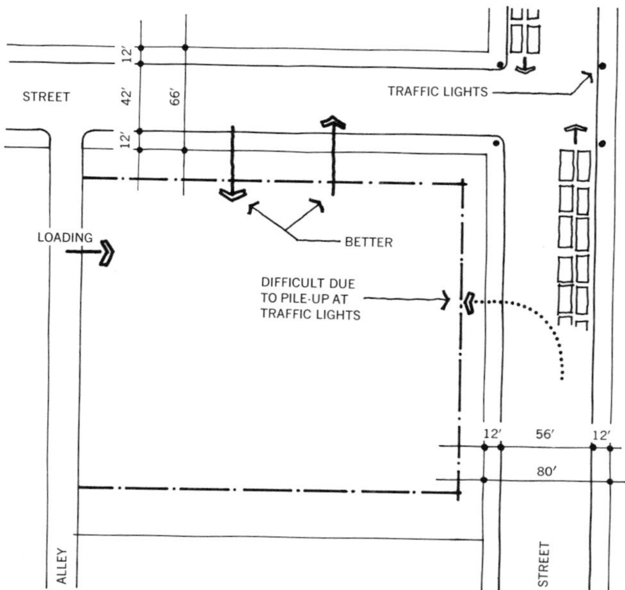

Further testing—in scheme A—of the interrelations of parking, loading, exit, and entrance seems to present no difficulties. Considering the possibilities of integrating the vertical tower and the horizontal parking volume, this scheme lends itself to a number of options that should be studied at this time, though for the sake of continuity in this illustration they can be deferred for the moment. There is adequate length for the ramps under the tower and the entire lower parking level can be located in the basement. Half-level depression of the parking volume to reduce ramp length is without advantage in this case (a high-water table could alter this decision).

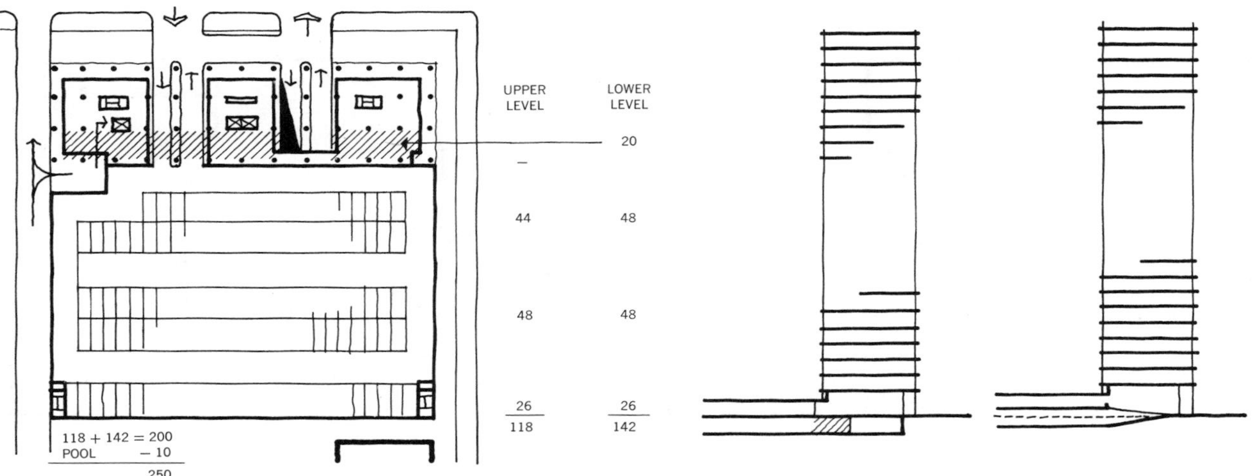

The next step in the investigation concerns the rest of the common spaces. Using criteria discussed in Chapter 2 and making some assumptions, we can establish space requirements for each need.

MECHANICAL AND STORAGE AREAS	
Electric gear and transformer	800 sf
Pumps and hot-water heater	500 sf
Building storage	300 sf
Refuse room	300 sf
Receiving room	400 sf
Tenant lockers (240 @ 25)	6000 sf
LOBBY AREA	
Lobby and mail room	1500 sf
Pram room	150 sf
RECREATION AREAS	
Pool (open) with deck area	6000 sf
Tennis courts	6200 sf
Sauna (and pool toilets)	1200 sf
Mtg room (and storage, kitchenette)	3000 sf
Game rooms	600 sf
Laundry	500 sf

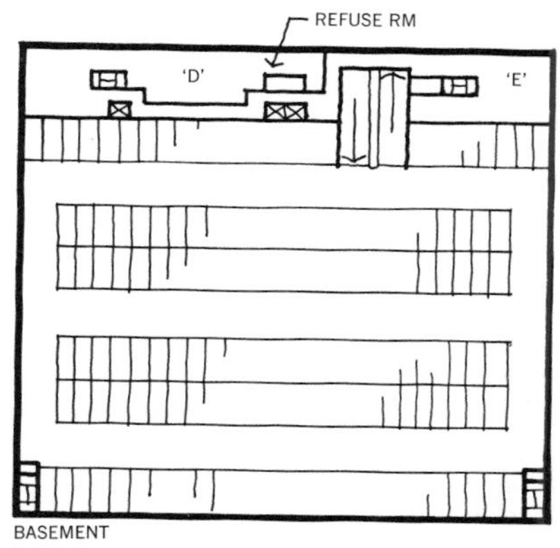

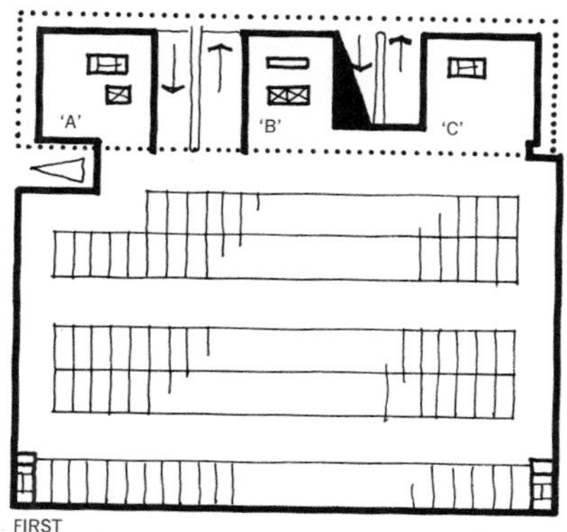

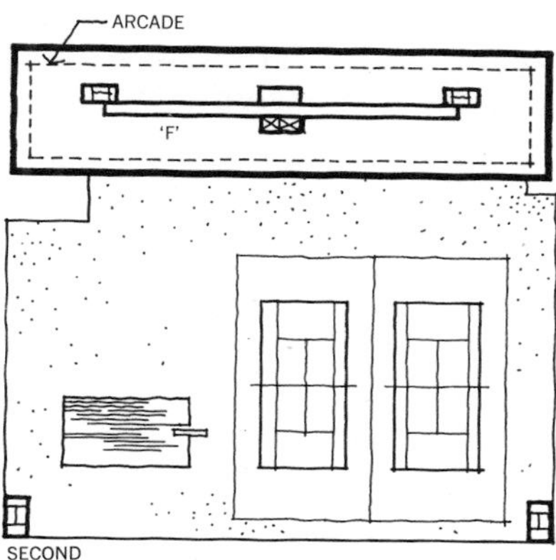

Examination of the spaces that are left after solving parking and loading will indicate that the center area B (approximately 1700 sf net) is about right for lobby and pram room in the proper location. Area A (approximately 2300 sf net) next to the service elevator is ideal for receiving room and building storage with the leftover space used for some of the tenant lockers. Area C (approximately 2400 sf net) is cut off from the service elevator and is not useful for tenant lockers; it is excellent, though, for electrical gear and transformer (with good access), for pump and hot-water heater, as well as for building storage. The spaces left in the basement, areas D and E (approximately 6000 sf net), are useful for the balance of the tenant lockers and refuse room.

The deck of the garage can comfortably accommodate tennis courts and open swimming pool with adequate space left for a sundeck. The indoor recreation spaces called for under the arbitrary program add up to about 5300 sf and the lowest typical floor provides 12,700 sf of useful area (area F), more than twice the amount needed. It is ideally located for recreational purposes near the pool and tennis courts.

Even if this floor were cut back to the arcade line of the first floor—assuming this is wanted for architectural form—it would still have a useful area of 9200 sf, more than is needed for the program. The surplus space can be utilized for tenant lockers, thus eliminating the need for space in the basement (see p. 240).

A similar investigation should be made for every possible scheme that answers the program's requirements. Only after the designer has been assured of the gen-

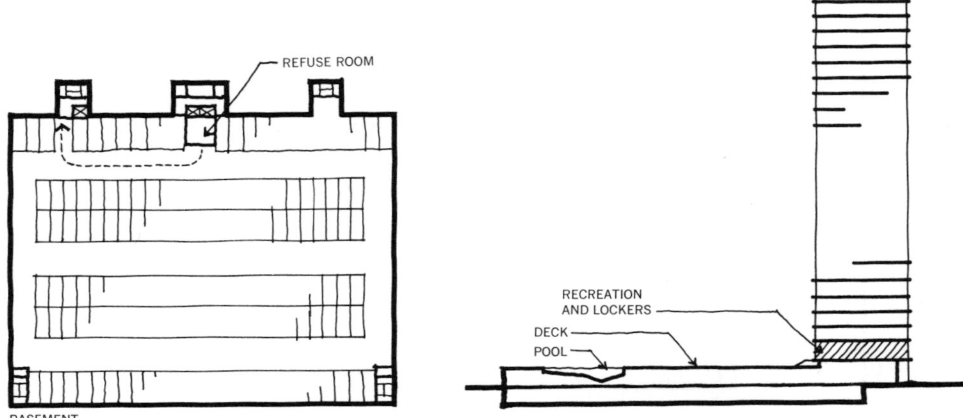

eral allocation of spaces and the working interrelations of volumes can detailed planning of the typical floors be more than wasted exercise.

MULTITOWER SITES

A site like the one analyzed in the preceding chapter is so circumscribed by its size that the single apartment tower it contains relates to its environment in a minimal sense. The options, within economic reality, are extremely limited. Large sites, for which several apartment buildings are planned, offer the designer an opportunity to deal with these volumes on additional levels.

On large sites the system selected for the organization of apartments is more the result of composition, form, site circulation, and environmental relations than of defined dimensions between setbacks as on restricted small sites.

1. The apartment-tower volumes enter into a more complicated *relationship with the lower volume*, the garage:

Placement of the towers often depends on the most efficient parking layout below. If there is a single entrance control for the security of an entire project, connection of the main lobby with the elevator lobbies of the individual towers becomes a complex problem.

Similarly, if there is a single loading area, its connection with the service elevators of the individual towers is also complex and so, in reverse, is the hook-up between the individual refuse rooms and the loading dock.

2. The *relation of the towers to the environment* can now be planned instead of dictated by zoning and setbacks:

The apartment volumes relate to an existing structure or group of structures to form continuity or contrast, to open up space or close it.

The shadows cast by the towers on the neighborhood are not disregarded; their effect on parks, vegetation, and play areas at particular times of day is to be considered.

Orientation—for sun, for wind—becomes a factor in siting the towers.

The views of or from existing structures and public spaces should when possible be respected.

3. Towers within the project gain another dimension in their *relation to one another:*

The aesthetic relation is a constantly changing one, depending on the observer's viewpoint, on the changing surfaces in sunlight or shade, and on the shadows cast by the towers. Towers overlap one another or open up unexpected vistas. They also reflect one another in their glass surfaces.

The position of the towers should be considered in relation to view and light for the majority of units. The distance between them is related to the amount of overlap and both are related to height. From the point of view of minimum overlap and maximum view the advantages of the point block become obvious.

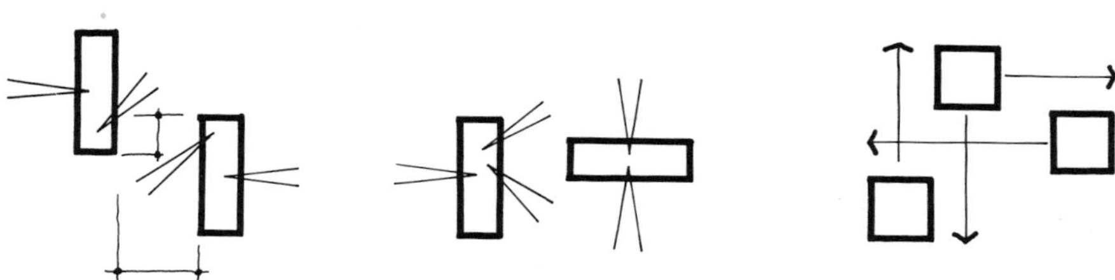

Minimizing the cross view from apartment to apartment is equally important to ensure privacy.

Individual towers can be linked together. They can be joined at end walls or by the vertical transportation core. Either way, especially when the site is large enough to provide multiple links, new possibilities open up for meandering volumes and exciting spaces created between them.

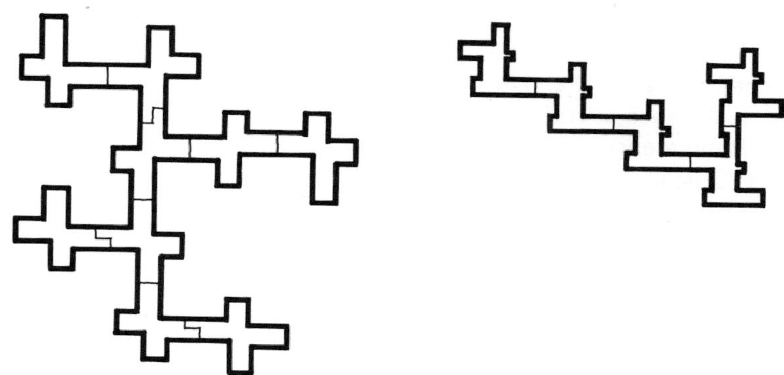

EXTERIOR

In the example that was analyzed to cast light on single tower sites each step was taken with a warning about exterior consequences, although these exterior issues were delayed for the convenience of illustrating a procedure. In reality that is not the case. The effect on exterior form is kept in mind as each step is analyzed.

The chart that compares the economic benefits derived from each of the four possible schemes would be a meaningless exercise without a simultaneous comparison of volumes. The question must be asked: is this the volume the designer wants? On multitower sites, when the designer's options are not so limited, the issue of the volume becomes crucial (see p. 242).

Once the mass is tentatively decided on—tentatively because every decision must be subject to reevaluation as its effects are further realized—the most soul search-

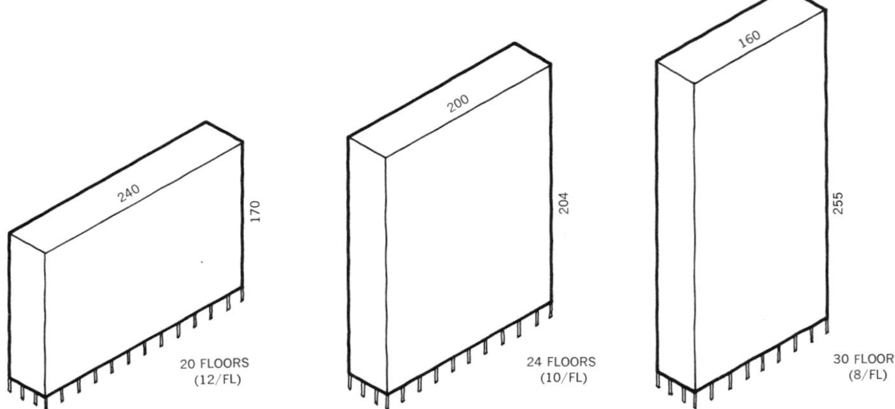

ing question faces the designer: the building exterior. Naturally, it was brought up earlier at the time the plan was conceived, but now it must be solved.

Budget, climate, and the availability of construction technology and materials are factors, as is the architect's philosophy of form. Although philosophical approaches to exteriors can be discussed, it must be conceded that many, or even all, may be valid under certain conditions. Paul Rudolph's statement that architects wish to build "dominant buildings" and to maintain "intimate scale"[26] is nowhere truer than in the field of highrise housing. The designer strives for the human, residential, or "intimate scale" against many odds, one of which is the sheer volume of the tower. We do not need to strive for dominance in highrises; it is there whether we want it or not. The dichotomy of highrise residential exteriors lies in just this: the higher the rise, the more dominant the mass, and the harder it is to achieve intimate scale.

On the one hand, we find the designer whose goal is to give clear exterior presence to the structure. The Chicago group—if such gross oversimplification is permitted—under the influence of Mies van der Rohe's early highrises and with the strong presence of buildings by members of the Chicago School, has been the main advocate of the expressed frame. The New York group—another oversimplification—heir to a long tradition of brick-clad highrises, deals with large masonry surfaces where the graphics of the punched openings and sculpturing of brick volumes are the dominant aim, and exterior rhythm does not necessarily require structural purity.

Expressing the structure is not limited to exposed frame. Cladding—brick or other—will also suggest structural reality but less explicitly. In any case, "a structure makes us uncomfortable if we can't somehow see or sense what supports it. Expressing the structure is by no means an architectural whim but, I believe, a psychological necessity of good design."[27]

Parallel with the urge to express structure is the desire—except in the purest of formalists—to express what the building really is, a hive of human habitation. The designer has the option to deny that individual dwellings exist by using completely anonymous curtain walls; he can disregard the issue in preference for the superimposed structural grid or he can give "tangible presence to people," to use the phrase coined by Donlyn Lyndon. Whatever the means, particularized rhythm, balconies, or bays, the intent is to give real manifestation to the existence of someone in the rooms. The tendency is from the general to the particular or, as Charles Jencks said, "the general, repetitive geometry is made more particularized by being changed where a bedroom differs in size."[28] Proceeding from inside out, from plan to exterior form, the plan is organized to take advantage of every expressible particularity within economic realities.

Expressing the particular does not have to deny the existence of structure, nor must it lead to structural disorder. The work of Sert, Corbusier, and many British architects is proof.

Thus there is the structure that wants to dominate and there is the human dwelling that wants to be recognizable. It is the exterior wall that will hide or express, emphasize or quietly deny one or the other of these aspects. The wall, in fact, to quote Venturi, "becomes the special record of this resolution and its drama," or, differently stated by him in the same book,

> Louis Kahn has referred to "what a thing wants to be," but implicit in this statement is its opposite: what the architect wants the thing to be. In the tension and balance between these two lie many of the architect's decisions.[29]

EXPOSED FRAME: COLUMN BAYS

The importance of the rhythm created by bay sizes and by the order of living rooms and bedrooms cannot be overemphasized. Though this issue has already been amply covered in earlier chapters, no discussion of exposed frame would be complete without it **(2, 4, 6, 16, 17, 19, 20, 24, 35).**

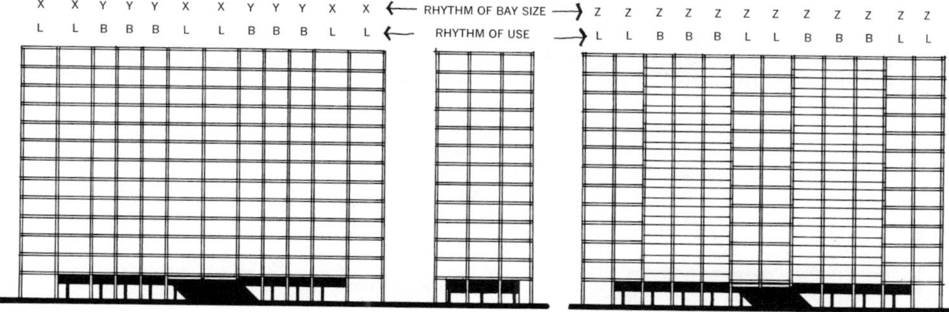

Beyond rhythm, the issue *par excellence* is proportion: the proportions of the negative space or void between slabs and columns; the proportions of the framing members themselves; the proportion of the slab thickness and the column width.

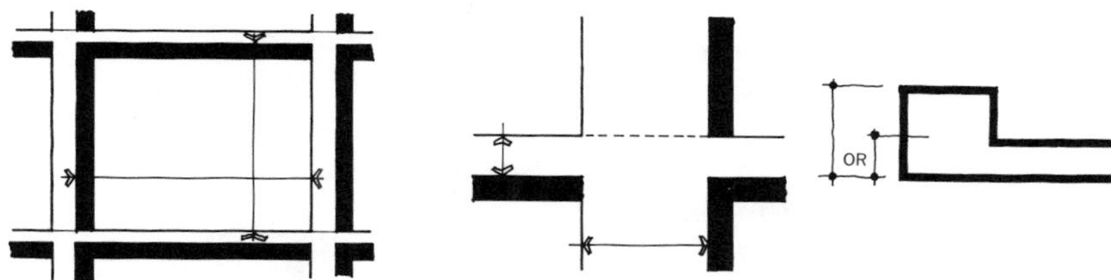

When the required structural slab is thin, the issue of real versus apparent structure emerges and the slab edge must often be made heavier than needed to achieve proper proportions at a cost that should be taken into consideration **(22).** To quote Rudolph:

The actual structural members of this tower are so small that they would never read from a distance . . . . If you should expose the actual structural members, you would not have the apparent sense of structure.[30]

Or Scott:

In the first place, it is clear that the vivid constructive properties of a building, insofar as they are effectively constructive, must exist as *facts*. The security of the building and hence also of any artistic value it may possess, depends on this; and a support which seemed to be adequate to its load, but actually was not, would, as construction, be wrong. But insofar as they are vivid, they must exist *as appearances*. It is the effect which the constructive properties make on the eye, and not the scientific facts that may be intellectually discoverable about them, which alone can determine their vividness.[31]

To achieve the desired proportions columns can be molded according to the architect's design: square, broad, narrow, and deep. **(4, 6, 16).** The designer's ability to mold columns, however, will be affected by the mechanical system of the building, by pipe risers, vertical fan-coil units, and so on.

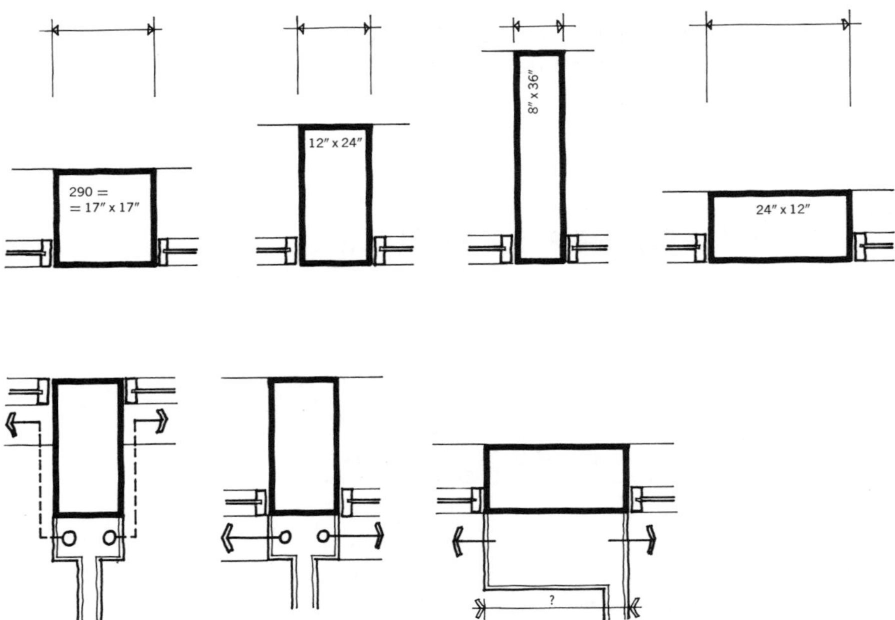

The concrete frame can be thought of as continuous and flowing, in which necessary joints are de-emphasized or as elements erected one after the other in a series of pours in which pour joints are deliberately expressed. These rustications are especially helpful in identifying main frame from secondary-pour spandrels. When rustication deteriorates into decoration, when pouring sequence is disregarded, "joints" are self-willed.

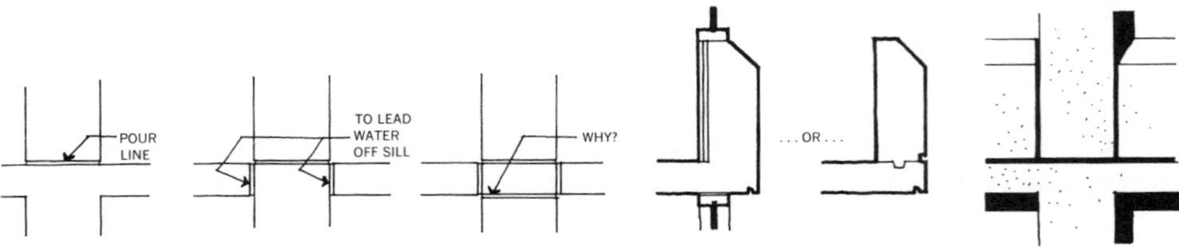

Spandrels can be made of a variety of materials in addition to poured concrete: expressed, such as precast concrete panel and masonry infill, or camouflaged, such as masonry behind structural glass or porcelain enameled-metal panel, simulating the fenestration above **(19, 20).** The height of the spandrel can be determined by several factors besides the sense of proportion; factors such as the furniture to be placed against it in bedrooms and the dimensions of the horizontal heating/cooling element. Fire codes may also determine spandrel height to minimize the potential flame spread.

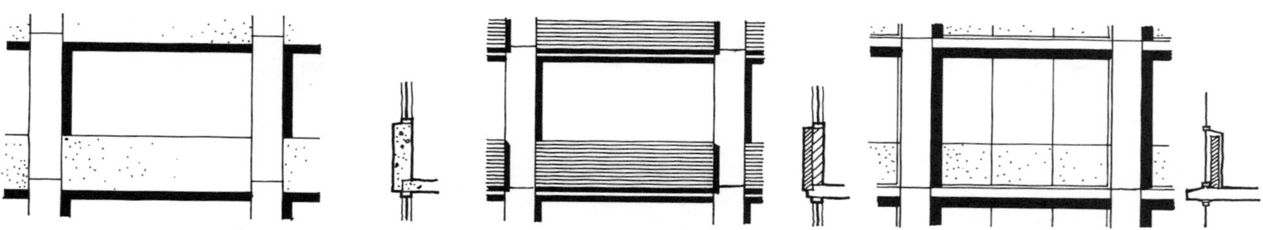

In addition to spandrels, solid elements can be used within the structural frame not only to cut down on the glass area but to accommodate partitions **(17).** Partitions that do not occur on column line can be lined up with mullions. Far more leeway in locating partitions is provided by solid vertical panels that also create a secondary rhythm on the elevation. Recent attempts to deal with energy conservation by increasing the insulating properties of the building envelope are likely to lead to the introduction of more and more solid panels within the structural frame.

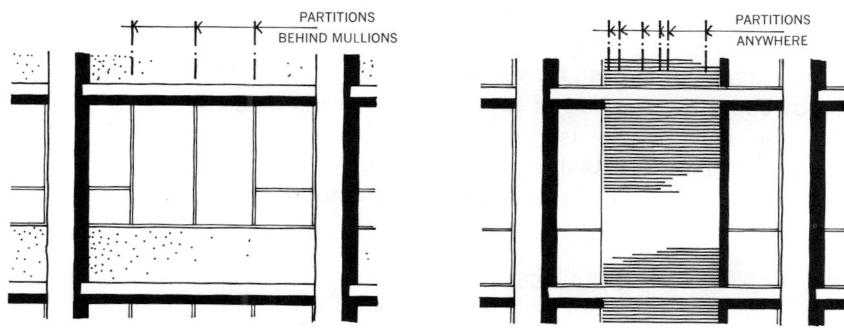

In the ideal sense the structural frame ought to be filled with glass to express what indeed it surrounds: void. The use of dark anodized aluminum, tinted glass, and toned window shades or curtain liners help to heighten this effect. The more the glass wall recedes in relation to the column and slab edge, the more voidlike the fenestration appears. This relation of glass to frame edge is a critical one and the accumulated dirt on horizontal surfaces should be spilled or lead off in such a way that it does not dirty the frame.

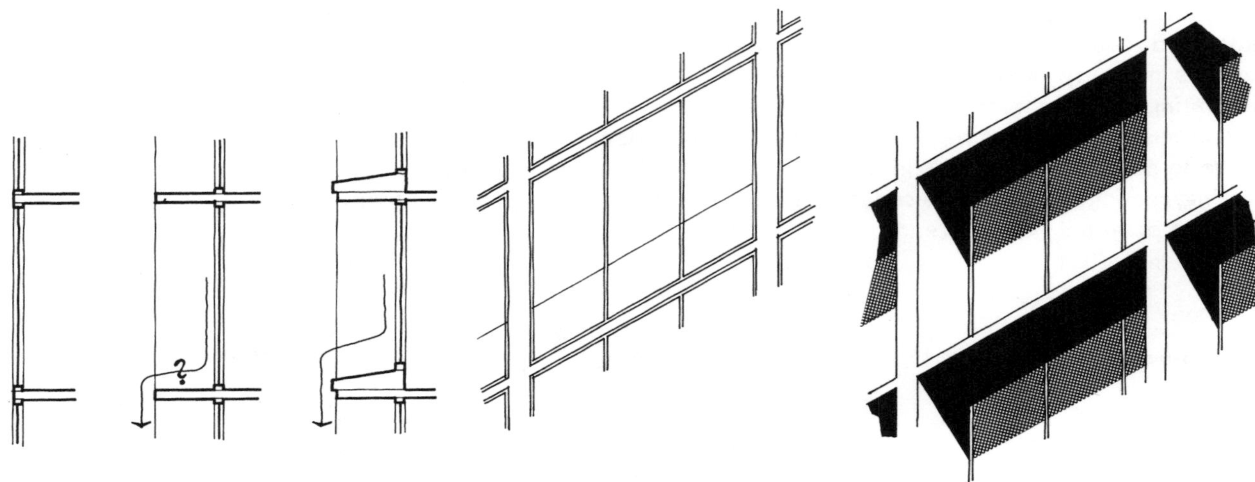

When heating and cooling elements require it, exterior air intake grills can be integrated into the skin or they may lead to further articulation of the exterior **(4, 17).**

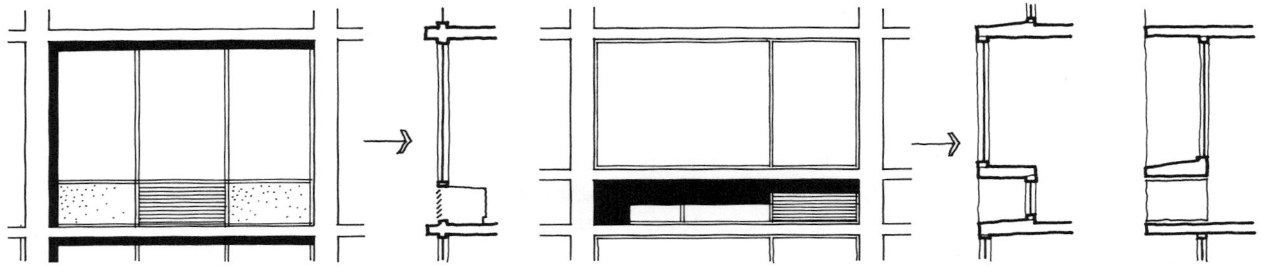

Ultimately the glass area itself, in spite of dark anodized aluminum frames becomes a network of horizontal and vertical mullions, the proportion of which critically affects the exterior. Other issues must also be faced: the amount of light and natural ventilation required by code; the method of exterior window washing (the window washer climbs out of the apartment or is raised on the outside in a scaffold); possibilities of draping (will operating sash interfere with drape?); screens (if on the exterior, the screens will create a rhythm that must be planned).

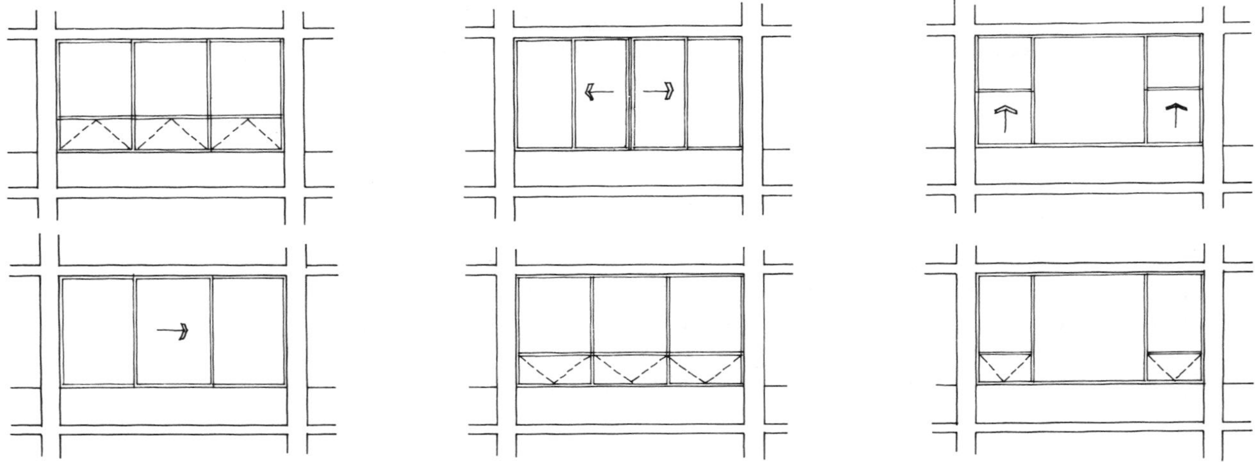

Three special parts of the apartment tower need additional attention: the corner, the top, and the bottom.

It has been said that one of the most difficult issues facing the architect is the turning of the corner on a building. Here the "facades" meet and become volume or three-dimensional reality. In a four-directional tower, when adjoining walls are similarly fenestrated, the issue revolves around the articulation of the corner column **(2, 6, 22).** In a perspective view it appears heavier than the rest, though in truth it carries less load.

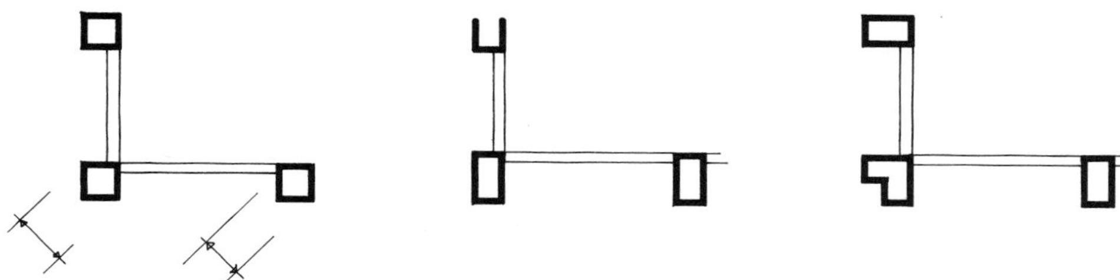

When the tower is two-directional the end wall may be a concrete shear wall with a pattern that expresses the floor slabs behind, thus providing continuity with the expressed frame on the main elevation **(4, 16, 17, 20).** (The cost problem of end shear walls and their contribution to the racking action due to exposure to low temperatures has already been covered elsewhere.) The end wall may also be filled, completely or partially, preferably with the same material that served as filler for the spandrels.

The bottom floor of the tower, whether on grade or on top of the "parking box," usually houses different functions than the typical floors and consequently is treated differently. The bays are filled—glass or solid—or indented to form an arcade. The floor above the arcade requires insulation which is achieved by a furred-down volume that also serves as a gathering space for plumbing stacks and heating risers. The articulation of this furred element needs sensitive handling **(20),** as do canopies, in their relation to columns and arcade.

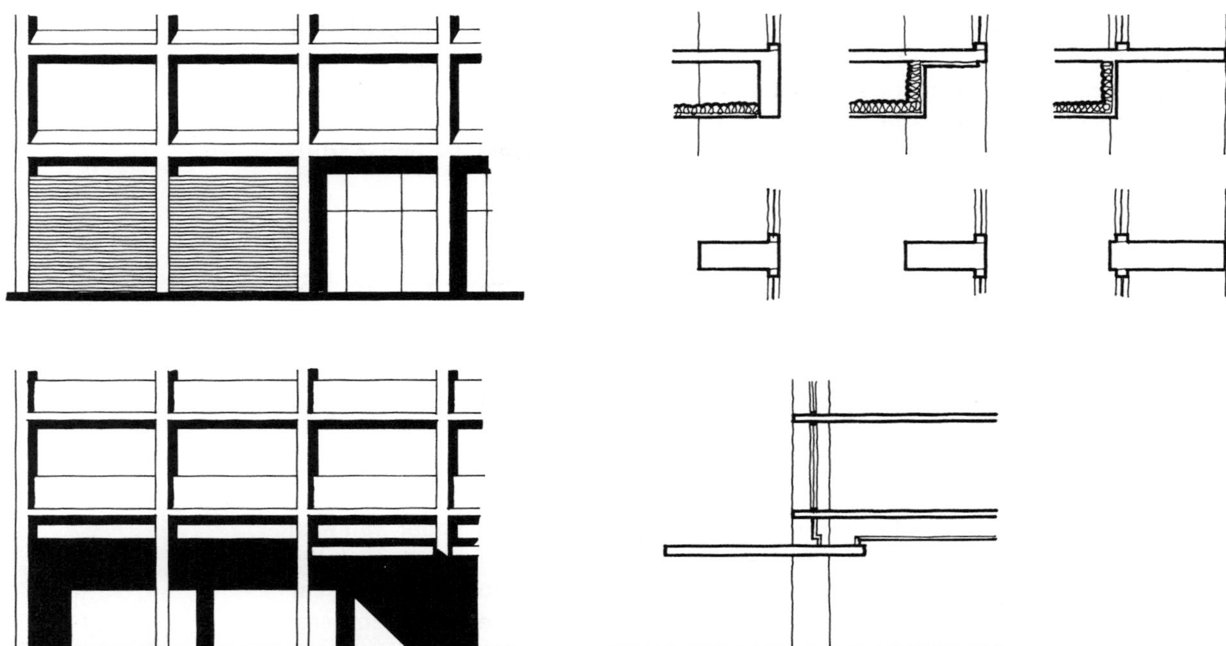

In a manner similar to gathering pipes in a space below the tower, a space is required above the top floor of the building where bathroom and kitchen exhaust ducts and corridor air supply ducts can turn horizontal to reach the proper location of the fan equipment. This space is generally located above the inner zone. It may also be carried to the edge of the tower, especially when a heavy horizontal element is needed aesthetically or to repeat the rhythm of spandrels at the top **(2).** The handling of the roof flashing detail may result in an added closure element over the top slab and will require careful articulation.

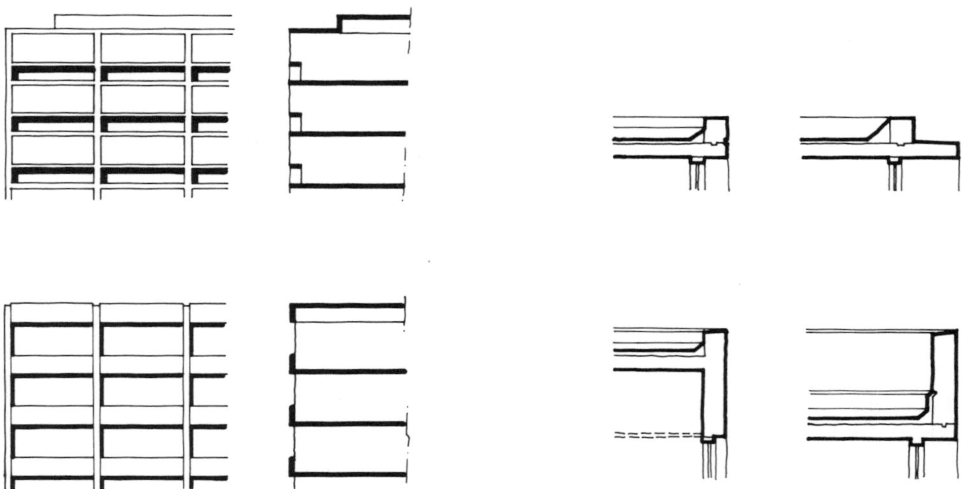

EXPOSED FRAME: LOAD-BEARING MULLIONS

The discipline imposed on the designer by the exterior columns is not an easy one, though most satisfying when successfully adhered to. This discipline demands that rooms do not straddle column lines. When the columns are replaced with load-bearing mullions (a series of small columns), almost unlimited flexibility of planning is attained **(5, 21).**

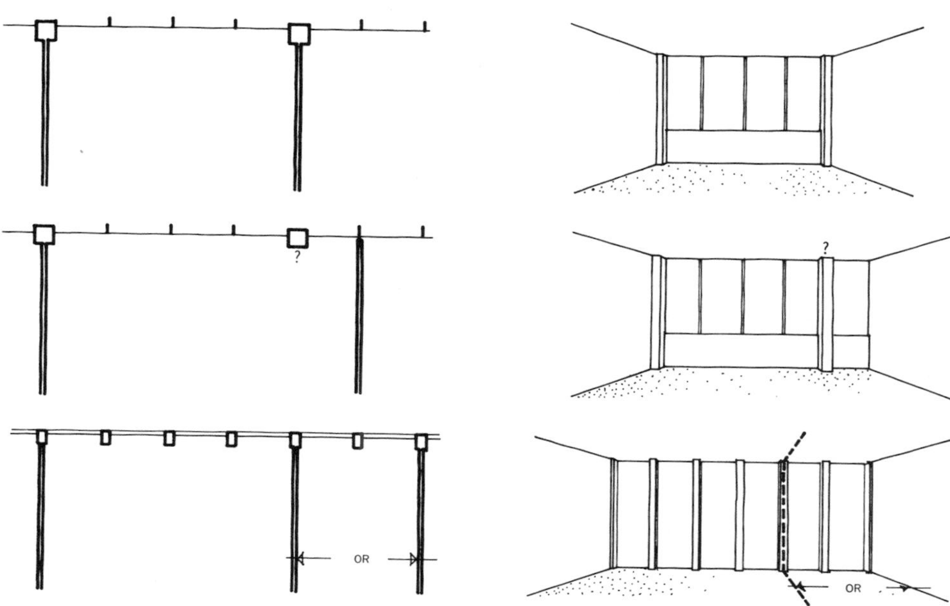

The grid system has its shortcomings. If the exterior column bay is considered less than ideal to express the particular of the human habitation, the grid system is completely unconducive for bays, balconies, or any kind of expression of different spaces. Its beehivelike grid camouflages instead of expresses the particular.

If this hindrance is accepted, it can be handled elegantly. Much of its elegance lies in details and proportions, in the articulation of its elements. The space between the load-bearing mullions and the slabs wants to be a void, far more than in bay system structures. Therefore, if a spandrel is required, it is either a concrete extension of the slab or is made to look like glass by using for the facing of the solid spandrel some kind of glassy-appearing material, but not a new material like brick.

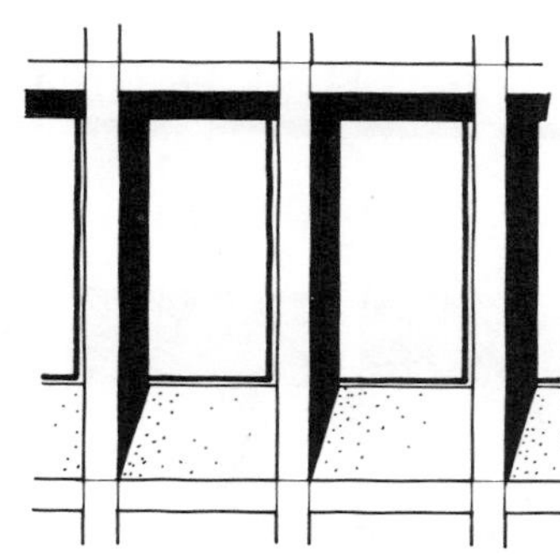

When the load-bearing mullion system is used on a four-directional structure, the handling of the corner detail demands acute sensitivity. Unless the corner is liberated from the mullion (glass butts glass) or the building is "soft cornered" (in fact has no corners), the corner mullion will appear to be clumsy and heavy, regardless of its articulation.

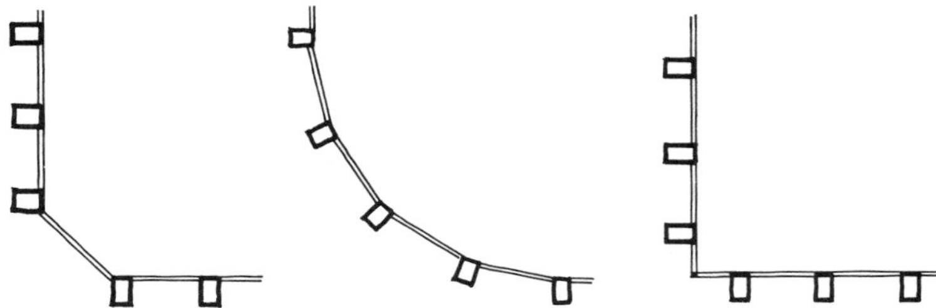

In most cases, either for the sake of openness or because it would otherwise interfere with parking, the load-bearing mullions cannot run down to the ground. They will have to be supported on girders, whose articulation is a challenging problem. The height required for these girders can easily accommodate the furred space needed above arcades. When the height of the girder is increased because of the span, it can accommodate a complete floor behind it.

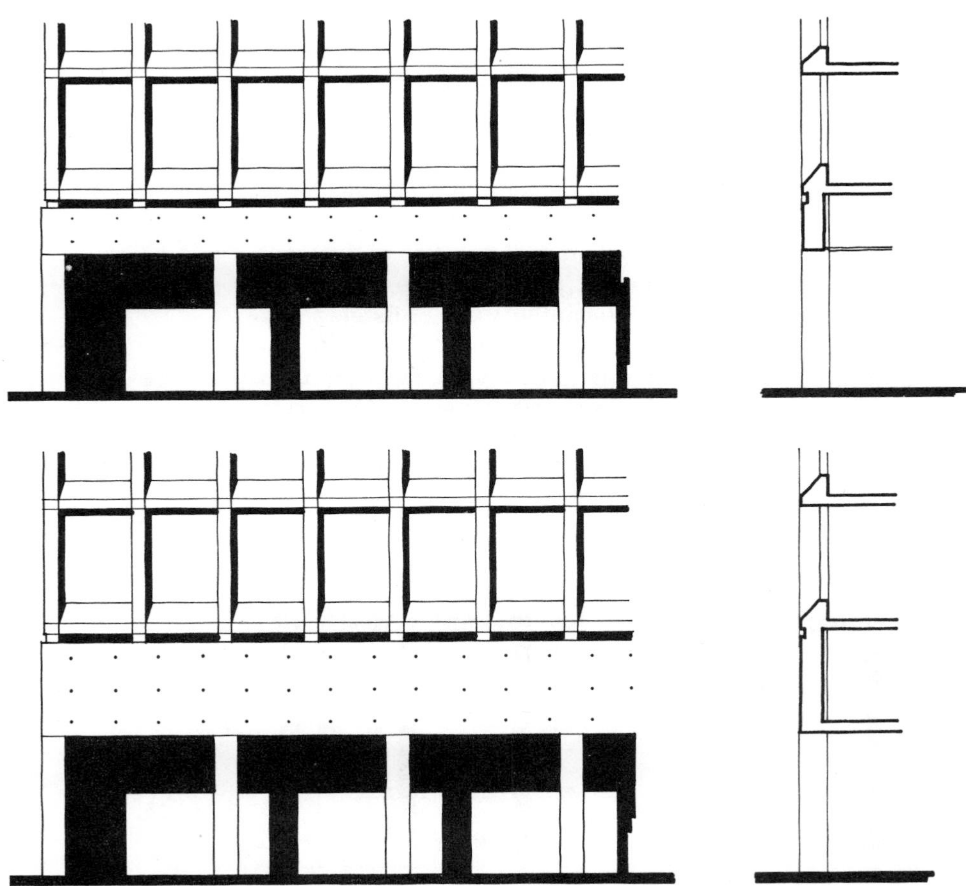

CLADDING: CURTAIN WALL

Curtain-wall cladding of the structural frame provides the designer—by its relatively small modules of vertical elements—with planning flexibility similar to the load-bearing mullion system **(1, 3, 25).** However, although the load-bearing mullion system is still a structural grid, the cladding by curtain wall completely covers the structural frame; at best, when well handled, it "suggests" the frame. In losing much of the strength of the exposed framing, nothing is gained in expressiveness of human habitation. If there is anything that neglects the variable, the particular, it is the curtain wall.

Its beauty is in its uninterrupted reflective quality, which mirrors the intricate, varied, and often bizarre silhouette of old buildings and the simple geometry of the new. The reflections of sky and clouds, of sunshine and storm make it an ever-changing prism of atmospheric conditions. Strong, curving shapes—like the Lake Point Tower by Schipporeit & Heinrich in Chicago—change the reflected image as the observer travels around the building and lend the structure a kaleidoscopelike, dynamic quality.

Curtain walls of precast concrete are used less often in the United States than those of steel or aluminum framing. The easy availability of metal and the highly advanced metal industry would explain this phenomenon when it is compared with the infant status of concrete prefabrication for exterior wall elements.

Both precast concrete and metal curtain wall rely on the refinement of detail in their aesthetic appeal. Some of the key factors are the thickness and articulation

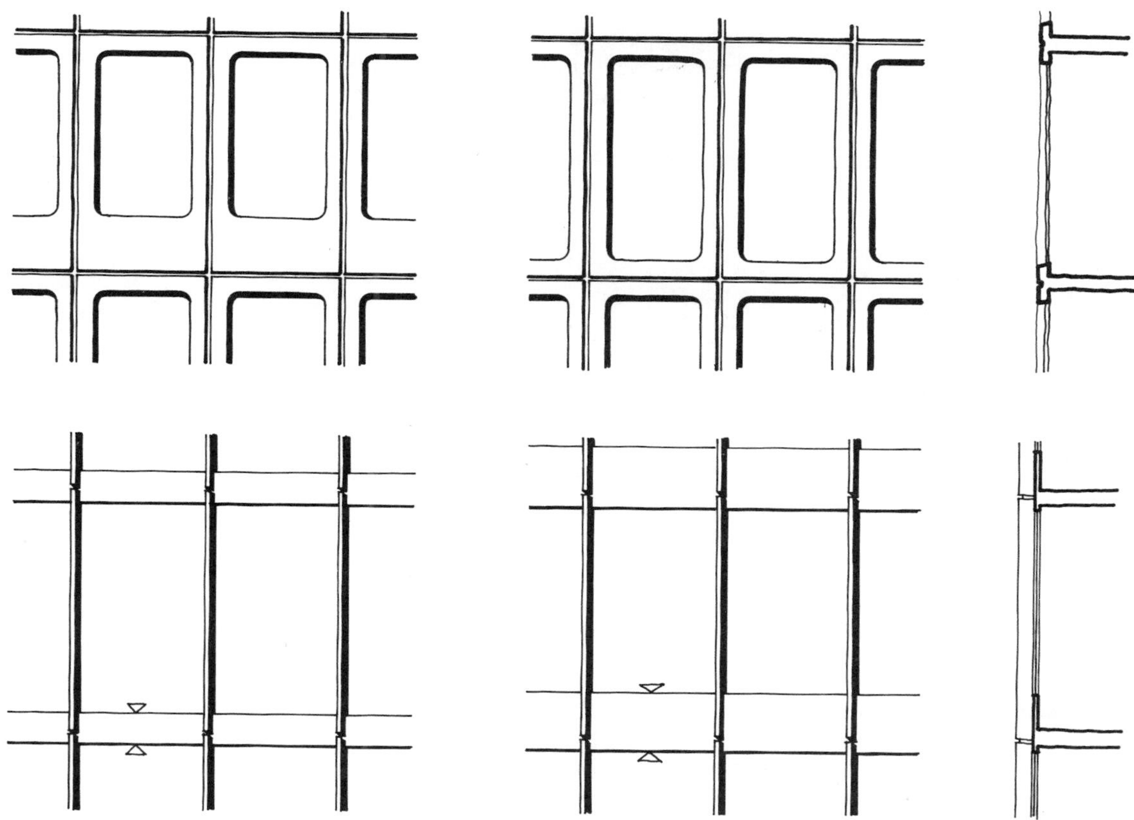

of members, the proportion of the module to floor height, the proportional relation of the glazed area to the cladded slab edge, especially when this edge is a heavy element that combines the cladding of slab and spandrel (see p. 251).

Curtain walls are particularly accommodated to mechanical systems. Vertical pipe risers do not have to be on the inside face of columns in which column-to-slab connection is most critical and in which horizontal piping must make tortuous turns around the columns. The space between exterior column face and curtain wall is ideal for risers and straightforward horizontal connections. The grills of horizontal heating/cooling elements can be made to fit in the grid of the curtain wall and will melt into the total pattern.

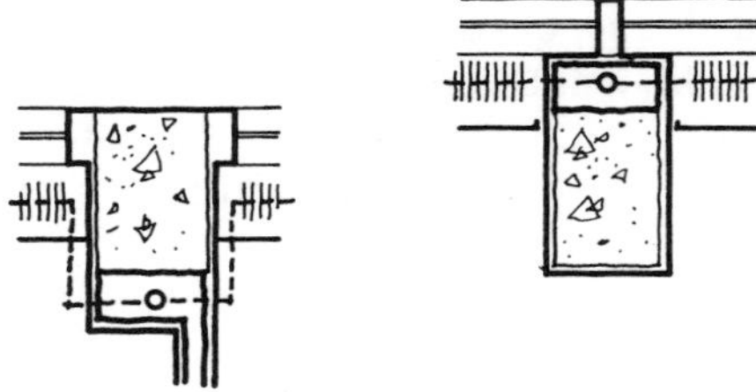

If the "turning of the corner" was difficult with exposed frame and especially with load-bearing mullions, it is almost an insurmountable aesthetic task with curtain walls. The curtain wall can cover all the columns except the corner one, and although Mies refined wrestling with this insoluble detail to an art, even he never succeeded. The corner column—which for load-carrying quality is the least important—is exposed not because the designer wants it to be, but because nobody has figured out a way to handle it. The best solution to the problem is to avoid it by cantilevering the corner—in fact, divorcing the curtain wall corner from the column.

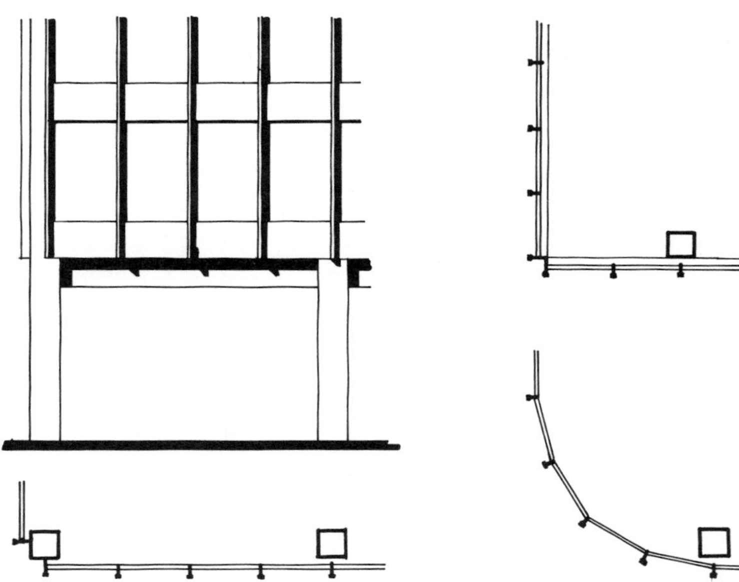

CLADDING: MASONRY

Masonry cladding liberates the inherent possibilities of the exterior wall from the limiting presence of the structural frame **(7 to 13, 15, 27 to 34, 36 to 40).** The breaking up of overwhelming surfaces, the interruption of the repetitive grid, all that is considered "human" in highrises, are readily achievable with masonry cladding. Cladding, however, is no license for undisciplined, nonrhythmic planning. Poor rhythm in living and sleeping spaces will show up as well on a masonry clad structure. If a brick exterior skin gives the designer a broader scope to shape openings freely to reflect the spaces behind it, the rhythm of these spaces becomes even more important.

The windows in the brick surface are the real issue in a masonry clad exterior. The choice of size and shape is almost unlimited because the number of openings in a highrise will permit custom-made rather than stock sashes without economic disadvantage. However, because of this freedom of choice, brick exteriors require sensitive treatment. Gone is the superimposed grid of the structural frame which in no way ensures good architecture but provides the unimaginative architect with a more or less acceptable crutch. Because success lies almost completely in proportions, in the rhythm of openings, we find that when the weight of solids is about equal to the weight of voids or when repetitiveness turns into unrelieved boredom the results are highly unsatisfactory.

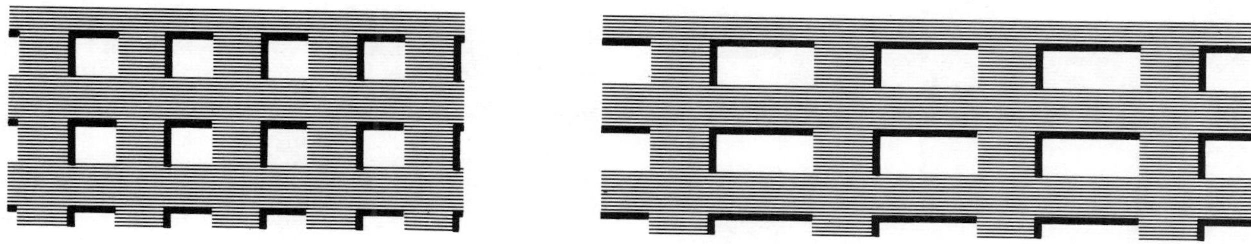

Masonry cladding lends itself to varied shapes and sizes of fenestration not only reflecting the character of the interior space (a solid spandrel for furniture placement in a bedroom, more glass in a living room, and so on) but also providing interrelations and juxtapositions of strong graphic quality **(10).**

The chances of expressing specific spaces differently—and thus creating rhythm—is considerably enhanced in skip-stop highrises with their multilevel apartments **(30, 33).** The vertical alternation of living and sleeping spaces adds a unique rhythm to the exterior.

What is also possible on masonry clad exteriors is the actual molding of openings for a variety of possible reasons: to integrate the grills of heating/air conditioning units; to combine regular windows (vision) with clerestories (light) in bedrooms that are short of furniture space.

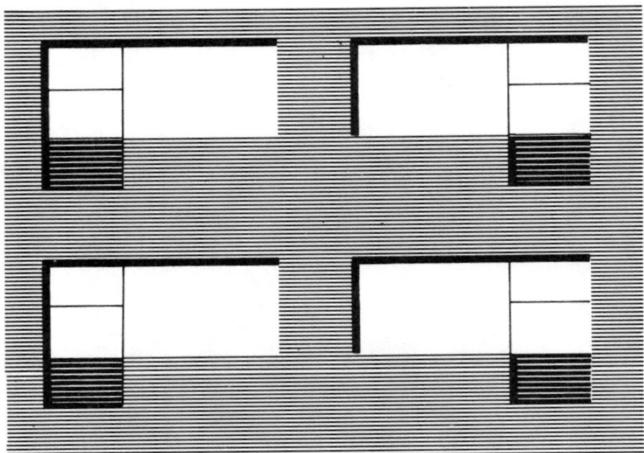
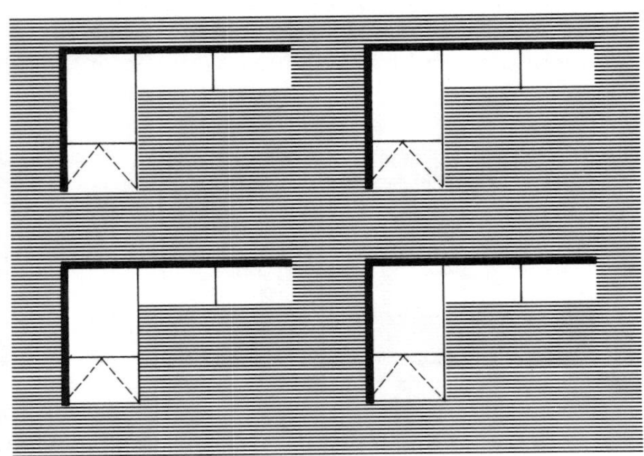

Cladding does not necessarily hide the structural frame that exists behind it. With enlarged openings, the masonry cladding can reflect the structural framework quite strongly. It is also possible to express the structure more explicitly by exposing the actual concrete members at least in part **(28, 36, 37)**.

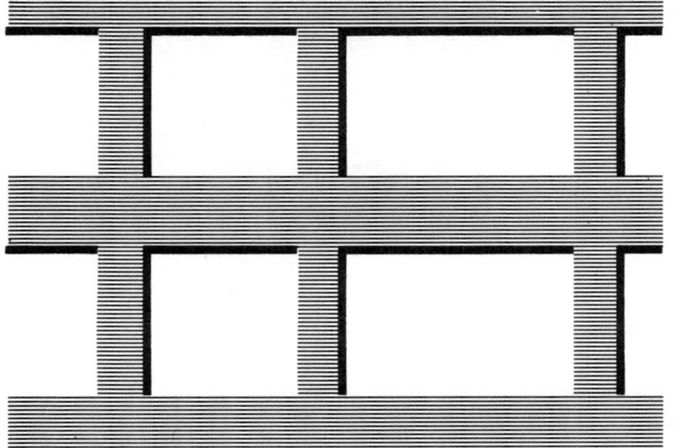
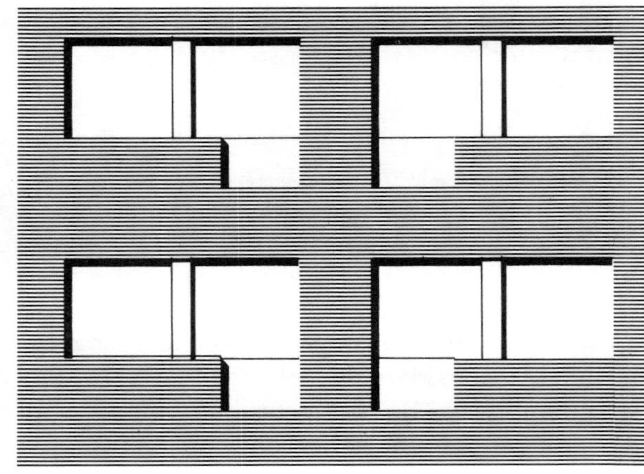

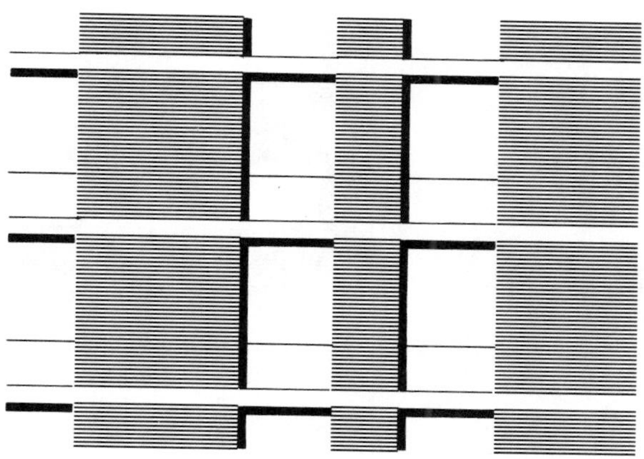

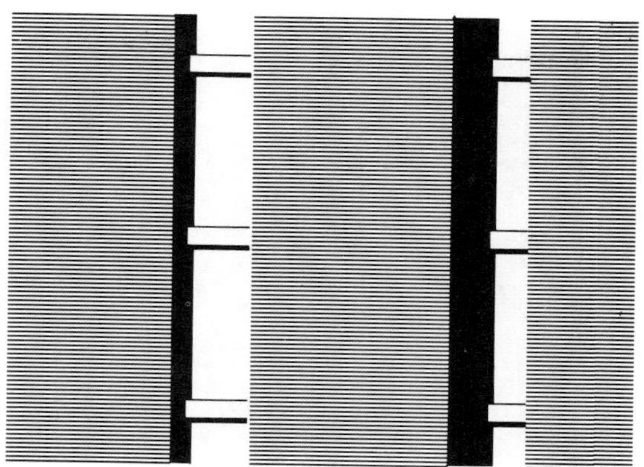

Exposed frames and curtain walls have their Achilles heels in the turning of corners. Masonry cladding has its own: the base, the way the building rests on the ground. Actually there is no problem when ground-level functions do not require opening up the volume at this level, when the entire masonry mass grows out of the ground.

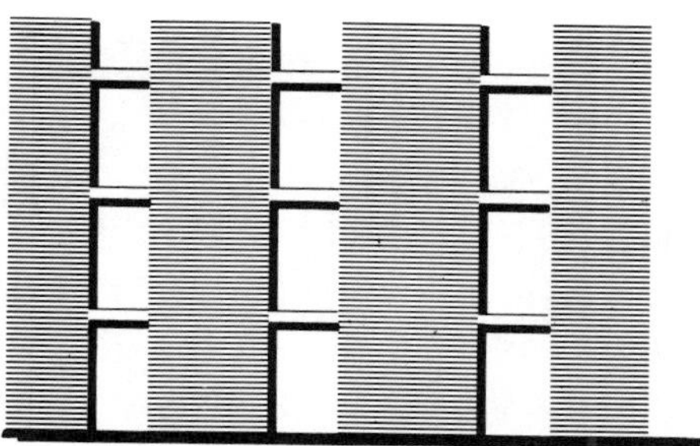

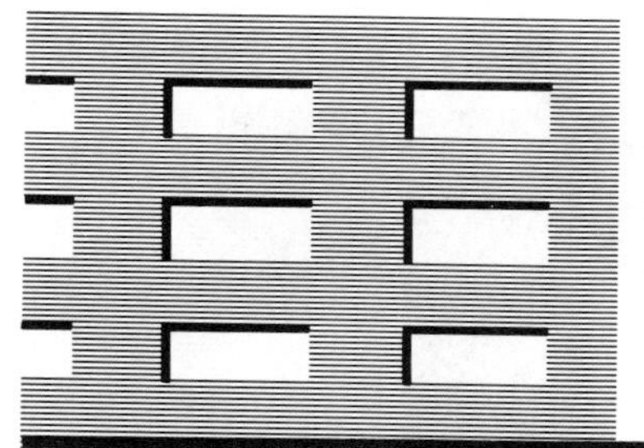

If an open ground floor becomes a necessity, cladding the supporting elements seems a more satisfactory solution than exposing them. The ''resting'' of the heavy masonry mass on seemingly spindly supports has the appearance of structural unstability, although in fact the cladding masonry is supported at each or every other floor level by shelf angles. Attempts to solve this problem by exposing the floor above the arcade—to give the impression of a single concrete slab supporting the entire masonry mass is equally incongruous. Truly load-bearing masonry wall construction obviously does not present a problem at its base (see p. 256).

The pattern of the masonry joints and the detail of the openings enhances the masonry clad building with rich texture and articulation, and sills, jambs, and window heads lend themselves to unlimited sculptural variety.

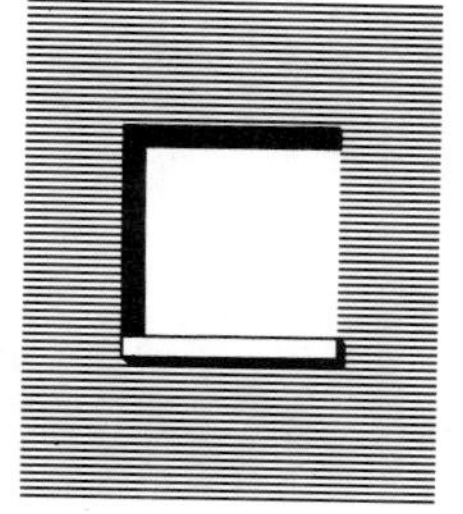

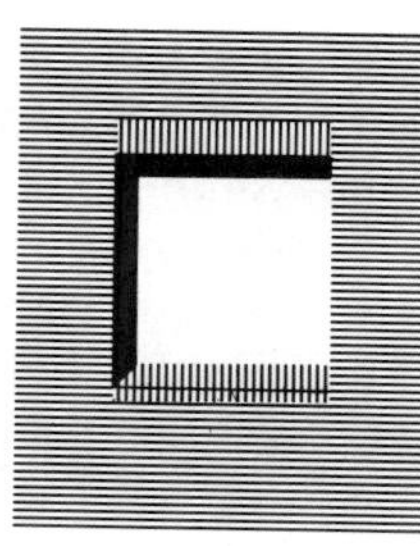

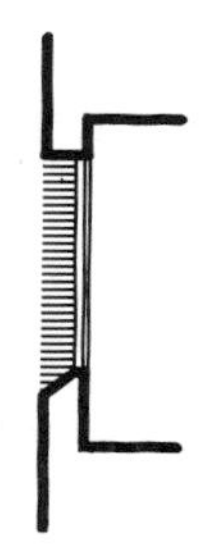

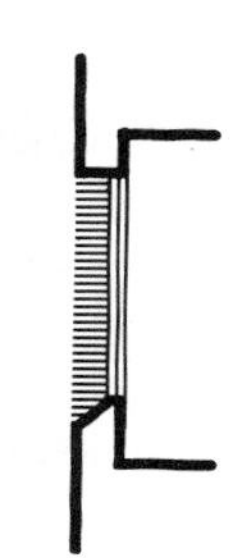

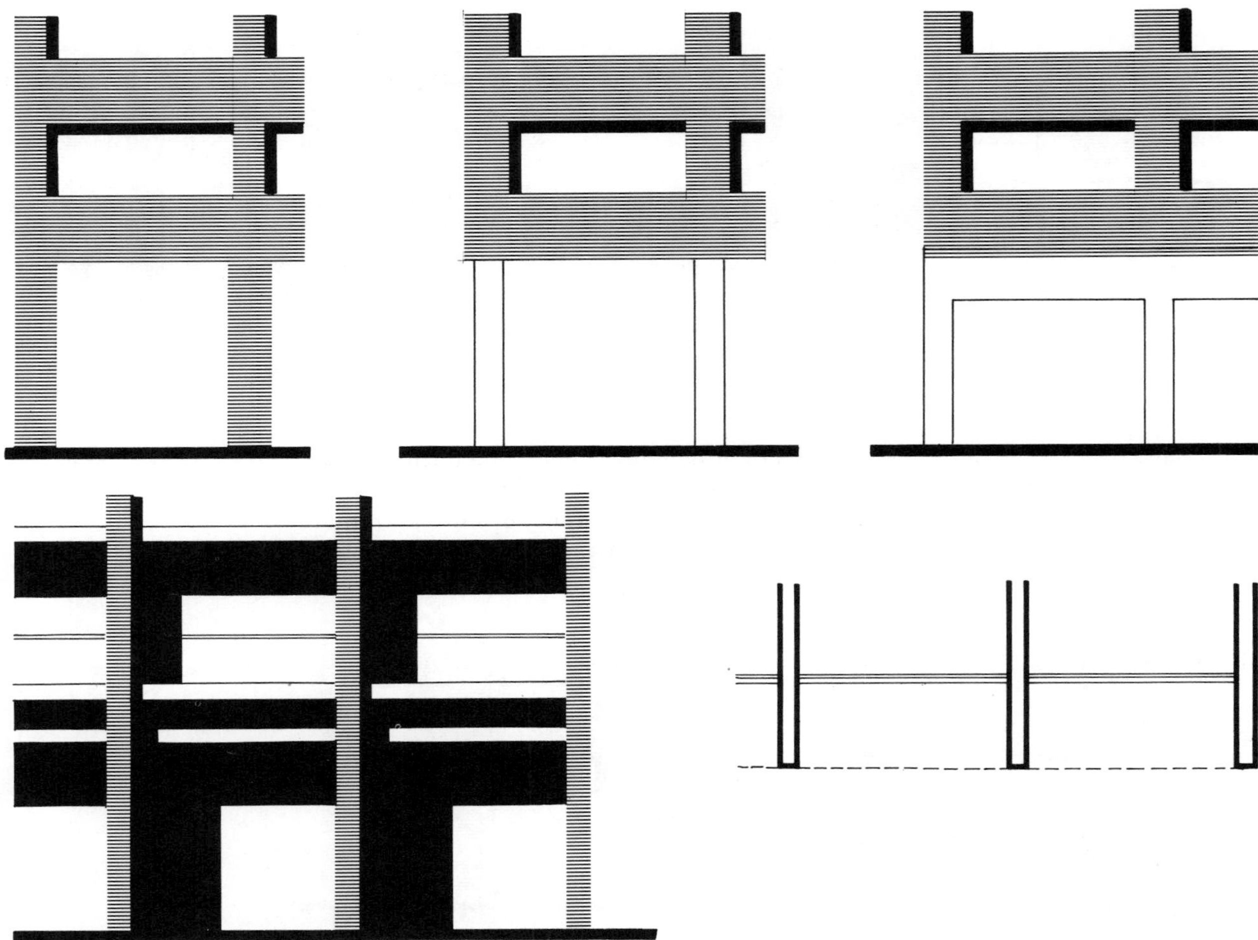

BALCONIES

Man's desire to decorate the box is ancient and no design philosophy of the machine age has succeeded in killing it. The major change is that today the designer looks for functional or technological requirements to achieve visual excitement. Inasmuch as an apartment building is a ''box,'' the structural frame and fenestration are used to ''decorate'' it.

When the program calls for balconies, the desire to decorate is satisfied in good conscience. Balconies and the shadows they cast can break up the monotony of the facade. Dressed with furniture and plants they add life and color to the appearance of the building, an excellent opportunity for individual human expression, which often disturbs the purist **(7, 11, 12, 15 to 19, 22 to 24, 31, 35, 36 to 39).**

A balcony can fit into the indentation of the building volume, can project from the exterior wall, or can be a combination of both. In any case, to be usable it should be not less than 5 ft deep, preferably 6. The dimensional criterion is the small conversation group—a table with chairs around it. The indented balcony has several advantages. It is wind protected and offers more privacy and security at highrise height. Being indented, it helps to break up the volume of the box. It also provides access from more than one room. With certain mechanical systems it can serve to locate the aircooled condenser or even larger equipment if its housing and the balcony are designed in an integrated manner.

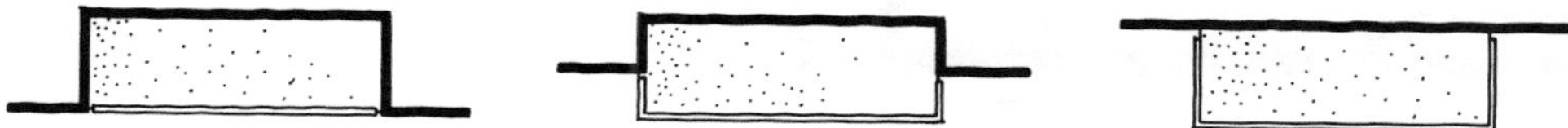

The rhythm of living and sleeping spaces is further emphasized by a balcony in front of the living room and makes good rhythmic design essential. It is important to realize that when two balconies are paired the sum takes on a different quality than the parts (*L* + *L* is not equal to 2*L* but becomes something new), regardless of how unobtrusively the high divider, necessary for privacy, is handled. Emphasizing their individuality by slight separation helps but does not answer the need for privacy. When the balconies are indented, the problem is removed because the rhythm created by the volumes between the recesses becomes more dominant.

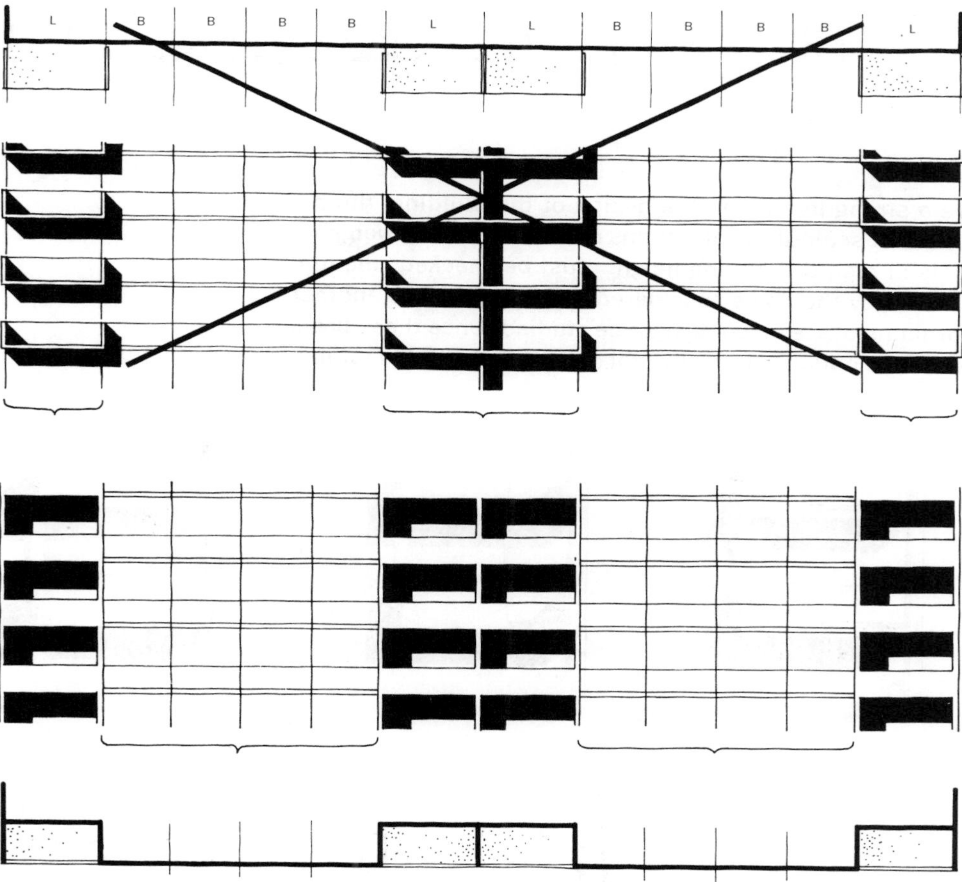

The question of rhythm cannot be avoided with continuous balconies. The dividers between apartments, no matter how thin and de-emphasized, will be apparent. Now, instead of just the living rooms, entire apartments will have to produce rhythm.

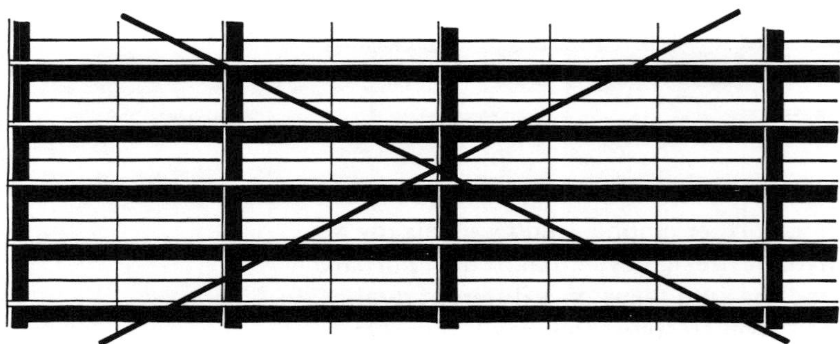

One of the problems created by sequence planning occurs when balconies are required. When the living room in one apartment is adjacent to the bedroom in the next, privacy is seriously jeopardized unless balconies are designed to discourage peepers.

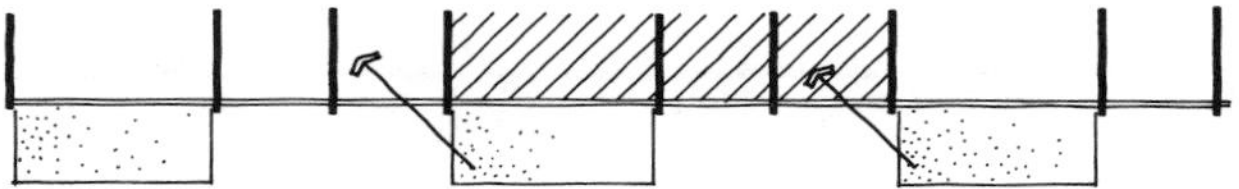

Because balconies have a strong impact on the design of the building, the decision to create lacy openness or sculptural solid forms must be carefully weighed. Building code requirements in regard to railing height must be checked; the tenant's sense of security and privacy should be considered; the view must be another deciding factor; and the draining of the balcony must be studied. Once these basic issues have been disposed of the options are many, not only in shape but in railing.

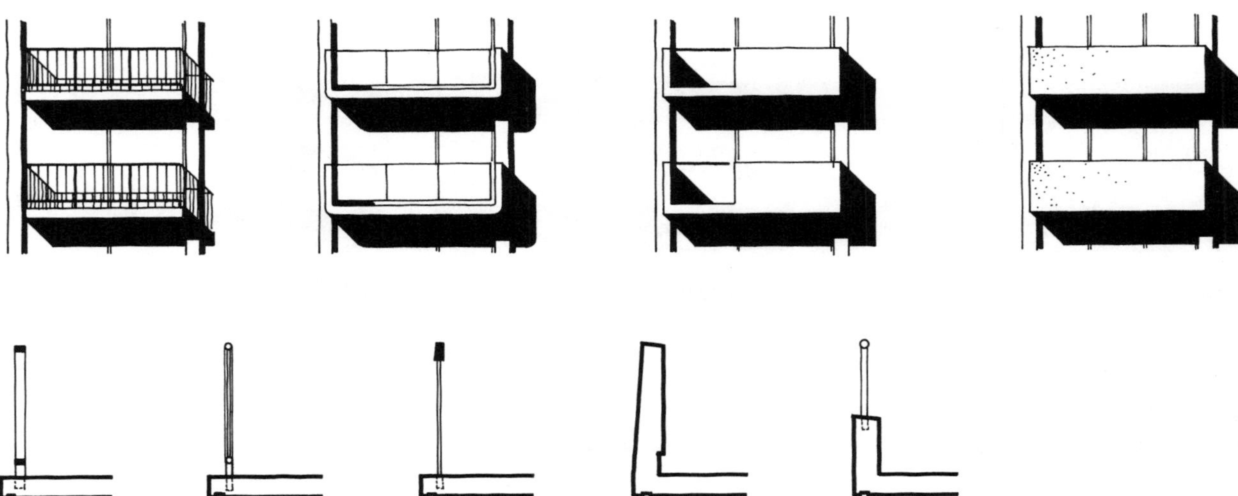

Because economy prohibits the installation of interior downspouts, balconies are generally drained outward. When the railing is open at the bottom and the balcony slab is not turned up at its outside edges, the chances are good that dirt will wash off and discolor the slab at unexpected spots. A solid balcony rail or upturned slab edges can provide the location for drain spouts that, when well planned, can become design elements.

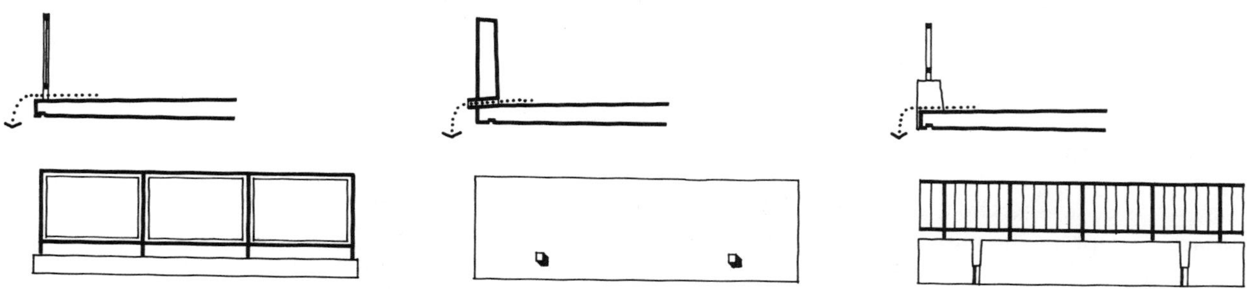

Doors to the balcony can be swinging or the more popular sliding. A 7- or 8-in. curb under the door, contrary to expectations, is accepted by most users who do not mind stepping over it. The curb gives protection against snow pile-up and an opportunity to place a heating element under the door. One of the advantages of continuous balconies is that sliding doors can be used as operating sashes to provide the occupant with an opportunity to wash his own windows.

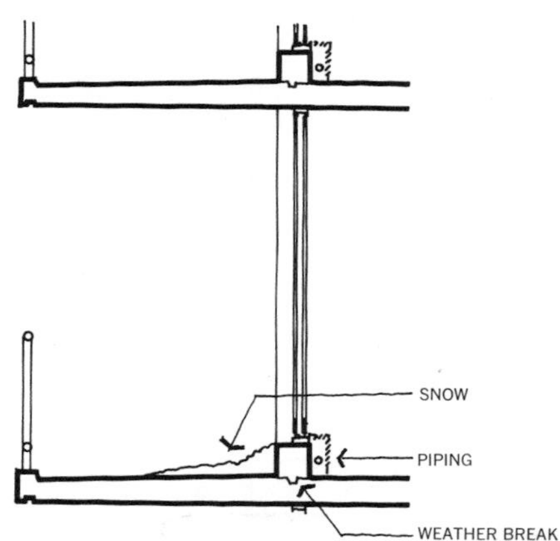

Balconies create a pattern. Quietly overall or dynamically moving, the reasons for the variation are many. A pattern may develop from the program that does not require a balcony for each apartment. A building type such as the multilevel in a skip-stop system may have an inherent pattern. Using alternating balcony sizes and locations may not have functional justification; it may be done simply to create visual variety or to strengthen and underline the designer's intent as in Rudolph's Crawford Manor in New Haven, Conn., in which balconies do not line up one above the other on one side because they ''otherwise would appear from a distance as a shaft vertically'' (see p. 260) **(7).**

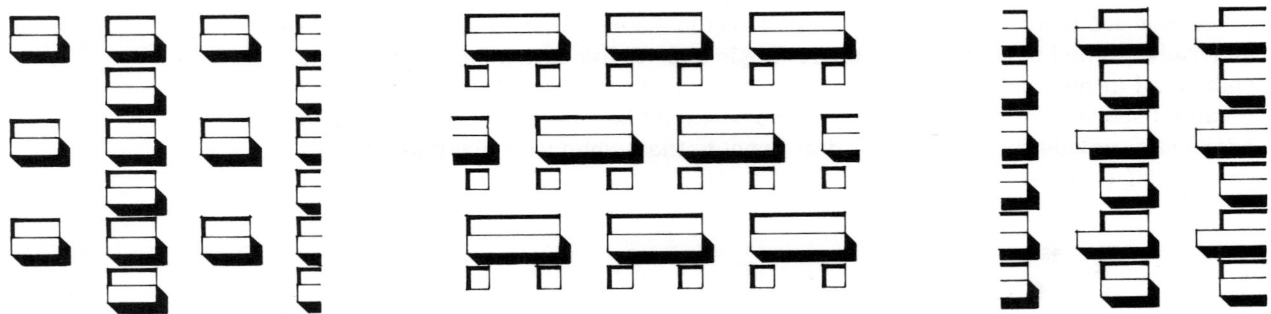

VOLUME BREAKS

Structural grid, fenestration, and balconies all give scale to the large masses of highrises. Except for the purest of purists, who seem to be satisfied with the gutsy strength of the expressed frame and the monumental simplicity of the volume, architects have been seeking logical reasons to articulate and break up the overwhelming mass of apartment buildings. The increased perimeter and cost do not seem to be enough of a deterrent to stifle this urge.

Several of the planning issues that become generators of breaks in the building volume have been discussed under various headings, such as indented balconies, pulled out living rooms, protrusions in the volume to accommodate vertical core elements, and breaks to introduce light into inside corridors **(11, 12, 14 to 16, 19, 34, 36 to 38).**

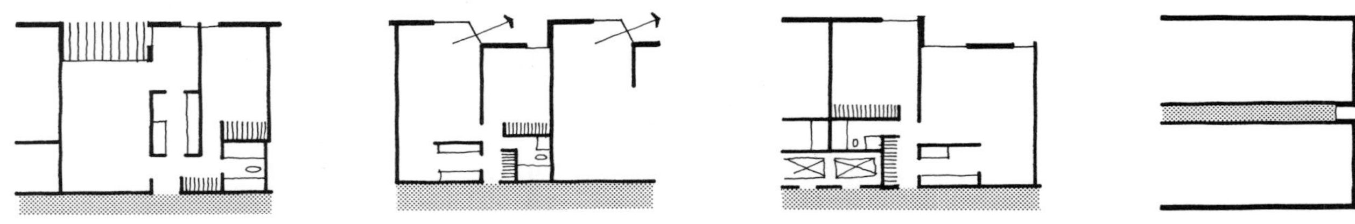

Link-generated volume breaks to interrupt very long corridors, to utilize vertical core elements in more than one building have also been mentioned **(6, 9, 24, 26, 32).**

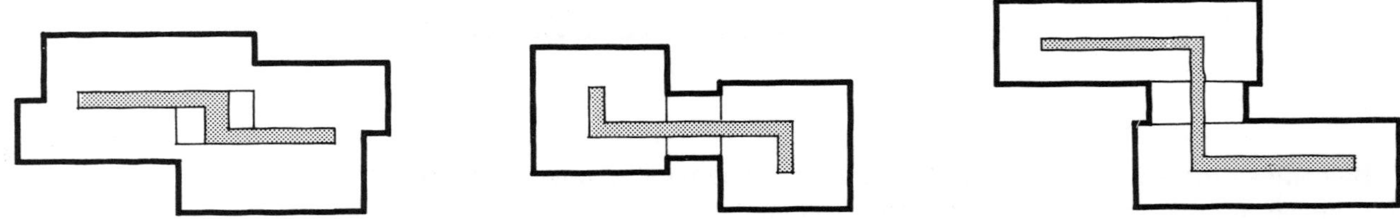

Additional molding of the building volume is the result of various planning problems. Bay windows not only add space to the living room in relatively narrow building volumes but also help to improve the view and catch sunlight on north elevations. Conversely, in deep buildings indentations bring daylight to interior spaces. In tight plans, in which storage requirements cannot be satisfied within their confines, closets projecting beyond the exterior walls may provide a solution in addition to helping modulate the volume **(7, 17, 23, 29, 39, 40).**

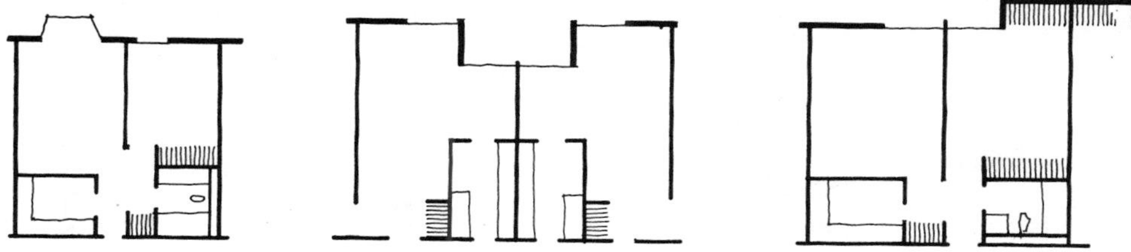

Site conditions also may generate volume breaks. Adaptation to diagonal property lines is the most obvious. Limitations in the length of the lot can be overcome by overlapping **(13, 38).**

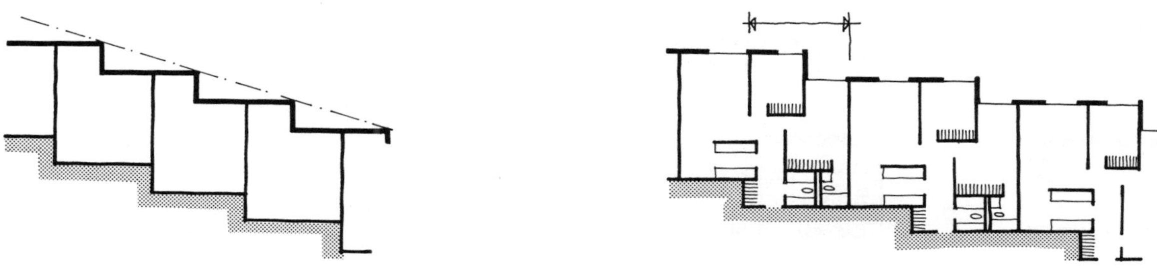

Major volume breaks in complex buildings of L, T, or other shapes present a special problem at the inside corner where the wings meet. Interior spaces created at the intersection are not easy to utilize and the possibility of cross view must be avoided **(8, 25 to 27, 38).**

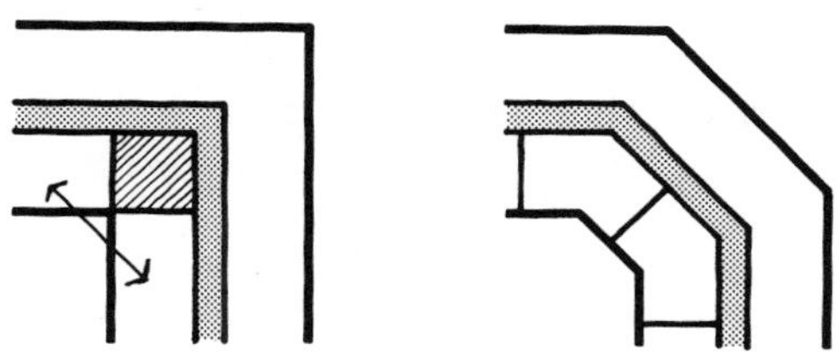

All the volume breaks mentioned have one thing in common: they occur on every floor and create a continuous vertical element. Volume breaks, however, can also be interrupted vertically.

The main generator of these breaks is the need for increased floor area in a particular group of apartments or increased space for corridor in skip-stop schemes **(14, 32, 34)** (see p. 262).

The projecting and recessed forms, angled at the corners and overhung at the top, both reflect and make possible a greater variety of apartment plans and sizes. The diagonal corners open vistas and rooms; the thrusting overhangs mean larger apartments. (Ada Louise Huxtable on the Waterside Apartments in New York, by Davis Brody & Associates *The New York Times*, February 10, 1974) **(27).**

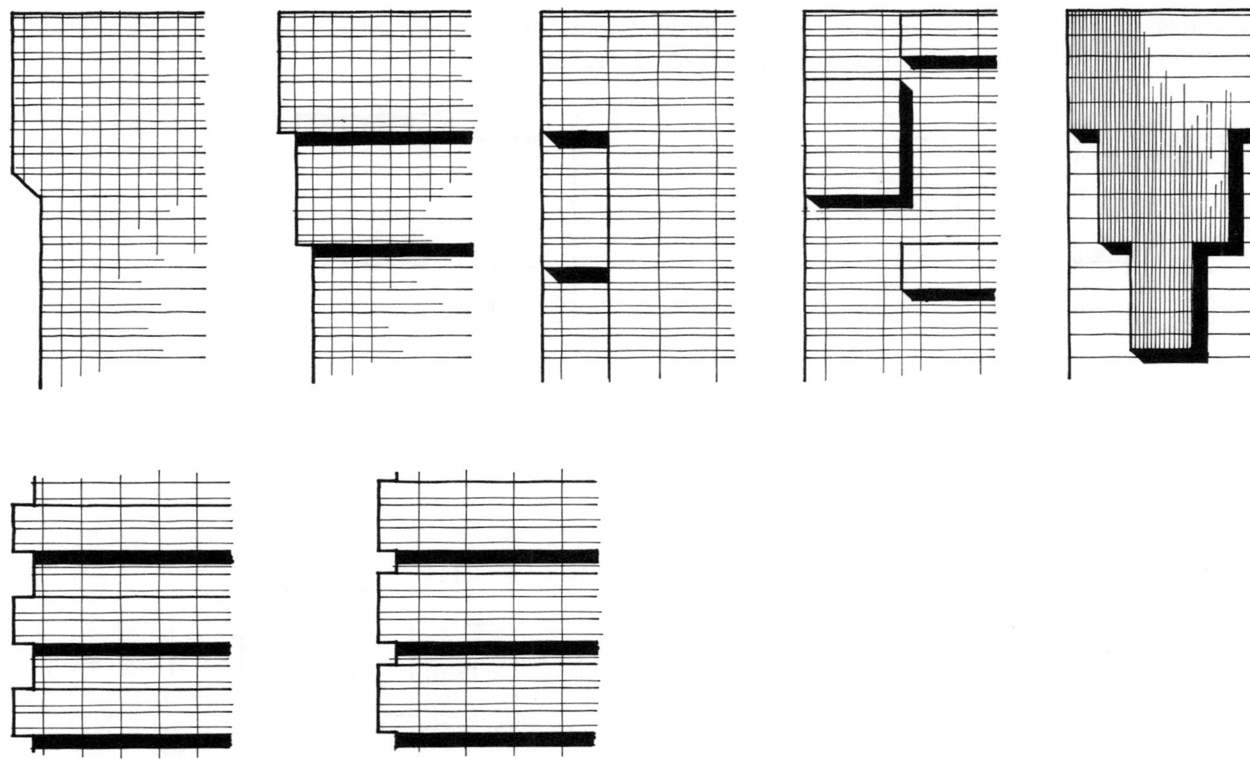

Terrace housing at the base of highrises or the attempt to integrate lowrise to apartment towers by gradually receding volumes is another form of vertical volume break which utilizes the breaks for terraces **(33).**

Because of the inherent cost problem, vertically interrupted volume breaks do not occur with great frequency. The underside of a volume projection requires thermal insulation. The top, in addition to being thermally insulated, will have to be roofed, and if it is used as a terrace membrane waterproofing and wearing slab or paving material will be required above the concrete slab. All this has to be done with high quality materials and workmanship, for it occurs above living spaces. The result is considerable cost, which explains the caution with which such volume breaks are handled.

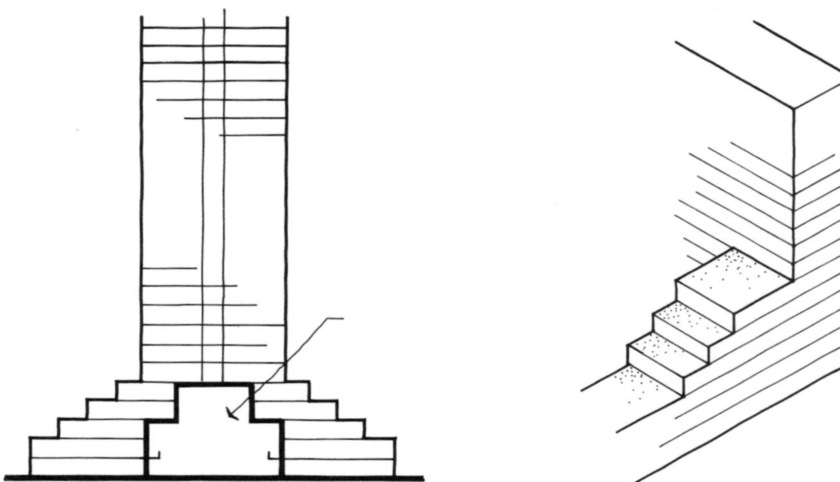

TOP AND BOTTOM

Most highrise apartment buildings (except those with on-grade, open parking, and minimal amenities) consist of two distinct volumes: the vertical tower and the horizontal base. Functionally these two are quite distinct, one for dwellings, the other for parking, commercial, storage, mechanical, and other spaces. When merged, however, there is a functional ambiguity—part of the vertical may be devoted to parking and part of the horizontal to apartments—and the articulation of the two is more of an aesthetic issue than is functionally self-evident.

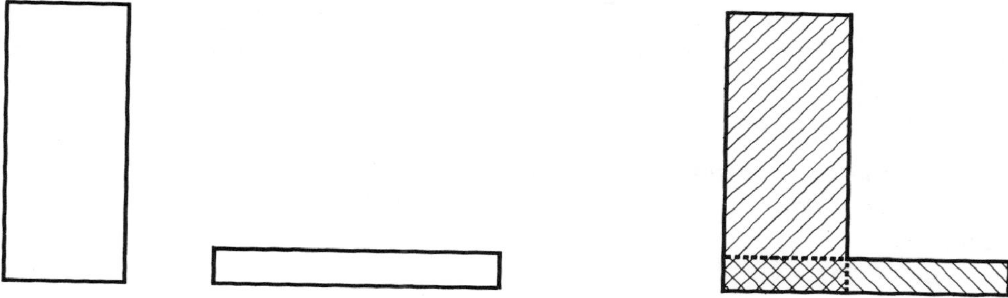

On closely built-in, tight sites without side yards there is little or no option for articulation because the merging of the two volumes stays unresolved, hidden behind adjoining structures.

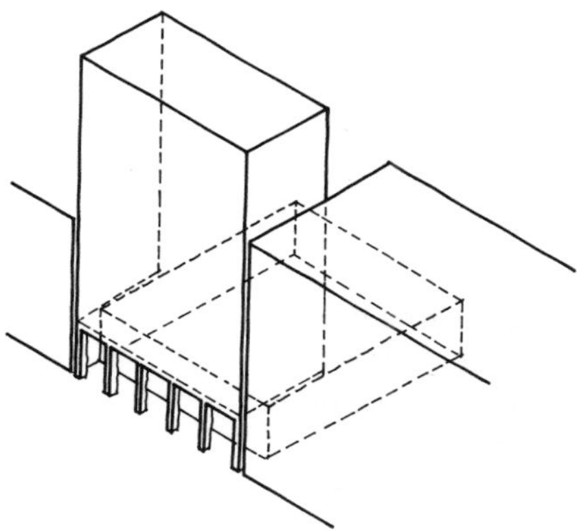

Larger sites present a multitude of options. The simplest, naturally, is presented when the property is large enough to handle the horizontal volume completely or in part as a separate element, and with the tower "resting" on grade the issue is purely that of linkage.

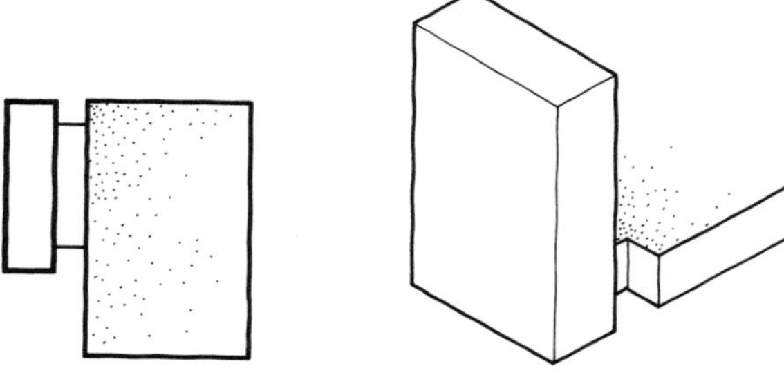

When the two volumes merge, the tower may still appear to be growing out of the ground, surrounded on two or three sides by the base; it might also become completely one with the base except on its end, where articulation is still possible.

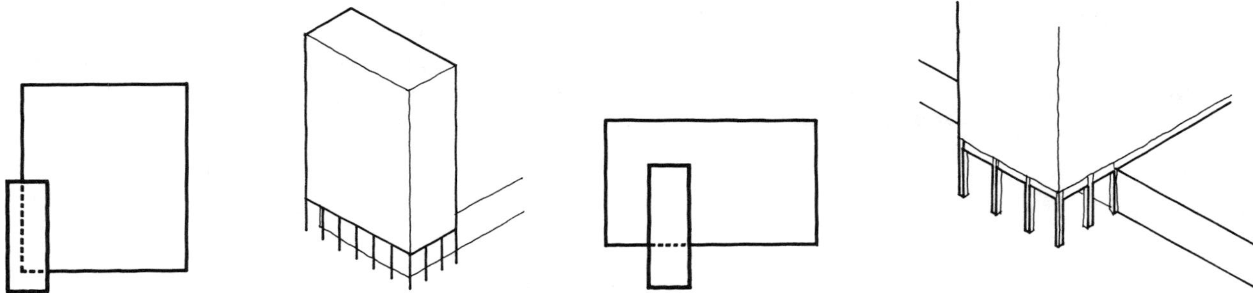

When the base is so large that the tower is set back a considerable distance from its edge it rests on the base as if it were sitting on the ground and there is no aesthetic question of intersection.

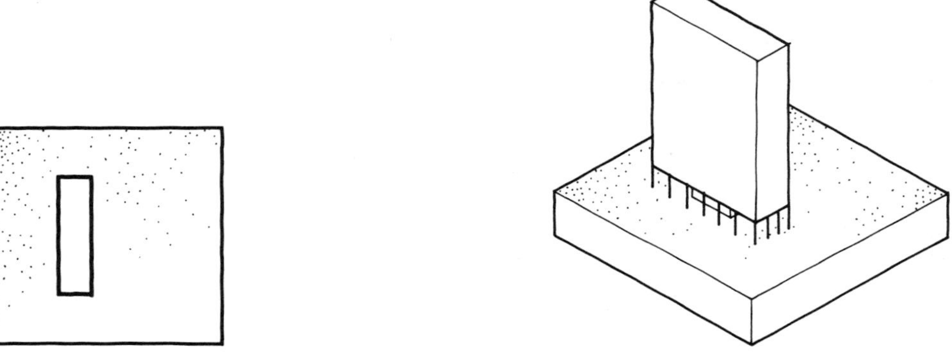

The most critical condition presents itself when the tower ends on the same plane as the base. Distinct separation can be achieved either vertically, suggesting a tower growing out of the ground surrounded by its base, or horizontally, suggesting a tower sitting on top of its base, by a reveal or preferably by a functionally justifiable separator such as differently expressed intermediary floor which houses a different function. Distinct articulation, however, is not the only option the architect has. Ambiguity where the two volumes intersect may be accepted or even exploited. Fusion of the two volumes can be achieved by using elements that make the transfer from horizontal to vertical a gradual one.

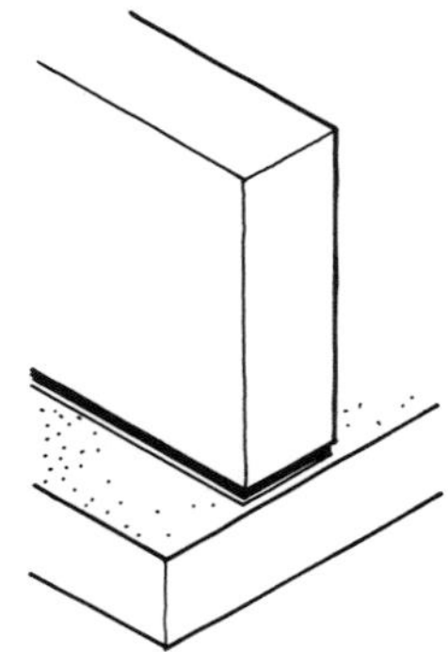

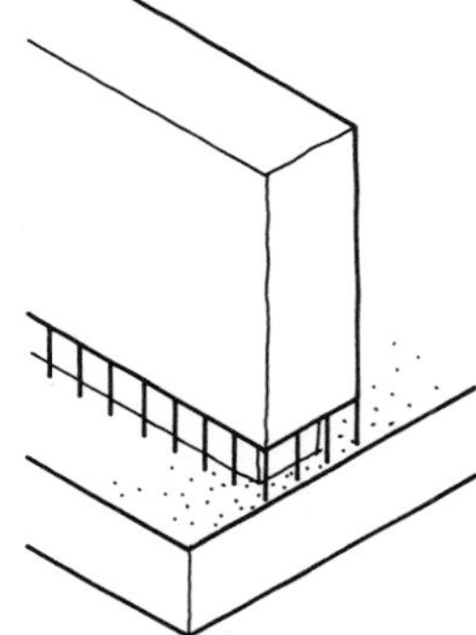

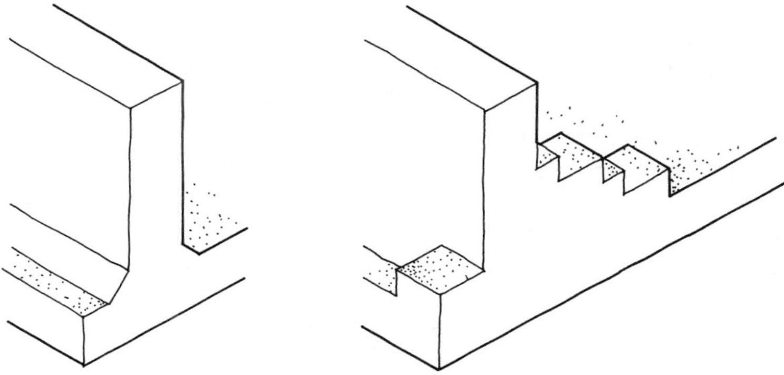

The base proper, an architectural problem that presents an unlimited number of choices, depends on issues such as exterior expression different from or continuing that of the tower, the amount of penetration required for the lobby, arcade, or vehicular access, the amount and kind of glazed area needed for the lobby, and commercial and recreational facilities. One of the difficulties is in the way the base grows out of the ground. Occurring at pedestrian level, its immediately visible presence fuses it with its environment, whether it is raised, depressed or on grade.

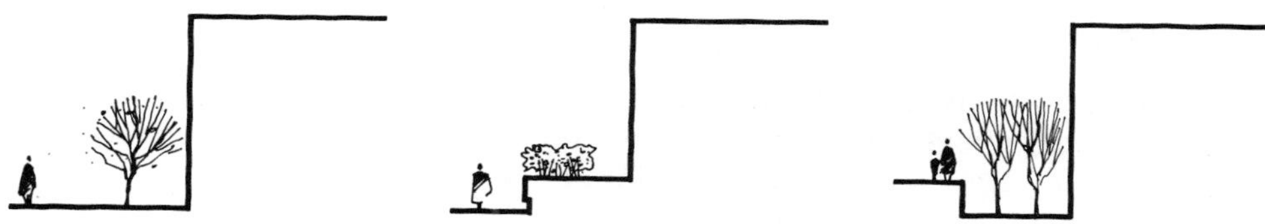

Somewhat less visible at the opposite pole—and therefore generally neglected—is the way the tower ends at the top. It is only less visible from ground level, however. From the upper floors of adjacent highrises it is quite significant, and considering the long vistas of the city it is an important element of the skyline.

Only thorough cooperation between the architect and the mechanical engineer and an awareness of the problem as soon as the typical floor is being planned will eliminate the incredible chaos occurring on our rooftops. The roof elements are admittedly not easy to organize. Some like the elevator penthouse, the stair penthouse, and the boiler stack are tied to the location of the vertical core, others like fan housings, cooling towers, or mechanical rooms can be located with more freedom. All require different heights: 9 ft is enough for a stair penthouse, 11 to 12 ft for a fan housing or mechanical room; the elevator penthouse should be 17 to 18 ft above the roof and the boiler stack must rise above that. If it is impossible to organize these elements into a well-conceived volume, it is at least possible to screen them from view with a fence or shield that shows as a simple mass on the roof.

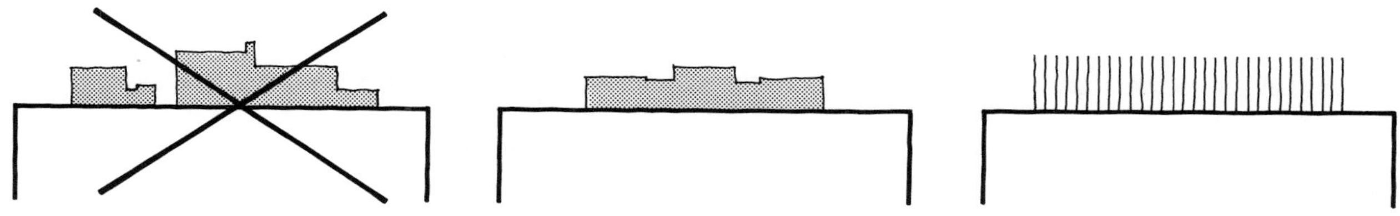

LOWRISE

The design of highrise apartment buildings is related to the limitations of the structural system, mainly concrete or steel, and the vertical core elements among which the elevators play a major role. Entering the world of lowrise, the designer finds himself in an entirely different atmosphere. Gone are the restraints of the structural frame. There are no elevators at all.

This is not to say that lowrise design is devoid of structural discipline. Within the limit of four floors, however, building codes are far more liberal, particularly in regard to fireproofing. A wide range of structural options, from wood frame to load-bearing masonry walls with wood, bar joist, or precast concrete floor framing and such hybrids as poured-in-place concrete slab resting on steel pipe columns are permitted.

In selecting a structural system, the maximum floor area permitted by the code for a particular construction type is the first determiner. This is followed by the skill limitations of local contractors or the available materials in the locality. Magnitude or volume also becomes a consideration, in contrast to highrise design in which height alone ensures a large enough volume. As the building volume increases, so does the likelihood that the budget will afford a more sophisticated construction type. Small jobs are likely to be built more simply of the well-tried exterior-protected wood frame, but, under any conditions, the designer has more options than on the design of highrises.

Exterior walls, which need a lesser degree of fireproofing, can also be more varied. Although masonry or stucco is the usual answer under city codes, a variety of wood sidings can be used in areas of lower density.

Greater options, however, do not negate the principles of apartment planning that we have discussed. Good function, circulation with a minimum amount of wasted space, and adequate room size are equally valid for dwellings in lowrises. The only major difference is that the 15% maximum nonrental space is reduced in lowrises because elevators, corridor supply ducts, stacks, or refuse chutes are not required and, in limited types, even one staircase is permitted. Obviously there is no nonrental space at all in townhouses. In duplex and quadruplex walk-ups with one staircase nonrental space may be as low as 5 to 6%; when there are two stairs, it may go up to 8 to 9%. In central corridor lowrises the nonrental should never exceed 12 to 14%.

Naturally the most significant difference between highrise and lowrise is their scale due to the reduced distance from which the lowrise is observed. Configuration and articulation become more important, and detail is brought closer, and texture is magnified. Not only is the intersection of building and ground immediately visible, but the way the building silhouettes against the sky is apparent. Details can be touched—or they produce the feeling that they could be—and therefore must be handled with increased attention.

As is true in highrises, the distribution system—horizontal and vertical—will help to group lowrises in distinct categories or types (see p. 267).

TOWNHOUSE

Row houses stand on the borderline between the single-family dwelling, which in fact they are, and the multifamily apartment building which they become because they are attached to one another **(41 to 47)**.

The earliest single-family housing found on the tells of Mesopotamia were attached dwellings that made use of common walls. This was necessary because of the limited space on the walled plateau of the tell. The ''row house'' continued in use in the densely built Greek and Roman cities and was neglected only in the rural,

TOWNHOUSE

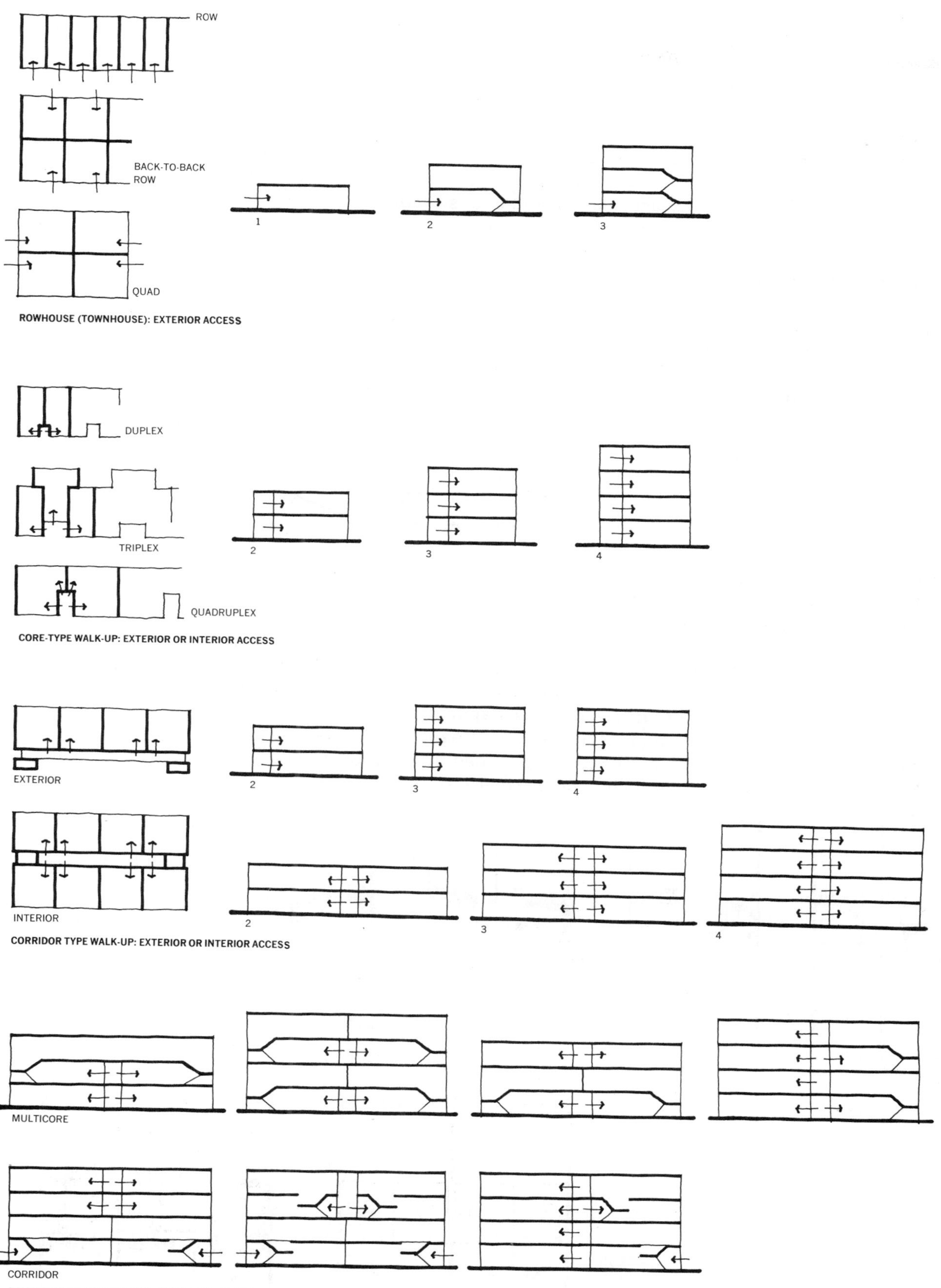

ROWHOUSE (TOWNHOUSE): EXTERIOR ACCESS

CORE-TYPE WALK-UP: EXTERIOR OR INTERIOR ACCESS

CORRIDOR TYPE WALK-UP: EXTERIOR OR INTERIOR ACCESS

COMPLEX WALK-UP: EXTERIOR OR INTERIOR ACCESS

feudal world of the Middle Ages, with its agriculture-oriented economy and lack of city life. The row house was reintroduced at the rebirth of cities in the commercially developing countries of northern Europe. A city dwelling (town house) *par excellence*: shop on the ground level, the apartment of the burgher above.

Townhouses—to use the popularly accepted terminology—are seldom seen in their one-story form because a two-story structure is more economical and occupies less land. The one-story form that occurs mostly as a court-house in connection with the matrix system is discussed at the end of this chapter.

The traditional two-story townhouse divides living zones on grade level and sleeping zones on the upper floors, though such clear demarcation is not always possible and bedrooms can be found on the first floor as well. On sloping sites, when both levels are grade-connected, the subdivision is reversed if the entrance is on the upper level. Although the bedrooms are generally located on the second floor, bathrooms—when more than one is called for—can be split between the two. The lower level bathroom then serves the living zone and guests and can be used also for the bedrooms above as long as it can be reached without crossing the living space.

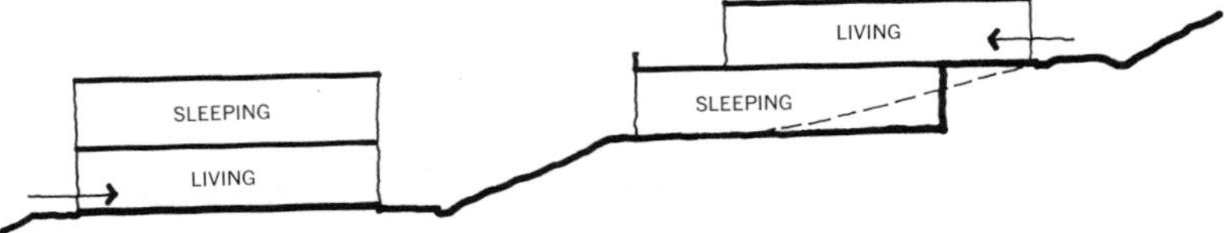

In most townhouses the number of bedrooms will determine the width of the structure, though as a second-dimension generator the stair also plays a significant role. Two- or four-bedroom townhouses have simple designs. Three-bedroom layouts pose problems. The third bedroom, because it occupies the same building width as the two bedrooms on the other side, has to be large, with its own bathroom and walk-through closet **(42, 43)**. When the program calls for three bedrooms of equal size, taut planning can be achieved by overlapping on the second floor. This overlap requires the careful study of fire and sound separation. When the site is narrow, the third bedroom (or fourth) can be provided by the addition of a full or partial third floor on top of a two-bedroom townhouse **(46)**.

The double-run stair, located in a central zone, allows maximum utilization of the two outer zones for bedrooms. What works so simply on the second floor, however, creates circulation problems on the first **(41, 44, 47)**. When the stair—the vertical connector—is in the center zone, the passage leading to it from the entrance bisects one of the living zones. If the townhouse is wide enough, this cut-off space can serve as a study or library. If it is narrow, the result is wasted space and traffic through the living zone. One way to eliminate the problem and still keep central, double-run stairs is to enter the townhouse in the middle, near the stairs **(43)**. This, however, is possible only in end townhouses and staggered rows. A better way to alleviate the problem, to shorten the distance from the entry to the stair, is to slide the two halves of the townhouse along the long axis to bring the entrance nearer to the stair. This sliding can occur on both floors or on the ground floor only.

The single-run stair, which originates on the first floor near the entrance and leads to the second floor landing in the central zone, seemingly eliminates these problems **(41, 46)**. Naturally it helps when the third bedroom is large enough to provide space for it. Otherwise, the townhouse—especially the two- and four-bedroom one—will have to be made wider to accommodate the stair. Nor is the first floor problem free. It is most difficult to create ideal circulation—from kitchen or backyard to basement—without having to cross the living space and a well defined entry hall with guest closet is hard to achieve. The problem is somewhat similar with pulled-out stairs handled as an independent volume (see p. 670).

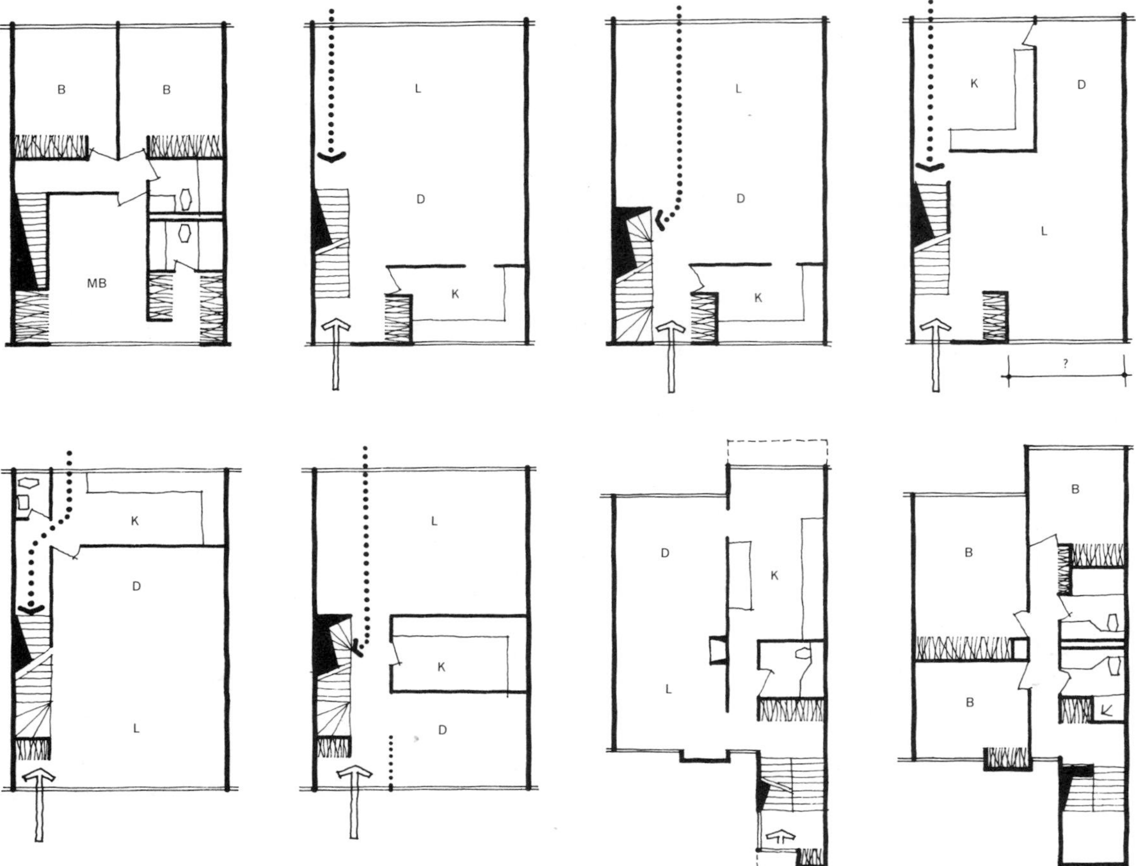

These difficulties encountered in connection with the single-run stair bring into focus some of the basic problems of the townhouse, the linkage to various exterior functions. The solution to all or some of the following linkages will profoundly influence the first-floor plan of the townhouse:

1. GARBAGE COLLECTION. Is it on the same side or on the opposite side of the main entrance? The kitchen should be on the garbage-collection side.

2. VISUAL SURVEILLANCE. This can be best achieved from the busiest part of the living zone, the kitchen or the family room. Where is surveillance important? On the yard side? (When the yard is fenced in, less surveillance is needed.) On the entry side where parking is generally located? Is there a common outdoor area that needs to be observed?

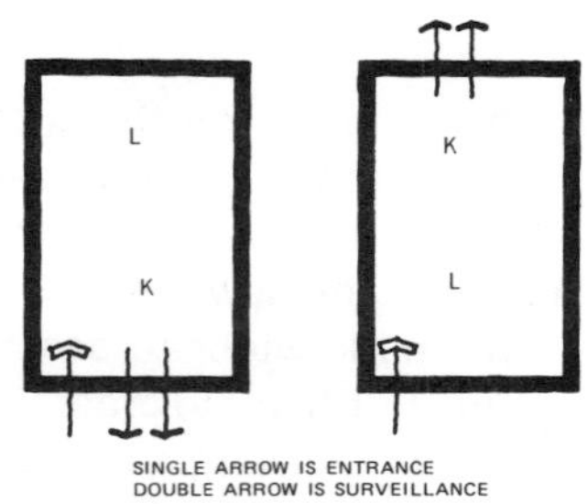

SINGLE ARROW IS ENTRANCE
DOUBLE ARROW IS SURVEILLANCE

3. GARDEN MAINTENANCE. Is there a tool shed in the yard? If tools are in the basement, is there an areaway stair directly to the basement or will passage with tools have to be made through the living zone? If there is a solution that works for the backyard, what happens in the front yard when garden tools are needed?

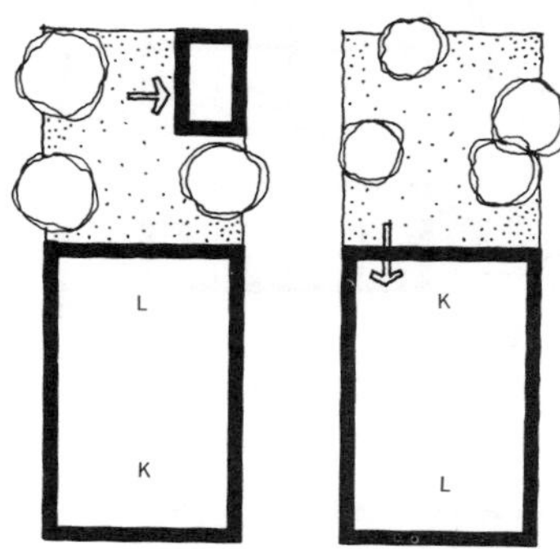

4. PARKING. Is there a lot on the entrance side for both guest and occupant parking? If only guest parking is on the entrance side, where is occupant parking: in a separate garage behind the unit, in an attached garage, or on sloping sites below the unit?

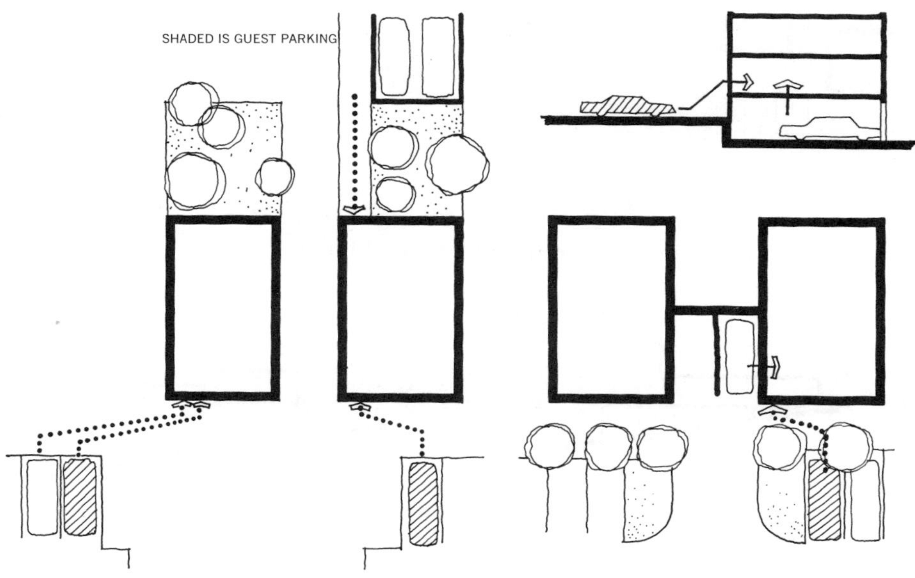

The clusters on p. 272 illustrate how under various site conditions these criteria will influence the location of the entrance, kitchen, and living room on the first floor of a townhouse.

Adaptation to significantly sloping terrain, unless adaptation is avoided, will influence the townhouse more than other multifamily housing types. Sliding the floors along a horizontal axis will result in terrace housing and sliding the elements along a vertical axis will lead to the split-level. To use the split-level townhouse on a level site may seem incongruous, but it does provide daylight for the basement **(41).** It works especially well with the adjacent ground depressed; that is, by adapting the terrain to the split-level unit. Another advantage of this scheme is its abil-

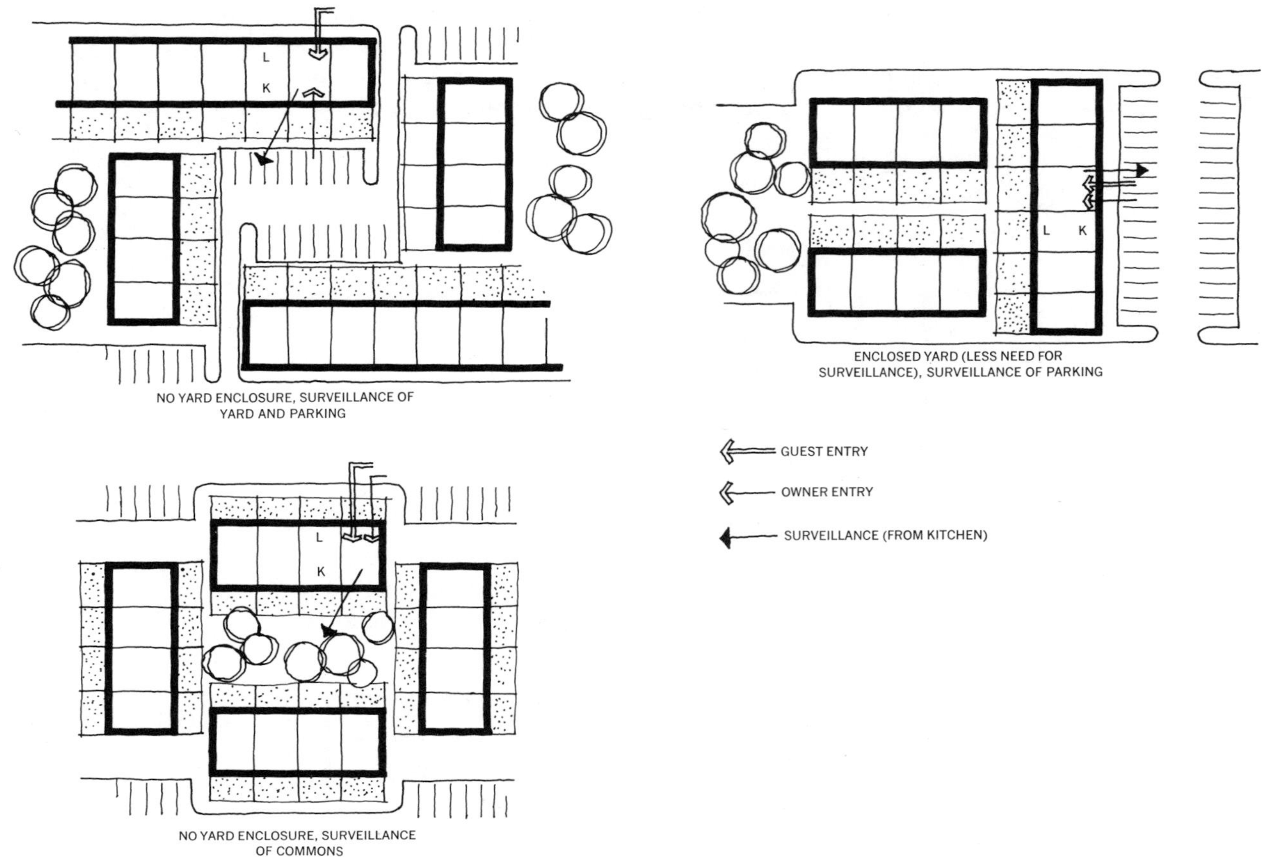

NO YARD ENCLOSURE, SURVEILLANCE OF YARD AND PARKING

ENCLOSED YARD (LESS NEED FOR SURVEILLANCE), SURVEILLANCE OF PARKING

NO YARD ENCLOSURE, SURVEILLANCE OF COMMONS

ity to create space a story and a half high in the living room while maintaining the regular ceiling height in the kitchen and other rooms.

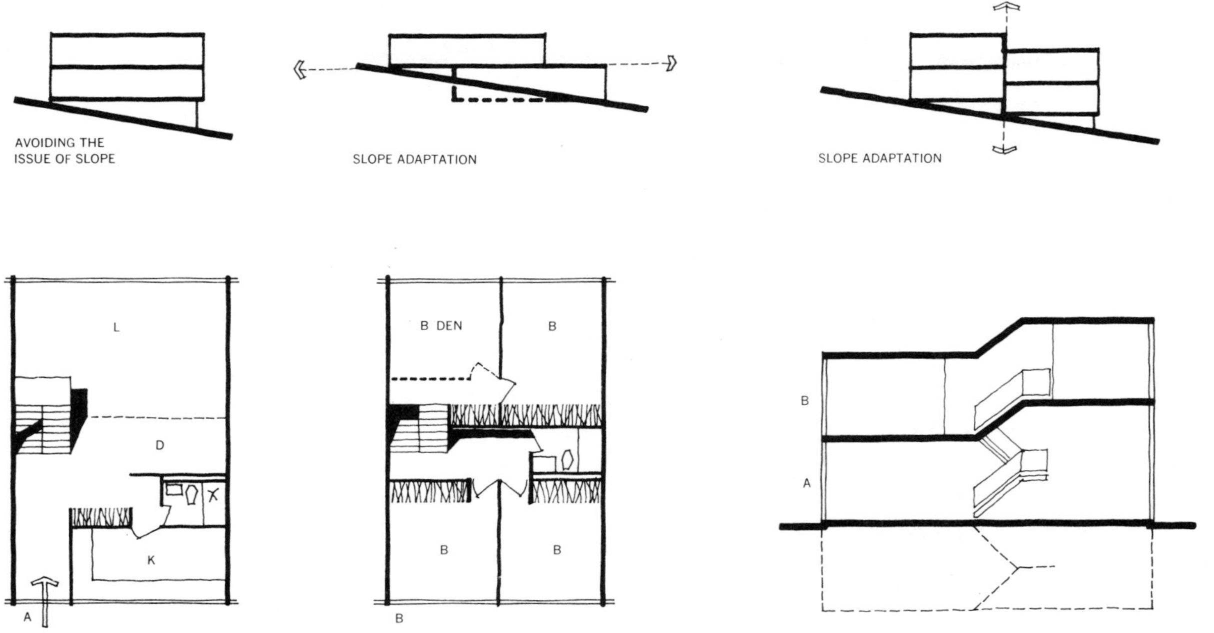

AVOIDING THE ISSUE OF SLOPE

SLOPE ADAPTATION

SLOPE ADAPTATION

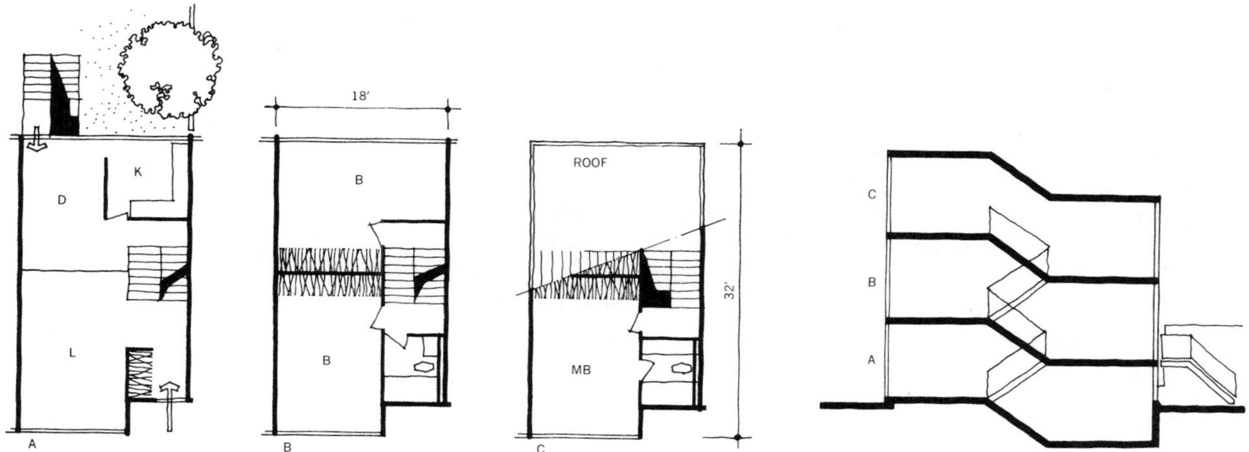

When the townhouse, due to site constraints, must be narrow, but the program calls for a large number of bedrooms, the solution is often a full or at least partial third floor as was previously discussed. Without increasing the number of floors and vertical travel, the extra bedroom, or bedrooms, can also be accommodated by the introduction of inner courts which increases the amount of exposed building surface and therefore the possible number of bedrooms.

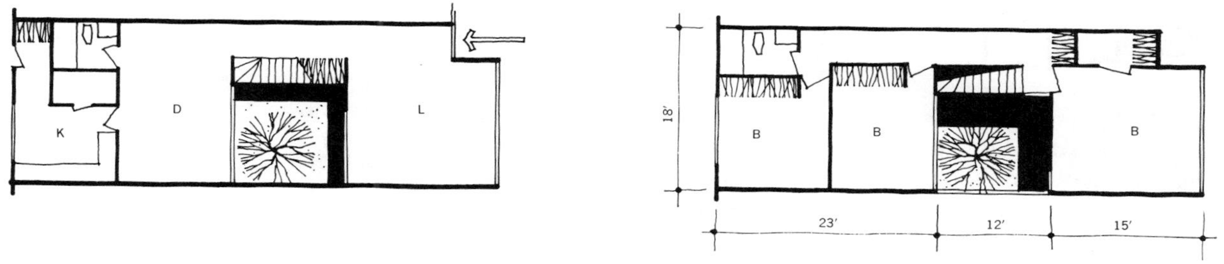

The back-to-back townhouse is not used as an independent building type except on the ground level of complex walk-ups and is discussed under that heading. A form of backing up townhouses is the recently popular arrangement of "quads" or "fourplexes" in suburban developments which result in construction economies, land saving, and higher densities.

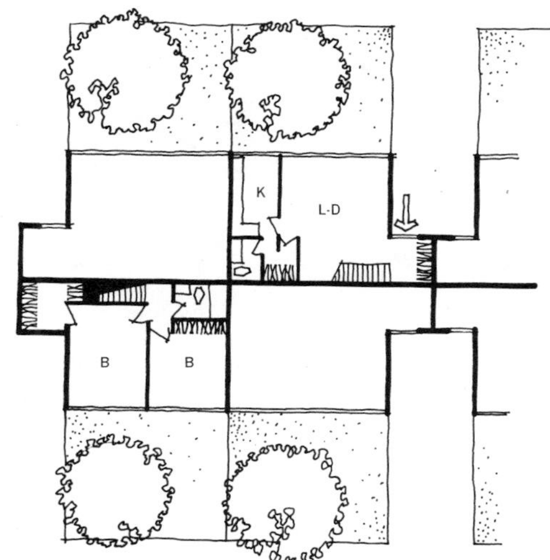

DESIGN METHODOLOGY

In addition to planning the individual unit, the real issue of townhouses is their attachment. The fundamental attachment methods are pairing and planning in sequence. Planning in pairs limits the rows to an even number. Except in condominiums, pairing permits backing up bathrooms and kitchens of rental units on common stacks. Walks to the entrances can also be paired, thus reducing the amount of pavement. When the number of units is uneven or a larger degree of articulation is desired, planning in sequence is the answer. In either case, end townhouses with their added exposure lend themselves to different treatment than those in the row. Neither pairing nor sequence planning is limited to straight-line demarcation between townhouses **(47).** A wide variety of overlaps and interlocks is possible. Staggering opens up unlimited possibilities to mold the row in order to meet site conditions or architectural preferences **(44, 45).**

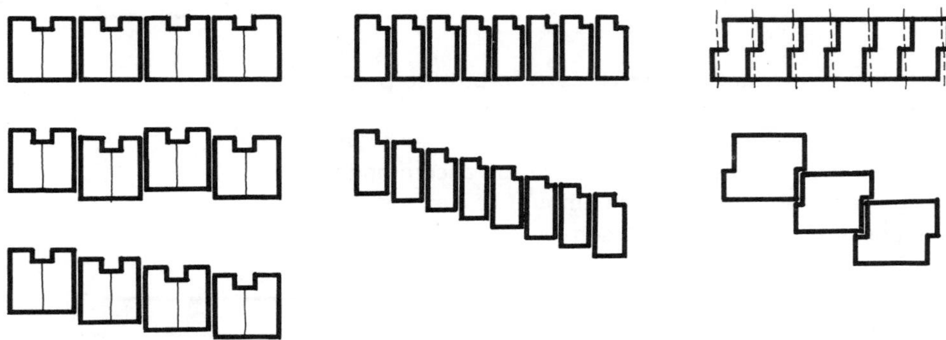

As part of planning the site in rows, groups, or clusters the townhouse, as the purest individual-access-type housing, poses special problems in relating the ground-level unit to public or semipublic spaces.

Open front yards can be defined and separated from public areas by a variety of means: hedges, fences, or a simple level change that provides, if not a physical, at least a psychological barrier. When the townhouse directly adjoins public space, at least a minimal definition and separation is desired.

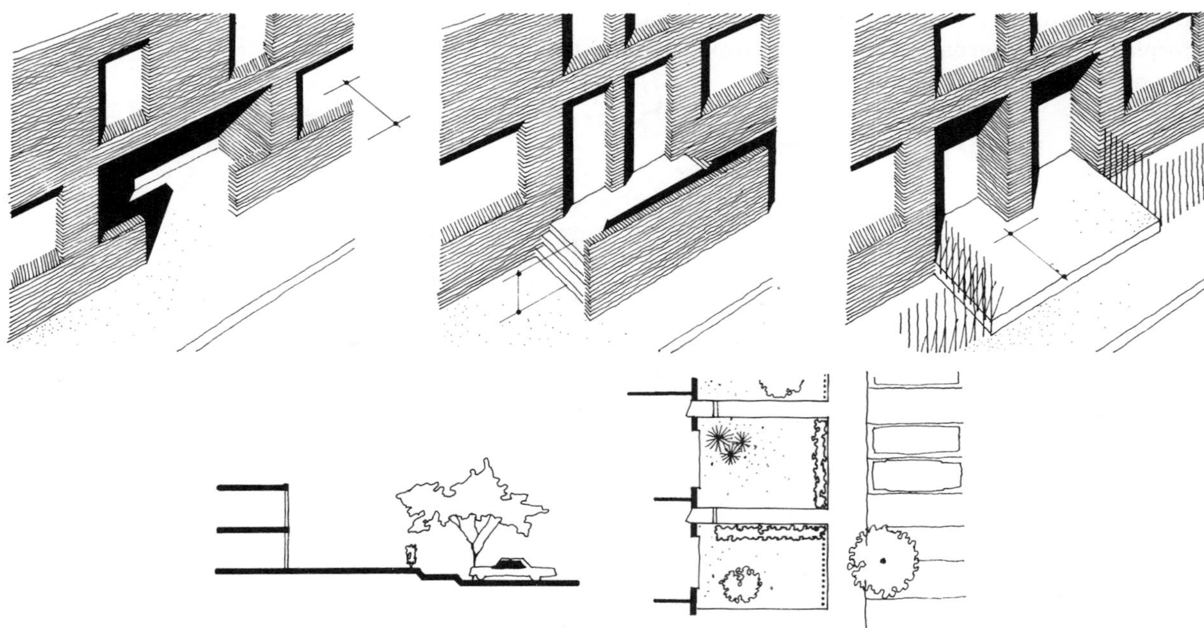

Rear yards can be fully private and completely fenced in. They can be semiprivate, separated from adjacent yards, but open or partly open to common areas. When they are fully open, at least some grade separation will define the private from the public.

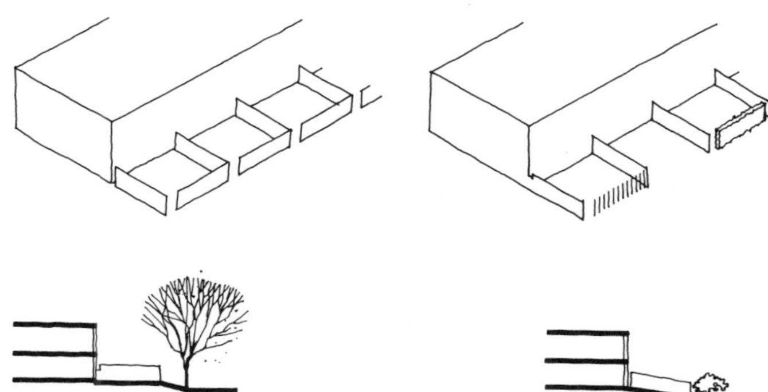

A most interesting application of the attached dwelling with private court is found in the matrix systems **(48, 49)**. The dwelling is arranged around an inner court or courts and maximum daylight penetration can be achieved for a one-story type. Two-story units tend to cut off sunlight and can be used only in bright, sunny climates. A good compromise is the partial two-story unit. Privacy in the relatively small court is essential and only one unit should face it. At first glance one would think that the matrix provides a higher density than the ordinary townhouse. This, however, is not the case except on sloping terrain when ''access from above'' becomes possible and walking passage is created on the top of units stacked on the hillside without having to provide space-consuming ''streets.'' (See density analysis in the chapter on Low and Midrise Sites.) The great attraction of the matrix lies in the unlimited combinations and permutations and the fascination of the resulting geometry.

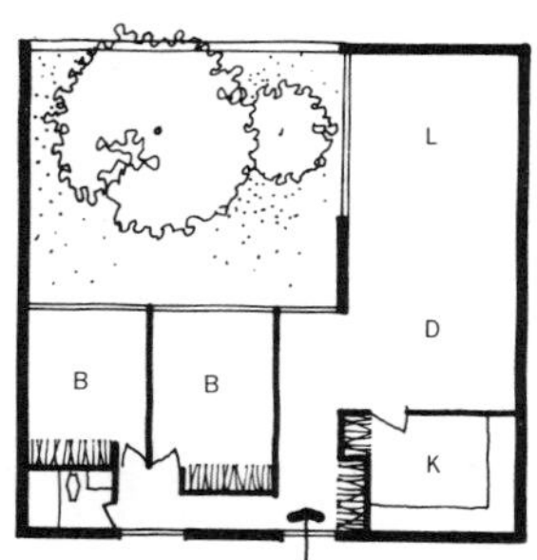

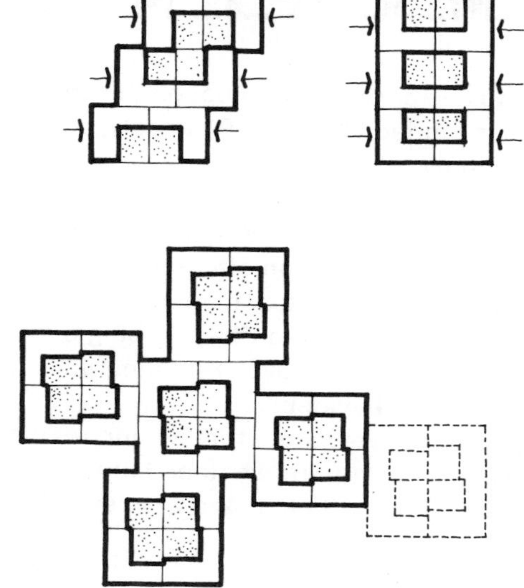

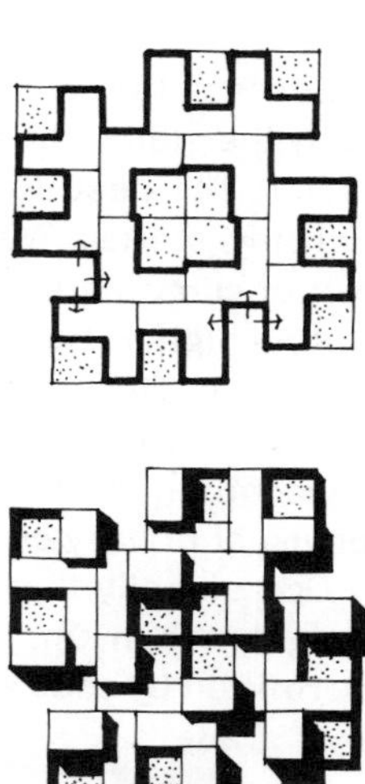

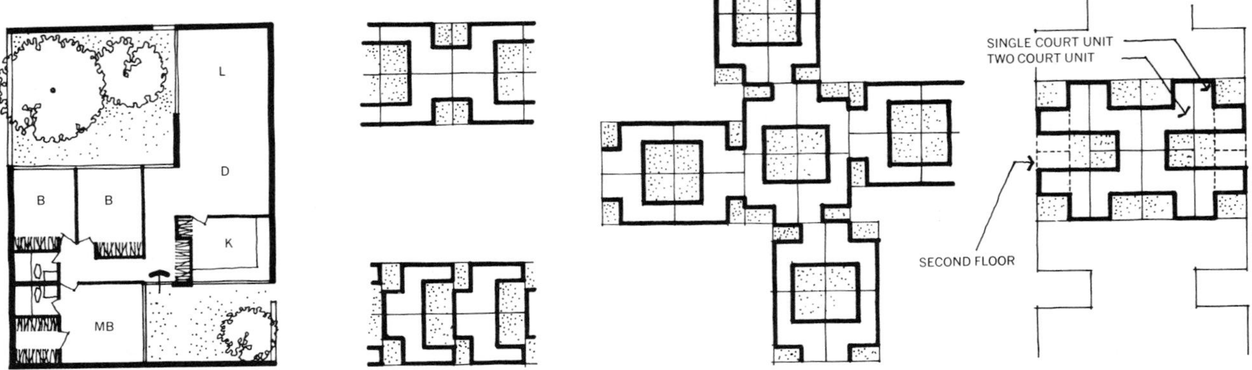

CORE-TYPE WALK-UP

Core-type walk-up buildings consist of a stair core (one or two stairs as required by code) serving a limited number of apartments on each floor **(50 to 54).** Depending on whether there are two, three, or four apartments around the stair, this type is called duplex, triplex, or quadruplex. The triplex is uncommon in the United States, though in Europe it is often seen. A series of cores forms a multicore walk-up, an economical option in contrast with high rises in which multicore means an increased number of elevators.

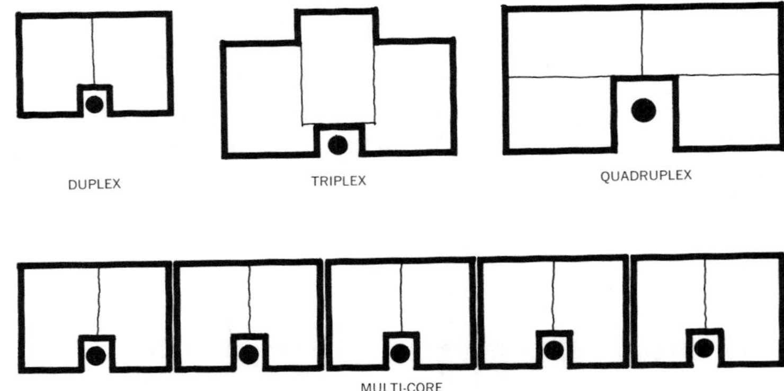

Because the sole means of access to an apartment—except on the ground floor—is by the stairs, the walk-up building is limited in height. Obviously, comfort is the factor. The need for density and economy generally does not permit the ideal of only two stories. Walk-ups are usually three stories high and, if the slight discomfort of climbing the stairs is accepted, the height can be stretched to four stories but no higher. Because of this discomfort, however, an attempt is made to reduce the climb. The building is often depressed by half a story in relation to the entrance elevation. Although this provides some amelioration of the climbing distance, the concomitant problems of depressed yards, snow removal, retaining walls, and lack of visual privacy on the depressed floor is self-evident.

Occasionally the building is depressed to overcome strict zoning regulations of height. When this happens it is prudent to inquire whether habitable space is permitted by code when it is below grade, how far below, and what exactly is meant by "grade."

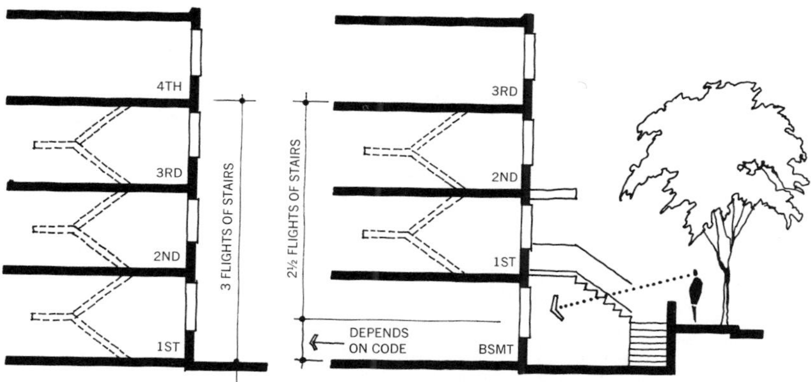

Exit requirements for walk-ups vary all over the map, and familiarity with the local code is essential. Some codes, depending on construction type, number of units served by a stair, and the size of the units, will allow a single means of egress in buildings of limited stories. A single stair is desirable not only because of economy but better chances of surveillance and less opportunity for prowlers. When codes permit a single stair to serve a limited number of floors, this number can be stretched by depressing the building, provided, however, that the code considers it a basement and thus it does not count as a floor when stair requirements are considered. Some building codes will permit a single stair for four-story or even taller buildings of duplex or quadruplex types as long as there is access to the roof from the apartments and the next stair—within permitted travel distance—can be reached via the roof.

Stairs play an important role in core-type walk-ups. How the problem is solved will have significant consequences for the apartment plan itself. In duplexes the stairs may force the location of the apartment entry near the end of the apartment oblong, thus creating internal traffic problems **(50, 51)**. Ideally, the stair should function so that the apartment entry is near the center of the apartment oblong, approximately between the living and sleeping zone to alleviate any difficult traffic patterns **(52, 53)** (see p. 279).

The stair is only one of the plan generators of duplexes. Bathrooms and kitchens also serve as generators of the plan. How they will be paired will determine whether the stair core can be moved to the center. Centrally located stairs will result in modification of the ground floor because passage to them will have to be borrowed from ground-level apartments **(52, 53).**

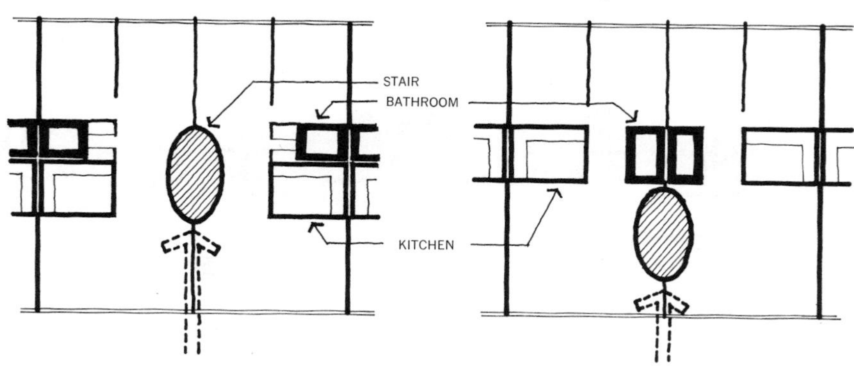

The number of bedrooms and the kind of dining space obviously influence basic duplex arrangements. The number of bedrooms determines the width of the units. Dining space and its relation to kitchen and living room will have a causative effect on the internal traffic pattern.

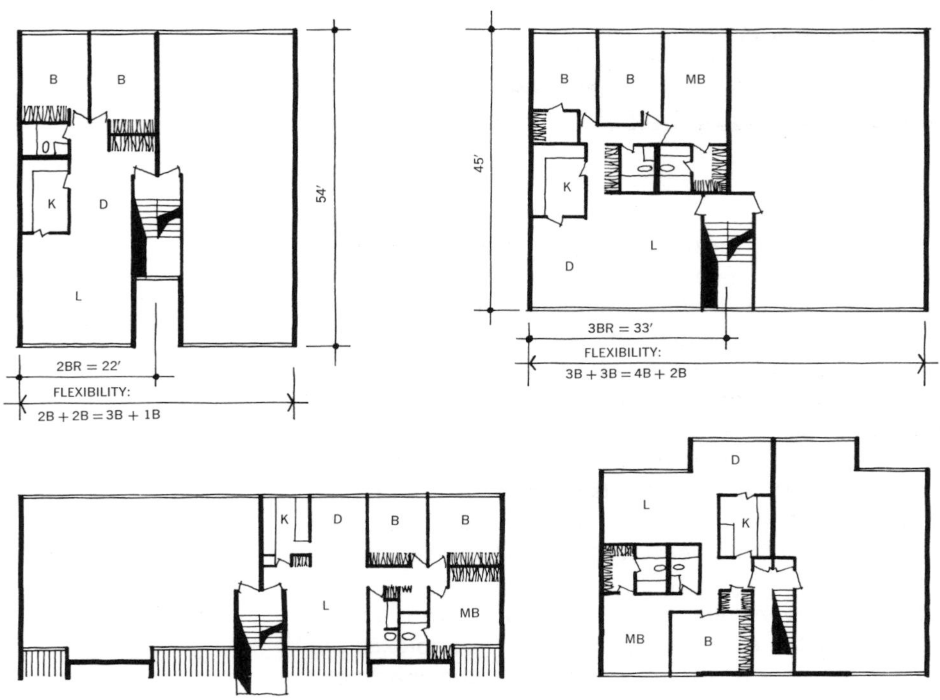

Quadruplexes, when the building code permits a single exit, must have the kind of stair arrangement that provides access to all four apartments from a single landing **(54).** When two means of egress—two stairs—are required, many arrangements are possible. In all cases it is important to determine whether the code requires the stairs—one or both—to be in a two-hour enclosure. Entry into the apartment oblong is preferred near the center rather than at the edge.

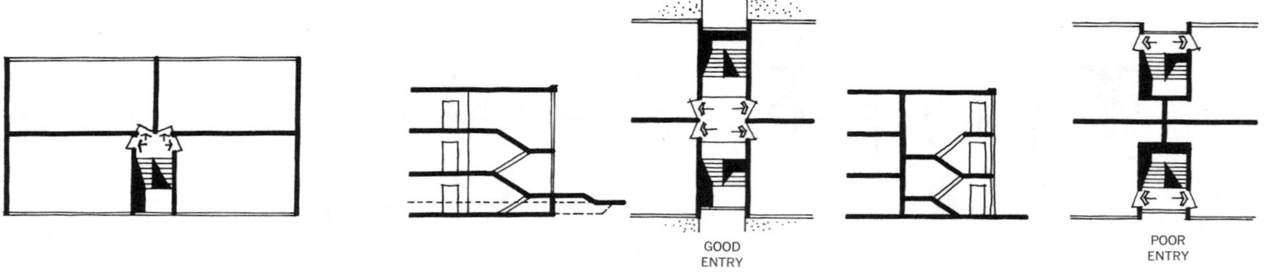

Quadruplexes with one means of egress can generate a variety of imaginative linkages, depending on site constraints and the acceptability of higher costs due to considerably increased building perimeters.

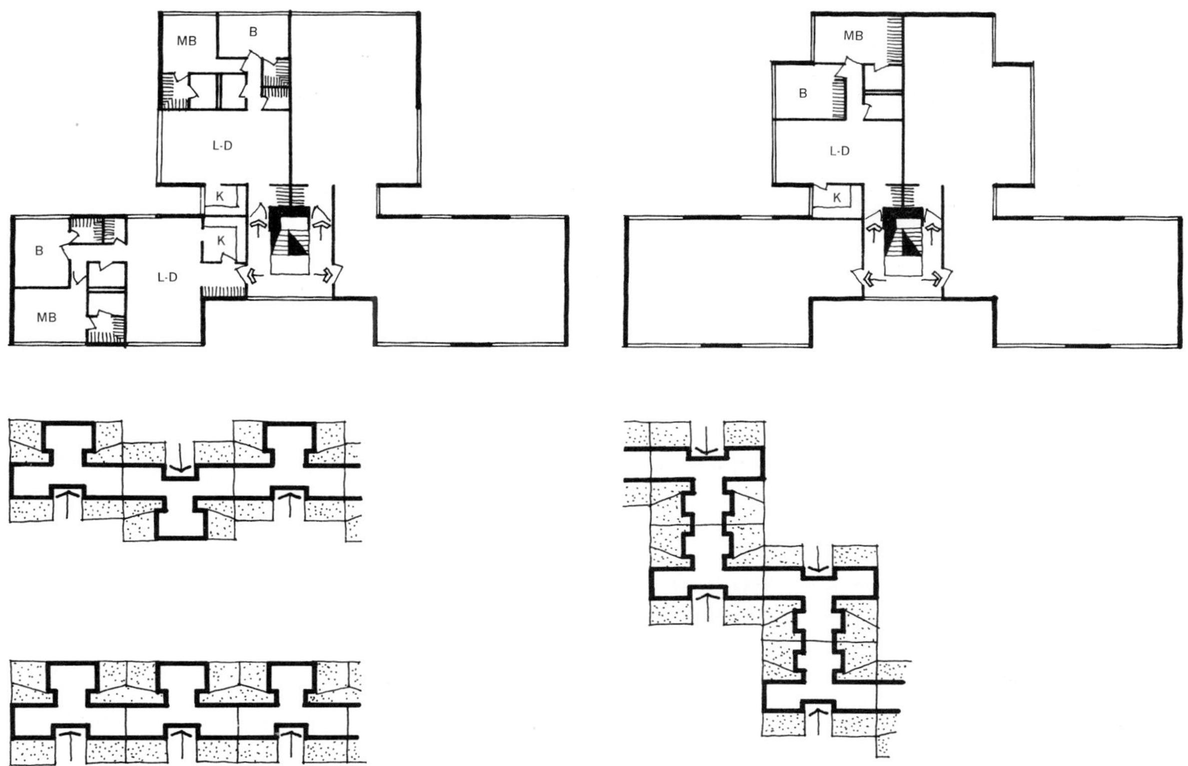

Core-type walk-ups, in contrast to townhouses whose laundry, tenant storage, and heating facilities are included in the unit, generally need a basement for the location of these common elements though combining them within the dwelling unit is also possible.

In spite of the popular term ''garden apartments,'' only the ground floor units can be directly connected to private yards; apartments on the upper floors are generally compensated with balconies or terraces, another strong form generator of this building type.

CORRIDOR-TYPE WALK-UP

The desire to maximize the number of units served by the stair core leads directly from the core-type walk-up to the corridor type **(55 to 60).** Four units are about as many as a stair core can handle; six units result in excessive dead-end corridor, unacceptable by most codes, and eight are possible only with a central corridor scheme.

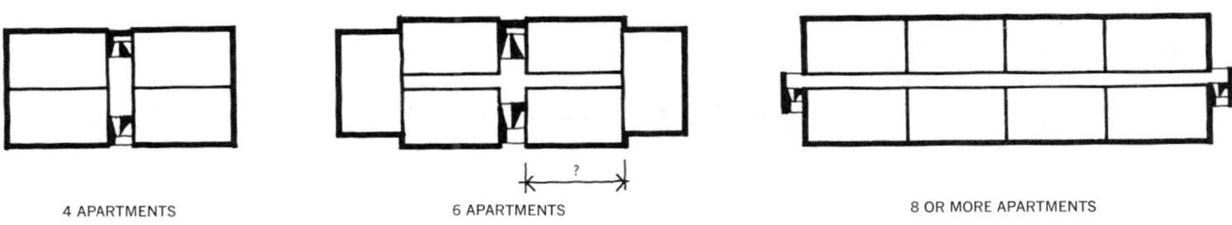

The outside corridor type—another possibility of increasing the number of units—has a low efficiency in regard to nonrental space and has limited climatic use. At this point a comparison between core-type, central corridor, and outside corridor designs will highlight the difference in efficiency.

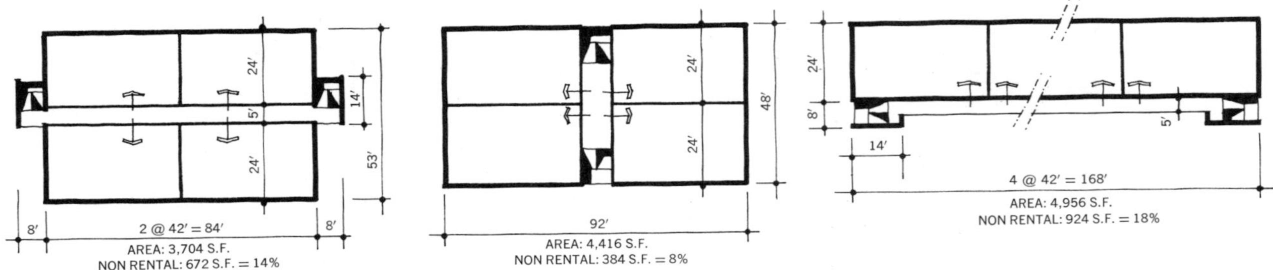

Building codes permit a lower rate of fire protection for lowrises. This low-rated construction type, however, has floor area limits, a problem that does not relate to core-type buildings which have inherently limited floor areas. When the corridor type walk-up has a larger floor area than permitted by code, a firewall of prescribed rating must subdivide it into sections, neither of which may exceed the code-allowed maximum. Depending on the local regulations, a simple set of smoke-stop doors may be acceptable when the firewall bisects the corridor; otherwise a double set of rated fire doors may be required. In either case doors must swing in both directions to prevent obstruction of travel toward the fire exit.

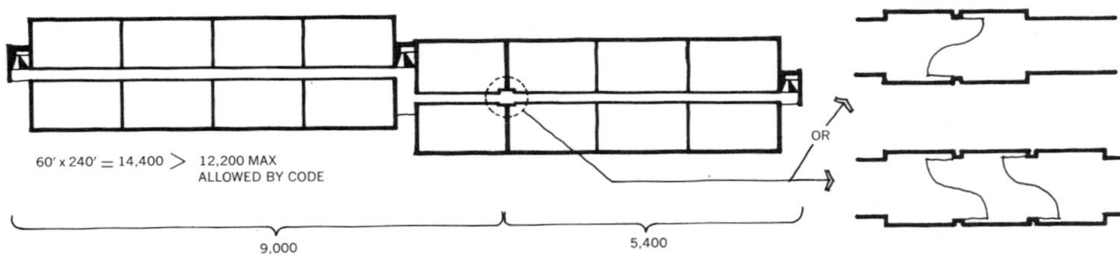

If the end stairs (required by code) are the sole means of vertical circulation, doubling of lobby-vestibules, no matter how small, splitting of mailboxes, and lessening of security may result. When a centrally located stair is provided, it is used mainly for circulation. The end stairs then become the fire stairs. A break in the building volume at this central staircase provides space for a small lobby on the first floor. Otherwise apartment space will have to be sacrificed, not to mention the difficult aesthetic problem when the lobby interrupts the window rhythm on the elevation.

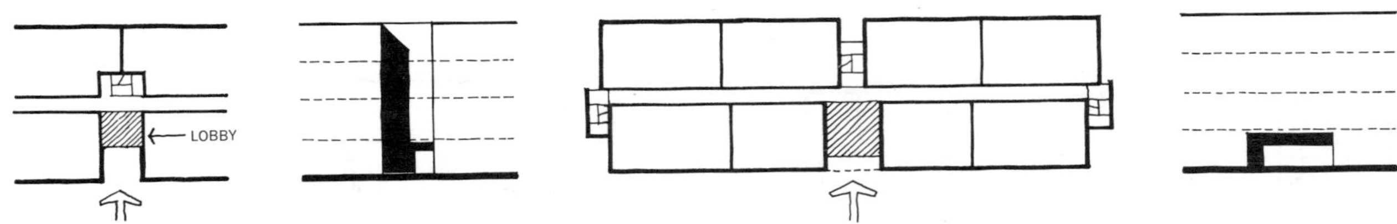

The central corridor walk-up is used less often than the exterior access type with its attached or bridgelike detached corridors. The advantages of the exterior corridor walk-up, especially under favorable climatic conditions, are obvious. The most significant is the double exposure of each dwelling unit. Because the framing system of lowrises is so much more economical than highrises, the poor ratio of nonrental space can be disregarded.

An increasingly common type of exterior-corridor walk-up is the "piggy back," in which townhouses are stacked one above the other **(55 to 57)**. Exit requirements of the building code must be carefully analyzed to ascertain whether direct egress is required from the bedroom level of the upper townhouse.

When the exterior and interior corridor systems are combined in clusters of interior corridor buildings connected with open galleries or in interior corridor building segments alternating with the exterior corridor type, strongly articulated building volume will result **(58, 60)**.

Another interesting application is the clusters of back-to-back units partly surrounded by and connected with an exterior gallery system that is greatly enhanced by varied handling of exterior stairs **(59)**.

In contrast to the highly clustered sculptured appearance of the preceding groups, the corridor type walk-up can have its aesthetic appeal in the low, long volume that results when a large number of apartments have to be contained **(56, 57)**. This powerful volume lends itself to periodic articulation that occurs at the stair cores, including adaptation to sloping terrain which will shift half a floor at the stairs.

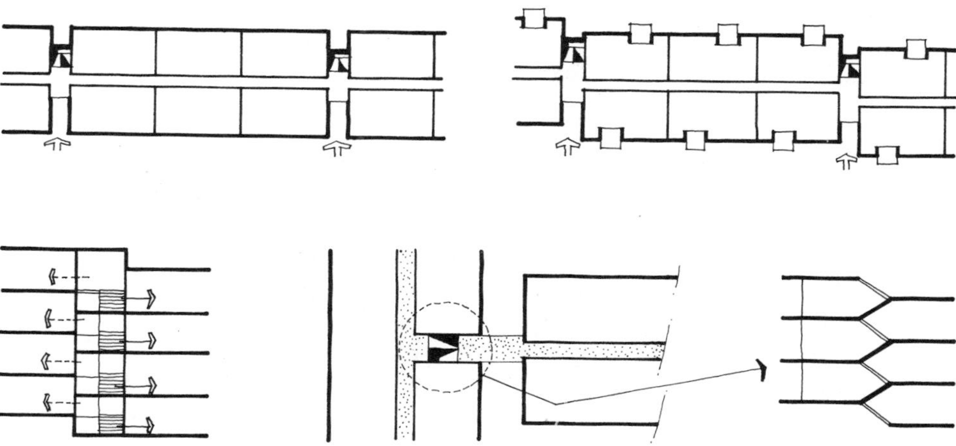

MIXED WALK-UP

The walk-ups discussed up to this point stack identical units above one another. To accommodate a complex mix in the client's program, to place family oriented units with large numbers of bedrooms on ground level and units for smaller households above, or to eliminate the necessity for the elderly to climb stairs in a walk-up vertical stacking of like units can be avoided. Instead of pure types, we are talking about mixed walk-ups containing townhouses, core-type units, and exterior or central corridor apartments in various combinations **(61 to 64)**.

The first group consists of all exterior access dwelling units. Townhouses and regular exterior corridor apartments can be combined in a variety of ways; the townhouse is usually on the top to minimize exterior stair height **(62)**.

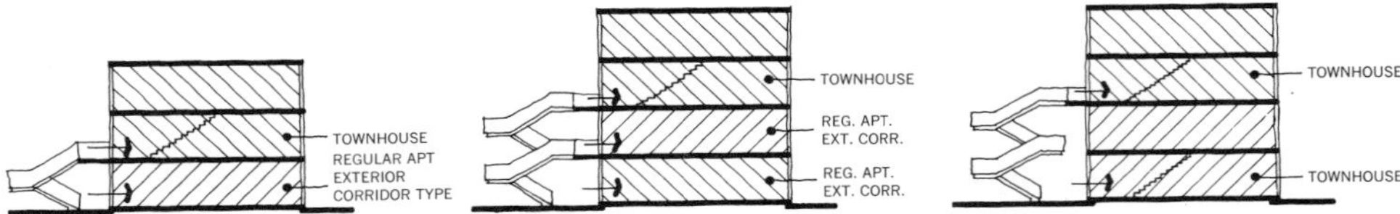

Core-type access characterizes the second group of combinations. Townhouse on townhouse can fall into this group as well, when the upper townhouse is reached by an inside stair. This is possible only when the building code does not require a second means of egress for the upper townhouse. The more common combination in this group consists of townhouses and duplexes **(61, 63, 64).**

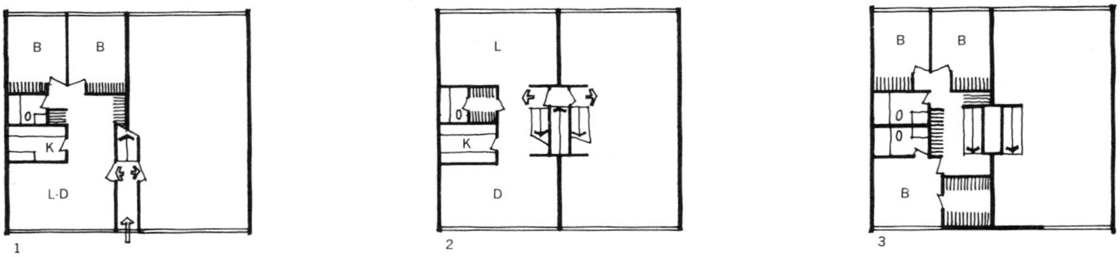

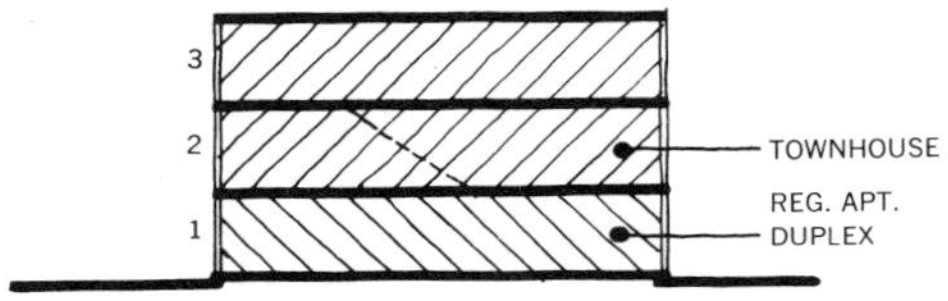

1 2 3

(THE INSTITUTE FOR ARCHITECTURE AND URBAN STUDIES: MARCUS GARVEY PARK VILLAGE, NEW YORK, N.Y.)

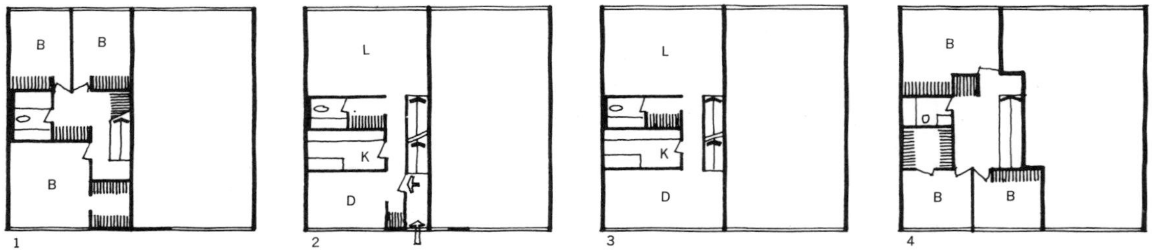

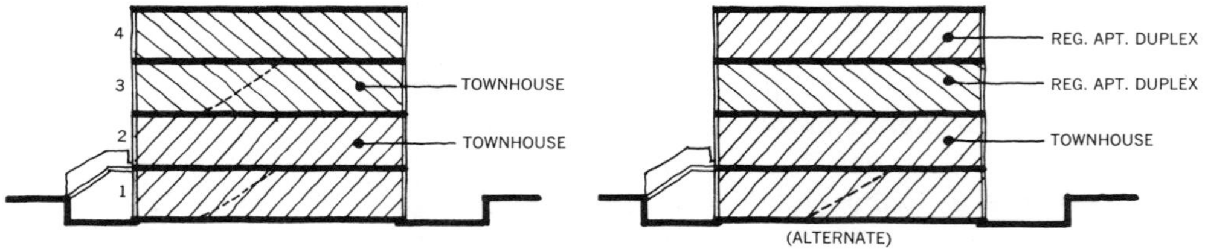

TOWNHOUSE
REG. APT.
DUPLEX

1 2 3 4

TOWNHOUSE
TOWNHOUSE

REG. APT. DUPLEX
REG. APT. DUPLEX
TOWNHOUSE

(ALTERNATE)

Combinations of exterior and interior access is also possible. To mention only the simplest form, back-to-back townhouses with ground level entry can be placed on the lower level of central corridor lowrises.

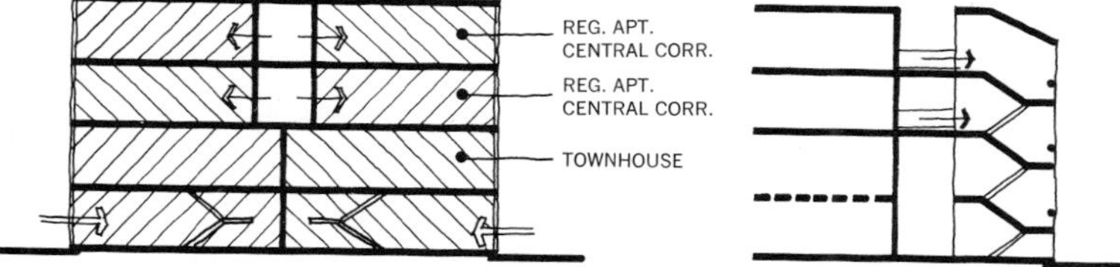

The possibilities inherent in stacking and attaching walk-ups are almost unlimited if structural framing, plumbing, and ventilation ducts can be properly aligned. Stairs pose a special challenge. Whether they are exterior or interior, a thorough understanding of the building code is necessary not only for compliance but because code provisions may generate novel solutions for stairs and exterior corridors or unusual combinations of dwelling units to solve exit problems.

Mixed walk-ups fascinate designers because their planning becomes truly three-dimensional. Planning not only horizontally but vertically adds the challenge the ordinary lowrise often lacks. The opportunity to change fenestration from floor to floor, completely justified because the apartment type itself changes, makes mixed walk-ups even more favored by the designer, for it allows the manipulation of the exterior not easily possible with pure types. Because the stacking of different units one above the other is likely to result in recesses for terraces, in projections of units, or in other volume breaks, the opportunities to mold the building form are further enhanced.

MIDRISE

Midrises start where walk-ups stop, at the five-story building height **(36 to 40).** Where the midrise ends is hard to agree on. According to the definition used in this book, the height of a midrise depends on how far a hydraulic elevator can be put to practical use. Not all will agree. Some consider an eight-story building midrise and there are five-story buildings that have electric elevators.

According to planning principles, there is little difference between highrise and midrise. All building types (central corridor, exterior corridor, multicore, and so on) can be adapted to midrises, and all highrise apartment types are valid.

Structurally, midrises are truly on the borderline. In some locations five- or six-story midrises can have wood framing with masonry exteriors. As the fireproofing requirements of the local building code increase, the framing system of the midrise changes from exterior-protected wood to poured-in-place concrete with all the possibilities between. When considering the structural options of midrises, the designer, accustomed to the simplicity of the highrise concrete frame, has to keep in mind that midrises require no shear walls; the load-bearing masonry system is a realistic possibility at this height; wood or bar joist floor framing, though suitable for midrises, will result in thicker floors and consequently longer stair runs; when parking is under the building, wood or steel floor framing does not provide adequate fire separation and a concrete deck will be needed above the parking level.

Most midrises, because of their limited number of apartments, cannot easily absorb the cost of a parking garage and are more often provided with open on-grade parking. When common elements are minimal or are located in a separate building, when the lobby is small and lockers and mechanical space are in the basement or on the roof, the ground floor of the midrise can be used for open but sheltered parking. Depending on the number of floors and apartment sizes, a good percentage, if not all, of the parking can be taken care of in this way.

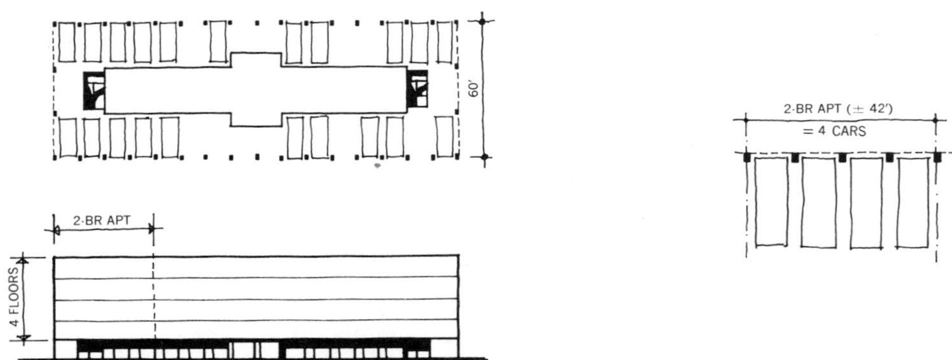

When the ground floor is used for lobby, lockers, and mechanical space, and the apartments start on the second floor, access to the elevator is simple. When the first floor is utilized for apartments, the more indirect access necessitates borrowing apartment space for lobby and loading and results in difficult volume penetration. In addition, the greater ceiling height required by lobbies must be considered.

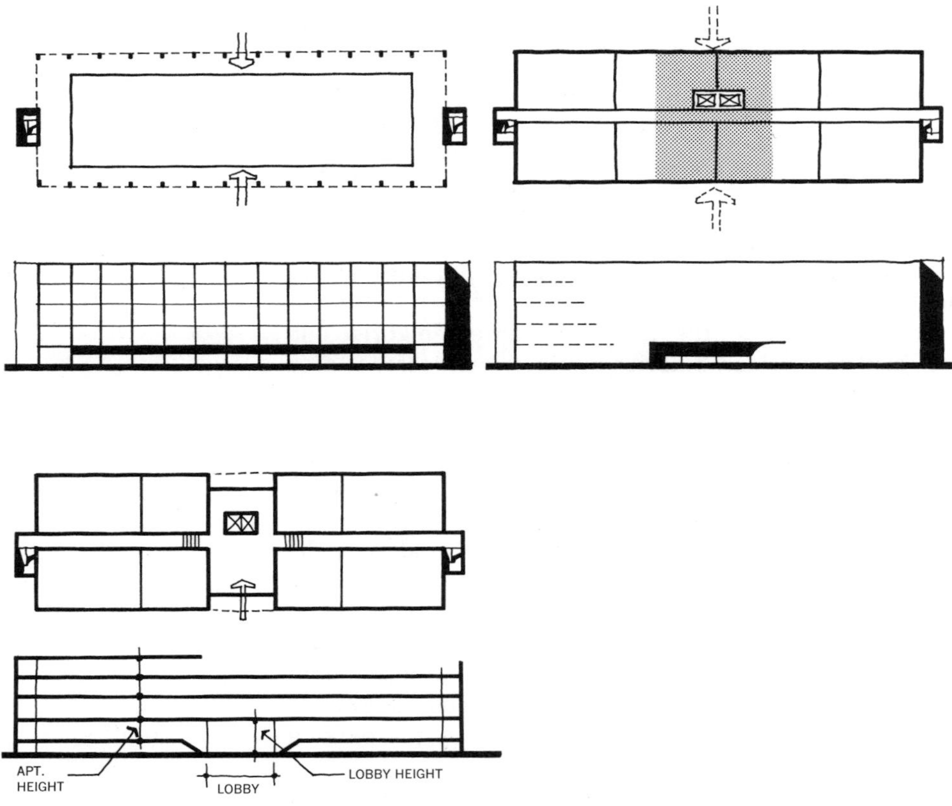

Midrises, like walk-ups, lend themselves to a wider range of linkage possibilities than highrises. Because they are low, complete or almost complete rings are possible as long as the sunlight can penetrate the court. Sometimes, to introduce more light and air, the exterior corridor is detached from the building itself to form a network of bridges.

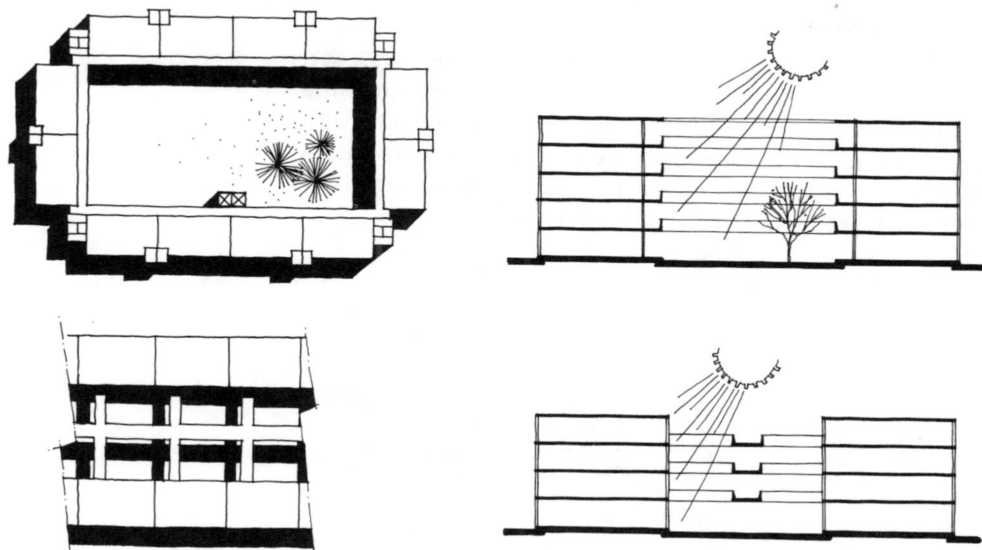

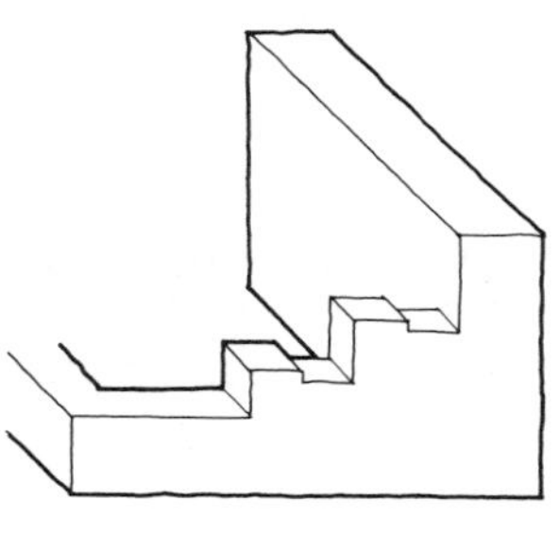

A logical use of the midrise is in low-income public housing. Compared with lowrise, it permits considerable density, compared with highrise, it is more economical to build. In its exterior corridor or multicore form it provides a high degree of surveillance.

Midrises in the context of large urban projects that incorporate buildings of various height can be used to serve as elements of transition and cease to be separate volumes. The highrise, instead of standing independently, becomes part of the total residential fabric growing gradually out of the low volumes. This gradual transition is a natural answer when high density development abuts parks, river edges, or seashores. Sometimes the transition is almost undetectable, high-, mid-, and lowrise melting into a sculptured residential matrix.

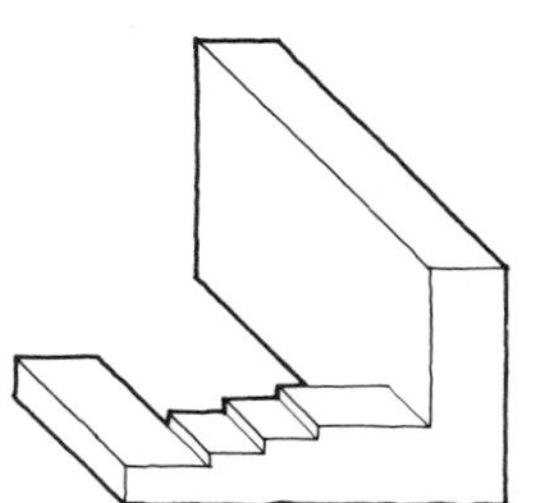

LOW- AND MIDRISE EXTERIORS

Lowrises and midrises, like highrise apartment buildings, reflect their particular structural system on their exteriors. Economy seldom permits—and the height of the building certainly does not warrant—pure skeletal structure for lowrises. Mies' townhouses in Detroit are the exception rather than the norm. Structural framing of lowrises is usually hybrid. The combinations and variations are many and complex, so that simple categorizations that are possible in highrise construction cannot be made here.

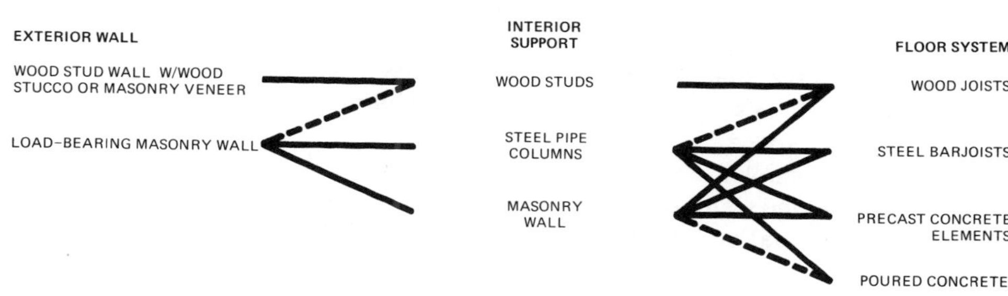

The large majority of lowrises are exterior clad structures—wood, stucco, and masonry—that emphasize the articulation of the building volume and the pattern of fenestration rather than the structural frame with any measure of purity **(55, 64).**

This is not to say that the lowrise structure cannot be expressed. When it is the intention of the designer, a degree of structural expressiveness can be achieved. If function permits large glass areas, the load-bearing masonry walls can be shown and further emphasized by extending them beyond the glass line. If floors are poured or precast concrete, they are readily expressible **(36, 37, 41).**

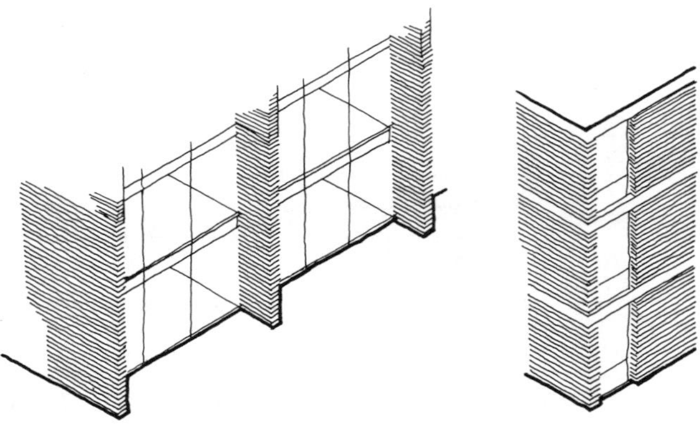

When floor framing is wood or steel bar joist, expressing the floor is not so easy. Both wood and steel require fireproofing on the exterior. In spite of this, the masonry cladding that acts as fire protection can suggest the floors. This is a good example of apparent structure instead of actual structure.

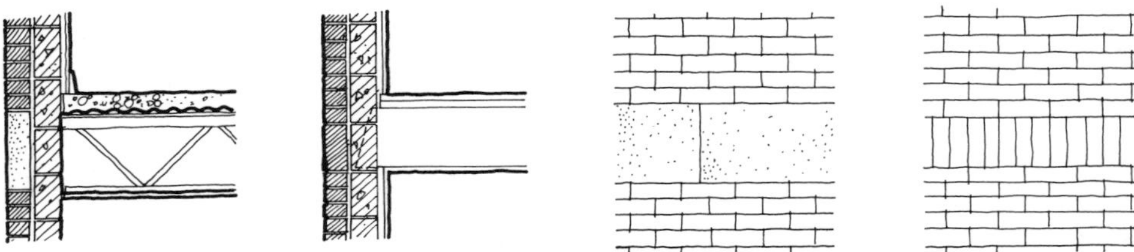

Whether the building is completely clad or tends to be structurally expressive or suggestive, the key issue is its scale, its closeness to the observer. Textures and details are experienced by the viewer as part of his visual environment instead of as an abstract pattern on a tower. Nuances are spotlighted and even such small items as the placement of a gas meter or a through-wall bathroom exhaust become extremely important.

The walls of lowrises, as the bordering and enclosing elements of an exterior space, are much more a part of that space than highrises, which are obelisks standing inside the space. The walls of the lowrise form the backdrop for the human interaction that takes place in the exterior space.

Because of this intimacy vis-à-vis the observer, not only the building but its relation to the ground and to the sky gains added significance. In referring to lowrises, Paul Rudolph once said—to paraphrase—that no one ever wrote a sonnet to the silhouette of a flat-roofed building.

Lowrises with their easily articulated volumes already tend to break up the straight-line intersection of building and sky and create a silhouette of interest, even with a flat roof. Two-story units extending above the roof line, mansards, and indentations for terraces are elements that can help to vary, intensify, and enhance the silhouette **(36, 40, 45 to 47)**.

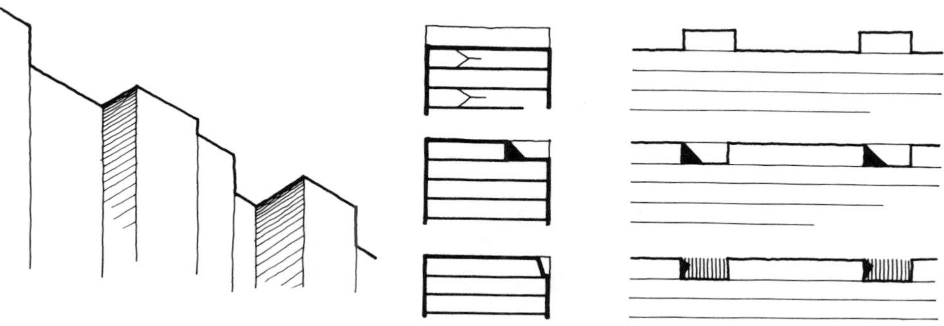

The termination of the wall, the edge detail, is so visible in lowrise distances that the various options demand far more scrutiny and sensitivity than in highrises **(42)**.

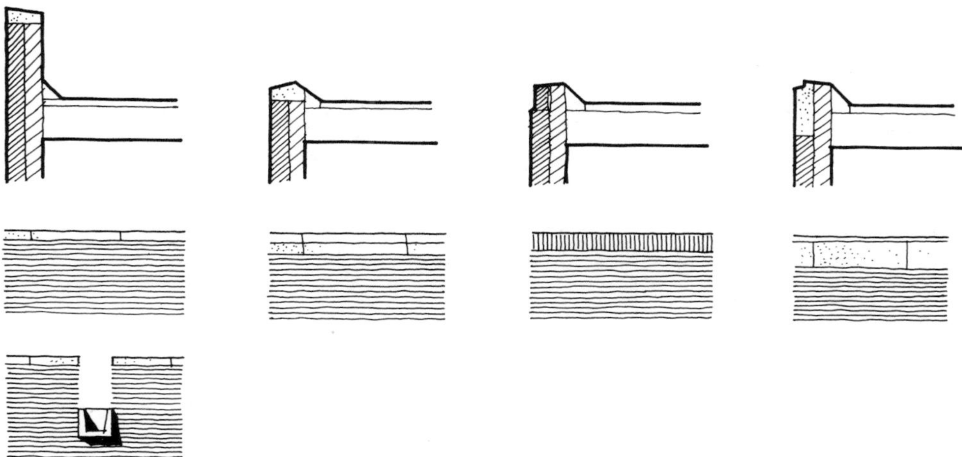

A unique problem is encountered when lowrises are part of a mixed development containing buildings of various heights. The view of the lowrise from the upper floor of a midrise or highrise is also an important one. The flat roofs of lowrises with vents, stacks, and condensing units scattered around do not present a pleasant picture. Unfortunately these tar-and-gravel flat roofs are still the most economical. When budget permits, however, the view from above can be improved with partial or full sloping roofs, which provide a rich vocabulary for varied volumes and silhouettes, not to mention the "residential character" they help to conjure in the mind of the user **(45, 52, 54, 59, 62)** (see p. 290).

The linkage with the ground is just as important as the silhouette. Though often covered by planting, it is the most closely observed border of the building. Whether

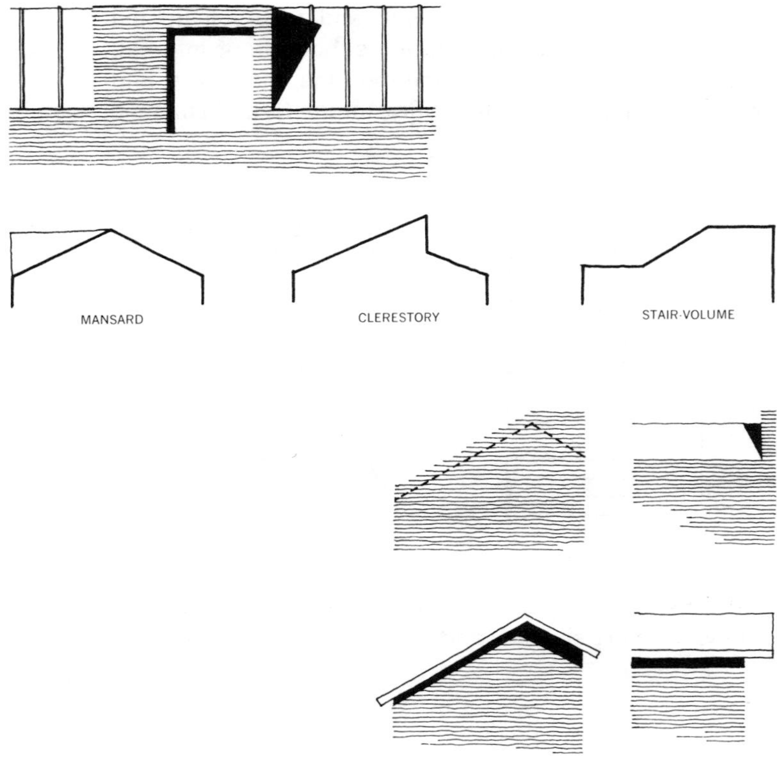

sitting on grade, lifted up on a plinth, or depressed, the meeting of wall and ground is a delicate problem **(43, 46, 48).**

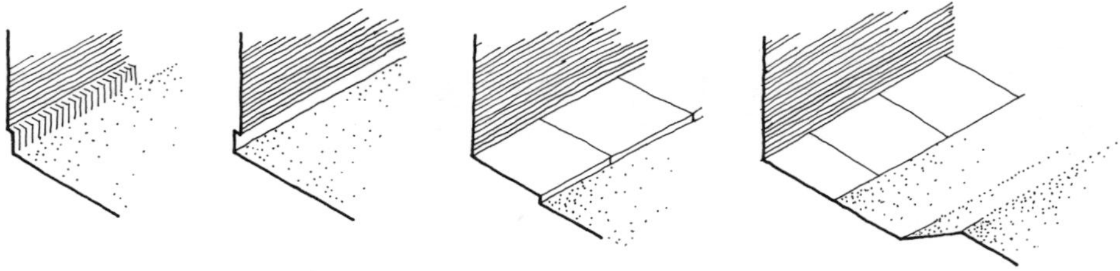

All other elements that serve as transition between the ground and the structure—stoops, steps, terrace platforms, stairs—are important. Similar sensitivity is needed for yard-enclosing structures—fences, garden walls, wing walls—in their method of attachment to the building **(46, 50, 53, 54, 59).**

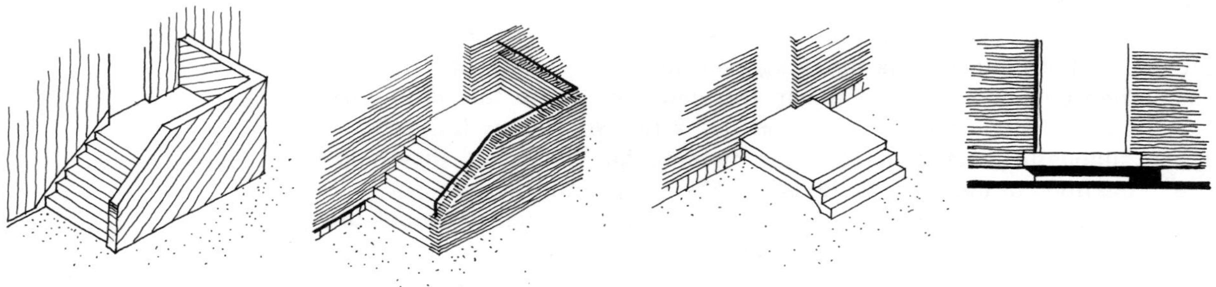

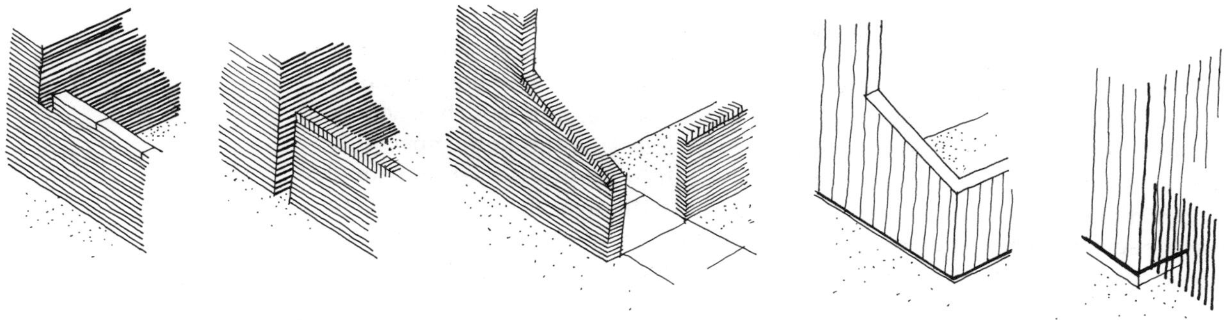

LOW- AND MIDRISE SITES

Site planning in small urban areas is a relatively circumscribed exercise. The limitations of the property and zoning regulations leave the architect with considerably reduced options. Traffic and vehicular servicing barely touches the site and from there on the distribution is vertical. Building volumes (if there are more than one) are placed with minimum choice.

As land increases, as the architect deals with more than one building, the situation changes completely, especially on really large sites. Site planning in this sense is beyond the scope of this book, for there is a growing, specialized literature that attends to site planning and that emphasizes an awareness of ecological and regional problems all the way to new towns with links to regional transportation networks and employment opportunities.

Here the issues of larger sites are merely called to the designer's attention. In one sense they are issues of movement systems: pedestrian movement across the property and pedestrian access to individual buildings; vehicular movement and vehicular storage (parking) linked to the dwellings (vehicles belonging to residents as well as to visitors); movement of vehicular services—delivery and pick-up of mail, refuse removal, fire fighting, and ambulance calls.

The placement of buildings along the movement system network is one site planning factor, their relation to common facilities and recreation areas is another. The opportunities for social contact is a major motivating force.

Buildings also relate to one another and to the environment surrounding the site. Through all these linkages—to movement systems, to other buildings, and to common facilities—some basic principles must be dealt with. One is the security to be achieved by a multitude of social contacts, observation or surveillance opportunities, discussed in detail by Oscar Newman.[32] Another is every resident's need to enjoy sunlight. Buildings should be oriented so that their windows and outdoor recreation areas are not "in the shadow of another structure more than fifty percent of the time they can be reached by sunlight."[33] The distance between balconies or windows and adjacent structures should be carefully considered. In housing for the elderly, often limited in mobility, north orientation should be completely avoided. Last, beyond the promotion of social contact or the need for surveillance, every resident's right to complete privacy should govern. Keeping privacy in mind, distances between buildings should be analyzed and windows or balconies should be far enough from other buildings or places that would allow a view inside. Movement systems, pedestrian or vehicular, should not "get closer than eight feet from a place where it is possible to look into a window, balcony or private open area of any dwelling unit."[34]

After fulfilling the needs for social contact, proper orientation, security, and privacy, after solving the multitude of linkage problems, the "human linkage," the quality of the path traveled through the space defined by the buildings, should be considered. This open space, like the buildings themselves, is a creation of the architect and can be molded to serve a variety of purposes. Open space is perceived by all the senses: kinetic, as one walks through; audio, as one hears children at play, the rustle of leaves or the playing of water; tactile, as a bench is touched; olfactory, the fragrance of flowering shrubs; but primarily through a special kind of vision. Space "is seen, not as a single view, but in sequence over an extended period of time while the observer is in motion."[35] The eye, like a motion picture camera, registers a series of images. This serial vision which requires the study of outdoor space at human eye level makes the customary bird's eye view of architectural site studies highly inadequate.

Architects, planners, and landscape architects have written extensively about exterior space and have examined it from various vantage points. The following tabulation reflects many of these studies:

SPACE IS EXPERIENCED
by entering, passing (using), exiting

SPACE IS PERCEIVED
by all senses: kinetic, audio, tactile, olfactory, and visual (serial vision)

SPACE IS DEFINED BY THINGS

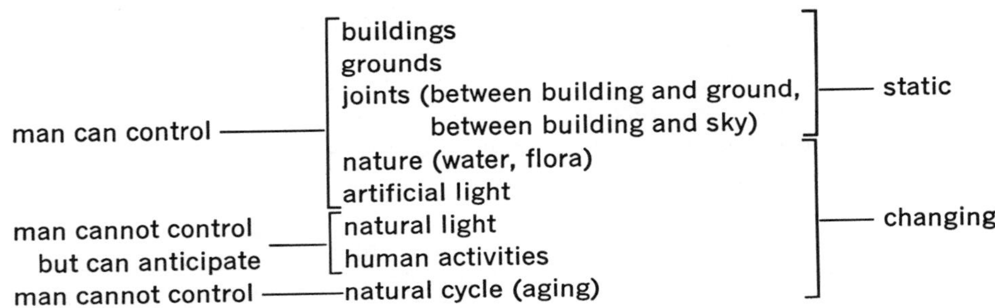

SPACE IS SENSED
in scale

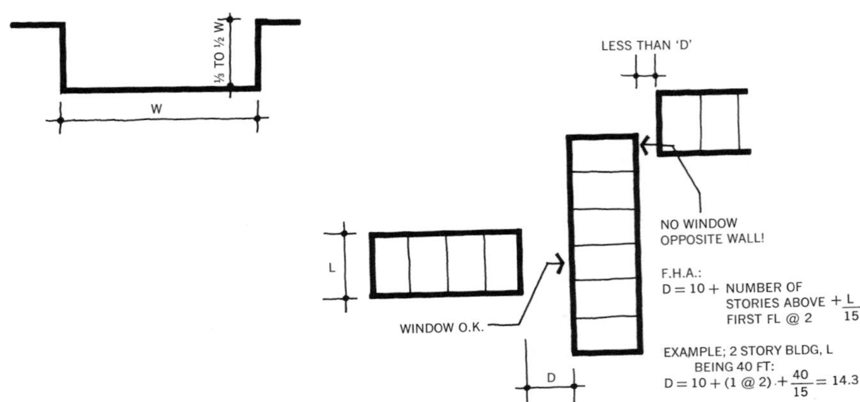

SPACE CAN BE MOULDED
to achieve goals

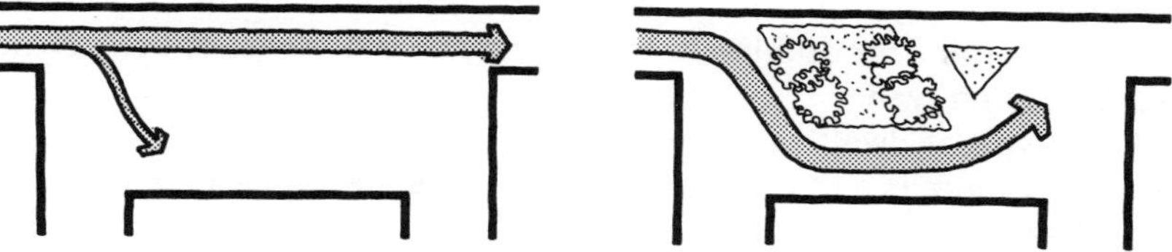

SPACE EXPRESSES MOODS

ANTICIPATION

SURPRISE

With urban land becoming scarcer and exurban land becoming more and more filled around the metropolitan areas, density has become a major issue in planning housing sites. Density, the number of dwellings per acre, is often part of the client's program. Zoning ordinances also include density to control land use. It is increasingly important for architects to understand the inherent density possibilities of each housing type.

Each type of dwelling—walk-up, midrise, highrise—suggests certain densities. Naturally there is a multitude of other factors that will influence the optimum density of each type: the size of the apartment and consequently the size of the building; the ratio of parking spaces required per dwelling; the type of parking, on-grade or stacked in several levels of garage; the amount of outdoor space assigned to private yard and common recreation areas; the location of recreation area, on-grade or on decks; the setbacks required by zoning. Beyond these are the restrictions of the site itself: odd angles and shapes that cannot well be utilized; natural features—lakes and woods—that are to be treasured and preserved; intrasite access roads that are needed on sites 5 acres or larger.

The variables are obviously so many that it is difficult to speak about fixed optimum densities for each housing type. If we were to make the statement that 15 units per acre is an ideal townhouse density, surely ingenious planning on urban sites without setbacks could raise it to 20 or even 25 if a low parking ratio is called for in the program, and in suburban situations, depending on land values and market requirements, an acceptable density might be 10 or even 7 units per acre.

The situation is further complicated by the fact that there are very few projects consisting of only one dwelling type. There might be a mixture of townhouses, five story midrises and a few highrise towers each with its own particular parking ratio.

While there are no prescriptions to achievable density, there are a variety of approaches based on assumed constants. The method can be varied for changing conditions. For sites with mixed building types—assuming the same constants—densities can be arrived at by interpolation.

The density studies are based on the following conditions: an urban block of 3.3 acres (535 × 270 ft), all two-bedroom units, 1:1.25 parking ratio with on-grade parking, and a 5-ft setback requirement along all property lines. Occasionally these conditions are changed to illustrate a point.

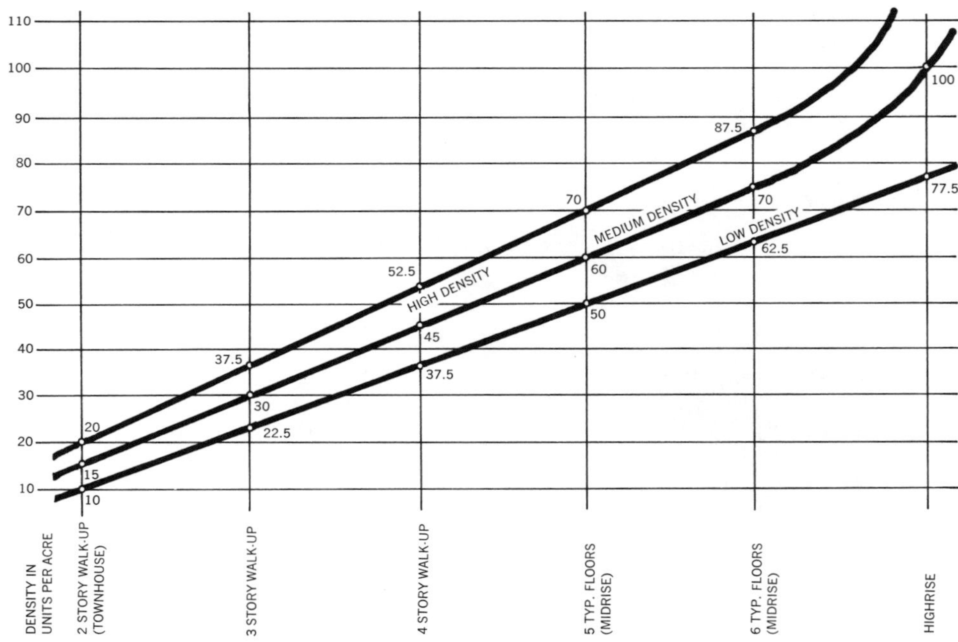

TOWNHOUSE

Assumed density: **20 units/acre**

Lot area: 535 × 270 ft = 144,450 sf = 3.3 acres.
Number of units: 3.3 acres @ 20 = 66 units.
Parking: 66 @ 1.25 = 83 cars.

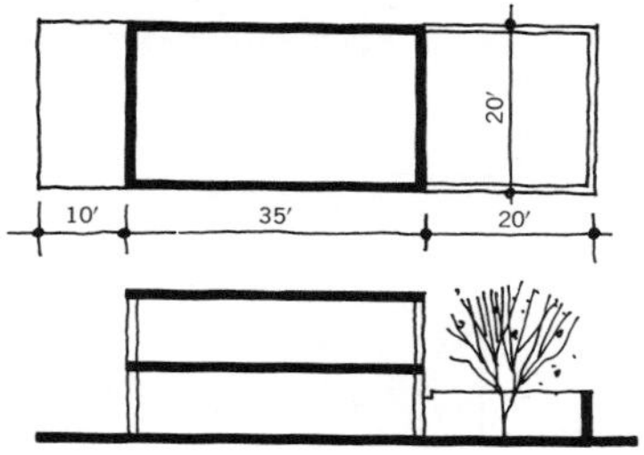

Ground utilization:

66 townhouses @ 700 sf	=	46,200 sf
66 yards @ 600 sf	=	39,600 sf
83 cars @ 300 sf	=	24,900 sf
		110,700 sf

144,450 sf — 110,700 sf = 33,750 sf (25%).
Open area left for circulation and outdoor recreation (approximately half for recreation).

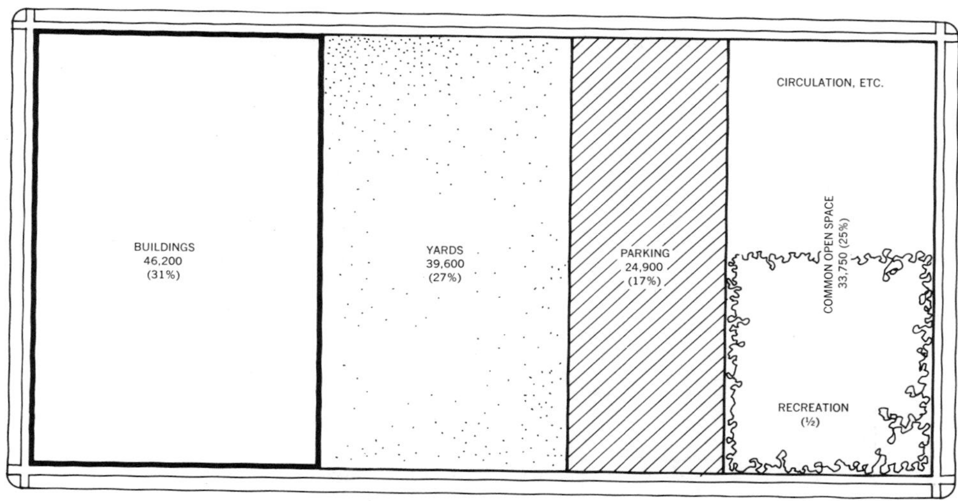

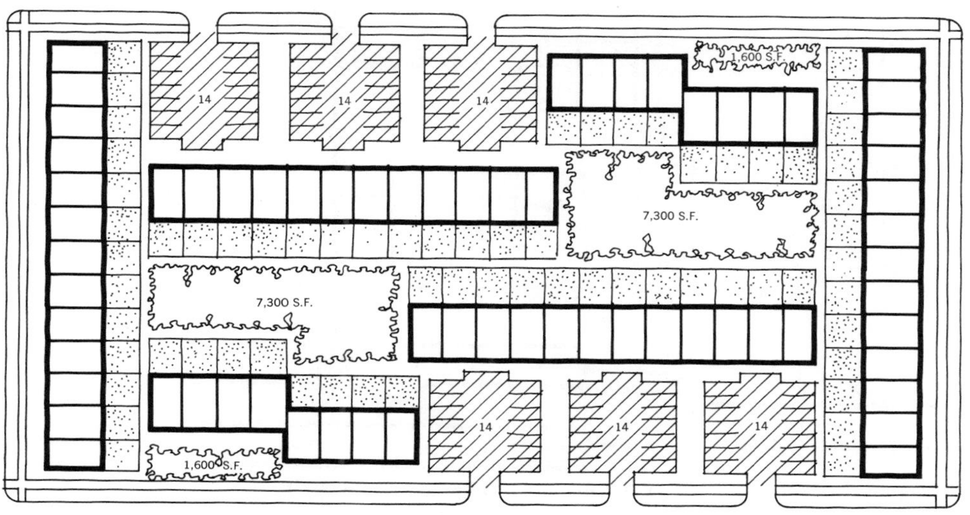

DESIGN METHODOLOGY

TOWNHOUSE

To improve outdoor recreation space start with 35% of the land to be left open (or approximately 50,500 sf).

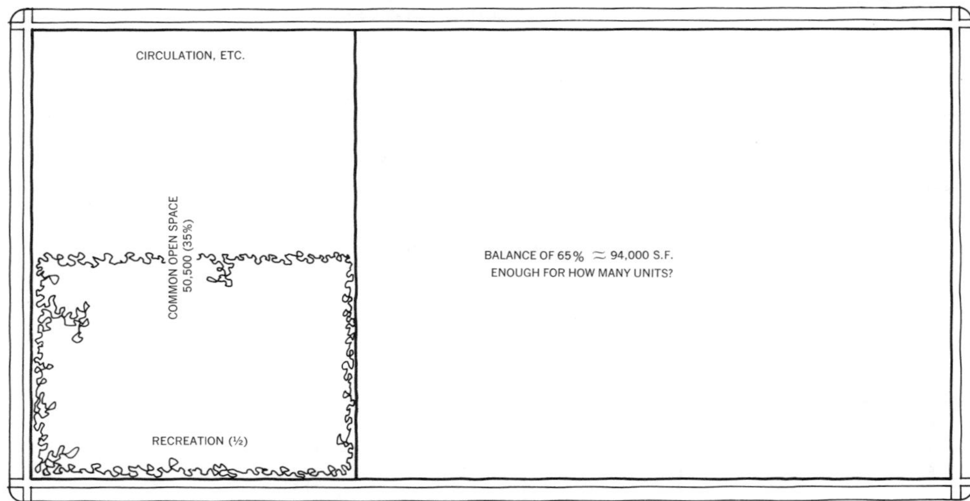

A single townhouse unit requires the following land:

Townhouse proper	=	700 sf
Yards	=	600 sf
Parking 1.25 @ 300 sf	=	375 sf
		1675 sf

94,000 sf ÷ 1675 sf = 56 units
56 ÷ 3.3 acres = **17 units/acre**

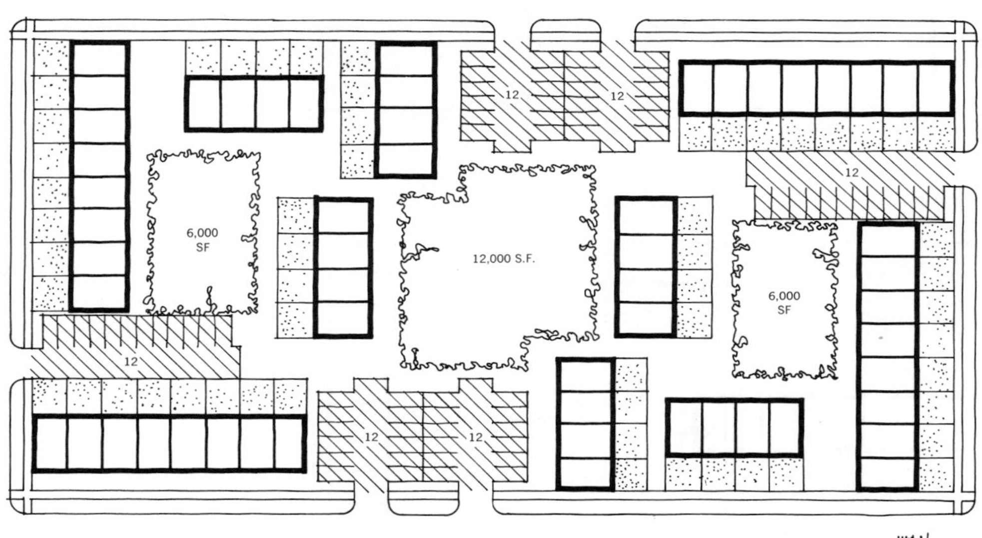

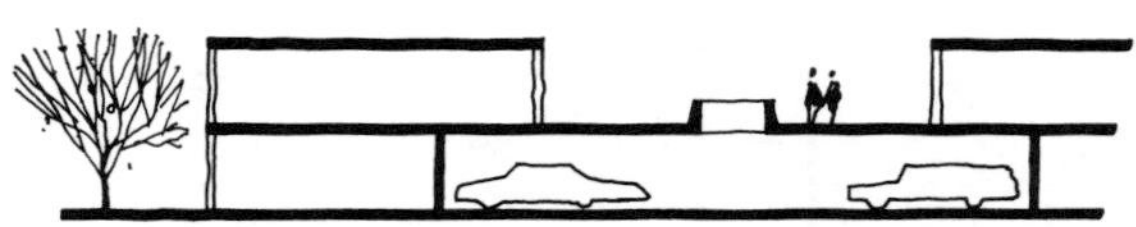

Partial decking of parking can increase density to **25 to 30 units/acre.**

Full decking of parking can increase density to **50 to 60 units/acre.**

PATIO TOWNHOUSE IN MATRIX

Lot area: 535 × 270 ft	=	144,450 sf
Less 15% of lot for circulation and recreation	=	−21,600 sf
Left for units and parking		122,850 sf
A single unit requires the following land:		
Townhouse proper	=	1,200 sf
Patio yard	=	400 sf
Parking 1.25 @ 300 sf	=	375 sf
		1,975 sf

122,850 sf ÷ 1975 sf = 62 units
Say 60 ÷ 3.3 acres = **18 units/acre**

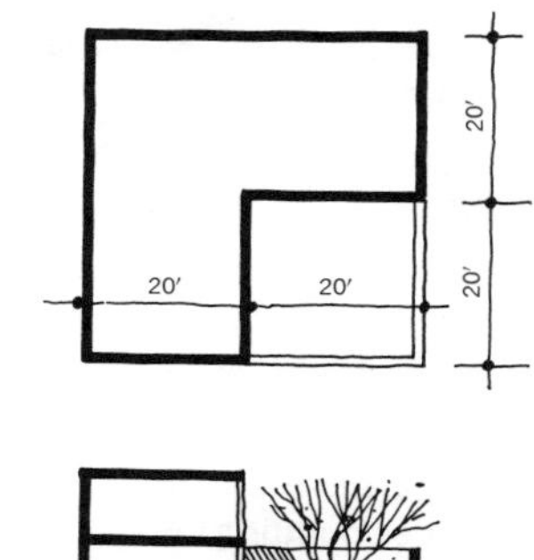

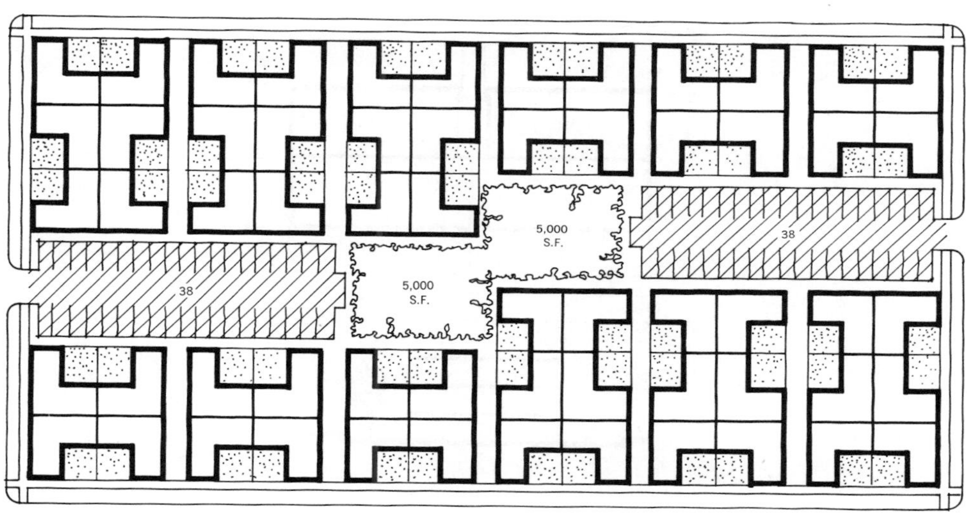

On sloping sites where units can slide above one another and patios or even walkways can occur above units (costly!) density can be increased to **30 to 35 units/acre.**

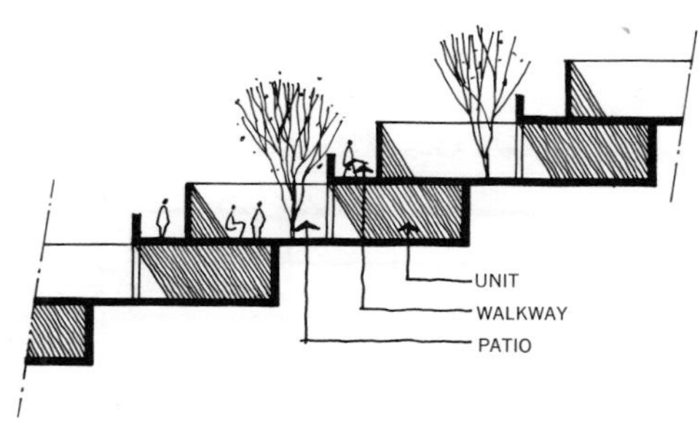

THREE-STORY WALK-UP

Lot area: 535 sf × 270 sf	= 144,450 sf
Less 25% of lot for circulation and recreation	= 33,750 sf
Left for units and parking	110,700 sf
Each apartment needs for ground coverage (114 × 48 ft) ÷ 12 (units per building) =	460 sf
Each apartment "carries" part of yards belonging to first floor apartments (114 × 30 ft) ÷ 12 (units per building) =	280 sf
Parking 1.25 @ 300 sf	= 375 sf
	1,115 sf

110,700 sf ÷ 1115 sf = 99 units
Because there are 12 units/building
99 ÷ 12 = 8 buildings
8 buildings @ 12 = 96 units
96 ÷ 3.3 acres = **30 units/acre**

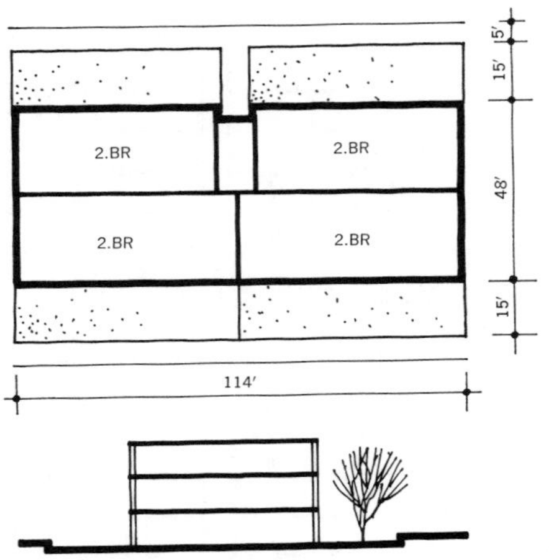

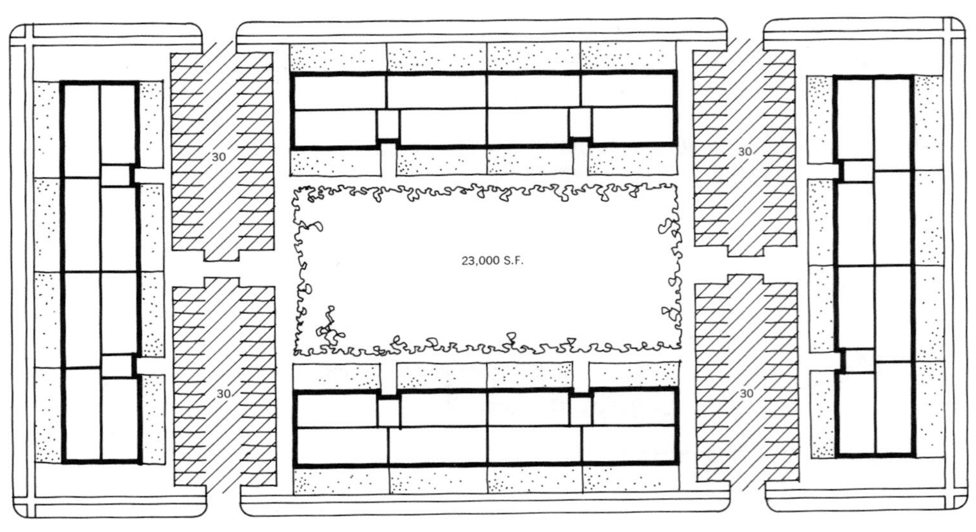

FOUR-STORY WALK-UP

Lot area: 535 × 270 ft	=	144,450 sf
Less 25% of lot for circulation and recreation	=	—33,750 sf
Left for units and parking	=	110,700 sf
Land required by each building:		
Building proper: 44 × 40 ft	=	1,760 sf
Yards: 30 × 44 ft	=	1,300 sf
Parking (1.25 @ 300 sf) × 8 units/building	=	3,000 sf
		6,080 sf

110,700 sf ÷ 6,080 sf = 18 buildings
18 @ 8 apartments = 144 units
144 ÷ 3.3 acres = **44 units/acre**

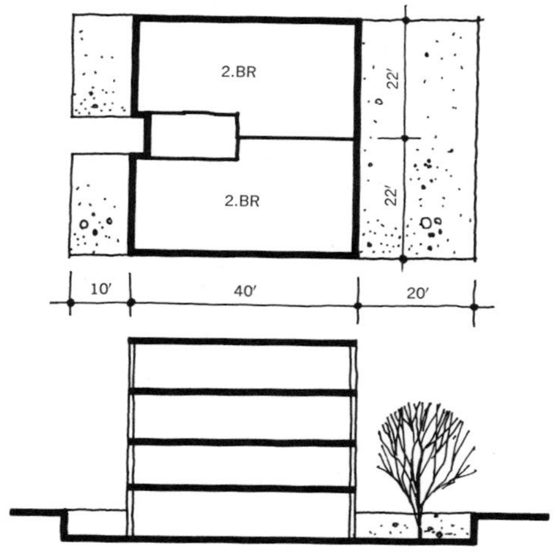

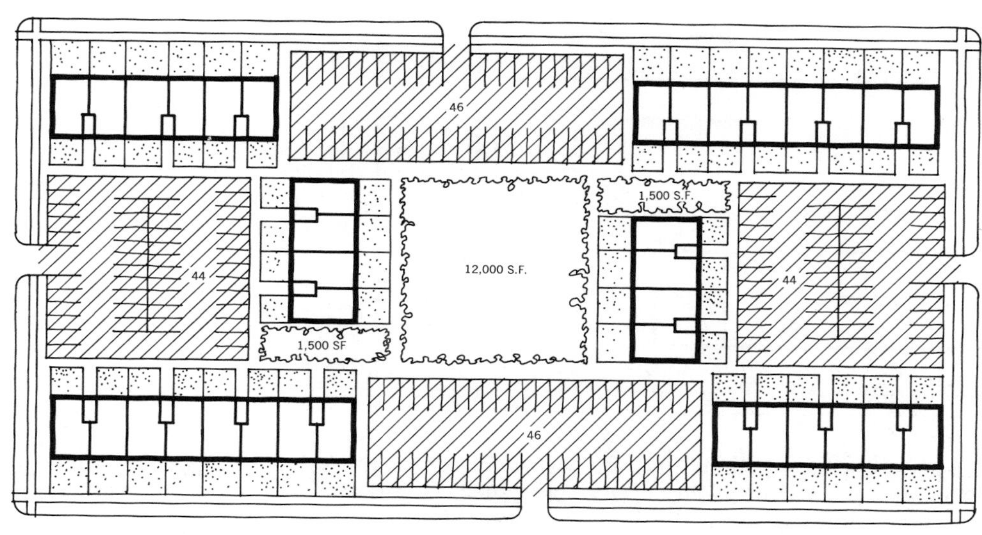

MIDRISE (Five Typical Floors)

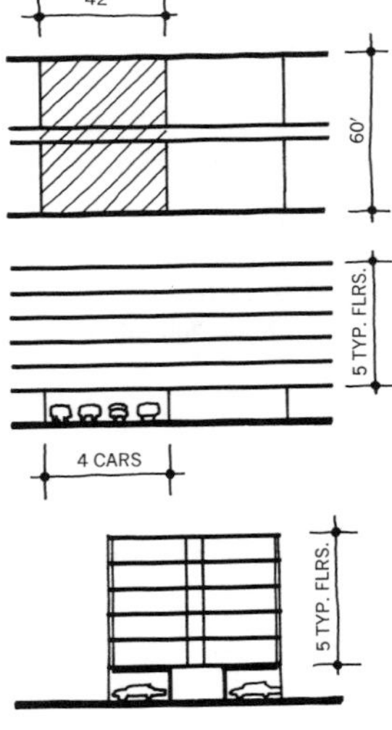

A. Land requirements (buildings) per unit:
(42 × 60 ft) — 10 (units per building segment) = 250 sf per unit

B. Land requirements (parking) per unit:

10 units @ 1.25 = 12.5 cars		
12.5 @ 300 sf	=	3750 sf
Less parking under building		
8 cars @ 200 sf	=	—1600 sf
		2150 sf
2150 sf ÷ 10 units	=	215 sf/unit

C. Land requirements (recreation) per unit:
Assumed criteria: all 2-BR units with 2 adults + 1 child

Child recreation: 1 @ 20 sf	=	20 sf
Adult recreation: 2 @ 100 sf	=	200 sf
Mixed recreation: 3 @ 25 sf	=	75 sf
		295 sf
Say recreational space per unit	=	300 sf
Less: Balcony 6 × 15 ft	=	—90 sf
Laundry	=	—10 sf
Roof deck	=	—40 sf
		160 sf/unit

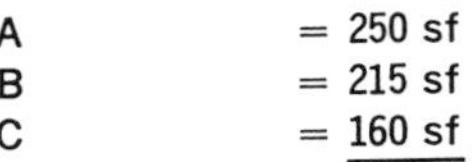

A = 250 sf
B = 215 sf
C = 160 sf

Total per Unit = 625 sf

Lot area: 535 × 270 sf	=	144,450 sf
Less setbacks	=	—14,450 sf
Left for units, parking, and recreation		130,000 sf

130,000 sf ÷ 625 sf = 200
200 ÷ 3.3 = **60 units/acre**

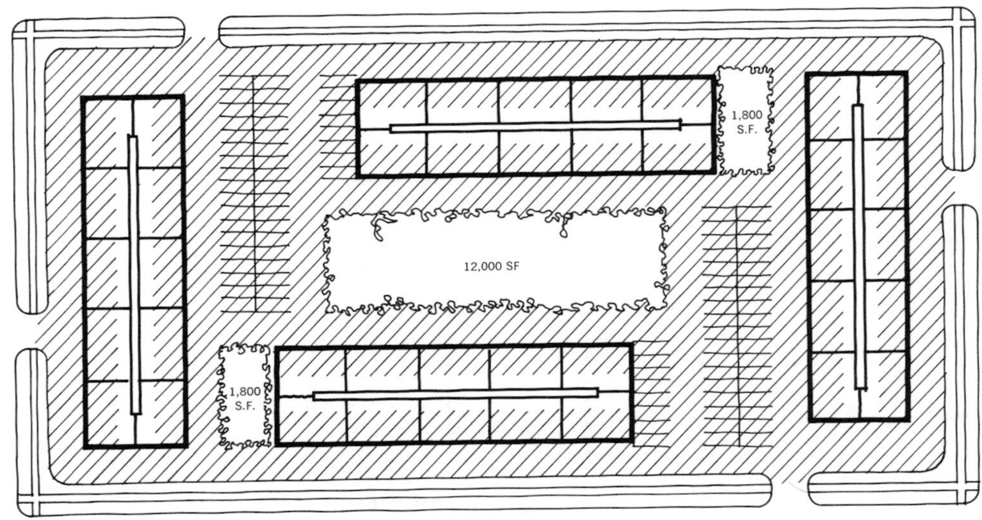

The 14,600 sf of outdoor recreation space is considerably less than called for by the criteria (200 units @ 160 sf = 32,000 sf) because much of the parking is on single-loaded driving aisles and carries disproportional amount of aisle space (car + aisle: 400 sf instead of 300 sf).

MIDRISE (Six Typical Floors)

To increase the outdoor recreation space lacking in the preceding study and to reduce "sea of asphalt" appearance, assume parking in two-level structure, the top of which is developed for recreation. Eliminating parking under the buildings, there are six typical apartment floors.

A. Unit:

6 apartment floors @ 40 units	=	240 units
Less 2 units per building for lobbies	=	—8 units
		232 units

232 ÷ 3.3 acres = **70 units/acre**

B. Parking:

2 parking levels in each garage @ 2 = 4 levels
4 @ 72 cars = ±290 cars = 232 apartments
@ 1.25

C. Recreation:

2 decks @ 21,000 sf	=	42,000 sf
On grade	=	11,000 sf
		53,000 sf
Required as per preceding study criteria (232 units @ 160 sf)	=	—37,120 sf
Overage		15,880 sf

If the 15,880 sf overage is used for 16 townhouses with private yards on top of the parking deck,
232 units + 16 units = 248 units
248 ÷ 3.3 acres = **75 units/acre**

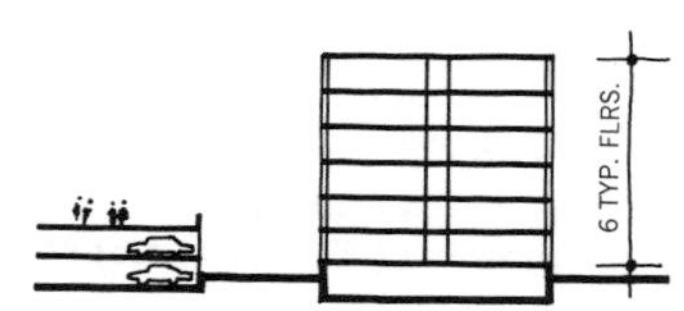

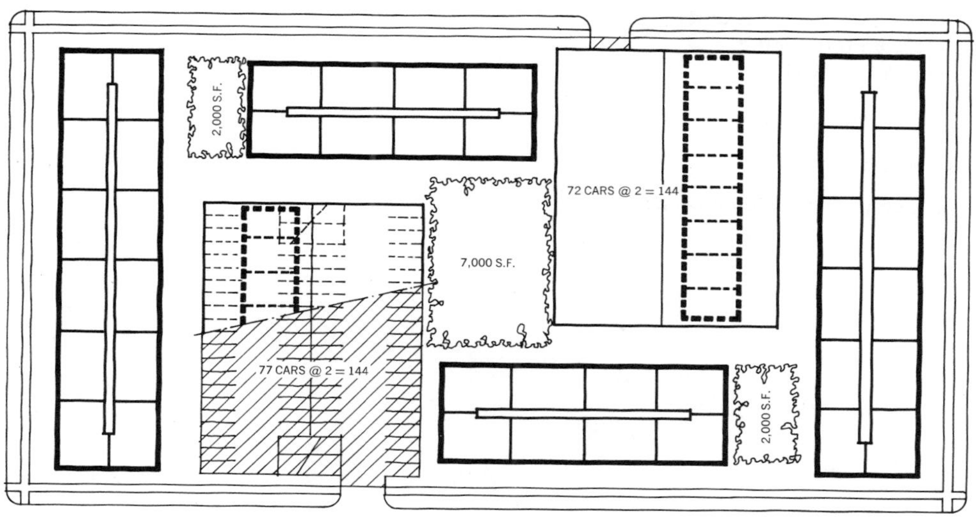

DESIGN METHODOLOGY

HIGHRISE

Using parking as a determiner of ultimate density on the site

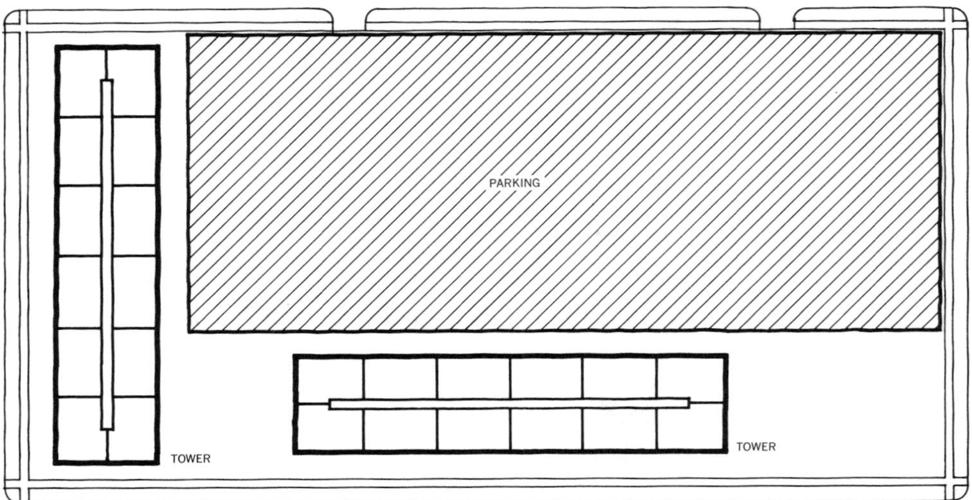

A. One-level parking in area shaded: 300 cars

Using 1:1.25 ratio, 300 cars serve 240 units
240 units ÷ 2 buildings = 120 units/building
120 units ÷ 12 units/floor = **10 floors**

240 ÷ 3.3 acres = **72 units/acre**

B. Two level parking in area shaded: 2 @ 260 = 520 cars

Using 1:1.25 parking ratio, 520 cars serve 416 units
416 units ÷ 2 buildings = 208 units/building
208 units ÷ 12 units/floor = 17.33, say **17 floors**
(17 @ 12 = 204 units/building
204 @ 2 = 408 units)

408 ÷ 3.3 acres = **123 units/acre**

C. Two-level parking over the entire site: 2 @ 400 = 800 cars

Using 1:1.25 parking ratio, 800 cars serve 640 units
640 units ÷ 2 buildings = 320 units/building
320 units ÷ 12 units/floor = 26.66, say **27 floors**
(27 @ 12 = 324 units/building
324 @ 2 = 648 units)

648 ÷ 3.3 acres = **200 units/acre**

. . . and so on upward depending on parking volume capacity.

FINANCING 8

Julius Y. Yacker

This chapter is being written in the Spring of 1975. If only it had been written three, even two, years ago, it would have been so academically satisfying to enunciate the truths and rules of our stable financial structure. We could have seemed so erudite by demonstrating with mathematical precision that the manner in which a housing development is financed will have a significant impact on the design.

We did not think then that our financing structure was stable. We were well aware of its ups and downs and fluctuations, but compared with the unprecedented and dramatic changes in interest rates and availability of financing during the last year the olden days before 1974 look like models of stability.

When change occurs so extensively and so rapidly, as it has during the last year, it is not easy to apply traditional rules and principles because we may no longer be dealing with any financing vehicle that will be relevant to a reader a year hence. That is to say, financing programs, as we have known them, may have been at relatively high costs or low costs or relatively hard or easy to obtain, but specific financing programs could be applied to a specific housing development with relatively predictable design results. If no available financing vehicle is likely to generate the housing development, then something other than traditional financing will bear on the design of housing.

Here is another way to say it. If we assume that a family should not pay more than 25% of its income for housing costs, including utilities, and that in a particular area nearly all of the families that will move into an average new two-bedroom apartment unit earn less than $12,000, we know that the rent, including utilities, for a new two-bedroom unit should be less than $250 per month. If the best financing program available will not permit the costs of the average new two-bedroom unit to be less than $270 a month, the architect will have to design a two-bedroom unit that will still be acceptable but less costly than average if the building is to be built. Even so, the family may be required, and willing, to pay somewhat more than 25% of its income to live in the new unit. If the unit costs $400 a month, regardless of how economically the building is designed and regardless of the financing programs that can be made available, we can be sure that few or no families in the market area will move into the building and pay 40% or more of their incomes for housing. If the building is to be built with $400 per month rentals, then we know that the financing, as we now understand it, is not relevant. On the assumption that private financing programs* will remain relevant at least until this is read, we shall continue with the chapter.

ASSUMPTIONS

For illustration we shall assume that we are dealing with a multifamily structure containing 100 dwelling units. There are some one-bedroom units, some three-bedroom units, with an average size unit of two bedrooms. The building is a high-rise elevator building, with approximately 80% net rental area and 20% public space. We shall also assume that the development is to be built and held for investment purposes. If the building were to be built for condominium or cooperative ownership, many of our examples would need to be altered only slightly.

We do not need to assume that our investor-developer is the legendary totally rational investor who will always seek the highest return on his investment commensurate with the risk. We do need to understand, however, that our investor-developer certainly will not be stupid enough to invest in a residential building with all its risks if he can get as good a return by investing in government bonds.

In all of our examples we shall assume that the investor is only willing and prepared to invest $100,000 of the cost of the development and will borrow the balance pursuant to a mortgage loan. The amount of investment ($100,000) is based on the expected yield with this particular type of development. Because our investor is at least reasonably sophisticated, as investors in residential real estate are in this day and age, he will tell the architect to design within the framework of a budget based on his financing, as we shall see.

Our investor ordered a good market survey and found that the 100 units could be rented within a reasonable time for average rentals not to exceed $350 per month, including all utilities. Of course, the one-bedroom units would be cheaper and the three-bedroom units more expensive, but for simplicity we shall assume 100 units at $350 per month. Thus our monthly income is $35,000 and our yearly income is $420,000. Prudence dictates that we allow at least 5% for vacancy and collection losses, leaving an effective gross income (EGI) of $399,000.

In the area in question utilities, maintenance, management, reasonable reserves, and all other operating expenses will cost the owner about $1400 per unit per year or $140,000 total. That leaves $259,000 to repay the mortgage loan and for a cash return on the investment. If the cash return on the $100,000 investment is calculated at $10,000 per year, that leaves $249,000 to pay back a mortgage loan.

Example 1

We shall assume that the investor is able to obtain a conventional loan with a rate of interest of 9½% and a term of 25 years. In all our examples the loans will be paid back with equal monthly installments so that the loan is completely amortized by the end of the term of the loan. The percentage of a loan needed for amortization is known as the constant annual percent (constant). Obviously the longer the

* Private financing programs for our purposes include any mortgage loans to nonpublic persons or associations, whether the loans are government or privately insured or issued. Public housing is not considered in this chapter.

term of the loan or the lower the interest rate, the lower the constant. In our first example the constant is 10.49%.

The amount available to amortize the loan is $249,000. The constant is 10.49%. The amount of loan is determined by dividing the amount available to amortize the loan by the constant, or approximately $2,374,000 ($249,000 ÷ 0.1049). By adding the cash investment ($100,000) to the loan we know that the total cost of our project can be $2,474,000 (replacement cost).

It will be reasonable to assume that nonconstruction items will cost approximately 20% of the replacement cost. These items will be land, interest during construction, taxes, insurance, legal and organizational costs, financing fees, and the like. Therefore there will be available for construction and architects' fees a total of $1,979,200. Using formulas established by certain governmental agenices, the design and supervising architects' fees would total $85,000 in this example; $1,894,200 would be left for construction.

Let us assume that the cost of construction, including the contractor's profit, is $22/sf. That would provide us with a building of approximately 86,100 ft. If 20% is public space, that leaves 68,880 ft of living area, or 689 ft per dwelling unit.

Now come the questions. Will people who can pay $350 per month rent two-bedroom apartments with only 689 sf? The answer is almost surely no. In the market area in question it will take a minimum of 850 ft to attract renters, or at least 25% more space. Can the architect design a structure with that much more space for the same amount? No, but he will be asked to. Can maintenance-free materials be used to cut the cost of maintenance so that more money will be left over to support a higher loan? A little help, perhaps, can be achieved, but not enough. Later we shall see that with more favorable financing a maintenance dollar saved will generate many dollars more of loan proceeds.

Next question. Can the rent levels be raised sufficiently to support a higher mortgage loan? With all our changes we still need at least another $500,000. That would mean more than $40 a month rent increase to repay the additional mortgage amount. Our market survey says we are already at the top of the market and we cannot risk such an increase.

The final question will be asked. Will the investor invest approximately $500,000 more so that we can offer 850 ft for $350 per month? Remember, he is receiving $10,000 as a cash return. That is 10% of his original investment of $100,000. With $600,000 invested, his cash return would be 1.66%. He is better off with government bonds. Of course, his real rate of return is more than 1.66% because he has tax benefits from depreciation and hopefully will gain equity and residual values. Nevertheless, the deal is too chancey and he will look to a better method of financing or forget the deal. If no other financing is available, we can say that financing affected the design totally. It eliminated the project.

Example 2

In today's market the next best financing is an FHA program with an 8% loan for 40 years. The constant, including a mortgage insurance premium of one-half of 1% of the loan, is approximately 8.80%. The rent remains the same. The operating costs, obviously, are the same regardless of how we finance. The cash return will also be the same. The amount available to amortize the loan remains $249,000. The amount of loan would be $2,830,000 ($249,000 ÷ 0.0880) with a replacement cost of $2,930,000 ($2,830,000 + $100,000).

By working backward, as we did in the first example, we find that the amount available for construction and architects' fees would be $2,344,000. The architects' fees in this case would be approximately $104,000, leaving $2,240,000 for construction. At $22/sf that would provide us with a building of approximately 102,000 ft, 81,600 ft of living area, or 816 ft per dwelling unit. Based purely on our financing, we have been able to increase the size of the dwelling unit from 689 to 816 ft.

The larger unit is certainly better but not good enough in this market. Now the architect will surely be asked to add about 4% to the space without increasing costs. By this time, if he has not already done so, the investor will ask the architect to work directly with the contractor. The contractor will be told that there will be $2,240,000 available. If he can bring the job in on budget, he may have the job. In an uncertain economy the most probable result will be that the contractor will need more not less. Therefore, unless the architect can affect significant savings in design, there will be no project.

Example 3

The next best financing is provided by many state housing finance agencies. The state agencies float issues of bonds at lower-than-market rates because they are tax exempt. The agencies make 40-year loans to developers at the favorable bond rate. A current rate is 7¼% with a constant of 7.68%.

Housing projects financed by state agencies are generally to be occupied by lower and moderate income families. For our purposes we shall assume that the families in our market area who will pay $350 per month rent for two bedrooms qualify under the state's definition of lower or moderate income families.

State agency financing, like other financing, does not change the operation costs or the amount available to amortize the loan. Wise readers may point out that state agencies usually restrict cash flow to 6% of assumed equity and that the equity is assumed to be 10% of the replacement cost. However, because of the manner of processing the loan, the actual equity is likely to be closer to $100,000 and the cash flow closer to $10,000 than the assumed figures.

The state agency loan could now be approximately $3,242,000 ($249,000 ÷ 0.0768). The replacement cost would be $3,342,000 ($3,242,000 + $100,000). The amount available for construction and architects' fees would be $2,673,600, with approximately $110,000 for the architects and leaving $2,563,600 for construction. At $22/sf that would provide us with a building of approximately 116,500 ft, 93,200 ft of living area, or 932 ft per dwelling unit.

Finally, we have alternatives available. Shall we decrease the unit size and provide more public space? Should we upgrade the units? Would the market be improved with more space and fewer amenities or vice versa? Should we maintain a moderate design with 850 ft and lower the rents somewhat?

At this point a caution is in order. The above examples and those to come are obviously greatly simplified and leave out many nuances and other variables and approaches. The examples, however, are reflective of the principles inherent in establishing budgets that will control the architectural design. The reader can "play" with the figures to obtain alternate results. The reader can add or subtract public space; he can raise or lower the amount of rents that can be obtained in an area (but they must be realistic). Our figures, for instance, include all utilities. Try taking them out of the operating costs, or better yet see what happens when utilities double in cost as they have in many areas. As another exercise, establish the replacement cost of a building and establish the operating costs; then determine what the different rental levels would be by changes in interest rates or terms of mortgage loans. You can find the constant in the tables at the end of this chapter.

Example 4

Let us now return to our original area in which the market is for families earning less than $12,000 per year. They can afford to pay up to $250 per month for a two-bedroom apartment. By going through the same exercises as above it will become apparent that none of the financing programs mentioned will come close to permitting us to build our project. Other financing must be made available.

By the early 1960s Congress recognized that the costs of new housing had exceeded the ability to pay for a large percentage of the population. In order to permit the private sector to serve the housing needs of lower and middle income families,* Congress provided for new methods of financing. First, government mortgage loans were to be made available at an interest rate of 3% for a term of 40 years [§ 221 (d) (3)]. Apply that constant and see what it does for the rents. That program was scrapped for a new one that provided for market-rate financing but with an interest subsidy that had the effect of a mortgage loan at 1% interest rate for 40 years with a constant of 3.03% (§236).

As a matter of social policy, Congress determined that only families below certain income levels would be eligible to move into the developments financed pursuant to §236. The income levels were determined for all sections of the country. In Chicago, for instance, the highest income level for families of three or four persons was $10,350 (exception limits). In most other areas of the country the income limits were much lower. Our $12,000 a year family was left out in the cold. The maximum rent that could be charged was 25% of the maximum income levels. In reality, the rent could not be that high because of marketing and FHA processing requirements, but for our example we shall deal with maximums.

We know our monthly rent levels. It is fixed at 1/48th of $10,350 (25% of $10,350 per year divided by 12) or approximately $215. Yearly income to the project would then be $258,000. Again, we assume a 5% vacancy and collection loss for an EGI of $245,100. Our operating costs are still the same ($140,000), leaving $105,100 for cash returns and debt payments.† The constant is 3.03%. We can now support a mortgage of approximately $3,139,000 ($95,100 ÷ 0.0303). The replacement cost could be $3,239,000. There will be $2,591,200 available for construction and architects' fees. If the architects' fees aggregate $110,000, there will be $2,481,200 for construction. At $22/ft we produce a building containing approximately 113,000 gross ft, 90,400 ft of living area, or a bit over 900 ft per dwelling.

If §236 financing is used, the economics will be only one factor to determine the budget. Another factor will be the FHA rules that dictate design of modest proportions and without unnecessary luxuries.

Of all the programs mentioned §236 provides the most startling example of the role that financing can have on design and use of materials; for instance, if an alternative design and use of materials would cost an additional $200,000 but would save $10,000 a year in maintenance cost, the project would be "ahead of the game." The additional $200,000 construction cost would generate an additional $220,000 replacement cost at a constant of 3.03%. That additional debt would cost $6666 for an overall savings in rent of $3334, or $2.80 per unit per month.

It should also be apparent that by adding $2000 to the cost of the unit with no savings in maintenance costs the rent increase will be only $5.05 per month ($2000 × 0.0303 ÷ 12).

* The lowest income families would continue to be served by public housing.

† Here again the assumed figures for processing will be quite different, but the end result will more probably be as shown.

FINANCING

As a further illustration, let us apply the same procedures to our conventionally financed building; the constant is 10.49% as in our first example. The additional $220,000 loan would cost approximately $23,000, a net increase in rent of $13,000, or approximately $11 per month per unit. Again, if we add $2000 to the cost of the unit without offsetting savings in maintenance, the rent increase would be more than $17 per month. Thus the improvements that we added to the building when financed under §236 resulted in a $3334 decrease in rent, but when financed conventionally it resulted in a $13,000 increase in rent. When one is already at the top of the market, the increase could well spell the difference between adopting the alternative design or not adopting it.

The §236 program has been all but suspended since January 1973. It is included here only as a dramatic example of the influence of financing.

OTHER CONSIDERATIONS

Housing is peculiarly dependent on developing budgets from available financing because the investment is reasonable only when there is a high ratio of loan to cost. This is especially true when the rents that can be obtained in the market leave only a small amount of cash flow as a return to the investor. The paradox is that during a time when available cash flow is at its lowest it is the most difficult to obtain a high ratio loan. As an illustration, let us assume that the investor decided to go ahead with the FHA financed development in our second example. The hope was to cut about 4% from the first estimate of cost to enable the construction of approximately 4% more space. If, after adding the space, there is still a 4% overrun, the investor would require $89,600 more cash. Thus with only a 4% overrun in budget the cash requirements would nearly double and cash return would be cut to 5.3%.

As the development and ownership of housing for investment purposes becomes less and less attractive, the development and ownership for use, such as condominiums or cooperatives, become more and more attractive. Nevertheless, condominium or cooperative ownership is still subject to many of the same rules that apply to investors. There may not need to be a cash return on investment and there may be a tax savings from the owner's share of real estate taxes and interest, but the owner is still subject to his ability and willingness to pay the total operating costs and to repay his loan. Also, the additional amenities almost always demanded by cooperative and condominium owners are likely to absorb a substantial part of the assumed savings. Remember, the cash return to our investor was only $10,000 of a total budget of $420,000, or about $8.30 of the $350 rental.

Architects who have not worked with housing development find the method of "working backward" to establish a budget puzzling if not downright irrational. Nevertheless, it is a discipline that will be increasingly forced on them. In a world of scarce money supply all but the wealthiest of institutions will need to determine the amount of funding that can be made available and the cost of the funding that can be made available and the cost of the funding. They will then set a budget and determine whether their desires can be accomplished within that budget, and if they cannot, at least if their needs can be.

Few, if any, investors in this day and age can hire an architect with instructions to design a 100-unit building with, for example, 20 one-bedroom units, 20 three-bedroom units, and 60 two-bedroom units, then determine the cost of the development, then determine how much money he will need to borrow to build the development, and then determine how much rent he will have to charge to operate the development, pay back the loan, and achieve a reasonable cash return. This rational "working forward" manner of development will almost invariably result in rent levels that will be much too high for the market to absorb. The investor-developer will be required to start with a rent level that the market in the area of development can absorb. He will then "work backward" as shown in the above examples.

There may have been a time when there was enough "play" in the market to permit rent levels to be established after all these economics were developed. If the project required $150 rentals, they could be obtained. If they required $165 rentals, they, too, could be obtained.

What happens when we are at the very top of the market, as we most surely are today? What happens when families simply cannot afford to pay more than $350 a month for rent and they need a minimum of two bedrooms? If a building will have too many vacancies if the rent level is more than $350 a month, there simply is no question that a developer will arrive at his construction budget before the architect places the first line on his drawing.

CONSTRUCTION FINANCING

We shall deal with construction financing only to determine the impact on the replacement cost and amount of cash investment. If our permanent mortgage loan presupposes a replacement cost of $3,100,000 with $100,000 of equity and $3,000,000 of loan, it is important that the construction budget be adhered to as has been shown. If it takes a year to build the project, and we assume that on the average approximately one-half of the loan is out during the course of the year, that means the developer will pay interest on approximately $1,500,000 during the year. If the interest rate is 10%, he will pay $150,000. There was a time when the developer knew what his interest rate would be and knew that the building could be constructed more or less on schedule. Recently, however, construction loans have been made at interest rates that fluctuated with the prime rate. During the course of the year the prime rate may have risen dramatically so that what started out as a 10% rate may have ended at 14% or higher. What started out as a one-year construction time may have ended up as an 18-month construction time because of material shortages. The interest budget could easily have doubled, which means that the cash investment would have more than doubled. It also means, of course, that the return on investment would be less than half the contemplated return.

Just a few years ago the interest during construction of our project may have been $120,000 or perhaps as much as $150,000. During the last year the interest could easily have been $250,000 or perhaps even $300,000. When the replacement cost is fixed at the beginning by the rent levels and financing, we need to contemplate the effect that such a large amount of interest has on an already tight construction budget.

SOME CONCLUSIONS

As we work with the figures and make certain assumptions about the future, we are led to the conclusion that the present financing methods will not permit the private sector to deliver new housing to persons with incomes under $12,000 per year and soon, perhaps, even $20,000 or $25,000 per year.

Assume that operating costs rise to $2000 per year, a figure already achieved in some areas with increased real estate taxes and fuel and maintenance costs. Assume also that construction costs rise only moderately to $25/sf to build our

100-unit apartment. Finally, assume that the very best financing available today will remain available; namely, state housing finance agency financing with a constant of 7.68%. The rent would be more than $400 per month. The state agency programs serve families whose incomes at 48 times monthly rental is assumed to be moderate or low. In this case that would mean a three- or four-person family with an income of more than $19,000 a year.

The Department of Housing and Urban Development (HUD) published in the March 31, 1975, Federal Register its estimates of the fair market rentals for all sections of the country. The rentals are for new or substantially rehabilitated buildings constructed by December 31, 1976. HUD's estimate of rent for a new two-bedroom unit in an elevator building in New York City is $622 per month. It would require an income just under $30,000 a year to support that rental. Even in New York and even by December 1976 it seems doubtful that more than a small percentage of families will be earning that amount.

If New York is not representative, surely Peoria, Illinois, is. In the same publication HUD estimated that the fair market rental for a similar unit in Peoria would be $329 per month. That assumes that families should earn nearly $16,000 per year to afford the rent.

Although the HUD estimates of fair market rentals are established for purposes of paying subsidies, they are indicative of the amount of rent that will be charged. Interestingly enough, many developers have stated that the HUD estimates are really too low to permit standard development.

POSTSCRIPT

The figures must say something to a designer of residential buildings. They tell the architect that families will need to settle for less space and fewer amenities than they are used to and at higher percentages of their incomes. The figures say something else. They tell us that we are at the limit of our ability to provide new housing on a private basis for the mass of our population. If the cost of producing and operating housing continues to escalate faster than the escalation in income levels, financing as we know it will not generate new or substantially rehabilitated housing.*

* It is not within the scope of this chapter to discuss the means by which new housing might be generated in the future. One recommendation is for the government to provide operating subsidies in addition to financing subsidies. The new Section 8 program comes very close to doing just that. We did not include this program in our examples because, as of this time, we do not know how the program will work. Essentially, the program establishes maximum fair market rentals that can be charged and the government will pay the difference between 25% of an eligible family's income and the fair market rental. That, of course, is the most startling example of the "working backward" method. A developer starts with a given rent level, not one developed from a market survey, but one prescribed by HUD. The developer will know the gross income. He can determine his operating costs and his minimum cash return. He will then know just how much loan he can support with the balance and whether he can proceed with construction.

TABLE OF CONSTANT ANNUAL PERCENT[a] NEEDED TO AMORTIZE A PRINCIPAL AMOUNT CALCULATED ON A MONTHLY BASIS. DIVIDE BY 12 TO DETERMINE MONTHLY PAYMENT

Interest Rate	2 Years	3 Years	4 Years	5 Years	6 Years	7 Years	8 Years
3	51.58	34.90	26.57	21.57	18.24	15.86	14.08
⅛	51.65	34.97	26.63	21.63	18.30	15.93	14.15
¼	51.72	35.03	26.70	21.70	18.37	16.00	14.22
⅜	51.78	35.10	26.77	21.77	18.44	16.06	14.29
½	51.85	35.17	26.83	21.84	18.51	16.13	14.35
⅝	51.91	35.23	26.90	21.90	18.57	16.20	14.42
¾	51.98	35.30	26.97	21.97	18.64	16.27	14.49
⅞	52.05	35.37	27.03	22.04	18.71	16.34	14.56
4	52.11	35.43	27.10	22.10	18.78	16.41	14.63
⅛	52.18	35.50	27.17	22.17	18.85	16.48	14.70
¼	52.25	35.57	27.23	22.24	18.92	16.55	14.77
⅜	52.32	35.63	27.30	22.31	18.98	16.62	14.84
½	52.38	35.70	27.37	22.38	19.05	16.69	14.91
⅝	52.45	35.77	27.44	22.44	19.12	16.76	14.98
¾	52.52	35.84	27.50	22.51	19.19	16.83	15.05
⅞	52.58	35.90	27.57	22.58	19.26	16.90	15.13
5	52.65	35.97	27.64	22.65	19.33	16.97	15.20
⅛	52.72	36.04	27.71	22.72	19.40	17.04	15.27
¼	52.79	36.10	27.78	22.79	19.47	17.11	15.34
⅜	52.85	36.17	27.84	22.86	19.54	17.18	15.41
½	52.92	36.24	27.91	22.95	19.61	17.25	15.48
⅝	52.99	36.31	27.98	23.00	19.68	17.32	15.56
¾	53.05	36.38	28.05	23.07	19.75	17.39	15.63
⅞	53.12	36.44	28.12	23.13	19.82	17.46	15.70
6	53.19	36.51	28.19	23.20	19.89	17.54	15.77
⅛	53.26	36.58	28.26	23.27	19.96	17.61	15.85

Interest Rate	9 Years	10 Years	11 Years	12 Years	13 Years	14 Years	15 Years
3	12.70	11.59	10.69	9.94	9.30	8.76	8.29
⅛	12.77	11.66	10.76	10.01	9.38	8.83	8.36
¼	12.84	11.73	10.83	10.08	9.45	8.91	8.44
⅜	12.90	11.80	10.90	10.15	9.51	8.98	8.51
½	12.97	11.87	10.97	10.22	9.59	9.05	8.58
⅝	13.04	11.94	11.04	10.29	9.66	9.12	8.66
¾	13.11	12.01	11.11	10.37	9.74	9.20	8.73
⅞	13.18	12.08	11.19	10.44	9.81	9.27	8.81
4	13.25	12.15	11.26	10.51	9.88	9.35	8.88
⅛	13.32	12.23	11.33	10.58	9.96	9.42	8.96
¼	13.40	12.30	11.40	10.66	10.03	9.49	9.03
⅜	13.47	12.37	11.47	10.73	10.10	9.57	9.11
½	13.54	12.44	11.55	10.81	10.18	9.65	9.18
⅝	13.61	12.51	11.62	10.88	10.25	9.72	9.26
¾	13.68	12.59	11.69	10.95	10.33	9.80	9.34
⅞	13.75	12.66	11.77	11.03	10.41	9.87	9.42
5	13.83	12.73	11.84	11.10	10.48	9.95	9.49
⅛	13.90	12.81	11.92	11.18	10.56	10.03	9.57
¼	13.97	12.88	11.99	11.25	10.63	10.11	9.65
⅜	14.04	12.95	12.07	11.33	10.71	10.18	9.73
½	14.12	13.03	12.14	11.41	10.79	10.26	9.81
⅝	14.19	13.10	12.22	11.48	10.87	10.34	9.89
¾	14.26	13.18	12.29	11.56	10.94	10.42	9.97
⅞	14.34	13.25	12.37	11.64	11.02	10.50	10.05
6	14.41	13.33	12.45	11.72	11.10	10.58	10.13
⅛	14.49	13.40	12.52	11.79	11.18	10.66	10.21

TABLE OF CONSTANT ANNUAL PERCENT[a] NEEDED TO AMORTIZE A PRINCIPAL AMOUNT CALCULATED ON A MONTHLY BASIS (*Continued*)

Interest Rate	2 Years	3 Years	4 Years	5 Years	6 Years	7 Years	8 Years
¼	53.33	36.65	28.32	23.34	20.03	17.68	15.92
⅜	53.39	36.72	28.39	23.41	20.11	17.75	15.99
½	53.46	36.78	28.46	23.48	20.18	17.82	16.07
⅝	53.53	36.85	28.53	23.55	20.25	17.90	16.14
¾	53.60	36.92	28.60	23.63	20.32	17.97	16.22
⅞	53.66	36.99	28.67	23.70	20.39	18.04	16.29
7	53.73	37.06	28.74	23.77	20.46	18.12	16.37
⅛	53.80	37.13	28.81	23.84	20.54	18.19	16.44
¼	53.87	37.19	28.88	23.91	20.61	18.26	16.52
⅜	53.94	37.26	28.95	23.98	20.68	18.34	16.59
½	54.00	37.33	29.02	24.05	20.75	18.41	16.67
⅝	54.07	37.40	29.09	24.12	20.83	18.49	16.74
¾	54.14	37.47	29.16	24.19	20.90	18.56	16.82
⅞	54.21	37.54	29.23	24.26	20.97	18.63	16.89
8	54.28	37.61	29.30	24.34	21.04	18.71	16.97
¼	54.41	37.75	29.44	24.48	21.19	18.86	17.12
½	54.55	37.89	29.58	24.62	21.34	19.01	17.28
¾	54.69	38.03	29.72	24.77	21.49	19.16	17.43
9	54.83	38.16	29.87	24.92	21.64	19.31	17.59
¼	54.96	38.30	30.01	25.06	21.78	19.46	17.74
½	55.10	38.44	30.15	25.21	21.93	19.62	17.90
¾	55.24	38.58	30.30	25.35	22.09	19.77	18.06
10	55.38	38.73	30.44	25.50	22.24	19.93	18.21

Interest Rate	9 Years	10 Years	11 Years	12 Years	13 Years	14 Years	15 Years
¼	14.56	13.48	12.60	11.87	11.26	10.74	10.29
⅜	14.64	13.55	12.68	11.95	11.34	10.82	10.38
½	14.71	13.63	12.75	12.03	11.42	10.90	10.46
⅝	14.79	13.71	12.83	12.11	11.50	10.98	10.54
¾	14.86	13.78	12.91	12.19	11.58	11.07	10.62
⅞	14.94	13.86	12.99	12.27	11.66	11.15	10.71
7	15.01	13.94	13.07	12.35	11.74	11.23	10.79
⅛	15.09	14.02	13.14	12.43	11.82	11.31	10.87
¼	15.16	14.09	13.22	12.51	11.91	11.40	10.96
⅜	15.24	14.17	13.30	12.59	11.99	11.48	11.04
½	15.32	14.25	13.38	12.67	12.07	11.56	11.13
⅝	15.40	14.33	13.46	12.75	12.15	11.65	11.21
¾	15.47	14.41	13.54	12.83	12.24	11.73	11.30
⅞	15.55	14.49	13.62	12.91	12.32	11.82	11.39
8	15.63	14.56	13.70	12.99	12.40	11.90	11.47
¼	15.78	14.72	13.87	13.16	12.57	12.07	11.65
½	15.94	14.88	14.03	13.33	12.74	12.24	11.82
¾	16.10	15.04	14.19	13.49	12.91	12.42	12.00
9	16.26	15.21	14.36	13.66	13.08	12.59	12.18
¼	16.42	15.37	14.52	13.83	13.25	12.77	12.36
½	16.58	15.53	14.69	14.00	13.43	12.95	12.54
¾	16.74	15.70	14.86	14.17	13.60	13.12	12.72
10	16.90	15.86	15.03	14.35	13.78	13.30	12.90

Interest Rate	16 Years	17 Years	18 Years	19 Years	20 Years	21 Years	22 Years
3	7.88	7.52	7.20	6.92	6.66	6.43	6.22
⅛	7.96	7.60	7.28	6.99	6.74	6.51	6.30
¼	8.03	7.67	7.35	7.07	6.81	6.58	6.37
⅜	8.10	7.74	7.43	7.14	6.89	6.66	6.45
½	8.18	7.82	7.50	7.22	6.96	6.74	6.53
⅝	8.25	7.89	7.58	7.29	7.04	6.81	6.61
¾	8.33	7.97	7.65	7.37	7.12	6.89	6.69
⅞	8.40	8.05	7.73	7.45	7.20	6.97	6.77
4	8.48	8.12	7.81	7.53	7.28	7.05	6.85
⅛	8.55	8.20	7.89	7.61	7.36	7.13	6.93
¼	8.63	8.28	7.96	7.68	7.44	7.21	7.01
⅜	8.71	8.35	8.04	7.76	7.52	7.29	7.09
½	8.78	8.43	8.12	7.84	7.60	7.37	7.17
⅝	8.86	8.51	8.20	7.92	7.68	7.46	7.26
¾	8.94	8.59	8.28	8.01	7.76	7.54	7.34
⅞	9.02	8.67	8.36	8.09	7.84	7.62	7.42
5	9.10	8.75	8.44	8.17	7.92	7.71	7.51
⅛	9.18	8.83	8.52	8.25	8.01	7.79	7.59
¼	9.26	8.91	8.60	8.33	8.09	7.87	7.68
⅜	9.34	8.99	8.69	8.42	8.18	7.96	7.76
½	9.42	9.07	8.77	8.50	8.26	8.04	7.85
⅝	9.50	9.15	8.85	8.58	8.34	8.13	7.94
¾	9.58	9.24	8.94	8.67	8.43	8.22	8.03
⅞	9.66	9.32	9.02	8.75	8.52	8.30	8.11
6	9.74	9.40	9.10	8.84	8.60	8.39	8.20
⅛	9.82	9.49	9.19	8.92	8.69	8.48	8.29
¼	9.91	9.57	9.27	9.01	8.78	8.57	8.38
⅜	9.99	9.65	9.36	9.10	8.86	8.66	8.47
½	10.07	9.74	9.44	9.18	8.95	8.75	8.56

Interest Rate	23 Years	24 Years	25 Years	26 Years	27 Years	28 Years	29 Years
3	6.03	5.86	5.70	5.55	5.41	5.29	5.17
⅛	6.11	5.93	5.77	5.63	5.49	5.37	5.25
¼	6.18	6.01	5.85	5.71	5.57	5.45	5.33
⅜	6.26	6.09	5.93	5.79	5.65	5.53	5.42
½	6.34	6.17	6.01	5.87	5.74	5.61	5.50
⅝	6.42	6.25	6.09	5.95	5.82	5.70	5.58
¾	6.50	6.33	6.17	6.03	5.90	5.78	5.67
⅞	6.58	6.41	6.26	6.11	5.98	5.86	5.75
4	6.66	6.49	6.34	6.20	6.07	5.95	5.84
⅛	6.74	6.58	6.42	6.28	6.15	6.03	5.92
¼	6.83	6.66	6.51	6.37	6.24	6.12	6.01
⅜	6.91	6.74	6.59	6.45	6.32	6.21	6.10
½	6.99	6.83	6.67	6.54	6.41	6.29	6.18
⅝	7.08	6.91	6.76	6.62	6.50	6.38	6.27
¾	7.16	7.00	6.85	6.71	6.58	6.47	6.36
⅞	7.24	7.08	6.93	6.80	6.67	6.56	6.45
5	7.33	7.17	7.02	6.89	6.76	6.65	6.54
⅛	7.42	7.25	7.11	6.97	6.85	6.74	6.63
¼	7.50	7.34	7.20	7.06	6.94	6.83	6.73
⅜	7.59	7.43	7.28	7.15	7.03	6.92	6.82
½	7.68	7.52	7.37	7.24	7.12	7.01	6.91
⅝	7.76	7.61	7.46	7.33	7.21	7.11	7.01
¾	7.85	7.70	7.55	7.42	7.31	7.20	7.10
⅞	7.94	7.79	7.65	7.52	7.40	7.29	7.19
6	8.03	7.88	7.74	7.61	7.49	7.39	7.29
⅛	8.12	7.97	7.83	7.70	7.59	7.48	7.38
¼	8.21	8.06	7.92	7.80	7.68	7.58	7.48
⅜	8.30	8.15	8.01	7.89	7.78	7.67	7.58
½	8.39	8.24	8.11	7.98	7.87	7.77	7.68

TABLE OF CONSTANT ANNUAL PERCENT[a] NEEDED TO AMORTIZE A PRINCIPAL AMOUNT ON A MONTHLY BASIS (*Continued*)

Interest Rate	16 Years	17 Years	18 Years	19 Years	20 Years	21 Years	22 Years	Interest Rate	23 Years	24 Years	25 Years	26 Years	27 Years	28 Years	29 Years
⅝	10.16	9.82	9.53	9.27	9.04	8.84	8.65	⅝	8.49	8.34	8.20	8.08	7.97	7.87	7.77
¾	10.24	9.91	9.62	9.36	9.13	8.93	8.74	¾	8.58	8.43	8.30	8.17	8.06	7.96	7.87
⅞	10.33	9.99	9.70	9.45	9.22	9.02	8.83	⅞	8.67	8.52	8.39	8.27	8.16	8.06	7.97
7	10.41	10.08	9.79	9.54	9.31	9.11	8.93	7	8.76	8.62	8.49	8.37	8.26	8.16	8.07
⅛	10.50	10.17	9.88	9.62	9.40	9.20	9.02	⅛	8.86	8.71	8.58	8.46	8.36	8.26	8.17
¼	10.58	10.25	9.97	9.71	9.49	9.29	9.11	¼	8.95	8.81	8.68	8.56	8.46	8.36	8.27
⅜	10.67	10.34	10.06	9.80	9.58	9.38	9.21	⅜	9.05	8.90	8.78	8.66	8.55	8.46	8.37
½	10.75	10.43	10.14	9.89	9.67	9.47	9.30	½	9.14	9.00	8.87	8.76	8.65	8.56	8.47
⅝	10.84	10.52	10.23	9.98	9.76	9.57	9.39	⅝	9.24	9.10	8.97	8.86	8.75	8.66	8.58
¾	10.93	10.61	10.32	10.08	9.86	9.66	9.49	¾	9.33	9.19	9.07	8.96	8.85	8.76	8.68
⅞	11.02	10.69	10.41	10.17	9.95	9.76	9.58	⅞	9.43	9.29	9.17	9.06	8.96	8.86	8.78
8	11.10	10.78	10.50	10.26	10.04	9.85	9.68	8	9.53	9.39	9.27	9.16	9.06	8.97	8.88
¼	11.28	10.96	10.69	10.44	10.23	10.04	9.87	¼	9.72	9.59	9.47	9.36	9.26	9.17	9.09
½	11.46	11.14	10.87	10.63	10.42	10.23	10.07	½	9.92	9.79	9.67	9.56	9.47	9.38	9.30
¾	11.64	11.33	11.06	10.82	10.61	10.43	10.26	¾	10.12	9.99	9.87	9.77	9.67	9.59	9.51
9	11.82	11.51	11.24	11.01	10.80	10.62	10.46	9	10.32	10.19	10.08	9.97	9.88	9.80	9.73
¼	12.00	11.70	11.43	11.20	11.00	10.82	10.66	¼	10.52	10.39	10.28	10.18	10.09	10.01	9.94
½	12.18	11.88	11.62	11.39	11.19	11.01	10.86	½	10.72	10.60	10.49	10.39	10.31	10.23	10.16
¾	12.37	12.07	11.81	11.58	11.39	11.21	11.06	¾	10.93	10.81	10.70	10.60	10.52	10.44	10.38
10	12.56	12.26	12.00	11.78	11.59	11.41	11.26	10	11.13	11.01	10.91	10.82	10.73	10.66	10.59

Interest Rate	30 Years	31 Years	32 Years	33 Years	34 Years	35 Years	36 Years
3	5.06	4.96	4.87	4.78	4.70	4.62	4.55
⅛	5.15	5.05	4.95	4.87	4.78	4.71	4.64
¼	5.23	5.13	5.04	4.95	4.87	4.79	4.72
⅜	5.31	5.21	5.12	5.03	4.95	4.88	4.81
½	5.39	5.30	5.20	5.12	5.04	4.96	4.89
⅝	5.48	5.38	5.29	5.20	5.13	5.05	4.98
¾	5.56	5.47	5.38	5.29	5.21	5.14	5.07
⅞	5.65	5.55	5.46	5.38	5.30	5.23	5.16
4	5.73	5.64	5.55	5.47	5.39	5.32	5.25
⅛	5.82	5.73	5.64	5.56	5.48	5.41	5.34
¼	5.91	5.81	5.73	6.65	5.57	5.50	5.43
⅜	6.00	5.90	5.82	5.74	5.66	5.59	5.53
½	6.09	5.99	5.91	5.83	5.75	5.68	5.62
⅝	6.17	6.08	6.00	5.92	5.85	5.78	5.71
¾	6.26	6.17	6.09	6.01	5.94	5.87	5.81
⅞	6.36	6.27	6.18	6.10	6.03	5.97	5.90
5	6.45	6.36	6.28	6.20	6.13	6.06	6.00
⅛	6.54	6.45	6.37	6.29	6.22	6.16	6.10
¼	6.63	6.54	6.46	6.39	6.32	6.25	6.19
⅜	6.72	6.64	6.56	6.48	6.42	6.35	6.29
½	6.82	6.73	6.65	6.58	6.51	6.45	6.39
⅝	6.91	6.83	6.75	6.68	6.61	6.55	6.49
¾	7.01	6.92	6.85	6.77	6.71	6.65	6.59
⅞	7.10	7.02	6.94	6.87	6.81	6.75	6.69
6	7.20	7.12	7.04	6.97	6.91	6.85	6.79
⅛	7.30	7.21	7.14	7.07	7.01	6.95	6.89
¼	7.39	7.31	7.24	7.17	7.11	7.05	7.00
⅜	7.49	7.41	7.34	7.27	7.21	7.15	7.10
½	7.59	7.51	7.44	7.37	7.31	7.25	7.20

Interest Rate	37 Years	38 Years	39 Years	40 Years	45 Years	50 Years
3	4.48	4.42	4.36	4.30	4.06	3.87
⅛	4.57	4.50	4.44	4.39	4.15	3.96
¼	4.65	4.59	4.53	4.48	4.24	4.05
⅜	4.74	4.68	4.62	4.56	4.33	4.15
½	4.83	4.77	4.71	4.65	4.42	4.24
⅝	4.92	4.86	4.80	4.74	4.51	4.34
¾	5.01	4.95	4.89	4.84	4.61	4.44
⅞	5.10	5.04	4.98	4.93	4.70	4.53
4	5.19	5.13	5.07	5.02	4.80	4.63
⅛	5.28	5.22	5.17	5.11	4.90	4.73
¼	5.37	5.31	5.26	5.21	4.99	4.83
⅜	5.47	5.41	5.35	5.30	5.09	4.94
½	5.56	5.50	5.45	5.40	5.19	5.04
⅝	5.65	5.60	5.55	5.50	5.29	5.14
¾	5.75	5.69	5.64	5.59	5.39	5.24
⅞	5.85	5.79	5.74	5.69	5.49	5.35
5	5.94	5.89	5.84	5.79	5.60	5.45
⅛	6.04	5.99	5.94	5.89	5.70	5.56
¼	6.14	6.09	6.04	5.99	5.80	5.67
⅜	6.24	6.19	6.14	6.09	5.91	5.78
½	6.34	6.29	6.24	6.19	6.01	5.88
⅝	6.44	6.39	6.34	6.30	6.12	5.99
¾	6.54	6.49	6.44	6.40	6.23	6.10
⅞	6.64	6.59	6.55	6.50	6.33	6.21
6	6.74	6.69	6.65	6.61	6.44	6.32
⅛	6.84	6.80	6.75	6.71	6.55	6.43
¼	6.95	6.90	6.86	6.82	6.66	6.54
⅜	7.05	7.00	6.96	6.92	6.77	6.66
½	7.15	7.11	7.07	7.03	6.88	6.77

TABLE OF CONSTANT ANNUAL PERCENT[a] NEEDED TO AMORTIZE A PRINCIPAL AMOUNT CALCULATED ON A MONTHLY BASIS (*Continued*)

Interest Rate	30 Years	31 Years	32 Years	33 Years	34 Years	35 Years	36 Years	Interest Rate	37 Years	38 Years	39 Years	40 Years	45 Years	50 Years
⅝	7.69	7.61	7.54	7.47	7.41	7.36	7.31	⅝	7.26	7.22	7.18	7.14	6.99	6.88
¾	7.79	7.71	7.64	7.58	7.52	7.46	7.41	¾	7.36	7.32	7.28	7.21	7.10	7.00
⅞	7.89	7.81	7.74	7.68	7.62	7.57	7.52	⅞	7.47	7.43	7.39	7.35	7.21	7.11
7	7.99	7.91	7.85	7.78	7.72	7.67	7.62	7	7.58	7.54	7.50	7.46	7.32	7.23
⅛	8.09	8.02	7.95	7.89	7.83	7.78	7.73	⅛	7.68	7.64	7.61	7.57	7.43	7.34
¼	8.19	8.12	8.05	7.99	7.93	7.88	7.84	¼	7.79	7.75	7.72	7.68	7.55	7.46
⅜	8.29	8.22	8.16	8.09	8.04	7.99	7.94	⅜	7.90	7.86	7.82	7.79	7.66	7.57
½	8.40	8.32	8.26	8.20	8.15	8.10	8.05	½	8.01	7.97	7.93	7.90	7.77	7.69
⅝	8.50	8.43	8.36	8.31	8.25	8.20	8.16	⅝	8.12	8.08	8.04	8.01	7.89	7.80
¾	8.60	8.53	8.47	8.41	8.36	8.31	8.27	¾	8.23	8.19	8.16	8.12	8.00	7.92
⅞	8.71	8.64	8.58	8.52	8.47	8.42	8.38	⅞	8.34	8.30	8.27	8.24	8.12	8.04
8	8.81	8.74	8.68	8.63	8.57	8.53	8.49	8	8.45	8.41	8.38	8.35	8.23	8.16
¼	9.02	8.95	8.90	8.84	8.79	8.75	8.71	¼	8.67	8.63	8.60	8.57	8.46	8.39
½	9.23	9.17	9.11	9.06	9.01	8.97	8.93	½	8.89	8.86	8.83	8.80	8.70	8.63
¾	9.45	9.38	9.33	9.28	9.23	9.19	9.15	¾	9.12	9.09	9.06	9.03	8.93	8.87
9	9.66	9.60	9.55	9.50	9.45	9.41	9.38	9	9.34	9.31	9.29	9.26	9.17	9.11
¼	9.88	9.82	9.77	9.72	9.68	9.64	9.60	¼	9.57	9.54	9.52	9.49	9.40	9.35
½	10.10	10.04	9.99	9.94	9.90	9.86	9.83	½	9.80	9.77	9.75	9.73	9.64	9.59
¾	10.31	10.26	10.21	10.17	10.13	10.09	10.06	¾	10.03	10.00	9.98	9.96	9.88	9.83
10	10.54	10.48	10.44	10.39	10.36	10.32	10.29	10	10.26	10.24	10.22	10.19	10.12	10.07

[a] Reproduced from Financial Constant Percent Amortization Tables, Publication No. 287, pages 146 through 151, copyright 1975, Financial Publishing Company, Boston, Mass.

NOTES

1. *Form in Civilization*, W. R. Lethaby, Oxford University Press, London, 1957.
2. *Conversations with Architects*, J. W. Cook and H. Klotz, Praeger, New York, 1973.
3. Theory in Practice, Robert Geddes, *Architectural Forum*, September 1972.
4. Beyond Golden Lane, Robin Hood Gardens, Anthony Pangaro, *Architecture Plus*, June, 1973.
5. *Apartments, Their Design and Development*, Samuel Paul, Reinhold, New York, 1967.
6. Zoning Laws: The Case for Repeal, David J. Mandel, *Architectural Forum*, December 1971.
7. *The Zoning Game*, Richard F. Babcock, University of Wisconsin Press, Madison. 1969.
8. *Housing Quality, A Program for Zoning Reform*, Urban Design Council of the City of New York, 1973.
9. *Death and Life of Great American Cities*, Jane Jacobs, Random House, New York, 1961.
10. *The Zoning Game*, Richard F. Babcock, University of Wisconsin Press, Madison. 1969.
11. *The Zoning Game*, Richard F. Babcock, University of Wisconsin Press, Madison. 1969.
12. *Housing Quality, A Program for Zoning Reform*, Urban Design Council of the City of New York, 1973.
13. *Housing Quality, A Program for Zoning Reform*, Urban Design Council of the City of New York, 1973.
14. *Apartments, Their Design and Development*, Samuel Paul, Reinhold, New York, 1967.
15. *Apartments, Their Design and Development*, Samuel Paul, Reinhold, New York, 1967.
16. *Experiencing Architecture*, Steen Eiler Rasmussen, M.I.T. Press, Cambridge, 1959.
17. *H.U.D. Minimum Property Standards for Multifamily Housing* (1973 Edition).
18. *H.U.D. Minimum Property Standards for Multifamily Housing* (1973 Edition).
19. *Multistory Housing*, Karl Wilhelm Schmitt, Praeger, New York, 1966.
20. What Should Chicago Do About High-rise Fires, Nory Miller, *Inland Architect*, August 1974.
21. *Defensible Space*, Oscar Newman, Macmillan, New York, 1972.
22. *Defensible Space*, Oscar Newman, Macmillan, New York, 1972.
23. *Complexity and Contradiction in Architecture*, Robert Venturi, The Museum of Modern Art, New York, 1966.
24. *Experiencing Architecture*, Steen Eiler Rasmussen, M.I.T. Press, Cambridge, 1959.
25. Beyond Golden Lane, Robin Hood Gardens, Anthony Pangaro, *Architecture Plus*, June 1973.

NOTES

26. *Conversations with Architects,* J. W. Cook and H. Klotz, Praeger, New York, 1973.
27. *A Place to Live,* Wolf von Eckardt, Dell, New York, 1967.
28. *Modern Movements in Architecture,* Charles Jencks, Anchor Press/Doubleday, New York, 1973.
29. *Complexity and Contradiction in Architecture,* Robert Venturi, The Museum of Modern Art, New York, 1966.
30. *Conversations with Architects,* J. W. Cook and H. Klotz, Praeger, New York, 1973.
31. *Architecture of Humanism,* Geoffrey Scott, Doubleday, New York, 1924.
32. *Defensible Space,* Oscar Newman, Macmillan, New York, 1972.
33. *Planning and Design Handbook for Community Participation,* Research Center for Urban and Environmental Planning, Princeton University School of Architecture and Urban Planning, 1969.
34. *Planning and Design Handbook for Community Participation,* Research Center for Urban and Environmental Planning, Princeton Univ. School of Architecture and Urban Planning, 1969.
35. *Site Planning,* Kevin Lynch, M.I.T. Press, Cambridge, 1971.

PROJECTS

HIGHRISE—CENTRAL CORRIDOR

1. Ludwig Mies van der Rohe: Lafayette Towers, Detroit, Michigan
2. Stanley Tigerman: Boardwalk, Chicago, Illinois
3. Skidmore, Owings & Merril: Lake Meadows, Chicago, Illinois
4. I. M. Pei & Partners: University Plaza, New York, New York
5. I. M. Pei & Partners: Washington Square East, Philadelphia, Pennsylvania
6. Solomon, Cordwell, Buenz & Associates: Hawthorn House, Chicago, Illinois
7. Paul Rudolph: Crawford Manor, New Haven, Connecticut
8. Prentice & Chan, Ohlhausen: Twin Parks Northwest Site 5–11, Bronx, New York
9. Davis Brody & Associates: 2440 Boston Road, Bronx, New York
10. Gruzen & Partners: Arthur Schomburg Plaza, New York, New York
11. Gilbert Switzer & Associates: Sbona Towers & Senior Center, Middletown, Connecticut
12. Keyes, Lethbridge & Condon: Tiber Island, Washington, D.C.
13. Ulrich Franzen & Associates: Williams Street Student Housing, Middletown, Connecticut
14. Backen, Arrigoni & Ross: 2000 Broadway, San Francisco, California

HIGHRISE—CENTRAL CORRIDOR AND EXTERIOR CORRIDOR

15. Davis Brody & Associates: East Midtown Plaza, New York, New York

HIGHRISE—MULTICORE

16. Hausner & Macsai: Harbor House, Chicago, Illinois
17. Hausner & Macsai: 1500 Sheridan Road, Wilmette, Illinois

HIGHRISE—POINTBLOCK

18. Bertrand Goldberg Associates: Marina City, Chicago, Illinois
19. Gruzen & Partners: Arthur Schomburg Plaza, New York, New York
20. Skidmore, Owings & Merrill: Dorchester Apartments, Chicago, Illinois
21. Hausner & Macsai: 1110 Lake Shore Drive, Chicago, Illinois
22. Ezra Gordon-Jack Levin: Newberry Plaza, Chicago, Illinois
23. Thorsen & Thorshov Associates: Ebenezer Towers, Minneapolis, Minnesota
24. Freerks/Sperl/Flynn: 727 Front Avenue, St. Paul, Minnesota
25. Schipporeit & Heinrich: Lake Point Tower, Chicago, Illinois
26. Hoberman & Wasserman: Southview Towers, Rochester, New York

PROJECTS

27. Davis Brody & Associates: Waterside, New York, New York
28. Conklin & Rossant: Two Charles Center, Baltimore, Maryland
29. Harry Weese & Associates and Ezra Gordon-Jack Levin: Lake Village, Chicago, Illinois

HIGHRISE—SKIPSTOP

30. Prentice & Chan, Ohlhausen: Twin Park Northwest Site 4, Bronx, New York
31. Davis Brody & Associates: Riverbend, New York, New York
32. Giovanni Pasanella Associates: Twin Parks West—Site 10–12, Bronx, New York
33. Hoberman & Wasserman: Coney Island—Site 5/6, Brooklyn, New York
34. Sert, Jackson and Associates: Roosevelt Island, Parcel 3, New York, New York
35. Ralph Rapson and Associates: Cedar-Riverside, Minneapolis, Minnesota

MIDRISE

36. Ezra Gordon-Jack Levin: South Commons, Chicago, Illinois
37. Solomon, Cordwell, Buenz & Associates: 1555 Sandburg Terrace, Chicago, Illinois
38. Hoberman & Wasserman: Agnes Morely Heights, Greenwich, Connecticut
39. Davis Brody & Associates: Lambert Houses, Bronx, New York
40. Hausner & Macsai: Winnetka House, Winnetka, Illinois

LOWRISE—TOWNHOUSE

41. Keyes, Lethbridge & Condon: Tiber Island, Washington, D.C.
42. Booth & Nagle: Atrium, Elmhurst, Illinois
43. Harry Weese & Associates and Ezra Gordon-Jack Levin: Lake Village, Chicago, Illinois
44. Ulrich Franzen & Associates: Williams Street Student Housing, Middletown, Connecticut
45. Burger and Coplans: Acorn Project, Oakland, California
46. Alden R. Berman: Sheffield Manor, New Haven, Connecticut
47. Louis Sauer Assoc.: Canterbury Garden Co-op, New Haven, Connecticut

LOWRISE—MATRIX

48. Backen Arrigoni & Ross: Tustin Apartments, Tustin, California
49. Werner Seligman and Associates: Elm Street Housing, Ithaca, New York

LOWRISE—WALK-UP/CORE TYPE

50. Joe J. Jordan: Reno Street Public Housing, Philadelphia, Pennsylvania
51. Harry Weese & Associates and Ezra Gordon-Jack Levin: Lake Village, Chicago, Illinois
52. Esherick Homsey Dodge and Davis: Banneker Homes, San Francisco, California
53. Marquis & Stoller: St. Francis Square, San Francisco, California
54. Paul Rudolph: Buffalo Waterfront Housing, Buffalo, New York

LOWRISE—WALK-UP/CORRIDOR TYPE

55. Booth & Nagle: Portals, Chicago, Illinois
56. Gruzen & Partners: Genesee Gateway, Rochester, New York
57. Werner Seligman and Associates: Elm Street Housing, Ithaca, New York
58. Brent Goldman Robbins & Brown: Esplanade Village, Redondo Beach, California
59. Martin/Soderstrom/Matteson: East Burnside, Portland, Oregon
60. Antoine Predock: The Citadel, Albuquerque, New Mexico

LOWRISE—WALK-UP/MIXED

61. Stanley Tigerman: Woodlawn Gardens, Chicago, Illinois
62. Collins & Kronstadt: Sursum Corda, Washington, D.C.
63. Charles W. Moore Associates: Church Street South, New Haven, Connecticut
64. The Institute for Architecture and Urban Studies: Marcus Garvey Park Village, Brownsville, New York

PROJECTS

1

LAFAYETTE TOWERS
Detroit, Michigan

Architect:
LUDWIG MIES VAN DER ROHE
Chicago, Illinois

Number of dwelling units: 292 @2 buildings
94—Efficiency @2
118—one bedroom @2
74—two bedroom @2
6—three bedroom @2
Gross floor area: 594,000 sf (including garage)
Construction cost: $8,000,000 approximately (including garage)
Year of bid: 1961
Site area: 9.5 acres
30.5 units/acre
User: middle income
Financing: FHA 220

Photo credit: Baltazar Korab

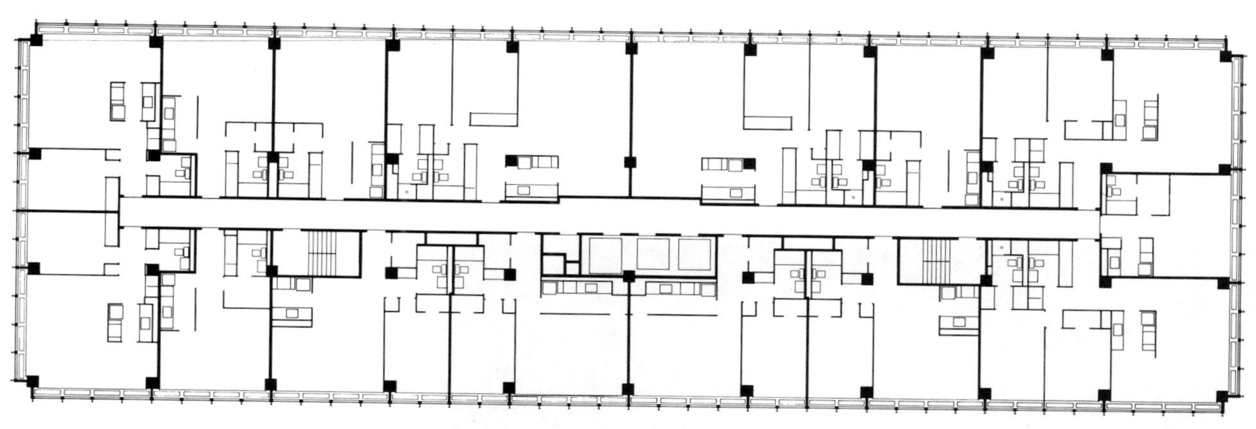

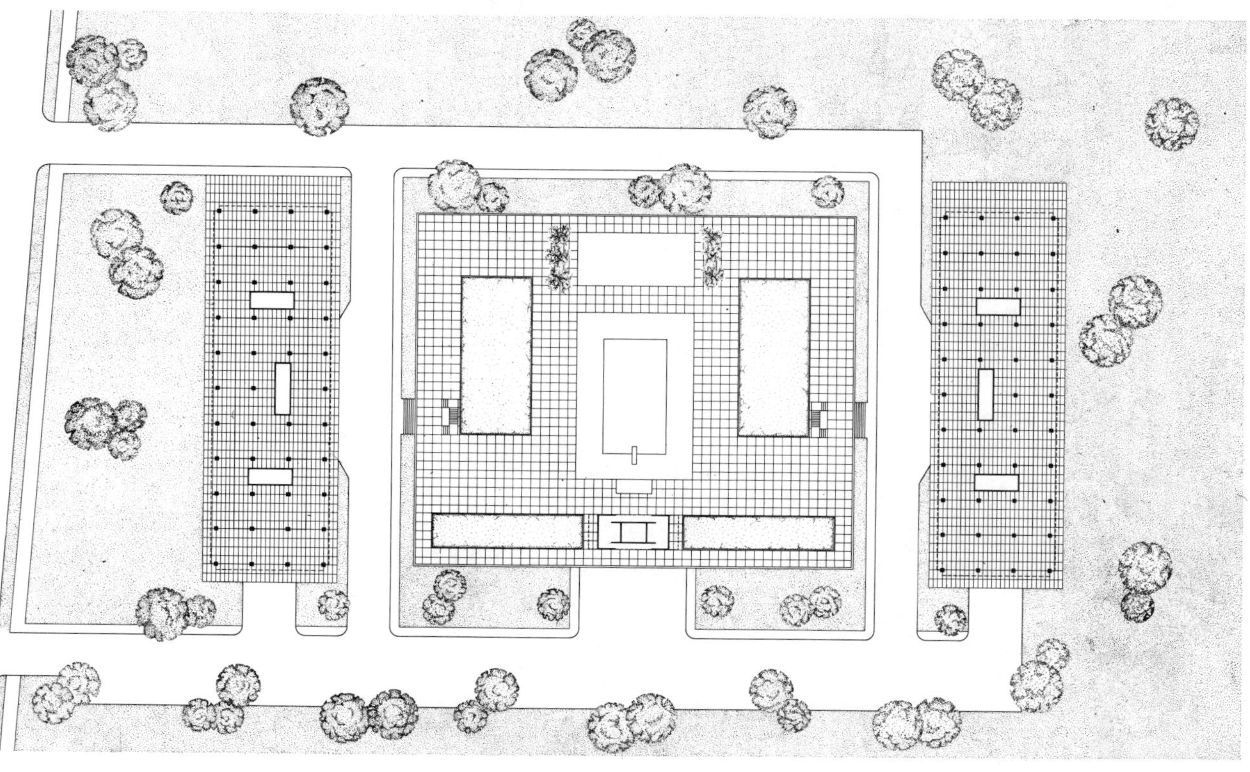

2 **BOARDWALK**
Chicago, Illinois

Architect:
STANLEY TIGERMAN
Chicago, Illinois

Number of dwelling units: 450
150—Efficiency
200—one bedroom
100—two bedroom

Gross floor area: 526,000 sf (including garage)
Construction cost: $8,500,000
$16.15/sf
$18,889/unit
Year of bid: 1972
Site area: 1.35 acres
333.5 units/acre
User: Middle income
Financing: FHA 221 (d) 4

Photo credit: Ruyell Ho

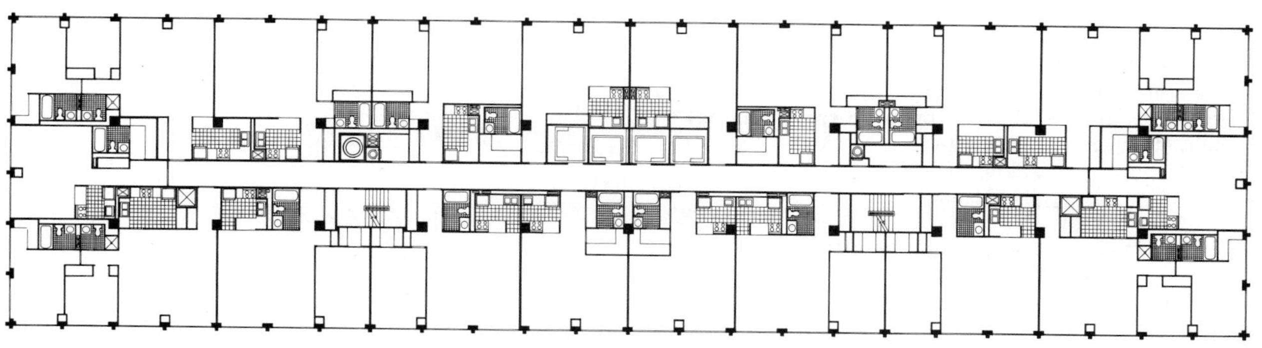

3

LAKE MEADOWS
Chicago, Illinois

Architect:
SKIDMORE, OWINGS & MERRILL
Chicago, Illinois

Number of dwelling units: 164
- 24—efficiency
- 48—one bedroom
- 48—two bedroom
- 24—three bedroom

Gross floor area: 187,000 sf (open, on grade parking)
Construction cost: $2,875,000
$15.36/sf
$17,530/unit
Year of bid: 1960
Site area: part of large complex
User: middle income
Financing: conventional

Photo credit: Ezra Stoller

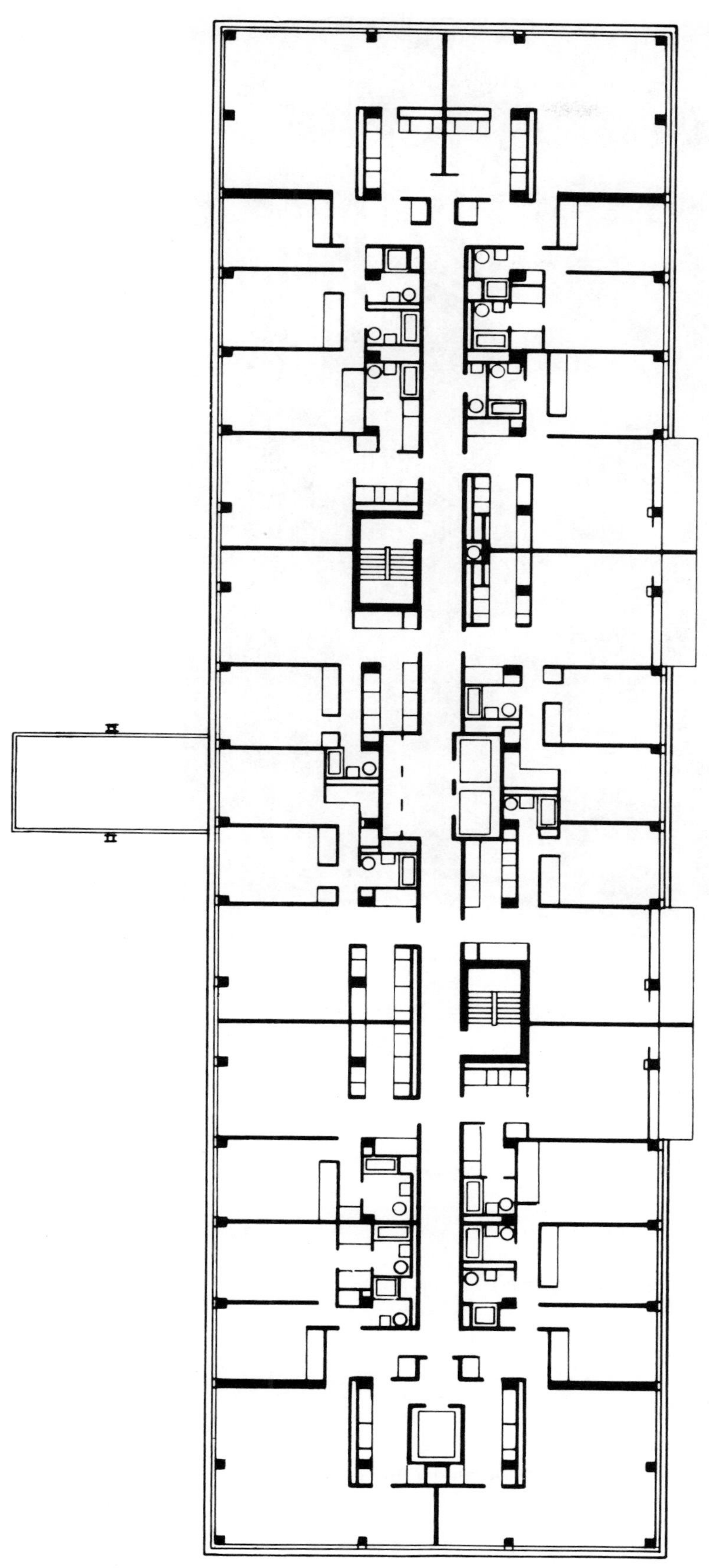

4

UNIVERSITY PLAZA
New York, New York

Architect:
I. M. PEI & PARTNERS
New York, New York

Number of dwelling units: 177 @3
2—efficiency @3
58—one bedroom @3
59—two bedroom @3
58—three bedroom @3
Gross floor area: 795,000 sf (including garage)
Construction cost: $11,367,000
$14.29/sf
$21,407/unit
Year of bid: 1964
Site area: 4.86 acres
109 units/acre
User: middle income
Financing: 2 towers—New York State Dormitory Authority
1 tower—New York City Mitchell-Lama

Photo credit: George Cserna

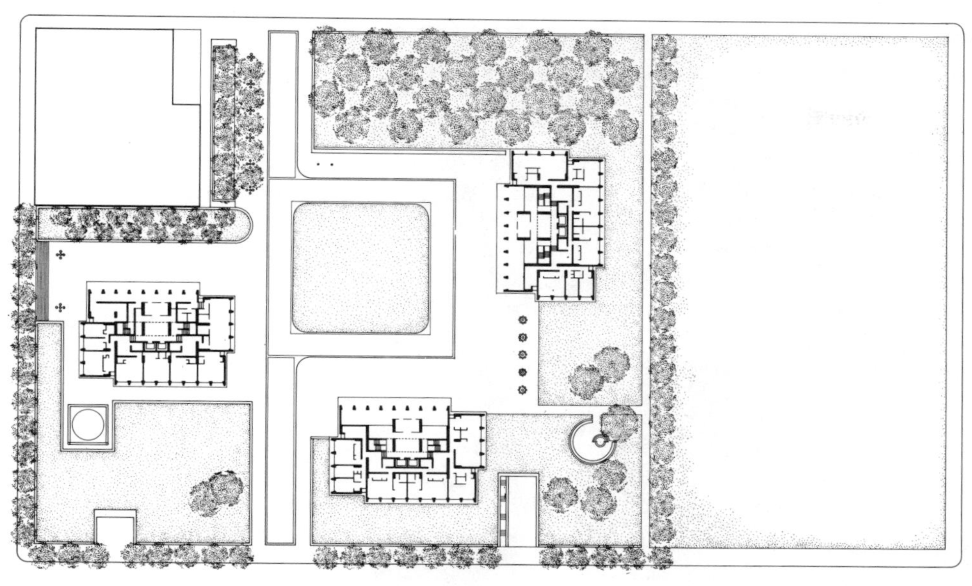

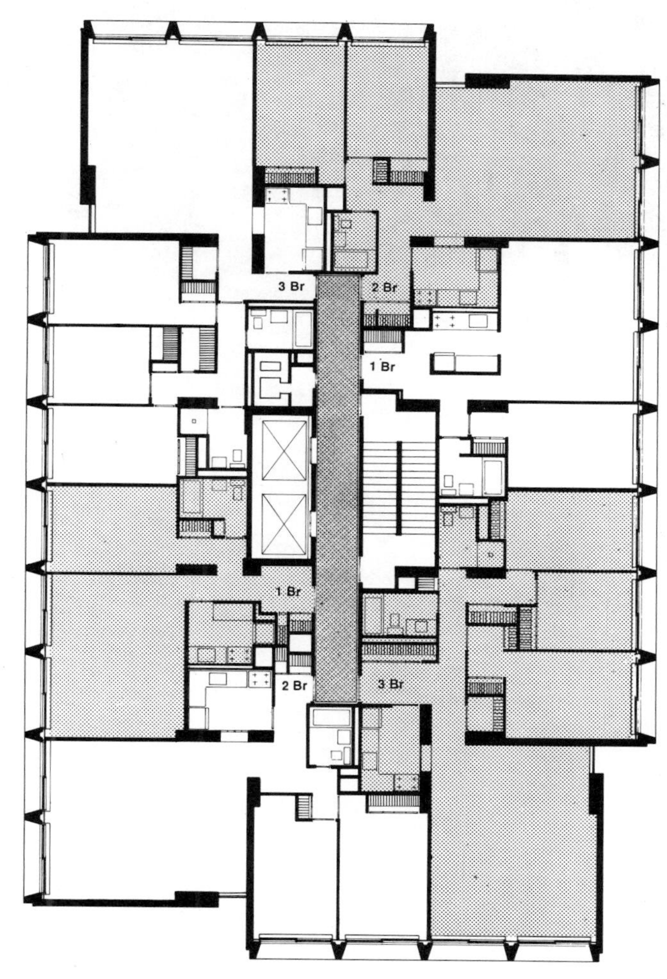
3 Br
2 Br
1 Br
1 Br
2 Br
3 Br

5

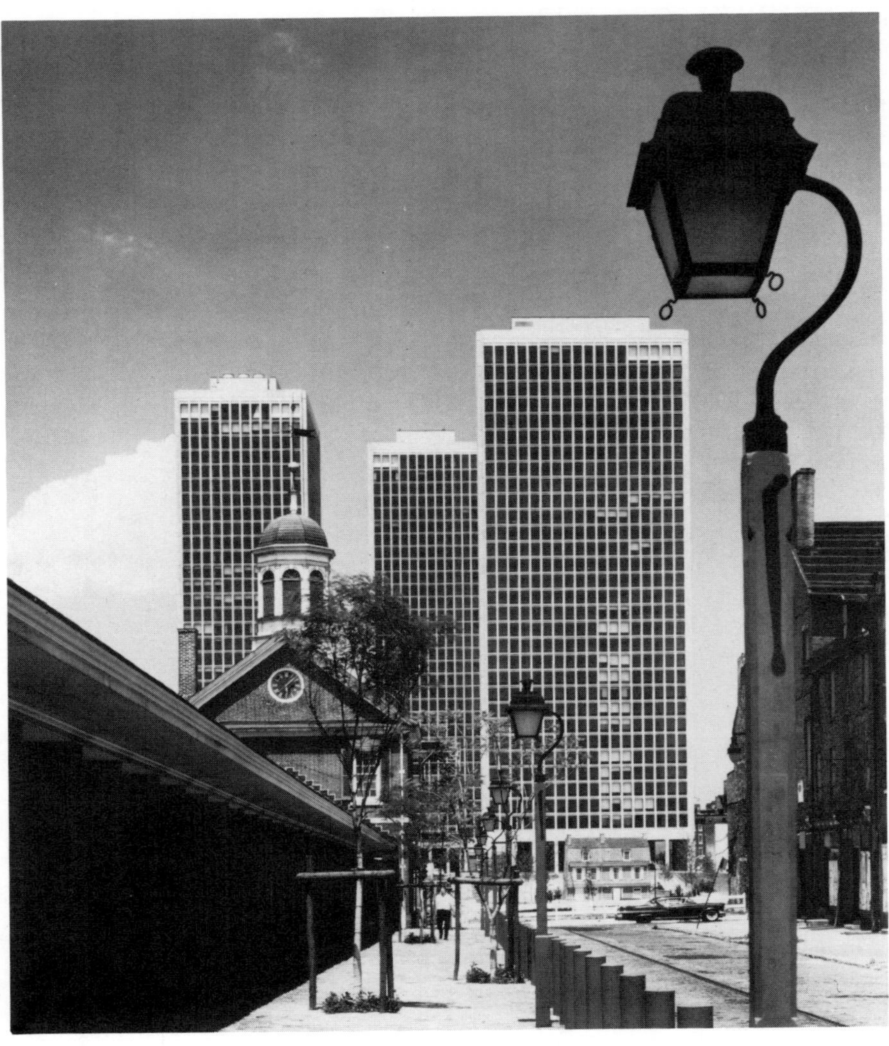

WASHINGTON SQUARE EAST
Philadelphia, Pennsylvania

Architect:
I. M. PEI & PARTNERS
New York, New York

Number of dwelling units: 240 @3 buildings
30—efficiency @3
150—one bedroom @3
60—two bedroom @3
Gross floor area: 937,350 sf (including garage)
Construction cost: $12,659,000
$13.50/sf
$17,582/unit
Year of bid: 1962
Site area: 4.2 acres
170 units/acre
User: middle income
Financing: FHA

Photo credit: George Cserna

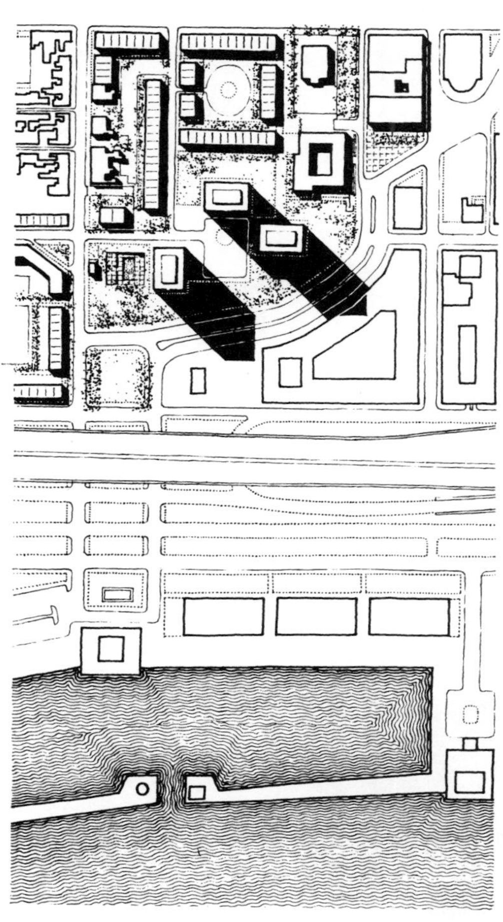

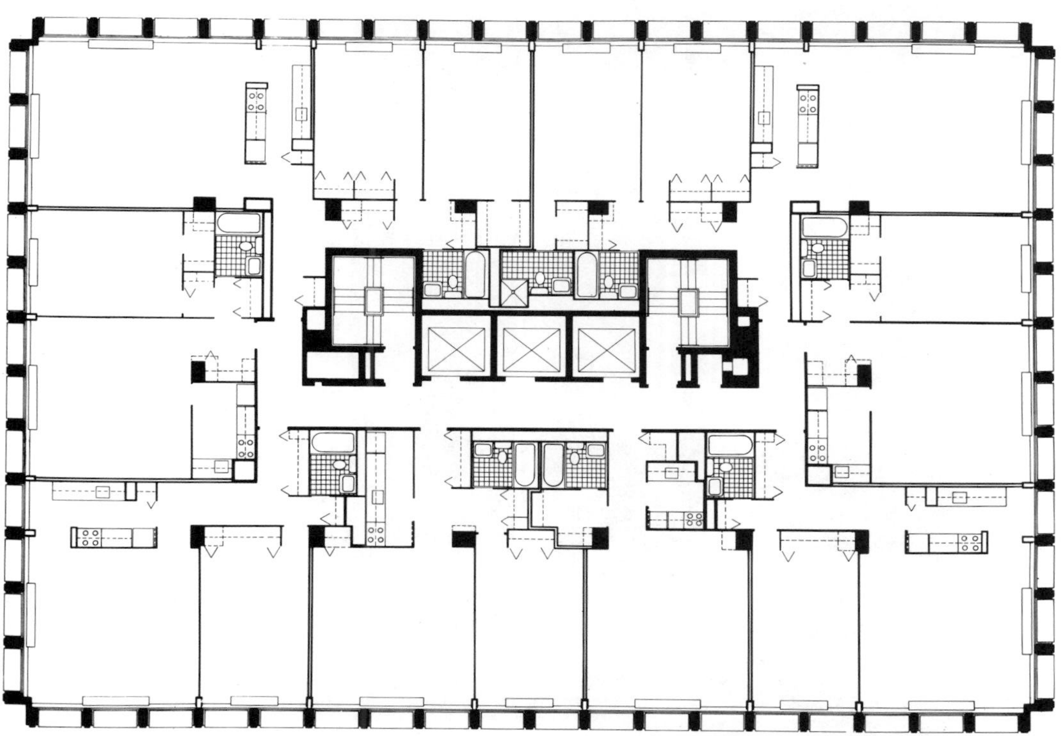

WASHINGTON SQUARE EAST 331

6 **HAWTHORNE HOUSE**
Chicago, Illinois

Architect:
SOLOMON, CORDWELL, BUENZ & ASSOCIATES
Chicago, Illinois

Number of dwelling units: 456
108—efficiency
240—one bedroom
108—two bedroom
Gross floor area: 508,700 sf (including garage)
Construction cost: $9,363,000
$18.40/sf
$20,533/unit
Year of bid: 1966
Site area: 1.28 acres
356 units/acre
User: middle to upper income
Financing: conventional

Photo credit: Orlando Cabanban

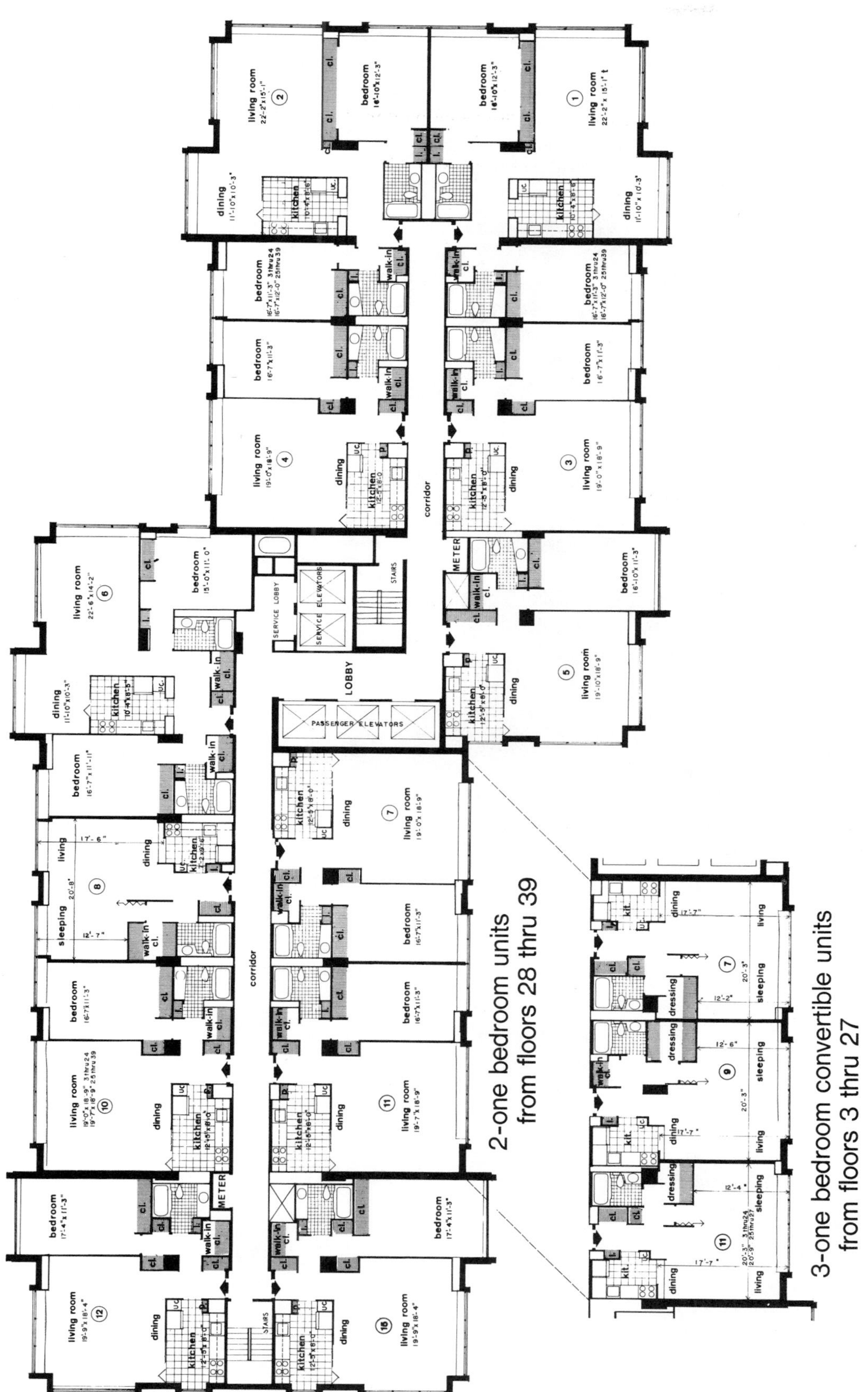

2-one bedroom units from floors 28 thru 39

3-one bedroom convertible units from floors 3 thru 27

7

CRAWFORD MANOR
New Haven, Connecticut

Architect:
PAUL RUDOLPH
New York, New York

Number of dwelling units: 109
52—efficiency
52—one bedroom
5—two bedroom

Gross floor area: 60,615 (open, on grade parking)
Construction cost: $1,003,000 (+ approximately $383,000 site work)
$16.55/sf (not including site work)
$9200/unit (not including site work)
Year of bid: 1964
Site area: 0.75 acres
145 units/acre
User: elderly
Financing: public housing

Photo credit: Robert Perron

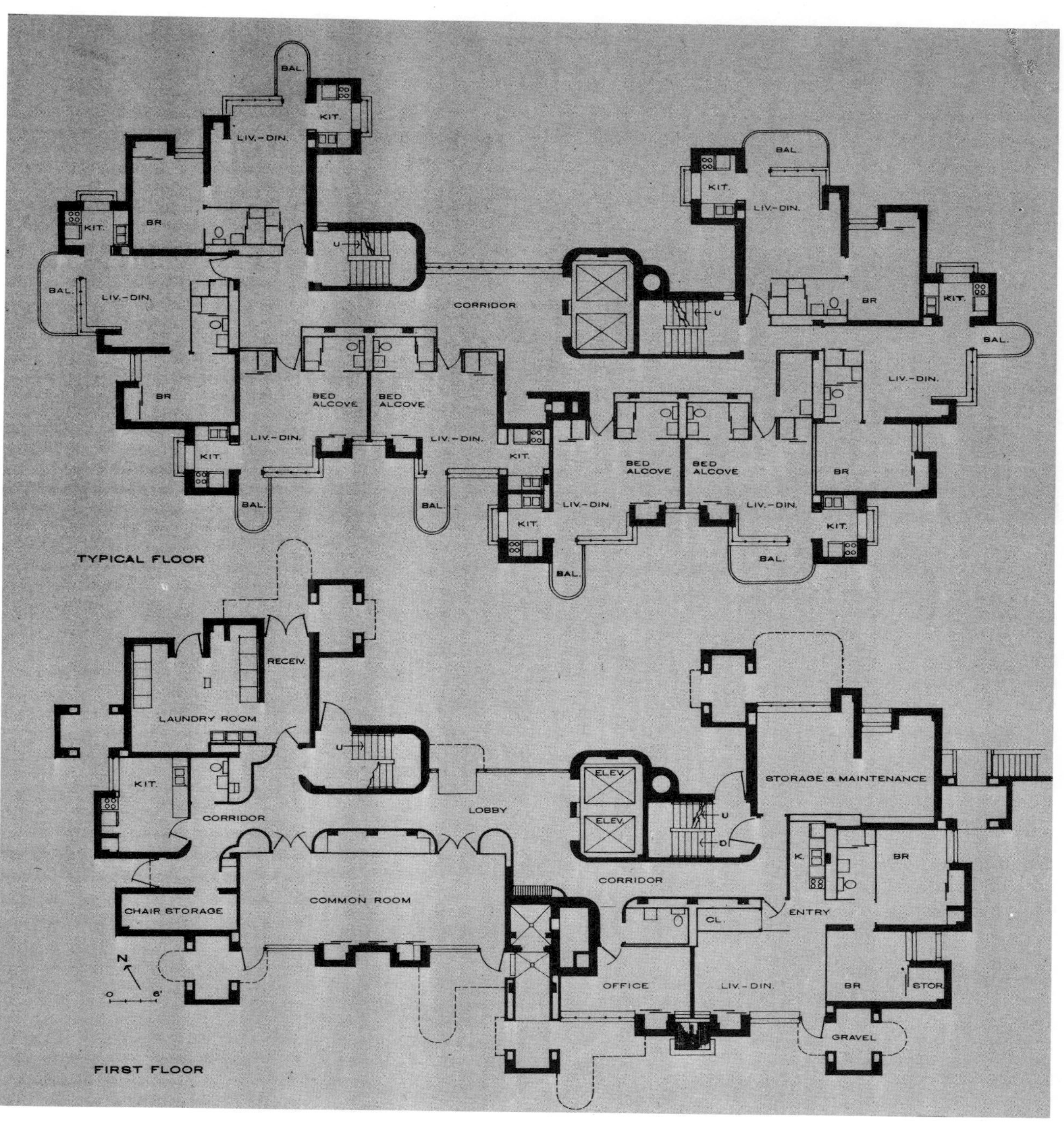
BAL.
KIT.
LIV.-DIN.
KIT.
BR
BAL.
LIV.-DIN.
U
CORRIDOR
BAL.
KIT.
LIV.-DIN.
U
BR
KIT.
BAL.
BR
BED ALCOVE
BED ALCOVE
LIV.-DIN.
LIV.-DIN.
LIV.-DIN.
KIT.
KIT.
BAL.
BAL.
KIT.
BED ALCOVE
BED ALCOVE
BR
LIV.-DIN.
LIV.-DIN.
KIT.
KIT.
BAL.
BAL.
TYPICAL FLOOR
RECEIV.
LAUNDRY ROOM
U
KIT.
CORRIDOR
LOBBY
ELEV.
ELEV.
U
D
STORAGE & MAINTENANCE
K.
BR
CHAIR STORAGE
COMMON ROOM
CORRIDOR
CL.
ENTRY
N
0
6'
OFFICE
LIV.-DIN.
BR
STOR.
GRAVEL
FIRST FLOOR

8

TWIN PARKS NORTHWEST—SITE 5-11
Bronx, New York

Architect:
PRENTICE & CHAN, OHLHAUSEN
New York, New York

Number of dwelling units: 213
- 10—efficiency
- 40—one bedroom
- 74—two bedroom
- 71—three bedroom
- 8—four bedroom
- 10—five bedroom

Gross floor area: 211,730 sf (including garage)
Construction cost: $7,136,000 (including garage)
$33.70/sf
$33,500/unit
Year of bid: 1970
Site area: 1.25 acres
170.5 units/acre
User: low to moderate income
Financing: FHA 236

Photo credit: Norman McGrath

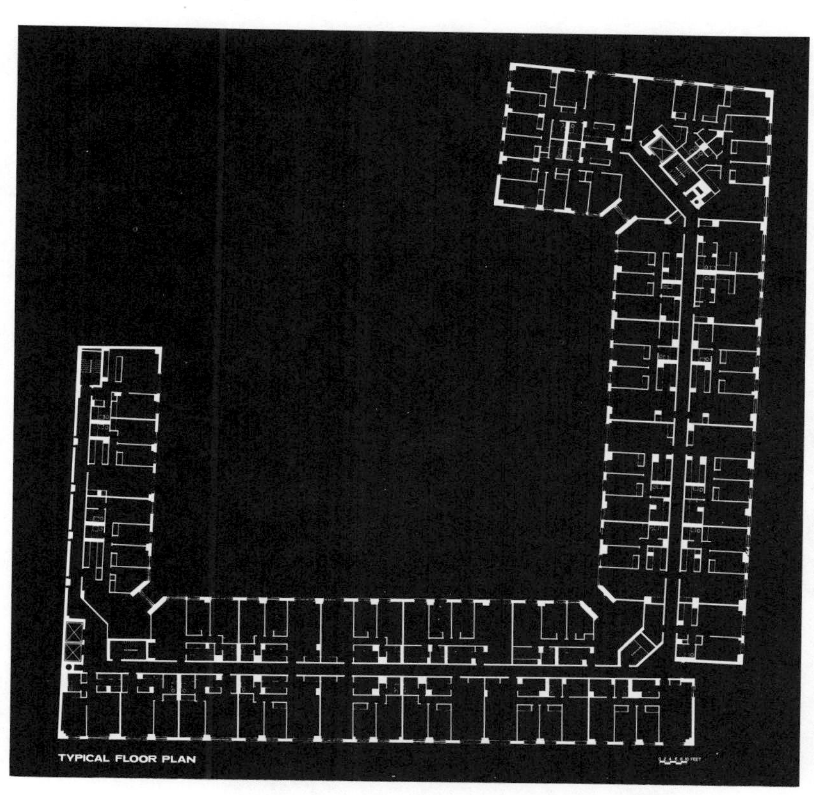
TYPICAL FLOOR PLAN

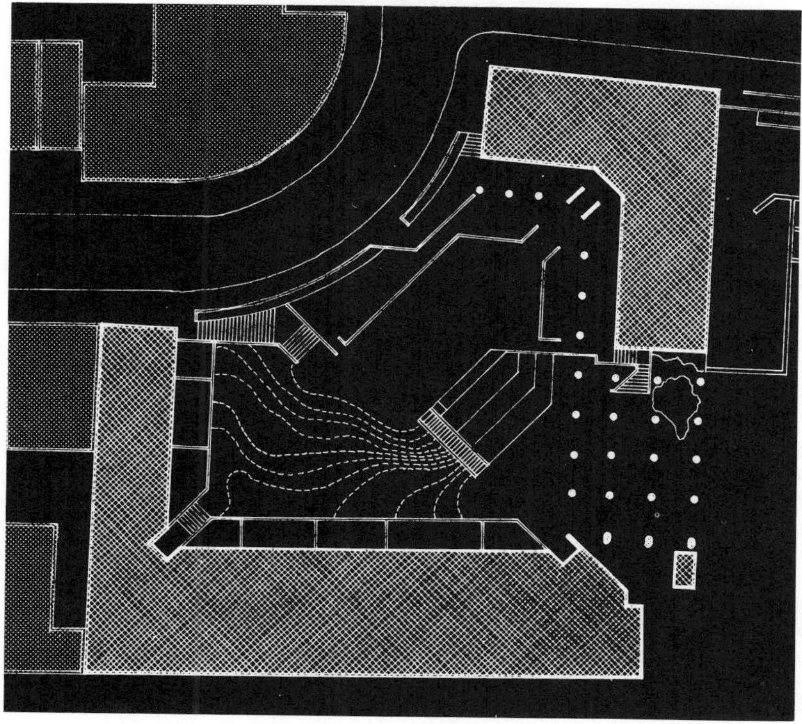

9

2440 BOSTON ROAD
Bronx, New York

Architect:
DAVIS BRODY & ASSOCIATES
New York, New York

Number of dwelling units: 235
39—efficiency (elderly)
156—one bedroom (elderly)
40—two bedroom
Gross floor area: 175,390 sf (on grade, open parking)
Construction cost: $5,200,000 (+ $400,000 site development)
$29.64/sf (+ site development)
$22,128/unit (+ site development)
Year of bid: 1970
Site area: 1.95 acres
120.5 units/acre
User: low income—elderly
Financing: state financed

Photo credit: Norman McGrath

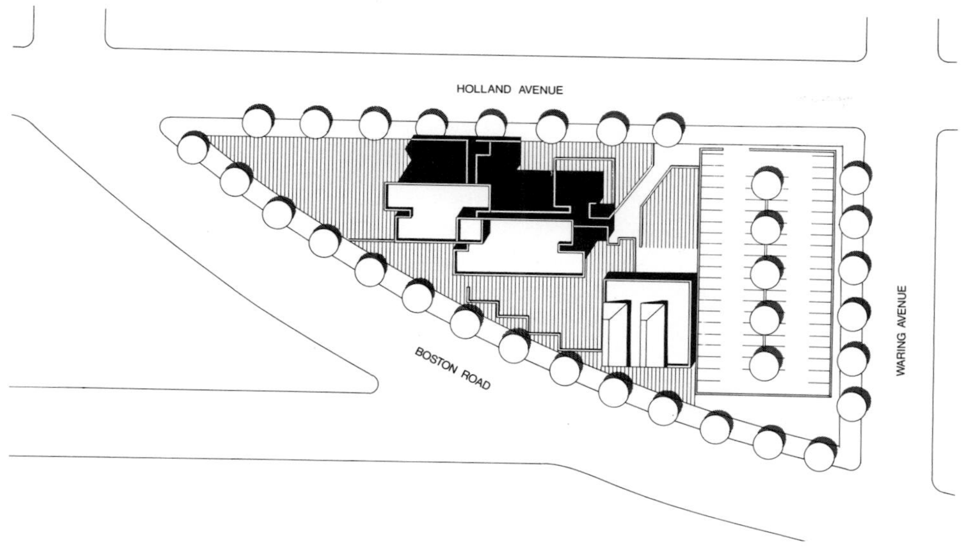

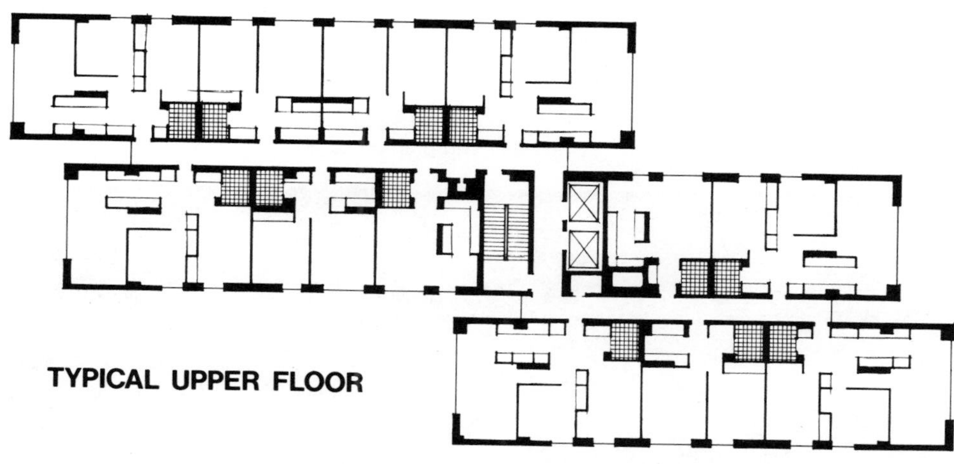
TYPICAL UPPER FLOOR

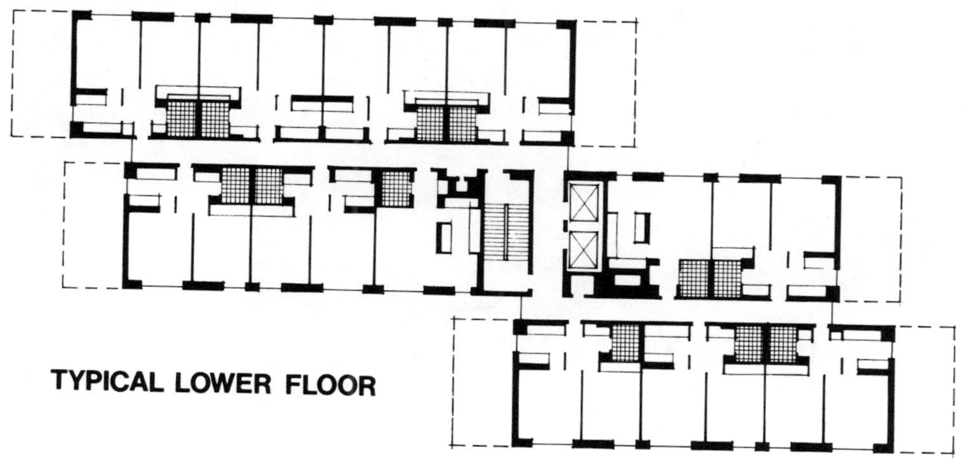
TYPICAL LOWER FLOOR

10 **ARTHUR SCHOMBURG PLAZA**
New York, New York

Architect:
GRUZEN & PARTNERS
New York, New York

Number of dwelling units: 600
Towers: 17—efficiency @2
68—one bedroom @2
102—two bedroom @2
Central Corridor: 85—three bedroom @2
28—four bedroom
28—five bedroom
Gross floor area: 585,530 sf
462,000 sf towers
85,460 sf central corridor
31,600 sf community
6,470 sf retail
Construction cost: $23,000,000 (including garage, community and retail)
$39.28 sf
$38,333/unit
Year of bid: 1971
Site area: 1.83 acres
328 units/acre
User: 60% moderate income
30% low income
10% elderly
Financing: New York State Urban Development Corporation

Photo credit: David Hirsch

See site plan on p. 359.

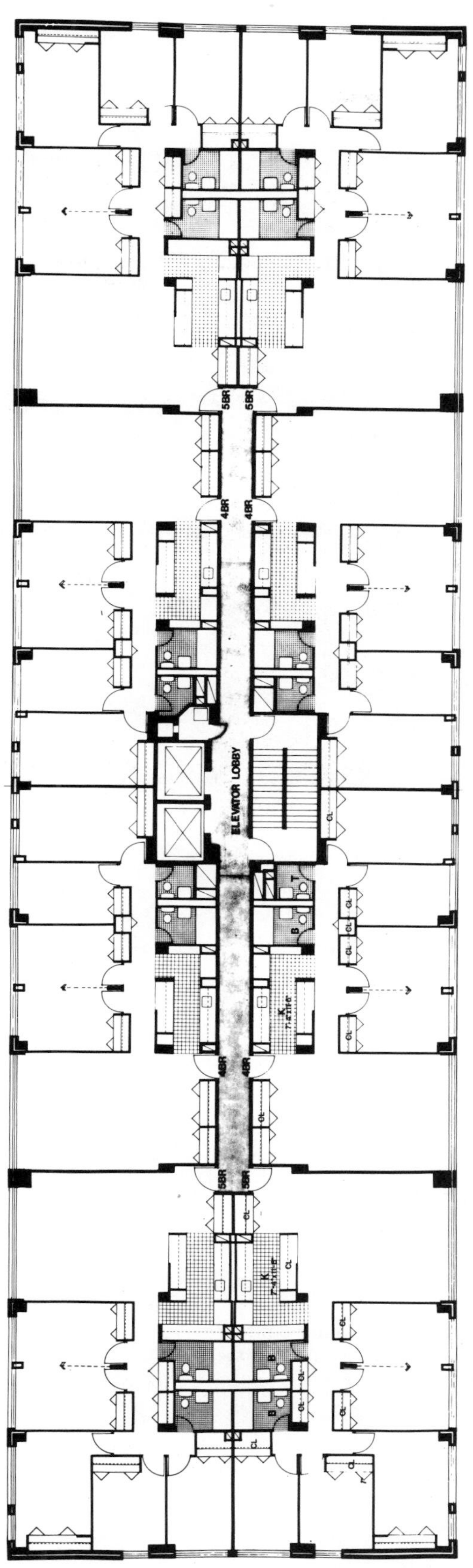
5BR
5BR
4BR
4BR
ELEVATOR LOBBY
4BR
4BR
5BR
5BR

11

SBONA TOWER AND SENIOR CENTER
Middletown, Connecticut

Architect:
GILBERT SWITZER & ASSOCIATES
New Haven, Connecticut

Number of dwelling units: 129
82—efficiency
47—one bedroom
Gross floor area: 95,730 sf (including Senior Center)
Construction cost: $2,132,000 (including Senior Center)
$22,27/sf
$16,527/unit
Year of bid: 1970
Site area: 2.23 acres
58 units/acre
User: elderly: low, middle, upper
Financing: HUD Turnkey

Photo credit: Thomas A. Brown

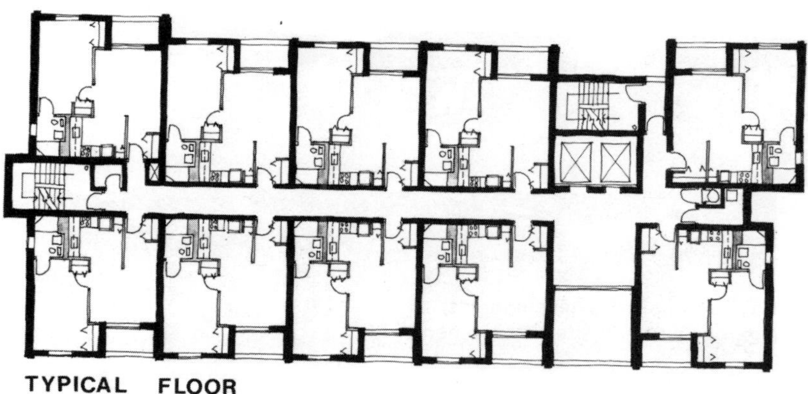

TYPICAL FLOOR

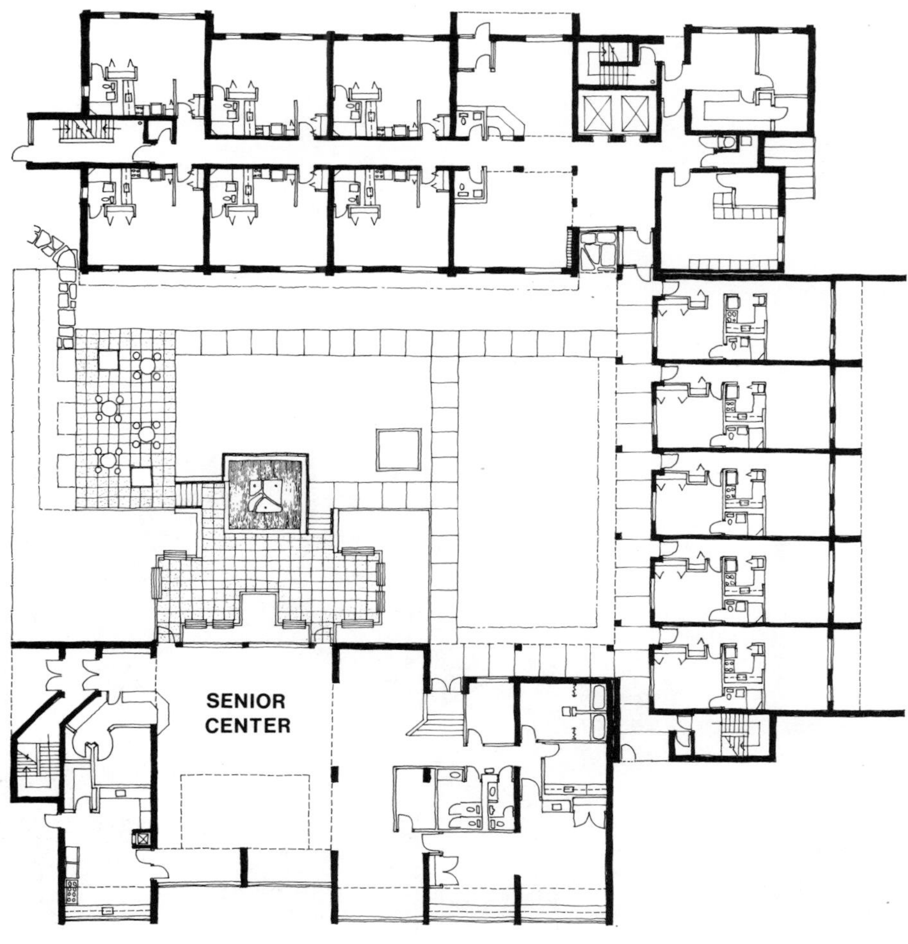

FIRST FLOOR

12 **TIBER ISLAND**
Washington, D.C.

Architect:
KEYS, LETHBRIDGE & CONDON
Washington, D.C.

Number of dwelling units: 453
Highrise: 160—efficiency
120—one bedroom
80—two bedroom
Townhouses: 60—two bedroom
25—four bedroom
Gross floor area: 446,000 sf highrises
186,000 sf townhouses
103,000 sf garage
Construction cost: $8,508,000
$5,670,000 highrise
$11.35 sf (including garage and half site development)
$16,937/unit (including garage and half site development)
$2,161,000 townhouses
$12.22 sf (including half site development)
$26,753/unit (including half site development)
$450,000 garage
$227,000 site development
Year of bid: 1963
Site area: 8.12 acres
56 units/acre
User: middle to upper income
Financing: FHA

Photo credit: J. Alexander

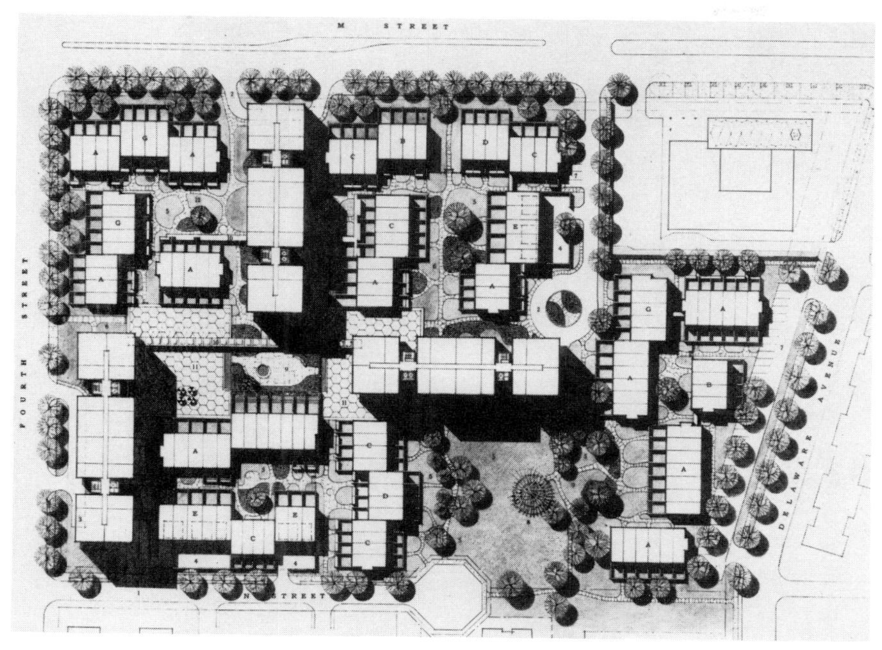
M STREET
FOURTH STREET
DELAWARE AVENUE
N STREET

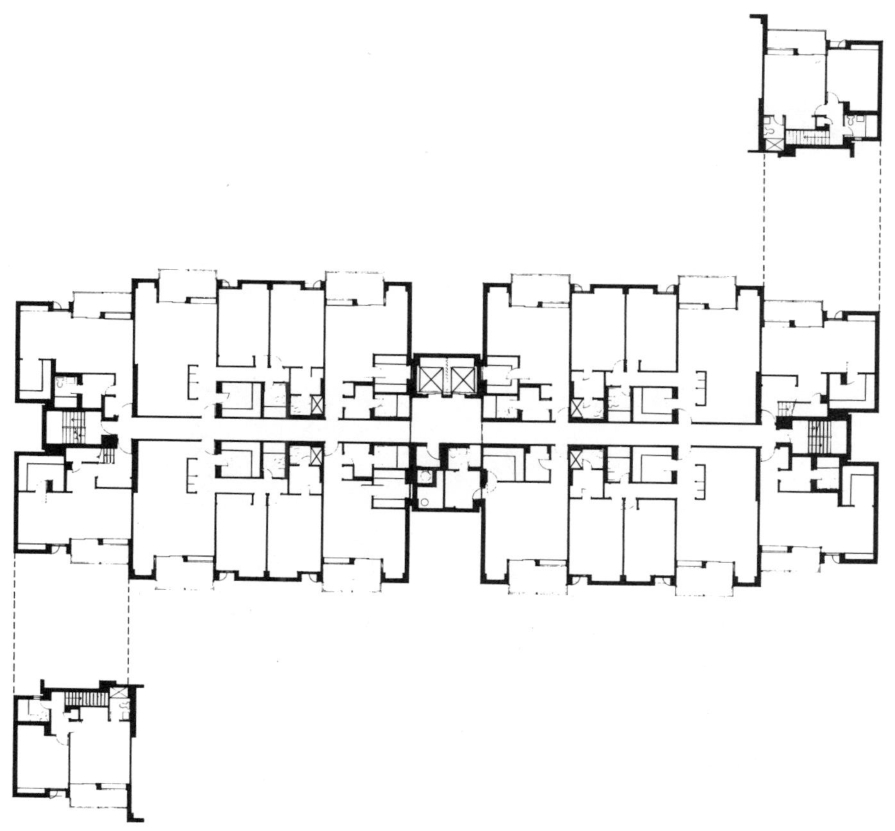

13

WILLIAMS STREET STUDENT HOUSING
Middletown, Connecticut

Architect:
ULRICH FRANZEN & ASSOCIATES
New York, New York

Number of dwelling units: 119
Highrise: 11—efficiency
72—one bedroom
1—manager
7—lounges
Lowrise: 20—four bedroom
8—ten bedroom
Gross floor area: 106,000 sf (open, on grade parking
Construction cost: $3,167,500 (including carpeting)
$396,000 (site work including abnormal soil conditions)
$29.87/sf (not including site work)
$26,618/unit (not including site work)
Year of bid: 1972
Site area: 3.45 acres
34.5 units/acre
User: students (middle income)
Financing: HUD College Housing Program Debt Service Grant

Photo credit: Norman McGrath

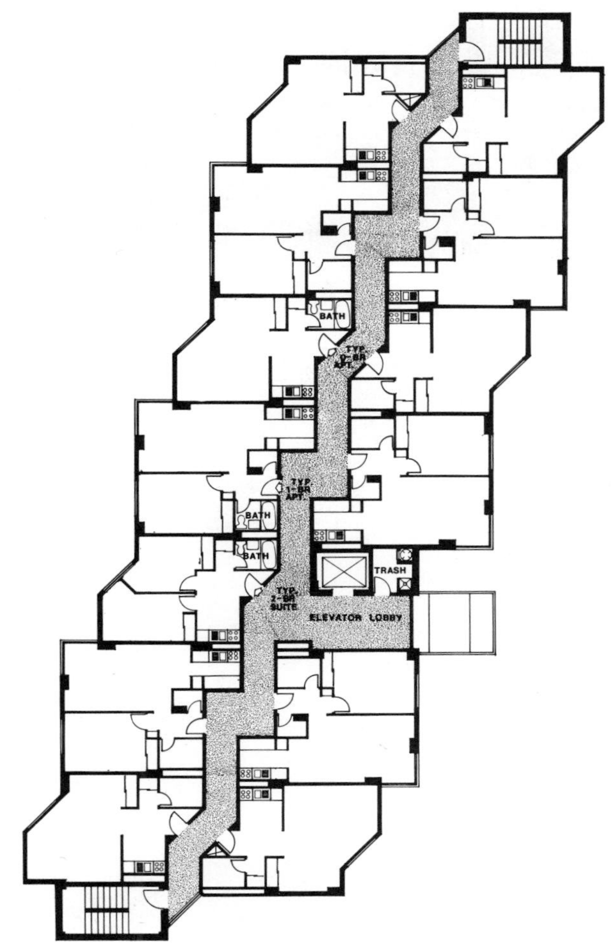

14

2000 BROADWAY
San Francisco, California

Architect:
BACKEN, ARRIGONI & ROSS, INC.
San Francisco, California

Number of dwelling units: 221
- 203—efficiency
- 6—two bedroom
- 6—two bedroom ("townhouse")
- 6—three bedroom ("townhouse")

Gross floor area: 245,180 sf (including garage)
Construction cost: $4,750,000 (including garage)
$19.37/sf
$21,493/unit
Year of bid: 1969
Site area: 0.51 acres
433 units/acre
User: middle income
Financing: FHA

Photo credit: Ed Stoecklein

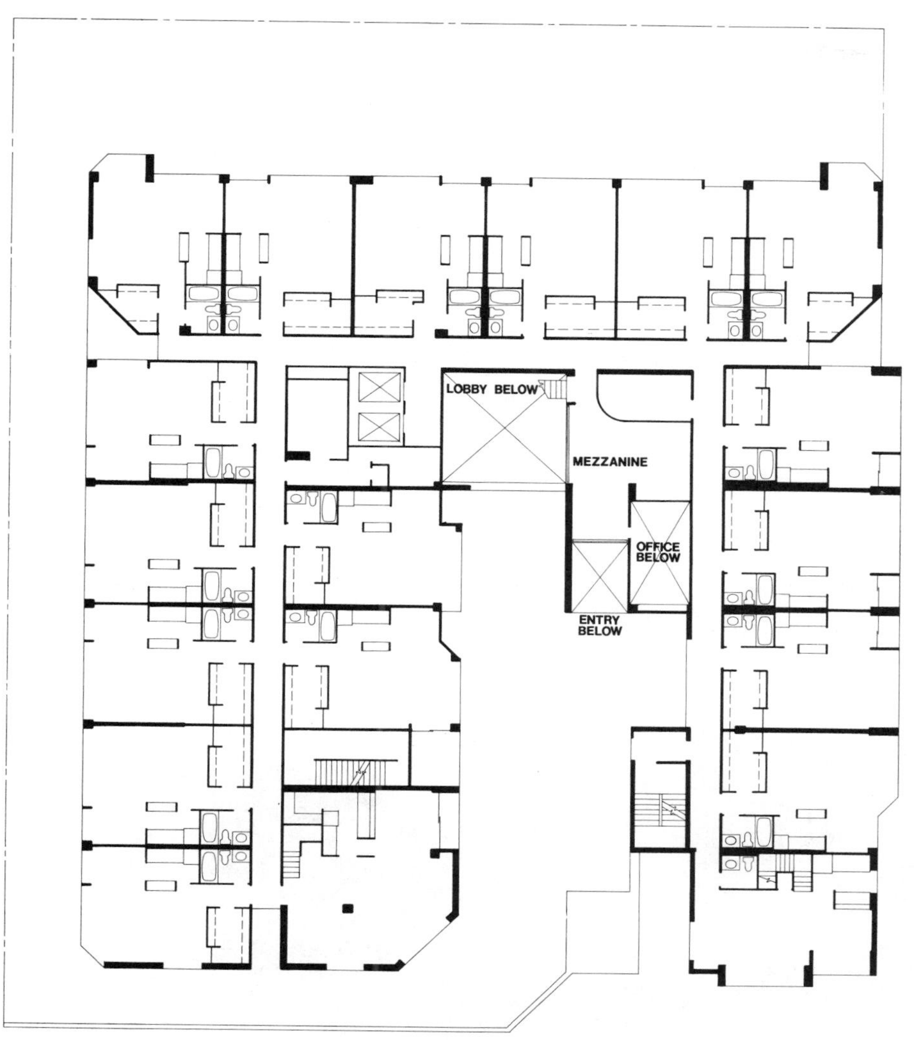
LOBBY BELOW
MEZZANINE
OFFICE BELOW
ENTRY BELOW

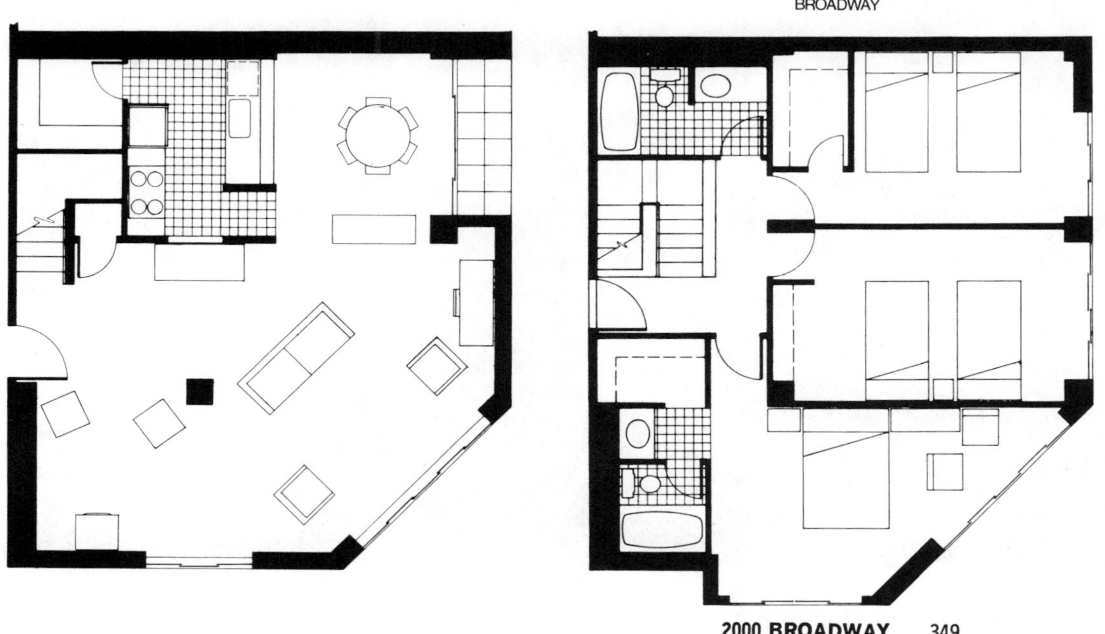
BROADWAY

15 EAST MIDTOWN PLAZA

New York, New York

Architect:
DAVIS BRODY & ASSOCIATES
New York, New York

Number of dwelling units:	737 (breakdown unavailable)
Gross floor area:	1,075,500 sf (including parking)
Construction cost:	$22,685,000 (including parking)
	$21.00/sf
	$30,780/unit
Year of bid:	1969
Site area:	3.5 acres
	210 units/acre
User:	middle income
Financing:	Mitchell-Lama

Photo credit: Robert Gray

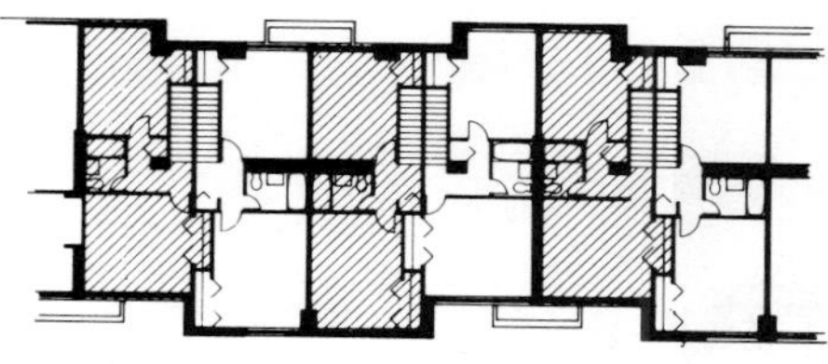

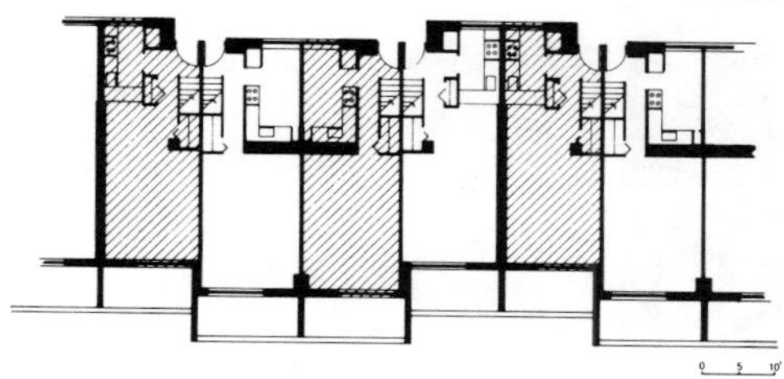

Typical duplex floors

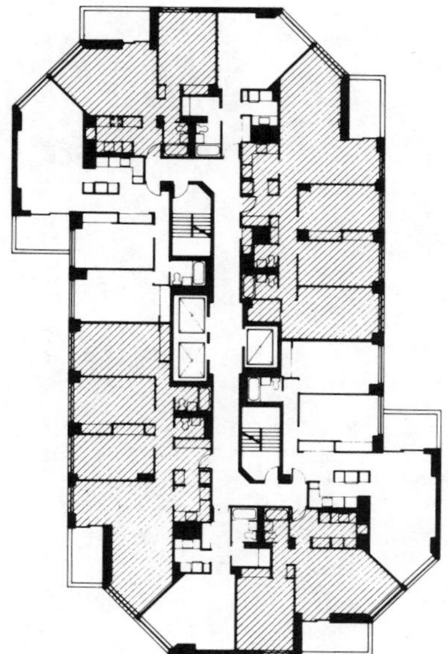

Typical tower floor

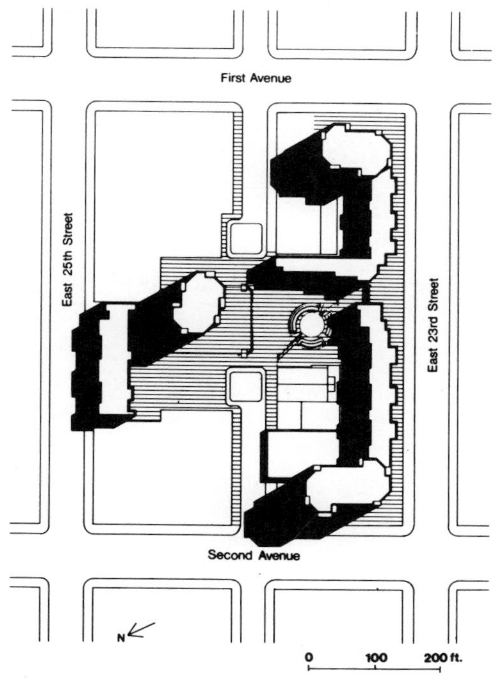

16

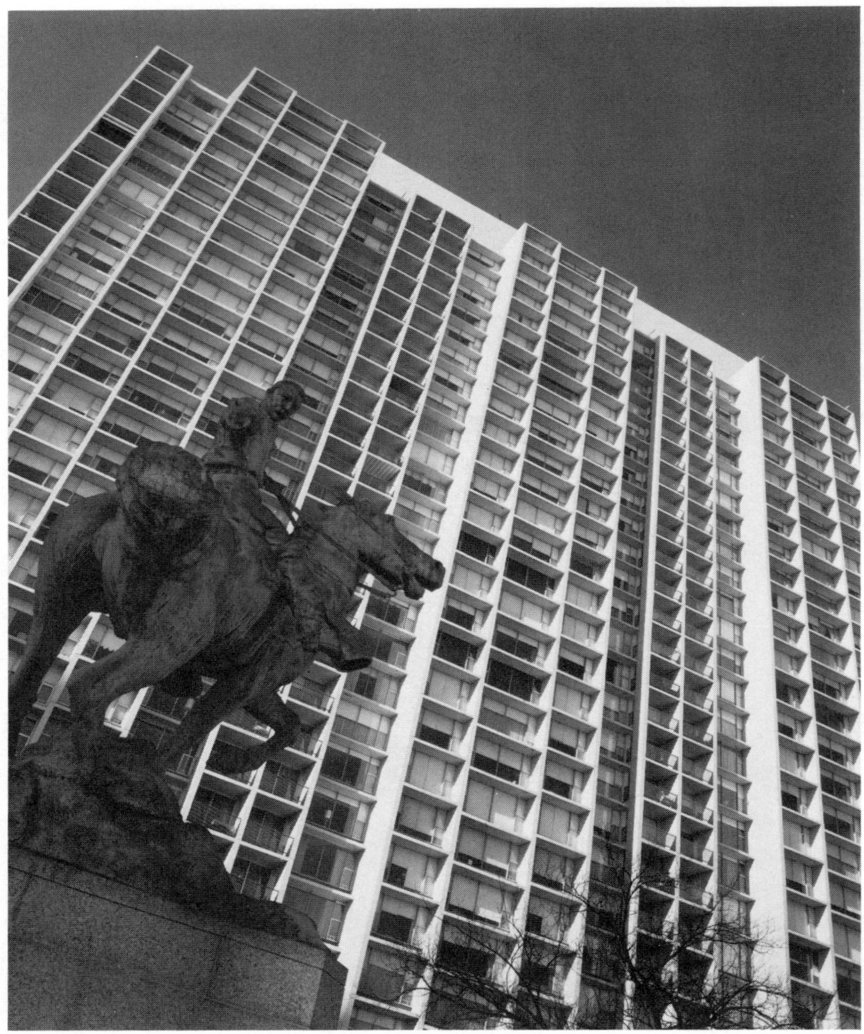

HARBOR HOUSE
Chicago, Illinois

Architect:
HAUSNER & MACSAI
Chicago, Illinois

Number of dwelling units: 278
50—one bedroom
175—two bedroom
53—three bedroom

Gross floor area: 488,000 sf (including garage)
Construction cost: $6,856,000
$14.00/sf
$24,662/unit
Year of bid: 1965
Site area: 1.08 acres
257.5 units/acre
User: middle to upper income
Financing: conventional

Photo credit: Bill Engdahl/Hedrich-Blessing

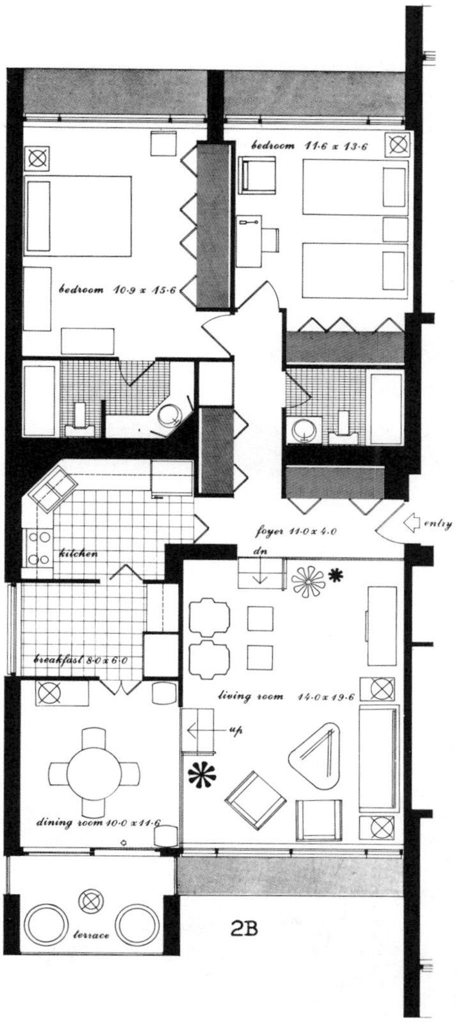

bedroom 11·6 x 13·6
bedroom 10·9 x 15·6
foyer 11·0 x 4·0
entry
dn
kitchen
breakfast 8·0 x 6·0
living room 14·0 x 19·6
up
dining room 10·0 x 11·6
terrace
2B

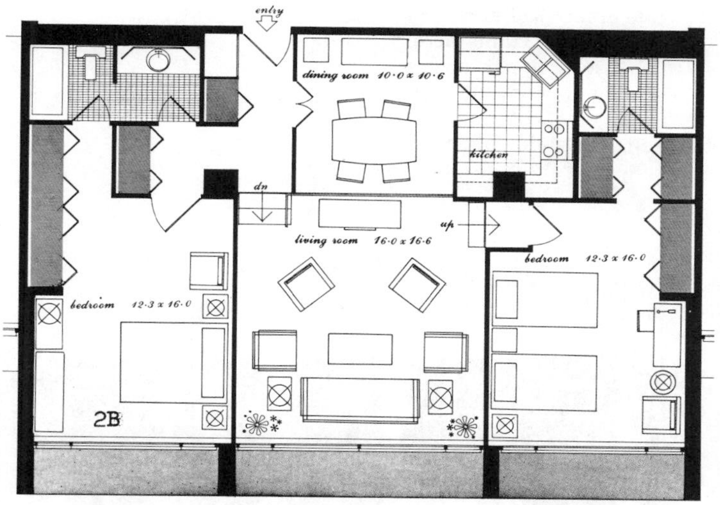

entry
dining room 10·0 x 10·6
kitchen
dn
living room 16·0 x 16·6
up
bedroom 12·3 x 16·0
bedroom 12·3 x 16·0
2B

1 B
2 B
2 B
2 B
3 B
2 B
3 B
2 B
1 B
2 B
2 B

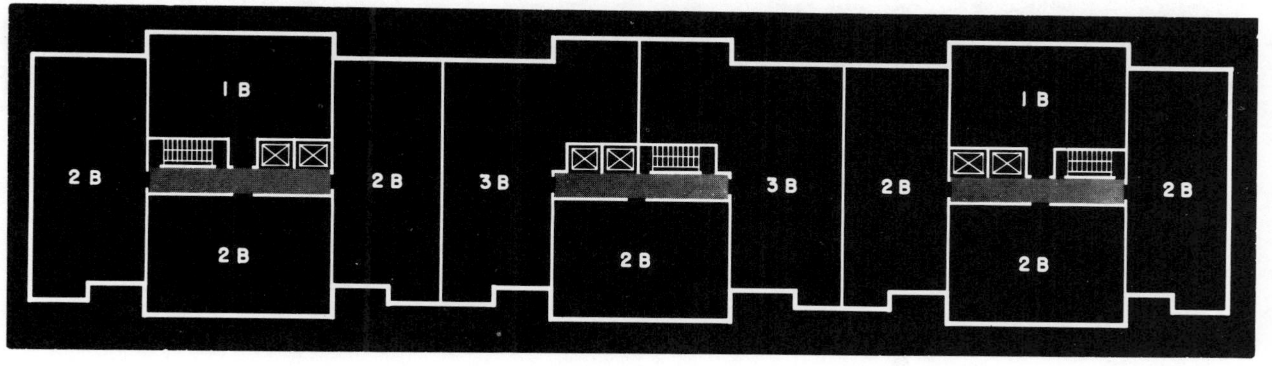

17 1500 SHERIDAN ROAD

Wilmette, Illinois

Architect:
HAUSNER & MACSAI
Chicago, Illinois

Number of dwelling units: 111 (condominium)
- 1—efficiency
- 1—one bedroom
- 38—two bedroom
- 40—three bedroom
- 21—four bedroom

Gross floor area:	326,500 sf (including garage)
Construction cost:	$4,770,000 (including garage)
	$14.63/sf
	$42,973/unit
Year of bid:	1968
Site area:	3.37 acres
	33 units/acre
User:	upper income
Financing:	conventional

Photo credit: Orlando Cabanban

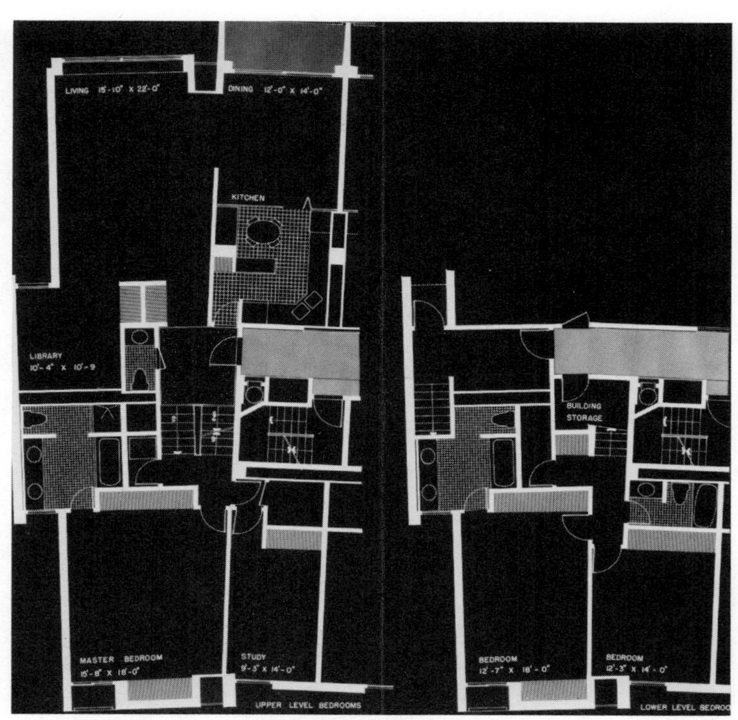

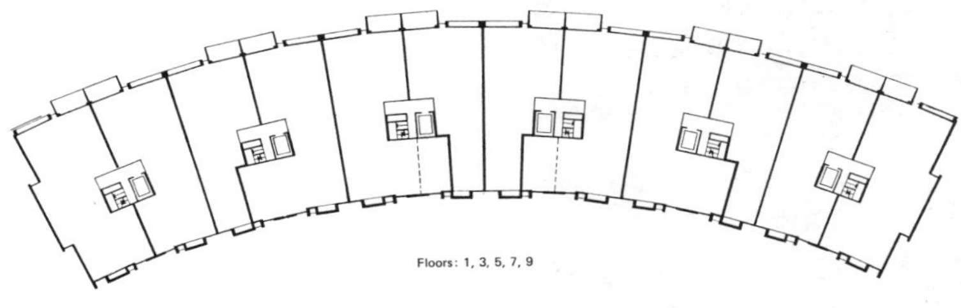

Floors: 1, 3, 5, 7, 9

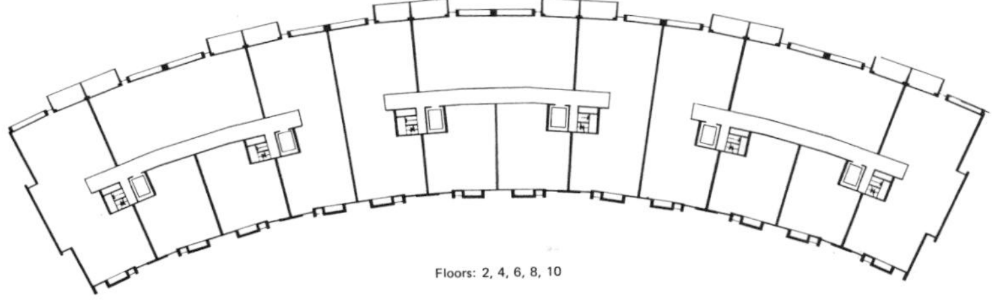

Floors: 2, 4, 6, 8, 10

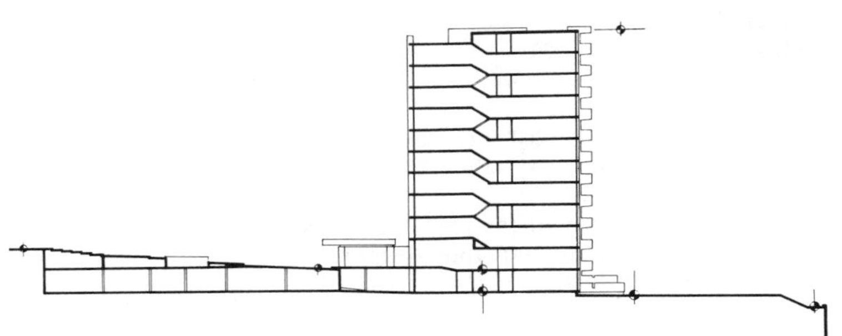

18

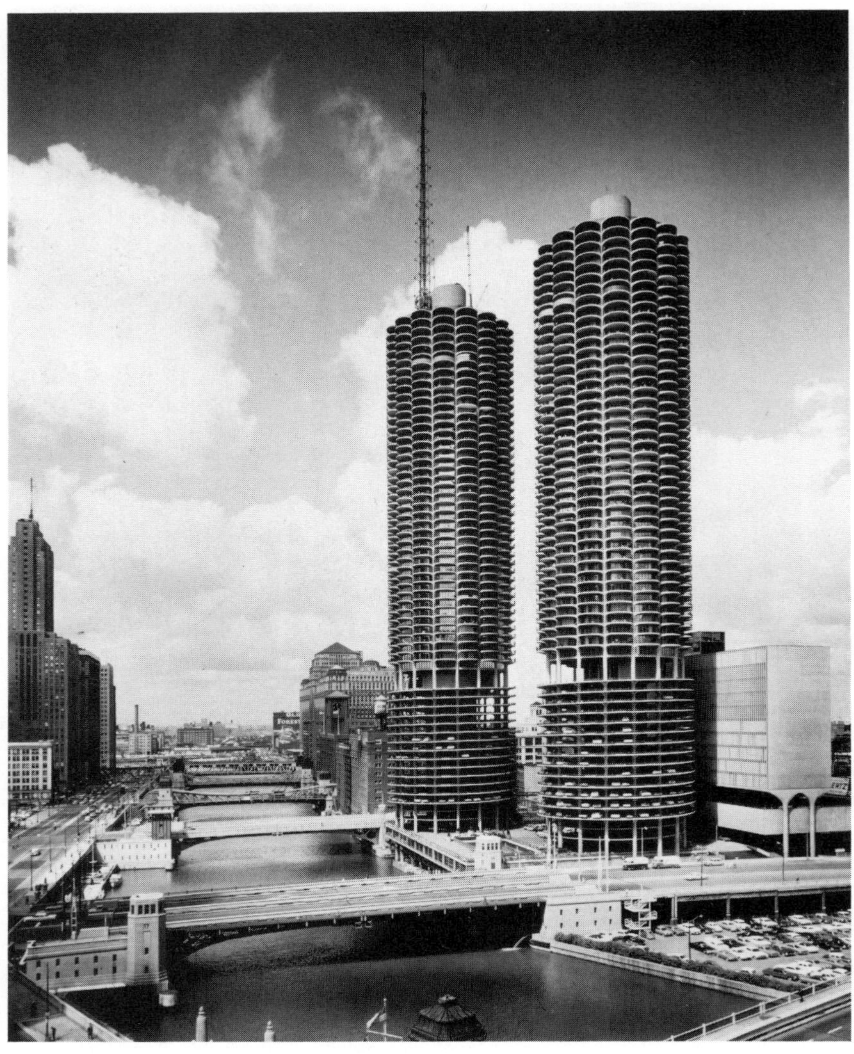

MARINA CITY
Chicago, Illinois

Architect:
BERTRAND GOLDBERG ASSOCIATES
Chicago, Illinois

Number of dwelling units: 896
128—efficiency @2—256
288—one bedroom @2—576
32—two bedroom @2—64

Gross floor area: 1,192,000 sf (towers only include parking and balconies @$\frac{1}{2}$)
Construction cost: approximately $11 to $13/sf
Year of bid: 1960
Site area: part of complex development
User: middle to upper income
Financing: FHA

Photo credit: Suter/Hedrich-Blessing

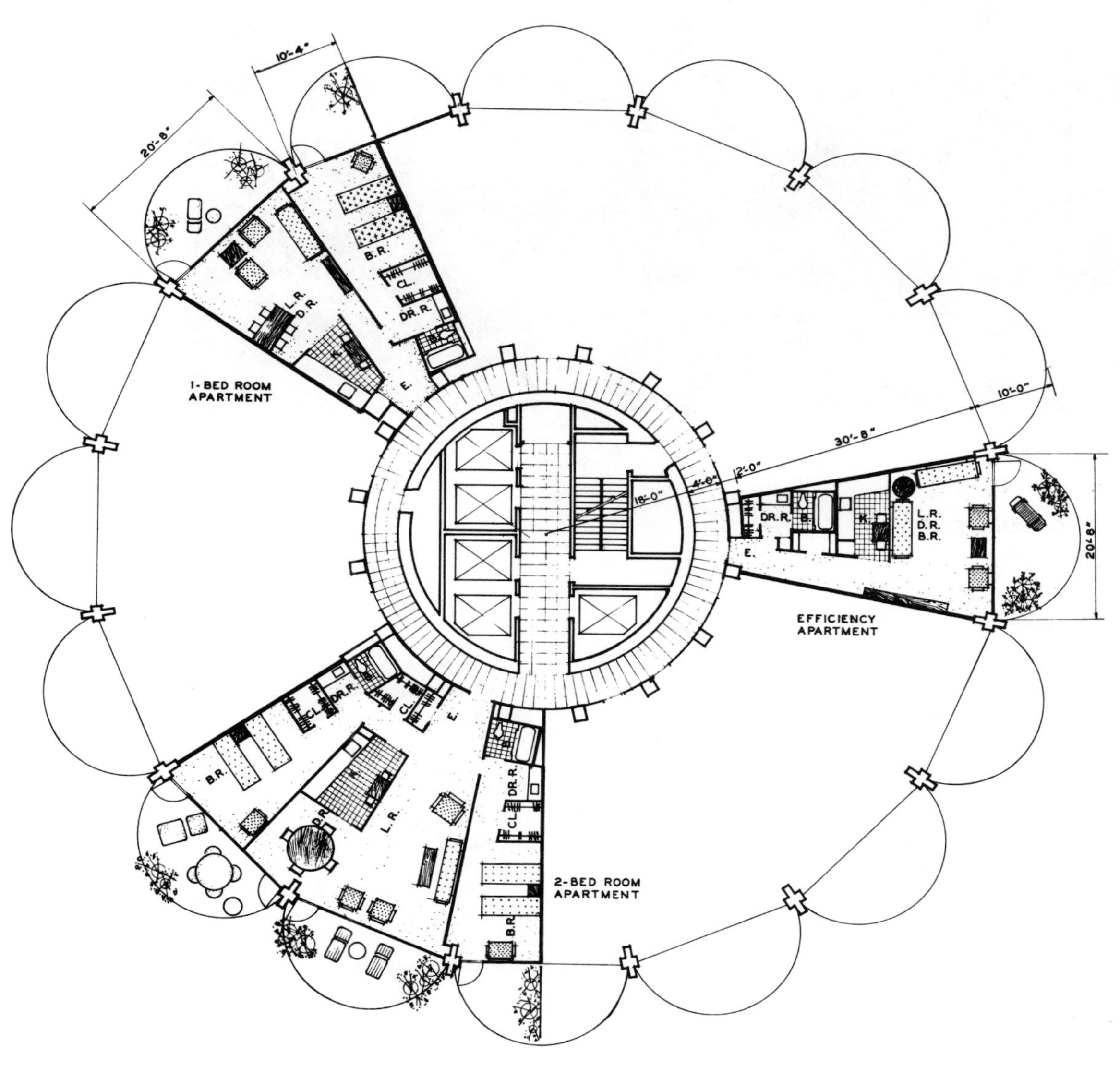
10'-4"
20'-8"
B.R.
CL.
DR.R.
L.R.
D.R.
K.
E.
1-BED ROOM
APARTMENT
10'-0"
30'-8"
2'-0"
4'-0"
18'-0"
DR.R.
K.
L.R.
D.R.
B.R.
E.
20'-8"
EFFICIENCY
APARTMENT
B.R.
CL.
DR.R.
CL.
E.
D.R.
L.R.
DR.R.
CL.
B.R.
2-BED ROOM
APARTMENT

19

ARTHUR SCHOMBURG PLAZA
New York, New York

Architect:
GRUZEN & PARTNERS
New York, New York

Number of dwelling units: 600
Towers: 17—efficiency @2
68—one bedroom @2
102—two bedroom @2
85—three bedroom @2
Central Corridor: 28—four bedroom
28—five bedroom
Gross floor area: 585,530 sf
462,000 sf towers
85,460 sf central corridor
31,600 sf community
6,470 sf retail

Construction cost: $23,000,000 (including garage, community, and retail)
$39.28 sf
$38,333/unit
Year of bid: 1971
Site area: 1.83 acres
328 units/acre
User: 60% moderate income
30% low income
10% elderly
Financing: New York State Urban Development Corporation

Photo credit: David Hirsch

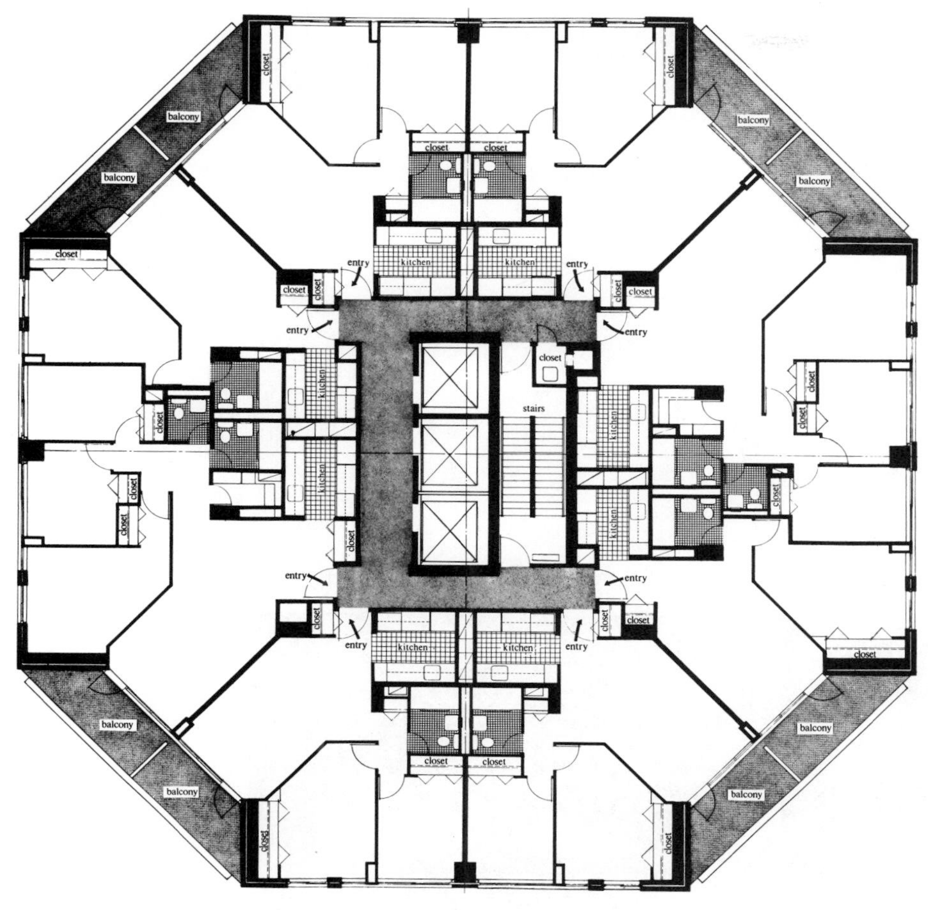

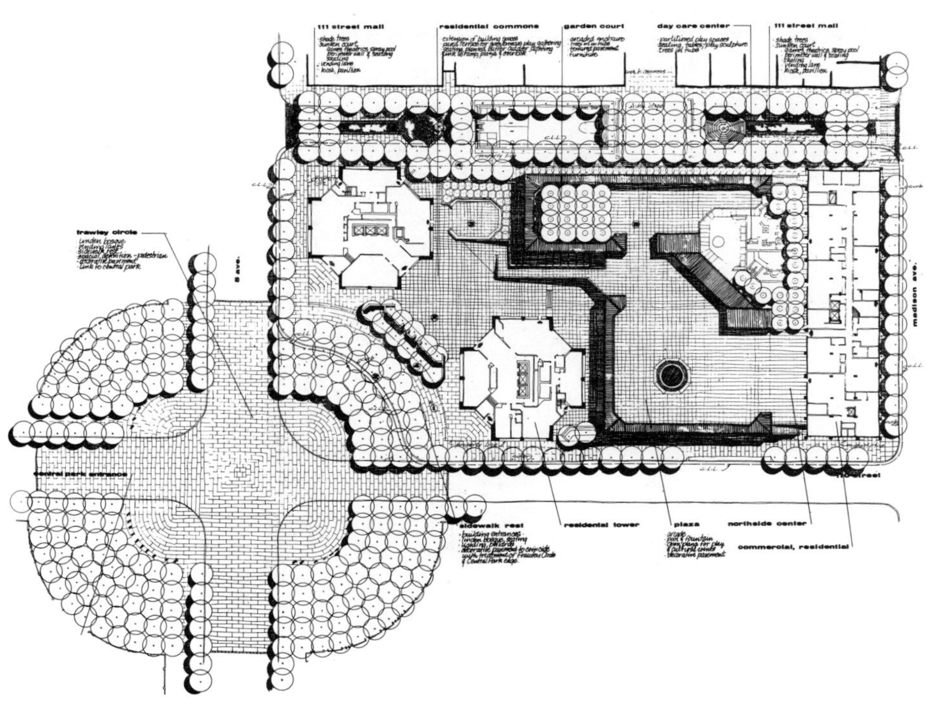

20 DORCHESTER APARTMENTS
Chicago, Illinois

Architect:
SKIDMORE, OWINGS & MERRILL
Chicago, Illinois

Number of dwelling units: 35
14—two bedroom
14—three bedroom
7—two bedroom townhouse

Gross floor area:	96,200 sf (including parking)
Construction cost:	$1,300,000
	$13.50/sf
	$37,140/unit
Year of bid:	1966
Site area:	0.51 acres
	69 units/acre
User:	upper income
Financing:	conventional

Photo credit: Ezra Stoller

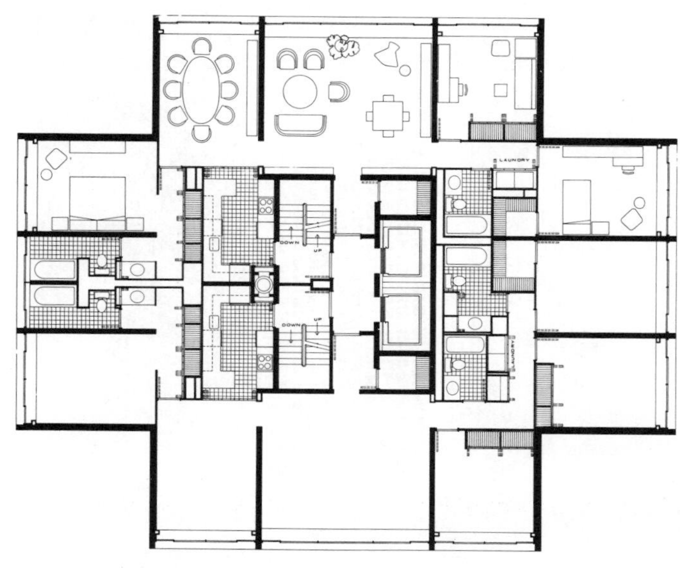
LAUNDRY
DOWN
UP
DOWN
UP

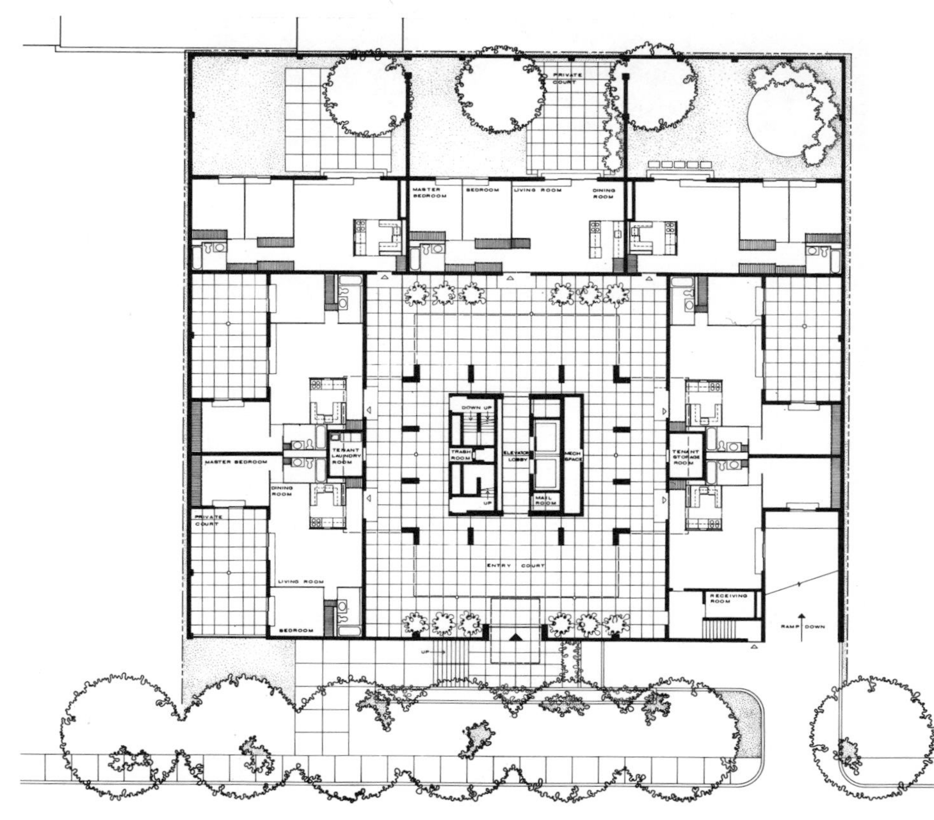
PRIVATE COURT
MASTER BEDROOM
BEDROOM
LIVING ROOM
DINING ROOM
DOWN UP
TENANT LAUNDRY ROOM
TRASH ROOM
ELEVATOR LOBBY
MECH SPACE
MAIL ROOM
TENANT STORAGE ROOM
MASTER BEDROOM
DINING ROOM
PRIVATE COURT
ENTRY COURT
LIVING ROOM
BEDROOM
RECEIVING ROOM
RAMP DOWN
UP

21

1110 LAKE SHORE DRIVE
Chicago, Illinois

Architect:
HAUSNER & MACSAI
Chicago, Illinois

Number of dwelling units: 74 two bedroom apartments (condominium)
Gross floor area: 166,000 sf (including garage)
Construction cost: $3,070,000
$18.49/sf
$41,496/unit
Year of bid: 1968
Site area: 0.25 acres
296 units/acre
User: upper income
Financing: conventional

Photo credit: Hedrich-Blessing

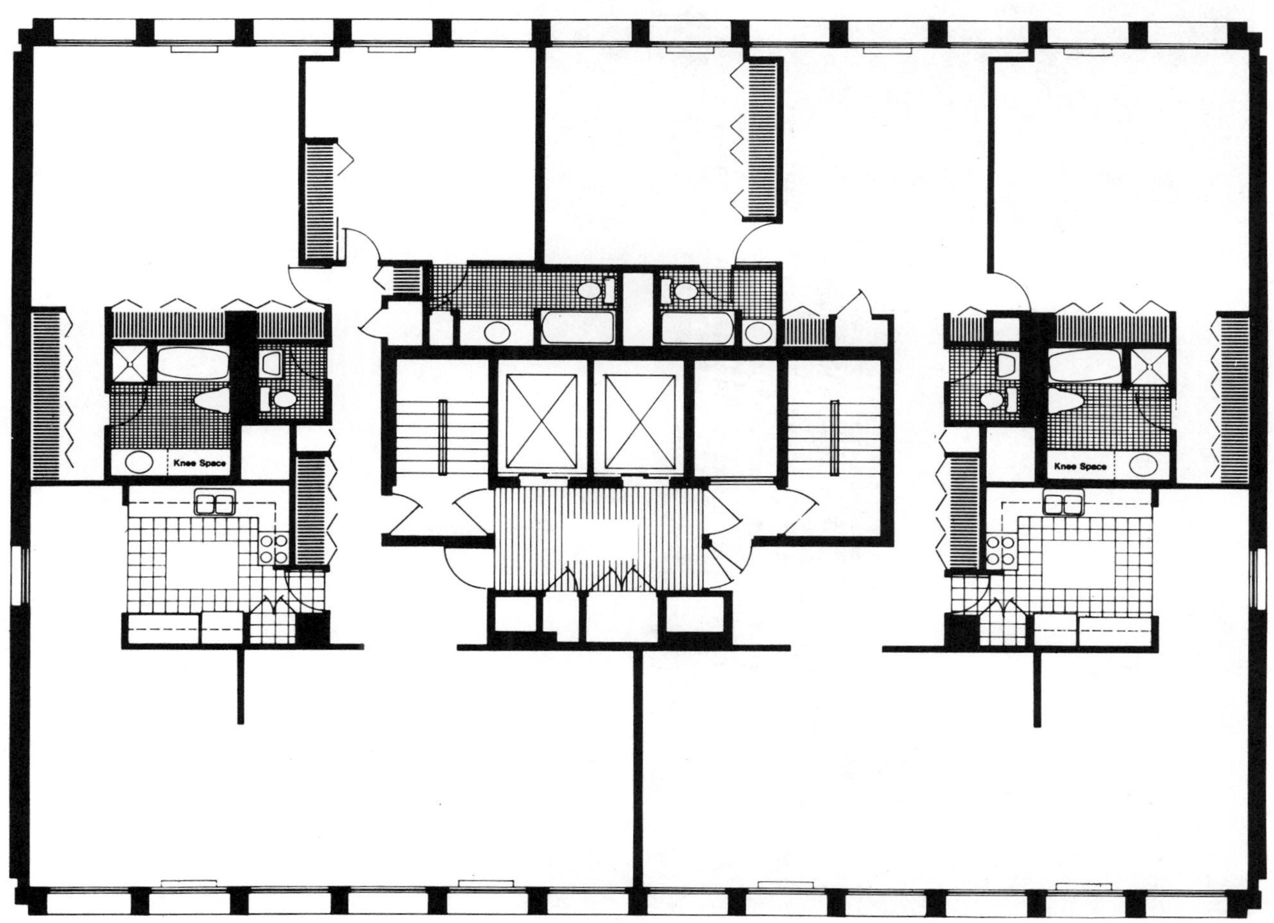

22 **NEWBERRY PLAZA**
Chicago, Illinois

Architects:
EZRA GORDON—JACK LEVIN & ASSOCIATES
Chicago, Illinois

Number of dwelling units: 624 apartments (+15 townhouses)
221—efficiency
234—one bedroom
143—two bedroom
26—three bedroom

Gross floor area: 930,000 ft (including garage + 80,000 commercial, not including townhouses)
Construction cost: $13,661,000 (not including townhouses)
$14.68/sf
$21,893/unit
Year of bid: 1971
Site area: 1.63 acres
392 units/acre
User: upper to middle income
Financing: FHA 207

Photo credit: Orlando Cabanban

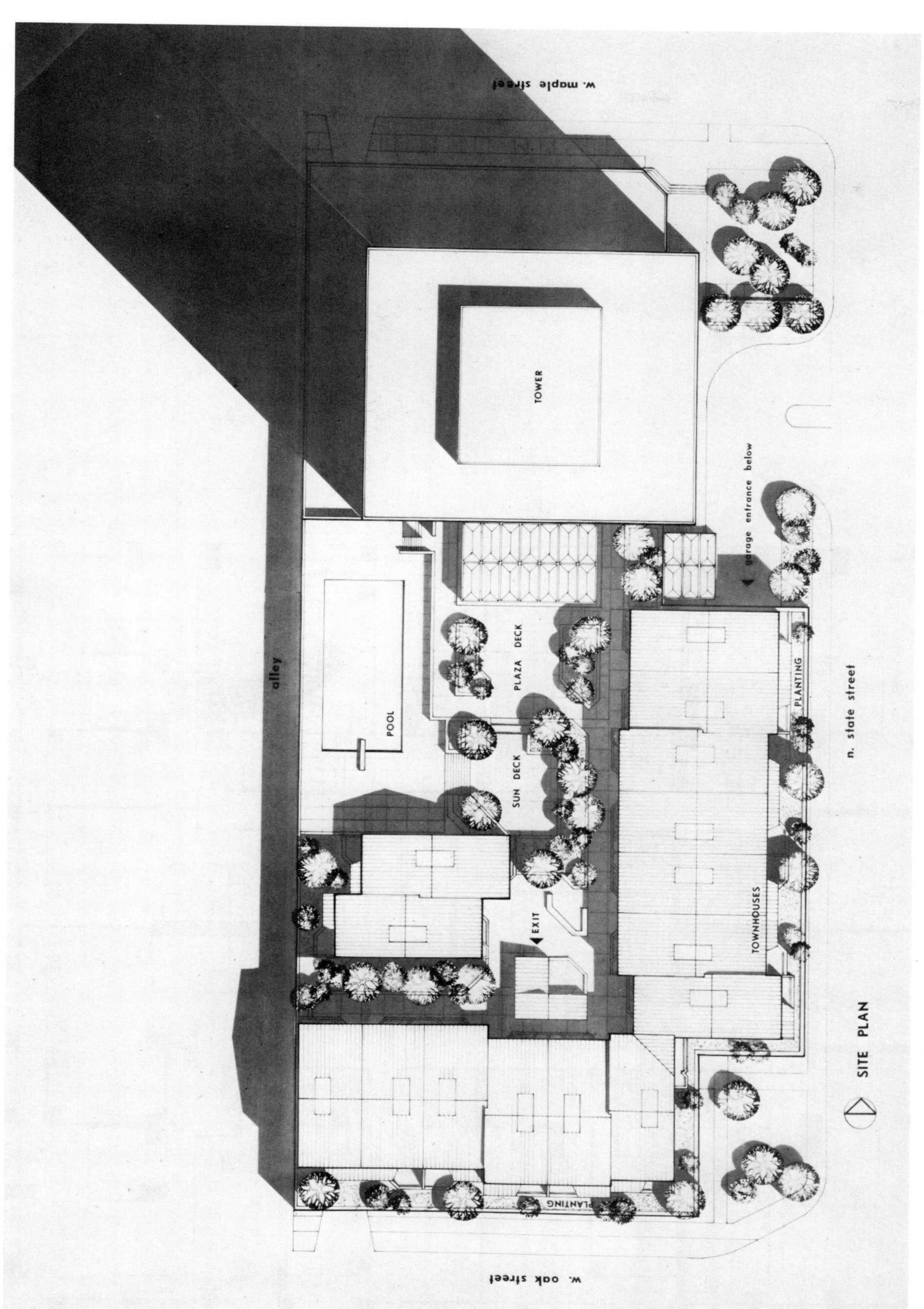
w. maple street
TOWER
garage entrance below
PLAZA DECK
POOL
alley
SUN DECK
EXIT
TOWNHOUSES
PLANTING
n. state street
PLANTING
w. oak street
SITE PLAN

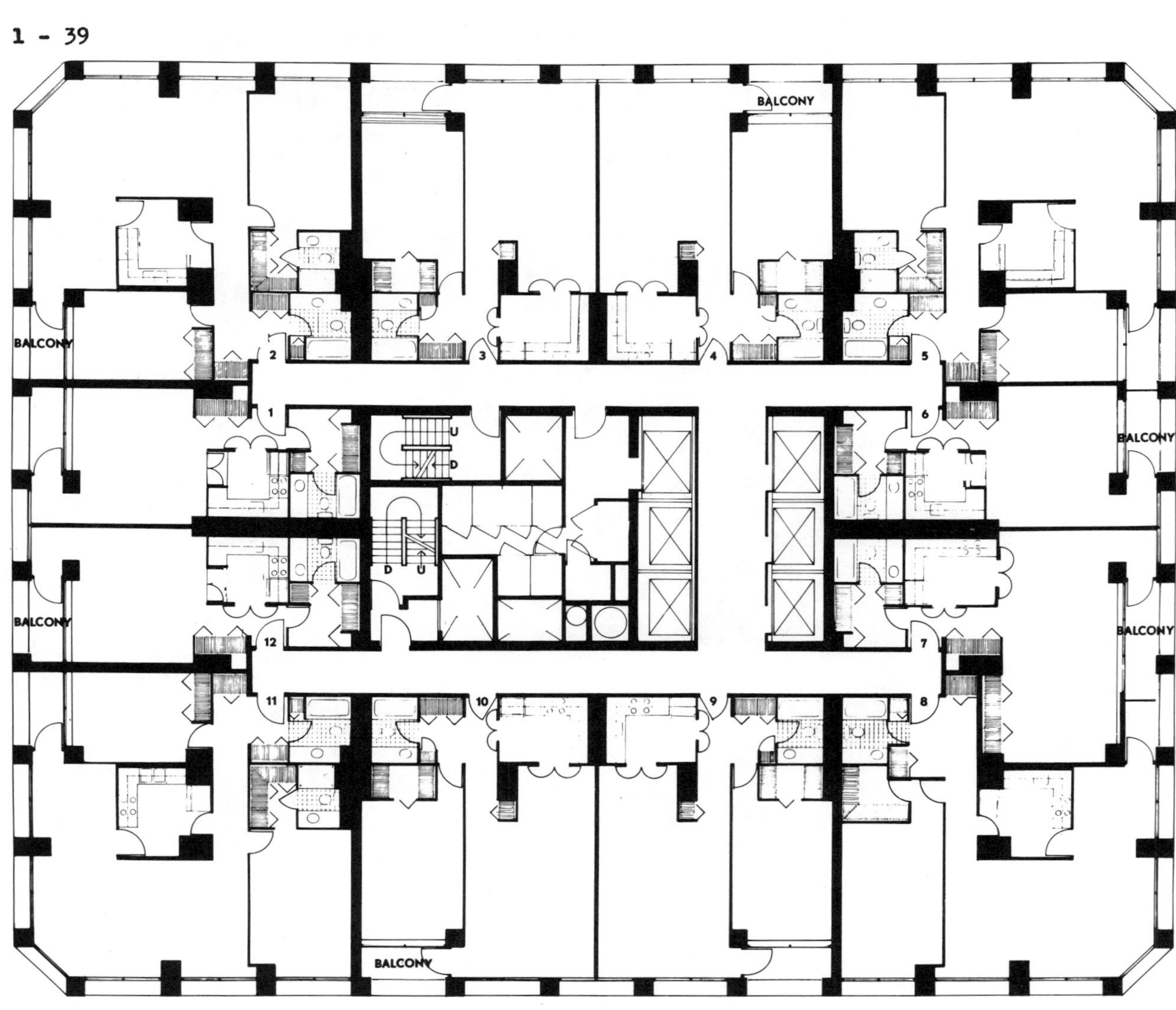
1 - 39
BALCONY
BALCONY
BALCONY
BALCONY
BALCONY
BALCONY
1
2
3
4
5
6
7
8
9
10
11
12
U
D
D
U

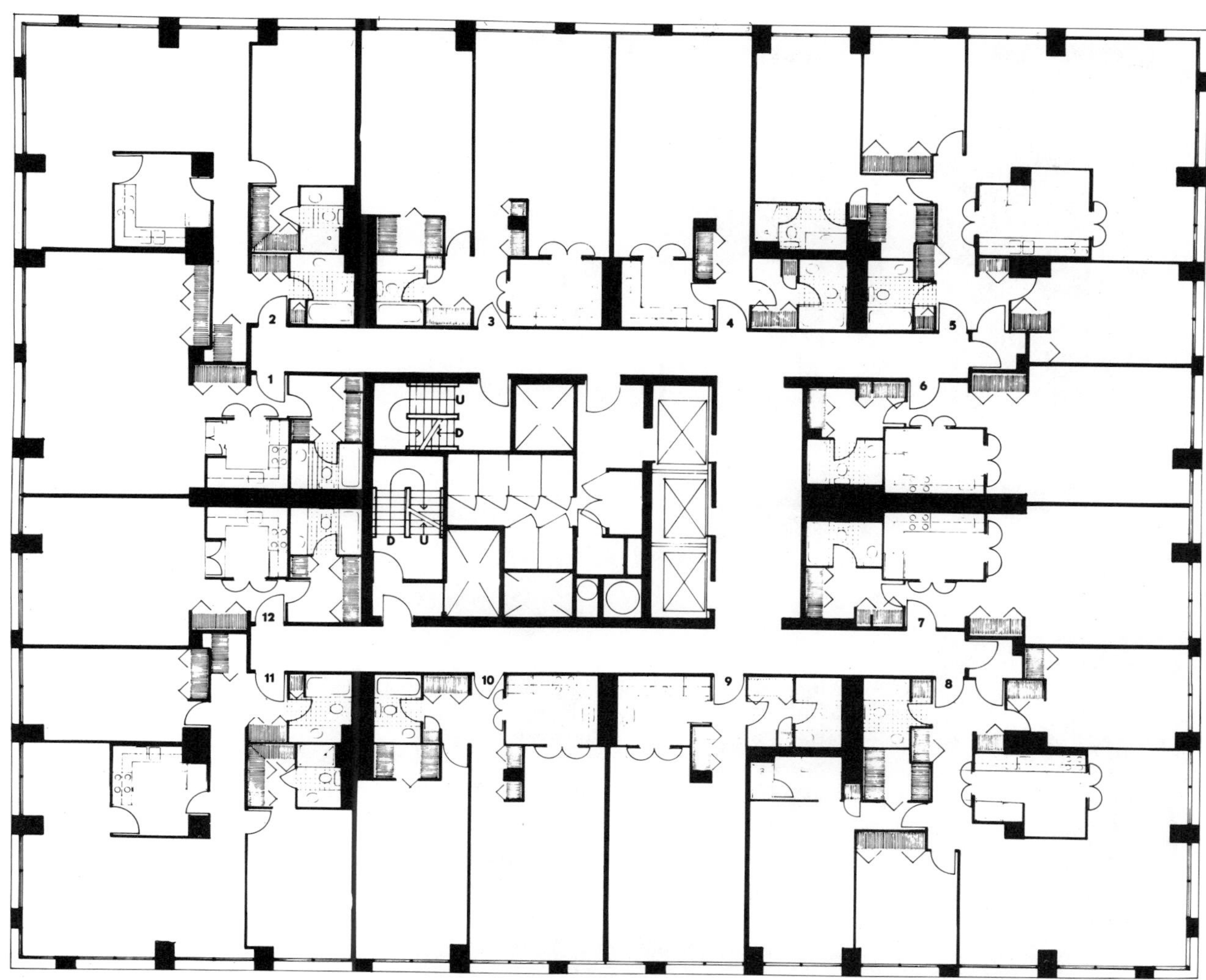

40 - 52

23

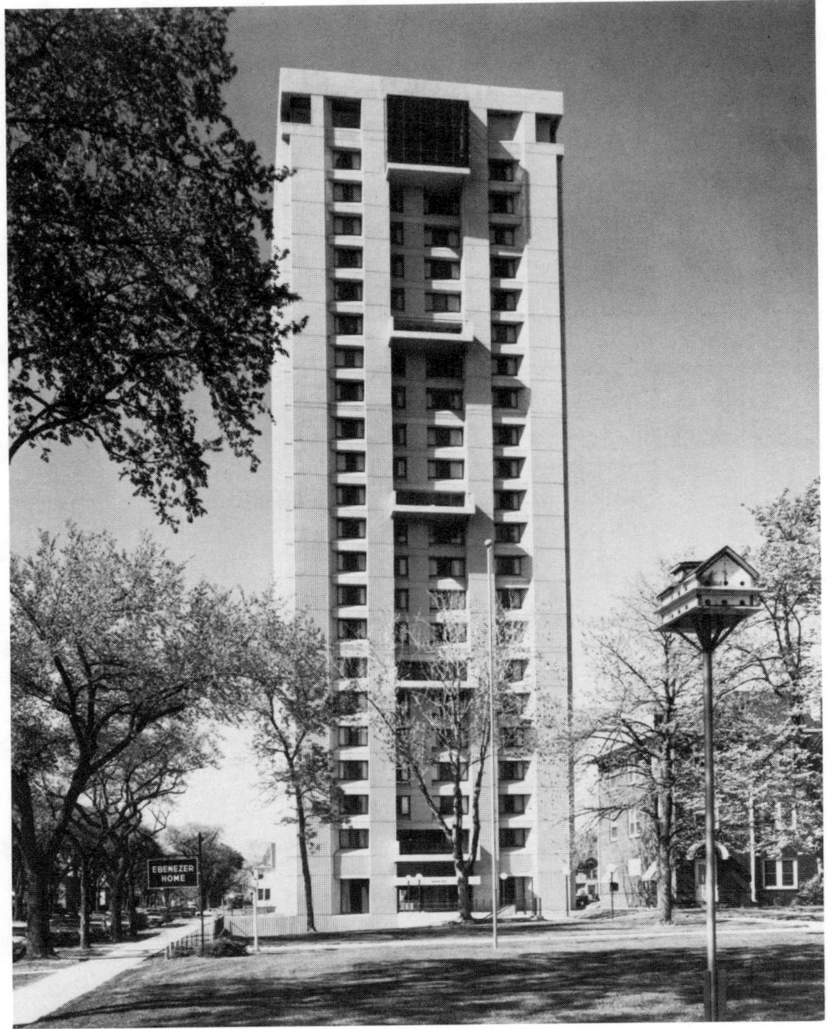

EBENEZER TOWER
Minneapolis, Minnesota

Architect:
THORSEN & THORSHOV ASSOCIATES, INC.
Minneapolis, Minnesota

Number of dwelling units: 200
84—efficiency
114—one bedroom
2—two bedroom
Gross floor area: 141,240 sf (open, on grade parking)
Construction cost: $2,739,000
$19.39/sf
$13,695/unit
Year of bid: 1969
Site area: 0.92 acres
217.5 units/acre
User: elderly
Financing: HUD Program No. 202

Photo credit: G. Edwards

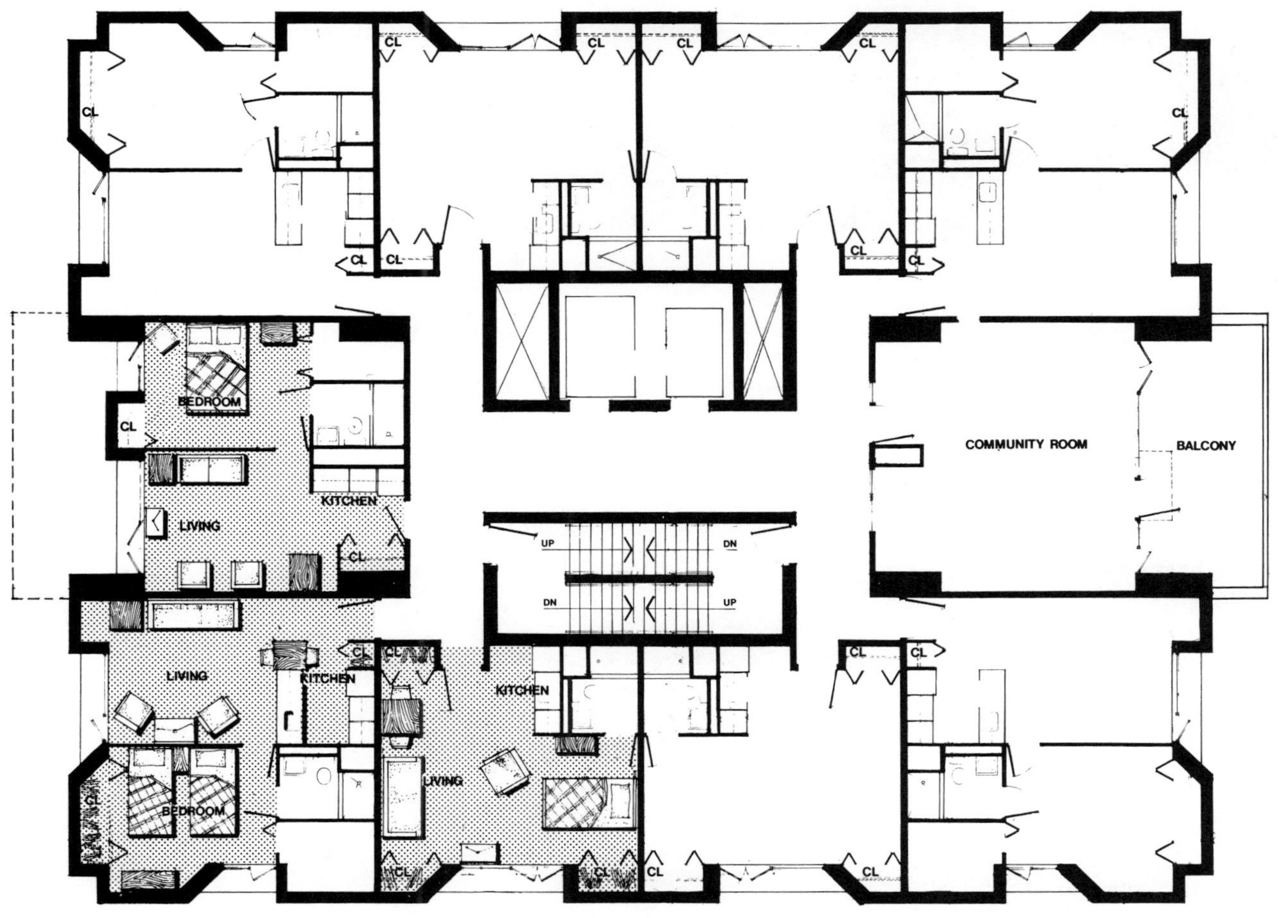
CL
CL
CL
CL
CL
CL
CL
CL
CL
BEDROOM
CL
KITCHEN
LIVING
CL
COMMUNITY ROOM
BALCONY
UP
DN
DN
UP
LIVING
KITCHEN
CL
CL
KITCHEN
CL
CL
BEDROOM
LIVING
CL
CL
CL
CL
CL

24

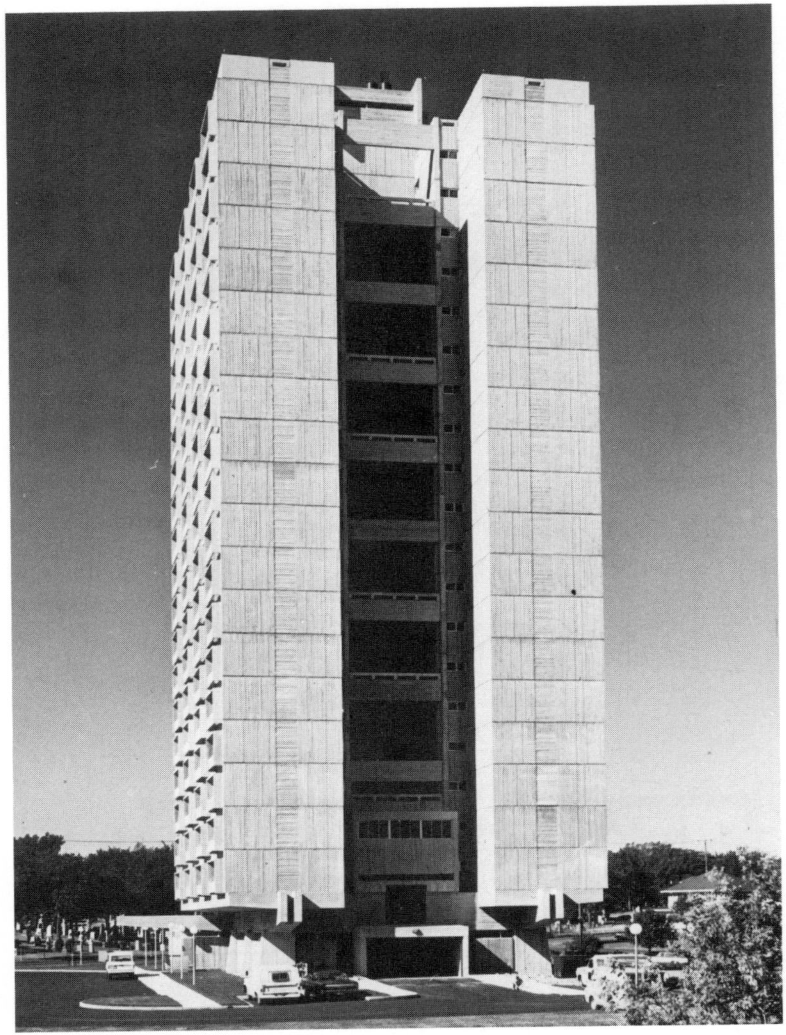

727 FRONT AVENUE
St. Paul, Minnesota

Architect:
FREERKS/SPERL/FLYNN
St. Paul, Minnesota

Number of dwelling units: 151
150—one bedroom
1—two bedroom
Gross floor area: 117,420 sf (open, on grade parking)
Construction cost: $1,954,000
$16.64/sf
$12,940/unit
Year of bid: 1967
User: low income (elderly)

Photo credit: Robert Sperl

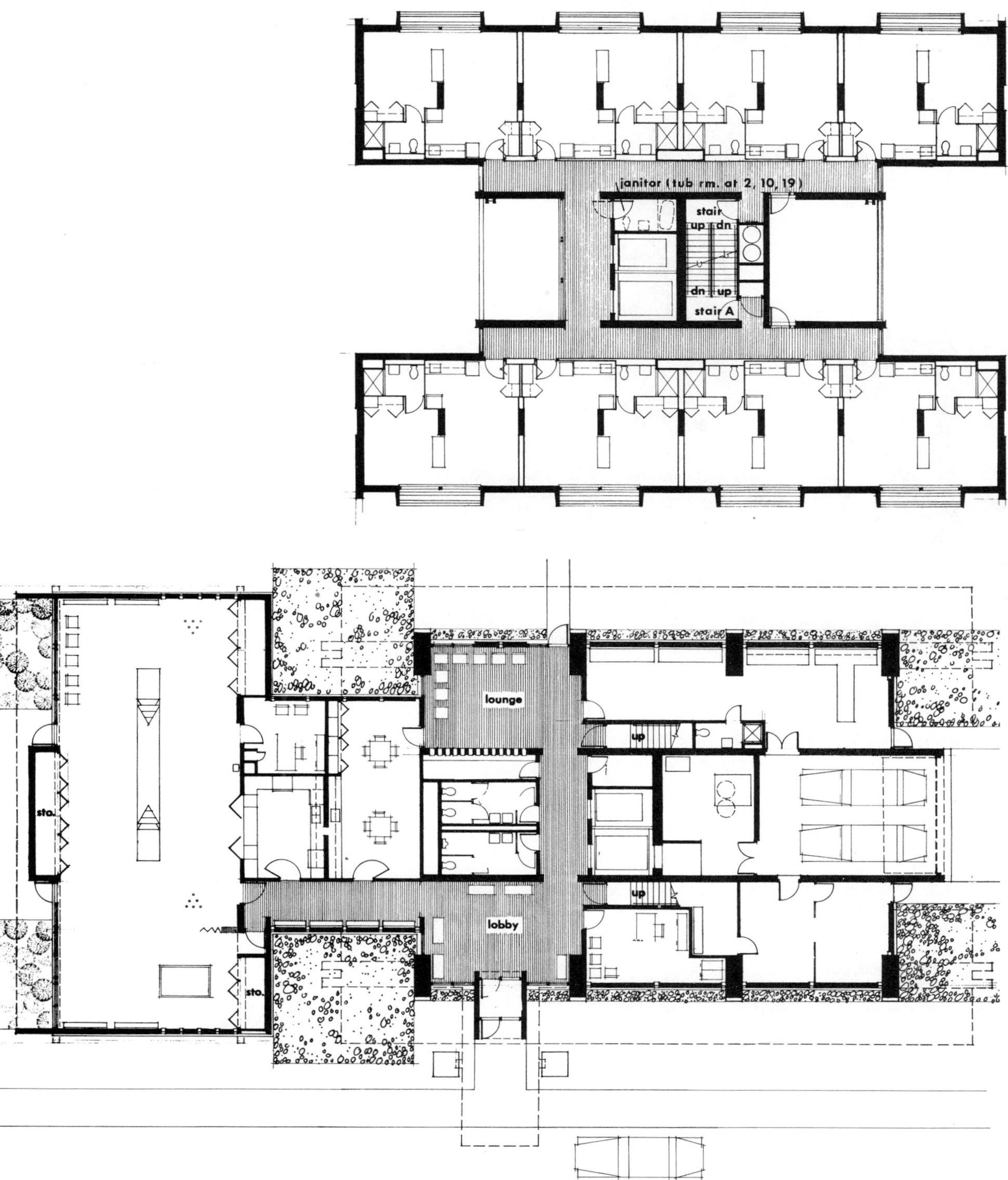

janitor (tub rm. at 2, 10, 19)
stair
up
dn
dn
up
stair A
lounge
up
sto.
up
lobby
sto.

25

LAKE POINT TOWER
Chicago, Illinois

Architect:
SCHIPPOREIT & HEINRICH
Chicago, Illinois

Number of dwelling units: 900
120—efficiency
360—one bedroom
300—two bedroom
120—three bedroom
Gross floor area: 1,732,000 sf (including garage)
Construction cost: not available
Year of bid: 1965
Site area: 2.92 acres
308 units/acre
User: upper income
Financing: conventional

Photo credit: Hedrich-Blessing

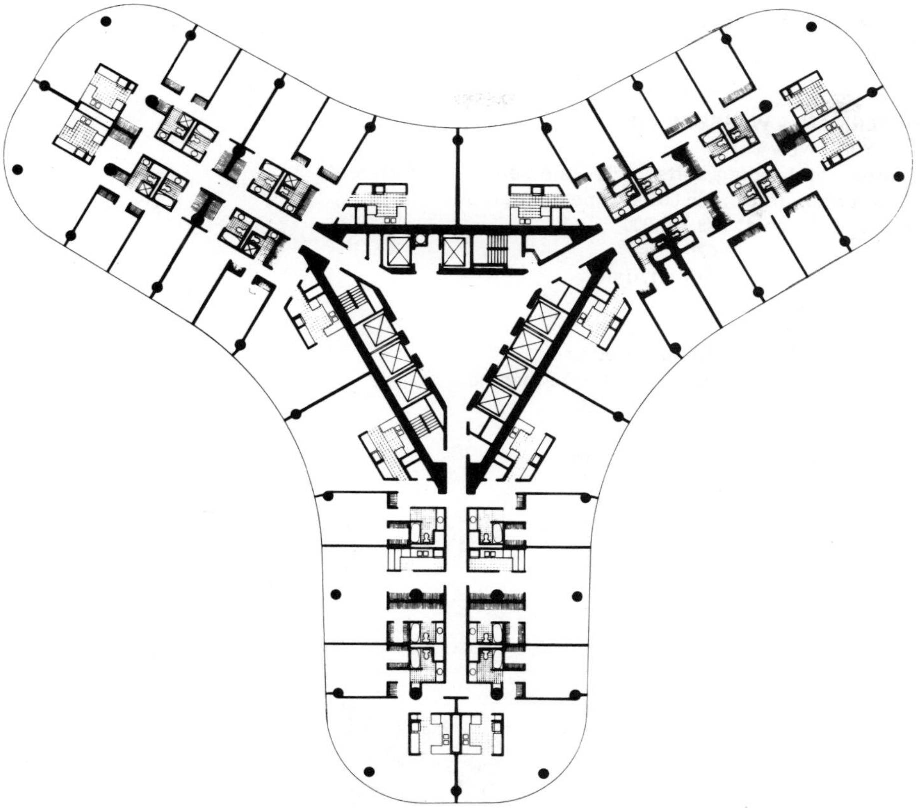

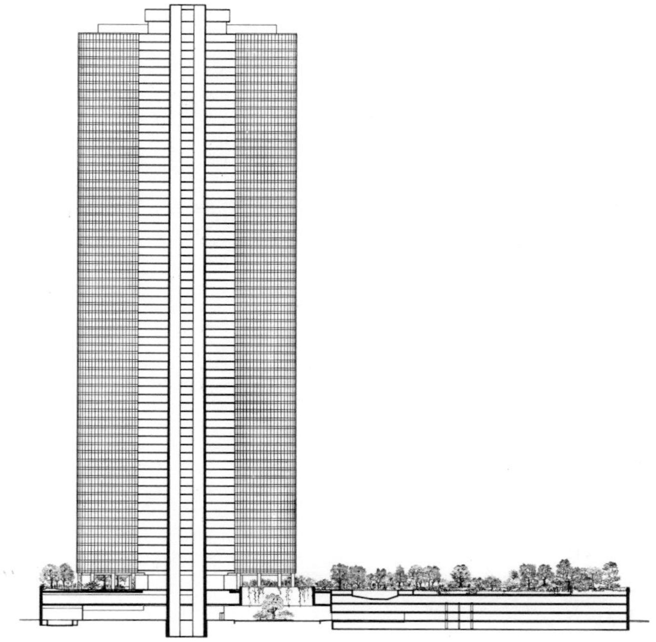

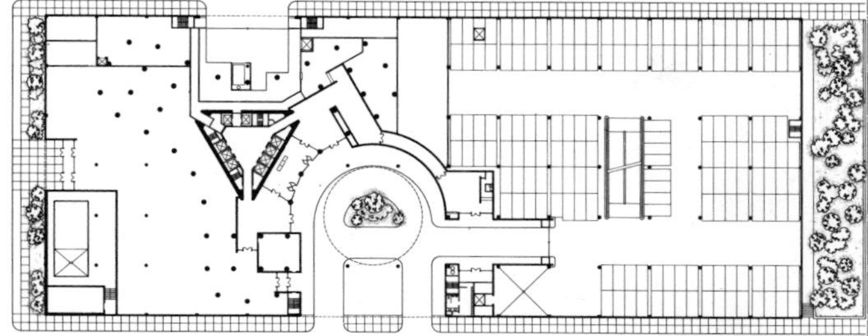

26

SOUTHVIEW TOWERS
Rochester, New York

Architect:
HOBERMAN & WASSERMAN
New York, New York
Number of dwelling units: 193—one bedroom apartments
Gross floor area: 145,000 sf (open, on grade parking)
Construction cost: $3,756,000
$25.00/sf
$19,461/unit
Year of bid: 1971
Site area: 1.6 acres
120 units/acre
User: low to moderate income
Financing: UDC, FHA 236

Photo credit: Norman Hoberman

27

Robert Gray

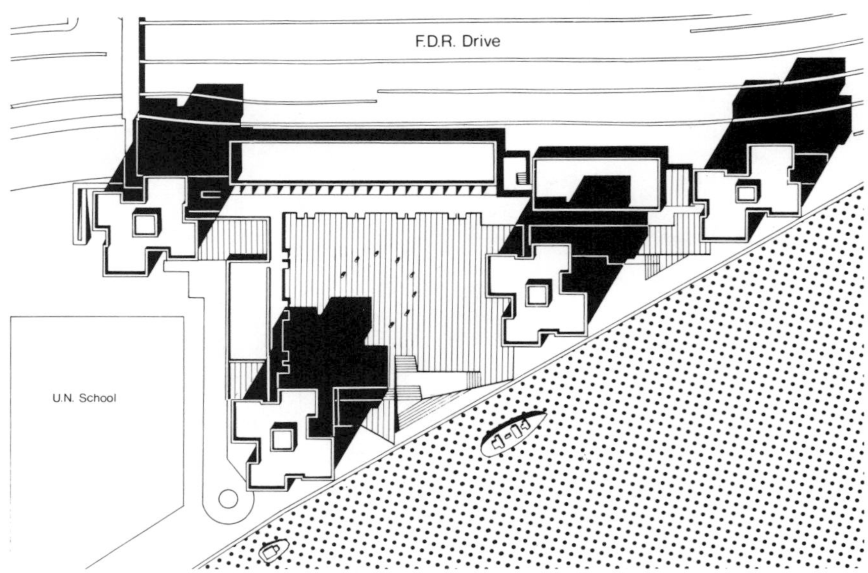

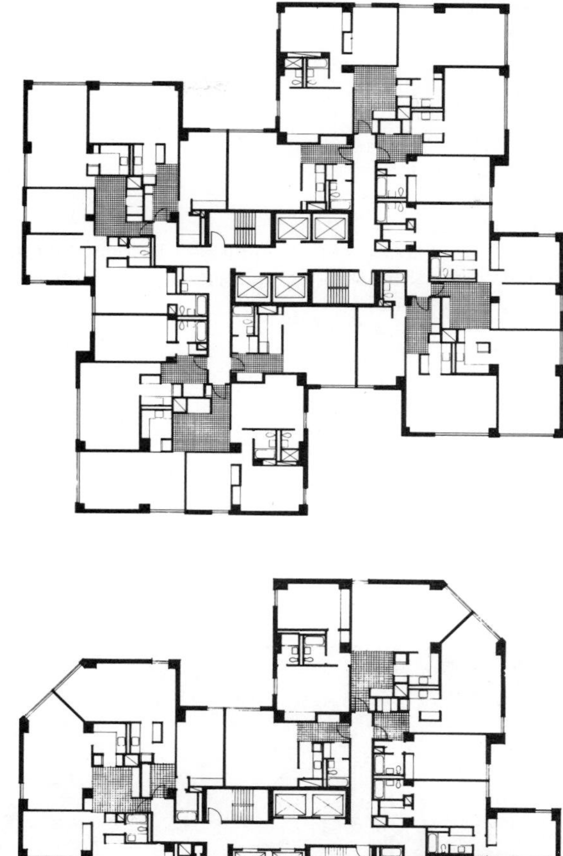

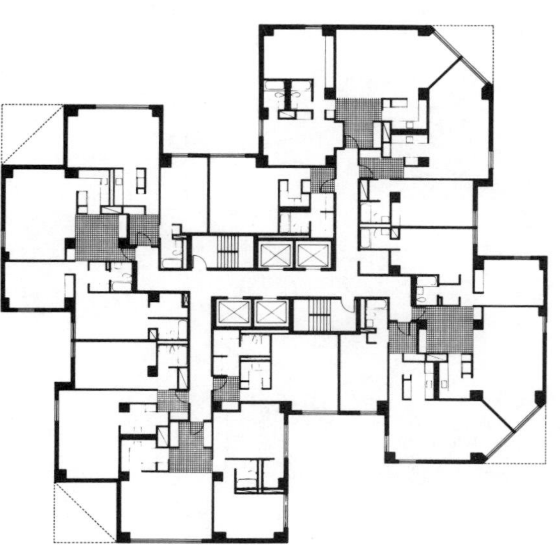

WATERSIDE
New York, New York

Architect:
DAVIS BRODY & ASSOCIATES
New York, New York

Number of dwelling units: 1470 (breakdown unavailable)
Gross floor area: 2,269,500 sf (including garage)
Construction cost: $54,800,000 (including garage)
$24.00/sf
$32,278/unit
Year of bid: 1971
Site area: 6 acres
245 units/acre
User: middle income
Financing: UDC—Mitchell-Lama

Photo credit: Robert Gray

28 **TWO CHARLES CENTER**
Baltimore, Maryland
Architect:

CONKLIN & ROSSANT
New York, New York

Number of dwelling units: 410
102—efficiency
308—one bedroom

Gross floor area:	717,852 sf (including 254,000 sf garage and 80,000 sf stores)
Construction cost:	$8,513,000 (including garage and stores)
	$11.85 sf
	$20,763/unit
Year of bid:	1964
Site area:	1.9 acres
	210.5 units/acre
User:	middle income
Financing:	conventional

Photo credit: J. Alexander

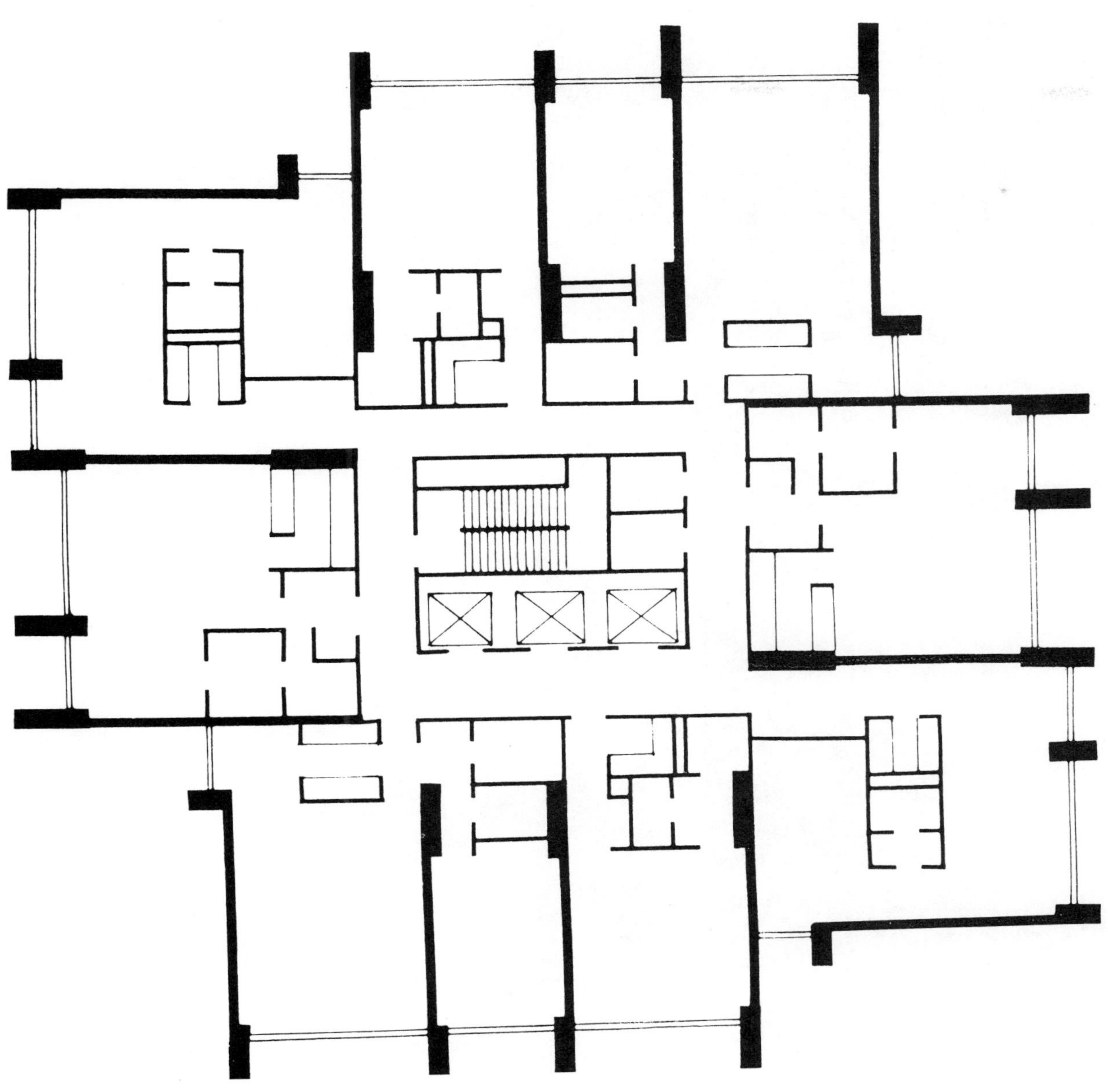

29

LAKE VILLAGE (highrise)
Chicago, Illinois

Architect:
HARRY WEESE & ASSOCIATES
EZRA GORDON—JACK LEVIN
Chicago, Illinois

Number of dwelling units: 200
50—efficiency
75—one bedroom
75—two bedroom
Gross floor area: 182,700 sf (open, on grade parking)
Construction cost: $3,091,000
$16.91/sf
$15,455/unit
Year of bid: 1971
Site area: part of large complex
User: moderate income
Financing: FHA 236

Photo credit: Philip Turner

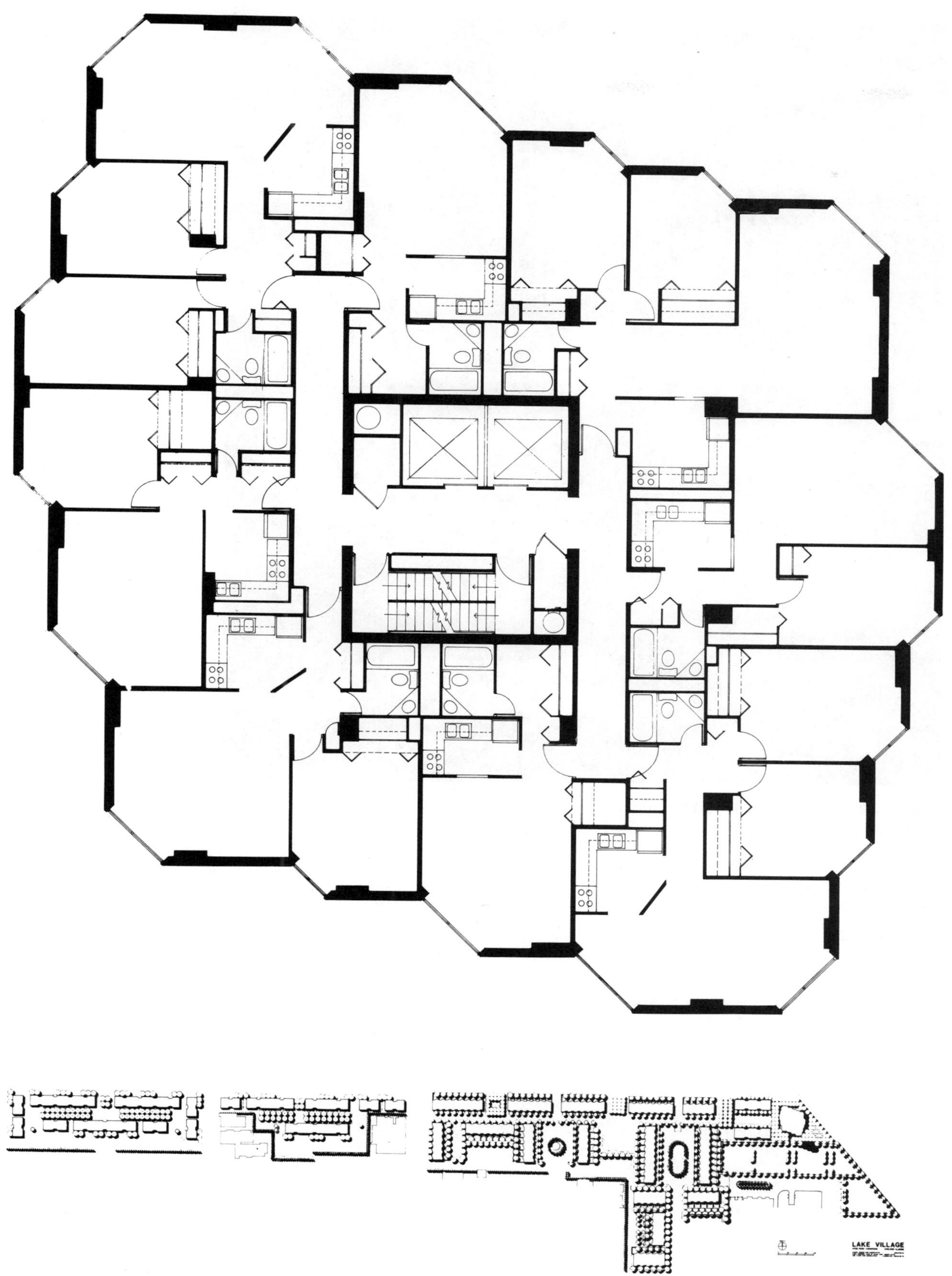
LAKE VILLAGE

30

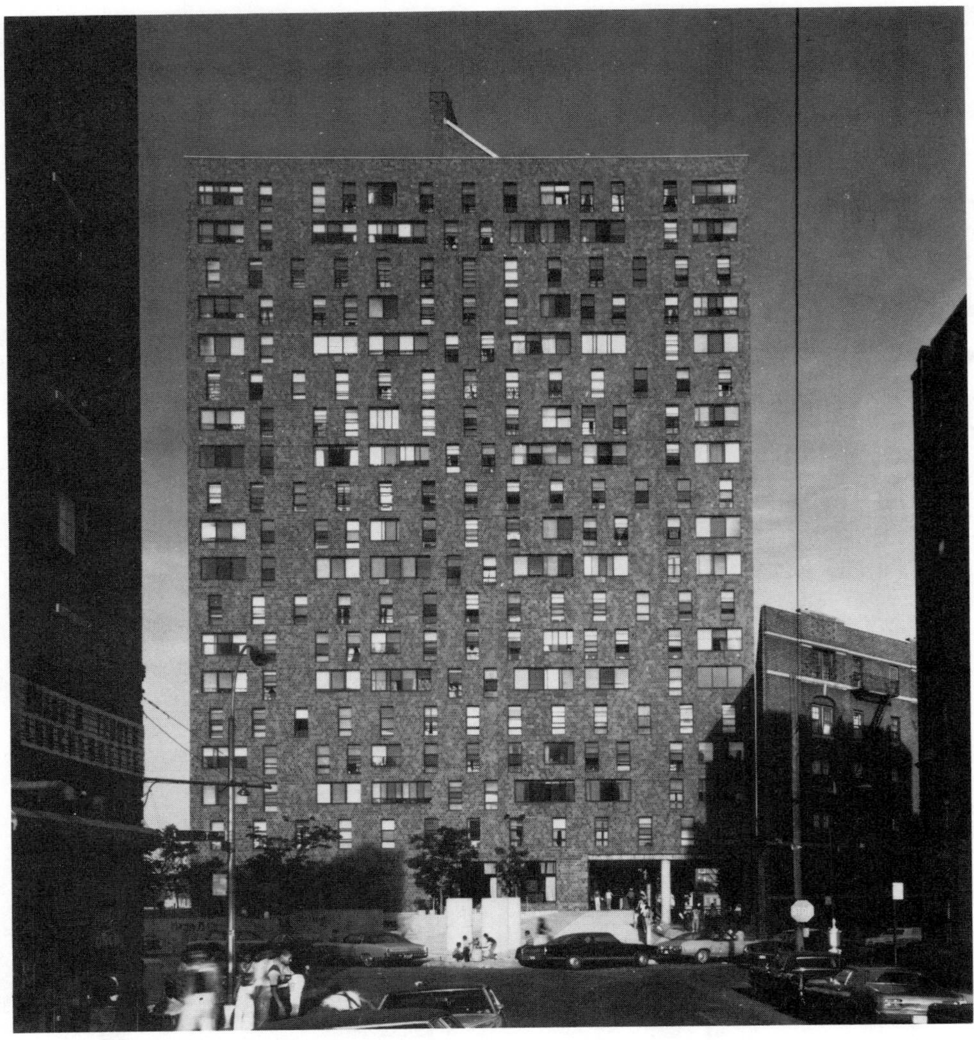

TWIN PARKS NORTHWEST—SITE 4
Bronx, New York

Architect:
PRENTICE & CHAN, OHLHAUSEN
New York, New York

Number of dwelling units: 120
- 6—efficiency
- 30—one bedroom
- 36—two bedroom
- 36—three bedroom
- 6—four bedroom
- 6—five bedroom

Gross floor area: 114,680 sf (open, on grade parking)
Construction cost: $4,047,000
$35.28/sf
$33,725/unit
Year of bid: 1970
Site area: 1.24 acres
96 units/acre
User: low and moderate income
Financing: FHA 236

Photo credit: Elliot Fine

A TYPICAL FLOOR PLAN
FLOORS 2,5,8,11,14 & 17

B TYPICAL FLOOR PLAN
FLOORS 3,6,9,12,15 & 18

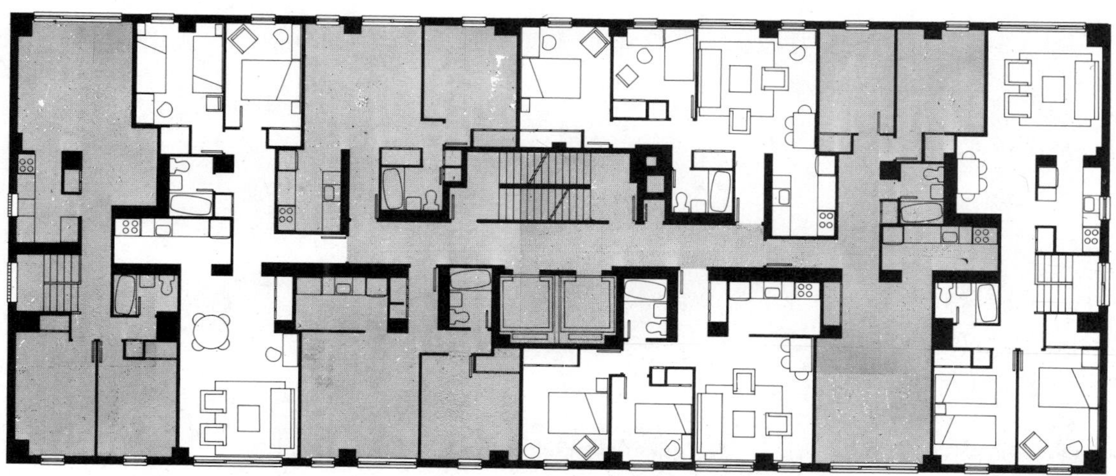

C TYPICAL FLOOR PLAN
FLOORS 4,7,10,13,16 & 19

31 **RIVERBEND**
New York, New York

Architect:
DAVIS BRODY & ASSOCIATES
New York, New York

Number of dwelling units: 625
32—efficiency
280—one bedroom
263—two bedroom
50—three bedroom

Gross floor area:	787,000 sf (including parking)
Construction cost:	$11,900,000
	$15.12/sf
	$19,040/unit
Year of bid:	1966
Site area:	3.7 acres
	169 units/acre
User:	middle income
Financing:	Mitchell-Lama

Photo credit: David Hirsch
Norman McGrath

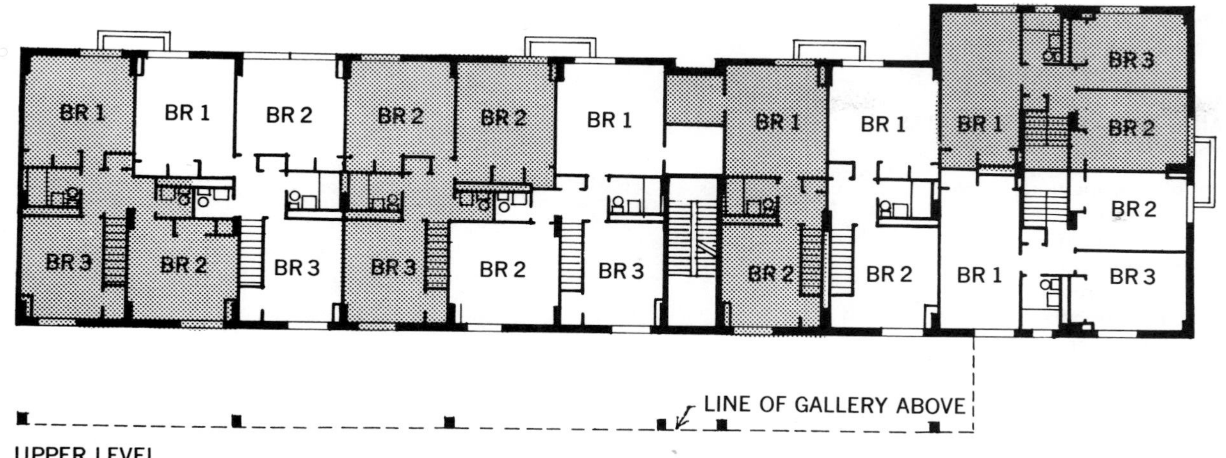

UPPER LEVEL

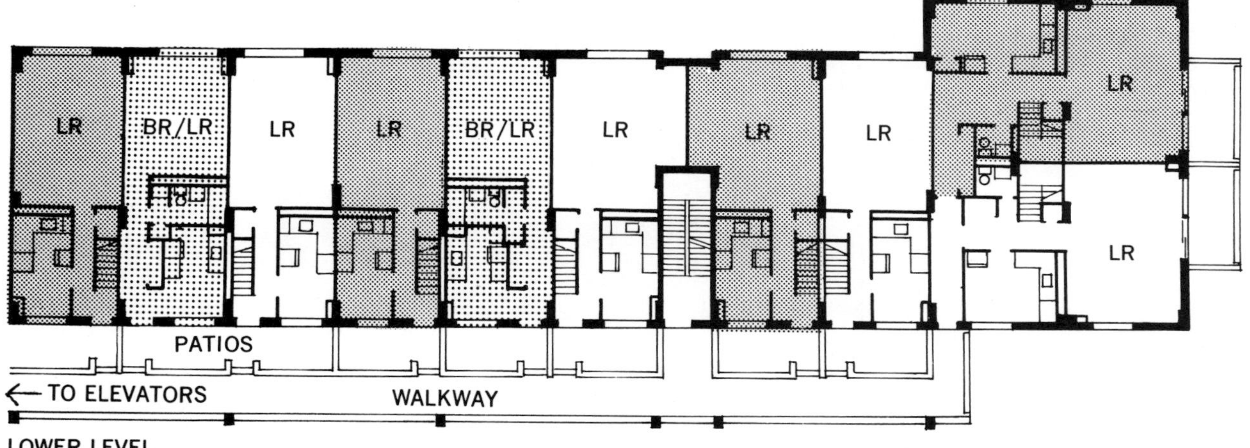

LOWER LEVEL

32 **TWIN PARKS WEST—SITE 10–12**
Bronx, New York

Architects:
GIOVANNI PASANELLA ASSOCIATES
New York, New York

Number of dwelling units: 186
5—efficiency
28—one bedroom
53—two bedroom
64—three bedroom
12—four bedroom
24—five bedroom

Gross floor area: 237,500 sf (not including parking)
Construction cost: $6,320,000
$26.61/sf (not including parking)
$33,978/unit (not including parking)
Year of bid: 1971
Site area: 1.5 acres
124 units/acre
User: low income
Financing: FHA 236

Photo credit: Giovanni Pasanella Associates

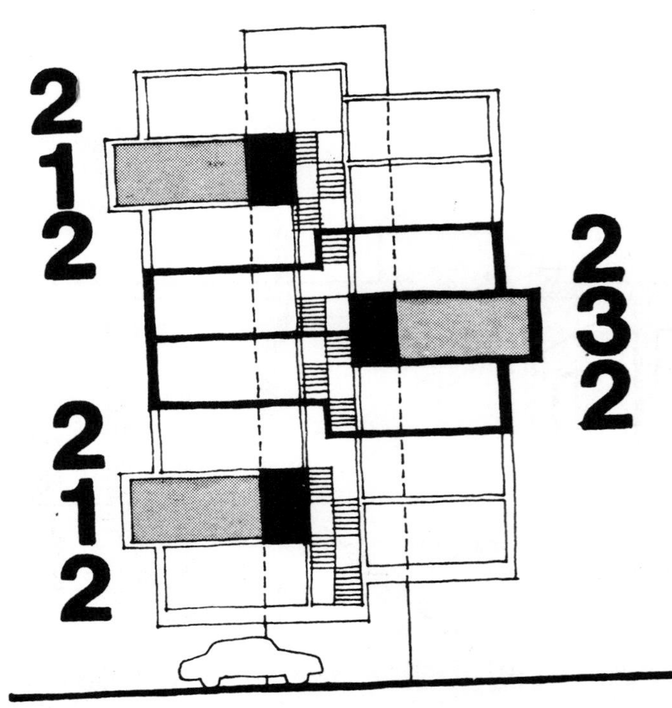

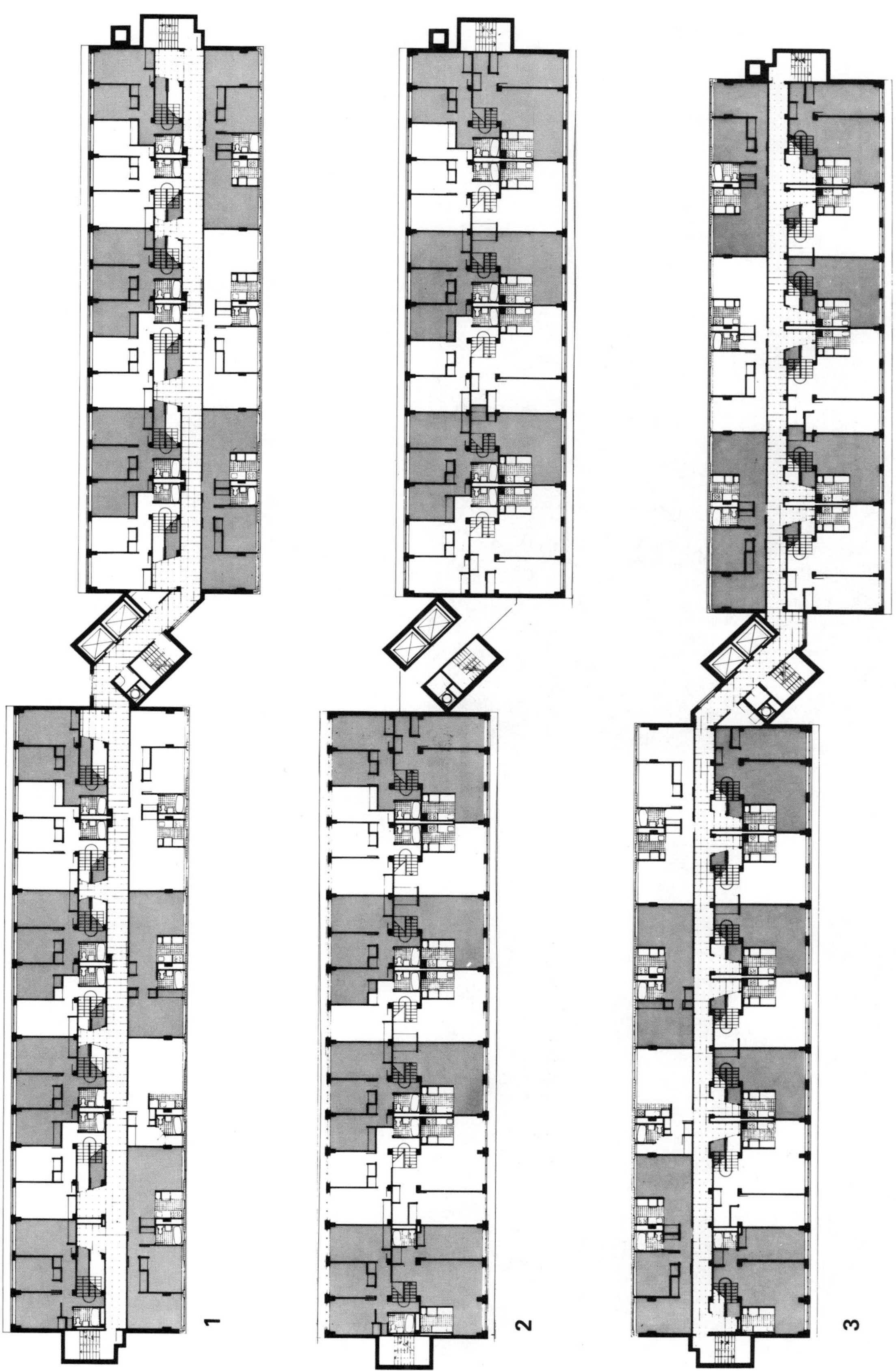
1
2
3

OTTO·WAGNER

33

CONEY ISLAND—SITE 5/6
Brooklyn, New York

Architect:
HOBERMAN & WASSERMAN
New York, New York

Number of dwelling units: 334
- 19—efficiency
- 45—one bedroom
- 132—two bedroom
- 105—three bedroom
- 22—four bedroom
- 11—five bedroom

Gross floor area: 379,650 sf (including garage)
Construction cost: $11,000,000
$28.97/sf
$32,934/unit
Year of bid: 1970
Site area: 3.5 acres
95.5 units/acre
User: low to moderate income
Financing: FHA 236

Photo credit: Norman Hoberman

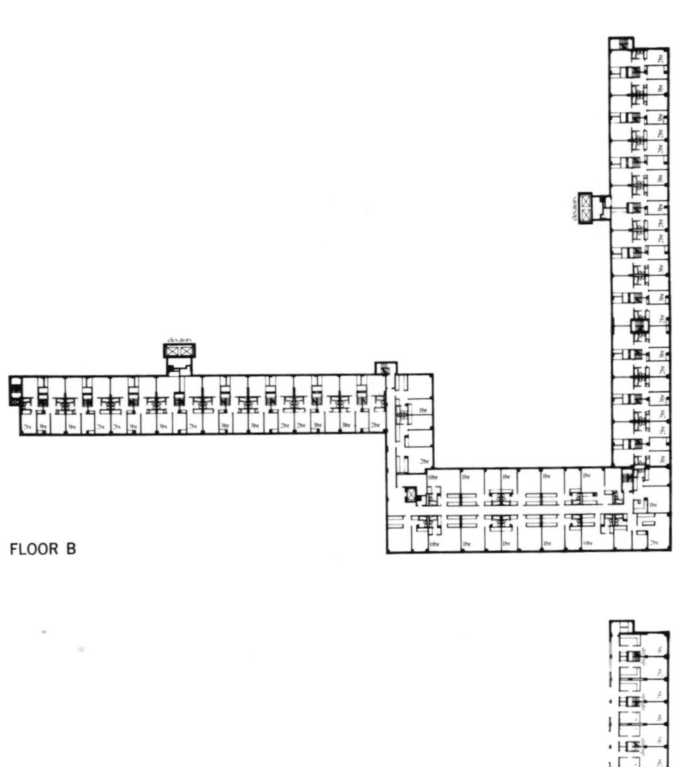

FLOOR B

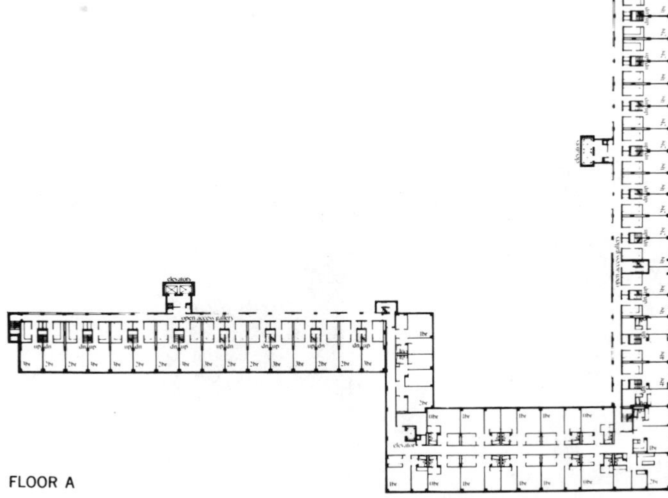

FLOOR A

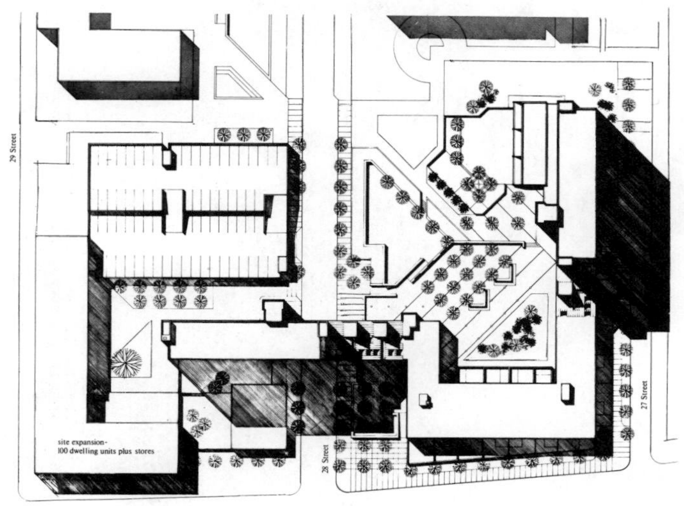

34 ROOSEVELT ISLAND, PARCEL 3

New York, New York

Architect:
SERT, JACKSON AND ASSOCIATES
Cambridge, Massachusetts

Number of dwelling units: 361
- 4%—efficiency
- 26%—one bedroom
- 45%—two bedroom
- 19%—three bedroom
- 6%—four bedroom

Gross floor area: 520,000 sf (including garage, 13,800 sf commercial, 17,300 sf school)
Construction cost: $15,000,000
$28.83/sf
$41,551/unit
Year of bid: 1972
Site area: 2.85 acres
126.5 units/acre
User: low to middle income
Financing: UDC and Mitchell-Lama

Photo credit: Steve Rosenthal

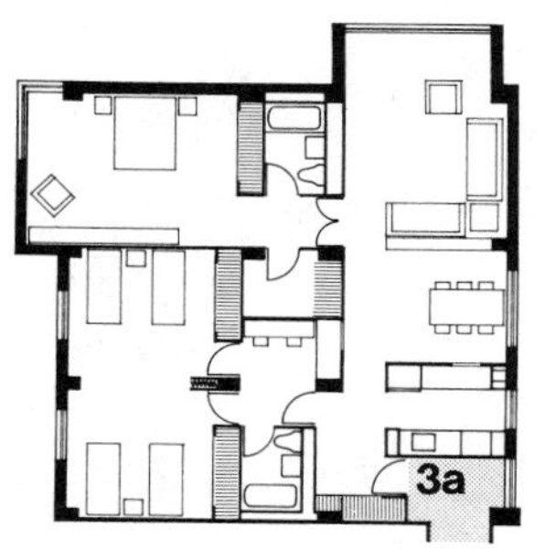

3 BEDROOM UNIT

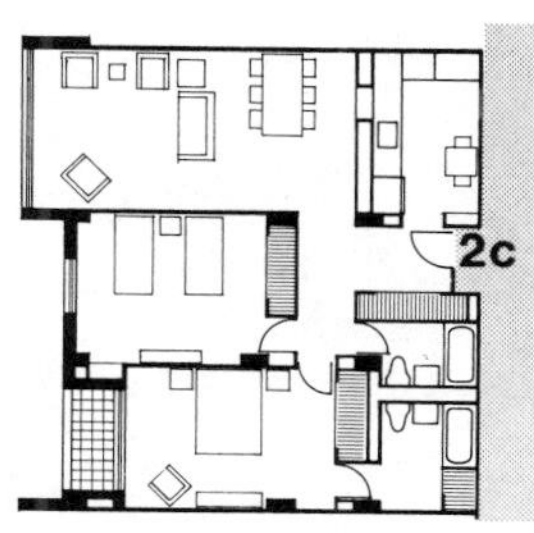

2 BEDROOM UNIT SOUTH

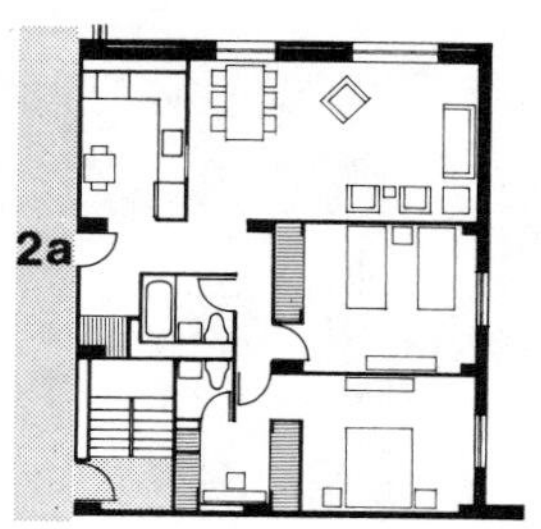

2 BEDROOM UNIT NORTH

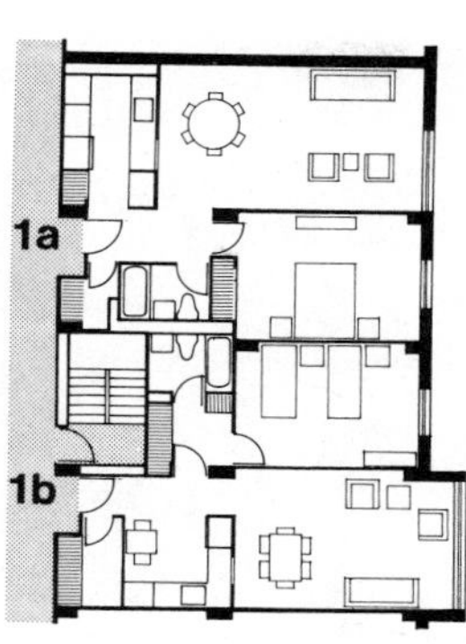

1 BEDROOM UNITS NORTH

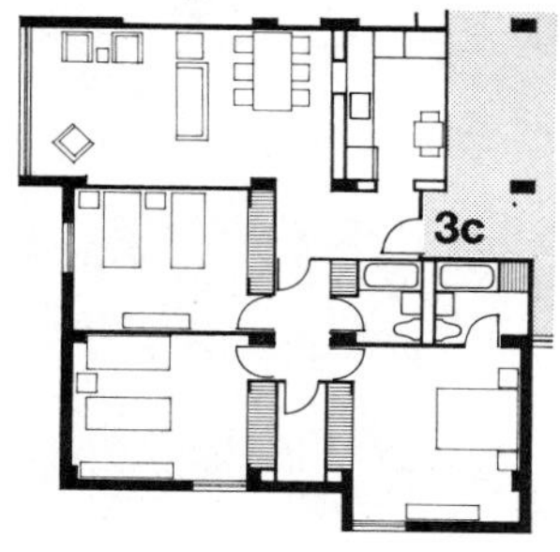

3 BEDROOM CORE UNIT

corridor level

noncorridor level

4 BEDROOM DUPLEX UNIT

3 BEDROOM CORE UNIT

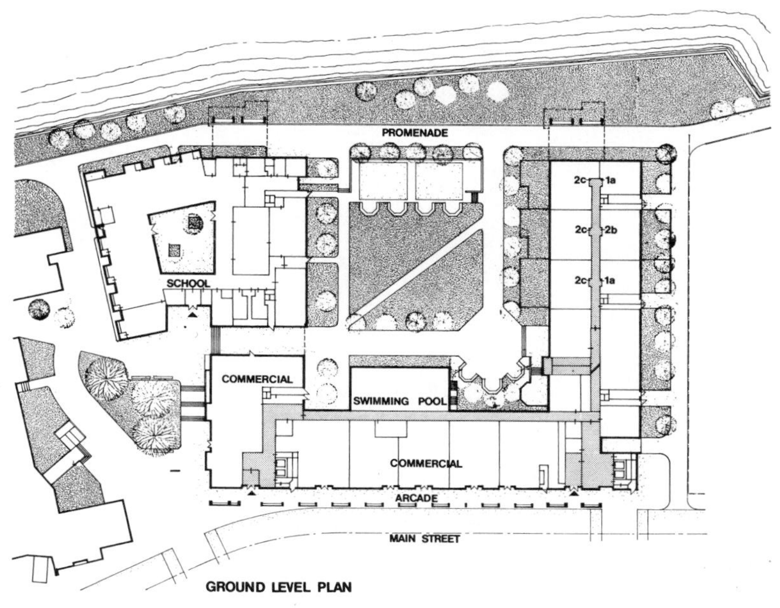

GROUND LEVEL PLAN

3a
2c 2a
2c
2c 1a
1b
2c 1c
2c 1a
1b
2c 1c
3c
4a 4a 4a 4a 4a 4a 4a
2d
3a
2c 2a
2c
2c 1a
1b
2c 1c
2c 1a
1b
2c 1e

LEVEL 6 AS A TYPICAL FLOOR PLAN

35

CEDAR-RIVERSIDE
Minneapolis, Minnesota

Architect:
RALPH RAPSON AND ASSOCIATES
Minneapolis, Minnesota

A complex development of which only a fragment (the Skip-Stop Scheme) is shown. Because of its complexity cost per single building would be meaningless.

Number of dwelling units: 1299

Gross floor area:	1,611,779 sf
Residential	1,200,897 sf
Ancillary functions	31,929 sf
Garage	290,086 sf
Plaza	88,867 sf
Construction cost (approximate):	$26,440,000
Residential buildings	21,990,000
Ancillary functions	590,000
Power and air conditioning	850,000
Landscaping	400,000
Plaza	610,000
Semienclosed garage	2,000,000
	$16.40/sf
	$20,354/unit
Year of bid:	1971–1973
Site area:	12.1 acres
	107.35 units/acre
User:	low to upper income

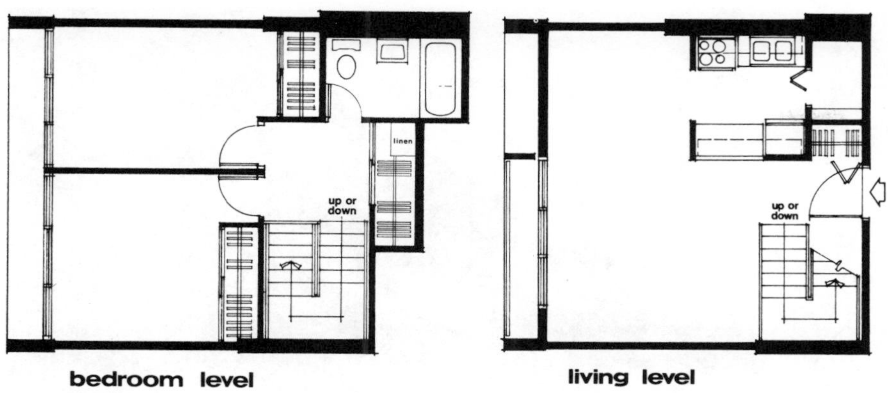

linen
up or down
up or down
bedroom level
living level

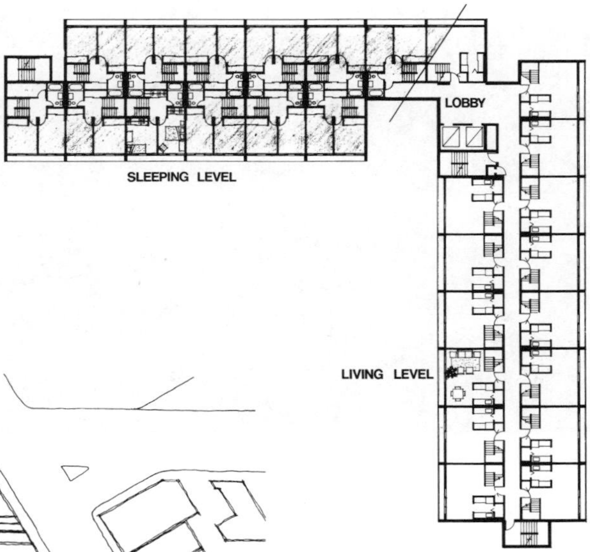

LOBBY
SLEEPING LEVEL
LIVING LEVEL

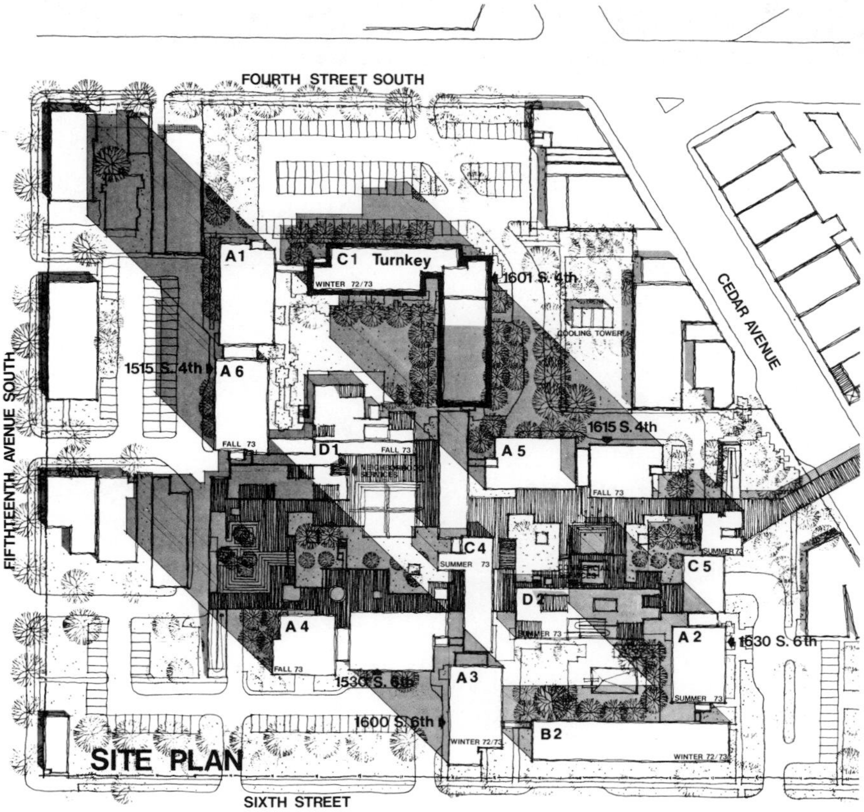

FOURTH STREET SOUTH
CEDAR AVENUE
FIFTHTEENTH AVENUE SOUTH
SIXTH STREET
SITE PLAN
A1
C1 Turnkey
WINTER 72/73
1601 S. 4th
COOLING TOWER
1515 S. 4th
A 6
FALL 73
D1
FALL 73
A 5
1615 S. 4th
FALL 73
C4
SUMMER 73
C 5
SUMMER 73
D 2
SUMMER 73
A 4
FALL 73
1530 S. 6th
A 2
1630 S. 6th
SUMMER 73
A 3
1600 S. 6th
WINTER 72/73
B 2
WINTER 72/73

36

SOUTH COMMONS (midrise)
Chicago, Illinois

Architect:
EZRA GORDON—JACK LEVIN
Chicago, Illinois

Number of dwelling units: 68
- 25—efficiency
- 28—one bedroom
- 11—two bedroom
- 4—three bedroom (two story)

Gross floor area: 70,942 sf (open, on grade parking)
Construction cost: $1,017,000
$14.33/sf
$14,956/unit
Year of bid: 1966
Site area: part of large complex
User: middle income
Financing: FHA 220

Photo credit: Orlando Cabanban

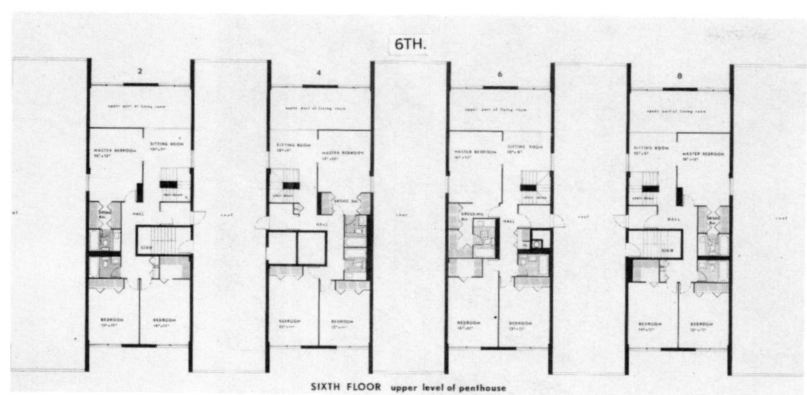

SIXTH FLOOR upper level of penthouse

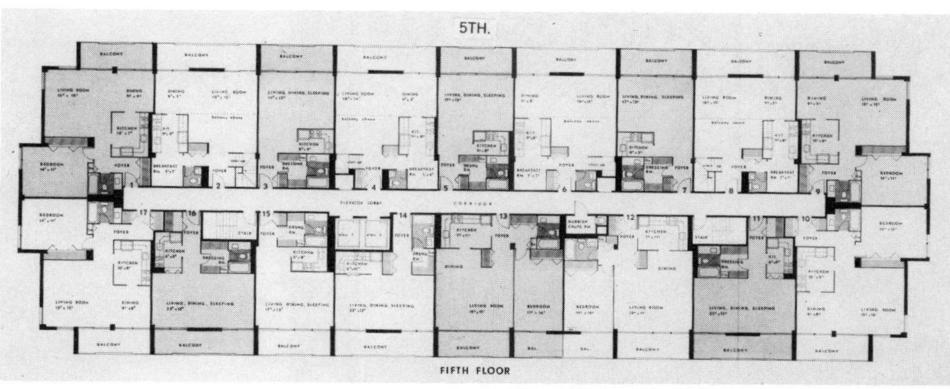

FIFTH FLOOR

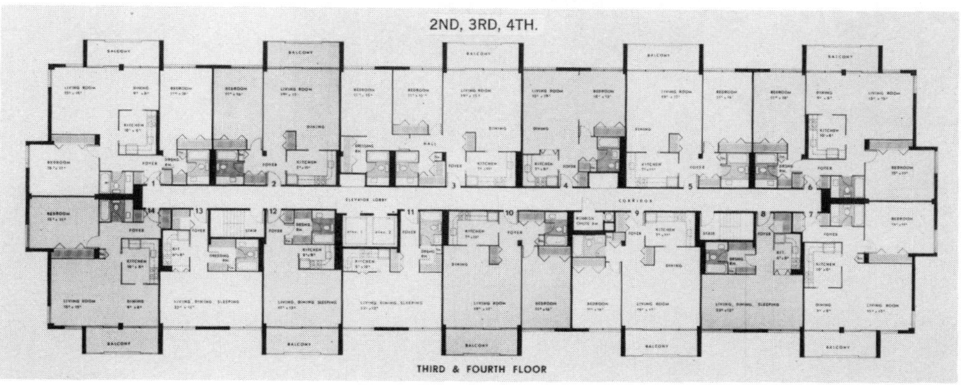

THIRD & FOURTH FLOOR

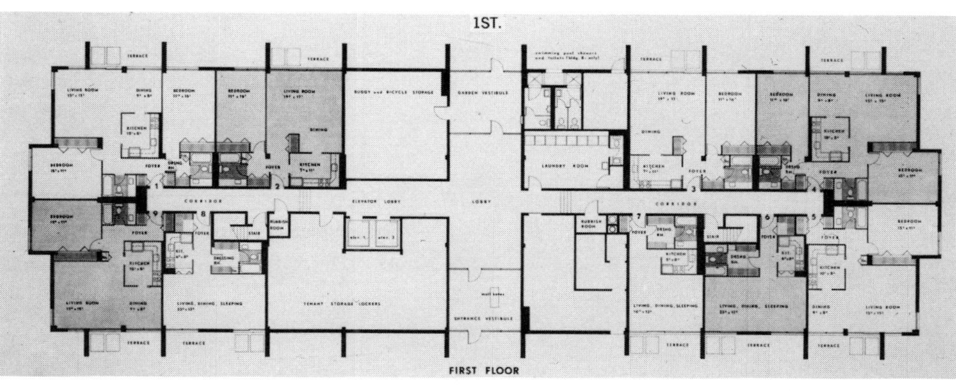

FIRST FLOOR

37

1555 SANDBURG TERRACE
Chicago, Illinois

Architect:
SOLOMON, CORDWELL, BUENZ & ASSOCIATES
Chicago, Illinois

Number of dwelling units: 96
48—one bedroom
36—two bedroom
12—three bedroom

Gross floor area: 158,100 sf (not including parking)
Construction cost: $1,617,000 (not including parking)
$10.22/sf (not including parking)
$16,844/unit (not including parking)
Year of bid: 1969
Site area: part of large complex
User: middle income
Financing: FHA 207

Photo credit: Henry Kluck

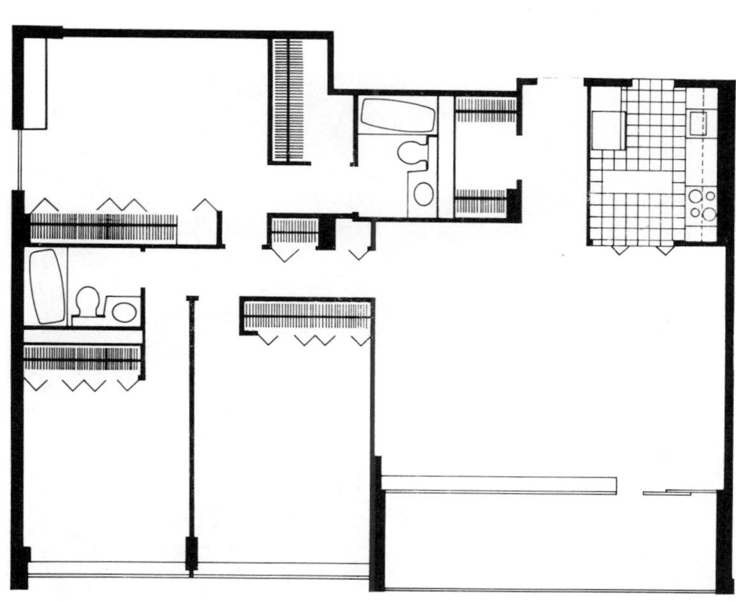

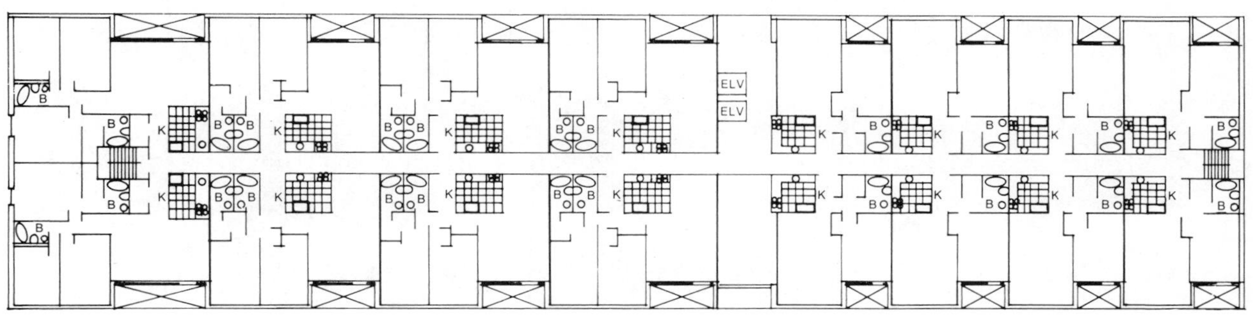
ELV
ELV
B
K

38 AGNES MORLEY HEIGHTS

Greenwich, Connecticut

Architect:
HOBERMAN & WASSERMAN
New York, New York

Number of dwelling units: 150
77—efficiency
73—one bedroom

Gross floor area:	112,000 sf (open, on grade parking)
Construction cost:	$3,100,000
	$27.67/sf
	$20,666/unit
Year of bid:	1971
Site area:	2.5 acres
	60 units/acre
User:	low income
Financing:	public housing

Photo credit: Norman McGrath

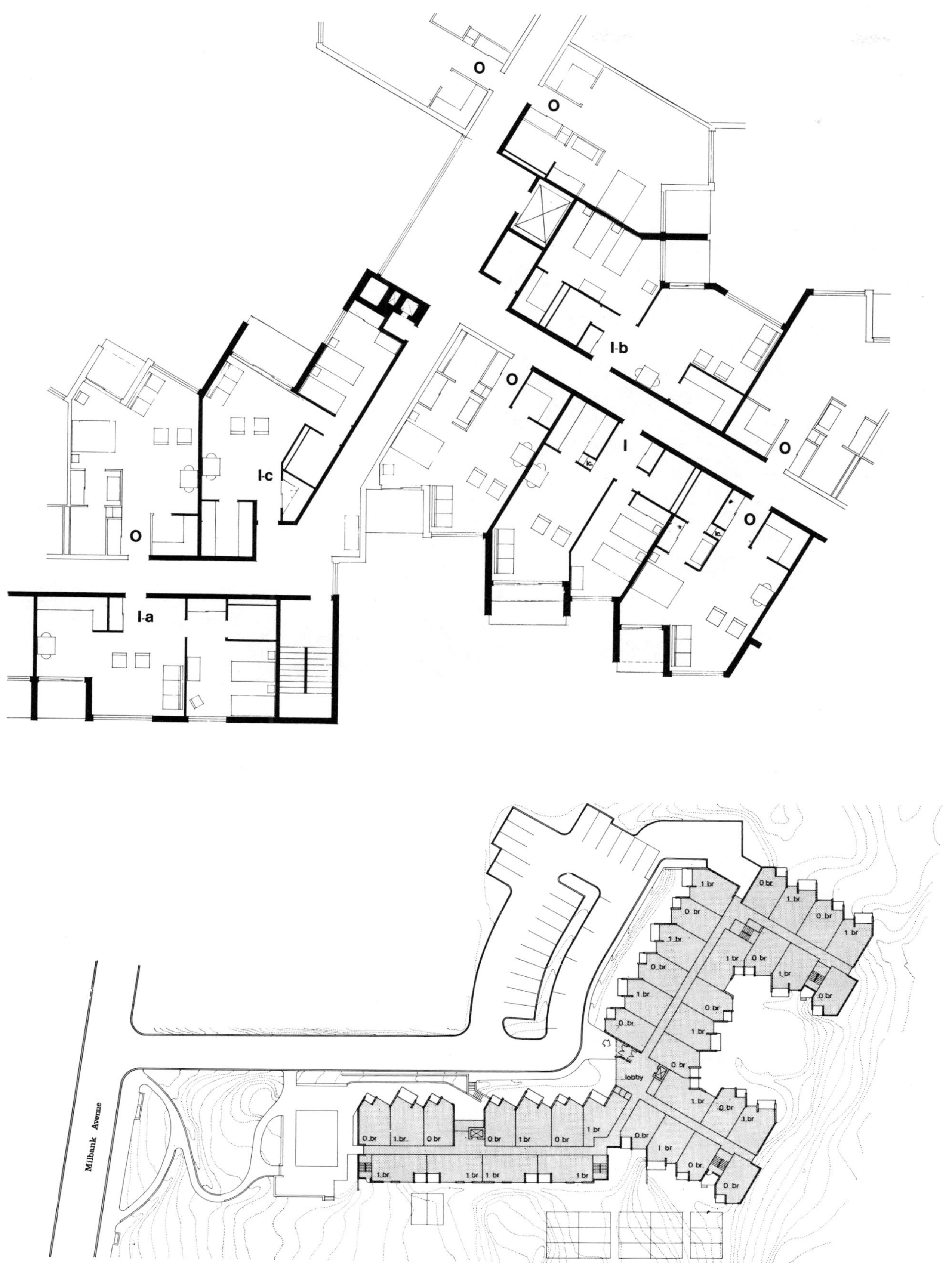
O
O
I-b
O
I-c
O
I
O
O
I-a
Milbank Avenue
lobby

39

LAMBERT HOUSES
Bronx, New York

Architect:
DAVIS BRODY & ASSOCIATES
New York, New York

Number of dwelling units: 731
18—efficiency
155—one bedroom
165—two bedroom
346—three bedroom
47—four bedroom

Gross floor area: 1,050,900 sf (no parking included)
Construction cost: $23,323,000
$22.19/sf
$31,905/unit
$31,905/unit
Year of bid: 1971
Site area: 11.73 acres
62.5 units/acre
User: moderate income
Financing: FHA 221 (d) 3

Photo credit: Robert Gray

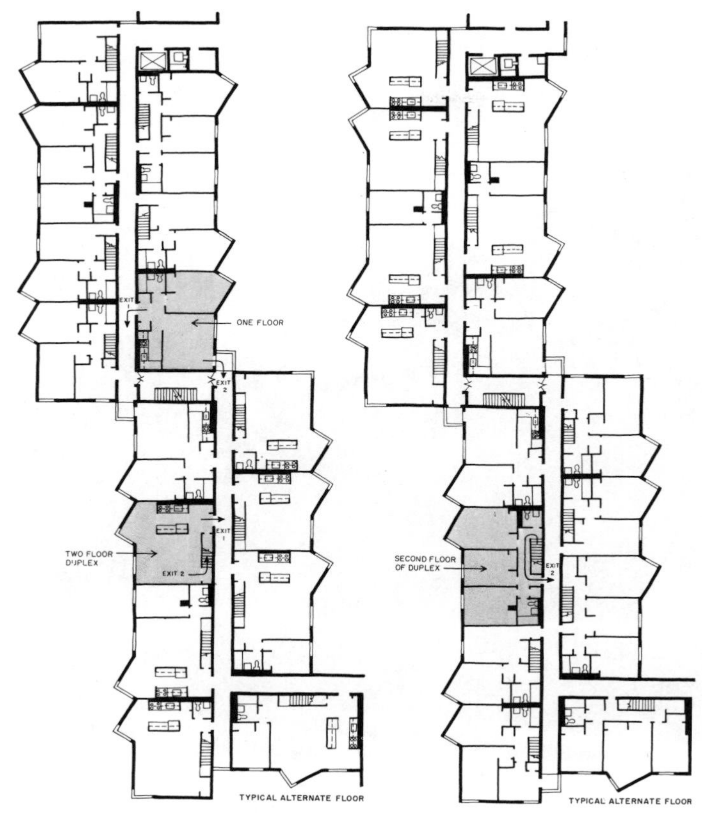
ONE FLOOR
EXIT 1
EXIT 2
TWO FLOOR DUPLEX
SECOND FLOOR OF DUPLEX
TYPICAL ALTERNATE FLOOR
TYPICAL ALTERNATE FLOOR

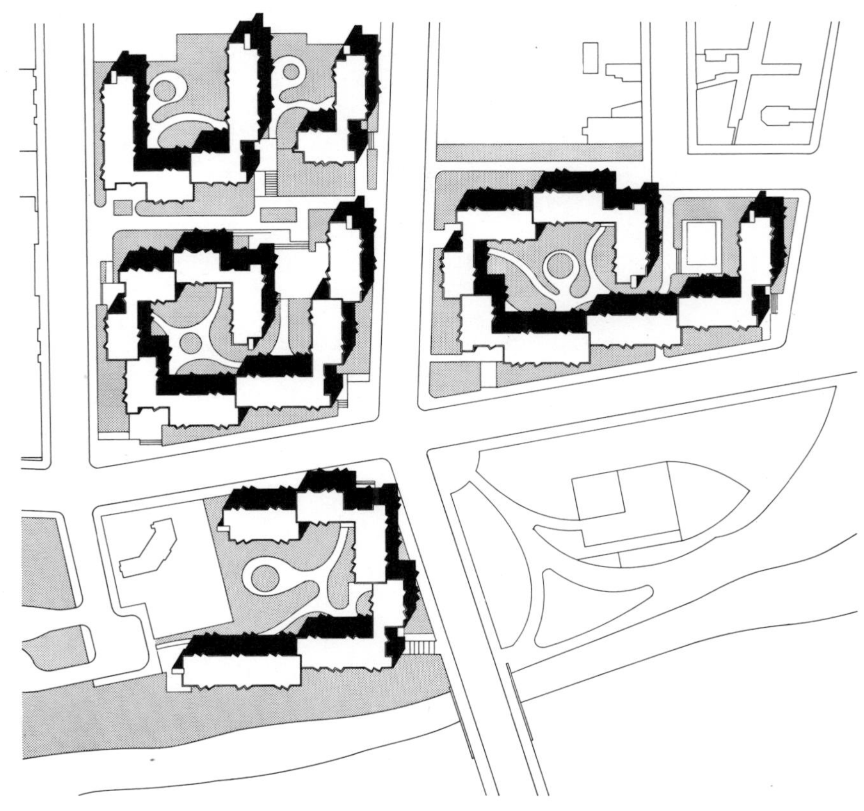

40

WINNETKA HOUSE
Winnetka, Illinois

Architect:
HAUSNER & MACSAI
Chicago, Illinois

Number of dwelling units: 64
12—two bedroom
40—three bedroom
12—four bedroom

Gross floor area:	177,300 sf (including garage)
Construction cost:	$3,050,000
	$17.20/sf
	$47,656/unit
Year of bid:	1970
Site area:	1.76 acres
	36.5 units/acre
User:	upper income
Financing:	conventional

Photo credit: John Macsai

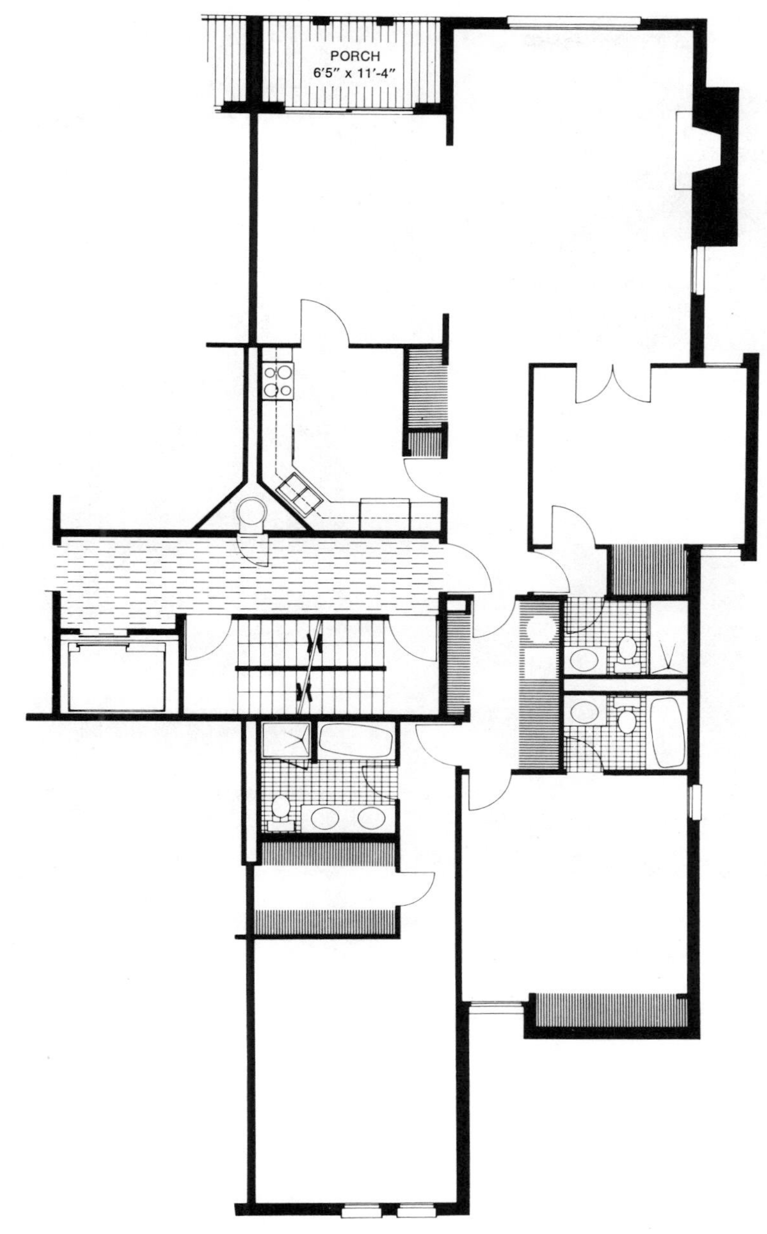
PORCH
6'5" x 11'-4"

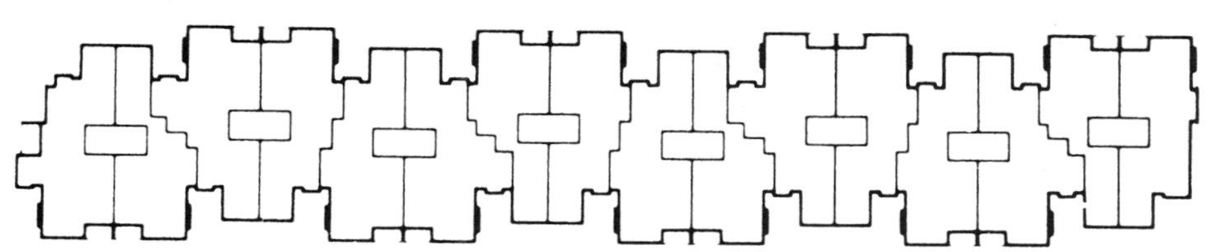

41

TIBER ISLAND
Washington, D. C.

Architect:
KEYES, LETHBRIDGE & CONDON
Washington, D. C.

Number of dwelling units: 453
Highrise: 160—efficiency
120—one bedroom
Townhouses: 60—two bedroom
25—four bedroom
Gross floor area: 446,000 sf highrises
186,000 sf townhouses
103,000 sf garage
Construction cost: $8,508,000
$5,670,000 highrise
$11.35 sf (including garage and half site development)
$16,937/unit (including garage and half site development)
$2,161,000 townhouses
$12.22 sf (including half site development)
$26,753/unit (including half site development)
$450,000 garage
$227,000 site development
Year of bid: 1963
Site area: 8.12 acres
56 units/acre
User: middle to upper income
Financing: FHA

Photo credit: J. Alexander

B
1ST
2ND
B
1ST
2ND

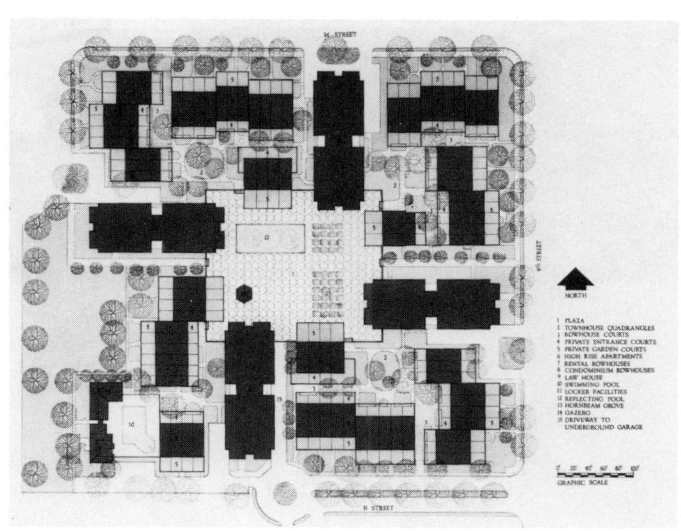
M STREET
N STREET
NORTH
1 PLAZA
2 TOWNHOUSE QUADRANGLES
3 ROWHOUSE COURTS
4 PRIVATE ENTRANCE COURTS
5 PRIVATE GARDEN COURTS
6 HIGH RISE APARTMENTS
7 RENTAL ROWHOUSES
8 CONDOMINIUM ROWHOUSES
9 LAW HOUSE
10 SWIMMING POOL
11 LOCKER FACILITIES
12 REFLECTING POOL
13 HORNBEAM GROVE
14 GAZEBO
15 DRIVEWAY TO
UNDERGROUND GARAGE
GRAPHIC SCALE

42 **ATRIUM**
Elmhurst, Illinois

Architect:
BOOTH & NAGLE
Chicago, Illinois

Number of dwelling units: 210 (+240 in midrises, not completed)
10—two bedroom
150—three bedroom
50—four bedroom
Construction cost: $19.00/sf (on grade, open parking)
Year of bid: 1972
Site area: 17 acres
12.5 units/acre
User: upper to middle income
Financing: conventional

Photo credit: Philip Turner

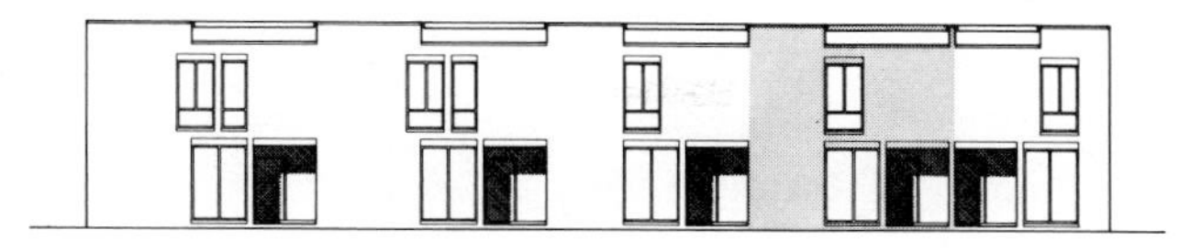

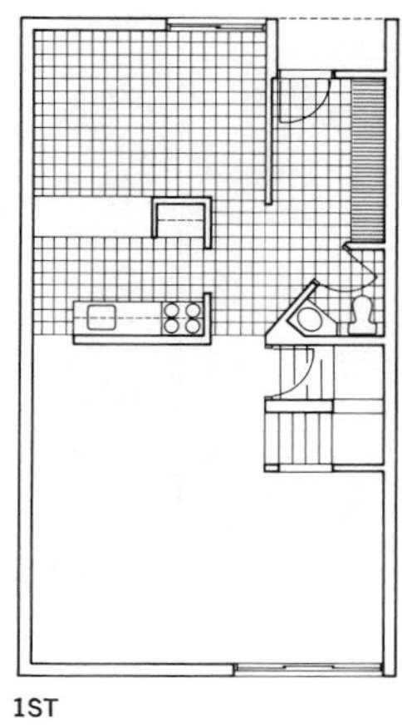
1ST

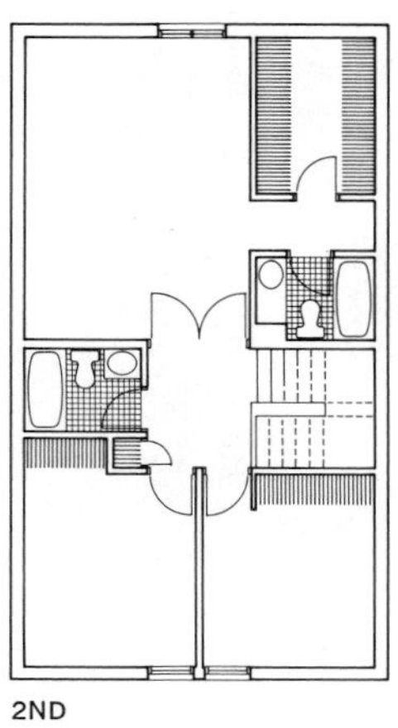
2ND

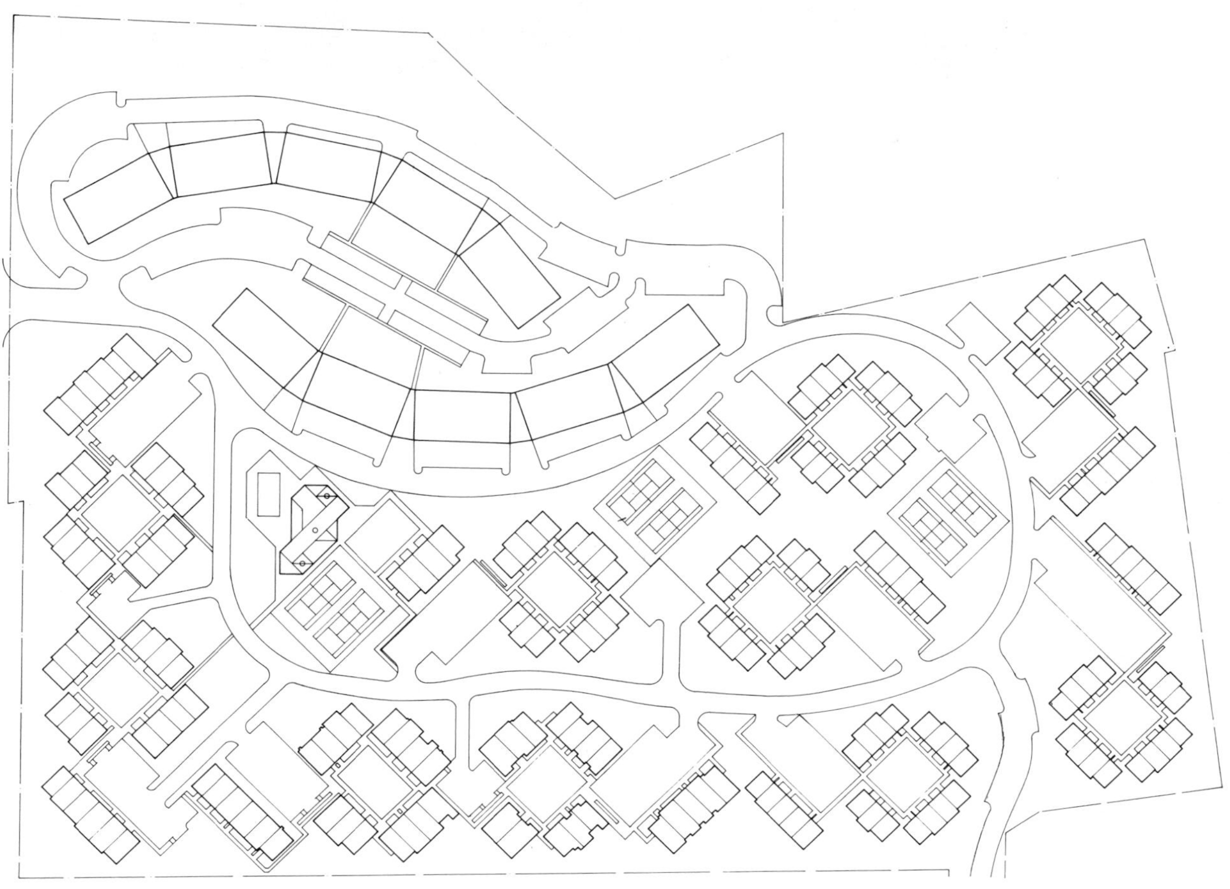

43

LAKE VILLAGE (townhouses)
Chicago, Illinois

Architect:
HARRY WEESE & ASSOCIATES
EZRA GORDON—JACK LEVIN
Chicago, Illinois

Number of dwelling units: 18
6—three bedroom
12—four bedroom
Gross floor area: 43,920 sf
Construction cost: $746,640
$17.00/sf
$41,480/unit
Year of bid: 1968
Site area: Part of large complex
User: upper income
Financing: conventional

Photo credit: Orlando Cabanban

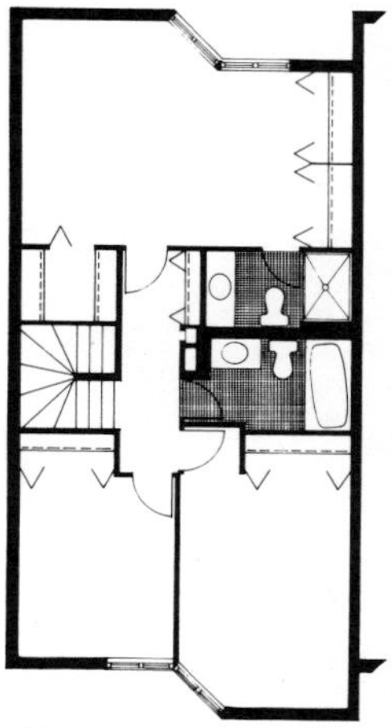

2ND

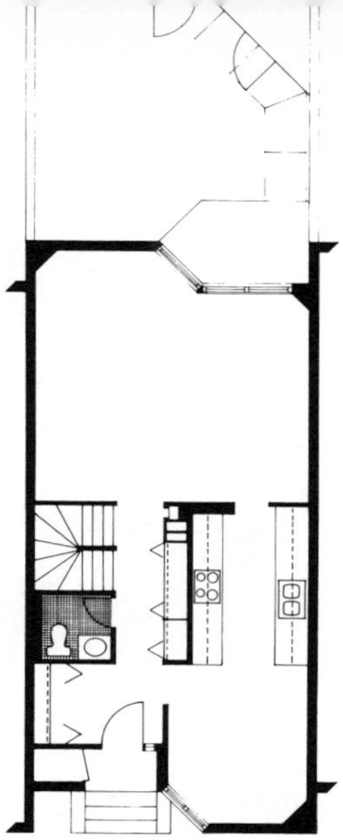

1ST

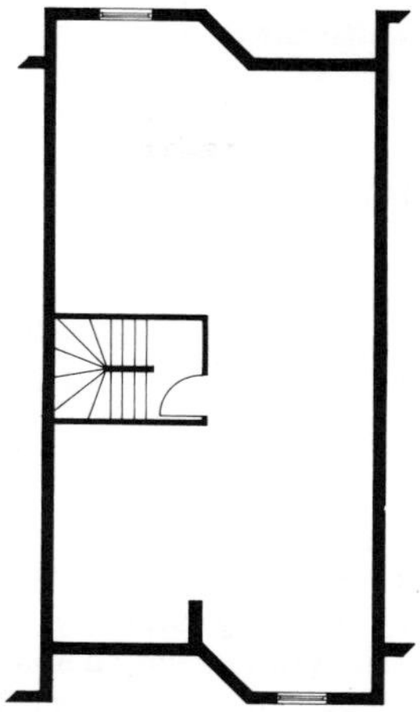

BSMT

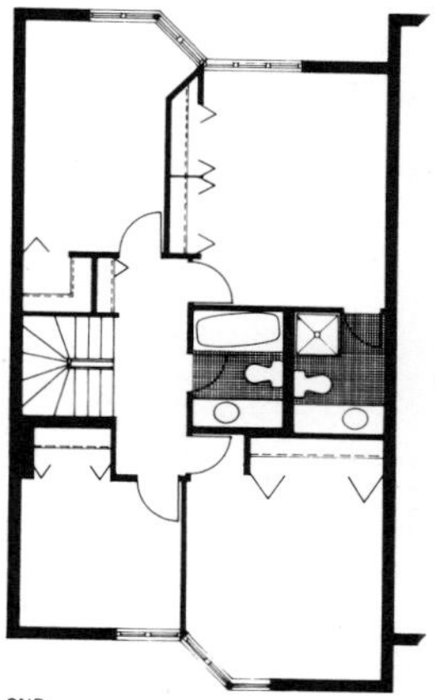

2ND

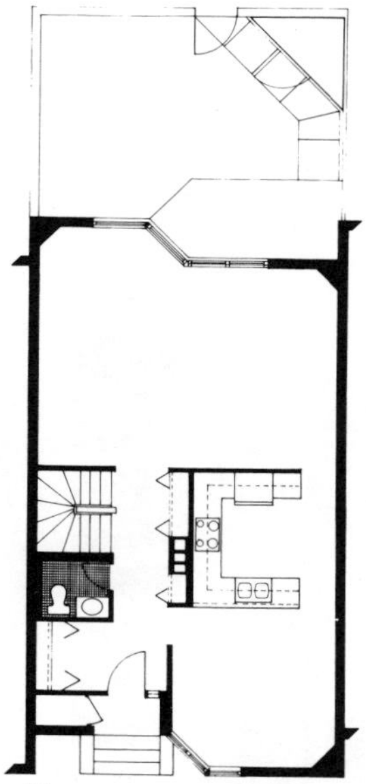

1ST

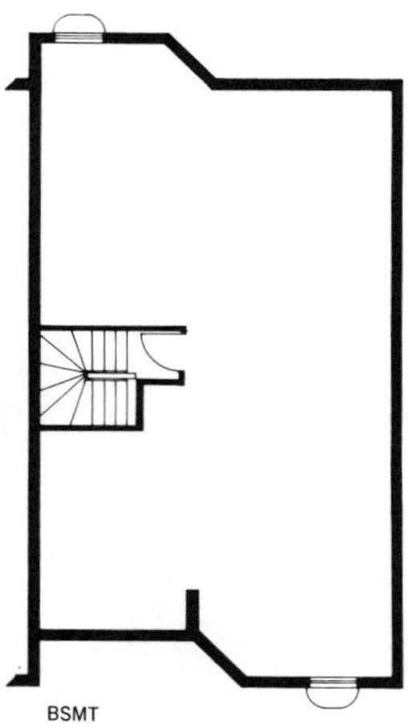

BSMT

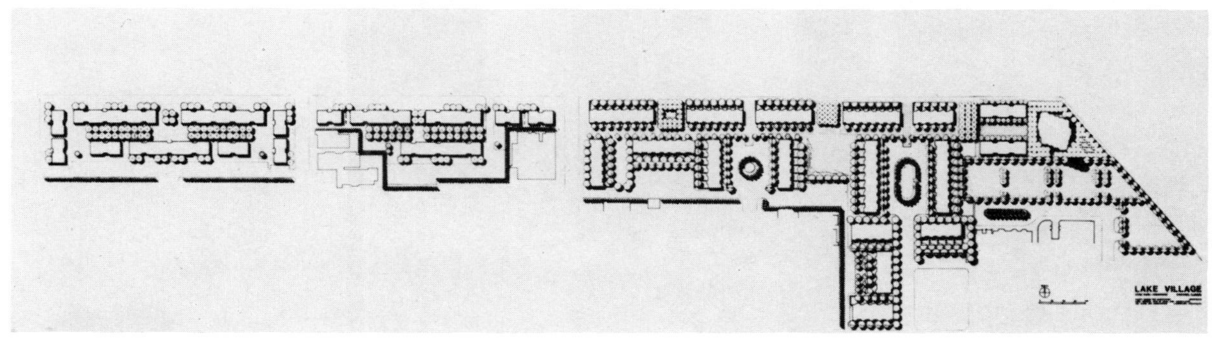

44 **WILLIAMS STREET STUDENT HOUSING**
Middletown, Connecticut

Architect:
ULRICH FRANZEN & ASSOCIATES
New York, New York

Number of dwelling units: 119
Highrise: 11—efficiency
72—two bedroom
1—manager
7—lounges
Lowrise: 20—four bedroom
8—ten bedroom
Gross floor area: 106,000 sf (open, on grade parking)
Construction cost: $3,167,500 (including carpeting)
$396,000 (site work including abnormal soil conditions)
$29.87/sf (not including site work)
$26,618/unit (not including site work)
Year of bid: 1972
Site area: 3.45 acres
34.5 units/acre
User: students (middle income)
Financing: HUD College Housing Program Debt Service Grant

Photo credit: Norman McGrath

2ND
1ST
BED ROOM
BED RM
DN
TRELLIS
ENTRY
KITCHEN
UP
STOR.
LIVING ROOM
STUDY
PATIO
2•BR
4•BR
10•BR

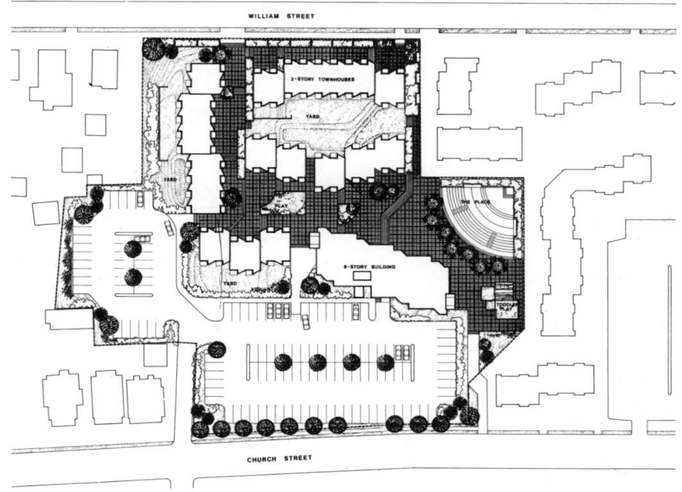

WILLIAM STREET
CHURCH STREET

45

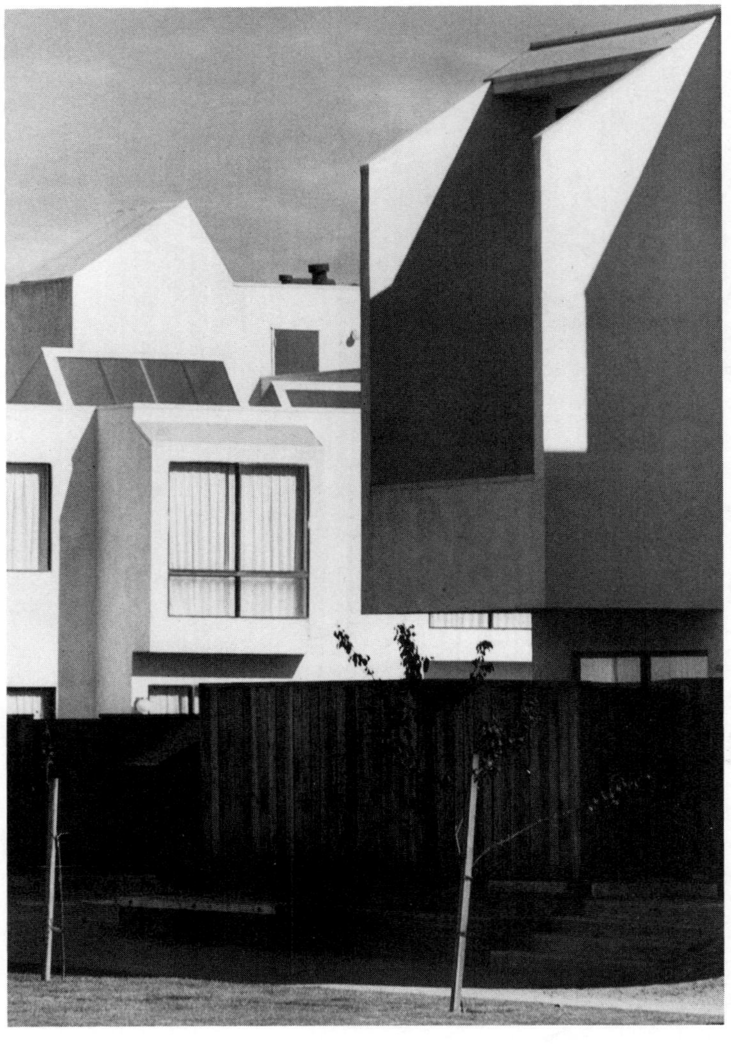

ACORN PROJECT
Oakland, California

Architect:
BURGER AND COPLANS, INC.
Oakland, California

Number of dwelling units: 479 in Phase I
23—efficiency
94—one bedroom
87—two bedroom
259—three bedroom
16—four bedroom
Gross floor area: 460,000 sf (open, on grade parking)
Construction cost: $5,950,000
$12.93/sf
$12,422/unit
Year of bid: 1968
Site area: 17 acres
28 units/acre
User: low income
Financing: FHA 221 (d) 3

Photo credit: Michelle Vignes

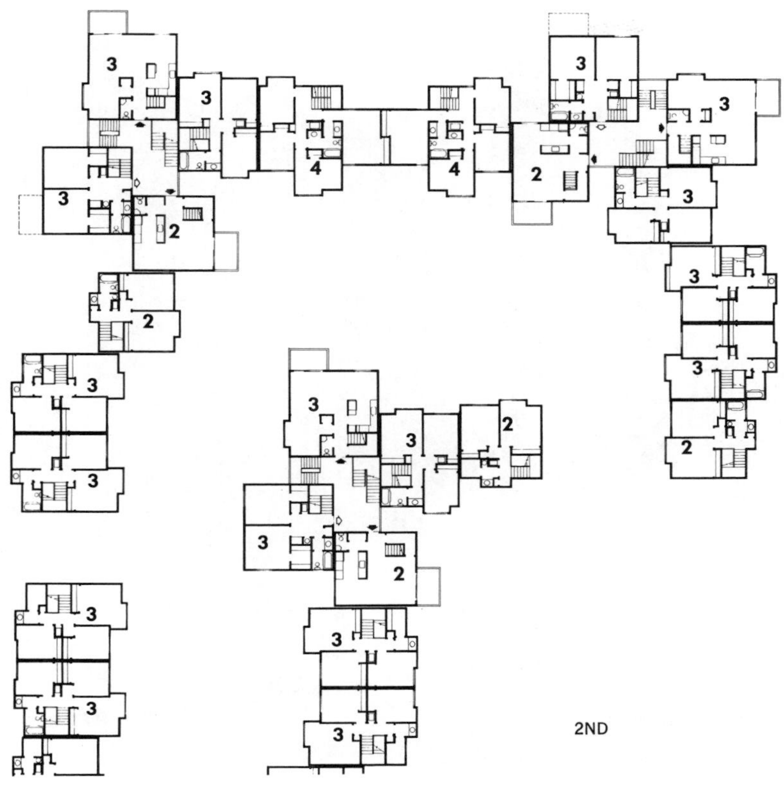
3
3
4
4
3
3
3
2
2
3
3
2
3
3
3
2
3
3
3
3
2
2
3
3
3
3
2ND

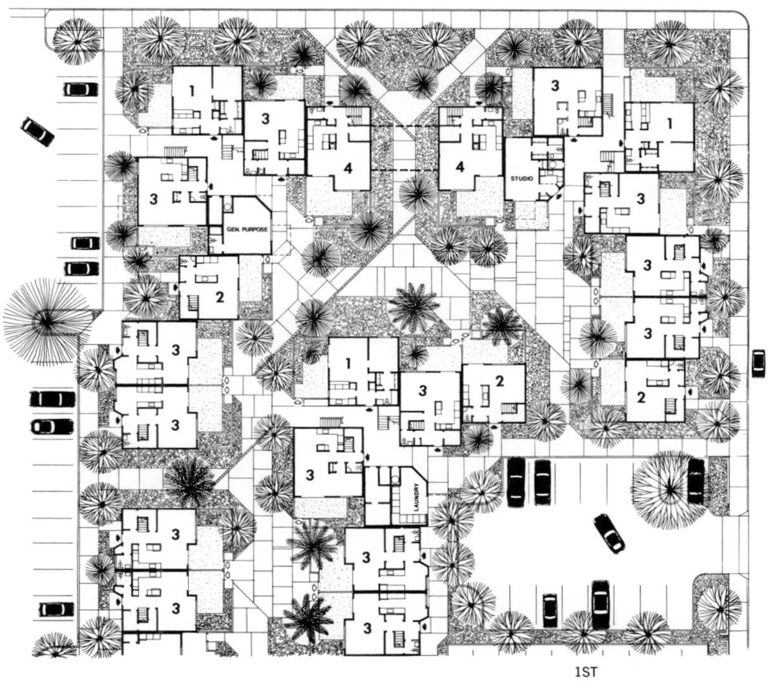
1
3
4
4
3
1
3
GEN. PURPOSE
STUDIO
3
2
3
3
3
1
3
2
3
2
3
LAUNDRY
3
3
3
3
1ST

46

SHEFFIELD MANOR
New Haven, Connecticut

Architect:
ALDEN R. BERMAN
Hamden, Connecticut

Number of dwelling units: 36
4—efficiency
12—two bedroom
8—three bedroom
12—four bedroom
Gross floor area: 36,200 sf (open, on grade parking)
Construction cost: $820,000
$22.65/sf
$22,778/unit
Year of bid: 1969
Site area: 1.06 acres
34 units/acre
User: low income
Financing: conventional

Photo credit: Jack Stock

1ST

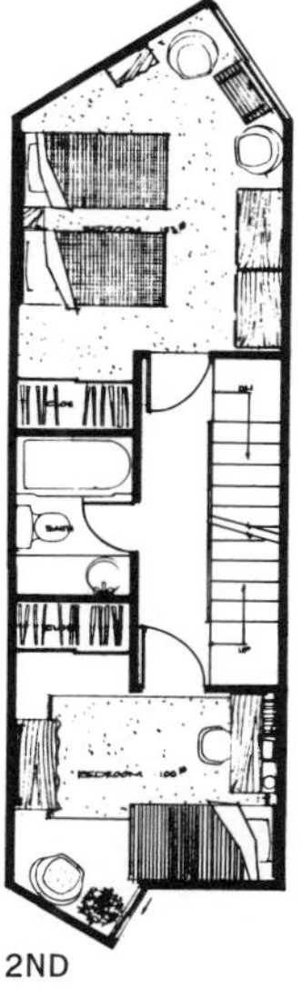
2ND

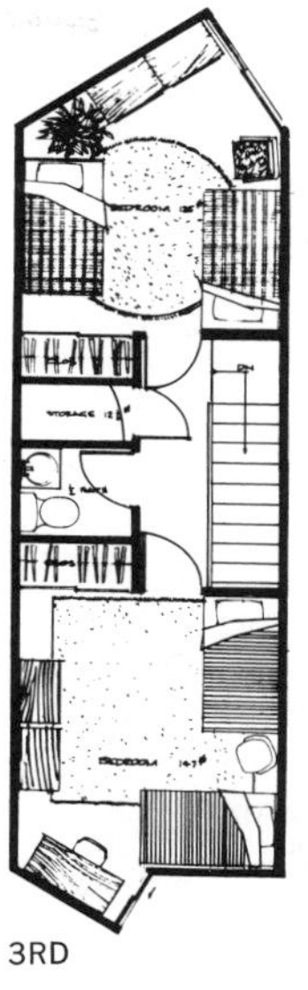
3RD

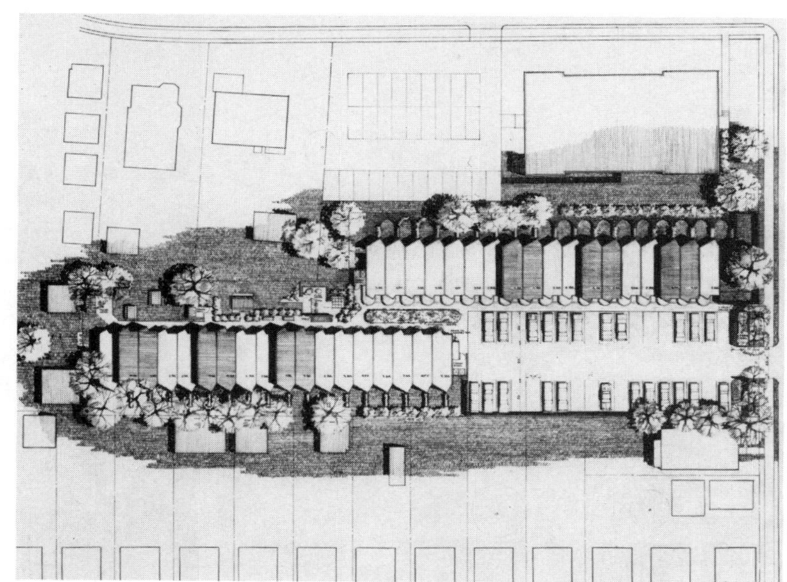

47 CANTERBURY GARDEN CO-OP

New Haven, Connecticut

Architect:
LOUIS SAUER ASSOC.
Philadelphia, Pennsylvania

Number of dwelling units: 34
16—four bedroom townhouses
12—one bedroom walk-ups
6—two bedroom walk-ups

Gross floor area:	38,000 sf (open, on grade parking)
Construction cost:	$850,000
	$22.36/sf
	$25,000/unit
Year of bid:	1970
Site area:	1.56 acres
	22 units/acre
User:	low income
Financing:	FHA 235

Photo credit: Otto Baitz

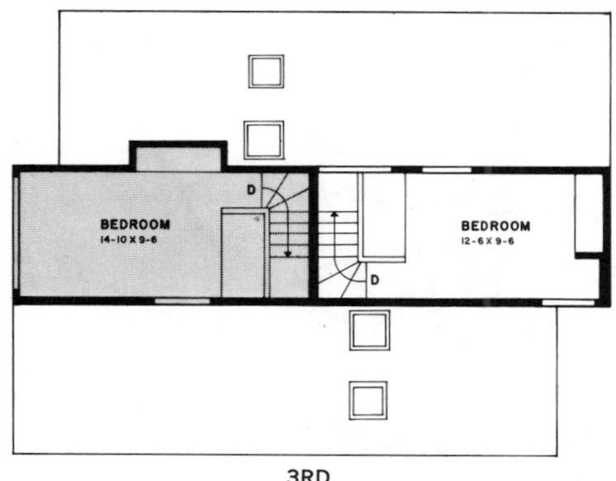

3RD

BEDROOM
11-5 X 11-5
BEDROOM
12-6 X 11-5
BEDROOM
12-10 X 9-6
BEDROOM
12-6 X 9-6
BEDROOM
12-10 X 11-5
BEDROOM
11-1 X 11-5

2ND

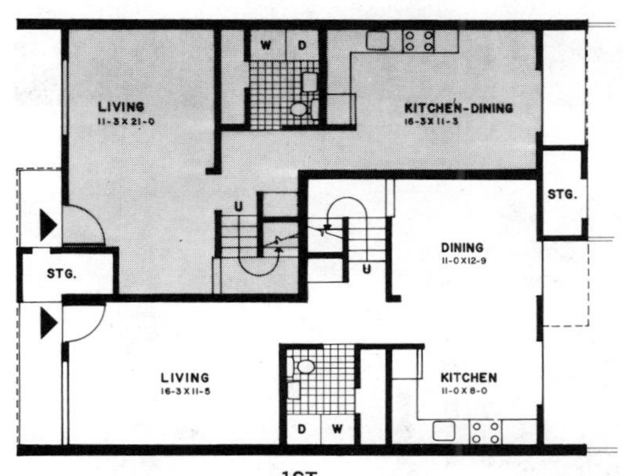

1ST

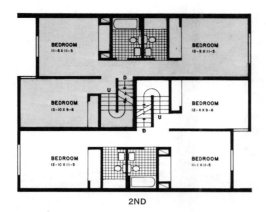

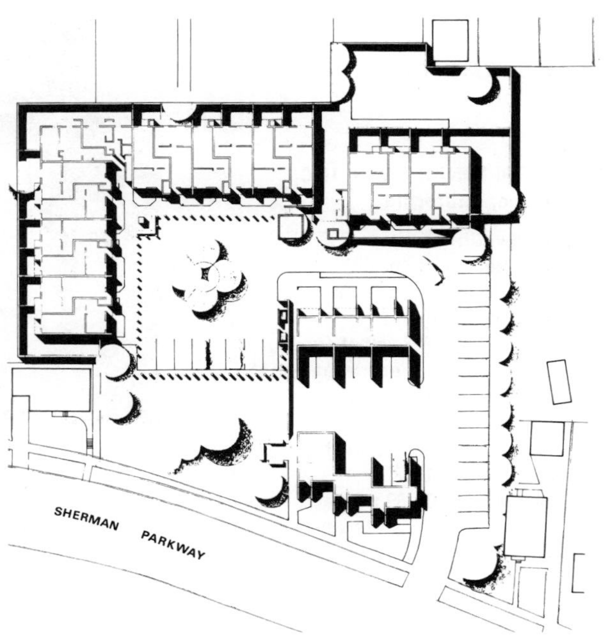

48

TUSTIN APARTMENTS
Tustin, California

Architect:
BACKEN ARRIGONI & ROSS, INC.
San Francisco, California

Number of dwelling units: 296
57—two bedroom (patio)
167—one bedroom (patio)
72—two bedroom (flats)
Gross floor area: 258,450 sf (open, on grade parking)
Construction cost: $2,580,400
$9.98/sf
$8,718/unit
Year of bid: 1968
Site area: 11.89 acres
25 units/acre
User: low to middle income
Financing: private

Photo credit: Ed Stoecklein

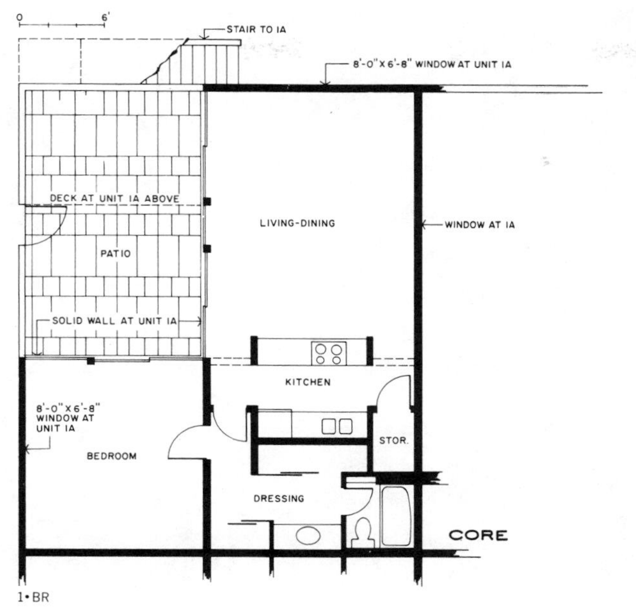

0
6'
STAIR TO IA
8'-0" X 6'-8" WINDOW AT UNIT IA
DECK AT UNIT IA ABOVE
LIVING-DINING
WINDOW AT IA
PATIO
SOLID WALL AT UNIT IA
KITCHEN
8'-0" X 6'-8" WINDOW AT UNIT IA
BEDROOM
STOR.
DRESSING
CORE
1•BR

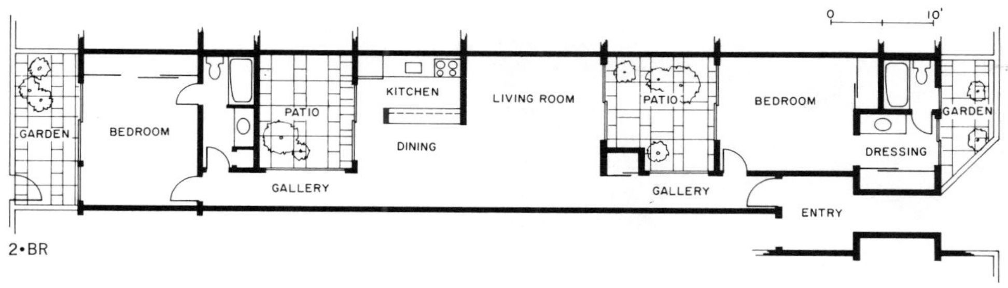

0
10'
GARDEN
BEDROOM
PATIO
KITCHEN
DINING
LIVING ROOM
GALLERY
PATIO
BEDROOM
GARDEN
DRESSING
GALLERY
ENTRY
2•BR

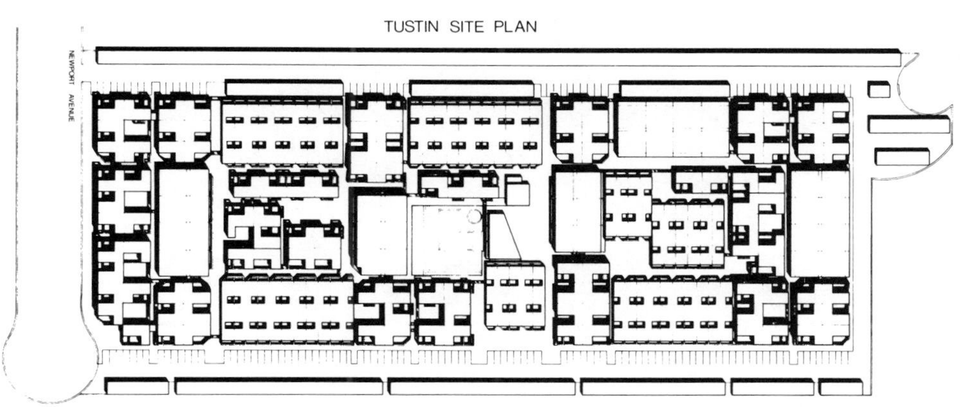

TUSTIN SITE PLAN
NEWPORT AVENUE

49

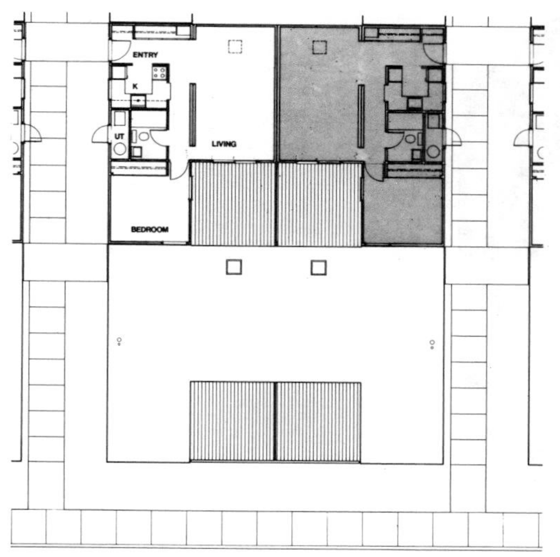

1 BR ATRIUM PLAN

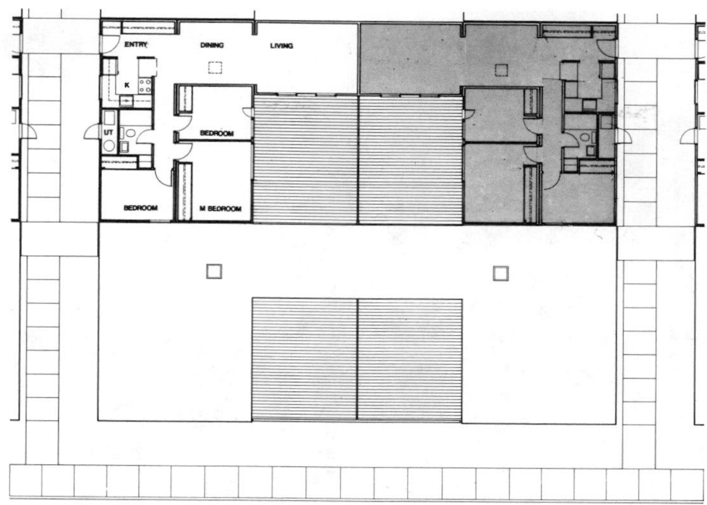

3 BR ATRIUM PLAN

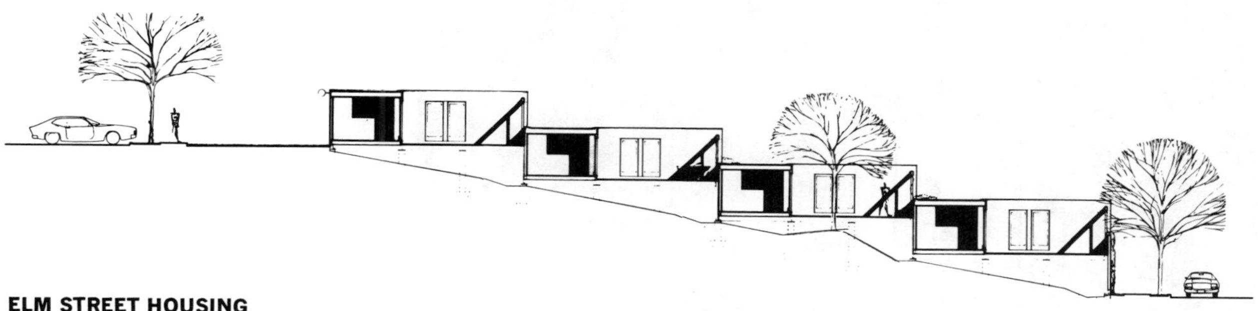

ELM STREET HOUSING
Ithaca, New York

Architect:
WERNER SELIGMAN AND ASSOCIATES
Cortland, New York

Number of dwelling units: 235
- 28—one bedroom atriums
- 72—three bedroom atriums
- 80—two bedroom in townhouse on townhouse walk-up
- 20—one bedroom in townhouse on townhouse walk-up
- 17—one bedroom in duplex walk-up
- 18—four bedroom in duplex walk-up

Gross floor area: 211,770 sf (on grade, open parking)
Construction cost: $5,173,000
$24.42 sf
$22.013/unit
Year of bid: 1970
Site area: 17.63 acres
13.5 units/acre
User: 70% middle income
20% low income
10% elderly
Financing: UDC (FHA 236)

Photo credit: Nathaniel Lieberman

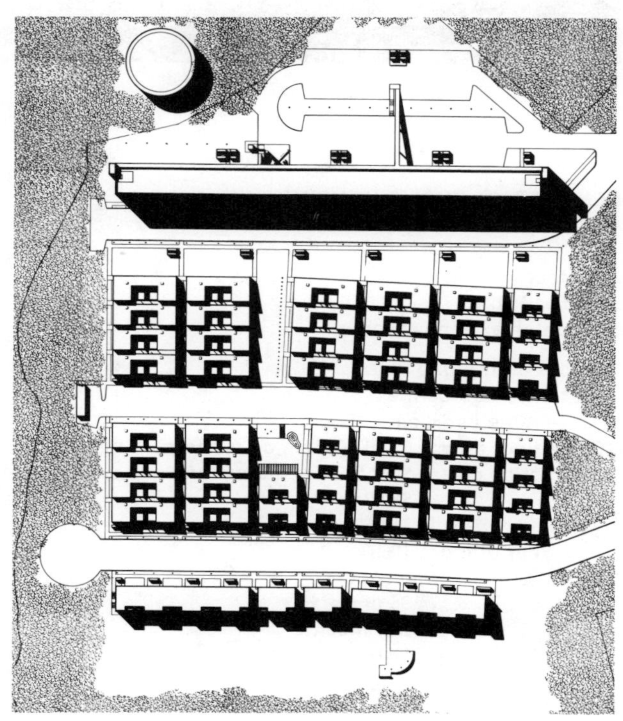

50

RENO STREET PUBLIC HOUSING
Philadelphia, Pennsylvania

Architect:
JOE J. JORDAN
Philadelphia, Pennsylvania

Number of dwelling units: 33
24—two bedroom
9—three bedroom
Gross floor area: 53,200 (open, on grade parking)
Construction cost: $478,500 (including land and architect fee)
$8.99/sf
$14,500/unit
Year of bid: 1965
Site area: 0.92 acres
36 units/acre
User: low income
Financing: HUD Turnkey

Photo credit: Lawrence S. Williams

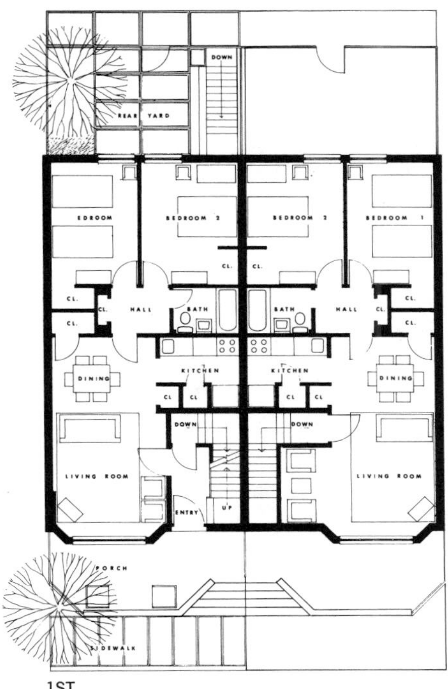
DOWN
REAR YARD
BEDROOM
BEDROOM 2
BEDROOM 2
BEDROOM 1
CL.
HALL
BATH
BATH
HALL
DINING
KITCHEN
KITCHEN
DINING
DOWN
DOWN
LIVING ROOM
LIVING ROOM
ENTRY
UP
PORCH
SIDEWALK

1ST

REAR YARD
UP
KITCHEN
CL
CL
BEDROOM 1
CL
CL
DINING
BEDROOM 2
HALL
DOWN
UP
CL
DOWN
LIVING ROOM
BEDROOM 3
BATH
PORCH
SIDEWALK

2ND

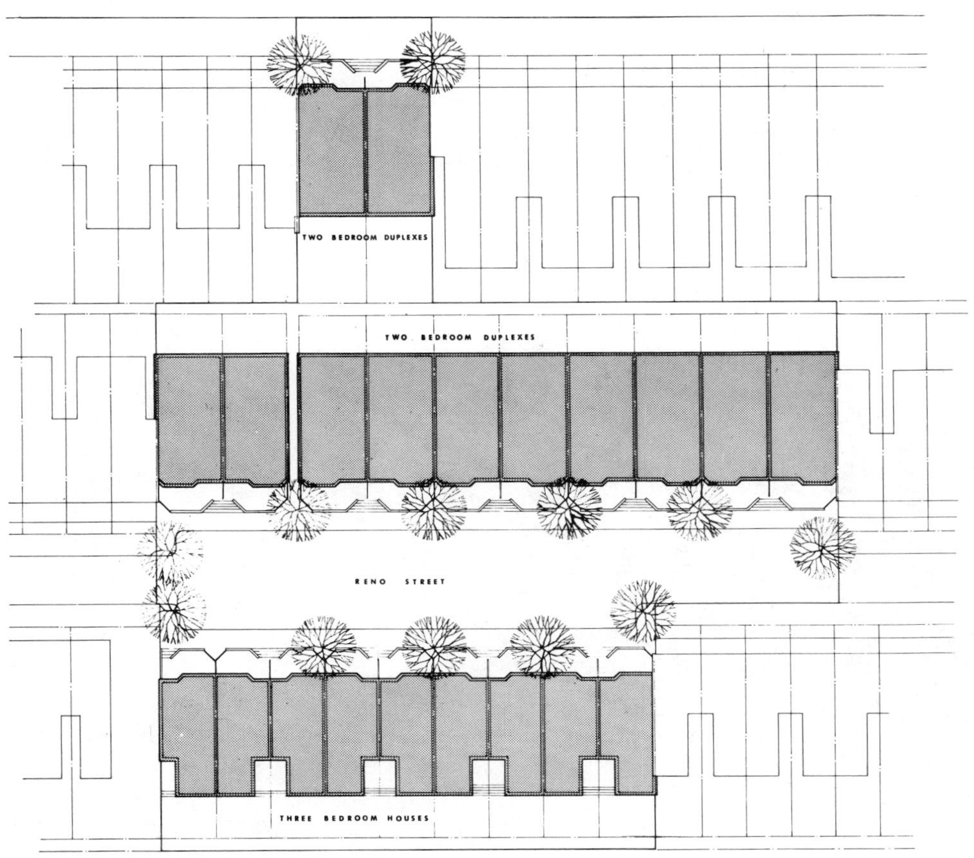
TWO BEDROOM DUPLEXES
TWO BEDROOM DUPLEXES
RENO STREET
THREE BEDROOM HOUSES

51 **LAKE VILLAGE (walk-up)**
Chicago, Illinois

Architect:
HARRY WEESE & ASSOCIATES
EZRA GORDON—JACK LEVIN
Chicago, Illinois

Number of dwelling units: 122
- 24—one bedroom
- 70—two bedroom
- 28—three bedroom

Gross floor area: 120,070 sf (open, on grade parking)
Construction cost: $1,615,550
$13.45/sf
$13,242/unit
Year of bid: 1968
Site area: part of large complex
User: moderate income
Financing: FHA 236

Photo Credit: Philip Turner

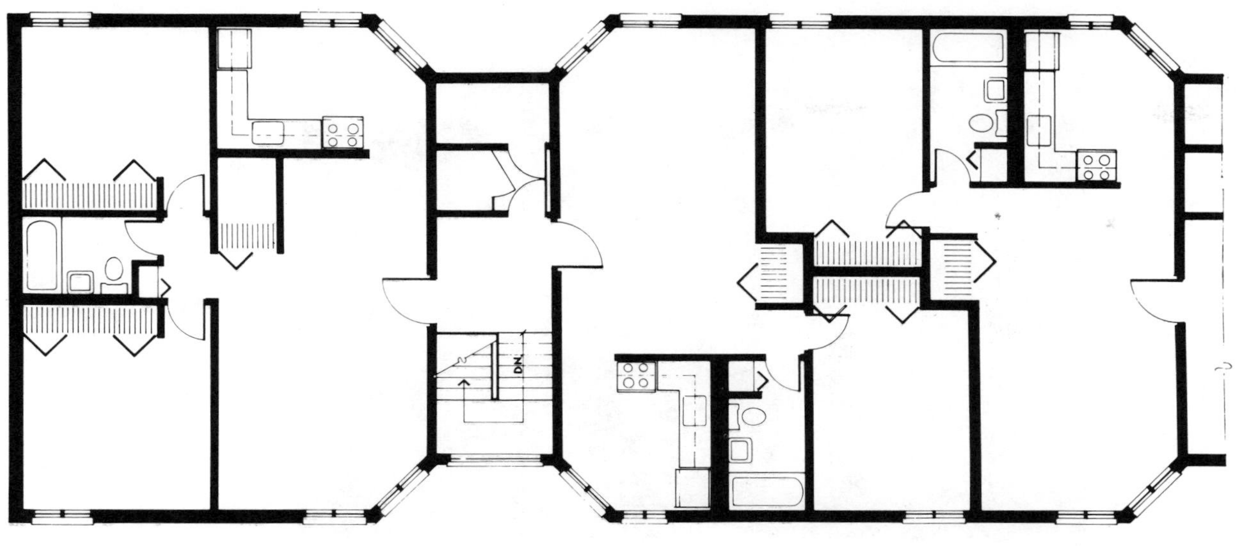

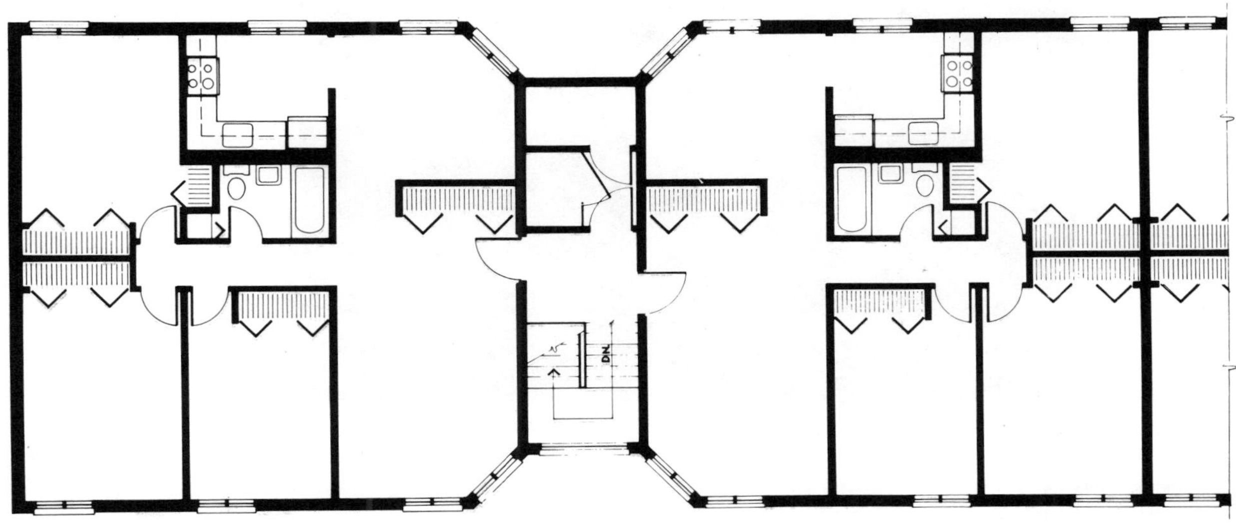

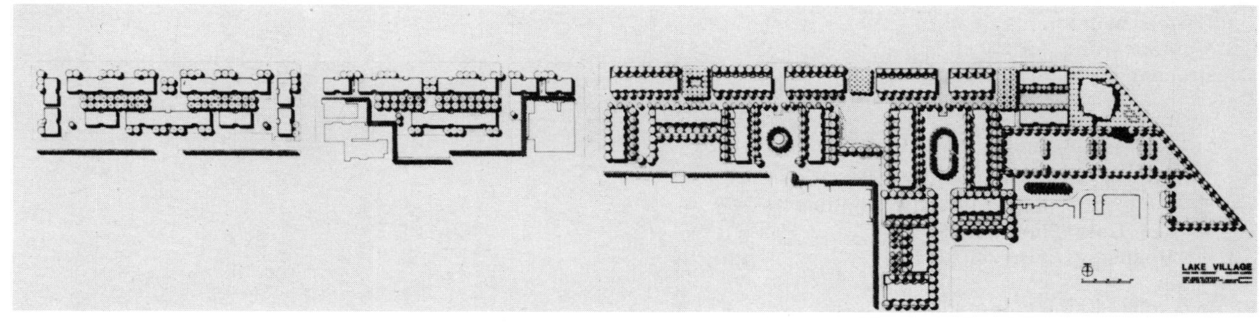
LAKE VILLAGE

52

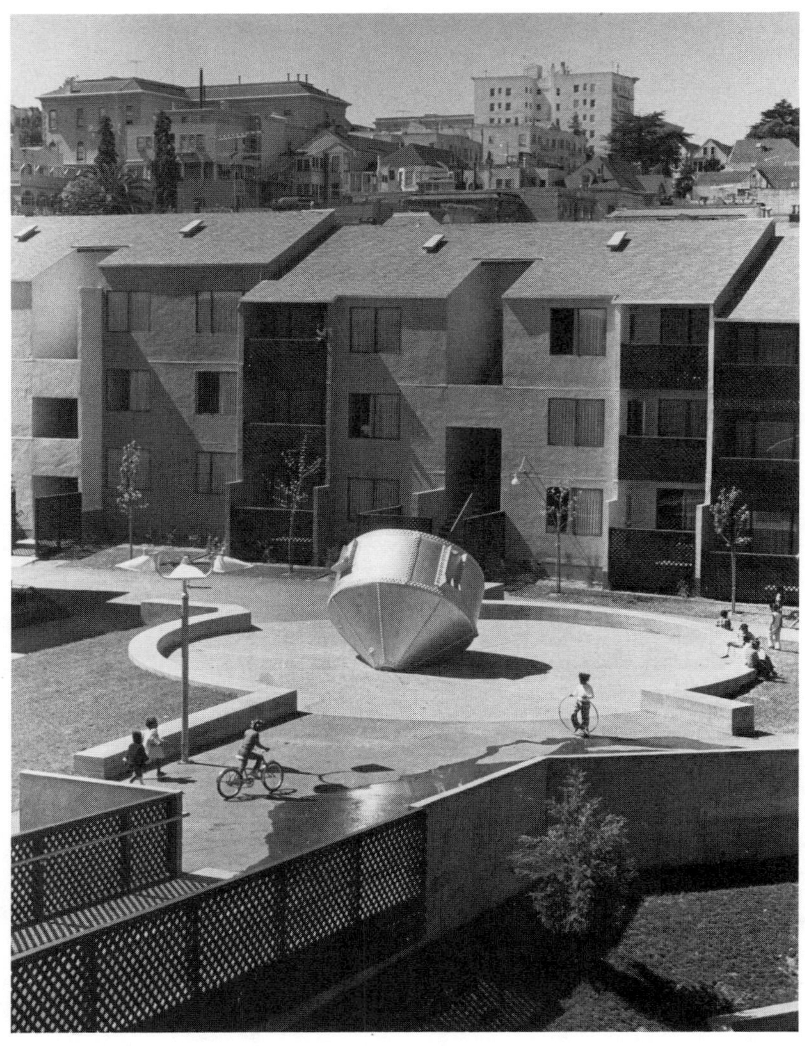

BANNEKER HOMES
San Francisco, California

Architect:
ESHERICK HOMSEY DODGE AND DAVIS
San Francisco, California

Number of dwelling units: 108
- 12—one bedroom
- 40—two bedroom
- 35—three bedroom
- 21—four bedroom

Gross floor area: 168,000 sf
Construction cost: $1,790,000
$10.65/sf
$16,574/unit
Year of bid: 1967
Site area: approximately 2.45 acres
approximately 45 units/acre
User: low income
Financing: FHA 221 (d) 3

Photo credit: Kathleen Kershaw

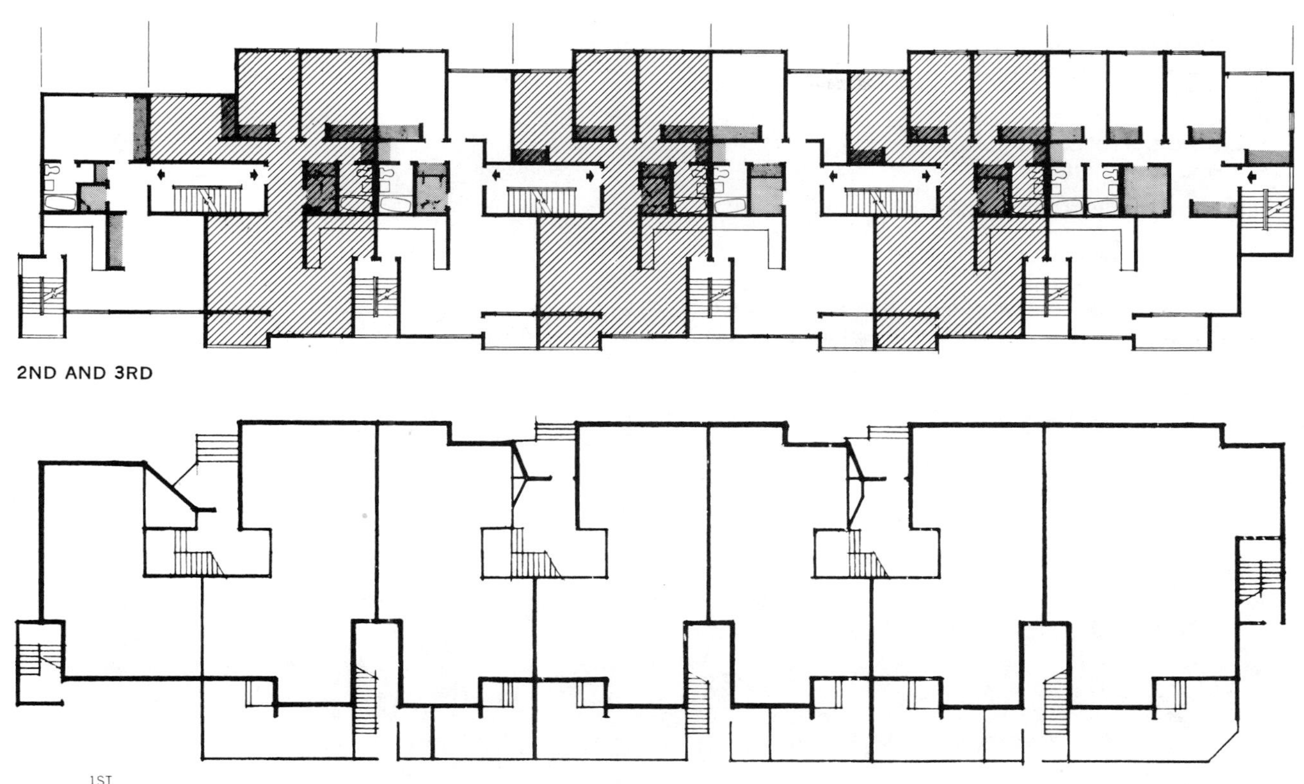
2ND AND 3RD
1ST

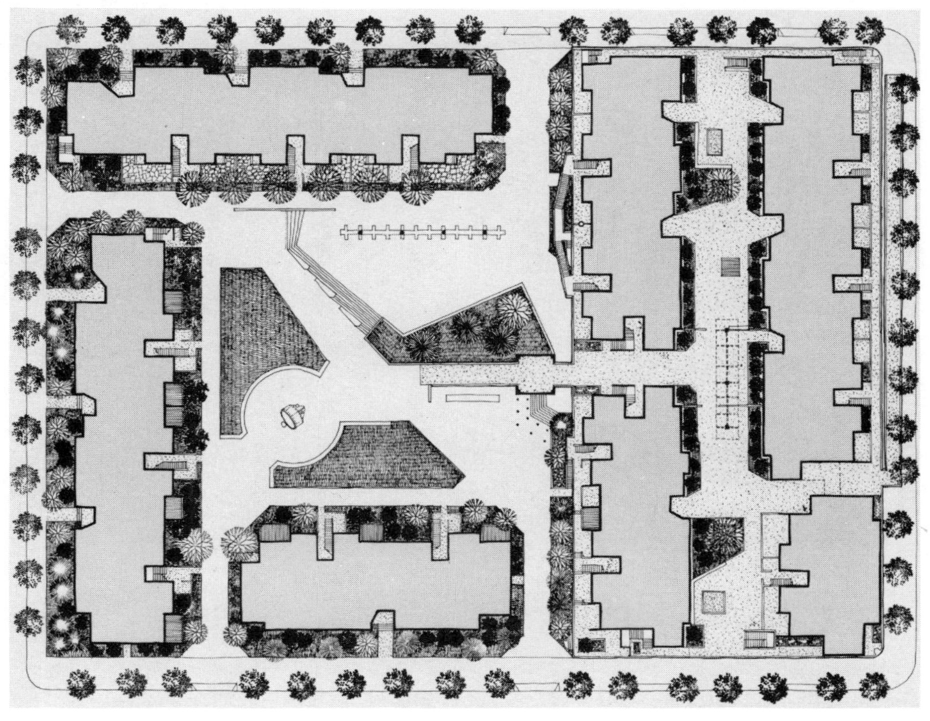

53 ST. FRANCIS SQUARE

San Francisco, California

Architect:
MARQUIS & STOLLER
San Francisco, California

Number of dwelling units: 299
14—one bedroom
107—two bedroom
178—three bedroom

Gross floor area: 305,600 sf (including approximately 20,000 sf parking structures)
Construction cost: $3,497,000 (including parking structures and site work)
$10.74/sf
$11,696/unit
Year of bid: 1962
Site area: 8.15 acres
36.5 units/acre
User: low income
Financing: FHA 221 (d) 3

Photo Credit: Karl H. Riek

UP
BATH
1•BR
UP
DN
BATH
2•BR
DN
UP
BATH 1
BATH 2
3•BR

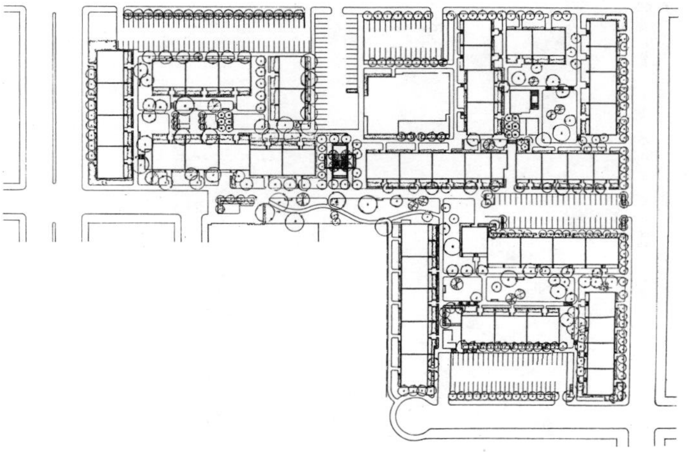

54 **BUFFALO WATERFRONT HOUSING**
Buffalo, New York

Architect:
PAUL RUDOLPH
New York, New York

The project, in addition to the walk-ups illustrated here, contains midrises and the data refer to the total project.

Number of dwelling units: 814
- 178—efficiency
- 197—one bedroom
- 287—two bedroom
- 152—three bedroom

Construction cost: $20,790,000
Year of bid: 1970–1972
Site area and density: not available
Square feet of buildings: not available
User: low income
Financing: U.D.C.

Photo credit: Donald Luckenbill

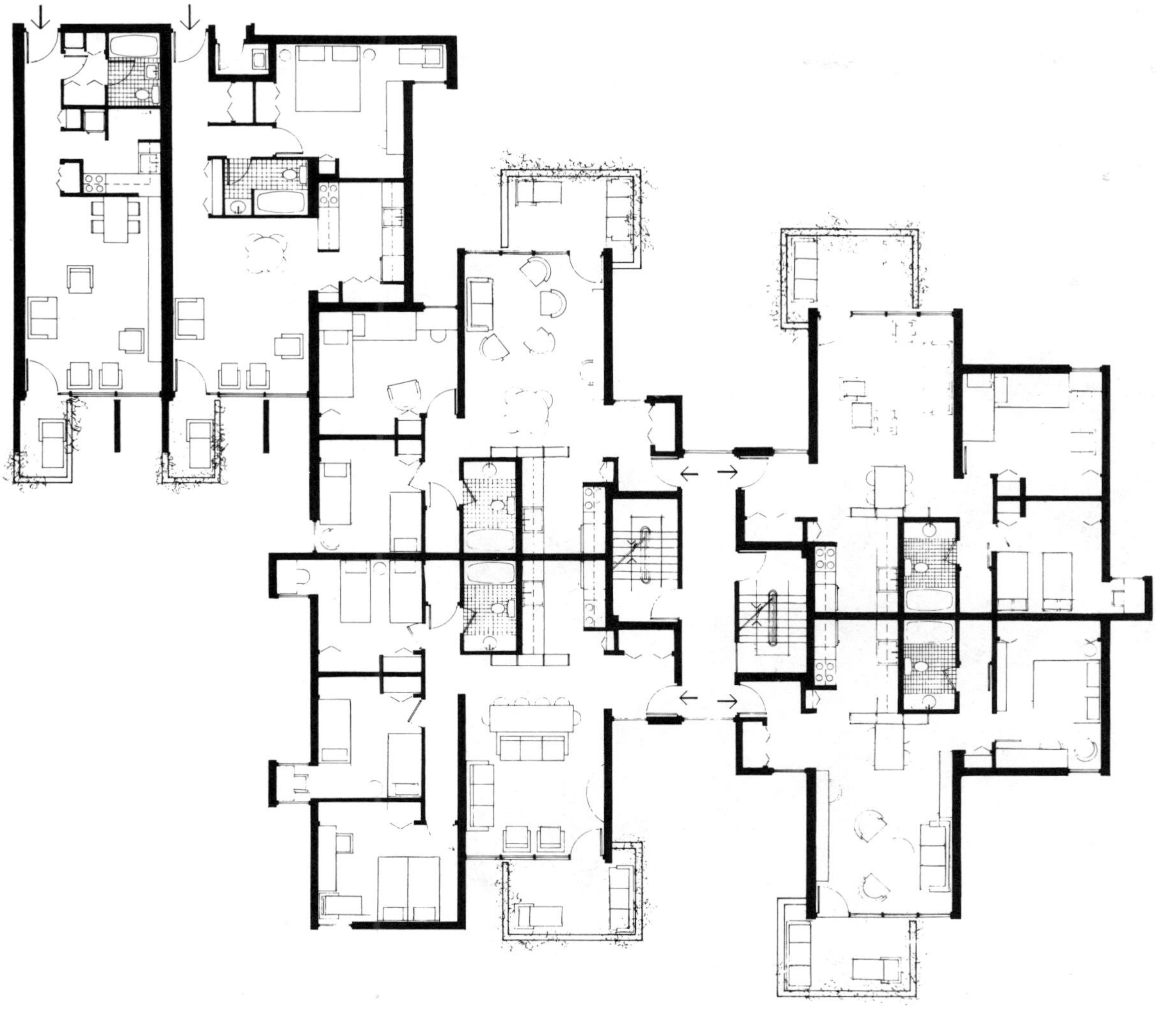

55

PORTALS
Chicago, Illinois

Architect:
BOOTH & NAGLE
Chicago, Illinois

Number of dwelling units: 50 three bedroom apartments
Gross floor area: 75,000 sf
Construction cost: $1,350,000 (open, on grade parking)
$18.00/sf
$27,000/unit
Year of bid: 1971
Site area: 0.94 acres
53 units/acre
User: middle income
Financing: conventional

Photo credit: Philip Turner

d.r. 10-0 x 12-7
l.r. 19-0 x 13-0
A
mbr. 13-0 x 13-0
br. 13-10 x 10-4
br. 9-0 x 12-7
A
l.r. 19-4 x 12-10
d.r. 12-7 x 10-7
B
br. 13-4 x 9-8
br. 10-7 x 9-3
mbr. 17-2 x 10-7
B

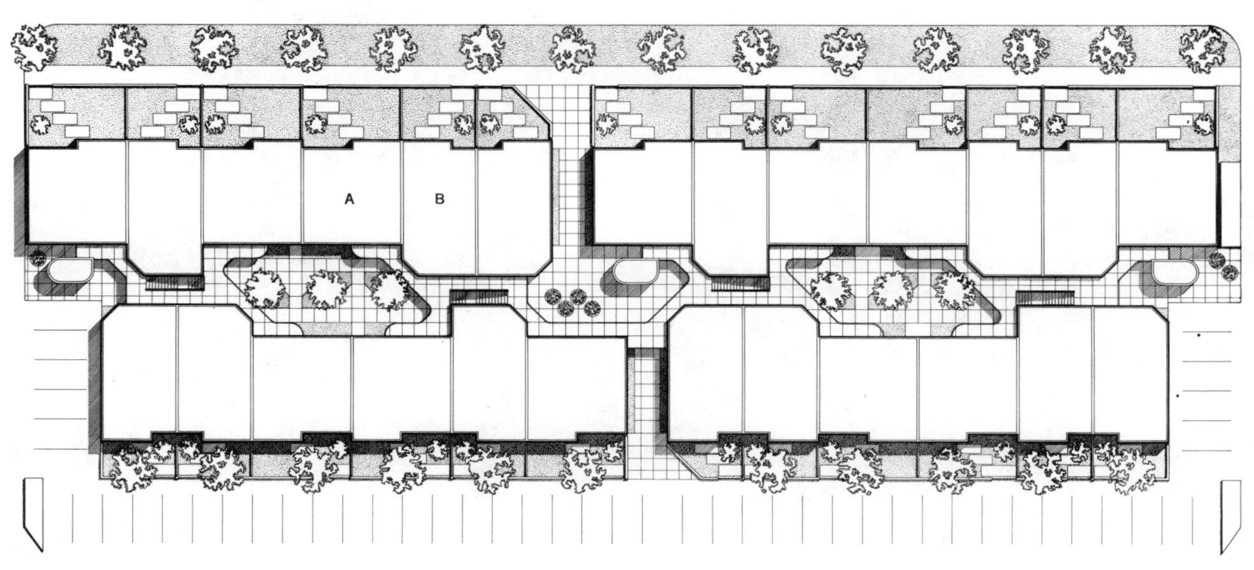
A
B

56 GENESEE GATEWAY
Rochester, New York

Architect:
GRUZEN & PARTNERS
New York, New York
Number of dwelling units: 1200
In lowrise: 480
240—two bedroom
180—three bedroom
60—four bedroom
Gross floor area: 1,036,000 sf
Construction cost: $24,000,000
$23.16/sf
$20,000/unit
Year of bid: 1973
Site area: 33 acres
36.5 units/acre
User: low and moderate income and elderly
Financing: New York State Urban Development Corporation

Photo credit: Robert A. Genchek

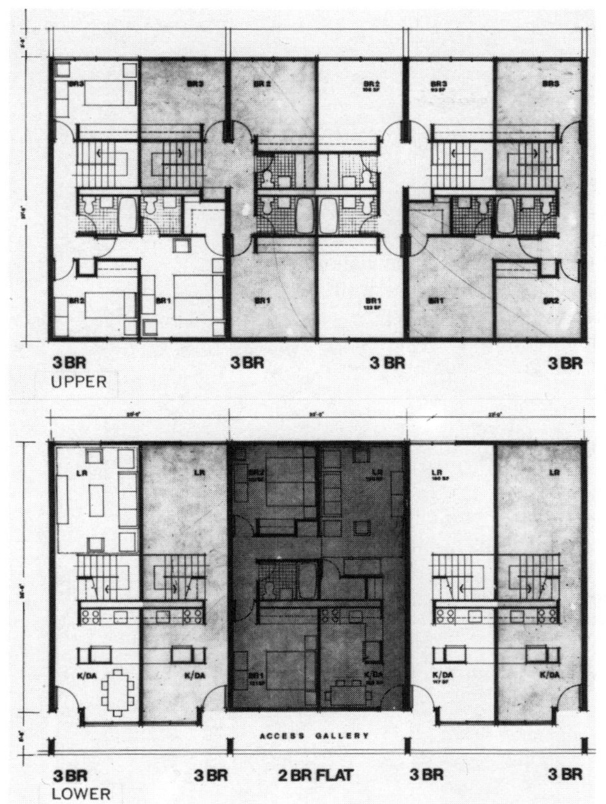
3 BR
UPPER
3 BR
3 BR
3 BR
ACCESS GALLERY
3 BR
LOWER
3 BR
2 BR FLAT
3 BR
3 BR

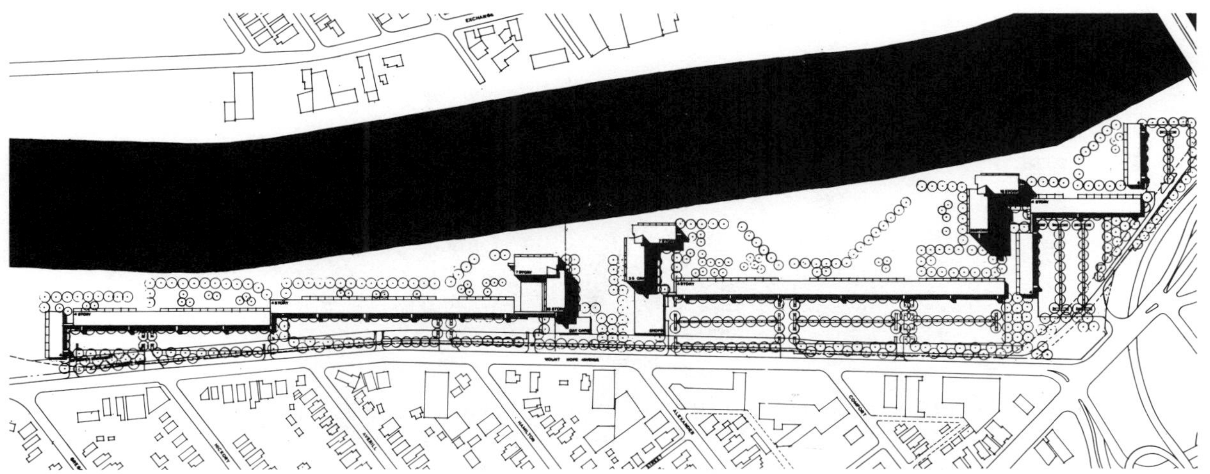

57 ELM STREET HOUSING

Ithaca, New York

Architect:
WERNER SELIGMAN AND ASSOCIATES
Cortland, New York

Number of dwelling units: 235

- 28—one bedroom atriums
- 72—three bedroom atriums
- 80—two bedroom in townhouse on townhouse walk-up
- 20—one bedroom in townhouse on townhouse walk-up
- 17—one bedroom in duplex walk-up
- 18—four bedroom in duplex walk-up

Gross floor area:	211,770 sf (on grade, open parking)
Construction cost:	$5,173,000
	$24.42 sf
	$22,013/unit
Year of bid:	1970
Site area:	17.63 acres
	13.5 units/acre
User:	70% middle income
	20% low income
	10% elderly
Financing:	UDC (FHA 236)

Photo credits: Nathaniel Lieberman; aerial: C. Hadley Smith

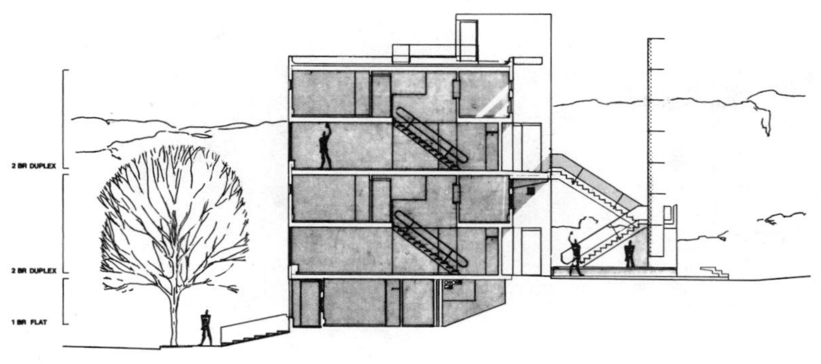
2 BR DUPLEX
2 BR DUPLEX
1 BR FLAT

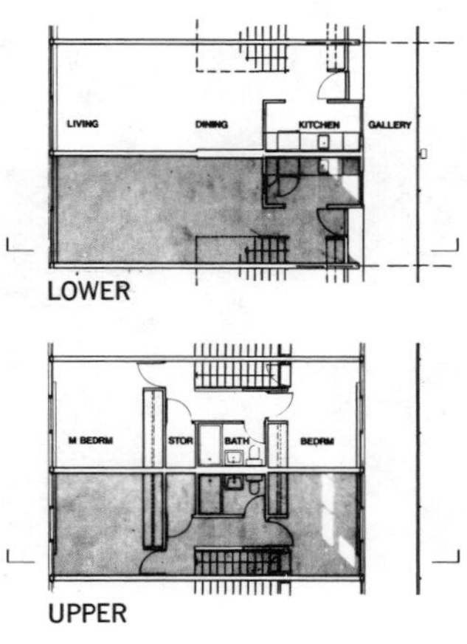
LIVING
DINING
KITCHEN
GALLERY
LOWER
M BEDRM
STOR
BATH
BEDRM
UPPER

58

ESPLANADE VILLAGE
Redondo Beach, California

Architect:
BRENT GOLDMAN ROBBINS & BROWN
West Los Angeles, California

Number of dwelling units: 105
29—efficiency
9—one bedroom
22—two bedroom
45—three bedroom
Gross floor area: 156,000 sf (including parking garage)
Construction cost: $1,400,000
$8.97/sf
$13,333/unit
Year of bid: 1971
Site area: 1.2 acres
87 units/acre
User: upper to middle income
Financing: conventional

Photo credit: Chuck Crandall

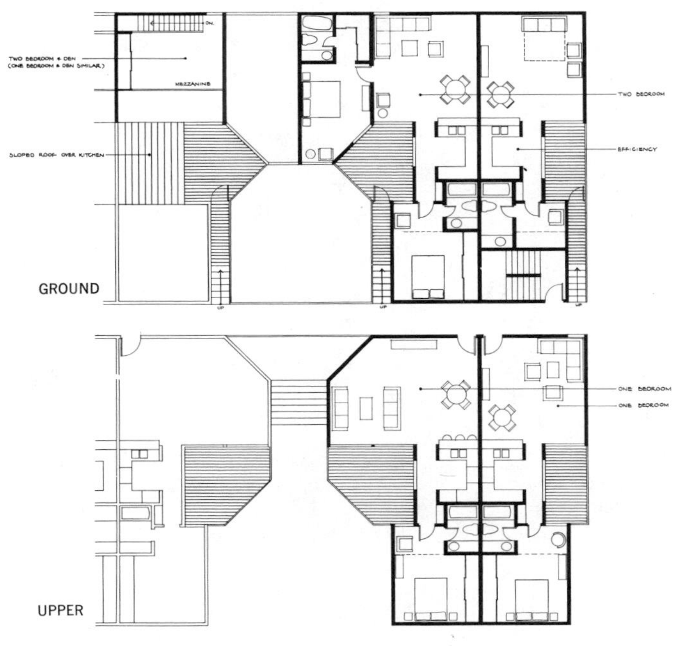
DN.
TWO BEDROOM & DEN
(ONE BEDROOM & DEN SIMILAR)
MEZZANINE
SLOPED ROOF OVER KITCHEN
TWO BEDROOM
EFFICIENCY
GROUND
ONE BEDROOM
ONE BEDROOM
UPPER

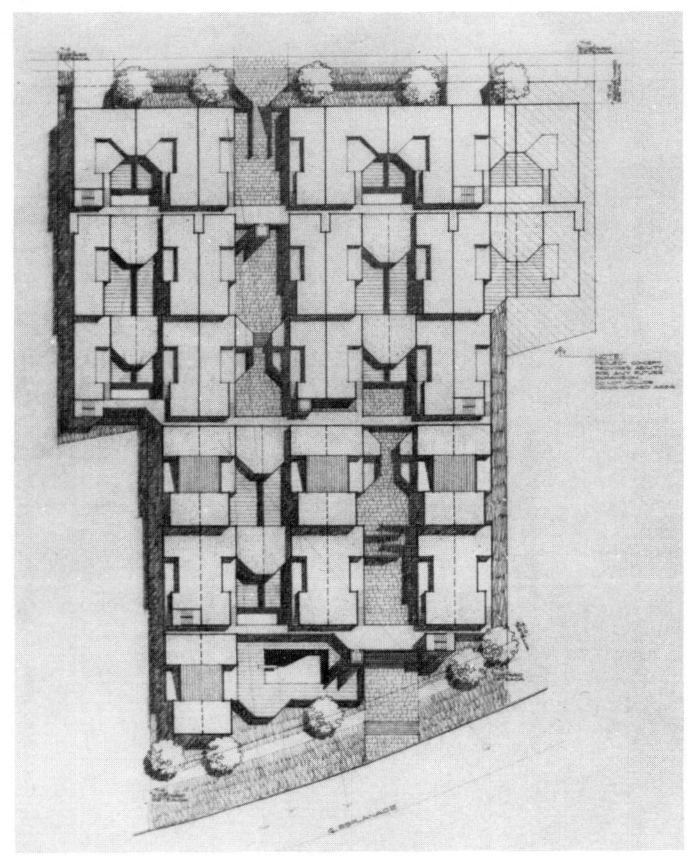

59

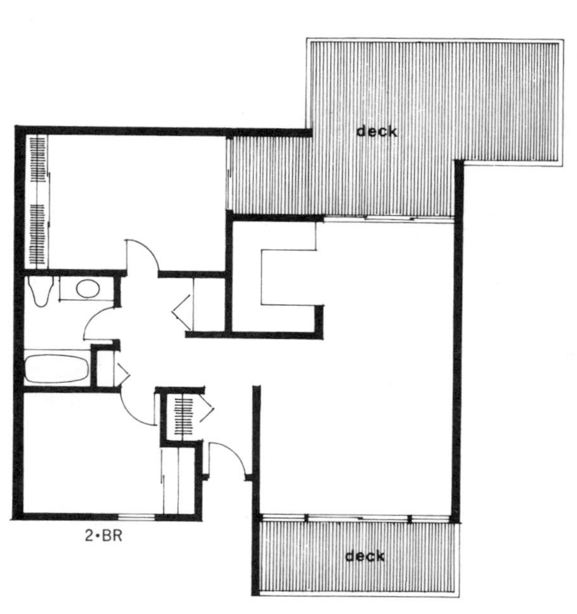

EAST BURNSIDE
Portland, Oregon

Architect:
MARTIN/SODERSTROM/MATTESON
Portland, Oregon

Number of dwelling units: 26
10—one bedroom
16—two bedroom
Construction cost: $10.00 sf
Year of bid: 1967
Site area: 0.78 acres
33.5 units/acre
User: middle income
Financing: conventional

Photo credit: Edmund Y. Lee

60

THE CITADEL
Albuquerque, New Mexico

Architect
ANTOINE PREDOCK
Albuquerque, New Mexico

Number of dwelling units: 232
102—efficiency
128—one bedroom
2—guest units
Gross floor area: 123,160 sf (open, on grade parking)
Construction cost: $2,000,000
$16.23/sf
$8,621/unit
Year of bid: 1972
Site area: 5.43 acres
43 units/acre
User: middle income
Financing: conventional

Photo credit: Joshua Freiwald

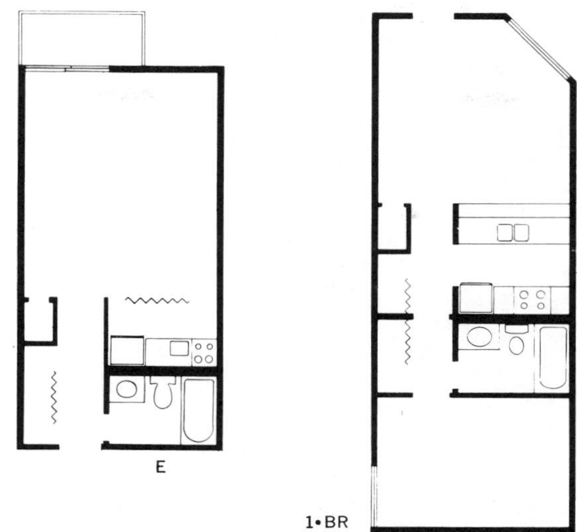

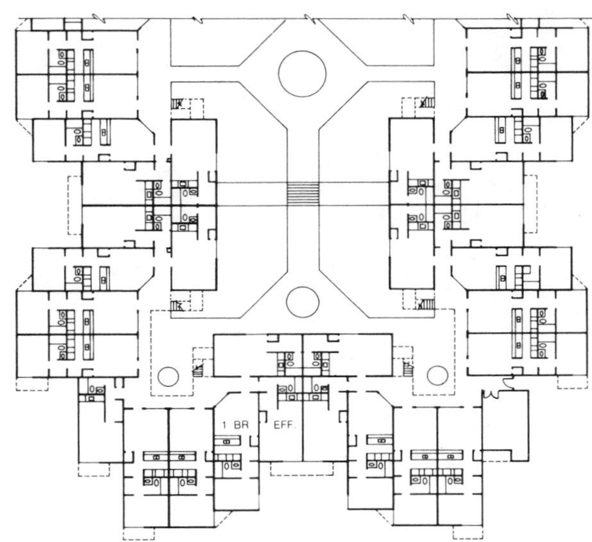

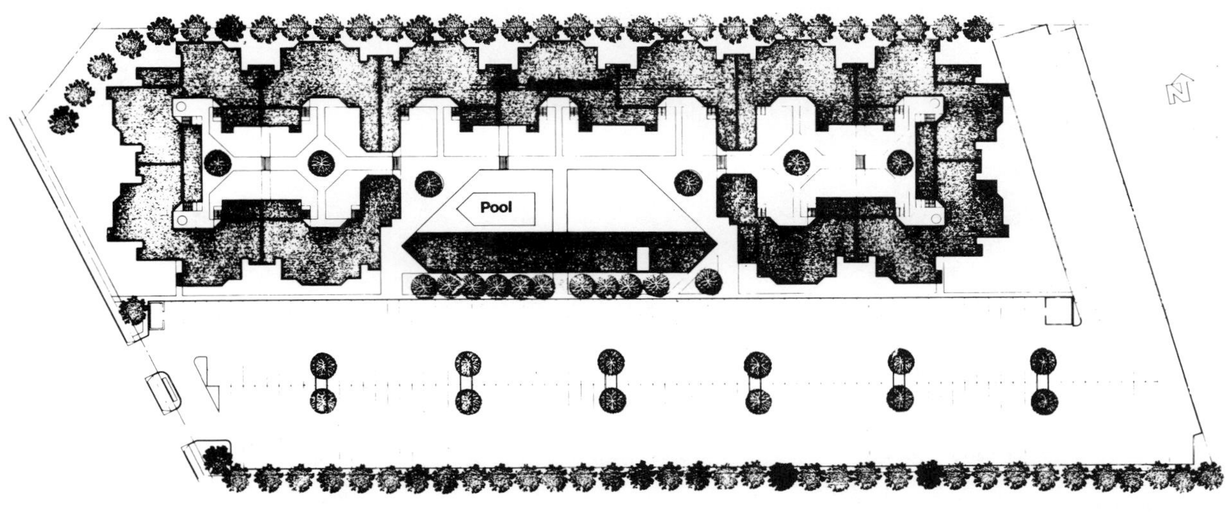

Site Plan

61

WOODLAWN GARDENS
Chicago, Illinois

Architect:
STANLEY TIGERMAN
Chicago, Illinois

Number of dwelling units: 504
Walk-up: 126—two bedroom
252—three bedroom
Midrise: 126 (not shown)
Gross floor area: 475,000 sf
Construction cost: $6,400,000
$13.47/sf
$12,698/unit
Year of bid: 1968
Site area: 11.27 acres
45 units/acre
User: low income
Financing: FHA 221 (d) 3

Photo credit: Philip Turner

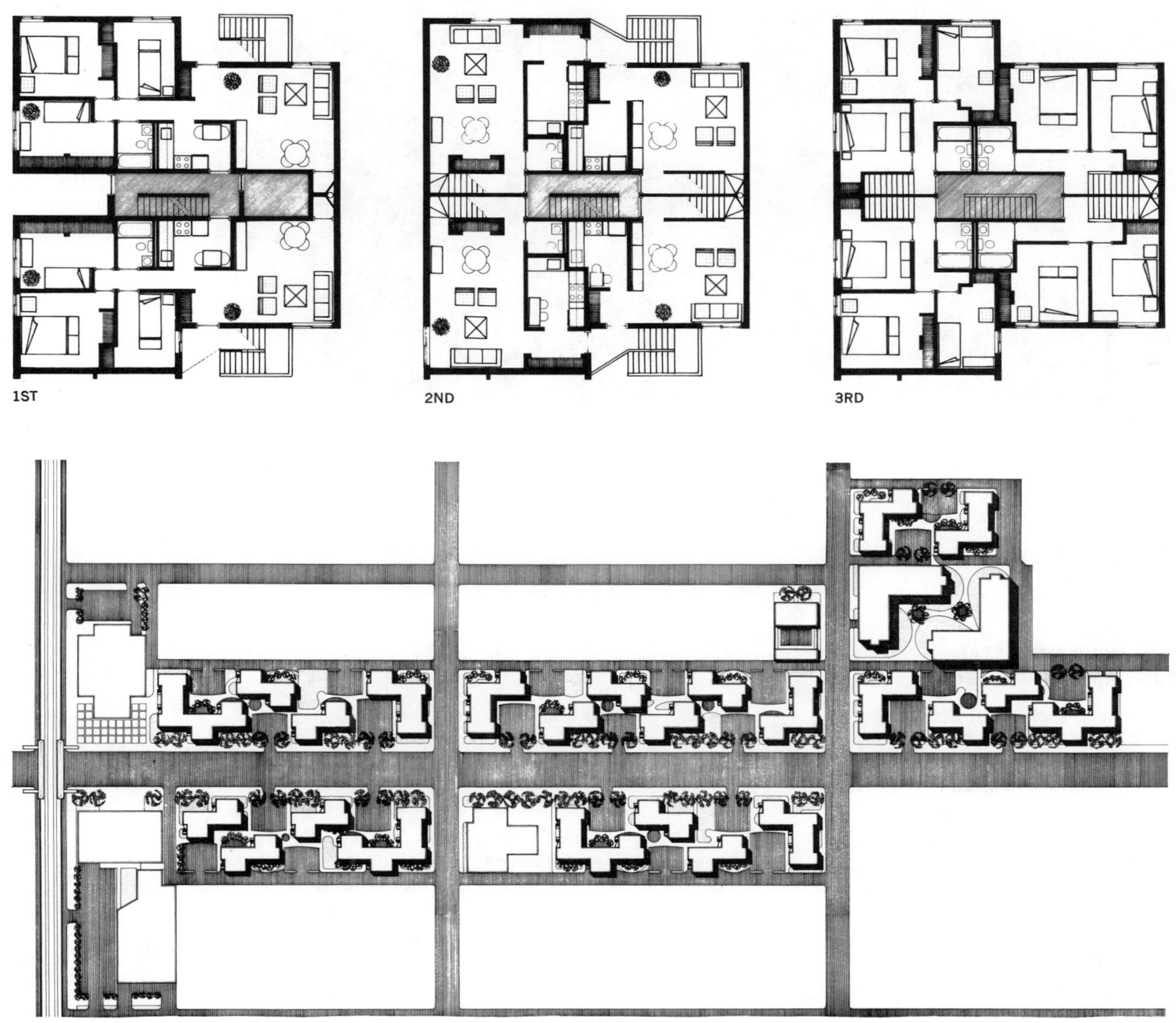
1ST
2ND
3RD

62

SURSUM CORDA
Washington, D. C.

Architect:
COLLINS & KRONSTAD
Silver Springs, Maryland

Number of dwelling units: 199
- Apartments
  - 30—efficiency
  - 14—one bedroom
  - 30—two bedroom
  - 14—three bedroom
- Townhouses
  - 25—three bedroom
  - 46—four bedroom
  - 20—five bedroom
  - 20—six bedroom

Photo credit: Mark G. Farris

Gross floor area: 193,000 sf (open, on grade parking)
Construction cost: $3,000,000
$15.53/sf
$15,075/unit
Year of bid: 1968
Site area: 5.63 acres
35.5 units/acre
User: low to moderate income
Financing: FHA 221 (d) 3

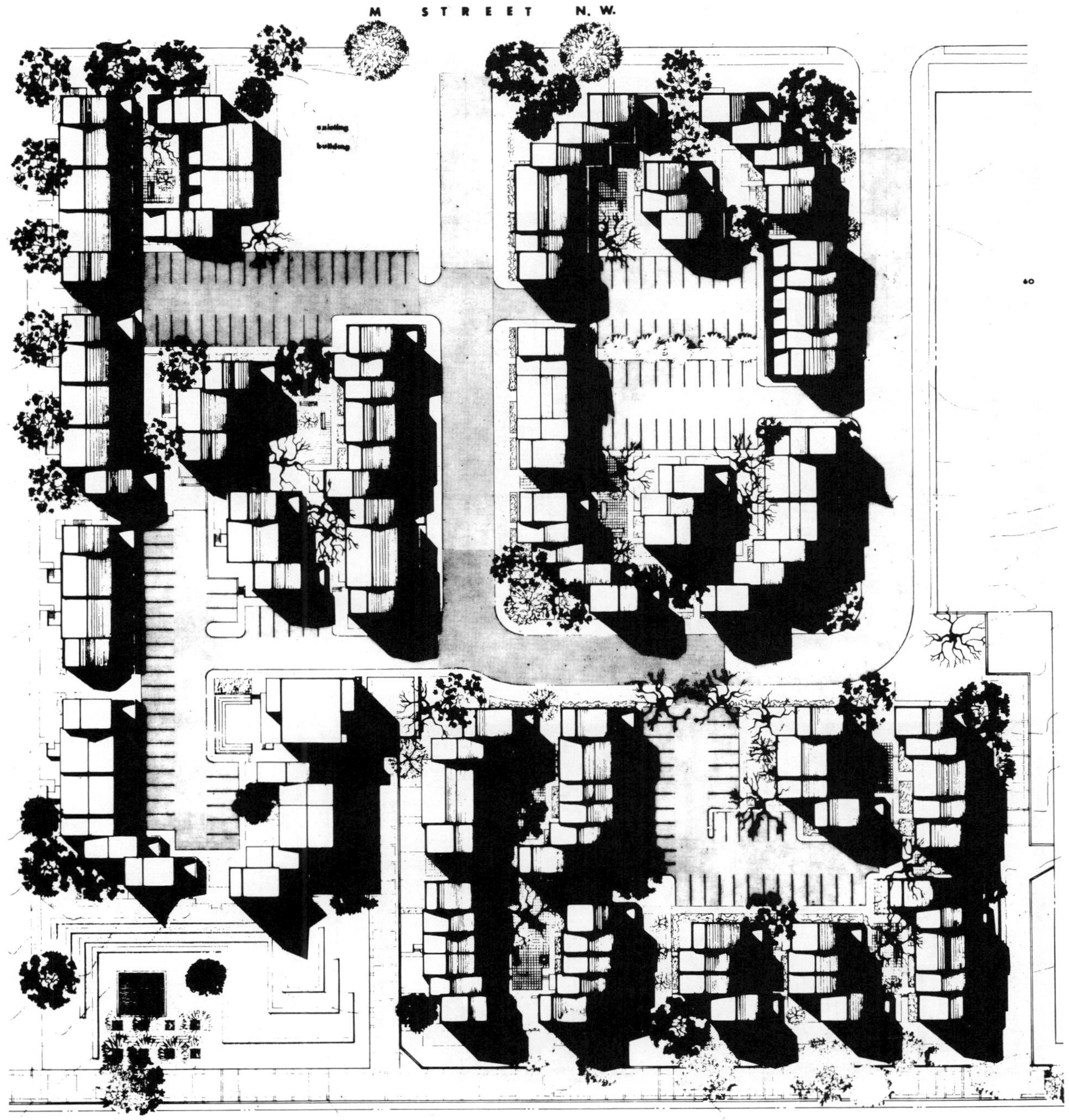
M STREET N.W.
existing
building

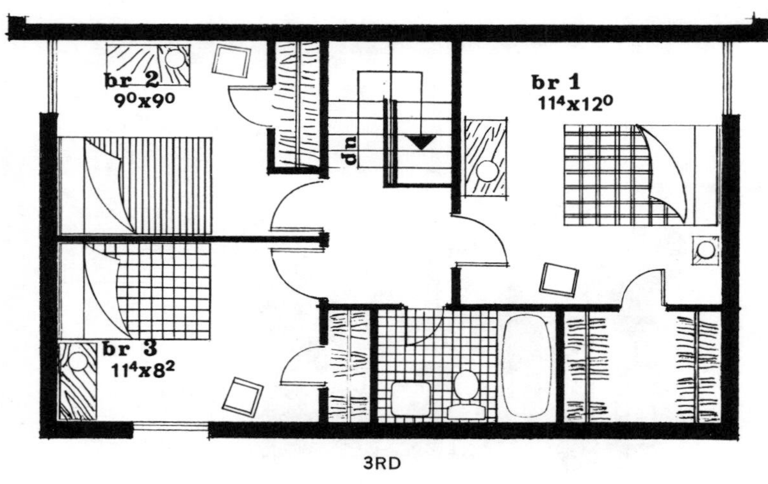
br 2
9^{0}x9^{0}
dn
br 1
11^{4}x12^{0}
br 3
11^{4}x8^{2}

3RD

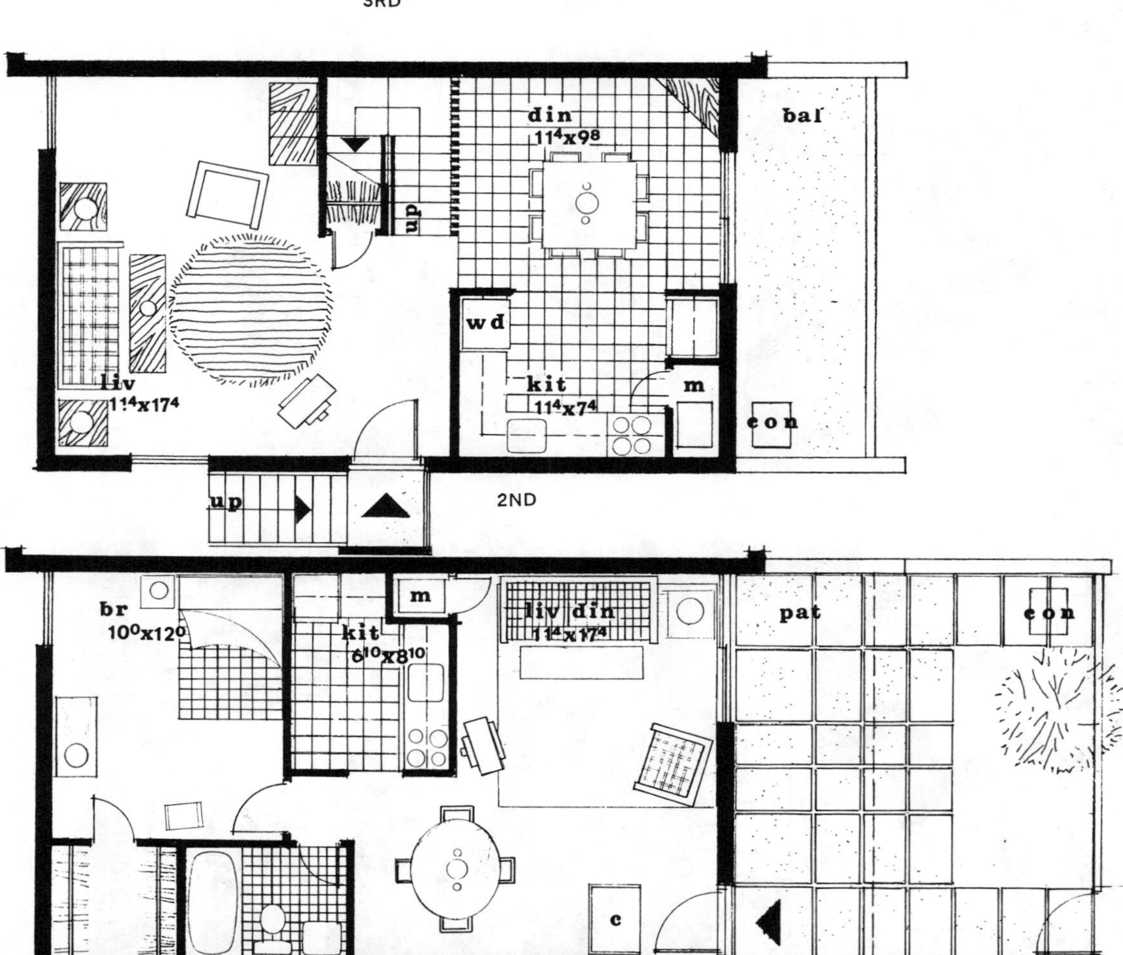
din
11^{4}x9^{8}
bal
up
wd
kit
11^{4}x7^{4}
m
liv
11^{4}x17^{4}
con
up
2ND
br
10^{0}x12^{0}
m
kit
6^{10}x8^{10}
liv din
11^{4}x17^{4}
pat
con
c

1ST

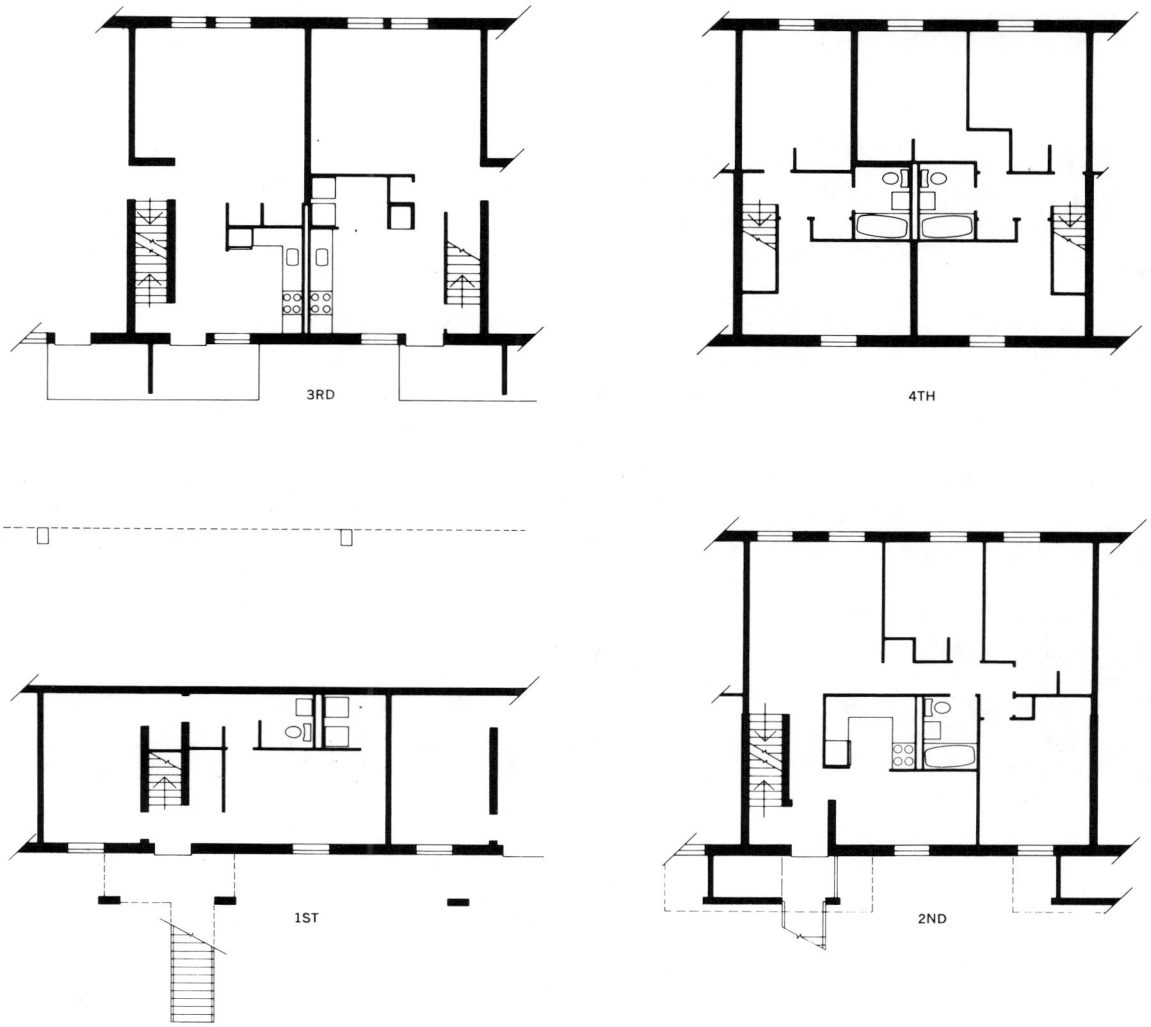

3RD

4TH

1ST

2ND

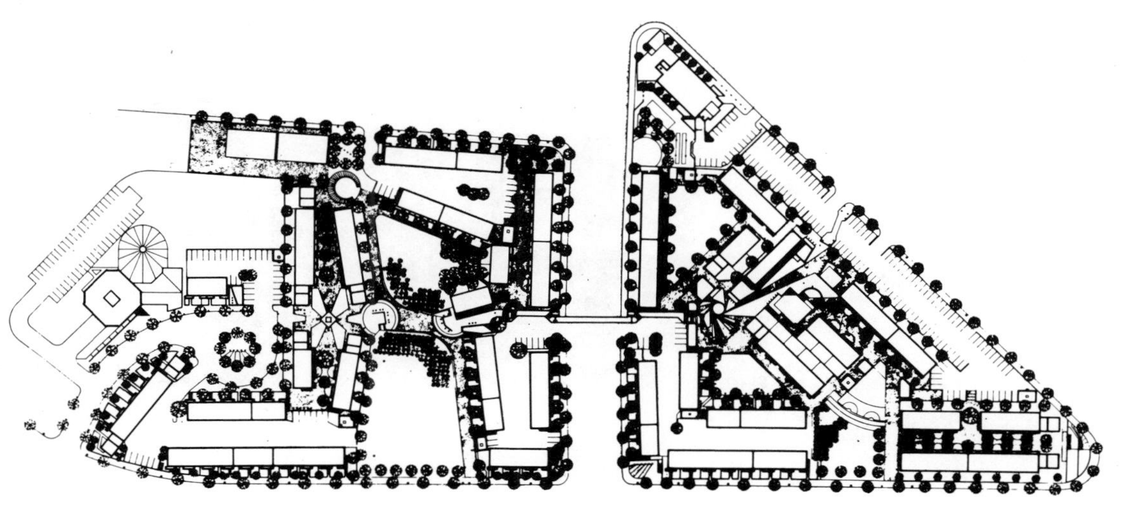

64

MARCUS GARVEY PARK VILLAGE
Brownsville, New York

Architect:
THE INSTITUTE FOR ARCHITECTURE AND URBAN STUDIES
(Architects: Arthur Baker, Kenneth Frampton; Planner: Peter Wolf; Supervising Architect: Leland Taliaferro)
New York, New York

Number of dwelling units: 625
- 23—efficiency
- 63—one bedroom
- 291—two bedroom
- 180—three bedroom
- 40—four bedroom
- 28—five bedroom

Construction cost: $22,650,000 (including 5000 sf community space; 8000 sf commercial; 12,000 sf day-care; open on-grade parking)
$36,240/unit
Year of bid: 1973
Site area: 12.5 acres
50 units/acre
User: low income
Financing: UDC

Photo credit: Sharon Lee Ryder

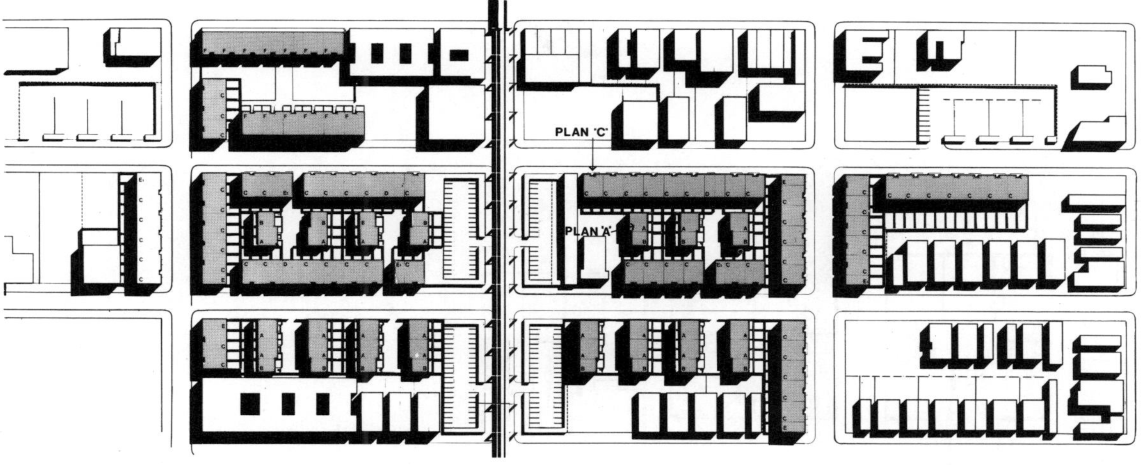

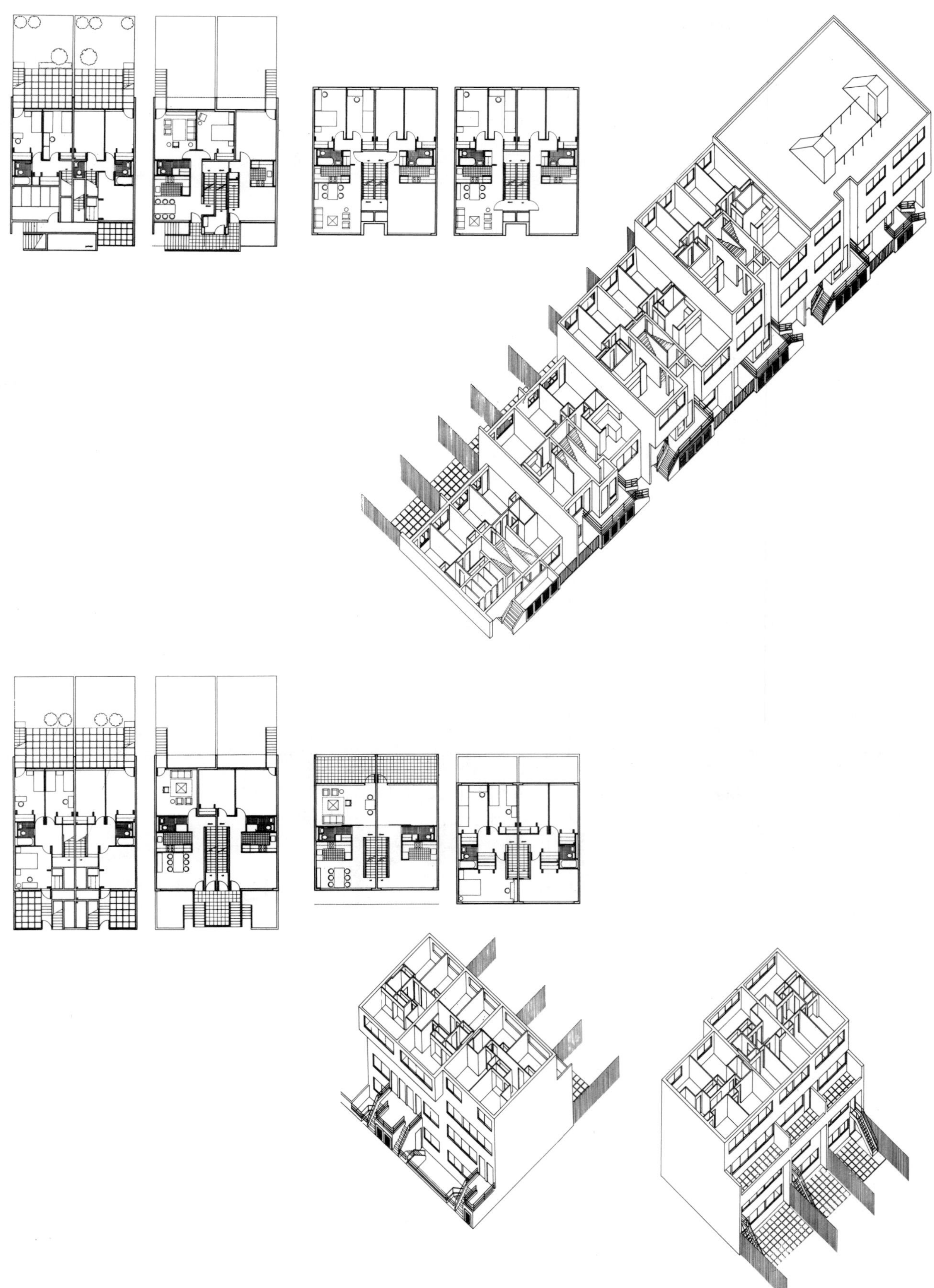

INDEX

Absorption refrigeration, 9, 121-122
Access to apt., 229
to distribution panel, 184
to electric box, 180
to electrical distribution, 181
to expansion-contraction devices in piping, 133
to sewers, 164
to transformers, 178
Access panels, 133
Accordion door, 37
Acoustical baffles, built into exhaust ductwork, 144
Actual heating load, 114
Adjustment of water distribution for heating, cooling, 132
Adult recreation facilities, 72
Africa, cooling in, 106
Air, as coolant, 120
as source of heat, 123
balancing connections, in venting systems, 165
chambers, protection of pipes, 159
change rate, 107
content, in ventilation, oxygen, fuel, odors, humidity, 140
cooling, 119
cushion, 154-155
distribution ductwork, 127
distribution system, advantages and disadvantages of, 113
in drainage pipes, 165
expulsion of, 107
filter, in furnaces, 112
in fuel conversion, 112
heat, 116-118
heating system, 113
intake grill, 246
leakage, as heat loss, 125
makeup, 145
passages, vertical, eliminating stack effect, 141
pockets, in piping systems, 161
removal of, 107
replacement, make-up, exhausted, 107
space, ductwork requirements, 118
spaces, 115
stream, outdoor, 120
supply, 146
supply duct, location of, 44
system, disadvantages and advantages of, 117
systems, space allowance for, 118
volume dampers, motor-driven, 139
in water pipes, 159
Airborne noise, 80
Air conditioning, 9, 105-139, 197
in estimated load, 182
Air passages, 135
Air-rights in zoning, 77, 90
Alarm, audible fire, location of, 188
Alarm system, for elderly, 66
Albuquerque, N. M., 445
Alcove, dining, 7, 27-28
Alternating current, 178
Aluminum, annodized, 245-246
Aluminum conductors, 178-179
Aluminum conduit, 179
Aluminum curtain wall, 251
Ambiguity, 264
Ambulance, 291
Amenities, 6, 263, 306, 308, 310
Amoritization, 305-306
Amount of loan, 305
Amperes, 177
service size, 182
Ancillary electrical systems, 187-192
Annunciator board, locating the fire, 189-190
Apartment feeder, 185
loads, 99
sizes of, 33
Apartment types, efficiency, 6, 20, 32-33, 37, 199, 215
elderly, 33
one bedroom, 6, 20, 33, 199, 205, 208, 210-211, 215-216, 225-226
two bedroom, 6, 26-29, 33, 199, 205-210, 216, 226, 235
three bedroom, 6, 33, 199, 205, 208-211, 214, 216
Apparent structure, 243, 288
Appliances, as heat producing

elements, 138
electrical, 175
estimated level (range, heat, air conditioner, clothes dryer), 182
Arcade, 20, 239, 247, 250, 255, 265
circulation of area, 21
for drive, 61
Areaway stair, 271
Armored cable, use of, 179
Artesian well, 151
Articulation, 210, 216, 223, 227, 229, 247, 249-251, 255, 263-264, 288-289
of balconies, 28
of lowrise, 266
by mechanical equipment room location, 110
of townhouses, 274
of walk-up, 279, 283
Asbestos-cement, as material for sewers, 164
Asbestos-cement pipe, water piping, 159
Asia, cooling in, 106
Assemblies of main switches, location in high-rises, 185
Assembly, boiler, 113
of a furnace, 112
Atmosphere, condensate in, 129
Attachment, of duplexes, 280
of quadruplexes, 280
of townhouses, 274
of walkups, 280, 285
Attendant parking, 68
Attics, location of furnaces in, 112
Auditory recreation, electrical service for, 175
Automatically operated cooling system, 139
Automatic controls, on pumping system, 155
Automatic sprinklers, for fire protection, 171
Automatic valve, for fire use of domestic water, 172
Auxiliary electrical systems, 187-192
Auxiliary fuel burners, necessity of in an owner-operated power plant, 177
Auxiliary plant, for emergency use, 187
Availability of natural water for cooling, 118
Aviation agency, 18

Babcock, Richard F., 13, 317
Baby carriage storage, 8. *See also* Pram room
Back siphonage, 161-162
Backen, Arrigoni & Ross, 348-349, 420, 421
Backyard of townhouse, 269
Balance of water heat systems, difficulty of, 117
Balancing cocks, 132
Balancing fittings, 132
Balcony, 14, 20, 28, 195, 204, 207-208, 211, 242, 249, 256-260, 281, 291, 300
in apartment size calculation, 33
in calculating volume, 21
cantilever for, 82
continuous, 258-259
convectors along, 134
data on, 7
divider, 257-258
door, 259
drainage, 258-259
exp. joints in, 85
in floor area calculation, 7
indented, 256-257, 260
lighting, 180
for location of refrigeration equipment, 127
for mechanical equipment, 127
railing, 258
for smoke proof tower, 18
structural considerations for, 83
Balloon framing, 92
Baltimore, Md., 378
Bar joist, 266, 285
depth, 102
framing, 288
Base, of building, 263-265
receptacle in, 181
Baseboard, 125
Baseboard convectors, 129, 133-134
with central hot water heating plant, 137
Basement, 11, 156, 238-239
below water table, 98
electrical conduit in, 178
of highrises, 68
influence of ground water on, 167-168
laundry room in, 69
lighting, 180
location of furnace in, 112
locker room in, 69
for mechanical equipment location, 110-111
of midrises, 285
of townhouses, 269, 271
of walkups, 277, 281
Basin, in siphonage, 162
Basketball, 71
Bathroom, 20, 24, 29, 122, 216, 220, 169
back-to-back arrangement of, 144
compartmentalization of, 7
data on, 7
door sizes for, 37
for elderly, 33
in efficiency apartment, 32
emergency intercom for elderly in, 189
exhaust equipment for, 143
exhaust of, ventilation of, 25, 52, 106-107, 137, 142-144, 146-147, 191, 248, 288
fixtures, 168-169
furred ceiling in, 136
light, connected to exhaust fan, 142
lighting, 180
of townhouse, 268, 274
of walkup, 277
plumbing, 170
window of, 140
Bathtub, 7, 169
Batteries, for emergency power, 186-187
Battery-switch lamp pack, 186
Bay, 78, 204, 206, 228, 242, 243, 247, 249
Bay window, 260
cantilever for, 82
Beam, 78, 87, 95, 195
concrete, 99-100
depth of, 101
edge, 78
flat, 86
ledger, 88
pipe opening near, 135
precast, prestressed concrete, 101
spandrel, 82-83
steel, 88, 89, 92
transfer, 84
Bearing elevation, of soil, 96
Bearing wall, 87-88, 92, 95
masonry, 91
as sound insulator, 34
Bedrock, 97
Bedroom, 24, 29, 202, 205-207, 209-210, 214, 217, 230, 242-245, 253-254
in apt. efficiency, 32
data on, 7
door sizes for, 37
elect. circuiting in, 184
emergency intercom for elderly in, 189
exit rhythm of, 204
lighting, 180
min. size of, 26
in narrow apartments, 198

second exit from, 32
television outlets in, 192
of townhouse, 268-269, 273
of walk-up, 278, 280, 283
zone control of, 139
Bell signal, 10
Bellows expansion joint, for risers, 133
Below-grade, code definition of, 17
Below-sewer drainage, 168
Berman, Alden R., 416-417
Bicycles, storage for, 8, 68
Blower, exhaust, in penthouse, 144
for exhaust systems, 142
in a furnace, 112
in a kitchen exhaust fan, 143
tandem, in electric furnace, 126
for ventilation, 148
Boiler, 10, 112-114, 156-157
capacity of, 113-114
location of, 52
malfunction, 113
plastic pipes for, 159
stack, 265
water heating, 158
Boiler room, 117
dimensions of, 114
space for, 114, 157
Boilers, heat pumps, in power failure, 187
Bond rate, 306
Bonds, 306
Bonus zoning, 14-15
Booth & Nagle, 408-409, 434-435
Borrowing, principle of, 199, 207-209, 216-218, 223, 229-230, 277, 286
Bottom, of building, 247, 263-265
Boundaries, of site, 11
Box type structure, 96
Braced bents, 91
Bracing, 76, 87, 96
Branch circuits, as safety feature, 183
Branch service, from total service to each dwelling, 183
Branch supply pipe, 132
Branch takeoff, 133
Branches, risers to fan coil units, 134
Brass, water piping, 159
Brass screen, 152
Breakers, part of distribution panel, 184
Brent Goldman Robbins & Bown, 440-441
Brick, 90, 249, 253
Brick cladding, 242
Brick Institute of America, 90
Bronx, N. Y., 13, 336, 338, 382, 386, 402
Brooklyn, N. Y., 390
Brownsville, N. Y., 455
BTU, 114
BTU/hr, 119
Budget, 5, 18-20, 65, 197, 242, 266, 289, 304, 306-309
Buffalo, N. Y., 432
Builder, developer, 106, 180-181
Building, multilevel, heating and cooling costs, 106
Building height, structural consequence of, 76
Building pressure, thru supply centilation, 146
Buildings, exposure, effect on heating, cooling, 131
Built-in thermostat, 125
Bulk, in zoning, 13, 15
Burger and Coplans, 414-415
Burglar alarm systems, 10, 189-190
Burner, in a boiler, 112
in a furnace, 112
Bus bars, 178-179
Bus duct, 179
cost of, 185
Bus duct risers, on distribution panels, 184

Cab, elevator, 49-50
Cables, as conductors-copper, aluminum, 178-179
electric conducting-resisting, 126
underground-TV, radio, 191
use of flexible, armored, 179
Cabs, 61
Caisson, 97-98, 220
bells, 97
steel liners, 97
Calculated heating load, 113
Calorific value of oil, 109
Camber, of slabs, 82, 85
Canada, 118
Canopy, 247
for drive, 61
Cantilever, 82, 229, 252
slab thickness, 82
span of, 82
Capacity, of air conditioning units, 121-122
of aluminum conductors, 179
of boiler, 113-114
of copper conductors, 179
electrical pumping fuel to equipment, 112
of fan coil units, 126
of overhead storage tanks, 154
of pumping system, 155
refrigeration, 119
Card room, 74
Caretaker, 8
Car washing, pressure needed for, 156
Carpet, 68, 232
corridor, 19, 218
discoloration through ventilation, 145
effect on sound insulation, 136
as sound isolator, 37
Cash flow, 306, 308
Cash investment, 305, 309
Cash requirements, 308
Cash return, 304-305, 308, 310
Cast, in place columns, 91
in place concrete, 77, 86
Casting beds, 87
Casting cycle, 85
Cast iron, enamel coated, as material for washbowls, 169
enameled, bathtubs, 169
as sink material, 170
housing for boiler assembly, 113
material for sumps, 168
as material for sewers, 164
used for radiators, 133
for venting pipes, 165
water piping, 159
Caulking, 35
around windows, 140
Ceiling, 7, 78-79, 87, 89, 92, 195
code, requirements for height, 16
of corridor, 218
dropped, for ductwork, 129
under overhands, 116
electric heat in, 126
exhaust duct in, 143
height of, 135-136, 147, 272
in midrise lobby, 286
joining w/partition, 35
lighting, 180
for sprinklers, 172
suspended, furred, 39, 195, 220
of top floor, 143
Central air units, filters for, 147
Central antenna, television, 10
Central boiler plant, in a combined heating/cooling plant, 137
Central cooling plant, location of, 111
Central cooling tower installation, in a combined heating/cooling system, 137
Central corridor, 198
Central corridor system, 197-198, 212, 217-218, 222-224, 227-231, 235, 284-285
Central exhaust system, 142-144

Central heating and cooling system, 129-137
Central heating plant, for water heating, 156-157
Central Mortgage and Housing Corp., Canada, 33
Central plant system, advantages in storing water, 158
Central system for cooling, 124
Central thermostat, 125
Central water distribution, in heating and cooling, 117
Central and Exterior Corridor Highrise Projects, 350-351
Central Corridor Highrise Projects, 332-349
Centrifugal refrigeration machine, 121-122
Chamber, combustion of a furnace or a boiler, 112
Charcoal, activated, 107
  in kitchen exhaust system, 143
Chase, for mechanical items, 79
Chemical spray, in a fire extinguisher, 173
Chicago, Ill., 14, 72, 242, 251, 307, 324, 326, 332, 352, 356, 360, 363-364, 372, 380, 396, 398, 410, 426, 434, 446
  fire statistics in, 40
  market in, 25
  requirements for smokeproof tower in, 76
  zoning in, 14-15
Child care, regulations for, 8
Children, 24
  recreational facilities for, 72
Chimney, expense of, 112
  for fuel, 110
  space allowance for, 111
  for water heating assembly, 158
China, as washbowl material, 169
Chlorine, 152
Circuit breakers, 176
  as a safety feature, 183
Circuits, in a distribution panel, 184
Circulation, 24-27, 31, 33, 266
  in apt. efficiency calculation, 33
  of hot water, 158
  site, 240
  in townhouse, 269
  in walkup, 280
  water distribution, 112
Circumference, of point block, 224
Cladding, 288
  curtain wall, 251-252
  masonry, 253-255
Clay tile, vitrified, as material for sewers, 164
Cleanliness, 105
Clerestory window, 230, 254
Climate, 11, 16, 157, 229-230, 235, 242, 275, 281, 283
  control, in condominium, 6
  factor in use of multiple boilers, 113
  history of, 106
Climatic experience, 105
Clogging of sewers, 164
Closed circuit TV, 8, 10, 65
Closets, 30, 33, 52, 122
  in apt. efficiency calculation, 32
  columns in, 80
  dimensions of, 31
  for doorman, 67
  door sizes for, 37
  elect. panel in, 185
  along ext. wall, 261
  for fan coil units, 127
  furred ceiling in, 136
  hall, 6
  as laundry location, 69
  lighting, 180
  location of furnace, 112
  for meeting rooms, 74
  of townhouse, 268-269
  ventilation of, 107
Clothes dryer, electric, in estimated load, 182
Coal, cost of for heating, 108
  efficiency of for heating, 108
  strengths and drawbacks to its use for heating, 108
  transportation to equipment, 111
Coal burning equipment, location of, 111
Code, 12, 15-18, 32, 75, 120, 124, 196, 202
  air chambers, 161
  auxiliary plants, 187
  construction type, 266
  dead end corridors, 226
  electrical, 178-179, 181-182, 186, 188
  electrical building inspection, 175
  electrical outlets, 180
  elevator, 50
  emergency systems, 10
  exhaust requirements, 142
  exit, 43, 45, 51, 61, 66, 219
    in walk-up, 277-278
  fire, 38-42, 78
  fire equipment, 171
  fireproofing, 88, 194, 285
  fire protection, 9, 171
  fire rating requirements, 34, 37
  fire separation of garage, 62
  garage headroom, 58
  garage ventilation, 62
  habitable space, 276
  highrise fire, 218, 222, 225
  lowrise, 266
  lowrise fire protection, 282
  material for sewer, 164
  multilevel apts., 232
  plumbing, 162, 165-168
  refuse chute, 51
  refuse room, 65
  restriction, 122
  revolving doors, 142
  smokeproof tower, 45, 195
  stairs, 47
    in walk-up, 278
  ventilation, 25, 106-107, 147
    of residential buildings, 140
  walk-up exit, 281-285
Coil, cooling, location of, 129
  finned tube, in electric furnaces, 126
Coin changer, for laundry room, 70
Collection, mail, 67
Collection loss, 304, 307
Collins & Kronstadt, 448-451
Column, 76, 111, 195, 203, 209, 228-229
  in apt. efficiency, 33
  arrangement, 76
  change in dimensions, 85
  concrete, 92, 100
  configurations of, 80, 82
  economy, 80
  electrical box in, 180
  exterior, 82
  formwork of, 80
  interior, 194, 220
  layout, 76, 78, 82, 88, 195, 206
    for parking, 55, 57, 59
    offset
    orecast, 88
  orientation of, 84
  placement of, 80, 220-221
  proportions of, 243-244
  rectangular, 80-81
  rigid layout, 76, 78, 80, 88
  round, 80
  scattered layout, 76, 78, 81
  semi-rigid layout, 80
  shapes of, 220
  size of, 79-80
  slenderness, 85
  square, 80
  steel, 88, 92
  steel pipe, 266
  transfer, 76-77, 83, 86, 221
  transition, 84
Combination exhaust systems, 142-145

INDEX

Combined heating and cooling systems, 137
Combined system for cooling, 124
Combustible elements, code definition of, 17
Combustion, 112-113
Combustion chamber, of a furnace or boiler, 112
Comfort, 9
Comfort level, steam heat, 116
Commercial air conditioning, multizone controls, 139
Commercial motors, standard, voltage in, 178
Commercial services, 12
Commercial space, 8, 231, 263, 265
Commercial use of central chilled-water plant, 137
Commissary, intercom in, 191
  music in, 192
Common areas, 221
  outdoor, 270, 275
Common elements, 236, 238, 291
  in condominiums, 6
  in midrise, 285
Common return mains, three pipe system, 131
Communication, in case of fire, 39-40
  emergency power for, 187
  facilities, 175
  light and power for, 187, 190-191
  for security at entrance, 189
  systems, 190-191
Community building, for laundry, 70
Community facilities, data on, 12, 231
Community room, columns in, 83
Compactor, 64
Compartmentalization, of bathrooms, 30
Compartmentation, for fire prevention, 40-41, 218
Complex walk-up, 273
Complex Walk-Up Projects, 446-456
Compression tank, for water heat, 117
Compression test cylinders, 85
Compressive strength, of concrete, 85
Compressor, 119
Compressor-condenser, refrigeration, 127
Compressor-part of hydropneumatic tank system, 155
Concentrator, 119
Concrete, 76, 266
  block, 44
  casting, 77
  cast in place, 77
  change in volume, 85
  compressive strength, 85
  construction, 235
  crews, 77
  deck, above parking, 285
  exposed, 82, 85
  fire rating of, 78
  flat plate, 76-77, 80
  floor construction for sprinklers, 172
  frame, 76, 285
  framing, 195, 212
  green, 85
  insulating quality of, 115
  lightweight, 77-78
  material for sumps, 168
  mullion, 207
  normal weight, 78
  on-site casting, 77
  post-tensioned, 86
  pouring, 205
    economy of, 196
    sequence, 195
  precast, 77, 266, 288
  radiant heat along, 126, 134
  reinforced, as material for sewers, 164
  rigid frame, 93-94
  slab, as sound isolator, 37
  structure, 78
Condensate, 128-129
  drain-riser pipes, 137
Condensation, of moisture on the furnace, 108, 129
  in summer, 138
  on water pipes, 161
Condensed steam, returning to the boilers, 116
Condenser, 119-120
  air-cooled, 121
    location of, 111
  evaporative, 120-121
  refrigeration, as part of a self-contained unit, 126
  watercooled and air-cooled, 120
Condensing agent, 120
Condensing unit, on roof, 289
Condominium, 6, 7, 33, 72, 123, 185, 203, 235, 237, 274, 304, 308
  common elements in, 6
  deliveries in, 47
  parking in, 53
Conductor run, size of, in relation to friction, 177
Conductors, 177
  in high rises, 178
  overloading of, 176
Conduit, 179
  cost of, 185
Configuration, 204
  of building, 199
  of lowrise, 266
Congress, U. S., 307
Conklin & Rossant, 378-379
Connections, of horizontal structural members with columns, illustration of, 133
  moment, 76
Conservation, of fuel, 115
Constant, annual percentage, 306-310
  tables to figure, 311-316
Construction, bulk, elimination of, 125
  cost, 19-21, 34, 38, 143
    by components, 20
    in relation to bldg. perimeter, 27
    by trades, 20
  financing, 309
  loan, 309
  procedures, 81
  provisions for fire safety, 171
  seasons, 77
  technology, 195, 242
  type, 196
    by code, 16-17
    lowrise, 266, 282
    walk-up, 277
Consumption, of energy, 115
  of water, meter requirements for, 174
Container, of a boiler, 112
Contents, total cubic of room, in expulsion of air, 107
Control, automatic on pumping system, 155
  cooling, 9
  factory built in thermo static control, 137-139
  fan speed for fan-coil units, 137-139
  on HVAC systems, 137-139
  manual valves, 137-139
  of materials, in electrical heat, 118
  of odors, 107
  remote room thermostats, 137-139
  self-actuating valves, 137-139
  state, of private waste disposal, 163
  of water in showers, 169
  water temperature, 137-139
  zone controls, 137-139
Convectors, baseboard, 134
  and standard, 129

in central heating cooling systems, 133
electric, 125
heating, remote thermostat on, 139
standard, with combined heating/cooling period, 137
steam heat, 130
Conventional loan, 304
Cook, J. W., 317-318
Coolant, 120
Cooling, 9, 106
with an air heat system, 117
coil, location of, 129
design temperatures, 106
equipment, 118-122
evaporative, 118
surfaces affecting, 116
system, effect on infiltration of, 141
use of electrical power, 177
water, 162
Cooling tower, 120-122, 265
location of, 110
Cooperative, 185, 304, 308
housing type, 6
Copper, conductors, 178-179
refrigerant lines, 127
rods, for grounding, 179
tubes, use in water heating, 157
tubing in concrete, 134
for venting pipes, 165
water piping, 159
Corbusier, 243
Core, 225-227, 241
elements, 207-210, 216-218, 223-224, 226, 228-230, 260, 266
structural, 228
vertical, 199, 222, 237, 260, 265
Core-type walk-up, 276-281, 283
Core-Type Walk-Up Projects, 424-433
Corner, apartment, 24, 225, 228
inside, 261
Corridor, 7, 45, 122, 185, 195, 197, 199, 212, 213, 218-219, 222-232, 236, 260-261, 281
air movement through, 140
air supply duct, 51, 195, 222, 266
air supply in case of fire, 41
air supply for, 52, 191
as horizontal exit, 18, 45
bedroom, 7, 24
in case of fire, 38-41
central, 91
dead end, 18, 226, 281
elect. load for lighting, 183
elevator, 50
exit from, 18
exit lighting in, 186
exterior, 83, 195, 197, 283, 285-286
interior, 283
pressurization of, 146
public, 32
fire protection, 171-172
ring, 226
service, 65
supply, in case of fire, 40
supply air through, 145-146
supply duct in, 52
of walk-up, 279-282
width of, 17
Corridor-type walk-up, 281-283
Corridor-Type Walk-Up Projects, 434-445
Corrosion, in venting pipes, 165
in water pipes, 159
Cost, 39-40
advantage of plastic piping, 159
of balancing devices, 132
of basement drainage, 168
of central exhaust system, 145
of coal use for heating, 108
of columns, 220
comparative, of bldg. systems, 235
comparison of copper, aluminum conductors, 179
consideration for energy, 108-109
construction, 75, 195, 305-309
advantages/disadvantages of locating equipment, 111
budget for controls, 138
in determining number of boilers, 113
of fenestration, 115
and operating, of exhaust systems, 144
of detergent stack, 167
of development, 308
of ductwork, 143
of electrical heat, 118
of electricity use for heating, 109
of evaporative condenser, 122
expense for special fittings, 155
of exterior corridor, 229
financing, 305
of fire insurance, 172
of fire sprinklers, 172
of fixtures, 170
of foundation, 77
of four-pipe, three-pipe installations, 131
fuel, 309
garage, 62, 285
influence of typ. floor on, 194
initial, of bathtubs, 169
of combined heating/cooling system, 137
of direct-return, 132
of electric heating, 185
exchangers for water heating, 157
of fixtures, 168-170
insulation of pipes, 161
operating of HVAC fuels, 149
of washbowls, 169
installation, 121
of cooling system, 106
of downfeel system, 161
of electrical equipment, 149
of hot water boilers, 157
and maintenance of private waste, 163
of manual valves, 138
of multiple boilers, 114
of one pipe systems, 130
and operating of electrical closets, 185
of steam, air water heat, 116
storage tank, 158
of insulation, 262
insurance, 305
of intercom systems, 191
investment of total energy plants, 177
legal, 305
of lighting fixtures, switches, 180
in locating equipment, 110
of locating mains underground, 178
in locating water lines, 110
of maintaining humidity, 108
maintenance, 305-309
of maintenance of fire equipment, 174
of materials for downspouts, 166
of mechanical ventilation, 143
of multicore system, 222
of multilevel apts., 232
operating, breaking down payments, 148-149
of combined heating/cooling system, 137
of cooling system, 106
of plumbing fixtures, 168-170
of three-phase current, 183
of water heating, 156
of operating ventilation systems, 144
organizational, 305
of parking, 55, 237
of piping of fuel supply, 112
of plumbing, 174

projects, planning for plumbing, 174
of receptacles, 181
of refrigerants, 119
of remote room thermostats, 139
rental level, 107
of riser systems, 135
of service on cooling system, 124
of shear wall, 197
of slabs, 78
of soundproof design, 111-112
of structure, 77
of supply ventilation ductwork, 146
of taxes, 305
of telephone equipment installation, 191
of transmission cables, 177
of use of oil for heating, 109
of use of solar energy for heating, 109
of vaults, 178
of ventilation ductwork, 147
of volume break, 260
of water distribution, 160
Court, 286
code definition of, 17
-house, 268
inner, 273, 275
private, 275
Craft room, 74
Crane, 195
Creep, deflections, 85
wood, 92
Cross ventilation, 229
Cross view, 261
Curb, at balcony, 83, 259
restrictions, 12
Current, 177
single phase, 183
three phase, 183
Curtain, liner, 245
Curtain wall, 203, 207, 242, 251-252, 255
aluminum, 251
metal, 251
precast concrete, 251
steel, 251
Cushion of air, 154-155

Day care, 71-72
Day care center, code requirements for, 18
Daylight, 225-226, 228, 230, 241, 246, 260, 271, 275, 280, 286
in kitchens, 28
in laundry room, 70, 72
Damage, caused by cooling system, 120
through fan coil unit ventilation, 145
from fire, 173
to water pipes, 161
Damper, air volume, motor driven, 139
for exhaust fan, 143
self-closing or motor-driven, in a combined exhaust system, 144
Davis Brody & Associates, 3, 227, 261, 338-339, 350-351, 376-377, 384-385, 402-403
Dead-end corridor, 226, 280-281
Debt payment, 307
Deck, 20, 231, 237, 239, 294
in calculating volume, 21
Deflection, creep, 85
of floors, 75
of forms, 85
of slab, 82, 85
Dehumidification, with air heat system, 117
in induction units, 137
Dehumidifying air, in cooling, 118
Delivery, 8, 24
through lobby, 66
mail, 67
Demand charge, electrical, 185-186
Density, 13, 15, 196, 235, 275-276, 287, 294
highrise, 302
matrix system, patio townhouse, 297
midrise, 300-301
townhouse, 295-296
walk-up, 298-299
Deposit, mineral, in water heater, 152
Depreciation, 305
Depressed building, 290
Depressed floor, 232, 234
Depressed grade, 271
Depressed ground floor, 276-277
Depressed yard, 276
Depth, of apartment, 199, 224, 228
of building, 198, 215
Desert, cooling in, 118
Design, mechanical, conformity to local sewer system, 164
conservation, 115
electrical, 175-192
elimination of stack effect, 141-142
heating temperature, 105-106
of HVAC systems, 148
in locating thermostats, 139
location of equipment, 110
placement of return risers, 132
of return risers, 132
for supply ventilation system, 146
temperature, 114
Detector meter, for fire system, 174
Detector, fire, 188
smoke and heat, 188
Detergent, effect on piping, 167
Detergent stack, 167
Detroit, Mich., 287, 322
Developer, 4-6, 8, 10, 14-15, 19-20, 26, 65, 72, 176, 191, 222, 306, 309-310
Device, metering, 119
Diaphragm, 87, 90, 94
Diesel engine, for fire pumps, 173
Dimensions, for open air sports, 73
Dining, 210
alcove, 7
along exterior wall, 209
combined with kitchen, 7
combined with living, 7
data on, 7
Dining room, dining area, dining space, 24-25, 27-28, 31, 202, 213, 234
door sizes for, 37
in efficiency apartment, 32
along exterior wall, 198
lighting, 180
minimum size of, 26
Direct and reversed return piping, 131-132
Direct current, 178
Direct exposure, 116
Direct return, 132
piping system, 129
Direction, compass, of exposures, 115
of building, effect on heat, 131
Directory, for intercom, 189
Discharge outlet, for water heating, 159
Discoloration of carpets through ventilation, 145
Discretionary review zoning, 14
Dishwasher, water connections to, 170
water temperature, 156
Disposal, of garbage, 110
Distance, between buildings, 17
Distributing ductwork, in heating and cooling, 117
Distribution, 105
and service, electrical, 181
electrical, systems for, 175-192
of steam heat, 116

supply risers, 132
of water heat, 117
Distribution panels, for electrical service, 184-185
Distribution pattern, vertical, in electrical service, 185
Door, 107, 219
apartment entry, 38, 145, 280
balcony, 134, 259
boiler room, 114
closer, 38, 40
double-acting, 37
elevator, 48-49
equipment room, 122
fire, 282
fire rating of, 41
fire vestibule, 61
infiltration through, 140, 145
garage, 64
kitchen pantry, 28
lobby, 141, 142
refuse chute, 51
revolving, 66, 142
screen, 230
security device for, 189-190
service entrance, 142
sizes, 37
sliding, 83, 259
smoke-stop, 282
smokeproof tower, 45
stair, 18, 40, 43, 141, 186
supply air through, 145
switch near, 180-181
width, 17
Door frame, heat loss through, 141
Doorman, 8, 61, 66-67
Double-loaded corridor system, 197-198
Double tee, 88-89, 101
Downfeed in water piping, 160-161
Downspout, interior, 165, 259
Drain pipe, 128
size of, 166
Drain plug, in washbowl, 169
Drain spout, balcony, 259
Drainage, 164-166
balcony, 83
location of fixtures, 170
outlet, 128
below sewer, 168
Drainpan, 119
Drapery, 246
Dressing room, of health club, 72
for open air sports, 73
ventilation of, 107
Drift, 75, 96
Drilled piers, 97
Driveway, drainage of, 163-164
Driving isle, 55
framing of, 86
"Dry bulb temperature," 106
Dryer, 8
Dryers, calculation for laundry room, 70
Dry standpipes, 172
Drywall, 92
Duct, 76
for air systems, 118
in exhaust systems, 142
in heating and cooling, 117
size planning, 147
sizes, 147
slab penetrations for, 78
supply, requirement in design, 129
Ductile moment resisting space frame, 96
Duct riser, 136
Duct space, planning, 129, 136
Duplex, 284
Duplex walk-up, 266, 276-278, 280
"Dutch door," 37

Earthquake, 96
Eccentric loads, 84
Ecology, 11, 291
Economy, 78
in column size, 101
in construction under water, 99
of deep apartments, 198
of footings, 97
in framing, 94
of midrise, 287
of shear walls, 95
of spans, 86
of structure, 75, 86
of typical floor, 198
in wind resistance, 93
Educational facilities, 12
Efficiency, of coal use for heating, 108
of electricity use for heating, 109
electrical, planning for, 149
of floor, 196
of floor plan, 213
of gas use for heating, 109
operating of several boilers, 113
ratio of floor in lowrise, 266
ratio of floor plan, 223-226, 236
ratio of walk-up, 280-283
of use of oil for heating, 109
of use of solar energy for heating, 109
E.G.I. (effective gross income), 304, 307
Egress, 219, 222
of walk-up, 277, 281, 284
Either-or control valve, 139
Ejector, for below sewer drainage, 168
Elastic deflections of slabs, 85
Elderly, 6, 10, 13, 131, 202, 283, 291
apt. types, 33
comfort temperatures for, 106
electrical distribution for, 184
elevators for, 50
emergency intercom for, 187, 189
handrail for, 219
laundry for, 69-70
needs for in lobby, 66
parking for, 53
receptacle height for, 181
recreational facilities for, 72
Electrical, 9-10
Electrical box as a serviceable arrangement, 184
Electrical capacity for pumping fuel to equipment, 112
Electrical charges and payments, 185-186
Electrical closet, 185
Electrical conducting-resisting materials, 126
Electrical conduits, 89
for structural consideration, 79
Electrical design, 175-192
Electrical distribution and service, 181
Electrical distribution systems, 175-192
Electrical efficiency, planning for, 149
Electrical equipment room, fire extinguishers in, 173
Electrical feeders, location of, 110
Electrical friction, 177
Electrical heating, 114, 124-125
Electrical installation, 175
Electrical provisions, 178-181
Electrical rates, 9
Electrical room, 195, 218, 222
Electrical runs of conduits, 78
Electrical service, 175-192
Electrical service entrance equipment, 110
Electrical service equipment, in relation to terminal grounding connection, 179
Electrical supply, location of equipment, 112
Electrical system, 123
Electrical systems, primary, ancillary, 187-188
Electrical transformer room, ventilation of, 148
Electric box, as a safety device, 179-180

INDEX

Electric central furnaces and boilers, 112
Electric gear and transformer, 238-239
Electric heat, in residential applications, 112
Electric heating, initial cost of, 186
Electricity, 175-192
  cost of use for heating, 109
  purchased, 177-178
  strengths and drawbacks of its use for heating, 109
Electric meter room, 51-52
Electric motor driven shaft, 152
  for fire pumps, 173
  fractional horsepower, 126
Electric operation of control valves, 139
Electric outlet as cause of sound transmission, 35
Electric power for heating and cooling, 10
Electric radiant panel heating, 125
Electric radiant panels, 126
Electric rises, 203
Electric valve on water supply line, 138
Electric vault, 178
Electrostatic charging, method of filtering, 146
Elements, heating, of electrical heat, 118
Elevation, 135
Elevator, 8, 10, 14, 47-48, 86, 92, 193, 195, 197, 199, 216-219, 222, 225, 227, 231, 235, 239-240, 266, 276, 285
  cab, 49
  car, 58
  in case of fire, 38-41
  cost of, 20-21
  door, 49
    air movement through, 141
  electric current for, 178
  electric loads for, 182
  electric service for, 184
  emergency power for, 187, 189
  framing of, 78-79
  hydraulic, 285
  for loading, 62-65
  lobby, security of, 68
  machine room, 173
  machinery, 49
  machinery penthouse, 111, 117, 120, 143, 154
    ventilation of, 148
  in midrise, 286
  motor, 191
  music in, 192
  panic alarm for, 10
  penthouse, 265
  proximity to laundry, 70
  proximity to tot-lot, 72
  for refuse removal, 63
  security of, 66
  selection of, 47
  shaft, re stack effect, 141
  rel. of to lobby, 65
  stop at laundry floor, 70
  stop at roof terrace, 72
  for tenant lockers, 69
  vestibule, 218
Elmhurst, Ill., 408
Emergency alarm, 10
Emergency circuitry, power for alarms, 189
Emergency light, 10
  and power, 186
Emergency lights, in power failure, 187
Emergency power, 10
  for fire, 40
Entrance, to apartment, 225, 228
  hall, 24-26, 31-32
    data on, 7
    for fan-coil units, 127
    in apt. efficiency calculation, 32
  switches at, 180
  of townhouse, 268-271, 274
  vestibule, 142
  of walk-up apartments, 277-278, 280
Environment, 240
Equipment, advantages of location of, 110
  coal burning, location of, 111
  electrical service, 110
  fuel converting, 112
  fuel utilization, 109
  gas-fired, for an independent cooling system, 124
  heating, 105
    location of, 109-110
    space considerations, 118
  HVAC, maintenance and operation of, 148-149
  installation, 128
  location of, 110
  and machinery for coal use for heating, 108
  nonrent paying, 110
  pumping, 110
  room, for meter location, 174
    layouts, illustrations of, 114
Equity, 305-306, 309
Erections, of frame, 77
Erosion, in water pipes, 159
Escalation, 310
Esherick Homsey Dodge and Davis, 428-429
Europe, 268, 276
  balconies in, 28
Evacuation, 39
Evaporation, 119-120
Evaporative condenser, 120, 122
Evaporative cooling, 118
Exchanger, heat, rusting, 129
  water heating, 157
Exercise room, of health club, 72
Exhaust, 203
  fans, 142-145
  grill, as cause of sound transmission, 35
  register, 144
  of smokeproof tower, 45
  synchronization with supply, 146
  systems, individual, central, combined, 142-145
    space for size of unit, 147
  ventilation, 142-147
Exhausted air, 107
Exit, 43, 45, 196, 202
  from apartment, 32
  capacity of, 17
  code requirements for, 16-17
  emergency lighting for, 186-187
  for fire protection, 170
  garage, 61
  from laundry room, 70
  lighting, 186
  from locker room, 69
  from multilevel apartments, 232
  number of, 17
  signs, 38, 40, 186
    in emergencies/power failure, 187
  of walk-ups, 277-278, 282, 285
Expansion joints, 85-86
  in piping, 132
Expansion provisions, piping length, 133
Expectation, use estimate factor in electrical service size, 182
Expectations of occupants, 105-106
Expenses and services, shared in condominium, 123
Exposed areas, regulation of electrical wires in, 179
Exposed concrete, 82, 85, 254
Exposed frame, 203, 220, 251-252, 255, 260
  column bays, 243-248
  load bearing mullions, 249-250
Exposed surfaces, 115
Exposure, of doors, windows, 140

effect on heat, 131
factor in water heating, 157
in heating and cooling, 115
in planning location of fan coil unit, 136
Expressed frame, 247
Expressed structure, 242
Expulsion of air, 107
Exterior, 82, 253
cost of, 20-21
effect of energy conservation, 18
quality of, 20
Exterior access, walk-up, 284-285
Exterior corridor, gallery, 195, 197, 25
Exterior corridor system, 8, 229-231, 235, 285, 287
Exterior entrance, light, 180
Exterior exposure, 198-199, 205, 226
Exterior form, 193, 241
Exterior protected construction, 266, 285
Exterior skin, 236, 246, 253
Exterior space, 288, 292-293
Exterior wall, 91-92, 95, 134, 195, 198, 202, 209, 221, 243, 251, 253, 256, 261, 266
in apt. area calculation, 33
of bathroom, 142
calculating of in floor area, 7
code control of, 16
downdraft near, 136
exhaust through, 143
fire code, 42
heat loss along, 125
of kitchen, 142
for Siamese fittings, 172
Exterior zone, 229
Extinguishers, fire, 173

FHA financing, 308
FHA program of financing, 305
FHA requirements, 307
Facilities during construction, 111
Failure, of bathroom exhaust fan, 143
of below sewer pump, 168
of independent air cooling system, 124
of electric power, 186
in water heat systems, 117
Fair market rental, 310
Family-living room, 7
Family room, 202
of townhouse, 270
Fan-coil unit, 126-127, 134
location of, 129
make up air entrance, 145
remote thermostat on, 139
vertical, 244
Fan equipment, 248
location of, 52
Fan housing, 265
Fan speed control, for fan-coil units, 138
Faucet, washbowl, 169
Faucets, on kitchen sinks, 170
pressure in, 153
in siphonage, 162
Federal agencies, 18
Federal Housing Administration, 113
Federal mortgage insurance, 18
Federal Register, 310
Feeder, apartment, 185
electrical, location of, 110
Fees, architects, 305, 307
financing, 305
for recreational electrical wiring, 192
Fence, 265, 274-275, 290
Fenestration, 9, 198, 204, 206, 213, 245, 247, 253, 260, 285, 288
for energy conservation, 115
relation of to window washing, 8
rhythm of, 220
Fiberglass, cast, material for sumps, 168
filter material, 146
forms, 86
Filter, air, in furnaces, 112
in electric furnaces, 126
electrostatically charged, 146
fiberglass, 146
in kitchen exhaust fan, 143
maintenance, 146
motor driven, 146
steel fiver, 146
for supply air systems, 146
Filtering, in air supply systems, 146
of swimming pools, 73
Financing, 5-6, 303-304, 306-308, 310
conventional, 308
data on, 3
effect on design, 303-310
program, 303-304, 307
structure, 303
subsidy, 310
vehicle, 303
verifying data on, 4
Finned coil, 134
Finned tube coils, in electric furnaces, 126
Fire, 34, 118, 145
automation of sprinklers, 171
with circuit breakers, 176
with electrical heat, 118
power interruption due to, 186
precautions against, 188
Fire alarm system, 10, 191
audible, 188-189
in power failure, 187
zoned, 188-189
Fire control, 39, 151
Fire department, 12, 18, 39-40, 42, 62, 170-171, 173-174, 188-189
Fire detection, 40
Fire door, 282
Fire equipment, cost of maintenance, 174
Fire extinguisher, 9, 173
Fire fighting, 291
data on, 12
installation, 171
water for, 174
Fire hose, 39
Fire hydrant, 42, 170
Fire lane, 42
Fireplaces, 106, 116
Fireproof construction, code definition of, 17
Fireproofing, 42, 88, 266, 288
code requirements for, 16
of midrise, 285
of steel frame, 89
of structural frame, 194
Fireproof steel housing, for a furnace, 112
Fire protection, 9, 188, 195, 288
of lowrise, 282
plumbing for, 170-173
Fire pump, 38, 40, 172, 173
in power failure, 187
Fire rating, 34, 39, 78, 89
of columns, 91
of doors, 37
of parking, 86
Fire requirements, 78
Fire safety, 17, 38, 218, 222, 225
Fire separation, 89, 129
code requirements for, 16
of garage, 61-62
of parking, 285
of townhouse, 268
Fire vestibule, 68
of garage, 61
Firewall, of lowrise, 282
Fit-casting, 87
Fittings, balancing, 132
pressure in, 153-154
selection for pressure, 155-156
Fixture, in siphonage, 162
Fixtures, as a factor in pipe size, 166
location of, 170

plumbing, 155
selection and purchase, exterion and interior, 180
Flame spread, 245
Flashing, roof, 248
Flat plate (flat slab), 76-77, 80, 87-88, 97, 100, 194-195
and pipe column, 91
casting cycle of, 85
forming and shoring of, 85
for parking, 57
post-tensioned, 86
Flexibility of slab, 82
Flexible cable, use in wiring, 179
Floor, 7, 34, 87
area of, 195-196
configuration of, 194-195
of corridor, 219
covering of, 80
deflection, 75
depth of, 195, 214
draft along, 136
for fan-coil units, 127
fire rating of, 34
framing, 90, 92
insulation of overhangs, 116
joint w/partition, 35
leak through, 138
length of, 195, 214
leveling of, 89
number of, 194-196
receptacle height above, 181
unlevel, 85
Floor area, code requirements for, 17
for furnace, boilers, 114
method of calculation, 21
ratio, 15
structural consequence of, 76
Floor construction, for sprinklers, 172
IIC ratings of, 36
STC ratings of, 36
Floor mounted fan coil units, access to, 136
Floor plan, for plumbing fixtures, 170
Floor slabs, 84
Floor space, in locating furnaces, 112
Flow, sewage, 164
Flue, with a furnace, 112
location of plastic pipes, 159
problem with natural fuel furnace, 127
Fluorine, 152
Flush tank, 168-169
Flush valve, 168-169
"Flying forms," 220
Folding table, for laundry room, 70
Foot bath, of swimming pools, 73
Footing, continuous, 97
drainage of, 168
plain concrete, 97
reinforced concrete, 97
spread, 97, 220
Forced water systems, 117
Form, 80, 85-86, 95
concrete, 191
cost of, 86
deflections, 85
fiberglass, 86
"flying," 76, 80
sets of, 85
steel, 86
Fossil fuels, 112
Foundation, 11, 20, 76-78, 94-99
along property line, 84
deep, 98-99
drainage of, 168
influence of ground water on, 167
mat, 97
Four directionality, 204, 219, 224, 247, 250
Four pipe system, 131-132
"Fourplex," 273
Frame, concrete, 76
selection of, 75-77
steel, 76
wood, 75
Frame construction, code definition of, 17
Framing, 90, 219-220
of garage, 86
of level changes, 232
midrise, 285
Franchised power companies, 177-178
Franzen, Ulrich & Associates, 346-347, 412-413
Freeks/Sperl/Flynn, 370-371
Friction, flow, pressure in regards to, 153-154
Front yard, of townhouse, 271, 274
Fuel, burning furnace, location of, 129
and energy supplies, diminution of, 106
converting equipment, 112
cost of, 9
efficiency, in heating system, 116
fossil, 112
for heating, 118
natural, 108-109
and electrical, conversion of, 112-114
transportation to equipment, 111
pumping to equipment, 112
source, 116
storage space, 109
supply, piping of, 112
restrictions of use, on air treatment, 107
use of, 108-109
for water heating, 156-157
utilization equipment, 109
Furnace, natural fuel, 127
Furnaces, 112-113
electric, 126
filtering in, 146
Furnace system, outdoor air connection, 145
Furniture, 253-256
for bedrooms, 29
for dining room, 27
for living room, 26
layout of, 25
lobby, 65
Furring, of arcade ceiling, 247, 250
around electrical box, 180
of hall ceiling, 136
Fuse as a safety feature, 183
Fused switches, part of distribution panel, 184
Fuses, 176
switches, 182

Gallery, 230-231, 283
Game room, 74, 238
Garage, 17, 20, 55-62, 220, 240, 294
connection to lobby, 68
cost of, 285
electrical conduit in, 178
enclosing of, 62
exit from, 18
exit requirements, 58, 61
fire dept. access to, 62
framing of, 86
as hazardous use, 16
heating and ventilation of, 148
heating of, 62
intercom in, 191
lighting, 62, 180
loading through, 63-64
for locker room, 69
of townhouse, 271
sprinklers in, 171
ventilation of, 62
below water table, 98-99
Garbage, 24
collection, townhouse, 270
disposal, 51, 110
see also Refuse
Garbage disposal units, 167
in kitchen sink, 170
Garden apartment, 280-281

Garden plots, for elderly, 72
Garden wall, 290
Gas, cost of for heating, 109
efficiency of for heating, 109
full of water heating, 157
pumping to equipment, 112
strengths and drawbacks of use for heating, 109
transportation to HVAC equipment, 111
Gas and water, compared to electrical power, 175-176
Gas engine driven pump shaft, 152
Gas engine or turbines, for fire pumps, 173
Gas fired system, 124
Gas meter, 288
Gasoline engines for fire pumps, 173
Gas service entrance piping and meter, 110
Geddes, Robert, 317
Generating plant, 176-177
Generators, emergency, storing of, 187
testing of, 187
Girder, 250
depth, structural steel, 101
steel, 89, 96
Glass, 16, 18, 45, 135, 139, 245-247, 249, 252-253, 288
corner detail, 250
downdraft near, 136
in energy consumption, 115
insulating, 108, 115
reflective quality of, 116, 241
as source of heat loss, 125
structural, 245
tinted, 115, 245
Glazing, lobby, 265
Goldberg, Bertrand & Associates, 356-357
Gordon, Ezra-Jack Levin, 364-367, 380-381, 396-397, 410-411, 426-427
Governmental agencies, 305
Government insured loan, 304
Government mortgage loan, 307
Government role w/electric company, 176
Government subsidy, 310
Grade, 290
definition, 276
separation, 275
Gradual acting, control valve, 139
Gravity, effect on water circulation, 158
in below sewer drainage, 168
Gravity air systems, 118
Gravity flow installations, water heat, 117
Gravity load, 94-95, 98
Grease, removal from plumbing (traps), 167
Great Lakes, 118
Greek cities, 268
Greenwich, Conn., 400
Greenwich Village, N. Y., 13, 33
Grill, of heating/air conditioning units, 254
Grille, corridor for ventilation, 145
Ground, 290
Ground coverage, in zoning, 15
Grounded receptacles, 181
Ground-floor, 116, 221, 255
depressed, 276
for equipment, 110
of midrise, 285-286
Grounding, of electrical systems, 179-181
Ground rods, 179
Ground water, drainage of, 167-168
Grout key, 87
Gruzen & Partners, 340-341, 358-359, 436-437
Guest, 268
Gutters, of swimming pools, 73
Gymnasium, intercom in, 191
Gypsum board, 16, 45, 89, 91
Gypsum plank, 89

Habitable space, code definition of, 16
Hall, 122
furred ceiling in, 136
lighting, 180
Hammering of water, 161
Handball, 71
Handicapped, code for, 18
elevators for, 50
lobby entry of, 66
Handrail, for elderly, 219
Hard water, 152-153
Hardpan, 97
Hausner & Macsai, 352-355, 362-363, 404-405
Hazards of direct-return piping system, 132
Head, window, 255
Headroom, stair, 44
Health club, 71-72
proximity of to swimming pool, 72
sizing of, 72
Health facilities, 12
Health regulations for swimming pool, 73
Heat, absorbing of, 119
in absorbtion refrigeration machine, 121
air, 116-118
availability of for heat pump, 123
electric, *n* estimated load, 182
steam, 116-118
water, 116-118
Heat detector, 188
Heat exchange, 134
Heat exchanger, in power reclamation, 177
rusting, 129
water heating, 157
Heat gain, recirculated air for, 136
Heat loss, 125
recirculated air for, 136
Heat producing functions, cooking, lights, TV, 138
Heat pump, 9, 122-123, 127
Heaters, local booster, required for dishwashers, 156
water, 156-157
Heating, 9, 105-139
central plant, 122
effect on electrical receptacles, 181
pump, 10
use of electrical power, 177
Heating and cooling system, central, 129-137
independent, 124-125
Heating/cooling elements, 245-246, 252
Heating design temperature, 105-106
Heating domestic water, use of electrical power, 177
Heating, electrical, 124-125
element, 259
elements of electrical heat, 118
facilities in walk-up, 281
load, calculated, 113
media, 116
medium, water heating, 157
of water, 156-158
pumps, boilers, in power failure, 187
riser, 247
steam, 130
system, effect of infiltration on, 141
water, 162
expansion space in pipes, 161
Hedges, 274
Height, 196
absorbing tank weight, 154
of building, 226
consideration of location of equipment, 110
effect, on fire protection planning, 171

on pressure and pipe fittings, 155-156
factors influencing, 195
limitation by code, 16
in planning water piping, 160
as pressure factor, 153
of receptacles, locating them, 181
of rooms, 7
by zoning, 15
High cost apartments, 107
High exposure apartments, cooling and heating costs, 106
High rental apartments, 107
High rent housing, 232
Highrise, 7, 15, 65, 77, 86-88, 90, 110, 127, 134, 136-137, 153, 176, 178, 194-197, 222, 242, 253, 262-263, 265-266, 276, 283, 285-289, 294, 304
central exhaust in, 143
central mechanical system for, 123-124
communication systems in, 190
definition of, 193-194
density, 302
electrical distribution in, 184
electrical riser in, 185
fire codes, 40-42, 89
fire safety in, 38-39, 171, 189
foundations of, 98
locker location in, 69
mechanical equipment, 117
mechanical equipment room, 111
parking, 59
parking location in, 53
piping runs, 132
power failure in, 186
recreation space in, 62
refuse removal, 64
risers in, 165
security in, 190
shear resistance in, 95
site, 302
stack effect in, 141
stair construction in, 44
storage needs of, 68
structure system for, 220
water pressure in, 155-156
water systems in, 160-161
zoning district, 15
Highrise-Central and Exterior Corridor Projects, 332-349
Highrise-Central Corridor Projects, 332-349
Highrise-Multicore Projects, 352-355
Highrise-Point Block Projects, 356-381
Highrise-Skipstop Projects, 382-395
High strength sttls, 88
Highway department, 18
Hinged door, 37, 66
History of weather, 106
Hoberman & Wasserman, 227, 374-375, 400-401
Holland, Eugene P., 75
Hollow core plank, 89
Hollow core slabs, 88, 101
Home, tract, 123
Hood, kitchen exhaust fan, 143
Horizontal dimension of a furnace, 112
Horizontal exit, 45
lobby as, 66
Horizontal furnace, 114
Horizontal mains, U bends in, 132-133
Hose, for fire pumps, 173
fire, 171
Hose cocks, siphonage of, 162
Hose equipment, for fire protection, 170
Hot water, circulation, 158
distribution of, 160
heater, 238-239
storage, 158
Hotel, 131
House, heating of, 113
Housing, of boiler assembly, cast iron, 113
fire proof steel for a furnace, 112
rental, payment for cooling system, 106
steel, 113
Housing Authority, programs of, 4-5
standards of, 18
Housing site, tract, electrical power for, 176-177
H.U.D. (Dept. of Housing and Urban Development), 18, 310
furniture guidelines, 25
minimum apartment sizes, 33
minimum property requirements, 26-29, 34
parking data, 53
parking dimensions, 55
requirements for refuse chute, 52
standards of, 18
travel distance requirements, 43
Humidification, 9
Humidification, winter, 108
Humidity, 105-108, 119
air, 106
with air heat, 117
Huxtable, Ada Louise, 261
HVAC, controls on systems, 138
equipment, maintenance and operation of, 148-149
location of systems, 111
machinery, 110
pipe sizes for systems, 111
Hydrants, 170
Hydropneumatic tank system, 154-156
Hydrostatic Pressure, 98

I.I.C. (Impact Insulation Class), 34, 80
ratings, 36-37
Illinois, 10
Impact noise, 80
Incinerator, 64
Income, 303-304, 307, 309-310
Independent heating and cooling systems, 123-125
Indexed valves, 132
Individual exhaust system, 142-143
Induction system for ventilation, 146
Induction unit, 136-137
remote thermostat on, 131
Industrial process, cooling, 122
Infiltration, 140-142
effect on construction, 141
factor, 20
Inflow of cash during construction, 110
Initial cost, insulation, 9
Inner corridor system, 197-198
Input, electric, in heating, 126
Installation of equipment, 128
Installation cost, electrical, 9-10
Instantaneous system, pumping system for water pressure, 155-156
Institute for Architecture and Urban Studies, New York, N. Y., 454-456
Insulation, 9, 115, 125, 245
in arcade ceiling, 247
blanket, 36
of conductor cables, 178
of electrical wires, 179
of hot water piping, 161
of radiant panels, 126
thermal, 18, 85, 262
worn, effect on circuit breakers, 176
Insurance, reduction w/fire protection, 9
Intercom, 8, 10, 65, 189, 191
for elderly, 66
at loading, 64

in lobby, 68
systems, 191
Interest, 308-309
during construction, 305, 309
rate, 303-307, 309
subsidy, 307
Interior booster system for pressure, 154
Interior access, walk-up, 284
Interior areas, ventilation of, 106-107
Interior zone of apartment, 7, 25, 228, 234, 248
Interior occupied areas, ventilation of, 106-107
Interior spaces, closets, dressing rooms, ventilation of, 107
Intermediate weather, four-pipe system, 131
Investor, 304-306, 308-309
Investment, 304-305, 308
Ithaca, N. Y., 423, 438

Jacobs, Jane, 13, 317
Jamb (window), 255
Jenks, Charles, 242, 318
Jockey pump, 173
Joints, 83, 99
bellows expansion, 132-133
expansion, 85-86, 132-133
concrete, 244
masonry, 255
precast, 87
U bends, 132-133
Joists, metal, 92
steel, 89
wood, 92
Jordan, Joe J., 424-425
Junction, window and doors, 140

Kahn, Louis, 243
Keyes, Lethbridge & Condon, 344-345, 406-407
Kira, Alexander, 30
Kitchen, 6, 20, 24-25, 28, 202-203, 213, 216, 230, 232
back-to-back arrangement of, 144
counter space in, 29
data on, 7
door sizes for, 37
in efficiency apartment, 32
for elderly, 33
electrical panel in, 185
electric load in, 182
exhaust equipment for, 143
exhaust of, ventilation of, 25, 52, 106-107, 117, 137, 142-144, 146-147, 191, 248
exterior, 214
fixtures in, 29
for meeting rooms, 74
laundry in, 69
lighting, 180
minimum size of, 26
plumbing in, 167, 170
second exit from, 32
storage in, 29
telephone box in, 191
in townhouse, 269-272, 274
in walk-up, 277-278
window of, 140
Kitchen-dining room, 28
Kitchen-dining-family room, 6
Kitchen-family room, 28
Klotz, H., 317-318
Knockouts, for conductors, 180

Labor, 77, 87
Lake, as water supply for cooling, 118
Lake Shore Drive (Chicago, Ill.), 25
Lake Superior, 118
Lamp pack, battery-switch, 186
Land, 5, 305
Landing, scissor stair, 45
stair, 44, 46
width of, 18
Landscaping, 19
Land use, 15
Lateral load, 76, 78, 82, 87, 89-91, 93-95
resistance, 76, 78, 92-96
Lateral stability, 87
Laundry, 9, 69-70, 236, 238, 300
central, 69-70
location of, 6, 8, 69-70
as recreation space, 70
in walk-up, 281
water supply for, 156
Lavatory, 9
sink, placement of, 166
wash bowl, 169
Lawn mowers, storage for, 68
Lawn sprinkling, 153
pressure needed, 156
Lead pump, in pumping system, 155
Leakage, 107
air, 145
of current, in grounding, 179
from stack effect, 141
in ventilation, 140
water, 145
when system is off, 138
Leaks, with steam, water air heat, 117
Le Corbusier, 13
Length, of bathtubs, 169
of building, 198, 215, 218, 223
of piping, 133
Lethaby, W. R., 317
Level change, 230
cost of, 107
of floor, 232, 234
of ground, 274
Level, lowest, space for equipment, 110
Library, in townhouse, 269
Life Safety Code, 18
Life style, 202-203
Lift, lever operated, in washbowl, 169
Lift slab, 88
Light, bathroom, connected to exhaust fan, 143
natural, 24
by code, 16
in zoning, 15
zoning control of, 13
Light and power, emergency supply, 186
public, on separate meter, 185
Lightning, effect on circuit breakers, 176
Lighting fixture, 10
corridor, 218-219
for open air sports, 73
roof terrace, 72
Liner, for resilient floor, 232
Lines, copper refrigerant, 127
Link, 260
Linkage, 263, 281, 289, 291
of buildings, 227
of midrise, 286
Lining, of tanks, 154
Lintels, wood, 92
Living area, electric circuiting, 184
Living room, 6, 24-28, 31, 197, 202, 205-210, 214, 217, 221, 228, 230, 234, 243, 251, 253, 258, 260
data on, 7
in efficiency apartment, 32
exterior rhythm of, 204
lighting, 180
minimum size of, 26
projecting, 260
television outlets in, 192
of townhouse, 271-272
of walk-up, 278, 280
Living-dining room, 26
zone control of, 139
Living space, 232, 257, 262
of townhouse, 269
of walk-up, 280
Living zone, 24, 232
of townhouse, 268-271
of walk-up, 277, 280
Load, demands, radiant panels, 125

electric, in sizing of service, 181
in estimating service size, 182
water pressure, 155
wind, 78
Load bearing masonry, 255, 266, 285, 288
Load bearing mullion, 249-252
Load bearing walls, 90, 221
Loading, 8, 62-64, 238-240, 291
clearances, 63
in midrise, 286
in parking lots, 63
zoning control of, 13, 15
Loading dock, 212, 237
security of, 68
Loads, eccentric, 84
Loan, 304-310
processing, 306
Lobby, 7-8, 61, 65-68, 196, 218, 238-240, 265
columns in, 83
electrical load for lighting, 183
elevator, 50
as exit, 18
as fire command center, 40
as horizontal exit, 45
intercom in, 189
loading nearby, 64
in midrise, 285-286
music in, 192
security of, 68
as social center for elderly, 67
stack effect in, 141
of walk-up, 282
Local air supply, in heating and cooling, 117
Location, of electrical closets, in highrises, 185
of fire alarms, 188-189
of fire extinguishers, 173
of fixtures, 170
of heating equipment, 109-110
of hoses, 171
of thermostats, 139
Locker room, sizing and location, 69
Lockers, in midrise, 285-286
Loggia, 28
Logistics on construction, 8
London, 204
Louver, for natural ventilation, 106
Low cost housing, 190, 229
Lowest level, space for equipment, 110
Low income housing, 6, 66, 222, 287
philosophy of, 4
Lowrise, 7, 88, 115, 124, 262, 266, 282-289
central mechanical system for, 124
definition of, 193-194
fire safety, 42
horizontal mains in, 132
location of recreation space in, 62
parking location, 53
security of, 43
site, 291-299
stair in, 47
stair construction in, 44
Lowrise-Matrix Projects, 420-423
Lowrise-Townhouse Projects, 406-419
Lowrise-Complex Walk-Up Projects, 446-456
Lowrise-Core Type Walk-Up Projects, 424-433
Lowrise-Corridor Type Walk-Up Projects, 434-445
Luxury housing, 30
Lynch, Kevin, 318
Lyndon, Donlyn, 242

Machinery, elevator, 49
fuel burning, proximity to refrigeration plant, 122
HVAC, 110
Machinery and equipment for coal use for heating, 108
Macsai, John, 23, 193
Mail, 291
data on service, 12
methods of handling, 8
Mailboxes, 65, 67
combined with directory, 189
in walk-up, 282
Mailroom, 238
Main, distribution of water, 160
electrical, location of, 178
service, failure of, 186
in siphonage, 162
for ventilation, 147-148
vertical, 132
water, 152, 154
switch, for entering service, 183
switches, assemblies of, location in high rises, 185
Maintenance, 304
building, 68
cost, electrical, 10
mechanical, 9
of private waste disposal, 163
effect of location of equipment, 112
of fire equipment, cost of, 174
of HVAC equipment, 148-149
of independent cooling system, 124
location of equipment, 111
of manual valve controls, 138
of mechanical equipment, 9
of plumbing fixtures, 168-170
and replacement of parts, 121
storage, 8
of supply ventilation filter, 146
time and cost of central exhaust systems, 145
of wood construction, 92
Make-up air, 107, 145
in kitchen exhaust, 143
Make-up water, location of equipment, 112
Malfunction, of boilers, 113
Management, 304
Manager's office, 67
Mandel, David J., 13, 317
Manlift, 68
Mansard roof, 289
Manual pull stations, 188
Manual valves, controls of HVAC systems, 138
Manufacturer of plumbing fixtures, pressure recommendation, 153-154
Manufacturer, warning on equipment use, 131
Market, 19, 25, 71, 106, 202, 227-228, 232, 235-236, 305-309
analysis, 4
competition in, 6
data on, 6
in relation of laundry, 69
survey, 304, 310
Marketing-rate financing, 307
Marquis & Stoller, 430-431
Martin/Soderstrom/Matteson, 442-443
Masonry, 17, 78-79, 82, 88, 92, 129, 221, 242, 245, 285
bearing walls, 90-91
cladding, 203, 206, 253-255, 288
design of, 90
electric box in, 180
electric conduit in, 178
joint, 90, 255
load bearing, 255, 266, 285, 288
materials, 90
nonreinforced, 90
openings in, 255
reinforced, 90
specifications for, 90
testing of, 90
veneer, 92
Material handling, 8
Materials, for electrical conducting-resisting, 126
for kitchen sinks, cast iron, enameled steel, stainless

steel, 170
for piping, cast iron, copper, brass, asbestos, cement, plastic, 159
for sewers, cast iron, vitrified clay tile, reinforced concrete, asbestos cement, plastic, 164
storage of, 77
structural, 77
for sumps, cast iron, fiberglass, concrete, 168
Mat foundation, 97-98
Matrix Projects, 420-423
Matrix system, 268, 275
density, 297
site, 297
Mechanical equipment, noise factor of, 34
Mechanical equipment area, planning for, 109
Mechanical equipment room, 122, 263
fire extinguishers in, 173
in highrises, 68
layout, 114
location of, 109-111
in midrise, 285-286
on roof, 265
water meter in, 174
Mechanical runs, of pipes, ducts, 78
Mechanical space, in suspended ceilings, 195
Mechanical system, 20, 193, 244, 252
cost of, 20-21
Mechanical ventilation, 106-107, 141, 202
Media, cooling, 119
heating, 116
Median strip, 11
Medicine cabinet, as cause of sound transmission, 35
Meeting rooms, 74, 238
sizes of, 74
Member size selection, 99-103
Mesopotamia, 268
Metal curtain wall, 251
Metal joists, 92
Meter, detector, for fire service, 174
for multiple residential project, 174
for power company charges, 185
Meter and piping, gas service entrance, 110
Metering, electrical, 10
of water, 9
Mezzanine, 232
Middle Ages, 268
Middletown, Conn., 342, 347, 412
Midrise, 65, 90, 127, 222, 285-290, 294
central mechanical system for, 124
definition of, 193-194
density, 300-301
economy of, 287
floor construction for sprinklers, 172
locker location, 69
parking location, 53
power failure in, 186
refuse removal, 64
site, 291-294, 300-301
Midrise Projects, 396-405
Midwest, 77
Mies Van Der Rohe, Ludwig, 3, 242, 252, 287, 322-323
Miller, Nory, 317
Mineral deposits in water heaters, 152
Minimum room sizes (H.U.D.), 26
Minimum standards of public housing, 4
Minneapolis, Minn., 368, 394
Mix, 4, 283
of apartments, 194, 204-205, 209-210
in programming, 6
Mixed walk-up, 283-285. *See also* Complex walk-up
Model apartment, 8
Modification of fan coil unit, 136
Moisture, 107
amount of in air, 106
concrete content, 85
on flush tank exterior, 169
removal of, 142
removal with piping, 137
storm plumbing waste, 163
in wood, 92
Moment connections, 76
Moore, Charles W., 452-453
Mortar cubes, 90
Mortar prisms, 90
Mortgage, 5, 304-305, 307, 309
Mortgage insurance premium, 305
Motor, in fan speed control for fan-coil units, 138
in a furnace, 112
Motor driven air volume dampers, 139
Motor driven damper, in combined exhaust system, 144
Motor overload protection, for exhaust fan, electrical safeguard, 143
Motors, electric, 121
voltage in, small appliances, commercial, 178
Mounting of electric boxes, 180
Movement systems, site, 291
Movement, of structure, 75
thermal, 82-83
Mud slabs, 87, 99
Mullion, 245-246, 250
concrete, 207
load bearing, 249-252
Multicore Highrise Projects, 352-355
Multicore system, 7, 197, 222-223, 227, 231-232, 235-236, 285, 287
Multicore walk-up, 276
Multilevel apartment, 7, 231-232, 253, 259
Multilevel building, heating and cooling costs, 106
Multiple boilers, use of, 113
Multiple residential buildings, heating in, 113
Multiple resident projects, water in, 174
Multizone systems, for commercial air conditioning, 139
Municipal sewers, 164
Municipal water system, 154
Municipality, as water source, 152
Music, in public areas, 192

Nachman, Harry S., 105, 151, 175
Nailing, 92
Narrow temperature range, of steam heat, 116
National Concrete Masonry Association, 90
National Electric Code, 182
National Fire Protection Association, 18, 182
National Loss Control Service Corp., 38
Natural fuels, 108-109
furnace, 127
transportation to equipment, 111
Natural ventilation, 106-107
Natural water, availability for cooling, 118
courses, 163-164
New Haven, Conn., 5, 259, 334, 416, 418, 452
New York, N.Y., 71-72, 227, 242 261, 310, 328, 340, 350, 358, 377, 384, 392
high rise fire code, 40
market, 25
zoning, 14

Newman, Oscar, 55, 66, 194, 291, 317-318
Noise, 11
  of air movement in ductwork, 147-148
  of exhaust fan, 144
  of fire pumps, 173
  function of rubber bumpers, 145
  in heating system, 116
  impact, 232
  of mechanical equipment, 120-121, 127
  transmission, 134
    through doors, 144
Noncombustible construction, code definition of, 17
Nonreinforced masonry, 90
Nonrent paying equipment, 110
Nuclear power, non-availability of, 109
Nursery, 71-72

Oakland, Cal., 414
Oak Park, Ill., 38
Occupancy, during construction, 110-111
  early, 77
  maximum by code, 16
Occupant, 9, 39, 43, 65, 107-108, 113, 131, 137-138, 140-141, 143-145, 148-149, 157, 167, 171, 180-181, 185, 187, 190, 192, 218, 230
  disability of, 189
  expectations of, 105-106
  interview with, 5
  learning about, 4
  notification in case of fire, 39
  payment for heat by, 137
Odor control, 107
Odor remover, in a kitchen exhaust fan, 143
Odors, removal of, 142
  in sewage disposal, 164
  in sewers, 165
  transmission of, 145
Office, for garage management, 68
  heating and ventilation of, 148
  intercom in, 191
Office building, 76
Ohms, 177
Oil, cost of for heating, 109
  efficiency of use of for heating, 109
  pumping to equipment, 112
  strengths and drawbacks of use of for heating, 109
  transportation to equipment, 111
Old Town, Chicago, Ill., 25
On-off valve, on thermostatic control, 139
One-pipe system, 129-130
Open space, 292
Operating condition of fire extinguishers, 174
Operating cost, 306-310
  electrical, 9
  mechanical, 9
Operating efficiency of several boilers, 113
Operating expense, 304
Operating life of an independent cooling system, 124
Operating sash, 16, 246
Operating subsidy, 310
Operation of HVAC equipment, 148-149
"Ordinary construction," 92
  code definition of, 17
Orientation, 11, 240, 291
  data on, 7
  for elderly, 33
  for emergency conservation, 115
  of open air sports, 73
Orifice, 73
Outage, electrical, 186
Out door lighting, 180
  electrical load for, 183
Outdoor space, 294
Outer zone, 228
  of apartment, 25
  of townhouse, 269
Outlet, for discharge of water pressure, 159
  part of boiler assembly, 113
  for smoke in a furnace, 112
Outlets, electrical, 175
Output, heat, in heating, 126
Overhang, 116
Overhead storage tanks, 154
Overhead tank, 160
Overloading, of electrical conductors, 176
  prevention of, 176
Owner, 9, 20, 106, 108, 174, 177, 185, 304, 308
Oxygen, in fuel conversion, 112
Oxygen replacement, in ventilation, 140
Ozone, 107

Pairing, planning by, 274
Panels, removable, for access to boilers, 114
Pangaro, Anthony, 4, 317
Panic alarm, for elevators, 10
Pan joist, 86, 100
Panorama, data on, 12
Pantry, kitchen, 28
  for meeting rooms, 74
Park, 12, 240, 287
Park district, 18
Parking, 12, 53-62, 76, 90, 92, 207, 220-221, 236-240, 247, 250, 263, 291, 294-302
  columns in, 83
  commercial, 8
  in condominiums, 6, 53
  cost of, 55
  distance to dwelling, 55
  elderly, 53
  fire extinguishers for, 173
  floor area required for, 56
  for model apartments, 8
  framing for, 86
  garage, 55-62
  on grade, 20, 53-55
  location for low-, mid- and high-rise, 53
  midrise, 285
  requirements for, 7
  sprinklers for, 171-172
  steel framing for, 88
  structure, 20
  systems, 55-56
  townhouse, 270-271
  zoning control of, 13, 15
Parking lot, 87
  drainage, 53-54
  fire lanes, 42
  lighting, 53-54
  loading through, 63
  sheltering, 53-54
  shielding, 53-54
Partition, 20, 34, 87, 92-93, 206, 209, 245
  between apartments, 33
  calculating of in floor area, 7
  corridor, 33
  cost of, 20-21
  electric conduit in, 178
  electric panel in, 184
  fire code, 42
  fire rating of, 34, 41
  layout of, 78
  location of, 82
  movable for meeting rooms, 74
  pipe riser in, 111
  risers in, 134
  STC ratings of, 34
  as sound insulators, 35
  structural interfacing of, 85
  television outlets in, 192
Parts per million (PPM), as water hardness measurement, 153
Party walls, 11, 34, 91

as sound insulator, 35
Pasanella, Giovanni & Associates, 386-389
Passage, of steam and water in one-pipe system, 130
Passages, part of boiler assembly, 111-112
Patio townhouse, density, 297
site, 297
Paul, Samuel, 317
Pavement, 274
Paving, 262
drainage of, 164
Pedestrian movement system, 12, 291
Pei, I. M. & Partners, 18, 328-331
Penthouse, elevator, 265
elevator machinery, 143, 154
ventilation of, 148
for fan equipment, 144
sizes of, 154
stair, 265
Peoria, Ill., 310
Perception, of exterior space, 292
Percolation test, 163
Performance, of a heat pump, 123
Performance factor, 117
Perimeter, 260
of building, 24, 27, 135-136, 198, 202-203, 218, 236, 281
Perlite, 89
Philadelphia, Pa., 330, 424
Phosphorescent light, in power failures, 186
Piers, concrete, 97
"Piggy back" townhouse, 283
Piles, 77, 98
cast in place concrete, 98
composite, 98
precast, prestressed, 98
steel sections, 98
steel shell, 98
timber, 98
Ping pong, 74
Pipe, 152
chase, slab penetrations for, 78
columns, 91-92
configuration, 132
length expansion and contraction, 132
riser, 244, 252
riser spaces, 111
sizes, for HVAC, 111
in water heat, 117
sleeve for, 79
space, for plumbing fixtures, 170
structural considerations for, 93
systems, one-pipe, two-pipe, three-pipe, four-pipe, 129-137
Pipes, condensate drain-riser, 137
corrosion from steam, 117
gathering of, 248
pressure in, 153-154
selection for pressure, 155-156
in tile field, 163
Piping and meter, gas service entrance, 110
horizontal, 252
length, 133
location of, 160
materials, copper, brass, cast iron, asbestos-cement, plastic, 159
and pumps, project, 131
sprinkler, 172
system, 116-118, 160-161
secondary, for water circulation, 158
tile, in basement drainage, 168
water, selection of, 159-160
Planned unit development zoning, 14
Planning, choosing fuses or circuit breakers, 176
concern with water pressure, 153
cost of sprinklers, insurance, 172
for fire protection, 170
of HVAC systems, 148
infiltration as a factor, 141
of residential building needs, 151
for pipe placement, 135
projecting costs of plumbing, 174
for ventilation space requirements, 147
Plant precast, 76, 88
sewage disposal, private, 164
Plants, heating, 113
Plaster, 78, 89
around electric box, 179
for electric radiant heat, 126
for radiant heat, 134
Plastic, pipe, water piping, 159
piping, material for sewers, 164
for ventine pipes, 165
Play areas, 230, 240
Playground, 12, 71-72
Plinth, 290
Plumbing, 9, 151-174, 203, 285
for craft shops, 74
fixtures, 165, 168-170
aesthetics of, 168-170
manufacturer, pressure recommendation, 153-154
water distribution for, 160
space, 174
stack, 247, 274
structural considerations for, 79
trap, 220
wastes, storm and sanitary, 163
Point Block Highrise Projects, 356-381
Point block system, 224-228, 231, 235-236, 241
Point system zoning, 14
Pollen, filtering, 146
Pollutants, 11
Pollution, air, 64
control, 18
of natural water supplies, 163
of water, 151
Ponds, 164
Pool, 238-239
Poolroom, 74
Population, for elevator selection, 48
for exits, 43
Porcelain enameled metal panel, 145
Porch, 230
Portland, Ore., 443
Post-tensioned flat slabs, 86
Pounds per square inch (psi) as pressure measurement, 153-154
Poured concrete, 245
Pouring sequence, 195
Powder room, 30
Power, aspirating, 136
companies, franchised, 177-178
company, privately and publically owned, 176
overloads in lines, 176
payments, 185
creation of, 177
failure, 186-187
PPM, parts per million, as water hardness measurement, 153
Pram room, 68, 238-239
Precast, 86-89
columns, 87, 91
concrete, 77, 82, 221, 245, 251, 266, 288
curtain wall, 251
double tees, 87
floor panels, 87
joints, 87
planks, 87
plant, 76
prestressed concrete, 101
site for, 76, 87
slabs, 91
wall panels, 88
Predock, Antoine, 444-445
Prefabricated structure, 76

Prentice & Chan, Ohlhausen, 336-337, 382-383
Pressure, 177
 air, in elimination of transmission of odors, 145
 in aluminium conductors, 179
 automatic, valve for, relieves hot water pressure, 159
 boosting system, 155
 building, through supply ventilation, 146
 control of shower, 169
 in drainage, 165
 for fire equipment, 171
 for fire pumps, 173
 increasing system, 154
 in piping systems, 132
 planning water piping, 160
 in reciprocating machines, 123
 in siphonage, 162
 in toilet operations, 169
 of steam heat, 116
 water, 153-156
  boiler capacity, 113
Prestressed, 86, 89
Prevention of overloading, electrical systems, 176
Primary air, 137
Prime rate, 309
Privacy, 7-8, 14, 24, 34, 202, 230, 241, 256-258, 275-276, 291
 of balconies, 28
Privately insured loan, 304
Private sector, 307, 309
 sewage disposal plant, 164
 waste disposal, 163
Process of refrigeration, 119
Process water, 162
Profit, 305
Program, 3, 5, 10, 23, 25, 30, 75, 193-194, 209, 216, 220, 239, 259, 283, 294
 preparation of, 4
Project piping and pump, zoned, 131
Project plant, 124
Property line, 84, 168, 261
Property selection, 163
Protected exterior, code definition of, 17
Protection, motor overload, for exhaust fan, 143
 of wires, codes concerning, 179
Provisions for expansion, in piping length, 133
PSI (pounds per square inch), 155
 as pressure measurement, 153-154
Public agencies, 19
Public area, light, 180
 music in, 192
Public housing, 10, 71, 287, 304, 307
 minimum dimensions, 25
 programming in, 5
 standards of, 4
Public light and power, separately metered, 185
Public lighting, on distribution panel, 184
Public space, 306
 outdoor, 274
Public transportation, 53
Public waste disposal, 163-164
Pump, booster, 156
 for fire equipment, 172
 heating, 123
 lead, in pumping system, 155
 sump, 168
 for water circulation, 158
 for well, 152
Pumped water systems, 117
Pumping equipment, 110, 171
 for fire protection, 170
 in sewage flow, 164
 system for water pressure, 155
Pumps, 238-239
 electric motors, gas engines or turbines or steam engine driven, 154
 motor driven, 121
 water, 155
Purchased electricity, 177-178
Putting green, 73

"Quad," 273
Quaduplex walk-up, 266, 276-281

Racking, 247
Racking movement, of columns, 35
 of partitions, 35
 of slabs, 35
Radiant panel heating, with combined heating and cooling systems, 137
Radiant panel heating, electric, 125
Radiant panels, in central heating-cooling systems, 133-134
 electric, 126
Radiation, solar, 116
Radiators, 125
 in central heating-cooling systems, 133
 steam heat, 130
Railing, 234
 balcony, 83, 258-259
 ramp, 66
 stair, 44
Rain cistern, as water supply for cooling, 118
Ramp, 58-59, 238
 as exit, 18, 58, 61
 dimensions of, 58-59
 for handicapped, 66
 space in parking, 56
Ramsey & Sleeper: Arch. Graphic Standards, 28, 30
Range, 10
 electric, in estimated load, 180
 sizes, 29
Rapid transit, 13, 53
Rapson, Ralph and Associates, 394-395
Rasmussen, Steen Eiler, 204, 317
Rate of interest, 304
Rate of return, 305
Rating, safe pressure, 155
Ratio of loan to cost, 308
Real estate tax, 308-309
Rear yard, of townhouse, 275
Receiving room, 64, 67, 238-239
Receptacle, 10
 codes for, 181
 cost of, 181
 grounding of, 181
 location of, 181
Reciprocating refrigeration machine, 121-123
Recirculated air, 137
 for heat gain, 136
 for heat loss, 136
Reclamation, of electrical power, 177
Recreation, 71-74, 191, 236, 291, 295-301
 criteria for, 8
 roof location of, 144
Recreation area, 196, 294
 drainage of, 163
 fire lanes in, 42
Recreation building, 68
Recreational facilities, 12, 265
 adult, 72
 children, 72
 mixed child-adult, 73-74
Recreation space, 14, 239
 computation of by occupation, 71
 on garage deck, 62
 locations for, 74
Redondo Beach, Cal., 440
Reflective surfaces, 116
Refrigerant, 119
 gaseous to liquid, 120
 lines, copper, 127
Refrigeration, machine, 127
Refrigeration compressor, condenser, 127
Refrigeration condensing water, 162

Refrigeration machinery, effect from exposure, 137
location of, 111
Refrigeration mechanical, basic cycle of, 119
Refrigeration process, 119
Refrigeration unit, planning for cost, 149
Refrigerator, sizes, 29
Refuse chute, 51, 62, 64-65, 195, 218, 222, 227, 266
sprinklers in, 171
Refuse, collection, data on, 12
handling, 8
removal, 62, 64-65, 291
see also Garbage
Refuse room, 63, 65, 110, 238-240
sprinklers in, 171-172
ventilation of, 148
Rehabilitated housing, 310
Reinforced concrete, 194
Reinforced masonry, 90
Reinforcing, 79, 81, 85, 93
Reinforcing bar, pipe openings near, 135
Reinforcing steel, 77-78
Relative humidity, 106-108
Religious institutions, 12
Remote room thermostats, 139
Removable panels, for access to boilers, 114
Removal of air, 107
Rent, 303-310
level, 309
structure, 6
Rentable space, location of HVAC systems, 111
Rental, housing type, 6
Rental housing, payment for cooling system, 106
Repair space, 8
Replacement, of parts, 121
storage tank, 158
Replacement air, 107
Replacement cost, 305-307, 309
electrical, 10
Research, architect's role in, 5-6
Research Center for Urban and Environmental Planning, Princeton University School of Architecture and Urban Planning, 318
Reserves, 304
Residence, single, heating of, 113
Residence, single and multiple, practicality in heating systems, 118
Resident, 122, 158, 173-174, 187-188, 191
Residential applications of steam heat, 130
Residential buildings, use of 4-pipe systems, 131
water supply for, 151
Residential electrical construction, use of circuit breakers, 176
Residential installation, 122
Residential occupancy, in boiler, furnace selection, 114
Residential project, life span for fuel use, 108
private waste disposal for, 163
Residential projects, multiple, plumbing for, 174
Resilient clip, 36
Resilient floor, 232
Resilient tile, effect on sound insulation, 36
Resistance heater, 127
Resistance to electrical flow, 177
Restaurant, 156
heating and ventilation of, 148
kitchen exhaust of, 52
kitchen sprinklers of, 171
Retaining wall, 276
Return, on investment, 304, 309
Return mains, 3 and 4-pipe systems, 131
Reversal, seasonal, on zone controls, 139
Reversed return, 132
piping system, 129
Rhythm, 202-212, 216-217, 222, 242, 245-246, 253, 257-258
of apartment doors, 219
of columns, effect on parking, 57
of exterior, 4
of windows, 253, 282
Riser, pipe, 130, 252
air pockets in, 161
condensate drain, 137
for distribution of water, 160
size, 132
systems, 135
in toilet operation, 169
ventilation, 147-148
vertical, 129
Riser, stair, 44, 47
height, 18
River, as water supply for cooling, 118
River edge, 287
Roads, 20
Roche, Kevin, 3
Rochester, N.Y., 374, 436
Rods, copper for grounding, 179
Roman cities, 268
Roof, 18, 52-53, 265
deck, 300
drainage of, 163-164, 166
exhaust equipment on, 143-144
exp. joints in, 85-86
flashing, 248
flat, 289
of garage, 62
heat loss through, 141
insulation of, 108
for laundry, 70
mansard, 289
for mechanical equipment, 120, 127
for mechanical equipment location, 110-111
of midrise, 285
recreation space on, 14, 71, 144
reflective quality of, 116
sloping, 289
tar and gravel, 289
for television antenna, 192
of walkup, 277
Roof framing, 92
Roofing, 262
Roofline, 289
Roof terrace, as recreation space, 72
Room-by-room thermostatic guidance, with electrical heat, 118
Room coolers, make up air entrance, 145
Room layouts, equipment, illustration of, 114
Rowhouse, 268
Rubber bumpers, on door frames, 145
Rudolph, Paul, 242-243, 259, 288, 334-335, 432-433
Rust, on electric box, 180
heat exchanger, 129
in water pipes, 159
Rustication, in concrete, 244

Safe pressure rating, 155
Safety, 13, 159, 187, 191
code requirements for, 15
electrical, 178, 183, 186
fire, 39
in fire protection planning, 171
lighting and power for, 187-189
precautions with electrical heat, 118
in wiring practice, 179-180
St. Paul, Minn., 370
Salts, used in water softening, 153
Samples, water, to determine softening, 153
San Francisco, Cal., 40, 348, 428, 430

Sanitary plumbing, wastes, 163
Sanitary sewers, 164
Sanitation, 151
Sash, operating, 8, 246, 259
  stock size, 253
Sauer, Louis, 5
Sauer, Louis Associates, 418-419
Sauna, 72, 238
Scaffold, window washing, 246
Schipporeit & Heinrich, 251, 372-373
Schmitt, Karl Wilhelm, 317
Scissor stair, 45, 222, 225
Scott, Geoffrey, 244
Screen, brass, 152
  window, 246
Screening of roof terrace, 72
Screens for filtering supply air, 146
Seashore, 287
Security, 7-8, 14, 55, 66, 86, 191, 240, 256, 258, 291
  control, in garage, 68
    at loading area, 64, 68
    in lobby, 65, 68
  facilities, 175
  light and power for, 187, 189-190
  in lowrise, 43
  system, 10
  in walk-up, 282
Seepage, in basements, 168
  in tile field, 163
Seismic regions, 96
Self-activating valves, 139
Self-closing damper, in a combined exhaust system, 144
Self-contained unit, independent element in a combined system, 137
  refrigeration condenser with fan-coil heating unit, 126
Seligman, Werner and Associates, 422-423
Semipublic space, outdoor, 274
Sensors, fire, 39
Septic tank, 163
Sequence, 216-217, 227, 258
  planning by, 274
Serial vision, 292
Sert, Jackson and Associates, 243, 392-393
Serve-through opening, 37
Service, hot water boilers, 156
Serviceability, of structure, 75, 82, 85, 92
Service areas, ventilation of, 148
Service calls, cost of, 124
Service conductors, at main switch, 183
Service and distribution, electrical, 181
Service entrance, water, 110
Service main, failure of, 186
Service size in amperes, 182
Service voltage, 183
Servicing, access to, 136
  blowers, 136
  coil, 136
  filters, 136
  of flush tank, 169
  motor, 136
Servicing area, boilers, furnaces, 114
  for evaporative condenser, 122
Setback, 15, 196, 235, 240, 294
Settlement, 86
  differential, 97
Sewage disposal plant, private, 164
Sewage flow, 164
Sewer facilities, public and private, 163-164
Sewer tax, 174
Sewers, common, 164-168
  municipal, 164-168
  sanitary, 164-168
  storm, 164-168
Shafts, in apt. efficiency calculations, 33
  slab penetrations for, 78
  of smokeproof tower, 18
Shaft wall, 78
Shape of buildings, effect on heat, 131
Shear core, 198
Shear head, parking, 57
Shear panel locations, 95
Shear panels, 87, 91, 94, 96, 198
Shear resistance, 95
Shear wall, 76, 94-96, 97, 197, 247, 285
  change in dimensions of, 85
  as sound isolator, 34
Sheet metal, aluminium, 166
  copper, 166
  for down spouts, 166
  galvanized steel, 166
Shelf angle, 255
Shielding, of sun deck, 73
Shocking, in grounding, 179
Shocks, electrical, 177-178
  voltage required, 182
Shop, 231
  craft, 71, 74
  fire extinguishers in, 173
  sprinklers in, 171-172
Shoring, 80, 85
  criterion, 85
  removal of, 85
  re-shoring, 85
  shortening of, 85
  of slabs, 85
  trapped, 85
Short-circuit, 176
Shower, 9, 169
  of health club, 72
  for open air sports, 73
  pressure in, 153-154
  stall, 7
  for swimming pools, 73
Shrinkage, wood, 92
Siamese connection, 39
Siamese fitting for fire hoses, 171
Sidewalk, 14
Side yard, 263
Siding, wood, 266
Silhouette, of building, 266, 288-289
Sill, window, 255
Single family dwelling, 268
Single-phase current, use and cost of, 183
Sink, Kitchen, 9, 167, 170
  laundry, 70
  sizes, 29
Siphon, 162
  in drainage pipes, 165
Siphonage, 161-162
Site, 10, 20, 75, 195-198, 204-205, 209, 214, 216, 222-223, 235, 237, 240-241, 261, 263, 268, 273-274, 281, 294
  boundaries of, 11
  data on, 3
  ecology of, 11
  highrise, 302
  limitations of, 5
  lowrise, 291-299
  matrix system, 297
  midrise, 291-294, 300-301
  patio townhouse, 297
  for precasting, 76, 87-88
  sloping, 268, 271, 275, 283, 297
  survey of, 11
  topography of, 11
  townhouse, 295-296
  verifying data on, 4
  walk-up, 298-299
Sitting area, for laundry room, 70
Size, of conductor run, in relation to friction, 177
  as determinant of sewage disposal system, 164
  of evaporative condenser, 122
  riser, 132
  of a self-contained heating-cooling unit, 126
  and space requirements of boilers, 113
  of unit, air conditioning, 117

water boiler, 157
Sizes of pipes, in water heat, 117
Sizing of electrical distribution and service, 181-186
Skidmore, Owings & Merrill, 326-327, 360-361
Skipstop Highrise Projects, 382-395
Skip-stop system, 231-235, 254, 259, 261
Skyline, 265
Slab, 78, 220-221, 247, 249, 255
balcony, 259
camber of, 82, 85
capacity of, 79
cast in place, 91
cladding of, 252
concrete, 97, 99, 262
conduit in, 191
construction, 85
deflections of, 82, 85
edge, 245, 252
elect. box in, 180
elect. conduit in, 178
fireproofing, 78
flexibility of, 82
forming of, 86
penetration of, 78-79
mud, 87
precasting on site, 91
proportions of, 243
shores, 85
reinforced, 86
sound transmission through, 80
span, 78, 80-82, 92
strength of, 86
thick, 80, 82, 96
thickness, 78-83, 92-93, 99-100
thin, 82, 86, 91, 96
wearing, 262
Sleeping area, 228
Sleeping space, 251, 253
Sleeping zone, 24, 207, 232
of townhouse, 268
of walk-up, 277, 280
Sleeves, 79
Sliding door, 37, 83
Slip forms, 95
Sloping site, 271, 275, 283
Sludge, in sewage disposal, 164
Smoke, 18, 38-40, 45, 142, 171, 191
alarm system, 10
containment in apartment, 145
detector, 188
inhalation, precautions against, 188
outlet, in a furnace, 112
Smokeproof tower, 18, 32, 39, 45, 79, 195, 217, 225, 236
in connection with stack effect, 141
Smoke-stop door, 282
Snow plows, storage for, 68
Snow removal, 276
Soap dispenser, for laundry room, 70
Soffit, for ductwork, 129
"Soft corner," 250
Softened water, 153
Soil, 20, 220
analysis of, 11
bearing capacity of, 96-97
borings, 167
boring logs, 96
conditions, 97-98
investigation, 5
pressure, 97
report, 96, 98
settlement, 96
water condition of, 110
Solar energy, cost of use of for heating, 109
efficiency in use of for heating, 109
strengths and drawbacks of use for heating, 109
Solar exposure, in heating, 115
Solar radiation, 116
Solomon, Cordwell, Buenz & Associates, 332-333, 398-399
Sound, airborne, 34
impact, 34
isolation of mechanical equipment, 110
of moving machinery, 111-112
separation, 7, 34
of townhouses, 268
in toilet flushes, 169
transmission, 79, 95, 111
Source of water, individual and communal, 151
Sources of energy, available to use, 108-109
South America, codes in, 15
South Bronx, N.Y., 13
Space allowance, mechanical, for central cooling equipment, 124
for central exhaust system ductwork, 143
for electrical service and distribution, 181
for expansion of heating water, 161
for four-pipe installation, 131
for fuel storage, 109
for furnaces, 112
for HVAC systems, 111
for layout of plumbing fixtures, 170
for mechanical and electrical equipment, 110
for pipe risers, 111
planning for risers, 132
in selection of boiler, 113
for sewage disposal plant, 164
for sprinklers, 172
tabulation for boilers, 114
in upfeeding or downfeeding, 160
for ventilation equipment, 147-148
water heating, 157
water storage tank, 158
Span, 220-221, 250
Spandrel, 244-249, 252, 253
Spandrel beams, 82-83, 85
Spandrels, 95
Spans, 220-221, 250
large, 83, 86
small, 86
Special use zoning, 14
Speeds, for fan speed controls, 138
Splice, in wiring, 180
Split independent system, for heating and cooling, 127
Split level townhouse, 271
Sponsor, 237
Sponsorship, data on, 6
Sports, open air, 73
Sportsfield, 12
Spread footings, 220
Sprinklers, 9, 17, 38-40, 43, 89, 172
for fire protection, 171
in garage, 58, 61, 171
in refuse chute, 171
in refuse room, 65, 171, 172
in restaurant kitchen, 171
setting off fire alarm, 188
in shops, 171-172
Sprinkling of lawns, 153
Stack, 195, 265-266
boiler, 51-52
plumbing, 80
on roof, 289
Stack effect, 141
in case of fire, 38
Staggered truss system, 90
Stainless steel, furnace material, 129
as sink material, 170
Stair, 32, 51, 122, 153, 195, 197, 199, 213, 219, 222, 224, 227, 225, 231, 235, 237, 266, 285
in apt. efficiency calculation, 33
areaway, 271
code requirements of, 18

in connection with stack effect, 141
construction of, 44-45, 47
dimensions of, 43-44
for elderly, 283
exit lighting for, 186
exterior, 45, 283, 285, 290
fire hose location in, 171
fire rating of, 44-45
first floor, 46
penthouse, 265
relation of to lobby, 65
in smokeproof tower, 45
of townhouse, 268-270
transfer of, 46
of walkup, 276-279, 282-285
width of, 17
within apt., 47
Stair core, of walk-up, 281-283
Stairs, 43
in case of fire, 38-41
framing of, 78-79
garage, 61
Stair shaft, 195, 212
Standard convectors, 129
with combined heating and cooling systems, 137
Standardization of voltage, 178
Standards, for electrical service, 181-182
of private waste disposal, 163
Standpipe, 9, 39-40
dry, 172
for fire hoses, 171
hose, setting off fire alarm, 188
State agency loan, 306
State control of private waste disposal, 163
State housing agency, 18
State housing finance agency, 306, 310
State regulations, of child care, 8
STC, ratings, 34, 36-37
sound transmission class, 34, 80
Steam, in absorption refrigeration machines, 121
type of boiler, 112
Steam bath of health club, 72
Steam heat, 116-117
by boiler, 113
in old buildings, 130
Steel, 195, 266
enamel coated, as washbowl material, 169
enameled, as sink material, 170
bathtubs, 169
floor construction for sprinklers, 172
galvanized, for venting pipes, 165
high strength, 88
reinforcing, 77-78
stainless, as material for kitchen sinks, 170
Steel beams, 89
Steel columns, 87, 91
Steel curtain wall, 251
Steel deck, 89
Steel fiber, filter material, 146
Steel forms, 86
Steel framing, 76, 86, 88-89, 95, 220, 285, 288
Steel housing, for boiler assembly, 113
Steel joists, 89
Steel piles, 98
Steel pipe, for sprinklers, 172
Steel pipe columns, 266
Steps, 290
Stiffness, 94
Stoop, 290
as recreation space, 71
Storage, 8, 27, 68-69, 236-239, 260, 263
baby carriage, 8
balcony as, 28
bicycle, 8
for craft shops, 74
of deck furniture, 73
in dwelling unit, 7
of fuel, 108-110
of hot water, 158
for kitchens, 28-29
maintenance, 68
for meeting rooms, 74
outdoor, 6
tenant, 8
Storage battery systems, for fire alarms, fire communications, 187
Storage tank, cylindrical steel for water, 158
Stores, heating and ventilation of, 148
Storm plumbing, wastes, 163
Storm sewers, 164
Storm windows, 140
Stoves, 116
Strata, subterranean, 151
Street, 13, 53, 61, 237, 275
cleaning of, 12
data on, 12
department, 18
drainage of, 164
lighting, 12
maintenance, 12
snow removal from, 12
widening of, 11
"Streets in the sky," 231
Streetscape, data on, 12
Structural action, two way, 87
Structural behavior, 87, 95
economy, 86
frame, 77, 203, 245, 251, 253-254, 266, 288
choice of, 77
cost of, 20-21
erection of, 77
of walkup, 285
frames, 77-92
glass, 245
grid, 260
members, 89
requirements for heating-cooling piping systems, 129
response, in concrete tubes, 95
slab, 85
steel, 77, 88, 90
system, 8, 75, 287
weight of equipment for, 111-113
Structure, 76, 193, 243
apparent, 243
appearance of, 244
limitations of, 5
movement of, 75
prefabricated, 76
variations in framing, 90
Stucco, 266
cladding, 288
Studs, of partitions, 92
Stud wall, elect. conduit in, 178
Study, in townhouse, 269
Subsidy, 310
by utility company, 9
Substructure, 96
Subterranean water table, 163
Sump pump, 168
Sun, in cooling, 115
Sun-deck, 73
Sunlight, 286, 291
orientation toward, 7
Superintendant's apartment, 67
Supply air, 146
Supply ductwork, requirement in design, 129
Supply of water, 151
for cooling well, river, lake, rain cistern, 118
in relation to pumps, 155
Supply risers, 132, 146
Supply ventilation, 145
Surfaces, exposed, 115
Surfacing, of roof terrace, 72
Surveillance, 13, 197, 222, 230, 277, 287, 291
by television, 189
in townhouse, 270
Survey, 5, 11
of utilities, 163
Suspended units, fan coil unit placement, 135-136
Swimming pool, 71, 73, 237

code governing, 18
intercom in, 191
music in, 192
Switch, 10
ampere sized, 182
light or ventilating, operates motor-driven damper, 144
on unit operation, 138
Switching, in a circuit breaker, 176
Switzer, Gilbert & Associates, 342-343
Symmetry, 208, 216-217, 227
System, central heating and cooling, 128-137
for venting in drainage, 165
instantaneous, pumping system for water pressure, 155-156
interior booster, for pressure, 154
municipal water, 154
of piping, 160-161
pressure boosting, 155
pressure increasing, 154
secondary piping, for water circulation, 158
water supply, 153-154
for fire protection, 170
Systems, air conditioning, 105
electrical distribution, 175-192
heating, comparison of, 118
HVAC (distribution) central, combination, independent, 123-125
refrigeration, direct or indirect, 119-120

Tank, compression for water heat, 117
cylindrical steel storage for water, 158
overhead, 160
overhead storage, 154
Tank system, hydropneumatic, 154-156
Tax, sewer, 174
Tax benefits, 305
Tee fitting, 129
Telephone, 10
equipment, 190
extensions, 191
installation, 190-191
intercom, 65
Television, 191-192
antennas, 192
closed circuit, 189
Temperature, 105-107, 117
change of, 85
changes, stack effect, 141
control of shower, 169
controlling, 139
design, 114
effect on heat, 131
between floors, 116
for freezing pipes, 152
in insulation of piping, 161
range of steam heat, 116
sensing devices on thermostatic devices, 139
in toilet operations, 169
variability, with water heat and air heat, 117
water, in cooling, 118
water heating, 156-159
Tenant, 14, 106, 258
directory, 65
education, fire, 40
lockers, 8, 69, 227, 238-239
storage in walkups, 281
Tennis court, 71, 87, 238-239
Term of financing, 307
Term of loan, 304-306
Terminal cabinet for telephone equipment, 190
Terminal connection, in grounding, 179
Terrace, 28, 262, 281, 285, 289-290
data on, 7
as recreation space, 71
Terrace housing, 262, 271
Test, percolation, 163
Test cylinders, 85
Testing of emergency equipment, 187
Thermal movements, 82-83
Thermostats, 106, 139
Thermostatic control, factory built-in, for through-wall room coolers, 139
Thermostatic guidance, room-by-room, with electrical heat, 118
Thorsen & Thorshov, 368-369
Three-phase current, 183
Three-pipe system, 131
Threshold of stair doors, 141
Through apartment, 222-223
Through-wall coolers with combined heating and cooling systems, 137
thermostatic control of, 139
Tigerman, Stanley, 324-325, 446-447
Tile fields, 163-164
Tile piping in basement drainage, 168
Timber piles, 98
Time delay relay on bathroom exhaust fan, 143
Tinted glass, 115
Toilet, water closet, 168-169
for garage managements, 68
of health club, 72
location, 166
for meeting rooms, 74
for open air sports, 73
pressure in, 153-154
proximity to laundry room, 70, 72
proximity to roof terrace, 72
for sauna, 74
below sewer drainage, 168
siphonage of, 162
for swimming pools, 73-74
Ton, 119
Tool shed, 271
Tool storage, for elderly, 72
Top of building, 247-248, 263-265
Topography of site, 11
Total energy, 9
Total energy plants, 176-177
Tot-lot, 71-72
Tower, 220, 236, 238, 240-242, 248, 262-265, 288, 274
Townhouse, 5, 24-25, 27, 266, 268-275, 280-281, 283-284, 294
back-to-back, 273
density, 295-296
end unit in, 269
four bedroom, 268, 269
laundry for, 69
loading for, 63
"piggy back," 283
refuse removal in, 64
site, 295-296
split level, 271
staggered row, 269
stair, 47
two bedroom, 268, 269
three bedroom, 268
Townhouse Projects, 406-419
Tract home, heating, cooling, 123
Traffic, 11, 291
conditions, 216, 237
interval for elevator selection, 48
vehicular, 61
Transfer beam, 84
Transfer column, 86
Transfer tree, 84
Transfer wall, 84, 92
Transformer, reduction of voltage, 175
replacement of, 187
spacing in highrise, 185
Transmission of heat, 118
Transmission cable, 177
location of, 178
Transmission of odors, air pressure in corridors, 145
Transportation, 12
consideration in location of

equipment, 110
network, 291
Traps, in plumbing fixtures, 165
structural considerations for, 79-80
Trapped water, 98
Travel distance, 43, 51, 196, 213, 219, 224, 227
code requirements for, 16, 18
in garage, 61
Treads, stair, 44
width of, 18
"Tree," transfer, 84
Triplex walk-up, 276
Trouble circuit for alarm trouble, 189
Truss, staggered, 90
Truss system, diagonal, 95
Tub, 9
in siphonage, 162
Tube, 95-96
finned, 119
servicing areas, 114
removal space, 122
Tubing, copper used in concrete, 134
Turbine, 121
Tustin, Cal., 420
Two directionality, 247
Two-pipe system, 129-131
Two-pipe water circulating system, in a combined system, 137
Two-position, valve for control, 139
Two story apartment, 33, 231, 232

Underground water pipine, 159
Underlayment, as sound isolator, 36-37
Underwriters' laboratories, 34
Unions, 77
Unit (dwelling), size of, 7
United States, 53, 77, 118, 251, 276
comfort temperatures in, 106
cooling in, 106
government standards, 155
housing in, 19
nuclear power in, 109
public housing in, 4, 10
zoning in, 13
Upfeed, in water piping, 160-161
Upflow, 152
Uplift, 94, 99
hydrostatic, 98
Upper income housing, 6, 222, 235
Urban Design Council of the City of New York, 14, 71, 317
Urban Design Group of the New York City Planning Dept., 232
Use, code limitations of, 17
estimate, for electrical service, 182
of water, 158
User, 8, 152, 159, 185, 202, 289
age of, 6, 24
characteristics of recreational needs, 72
choices for, 6
data on, 3-4
economic status of, 24, 53
education of, 6
ethnic background of, 6
family size of, 6
identification of, 5
income level of, 6
information about, 23
life style of, 6, 24, 53
occupation of, 6, 24
previous housing of, 6
responses by, 5
Utilities, 303-306
survey of, 11
underground, 96
Utility closet, location for fan coil unit, 129
Utility company, 9
Utility room, as laundry location, 69
lighting, 180

Vacancy, 304, 307, 309
Vacation, care of system, 138
Vacuum, 121
breakers, to prevent siphonage, 162
Value of residences, sales or rental, factor in use of multiple boilers, 113
Valve, automatic, for fire use of domestic water, 172
pressure, relieves pressure, 159
expansion, 119
flush, 168-169
in siphonage, 162
hose, 173
on hose connection, 171
indexed, 132
manual, controls on HVAC system, 138
pumping system, 155
standards, 155
for ventilation noise, 148
for water department, 174
water distribution, 160
water supply, 38
Valving, in piping, 134
Variability of temperature, with water heat and air heat, 117
Vault, electric, 178
water meter in, 174
Vehicular access, 265
movement system, 291
servicing, 291
Vehicle storage, maintenance, 8
Velocity, in ventilation ductwork, 147
Vending machine, for laundry, 70
Vent, pipes, sizes of, 166
sleeve for, 79
Ventilation, 9, 105
of bathroom, 9, 25
in case of fire, 38-40
code requirements for, 16
cross, 197
duct, 285
effect of air heat, 117
exhaust, 37
fresh air, 137
of garage, 62
of kitchen, 9, 25
mechanical, 202
natural, 246
and mechanical, 106-107
Venting pipes, cast iron, copper, galvanized steel, plastic, 165
Venting system, in plumbing drainage, 165
Vents, on roof, 289
Venturi, Robert, 204, 243, 317-318
Veranda, 230
Vermiculite, 89
Vertical core, 199
Vertical dimension, of a furnace, 112
Vertical distribution pattern, of electrical service, 185
Vertical furnace, 114
Vertical main, 132
Vertical passages of air, eliminating stack effect, 141
Vertical risers, 129-130
Vestibule, elevator, 218
to lobby, 66
in smokeproof tower, 45
to smokeproof tower, 18
Vibration, of air conditioning machines, 121
of machinery, 111-112, 121, 127
Vibrations, 75, 89
View, 7, 197, 208-212, 214, 217, 222, 225-226, 228, 232, 235-236, 241, 260, 289
between apartments, 261

Voice communication, 10
Volleyball, 71
Voltage, 177
  standardization of, 178
  standards on, 182
Volume, 197, 212, 218, 223, 230, 240-242, 247, 256, 260-264
  breaks in, 260-262, 285
  change, 85
  of building, 282, 287-289, 291
  of midrise, 286
  proportions of, 196
  of walkup, 283
Von Eckardt, Wolf, 318

Waffle slabs, 86
Waiting space, garage, 68
Walk, 153, 274
  drainage of, 163-164
  light, 180
Walk-up, 24-25, 65, 75, 90, 92, 110, 127, 266, 285-287, 294
  in case of fire, 38
  core type, 276-281, 283
  corridor type, 281-283
  definition of, 193
  density, 298-299
  duplex, 277-280
  exit regulations, 43
  loading, 62-63
  locker location, 69
  mixed, 283-285
  multicore, 276
  power failure in, 186
  quadruplex, 277-281
  refuse removal, 62, 64
  site, 298-299
Walkup/Complex Projects, 446-456
Walkup/Core Type Projects, 424-433
Walkup/Corridor Type Projects, 434-445
Wall, 18, 79, 91-92, 97, 100, 125, 177, 231
  in apt. efficiency calculation, 33
  bearing, 87, 221
  common, 268
  electric box in, 180
  exp. joints in, 85
  exterior, 17
  for fan-coil units, 127
  heat loss through, 141
  insulation of, 108
  of lowrise, 288
  reflective quality of, 116
  risers in, 134
  transfer, 84
Wallboard, around electric box, 180
Washbowl, lavatories, 169
Washer, 8
Washing machines, 8
  calculating of for laundry room, 70
  pressure for, 156
  in siphonage, 162
Washington, D.C., 344, 406, 448
Waste disposal, private and public, 163-164
Waste gases, in fuel conversion, 112
Waste, connections for disposal in kitchen, 170
  kitchen and food, 167
  plumbing, storm and sanitary, 163
Water, 119
  as heat source, 123
  circulation, hot, 158
  closet, 9, 168-169
    pressure in, 153-154
  company, 152
  connection in kitchen, 170
  control, 151
    in showers, 169
  as coolant, 120
  courses, natural, 163-164
  department, 174
  domestic, heating of, use of electrical power, 177
  in drainage of fixtures, 165
  in a fire extinguisher, 173
  and gas, compared to electrical power, 175-176
  hammering, 161
  hardness of, 152-153
  heat, 116-117
    by boiler, 113
  heater, 152-153
  heating, 9-10, 156-159
    expansion space in pipes, 161
  intrusion, on balconies, 83
  main, 154
  mains, location for fixtures, 170
    means of distribution, 152
  makeup, location of equipment, 112
  meter, pressure in, 153-154
  natural, availability of for cooling, 118
    for cooling, 119
  pipe damage, 161
  pipes, location, 160
  piping, selection of, 159-160
  piping distribution system, connection to central heating and cooling system, 129
  plant, central chilled water, 137
  pressure, 153-154
    boiler capacity, 113
  pressure pump, in power failure, 187
  pumps, 10
  quality, 152
  samples, to determine softening, 153
  service entrance, 110
  storing of hot, 158
  softening of, 153
  source, individual and communal, 151
  supply, 151
    in relation to pumps, 155
  supply line, electric valve on, 138
  supply system, 153-154
    for fire protection, 170
  systems, pumped or forced, 117
  table, 11, 96-99, 163, 238
  temperature control, for heating systems, 138
  use, 158
  vapor, 106
Waterproofing, membrane, 99, 262
  of garage deck, 62
Waterstops, 99
Watt, in electrical heating, 114
Weather, 28
  effect on heating, cooling, 131
  history, 106
  intermediate, four-pipe system, 131
Weatherstripping, of stair doors, 141
Weese, Harry & Associates, 380-381, 410-411, 426, 427
Weight, as a factor in sewer construction, 164
  of an aluminum conduit, 179
  in equipment location, 110
  in locating equipment, 111
  as a pressure factor, 153
  structural considerations of for water pressure, 154
  of unit, air conditioning, 121
  of water, boiler capacity, 113
Well, as water supply for cooling, 118
  artesian, 151-152
Well pump, 152
"Wet bulb temperature," 106
Whistle, from stack effect, 141
Wilmette, Ill., 354
Wind, 11, 142, 145, 256
  in cooling, 115
  effect on supply ventilation system, 146
  loads, 78, 96